ELIZABETH CATLETT

EDITED BY
DALILA SCRUGGS

WITH
MARY LEE CORLETT
J.V. DECEMVIRALE
JULIA FERNANDEZ
MELANEE C. HARVEY
MELANIE ANNE HERZOG
CATHERINE MORRIS
SARAH KELLY OEHLER
LOWERY STOKES SIMS
RASHIEDA WITTER

NATIONAL GALLERY OF ART
WASHINGTON
BROOKLYN MUSEUM
NEW YORK
THE UNIVERSITY OF
CHICAGO PRESS
CHICAGO AND LONDON

ELIZABETH CATLETT

A BLACK REVOLUTIONARY ARTIST AND ALL THAT IT IMPLIES

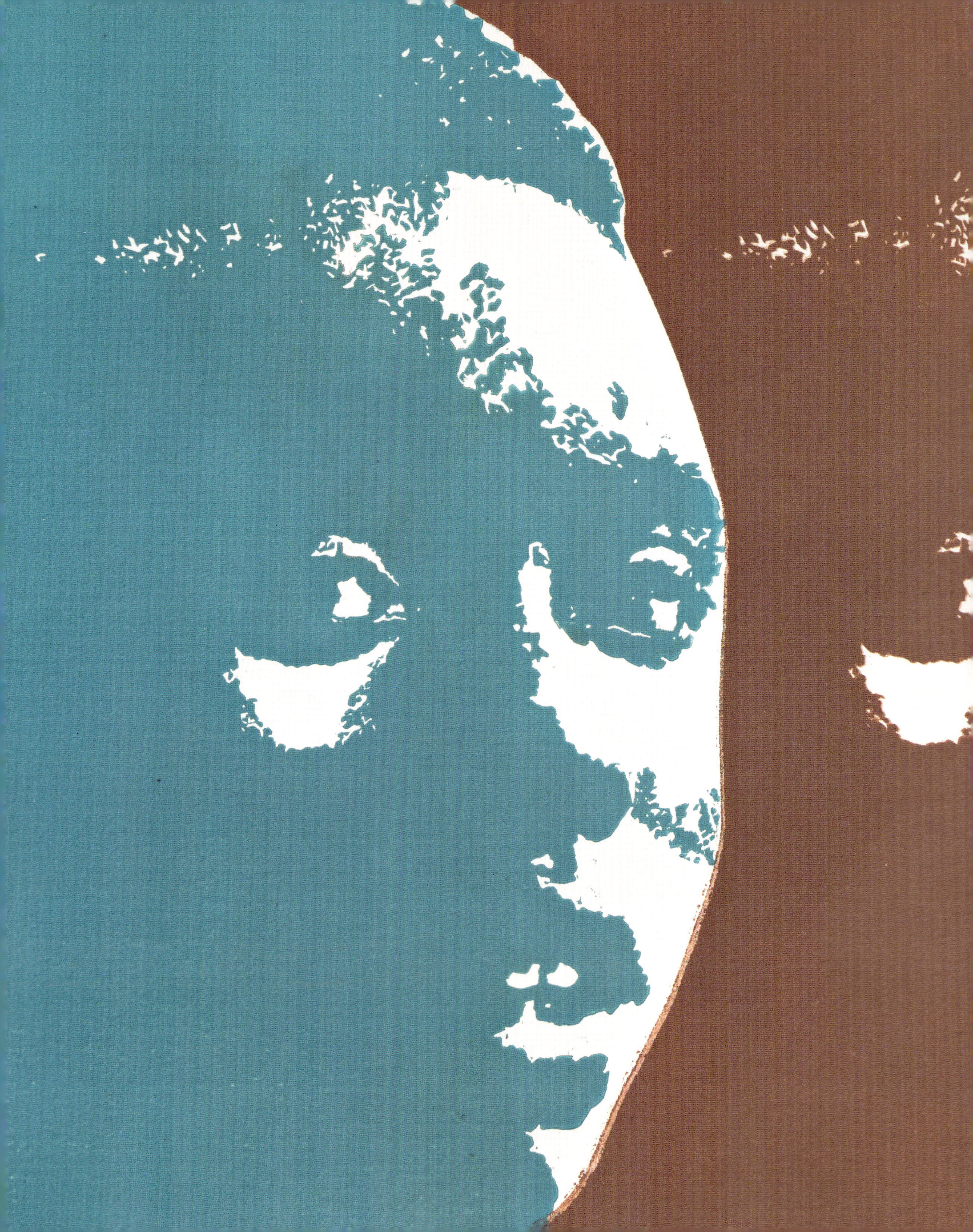

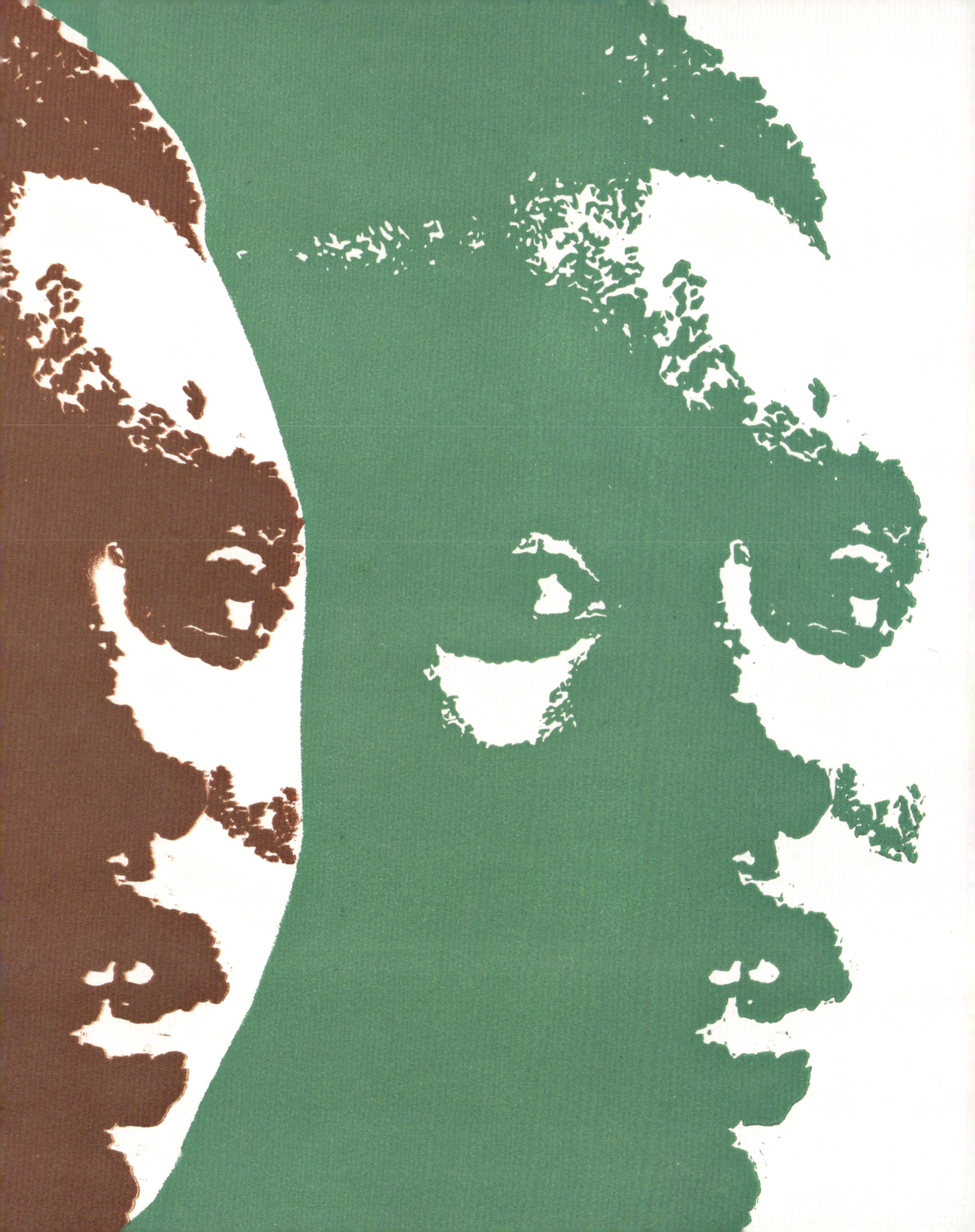

8 Foreword

11 TO THAT DEGREE AND MORE
Dalila Scruggs

17 PLATES: 1915–1947

67 BECOMING AN ARTIST-ACTIVIST AT HOWARD UNIVERSITY
Melanee C. Harvey

77 SOCIAL(IST) NETWORKS IN CHICAGO AND NEW YORK
Sarah Kelly Oehler

89 PLATES: 1947–1960

117 SHARECROPPER AND CAMPESINO
Julia Fernandez

123 AN ARTIST-ACTIVIST AT THE CENTER OF THE GLOBAL SIXTIES
Dalila Scruggs

137 LA MAESTRA'S FUGITIVE PEDAGOGY IN MEXICO
J.V. Decemvirale

145 PLATES: 1960–1975

177 PRESSING NARRATIVES
Mary Lee Corlett

187 "THINKING ABOUT WOMEN" THROUGH FORM, SUBSTANCE, AND RADICAL POLITICS
Melanie Anne Herzog

197 GIVING FEMINISM A SHOVE IN THE RIGHT DIRECTION
Catherine Morris

207 PLATES: 1975–2012

243 SHAPING PUBLIC SPACE
Dalila Scruggs

247 A WOMAN OF GREAT INTEGRITY, AND BRAVERY
Lowery Stokes Sims

255 CHRONOLOGY
Rashieda Witter

270 Notes
282 Acknowledgments
284 Index

FOREWORD

A dedicated artist-activist, Elizabeth Catlett (1915–2012) addressed societal injustices through art that deftly explores race, gender, and class. Centering the trials and triumphs of Black American and Mexican women, she drew on a wide range of influences—from African and Pre-Encounter art to Pop; from German expressionism to American and Mexican modernism. *Elizabeth Catlett: A Black Revolutionary Artist and All That It Implies* surveys her long career across seventy-five years of artistic production, highlighting iconic masterpieces alongside often overlooked works. We see Catlett as a skilled formalist, particularly in renowned prints from her *Sharecropper* and *Black Woman* series, while early paintings and drawings reveal her versatility as an artist and late public sculptures shape the very spaces around them.

The first-ever recipient of a master of fine arts degree, at the University of Iowa, Catlett became a creative cultural force. "The art world must be particularly active," she wrote in 1944 for the journal *American Contemporary Art*. "Think of an American culture with the full integration of the Negro people, and you can see how the art of our country and the world would be advanced through their participation." By celebrating Catlett and presenting the full range of her production, this book and the exhibition it accompanies seek to deepen our understanding of the true breadth of American art history, and the vital contributions of African American and African Diasporic art.

Projects such as *Elizabeth Catlett: A Black Revolutionary Artist and All That It Implies* are built on years of groundbreaking work undertaken by Black scholars and institutions who supported Catlett's career for decades—during her lifetime and after. Beginning with her days as an undergraduate at Howard University, Catlett consistently found encouragement for her work through a community of historically Black colleges and universities and other dedicated Black institutions. We are enormously grateful for the contributions of the Amistad Research Center, Dillard University, Hampton University, Howard University, Spelman College, the Schomburg Center for Research in Black Culture, and the Studio Museum in Harlem.

This collaborative project reflects the labor, care, and thoughtfulness of every person who played a part in its making, and we are grateful to each of them. Francisco Mora Catlett, Juan Mora Catlett, David Mora Catlett, and their families have been enthusiastic collaborators. We extend to them our sincere thanks for their generosity in sharing their mother's work and providing keen insights into the extraordinary life and legacy of both Elizabeth Catlett and their father, Francisco Mora. We also wish to express our appreciation for the dedicated vision of the exhibition's curators: Dalila Scruggs, Augusta Savage Curator of African American Art, Smithsonian American Art Museum; Catherine Morris, Sackler Senior Curator, Elizabeth A. Sackler Center for Feminist Art, Brooklyn Museum; and Mary Lee Corlett, associate curator, modern prints and drawings (retired), National Gallery of Art. This publication, edited by Dalila Scruggs, will undoubtedly frame Catlett scholarship for years to come, and we thank each of the contributing authors.

Because Catlett spent consequential years developing her artistic practice and her social awareness in Washington, DC, New York City, and Chicago, we are delighted that each city is a stop on the exhibition's tour, which concludes at the Art Institute of Chicago; our thanks go to James Rondeau, president and Eloise W. Martin Director, and curator (and contributing author) Sarah Kelly Oehler. The generosity of several donors has been instrumental. This exhibition is made possible through support from the Terra Foundation for American Art. Leadership support for the exhibition and this publication has been generously provided by the Henry Luce Foundation; we are grateful to its president Mariko Silver and program director for American art Teresa A. Carbone for their early enthusiasm. The exhibition was also supported by Christie's, the Every Page Foundation, the Maurer Family Foundation, and the National Endowment for the Arts at the Brooklyn Museum. We also extend special gratitude to our boards—chaired by Barbara M. Vogelstein at the Brooklyn Museum and David M. Rubenstein at the National Gallery. Last of all, we welcome this chance to thank the numerous institutions and private lenders whose meaningful loans made this project possible.

Kaywin Feldman
Director
National Gallery of Art

Anne Pasternak
Shelby White and Leon Levy Director
Brooklyn Museum

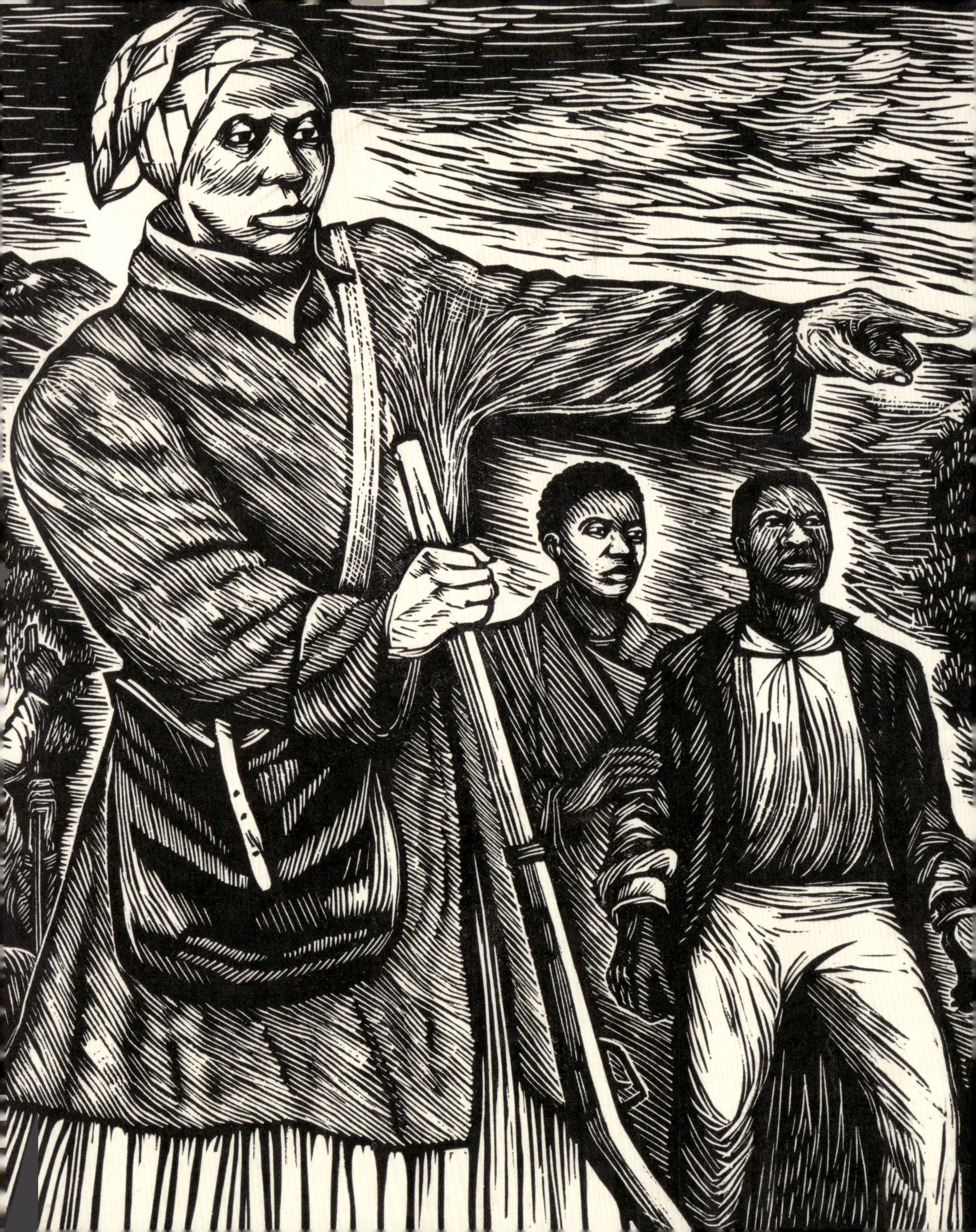

DALILA
SCRUGGS

TO THAT DEGREE AND MORE

In May 1970, denied a visa to enter the United States and speak at the Conference on the Functional Aspects of Black Art (CONFABA), Catlett remained undeterred. She delivered her speech from Mexico, over the phone, in the eighth year of her exile from the US—the country of her birth. "I was refused," she noted,

> *on the grounds that, as a foreigner, there was a possibility I would interfere in social or political problems, and thus, I constituted a threat to the well-being of the United States of America.*
>
> *To the degree and in the proportion that the United States constitute a threat to Black People, to that degree and more, do I hope I have earned that honor. For I have been, and am currently, and always hope to be a Black Revolutionary Artist, and all that it implies!*[1]

Recorded and played for the Black artists, art historians, and critics who had gathered at Northwestern University near Chicago for the conference—which became a landmark event in the Black Arts Movement (BAM)—these words are the conceptual North Star of this book, and the exhibition it accompanies.

Elizabeth Catlett (born Washington, DC, 1915; died Cuernavaca, Mexico, 2012) is admired as an avowed feminist, lifelong activist, and deft formalist. Over the course of nearly a century—from Jim Crow segregation and McCarthy-era persecution, through Cold War exile, and into the first term of the Obama administration—she built a life dedicated to the pursuit of formal rigor and social justice, which she understood to be mutually reinforcing. These two passions run throughout her career, across seventy-five years of artistic production.

The narrative on Catlett has solidified into well-rehearsed beats, assisted by the artist herself. She engaged in a kind of autobiographical canonization by telling the same stories in similar ways in countless interviews. We have come to know her as a social realist printmaker and sculptor employing a vocabulary of organic abstraction. *Elizabeth Catlett: A Black Revolutionary Artist and All That It Implies* aims to complicate, deepen, and extend these received narratives. When examining the archival record, alongside a close look at her work, what becomes clear is that her dedication to Black pride, revolutionary change, and artistic rigor were not inevitabilities, but born of a series of dogged, hard-nosed, and impassioned choices. We can take no part of it for granted.[2]

Encouraged, as she tells us, by artist Grant Wood to create work around "something you know the most about," she depicted Black women.[3] However, her commitment to depicting Black people as fine art was about more than self-representation—it was a profoundly political act. Light-skinned with mixed-race ancestry, Catlett could have passed for white. She flirted with that color line only once, sneaking into the white section of a movie theater in the South, before disavowing the practice altogether.[4] Instead of giving into society's pervasive anti-Blackness, she actively combated it. She had a clear-eyed view of colorism. Though she would be relegated to a lifetime of oppression, she proudly identified as a Black woman and made that subjectivity the leitmotif of her career.

Catlett navigated her artistry and politics with a Black feminist framework as her compass. Known as Betty Mora to friends and family, Catlett used her maiden name professionally—a common practice among Black Leftist women in the 1940s who asserted their independence while they addressed sexism within a larger class critique.[5] Long before Kimberlé Crenshaw coined the term, Catlett committed herself to examining Black women's intersectional identity. As she stated in her 1945 Rosenwald grant proposal:

> *Negro women in America have long suffered under the double handicap of race and sex. Because of subtle American propaganda in the movies, radio and stage, they have come to be generally regarded as good cooks, housemaids and nurses and little else. At this time when we are fighting an all out war against tyranny and oppression, it is extremely important that the picture of Negro women...be sharply drawn.*[6]

Attendant to this focus on Black women was her regard for family and her tender, if rare, depiction of men, guided by the womanist commitment to the "survival and wholeness of entire people, male and female."[7]

For Catlett, Black Power was only effective if it galvanized a broader commitment to transnational solidarity. Long before "revolution" became a keyword of the BAM of the 1960s and '70s, Catlett had embraced a political radicalism that merged the goals of the Black Left in the United States with those of the Mexican Revolution.[8] In New York in the 1940s, she may well have conceived or even executed her political cartoons for *Congress Vue*, the journal of the National Negro Congress, in its offices, where walls were papered with prints from the Taller de Gráfica Popular (TGP), a workshop based in Mexico City. Once in Mexico—Catlett arrived there in 1946—she saw and depicted "her two peoples" (Black Americans and Mexicans) as similarly bound by intersecting forms of oppression.[9] We thus emphasize the unified aesthetic and ideological lens Catlett used to critique US exceptionalism—highlighting the racist terror coercing many within its borders and decrying the racialized logic undergirding its imperial ambitions beyond them.

Catlett had a robust art education. She began her training at Howard University, where James A. Porter was a revered authority on African American art history. Later at the University of Iowa she took classes not only with Grant Wood but also with H. W. Janson, the author of the survey that solidified the canon of the Western tradition for decades. Catlett was ecumenical in her artistic references—Constantin Brâncuşi, Käthe Kollwitz and the German expressionists, Henry Moore, Barbara Hepworth, traditional African and Mesoamerican sculpture, Mexican muralists, Cuban graphic design, and even Andy Warhol informed her work. Over the years, Catlett repeatedly professed her love of abstract art. If we take her at her word, we can not only appreciate how clearly she understood the potential of her materials but also begin to see that underexamined aspects of her work are more central to her style. While the tale of how she evaded segregation policies to bring students to an exhibition in

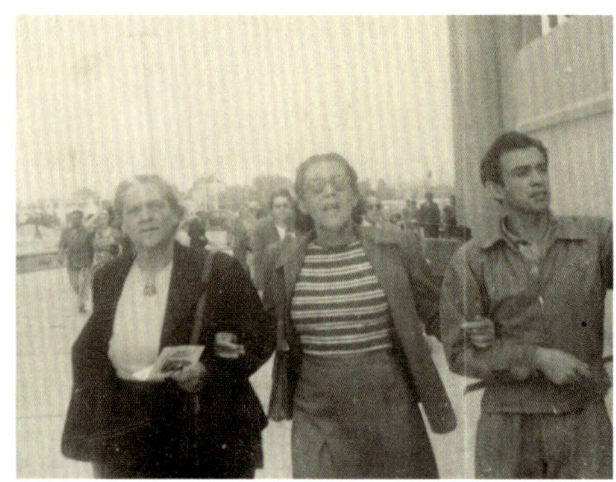

Fig. 1—Elizabeth Catlett with her mother (left) and husband, artist Francisco Mora (right), at a protest in Mexico, c. 1950, Photographs and Prints Division, Schomburg Center for Research in Black Culture, The New York Public Library

New Orleans is often repeated, few take stock of what motivated that feat of daring: it was Pablo Picasso's art.[10] Organized by Alfred Barr, the first director of the Museum of Modern Art in New York, the exhibition *Picasso: Forty Years of His Art* traveled the country starting in 1939; Catlett saw it in New York, Chicago, and New Orleans, and likely read its catalog—"a handbook for American artists throughout the 1940s and 50s."[11] This avid appreciation would not have conflicted with her Leftist politics. The journal *New Masses* praised the show, celebrating Picasso's blue and rose periods for their humanism and *Guernica*'s deft use of form to convey protest.[12] Catlett, for her part, experimented with the cubist vocabulary in New York in the 1940s. Though most of her work (p. 81) from this period is lost, photographs of her sculptures (p. 85, fig. 4) along with an exceptional surviving sketchbook (pp. 30–31) reveal the ways she experimented with clashing volumetric forms—cones, spheres, and cubes jutting up against one another capture multiple perspectives seen simultaneously.

For Catlett art was never just for art's sake. While she was most certainly committed to a rigorous exploration of form, she felt a moral obligation to work in a style that would be legible to all. "Let's...create the best art possible for the liberation of our beautiful Black People," she wrote in her 1970 CONFABA address.

> *Black Art is one media by which the masses of our people can be made aware, educated, and projected up to the summit of Black Liberation... we should learn all the techniques we can, make ourselves as professional as possible, so that we are prepared to be the best of functioning artists. Our people deserve no less. Let's dump that inferior stuff and raise our artistic standards, because racism is the white man's game.*[13]

Beauty, we see, is a lifeline in the struggle for justice. And expressed through art, Catlett's political views extended beyond it into direct action.

To convey the full sweep of her nearly century-long life, *Elizabeth Catlett: A Black Revolutionary Artist and All That It Implies* organizes her works along a linear, chronological backbone with each themed essay offering a discrete window into her practice. We begin with her political and aesthetic foundations. Placing Catlett at an epicenter of Black artistic and intellectual production, Melanee C. Harvey's insightful essay examines her matriculation at Howard University, where she benefitted from its innovative fine art curriculum and forward-thinking exhibition program. Sarah Kelly Oehler's chapter deftly illuminates the ways that Catlett earned her aesthetically modernist and politically radical bona fides in Chicago and New York's Black Leftist networks. The lifelong friendships she forged there helped hone the revolutionary outlook that would guide her for the rest of her career. And, as both authors show, Catlett's interest in Mexican art and culture began well before she arrived in Mexico City.

We then turn to Catlett's identity as an artist integrally embedded in the Mexican art world (fig. 1). Julia Fernandez explores Catlett's engagement with Mexican modernist campesino iconography, an intervention that disrupts the scholarly tendency to treat the artist's Black and Mexican subject matter separately. In my essay, I attend to the ways political exile, with its impediments to travel and communication, impacted her life and work in the 1960s and '70s. I also note the influence of Mexican artistic production, from student protest posters to a Pop art idiom expressing Third World solidarity. J.V. Decemvirale picks up a concurrent thread—Catlett's role as mentor to countless students as a professor at Mexico's premier institution of higher learning, the Universidad Nacional Autónoma de México (UNAM), and to a younger generation of artists within and outside of academe. She used, as he compellingly argues, a fugitive pedagogy to evade a white and mestizo male-dominated art world and guide her students toward a praxis of social critique and technical mastery.

We then attend to Catlett's commitment to formal rigor. Mary Lee Corlett's expert examination of Catlett's prints with the TGP artists' collective underscores her crucial role in their collaborative process. Melanie Anne Herzog encourages us to see the artist's choice of materials and materiality as indispensable to her articulation of a Black female subjectivity. Herzog's focus on sculpture, together with Corlett's rich assessment of Catlett's prints, ensures that aesthetics and politics are given equal weight within the publication.

Finally, we address Catlett's legacy. Catherine Morris examines Catlett's relationship to white, second wave feminism and her role as a trailblazer for Black contemporary artists, while Lowery Stokes Sims offers a reverential meditation that interweaves her personal relationship with the artist with larger trends in the scholarship on Catlett. Sims paints a picture of a formidable woman who sought connection to younger generations of artists and scholars, even when she fervently disagreed with them. Following Catlett's example, we selected contributors that cross generational divides and offer perspectives that challenge our preconceptions and deepen our understanding of this vital artist.

We hope to show Catlett as a master of her craft, highlighting overlooked works alongside her most iconic masterpieces. Her paintings, experiments with abstraction, and late public art (discussed in my second contribution) are particularly revelatory. She was an artist who created drawings with a profoundly steady hand, paintings that stylize the figure and compress the picture plane, linocuts incised with hatching that showcases the strength and vigor of a carver, and sculptures with curves so voluptuous they belie the power tools that hacked them into form. Three key throughlines—Blackness, radicality, and political solidarity—connect these works, and Rashieda Witter traces them in the thorough chronology of Catlett's life that rounds out this volume.

Catlett invariably argued for a public art—one that privileged community as its audience—and blazed a trail with a Black feminist framework as her torch. Many aspects of her life and work resonate with contemporary concerns, from recent conversations about anti-racist activism, intersectional feminism, and Black visibility, to the migrant crisis, essential workers who saw us through a global pandemic, and the Black Lives Matter movement. How she would have relished the discussion. She was and is a Black Revolutionary Artist, and all that it implies![14]

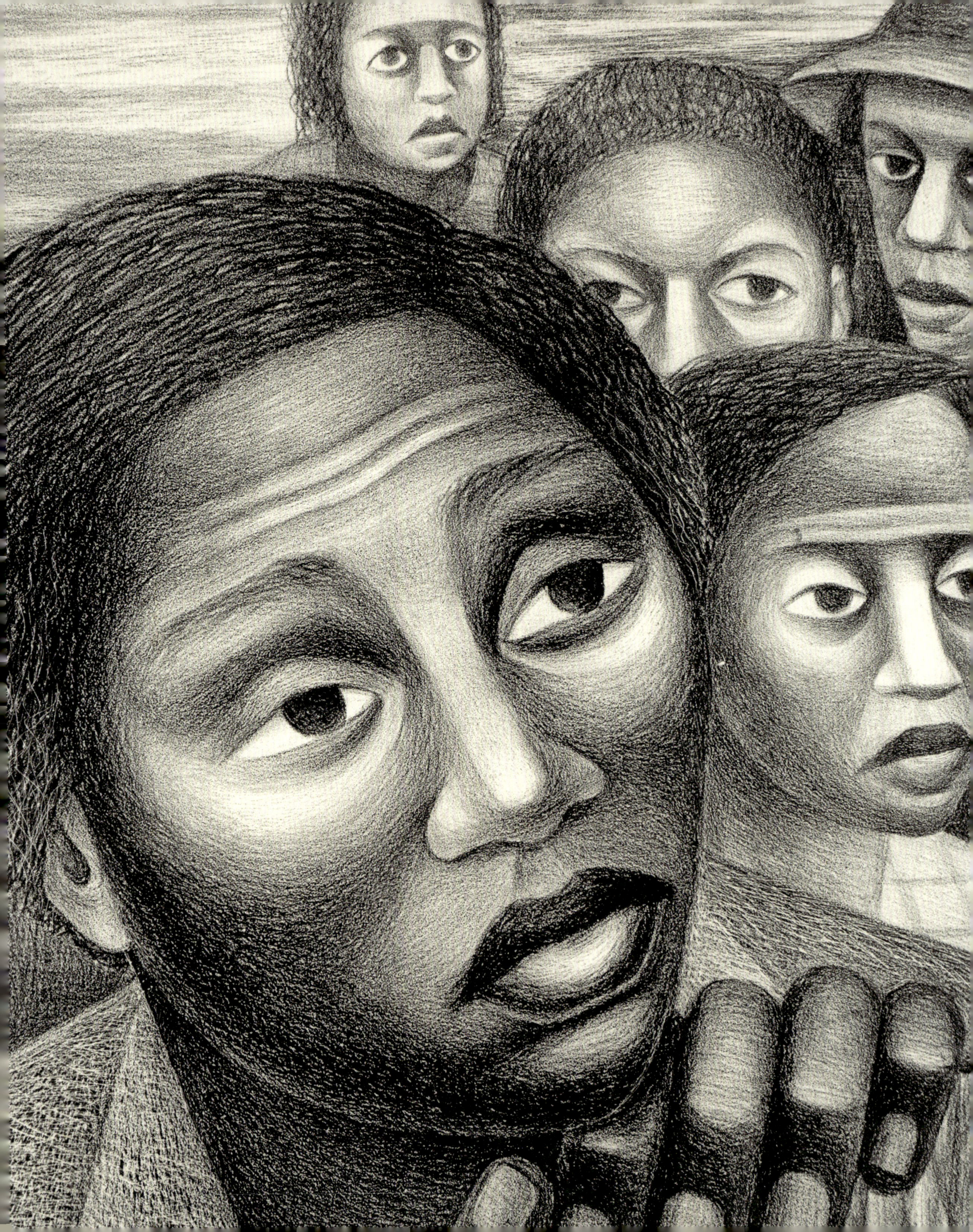

PLATES

1915–1947

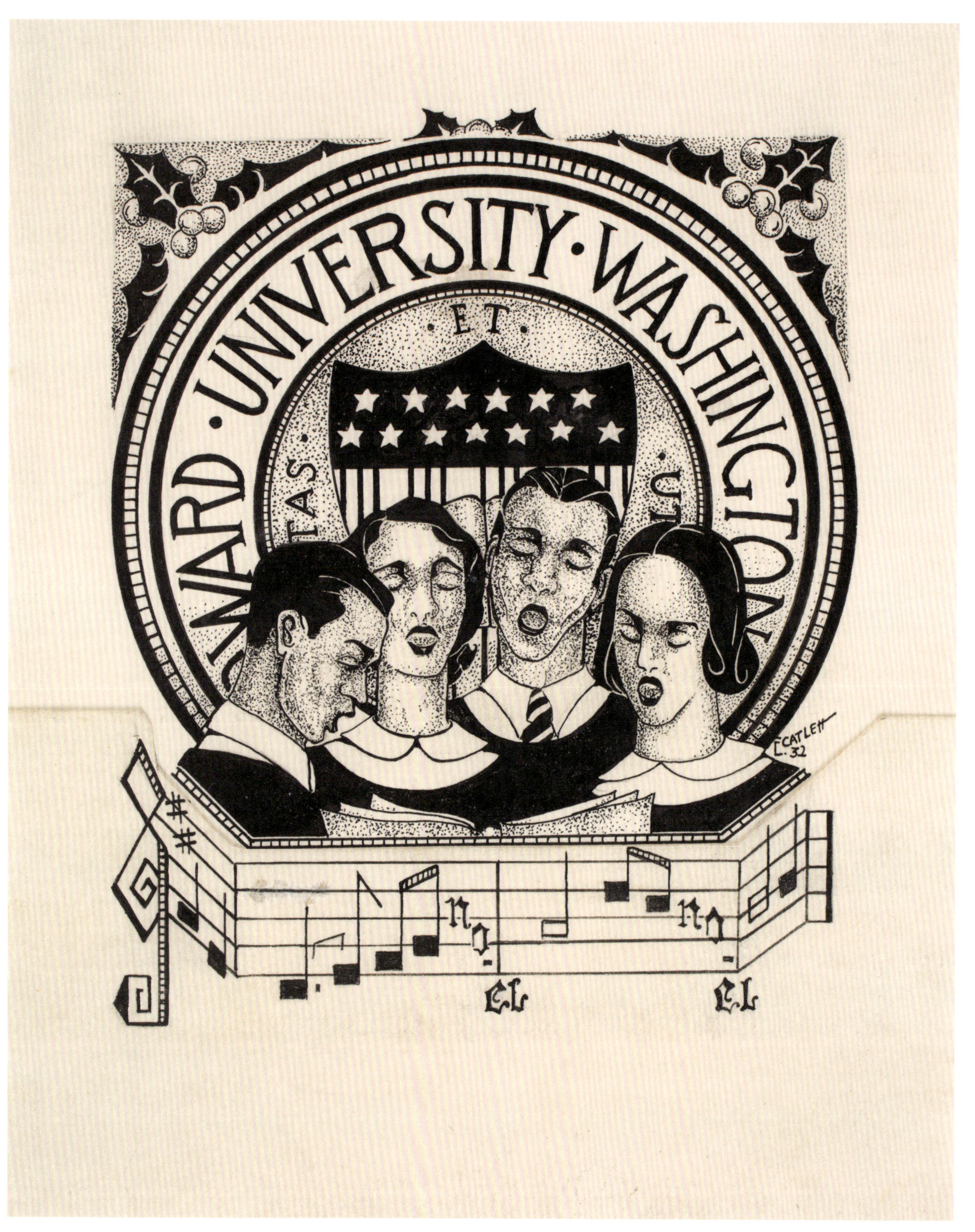

Howard University Choir, 1932, pen and ink, 10 1/16 × 9 5/8 in., Davis Museum at Wellesley College, Wellesley, MA, Gift of Jacqueline Loewe Fowler (Class of 1947)

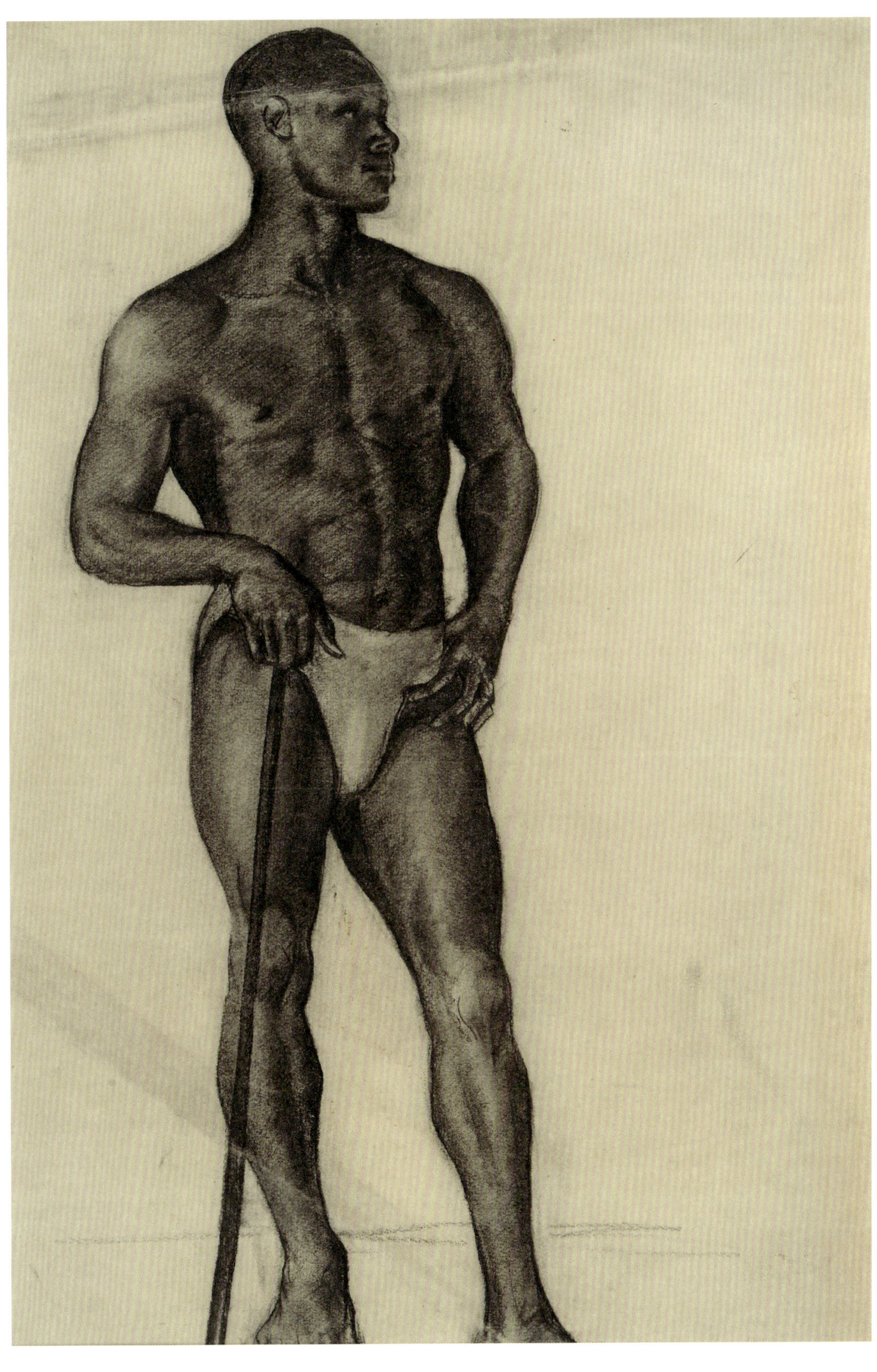

Untitled (student drawing—Standing Male Model), c. 1932, charcoal, 24 × 15 in., On loan from the Howard University Gallery of Art

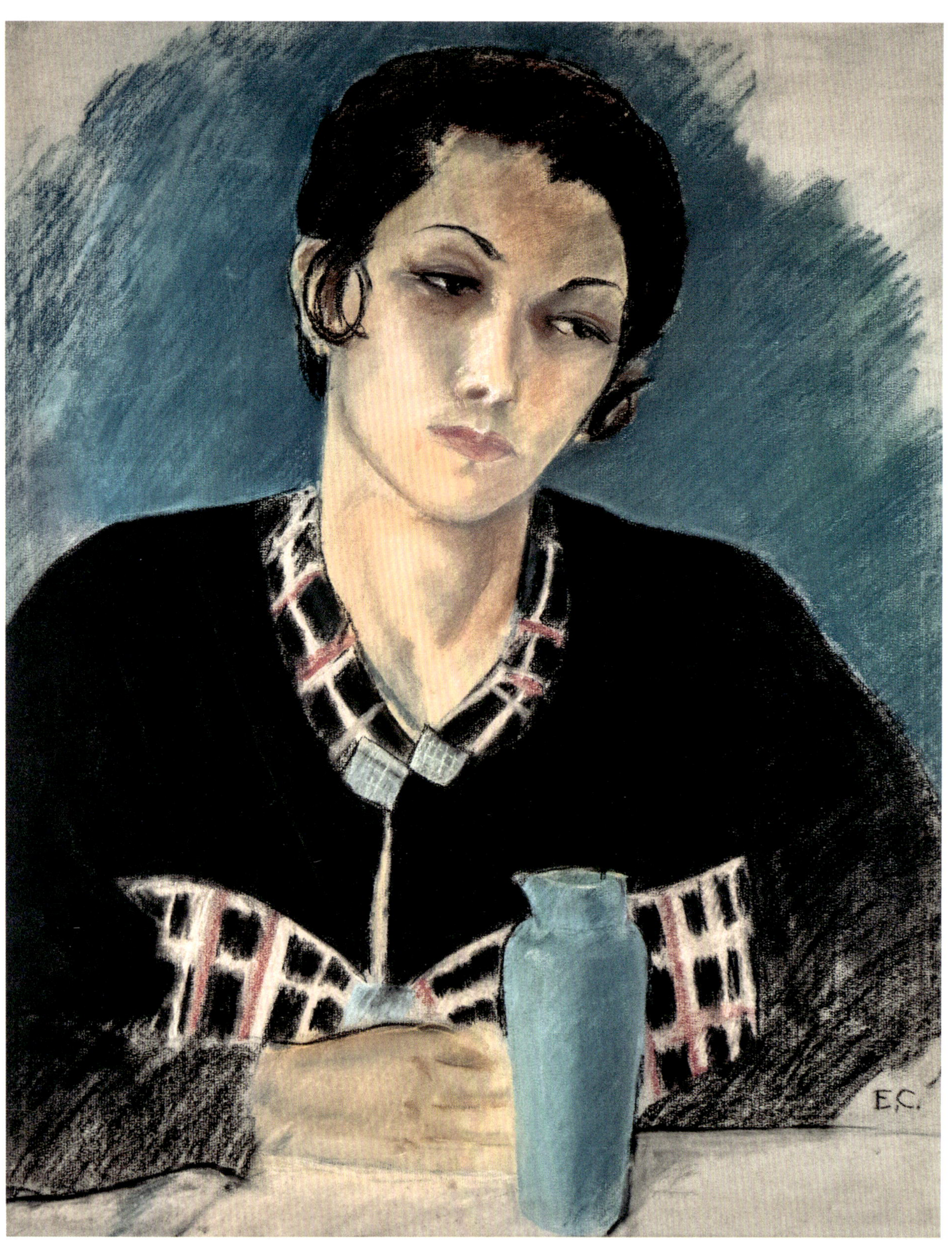

Untitled, c. 1935, pastel, 25 × 18½ in., Private collection, acquired through the Barnett Aden Collection

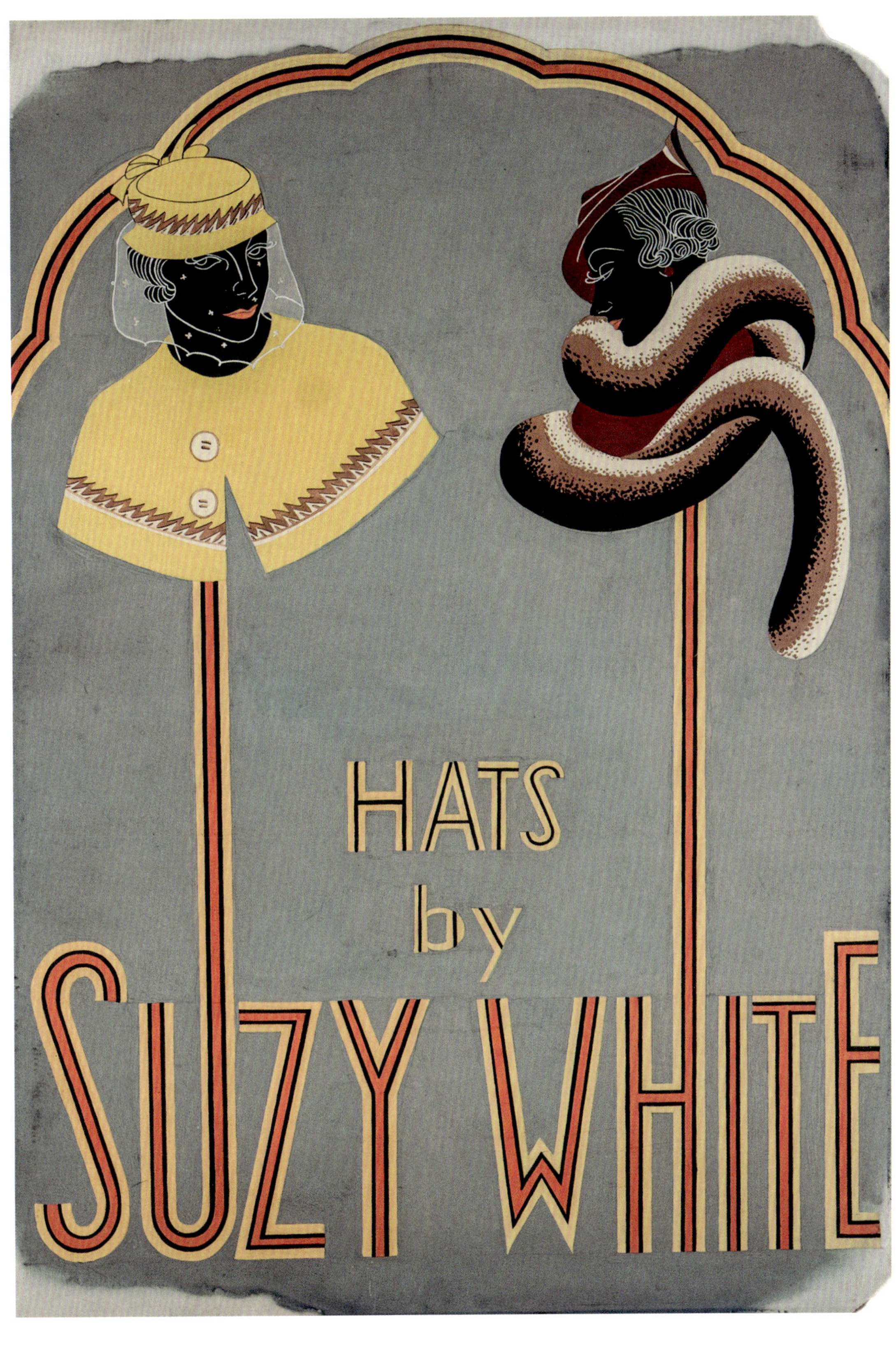

Hats by Suzy White, c. 1937, tempera and graphite on illustration board, 32 × 21 in., Private collection, acquired through the Barnett Aden Collection

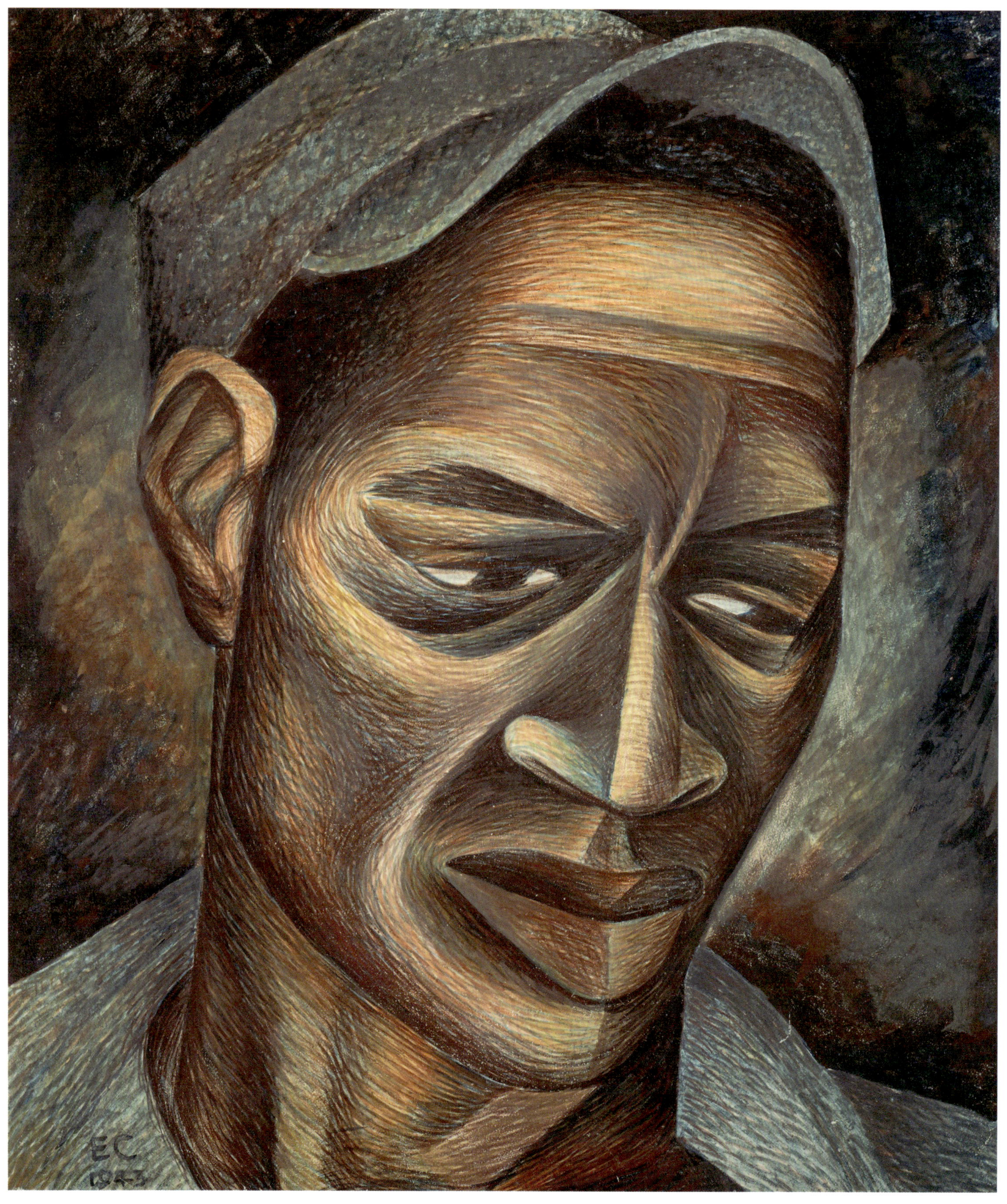

War Worker, 1943, tempera, 11 × 9¼ in.,
The Johnson Collection, Spartanburg, SC

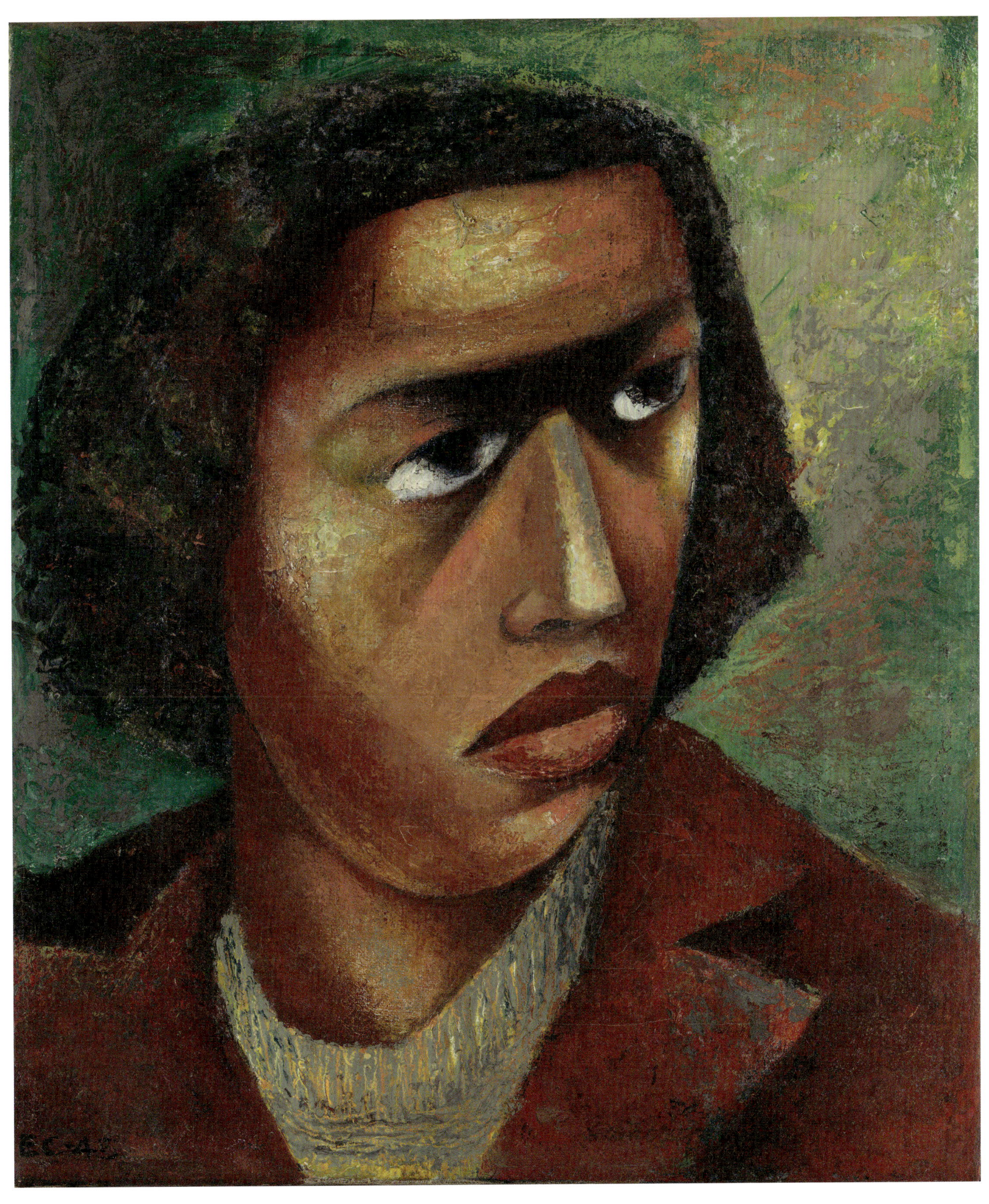

Head of a Woman (Woman), 1942–1944, oil on canvas, 12 × 10 in., Lent by The Metropolitan Museum of Art, Purchase, Gift of Continental Group, by exchange, 2018 (2018.157)

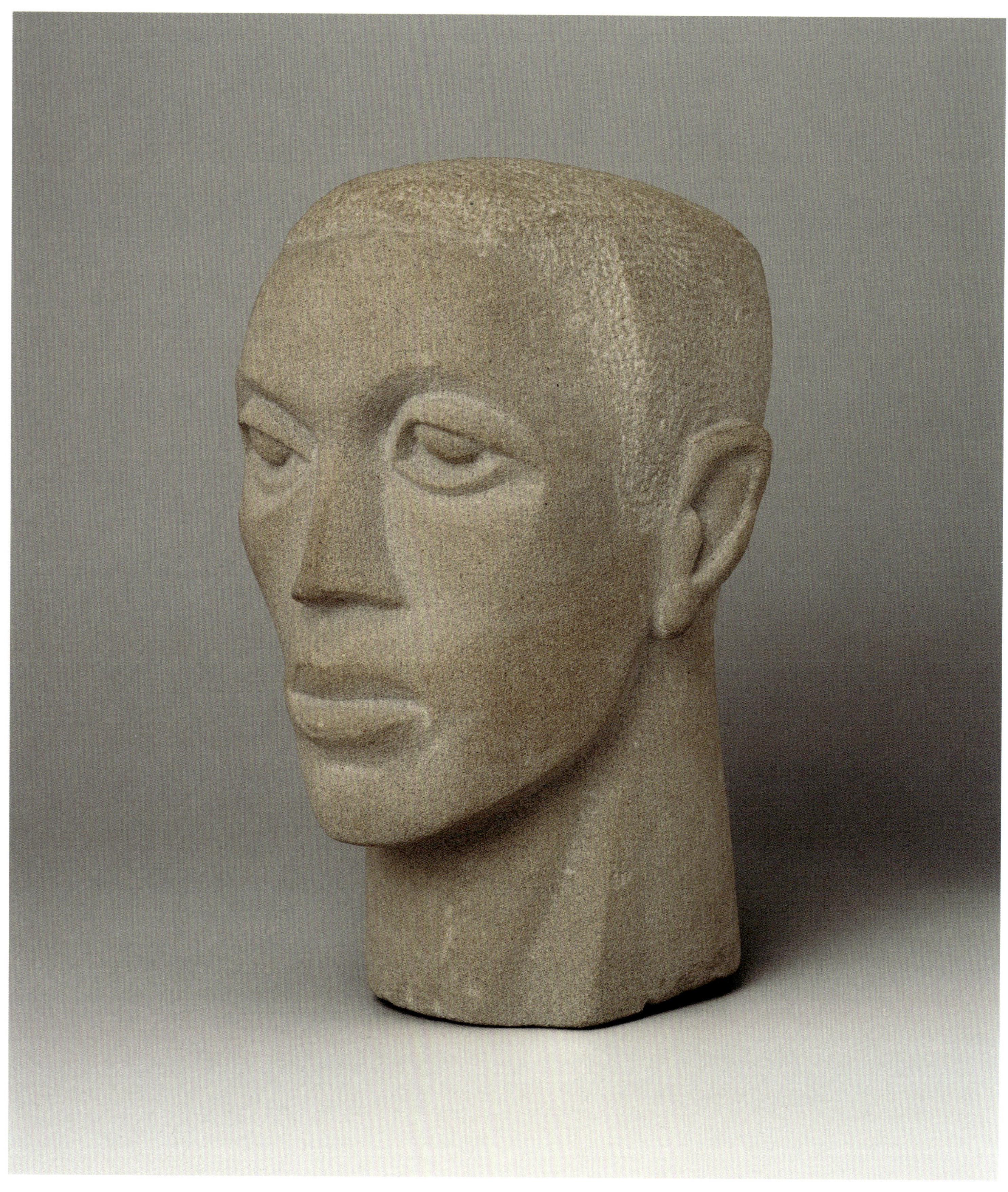

Head (Head of a Man), c. 1943, limestone, 13½ × 9½ × 7¼ in., The Art Institute of Chicago, Roger and J. Peter McCormick and Jane and Morris Weeden endowment funds, Arts of the Americas Discretionary Fund, 2021.413

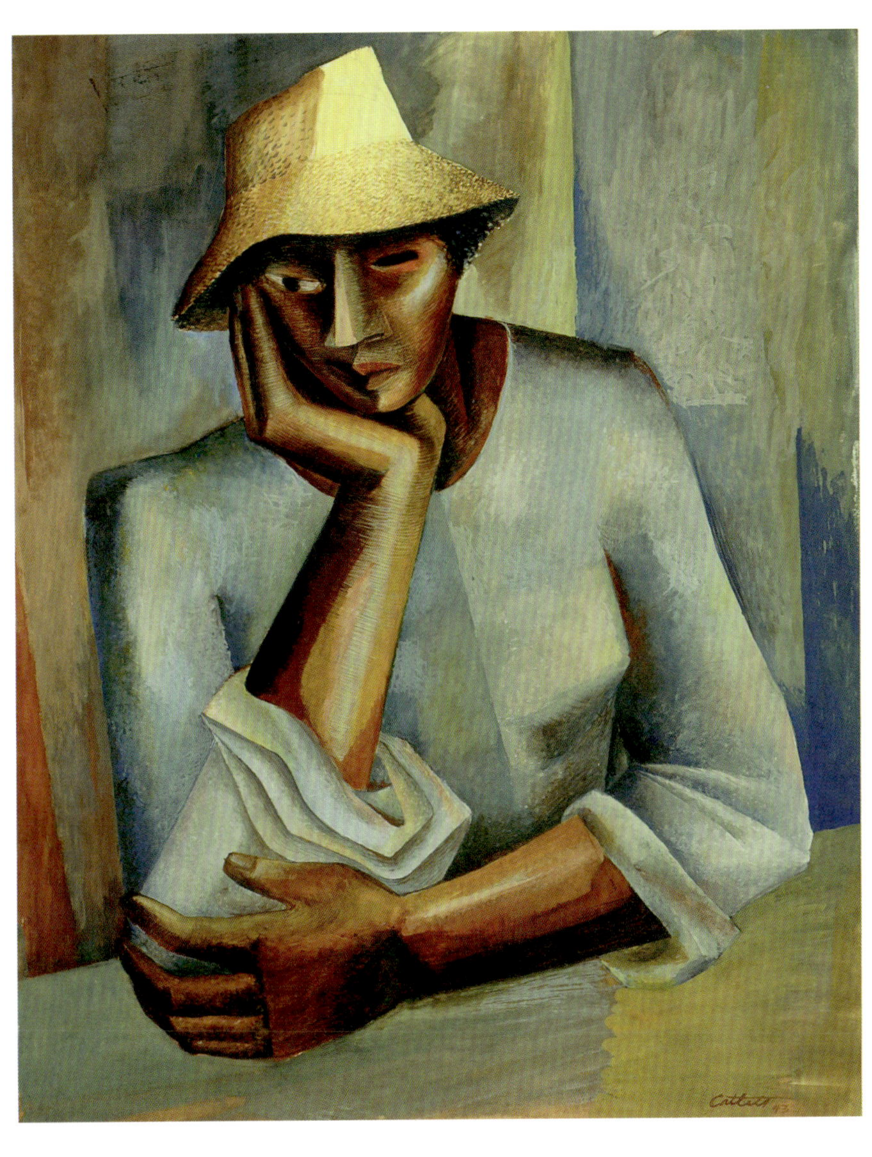

Untitled (Woman in a Yellow Hat), 1943, tempera, 22⅜ × 17⅞ in., JLW Collection

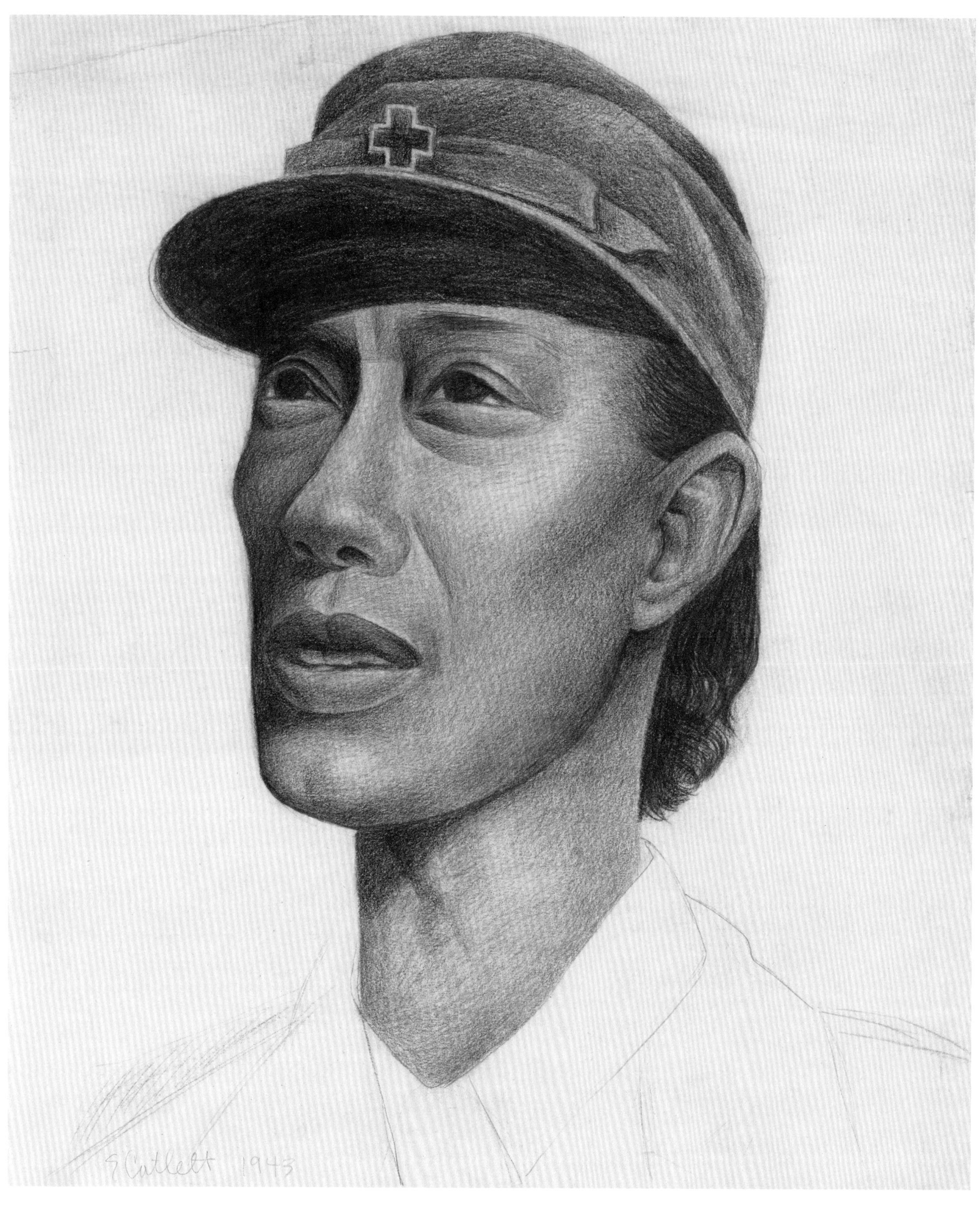

Army Nurse, 1943, graphite and black crayon with stumping and scraping, 16⅞ × 13¾ in., Philadelphia Museum of Art, Purchased with the SmithKline Beckman (later SmithKline Beecham) Fund for the Ars Medica Collection

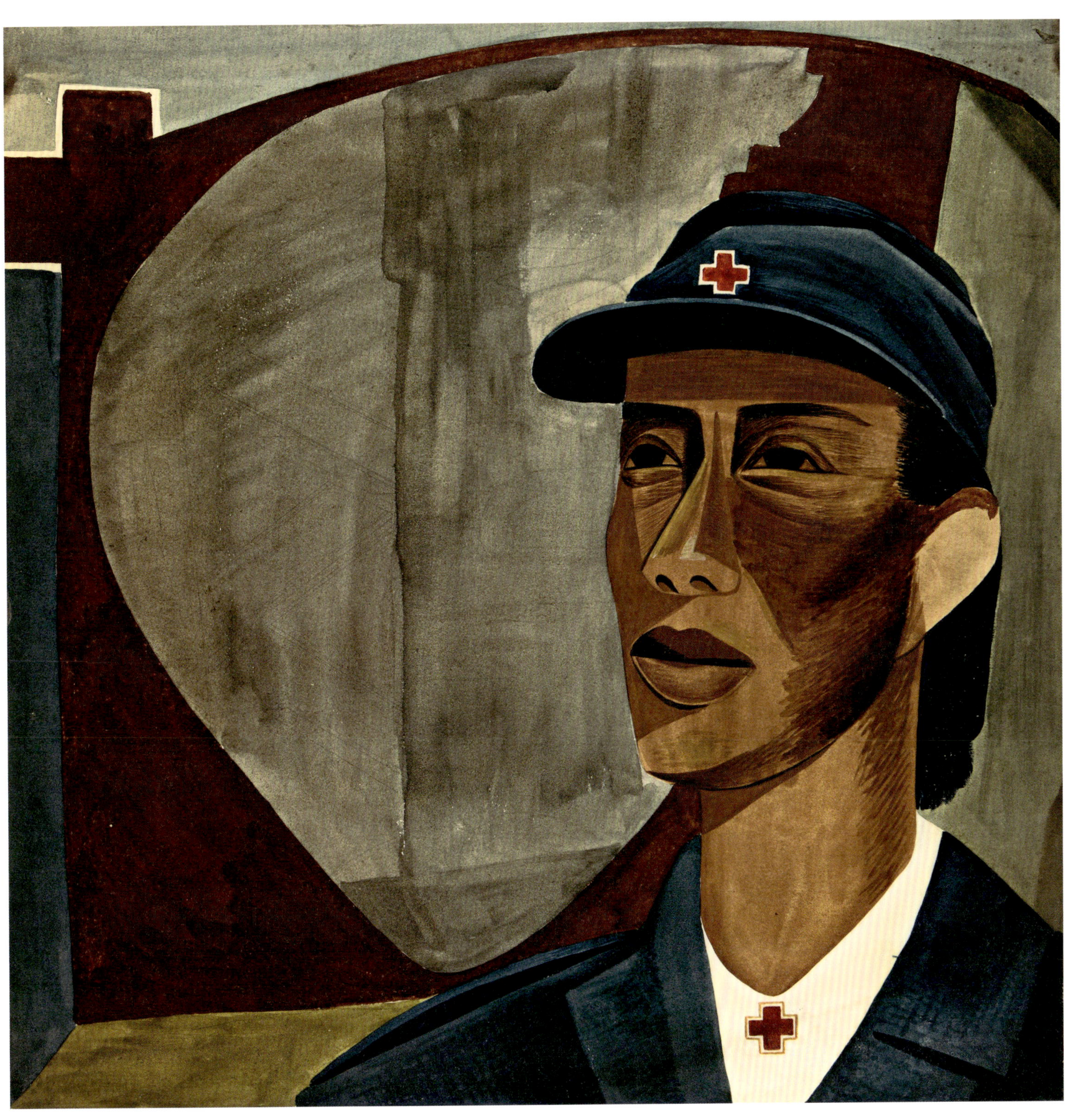

Red Cross Woman (Nurse), c. 1944, gouache, 20½ × 20 in., From the Hampton University Museum Collection, Hampton, VA

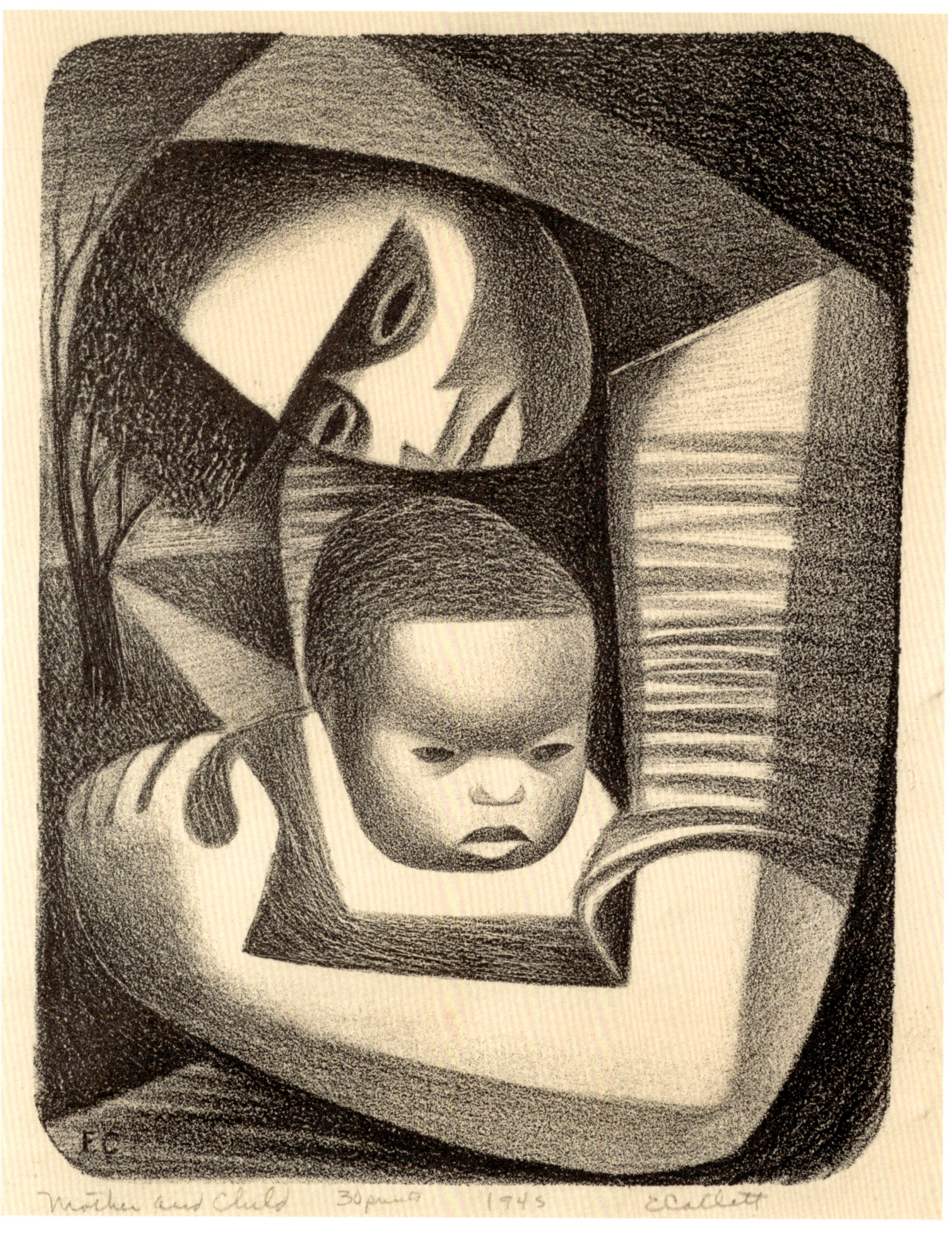

Mother and Child, 1944, printed 1945, lithograph, 12⅜ × 9⅜ in., Canton Museum of Art, Canton, OH, Gift of Louis Held

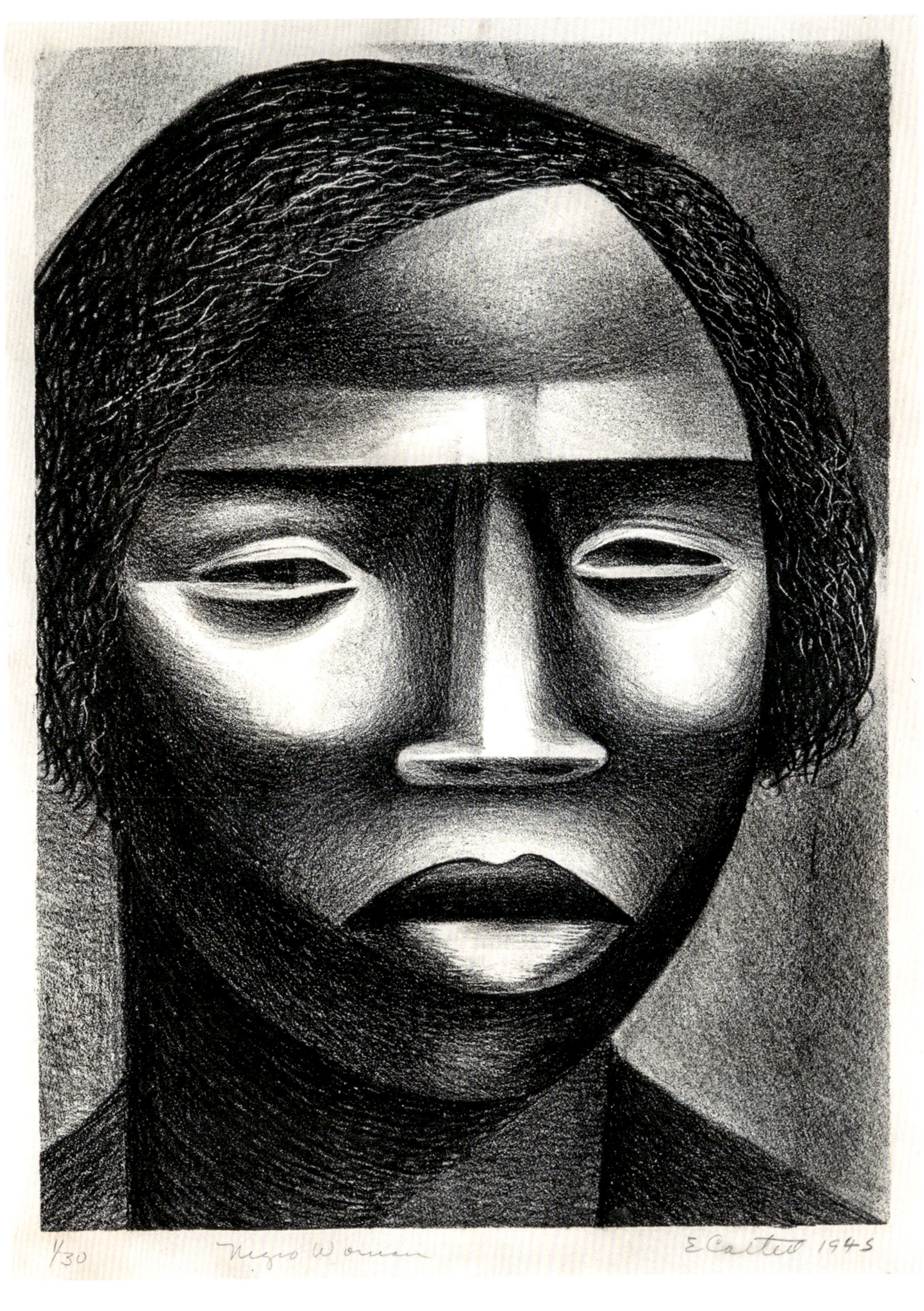

Negro Woman, 1945, lithograph, $18\frac{3}{4} \times 12\frac{11}{16}$ in., Private collection, acquired through the Barnett Aden Collection

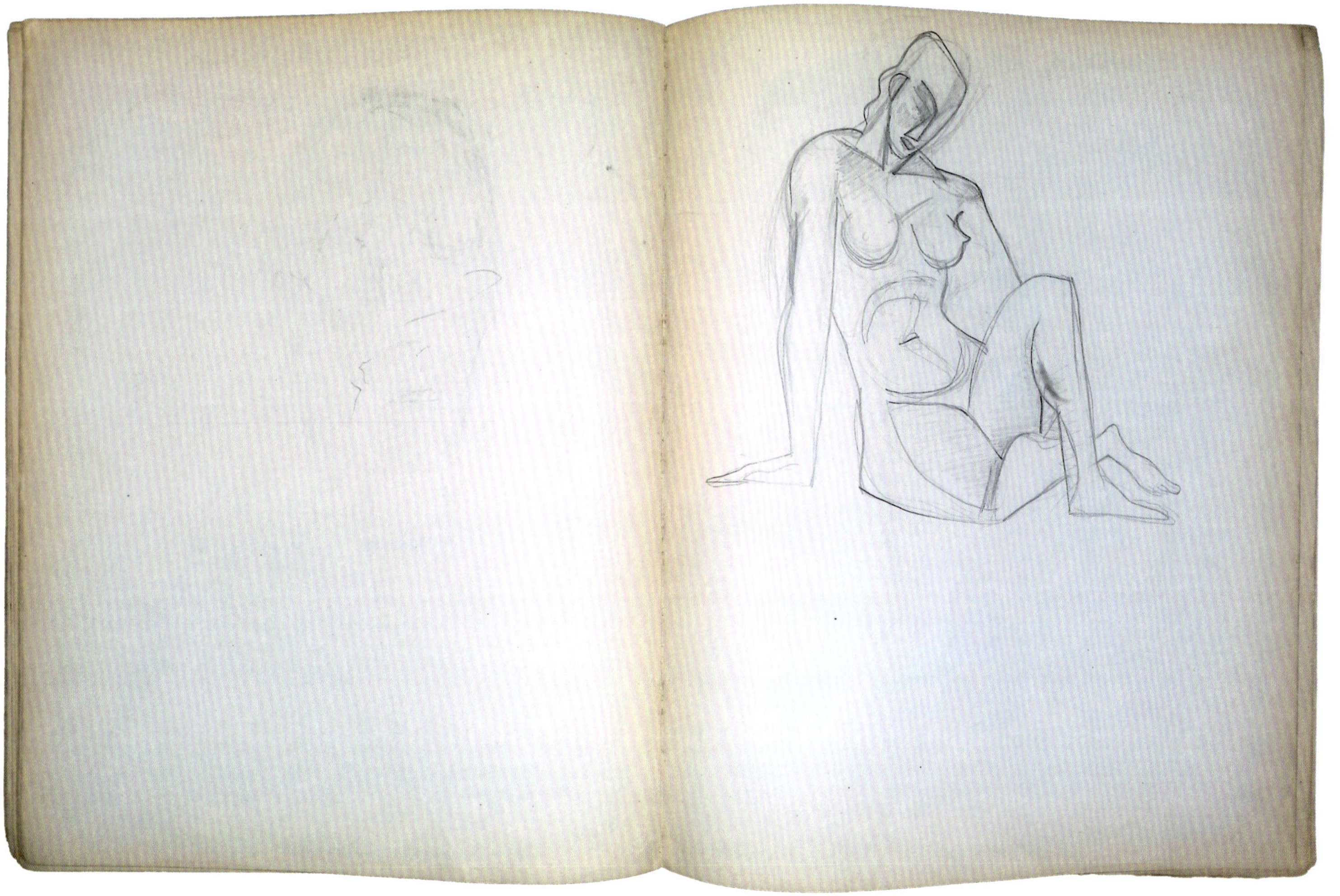

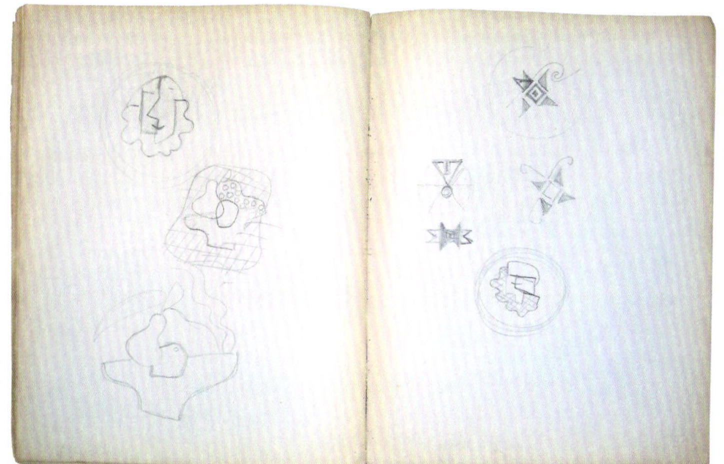

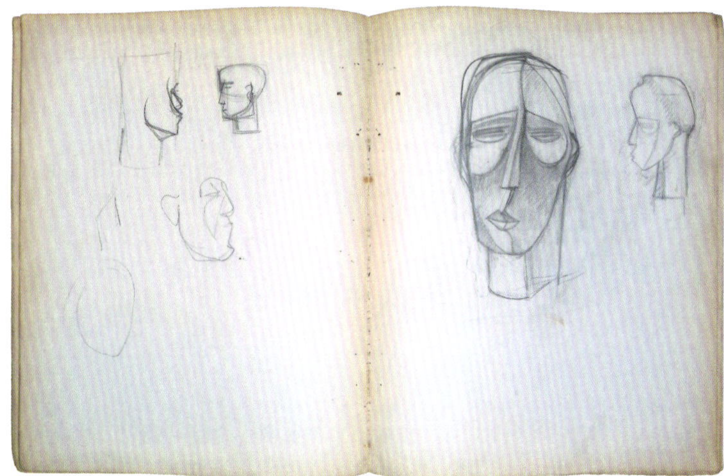

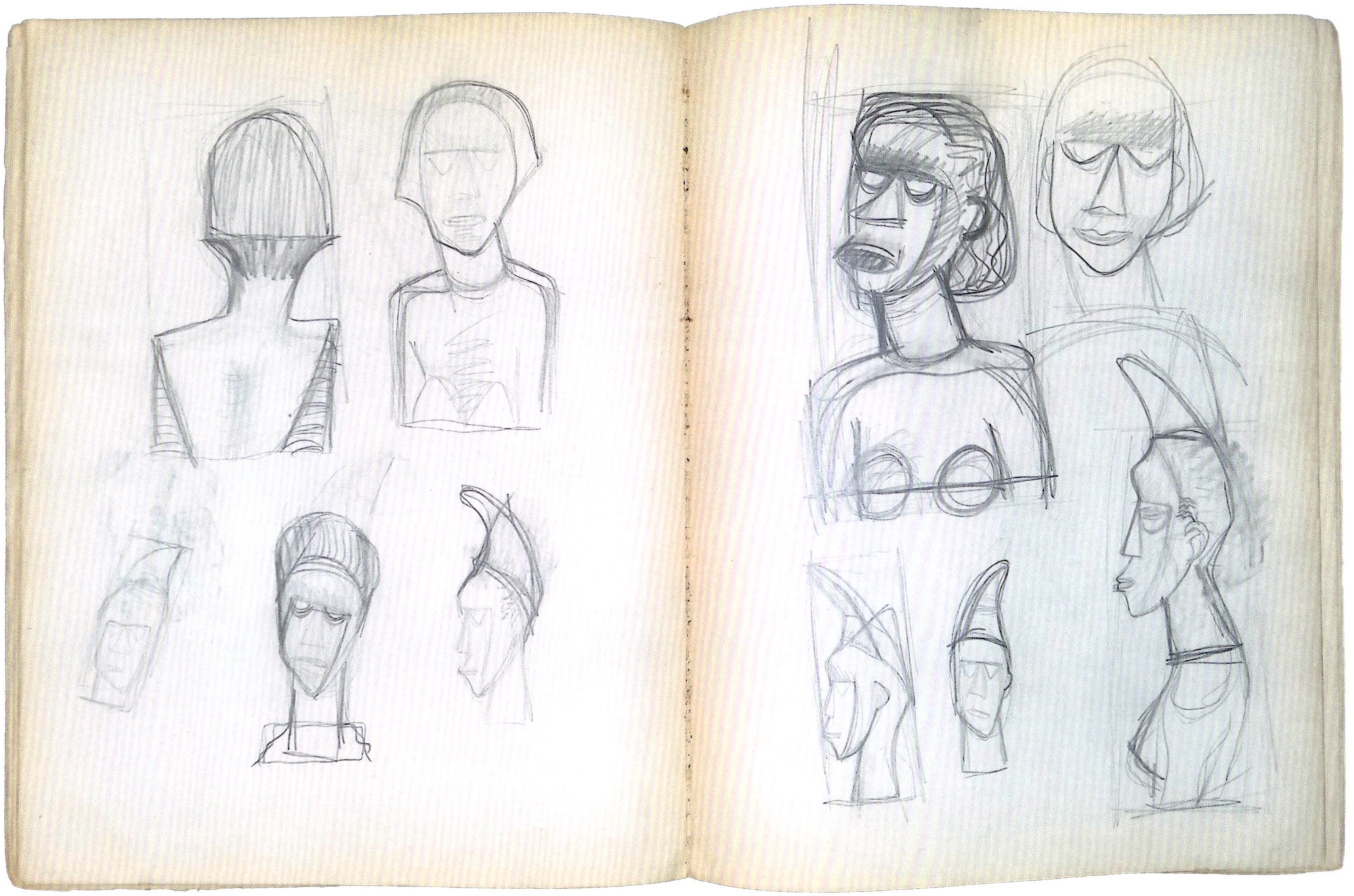

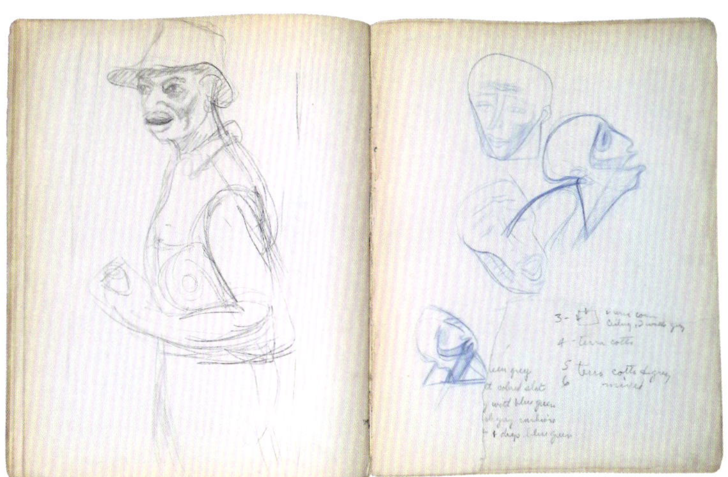

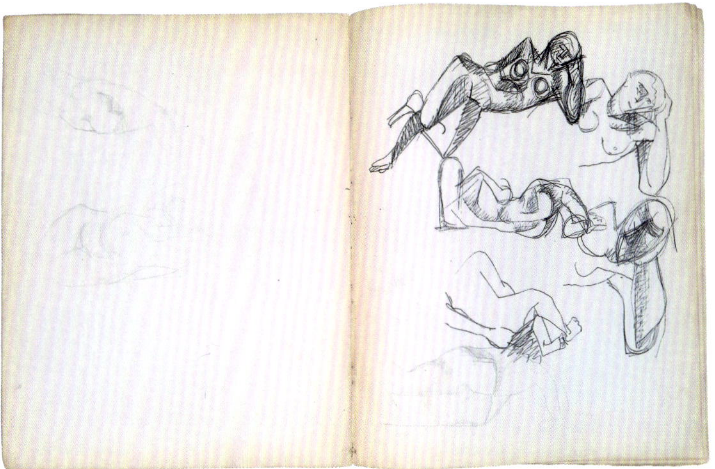

Early Sketchbook, before 1946, Private collection

THE BLACK WOMAN SERIES

I am the Negro Woman
I Have Always Worked Hard in America...
...In the fields
...In Other Folks Homes
I Have Given the World My Songs
In Sojourner Truth I fought for the rights of women as well as Negros
In Harriet Tubman I Helped Hundreds to Freedom
In Phillis Wheatley I Proved Intellectual Equality in the Midst of Slavery
My Role has been Important in the Struggle to Organize the Unorganized
I Have Studied in Ever Increasing Numbers
My reward has been bars between me and the rest of the land
I have special reservations
...Special houses
...And a special fear for my loved ones
My right is a future of equality with other Americans

— Elizabeth Catlett

Each print in Catlett's *Black Woman* series, which follows, depicts a line from Catlett's poem of resilience and resistance.[1]

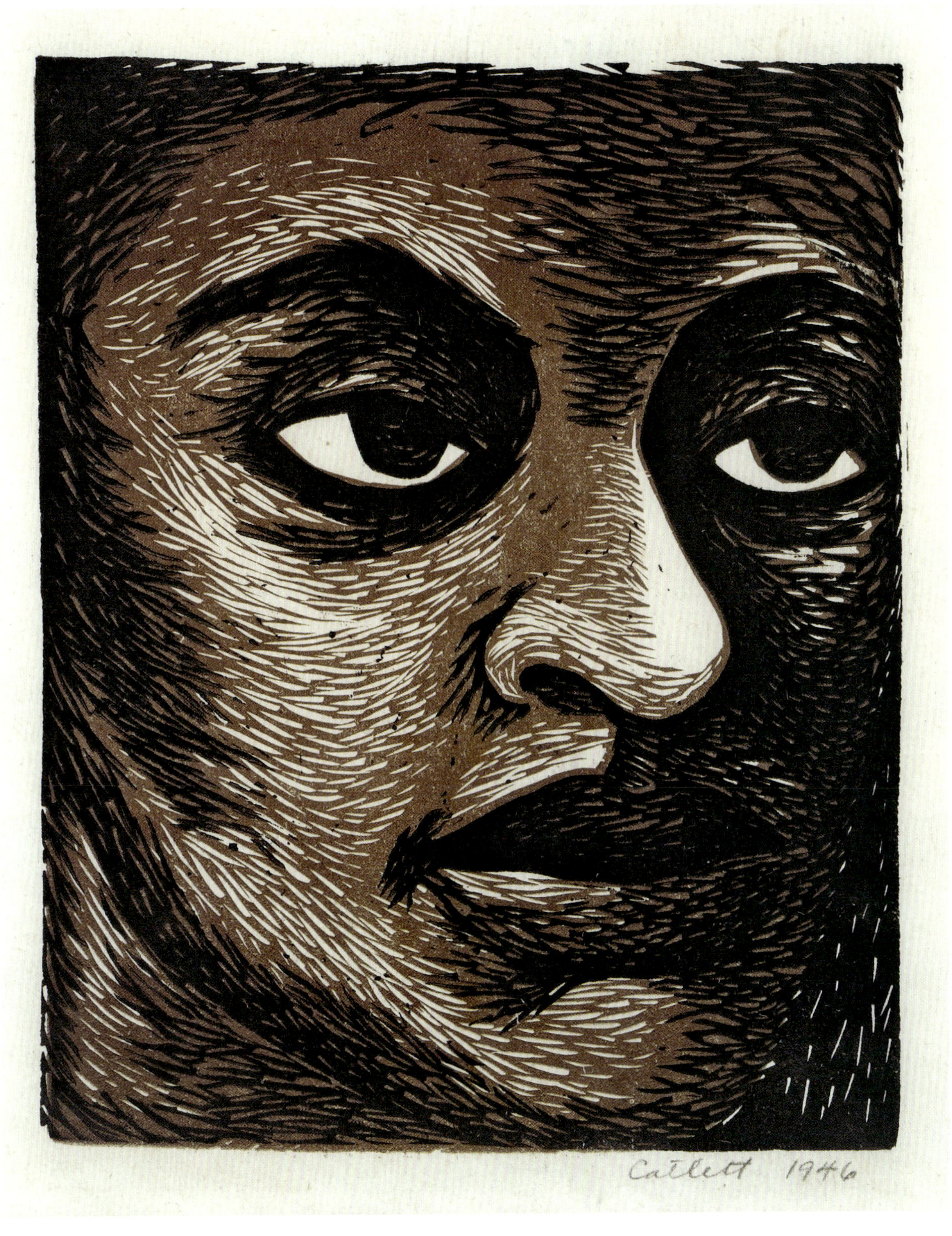

I am the Black Woman, from *The Black Woman* series, 1946, linocut, 6¾ × 5 in., On loan from the Howard University Gallery of Art

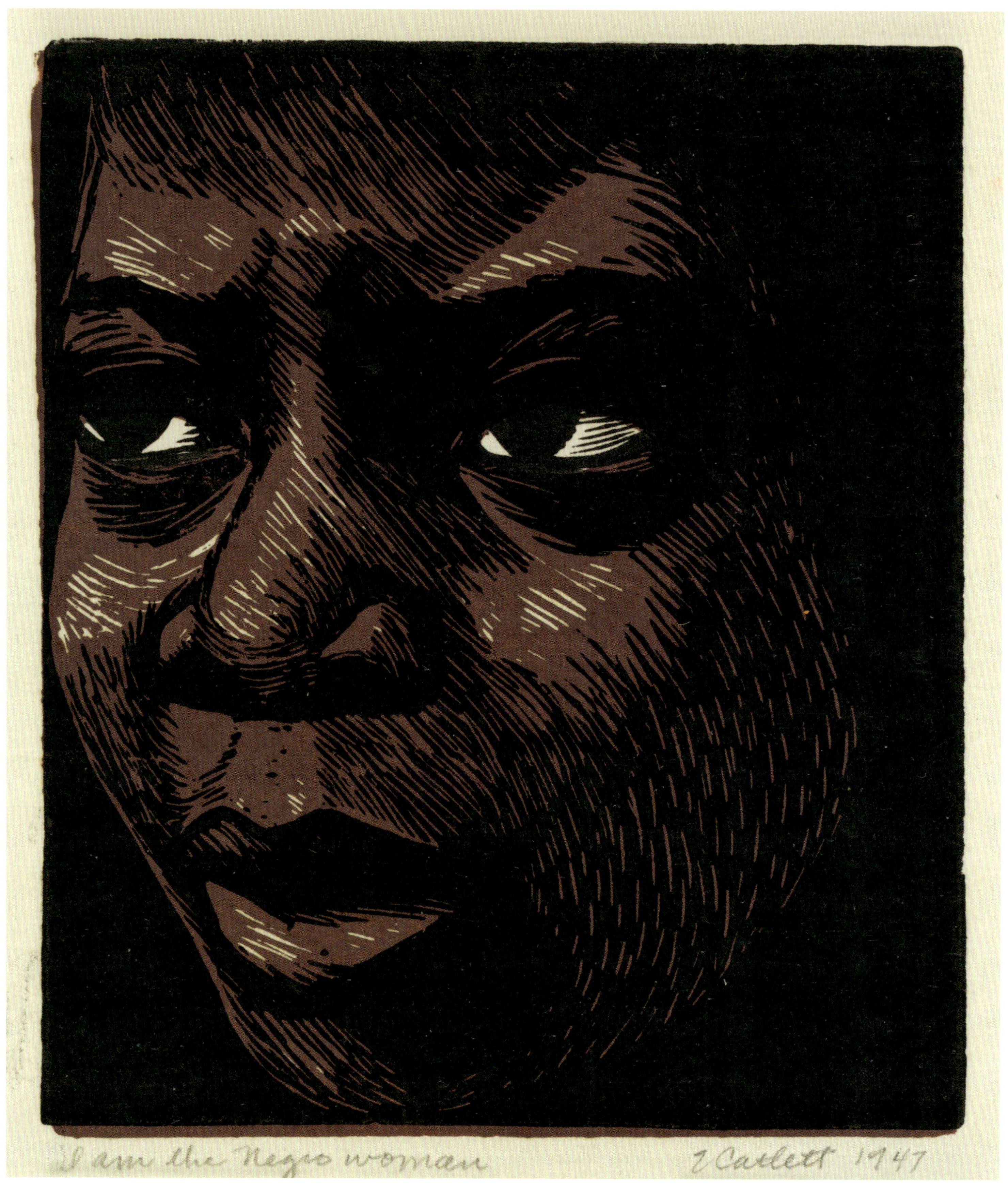

I am the Black Woman, from *The Black Woman* series, 1947, linocut, 5½ × 5 in., Courtesy of the Pennsylvania Academy of the Fine Arts, Art by Women Collection, Gift of Linda Lee Alter, 2011.1.172

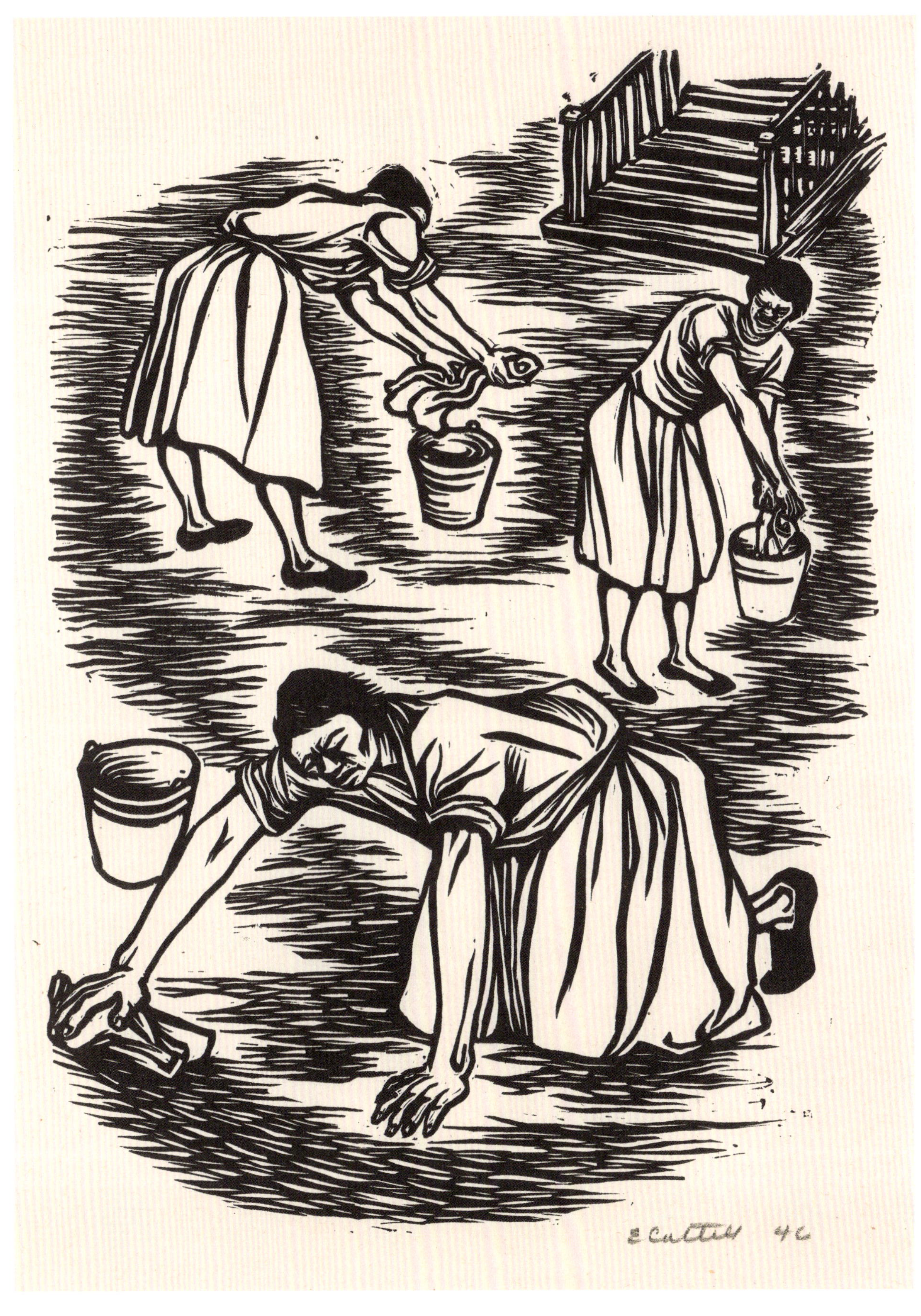

I Have Always Worked Hard in America..., from *The Black Woman* series, 1946, linocut, 11¼ × 9½ in., The Cleveland Museum of Art, Gift from funds of various donors to the Department of Prints and Drawings, 2000.95

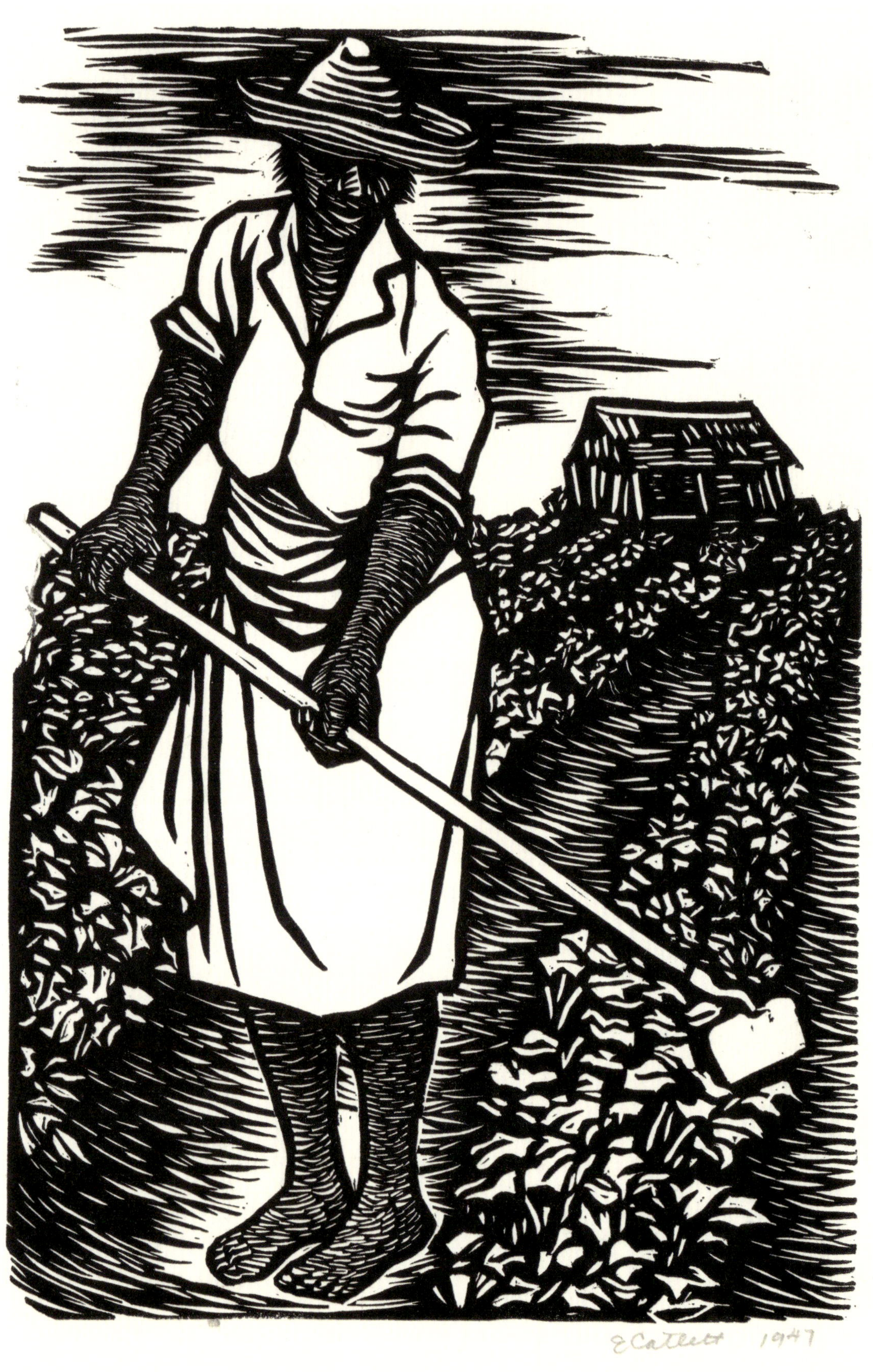

...*In the Fields*, from *The Black Woman* series, 1947, linocut, 18¾ × 12½ in., National Gallery of Art, Reba and Dave Williams Collection, Florian Carr Fund and Gift of the Print Research Foundation

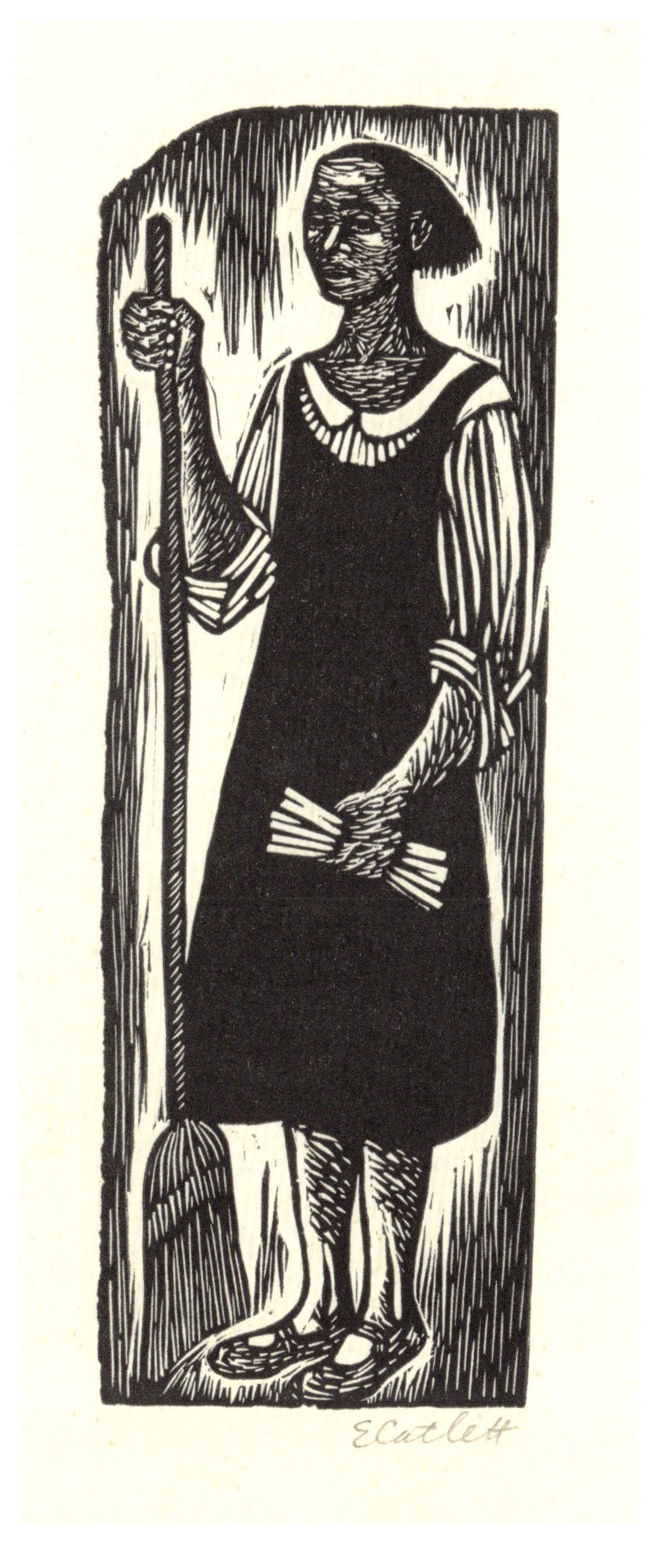

...In Other Folks Homes, from *The Black Woman* series, 1946, linocut, 9¹³⁄₁₆ × 6⅜ in., National Gallery of Art, Reba and Dave Williams Collection, Gift of Reba and Dave Williams

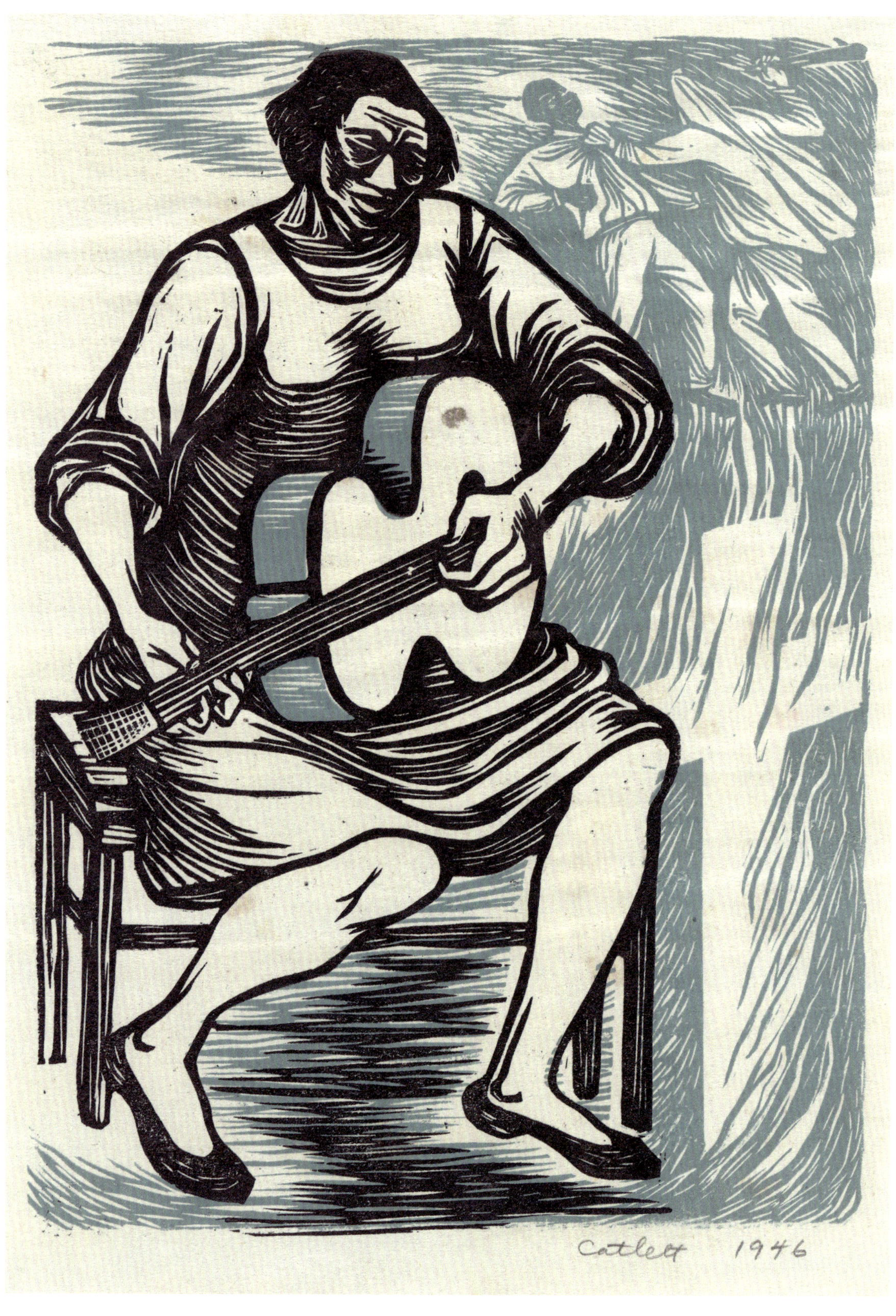

I have given the world my songs, from *The Black Woman* series, 1946, linocut, 12⅝ × 9⅜ in., Courtesy Virginia Museum of Fine Arts

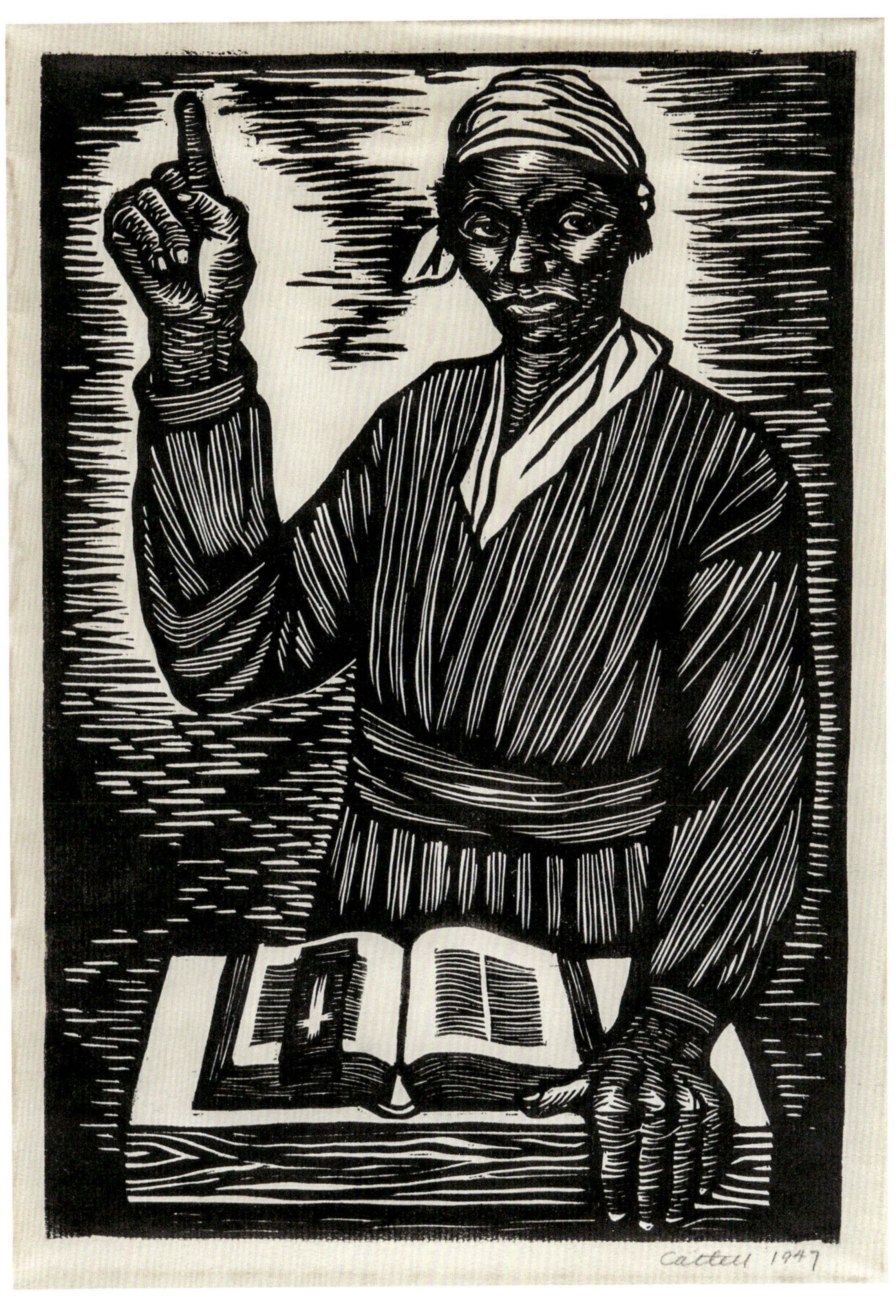

In Sojourner Truth I fought for the Rights of Women as well as Blacks, from *The Black Woman* series, 1947, linocut, 12⅝ × 9⅜ in., Private collection, acquired through the Barnett Aden Collection

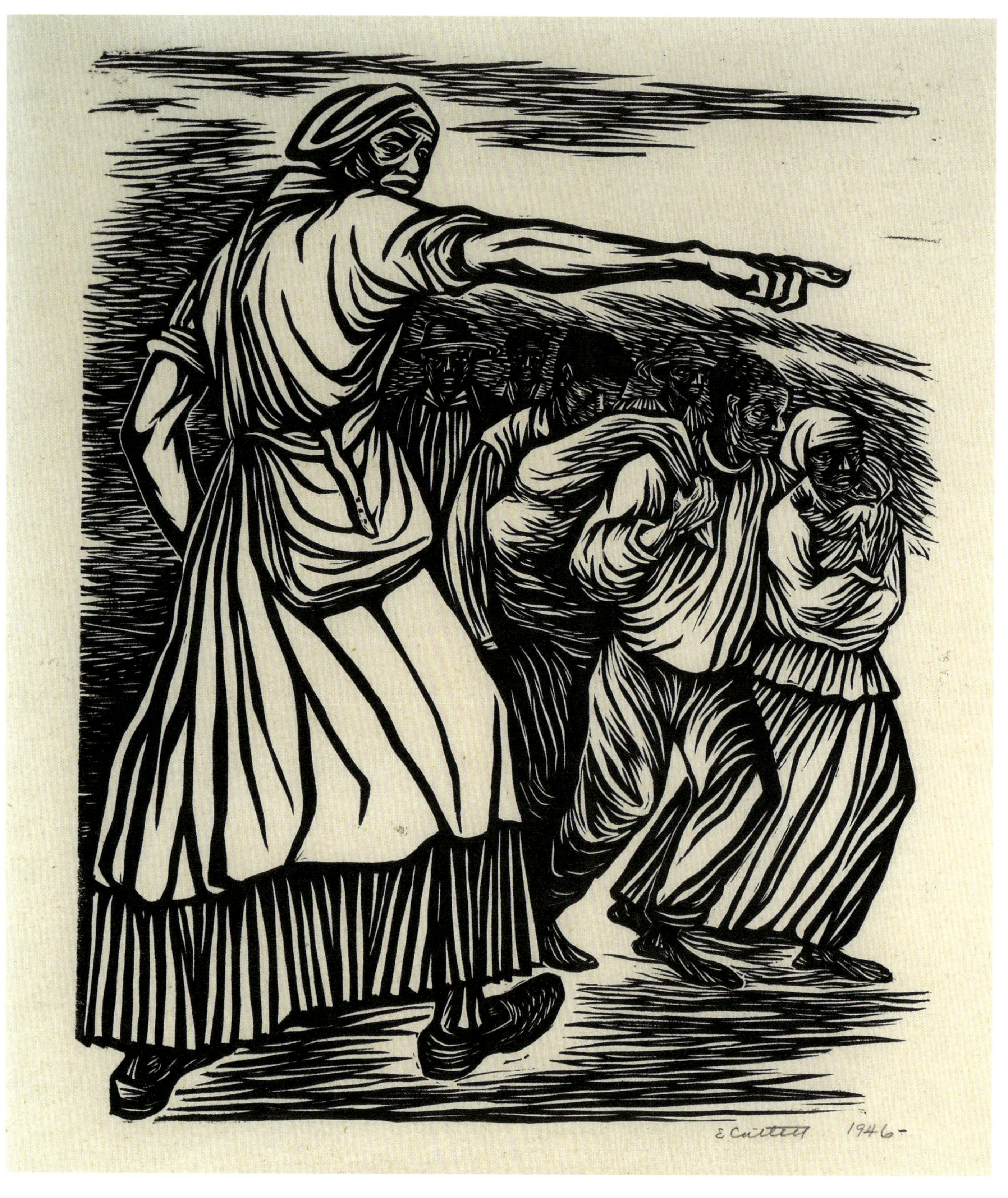

In Harriet Tubman I Helped Hundreds to Freedom, from *The Black Woman* series, 1946, linocut, 10 × 8¼ in., On loan from the Howard University Gallery of Art

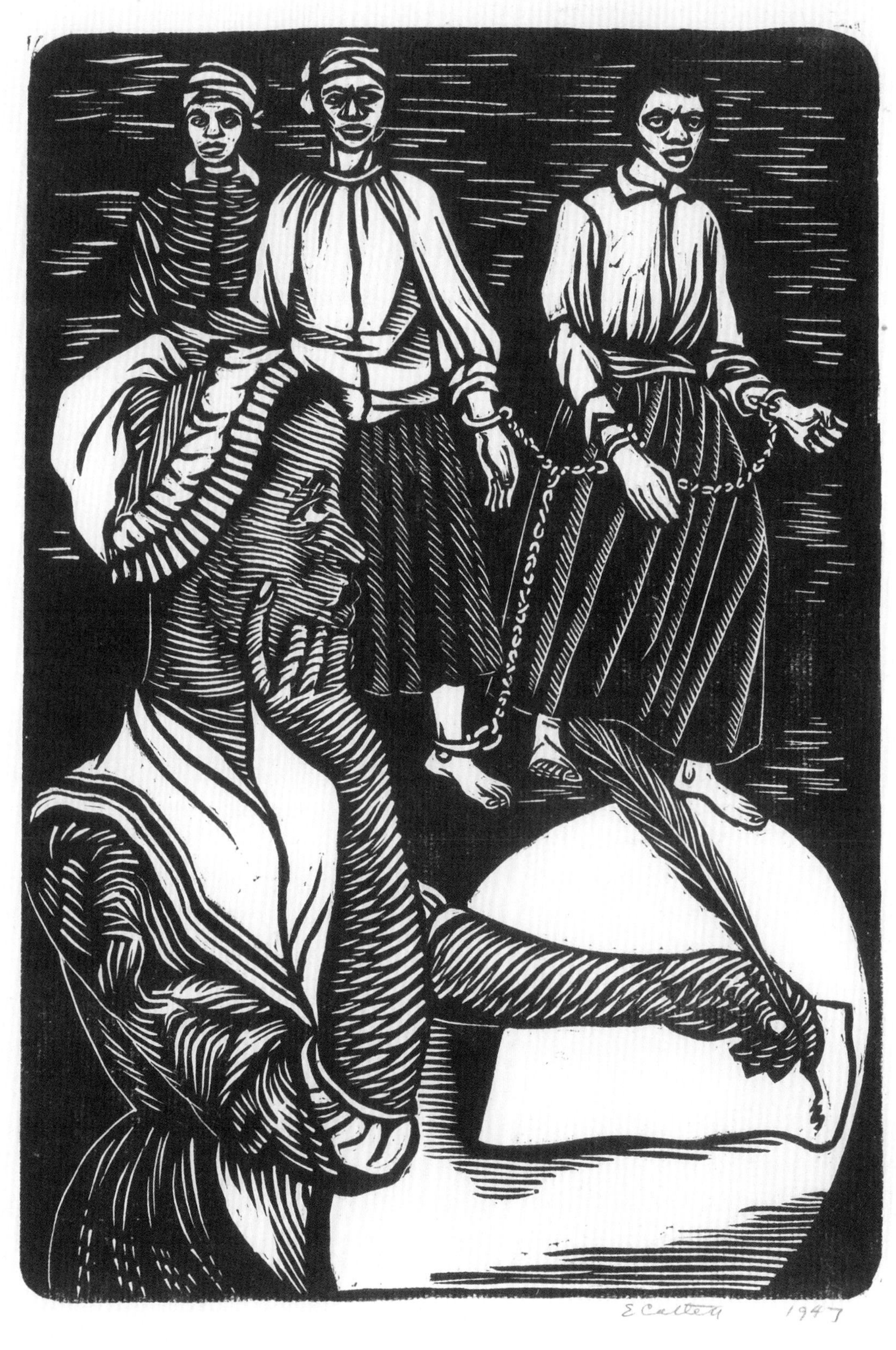

In Phillis Wheatley I Proved Intellectual Equality in the Midst of Slavery, from *The Black Woman* series, 1947, linocut, 11 × 8 in., On loan from the Howard University Gallery of Art

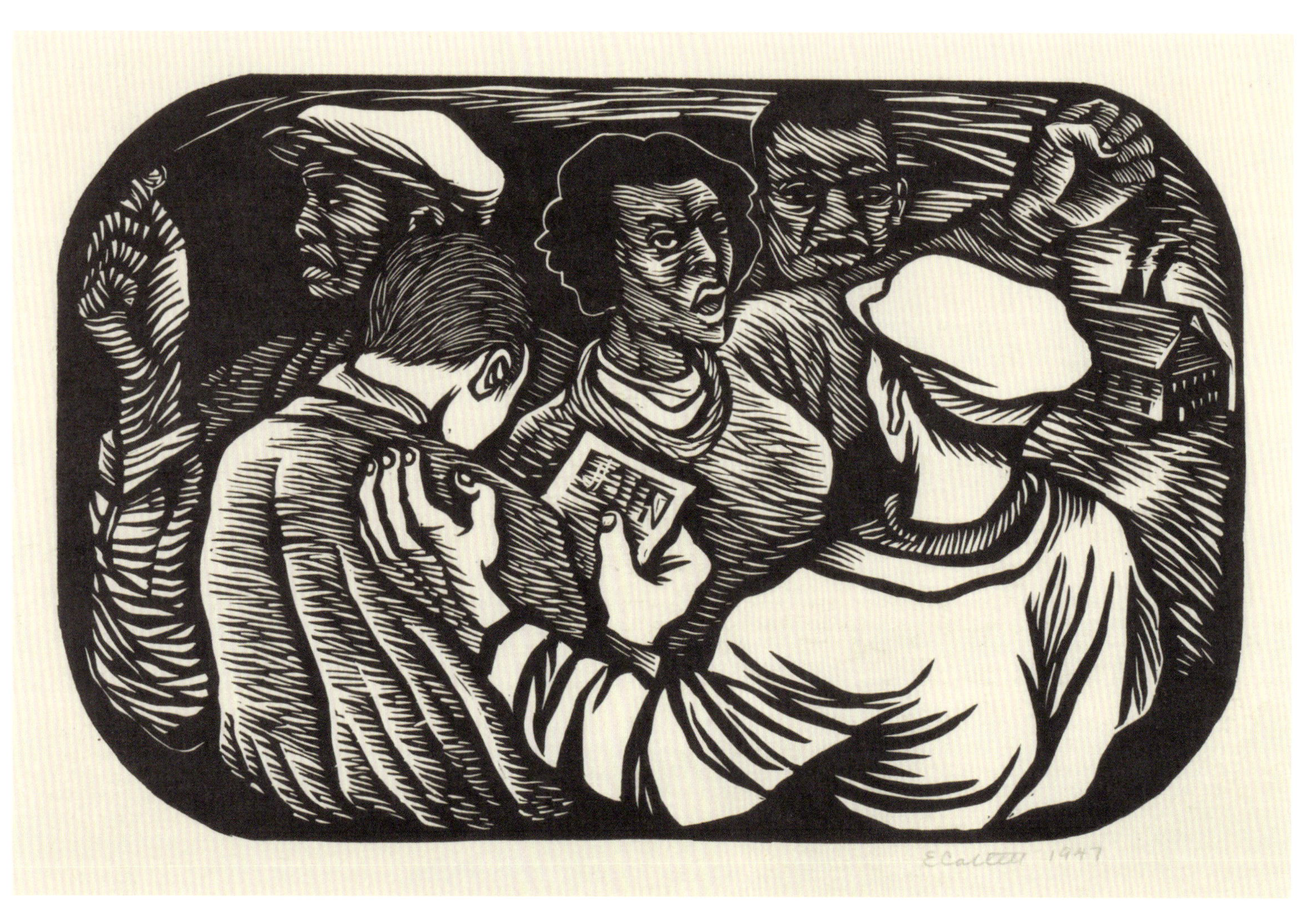

My Role has been Important in the Struggle to Organize the Unorganized, from *The Black Woman* series, c. 1946–1947, linocut, $12\frac{3}{16} \times 16\frac{1}{16}$ in., Peter Schneider and Susan DeJarnatt

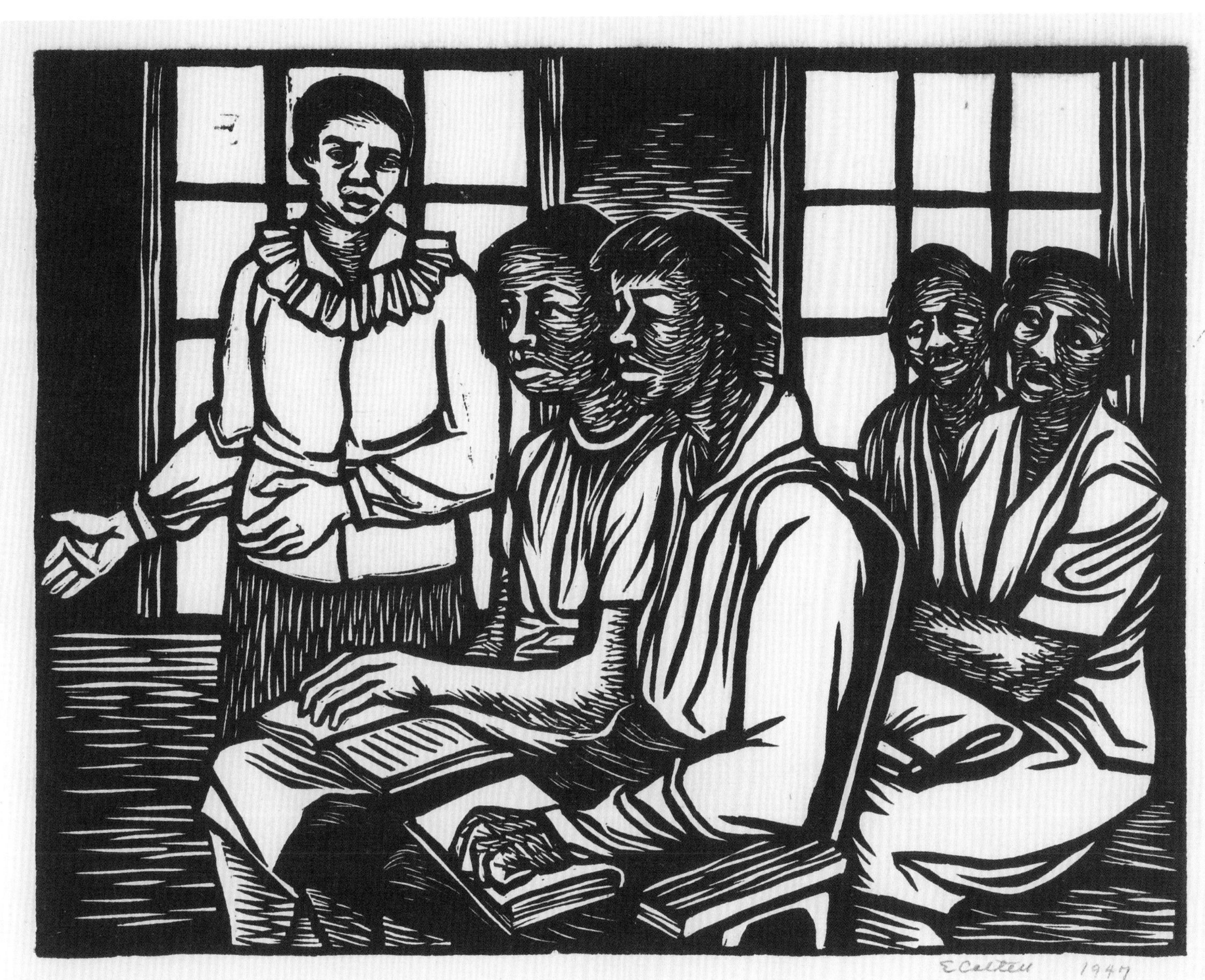

I Have Studied in Ever Increasing Numbers, from *The Black Woman* series, 1947, linocut, 8 × 10 in., On loan from the Howard University Gallery of Art

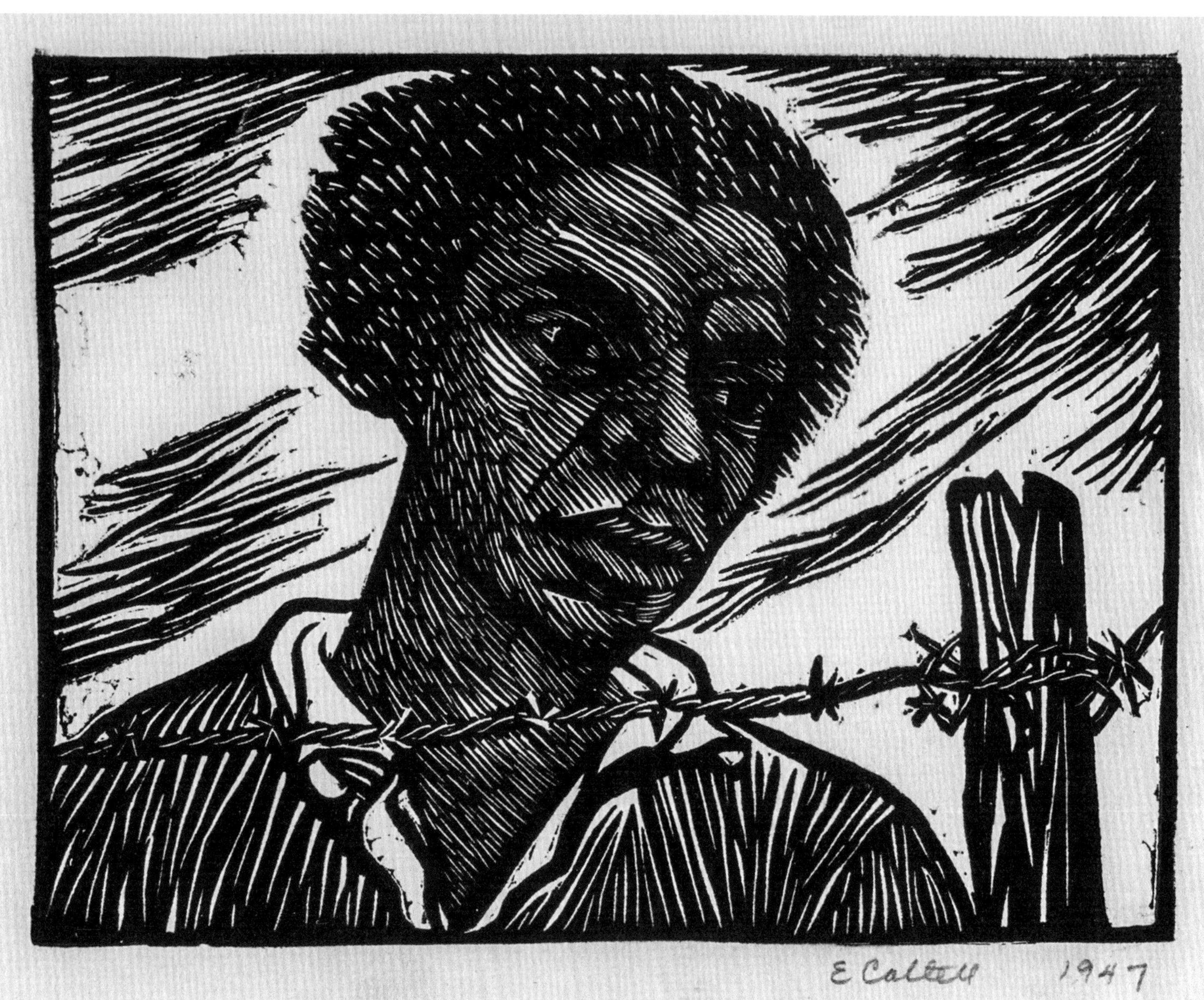

My reward has been bars between me and the rest of the land, from *The Black Woman* series, 1947, linocut, 8⅜ × 12½ in., Private collection, acquired through the Barnett Aden Collection

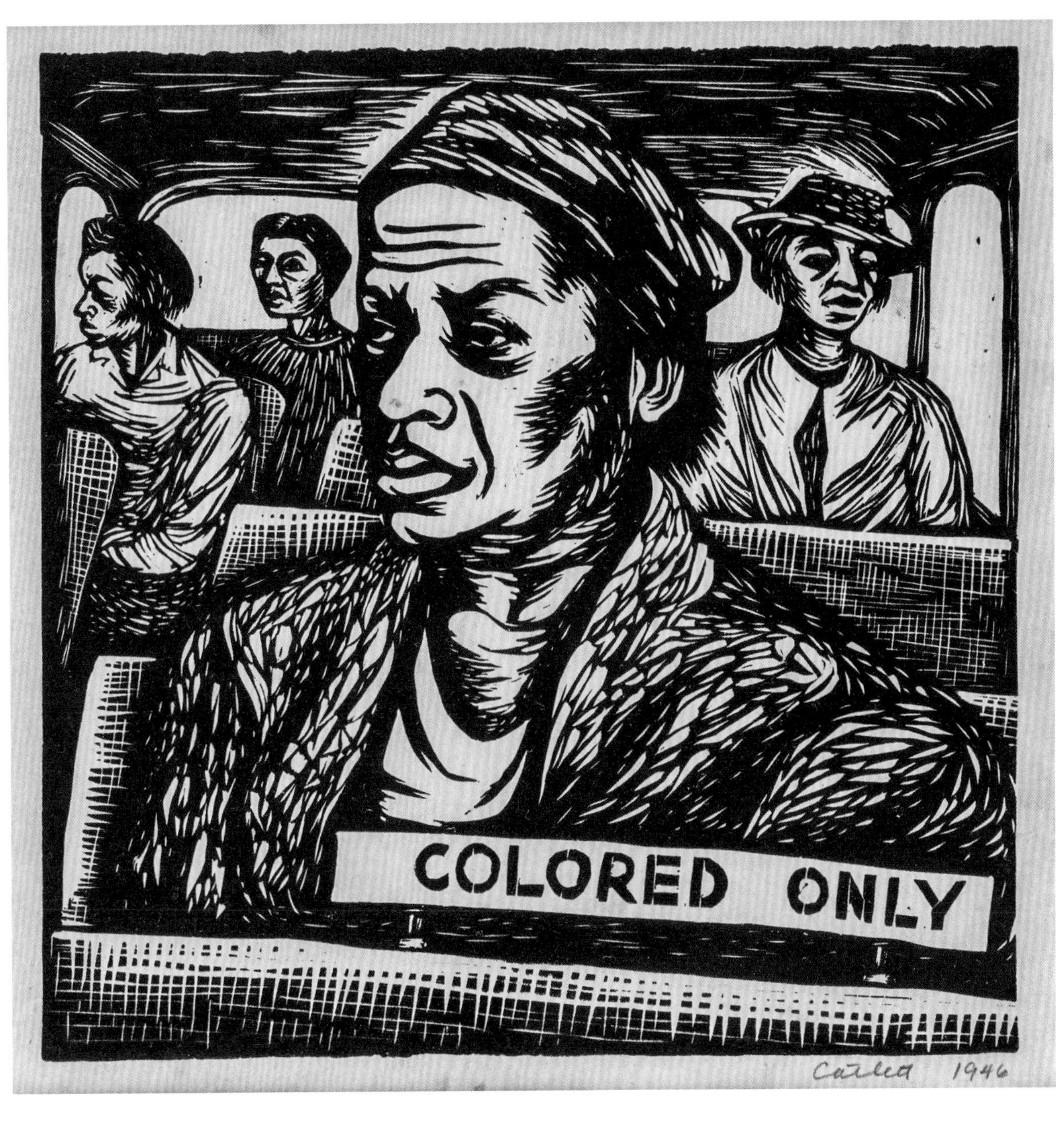

I Have Special Reservations, from *The Black Woman* series, 1946, linocut, 15⅛ × 11⅜ in., Private collection, acquired through the Barnett Aden Collection

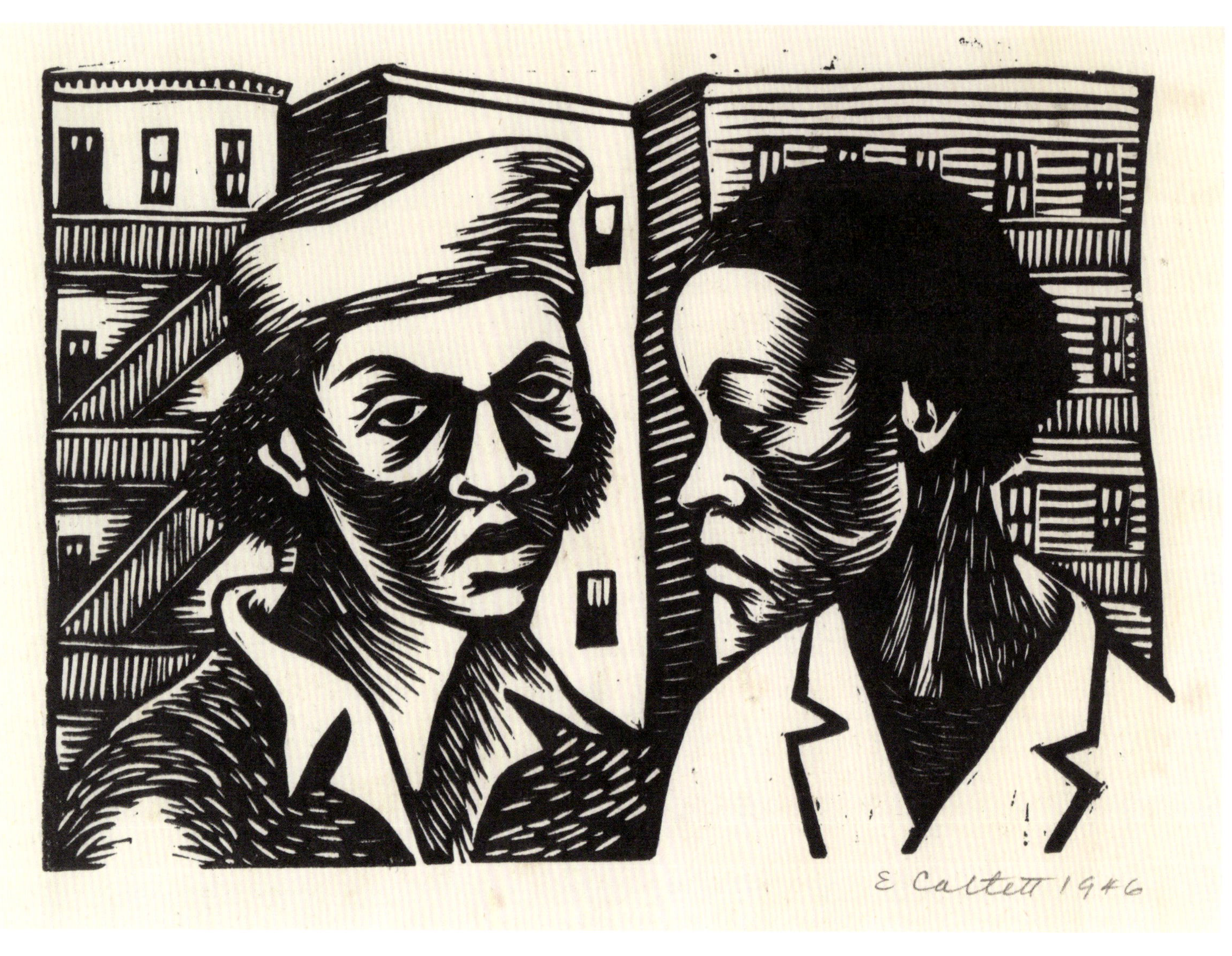

...Special Houses, from *The Black Woman* series, 1946, linocut, 8¼ × 9⅜ in., Private collection, acquired through the Barnett Aden Collection

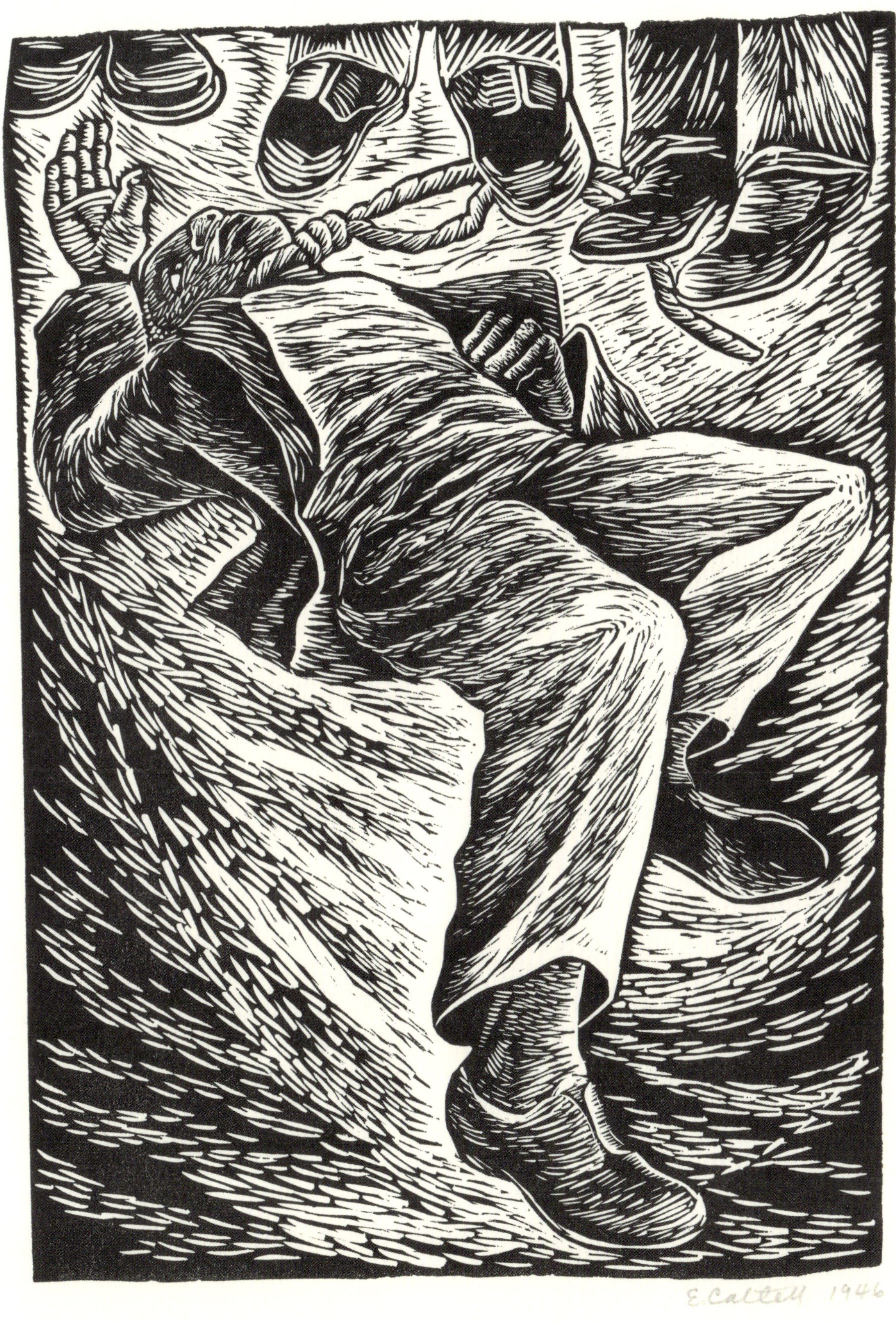

...And a special fear for my loved ones, from *The Black Woman* series, 1946, linocut, $18\frac{15}{16} \times 12\frac{1}{2}$ in., National Gallery of Art, Reba and Dave Williams Collection, Florian Carr Fund and Gift of the Print Research Foundation

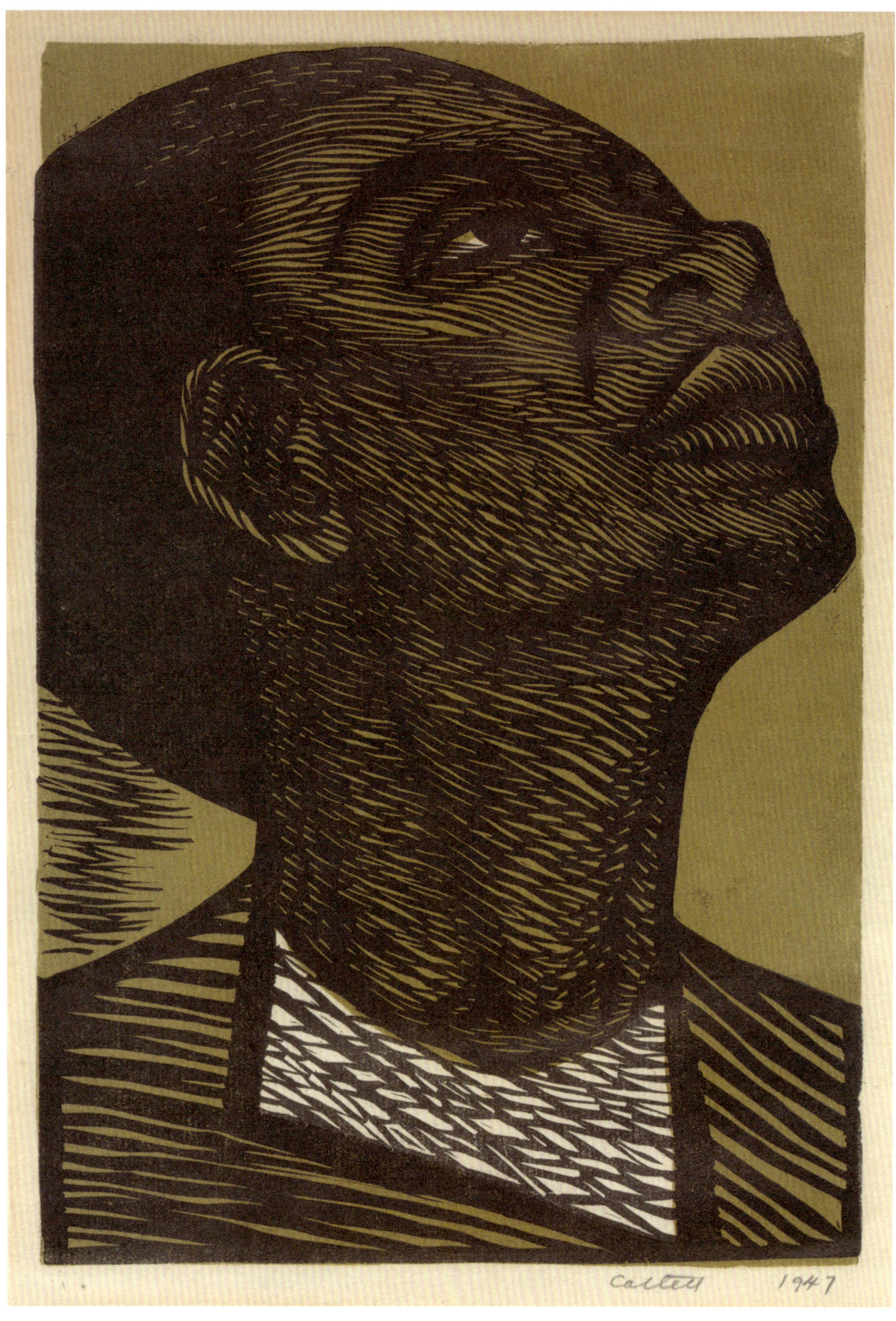

My right is a future of equality with other Americans, from *The Black Woman* series, 1946–1947, linoleum cut printed in green and black, 10¾ × 8⅛ in., The Baltimore Museum of Art, Purchased as the gift of Jeffrey A. Legum, Baltimore, BMA 2013.5

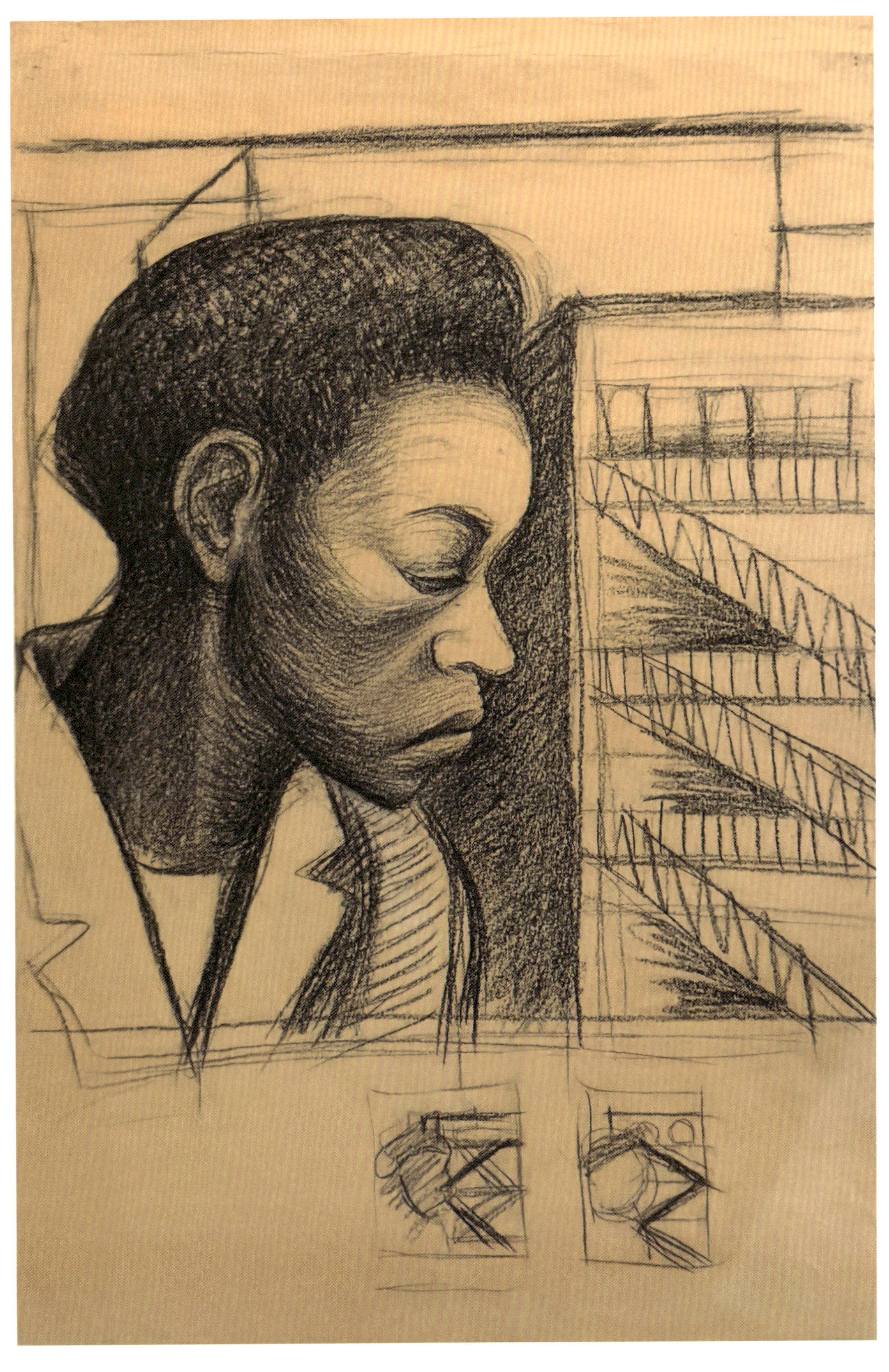

Head of a Woman, 1946, black crayon and brush and black ink, 12¾ × 9¼ in., The Morgan Library & Museum, NY, Purchase on the Manley Family Fund, 2022.162

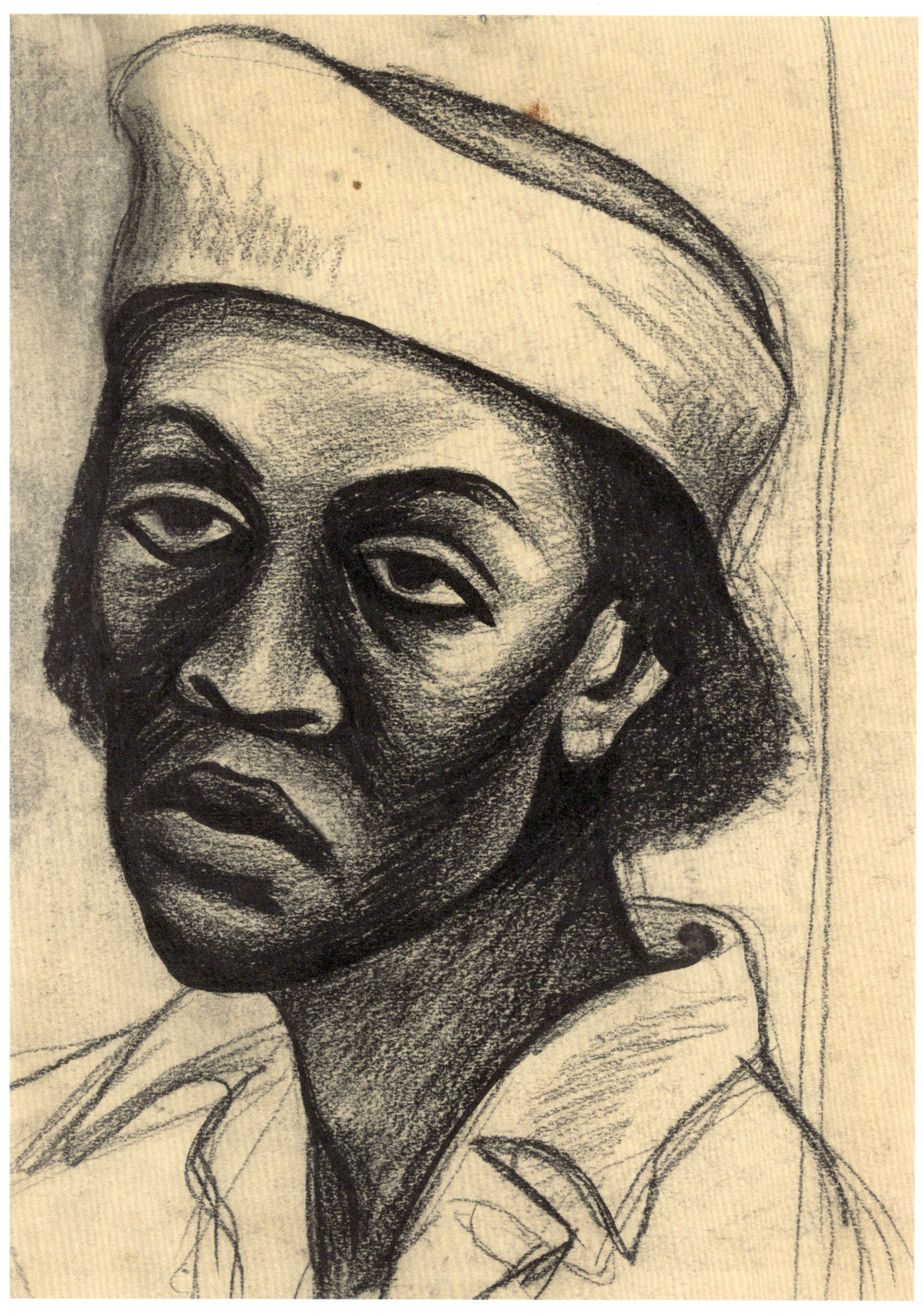

Study for Special Houses, c. 1946, litho crayon, 19½ × 12¾ in., Collection of Helen Nitkin, Courtesy of Conner-Rosenkranz

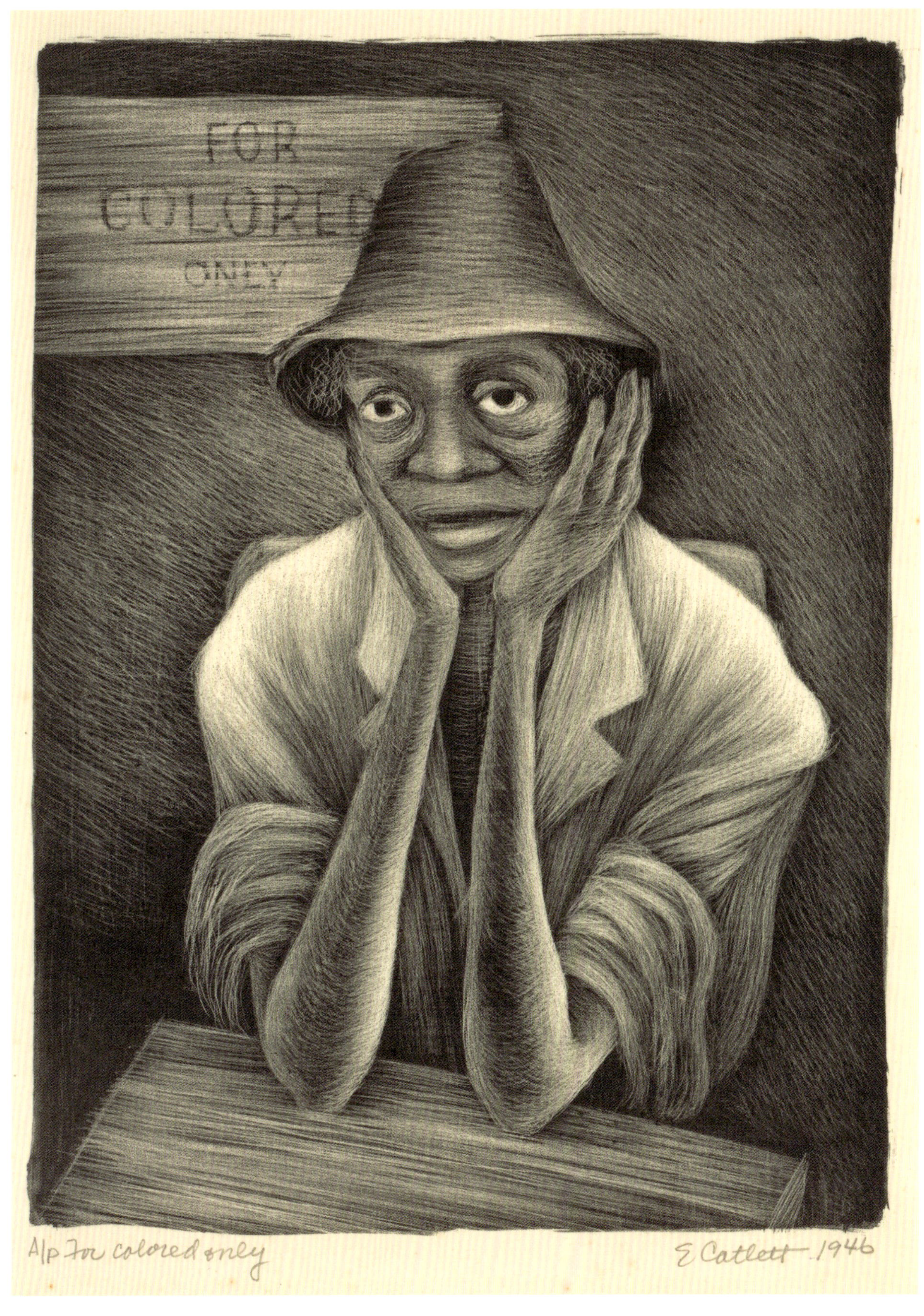

For Colored Only, 1946, tusche and crayon lithograph with scraping, $12\frac{11}{16} \times 9\frac{3}{4}$ in., The Baltimore Museum of Art, Dr. and Mrs. William W. Magruder Fund, BMA 1995.93

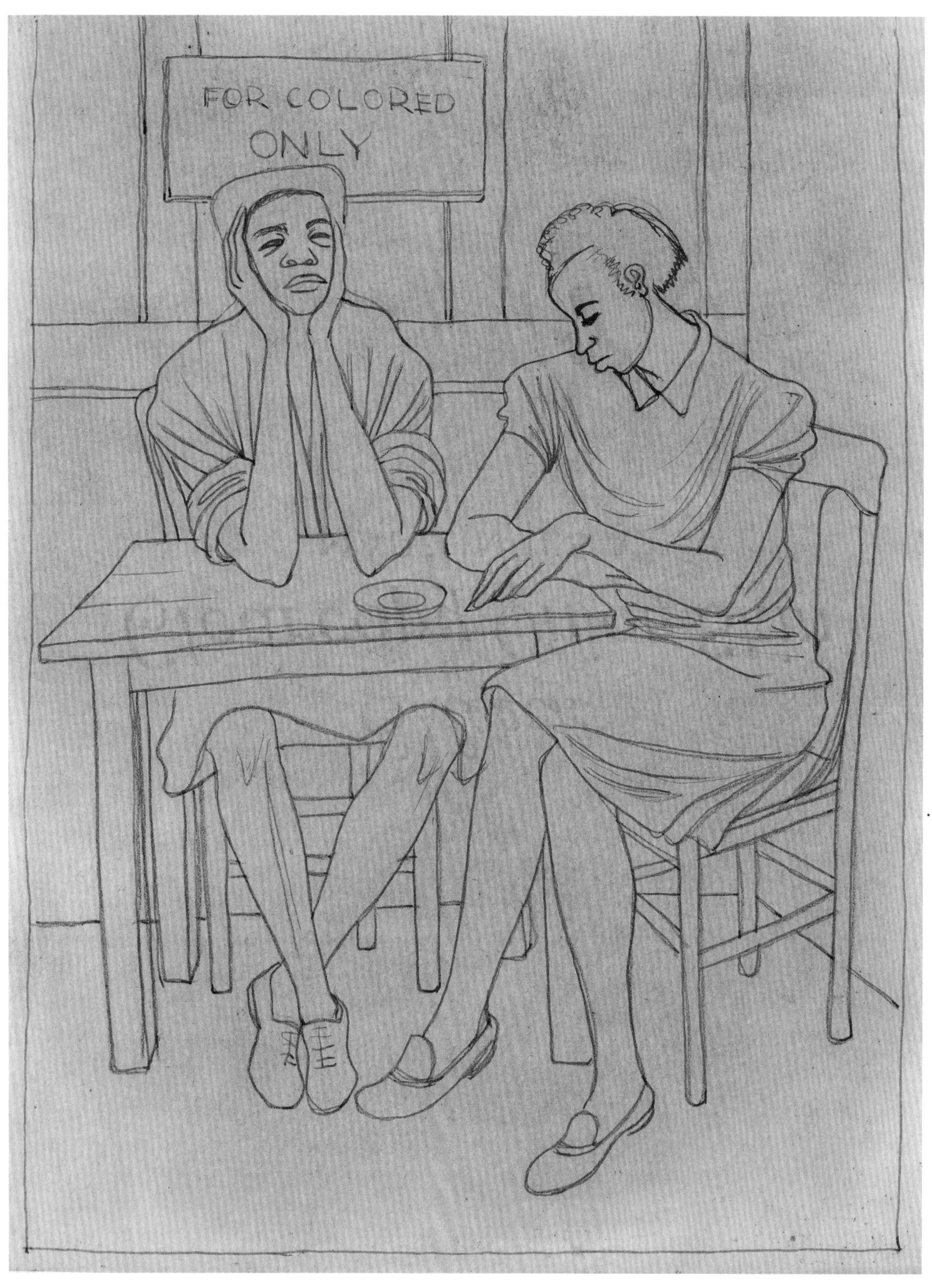

For Colored Only, 1946, ink and graphite on tracing paper, 11 × 8½ in., Williams College Museum of Art, Museum purchase, Joseph O. Eaton Fund, Wachenheim Family Fund, MacDonald Fund, Fogg Fund, Otis Family Acquisition Trust

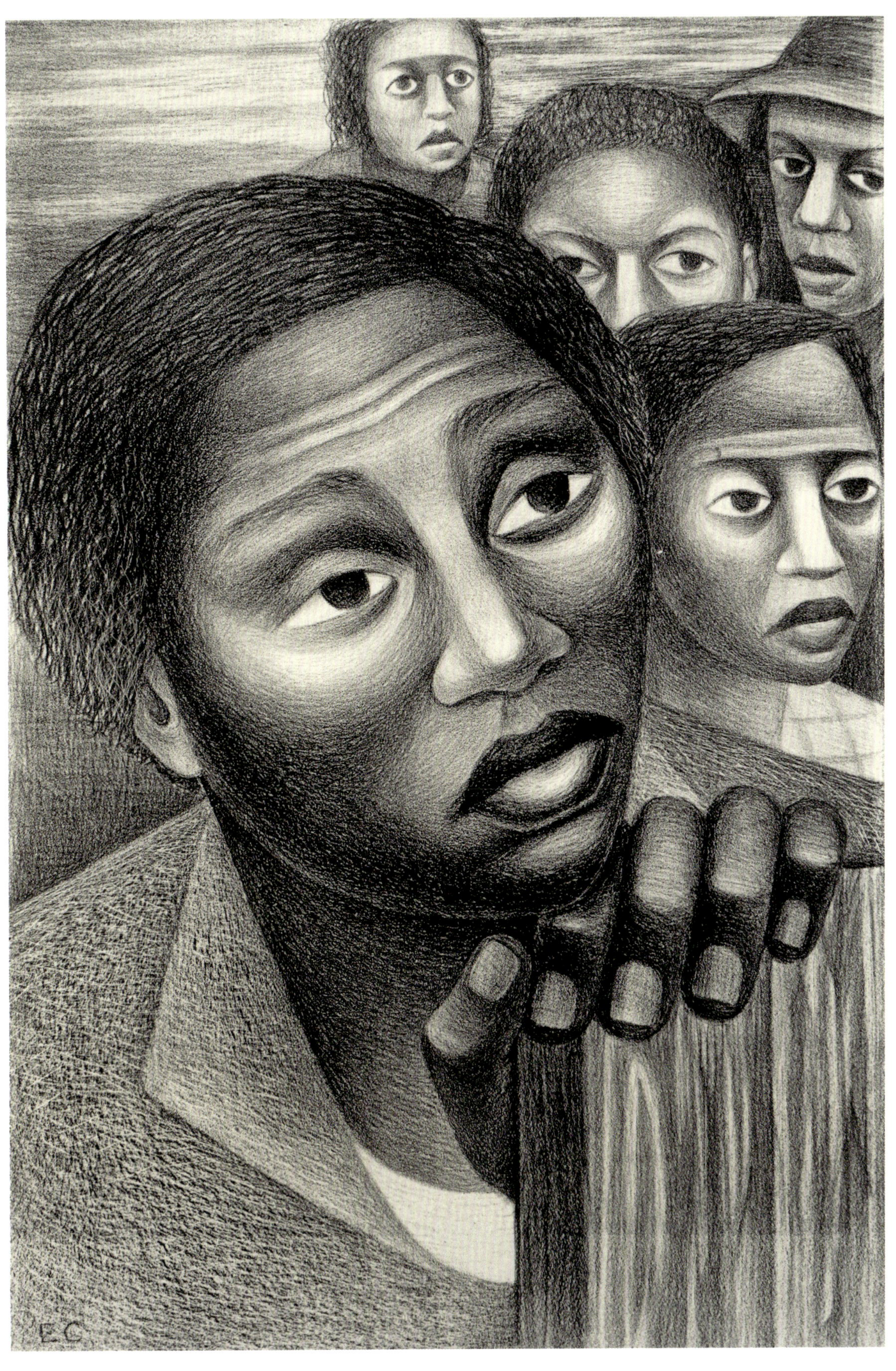

Mujer Negra, 1946, lithograph, $24\frac{7}{16} \times 19\frac{13}{16}$ in., Colección Academia de Artes, México

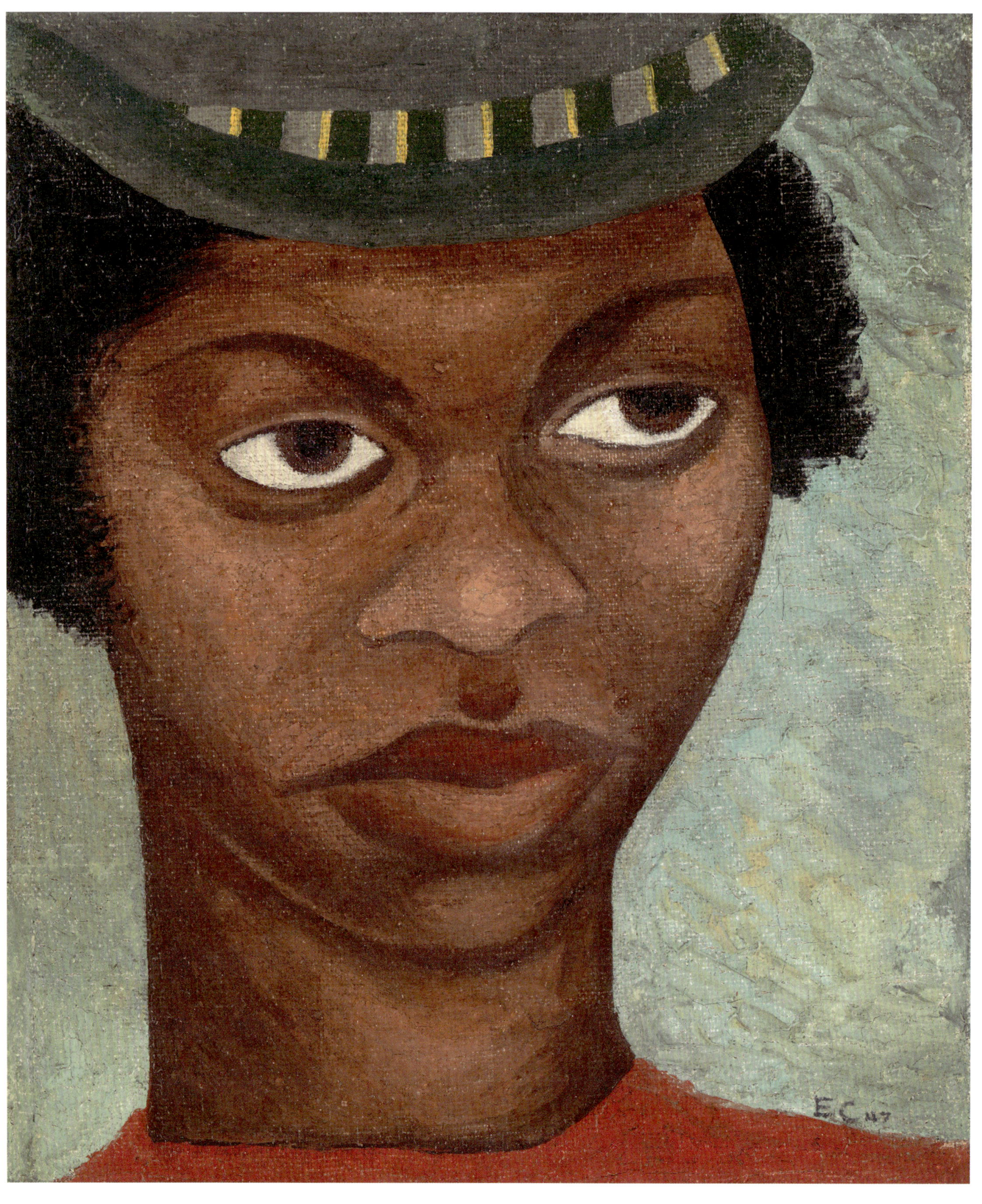

Untitled, 1947, oil on canvas, 10 × 8 in., Private collection, acquired through the Barnett Aden Collection

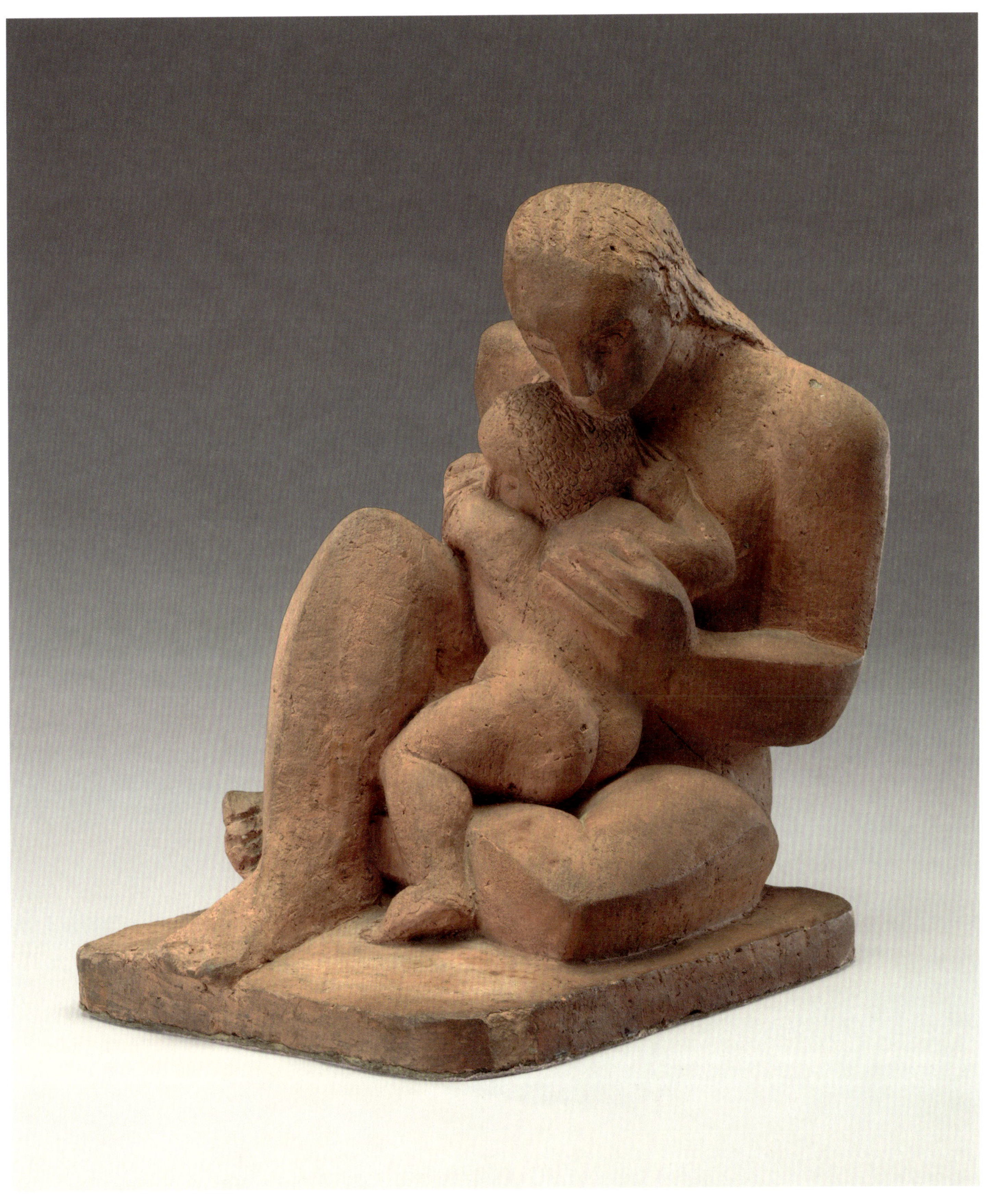

Mother and Child, 1942–1944, terracotta, 14 in., Private collection

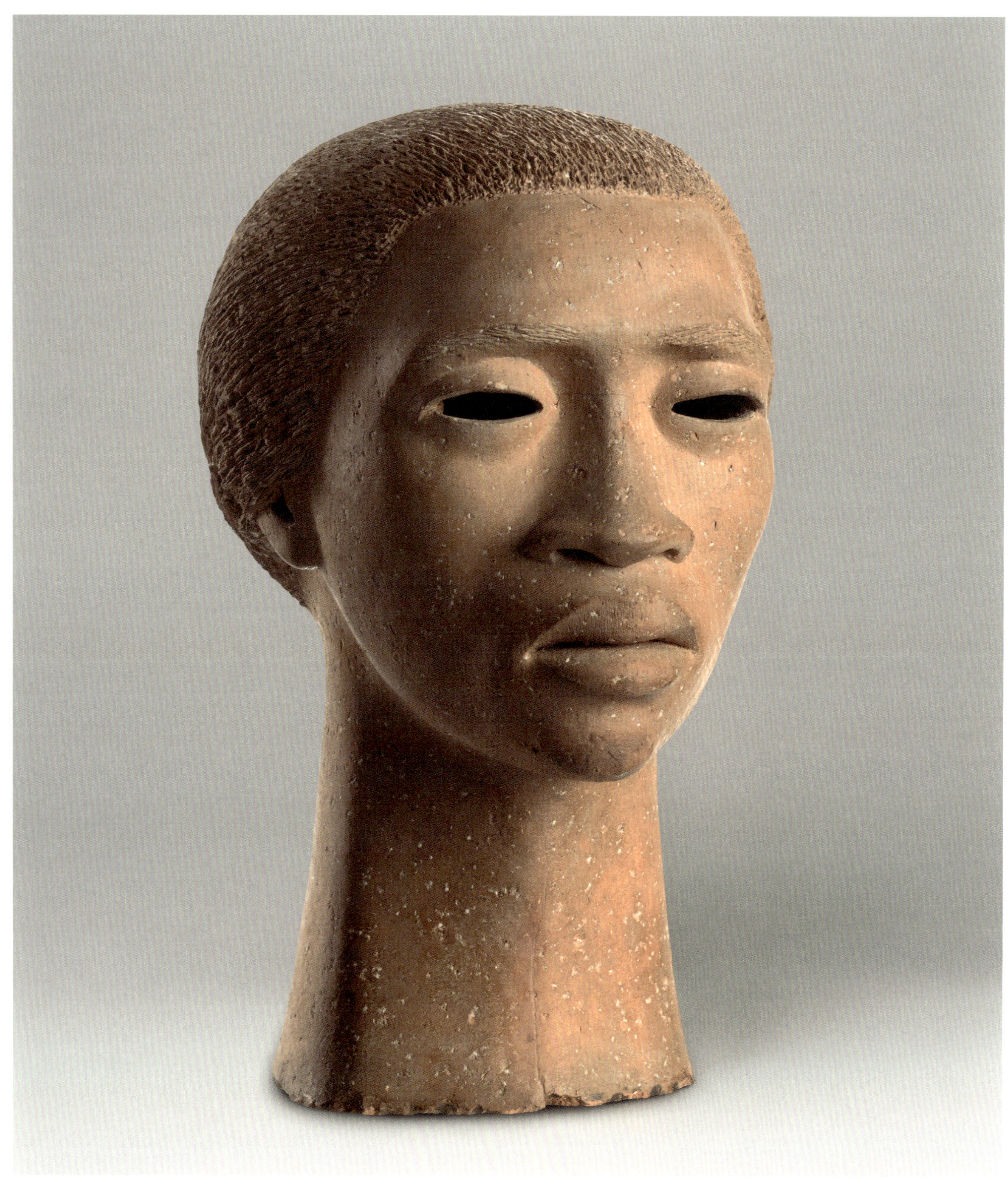

Head of a Negro Woman, 1946, terracotta, 12 × 7 × 9 in., Collection of the Smithsonian National Museum of African American History and Culture, Gift of Robert L. Johnson, 2015.2.4

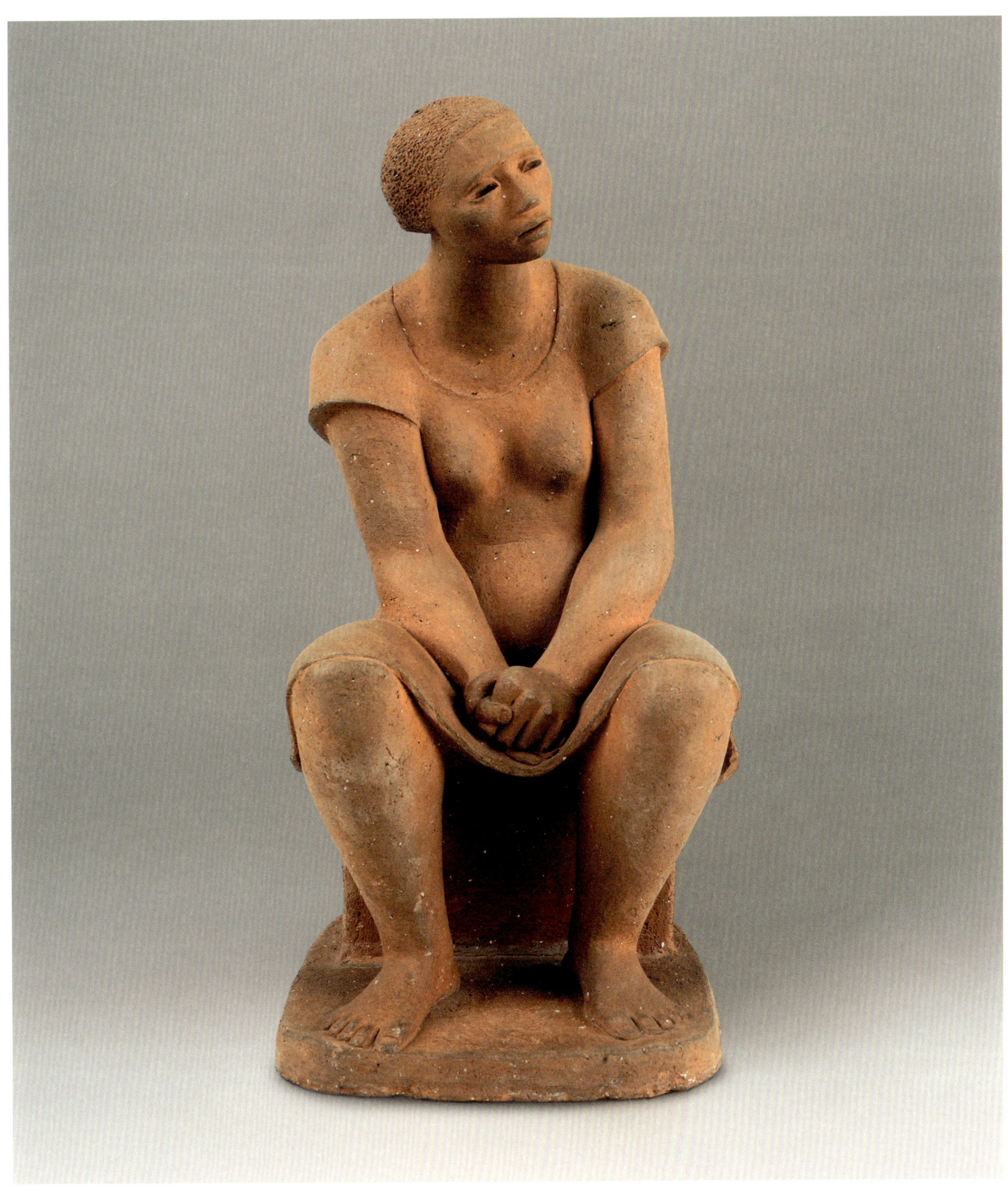

Tired, 1946, terracotta, 13½ × 6 × 7 in., On loan from the Howard University Gallery of Art

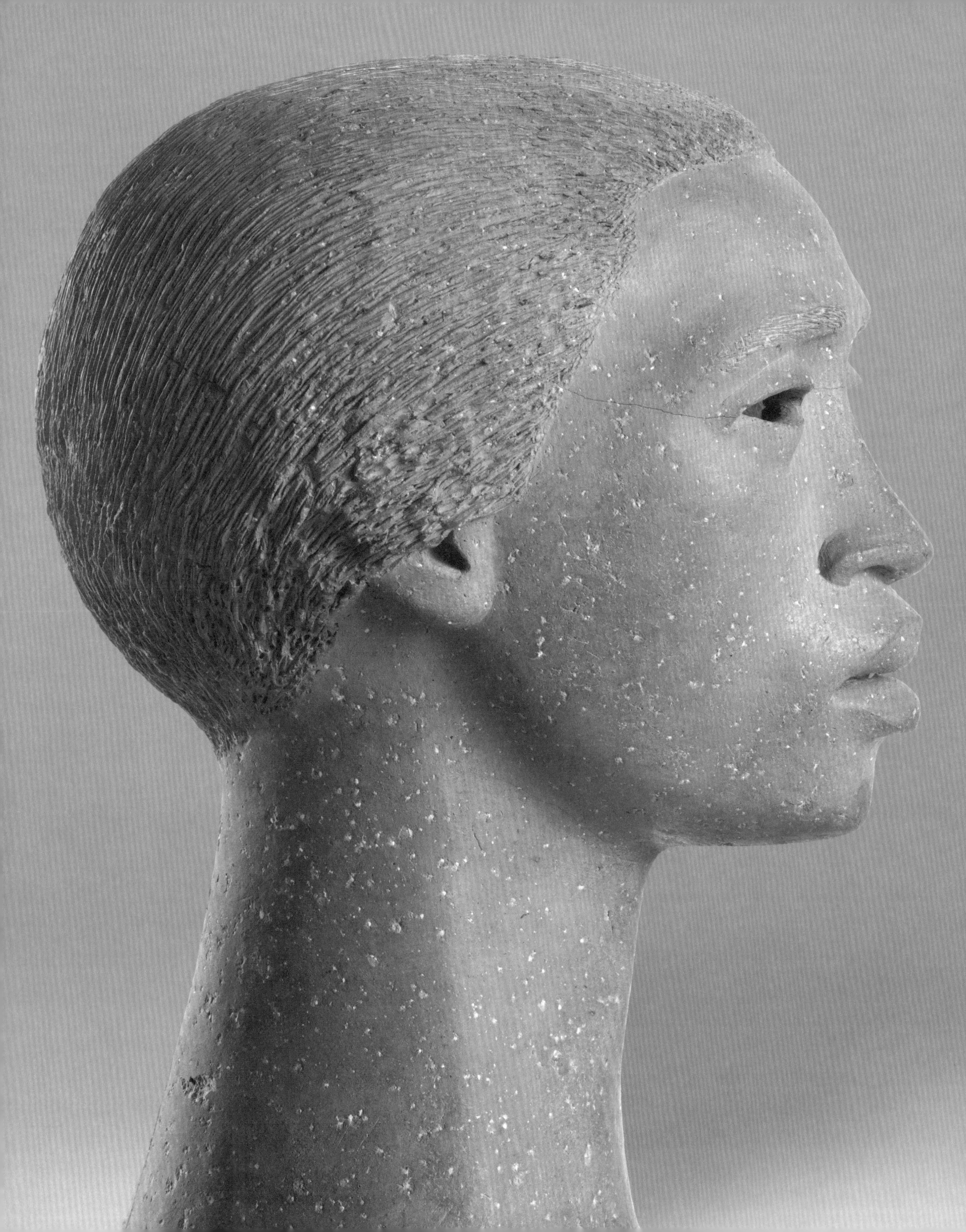

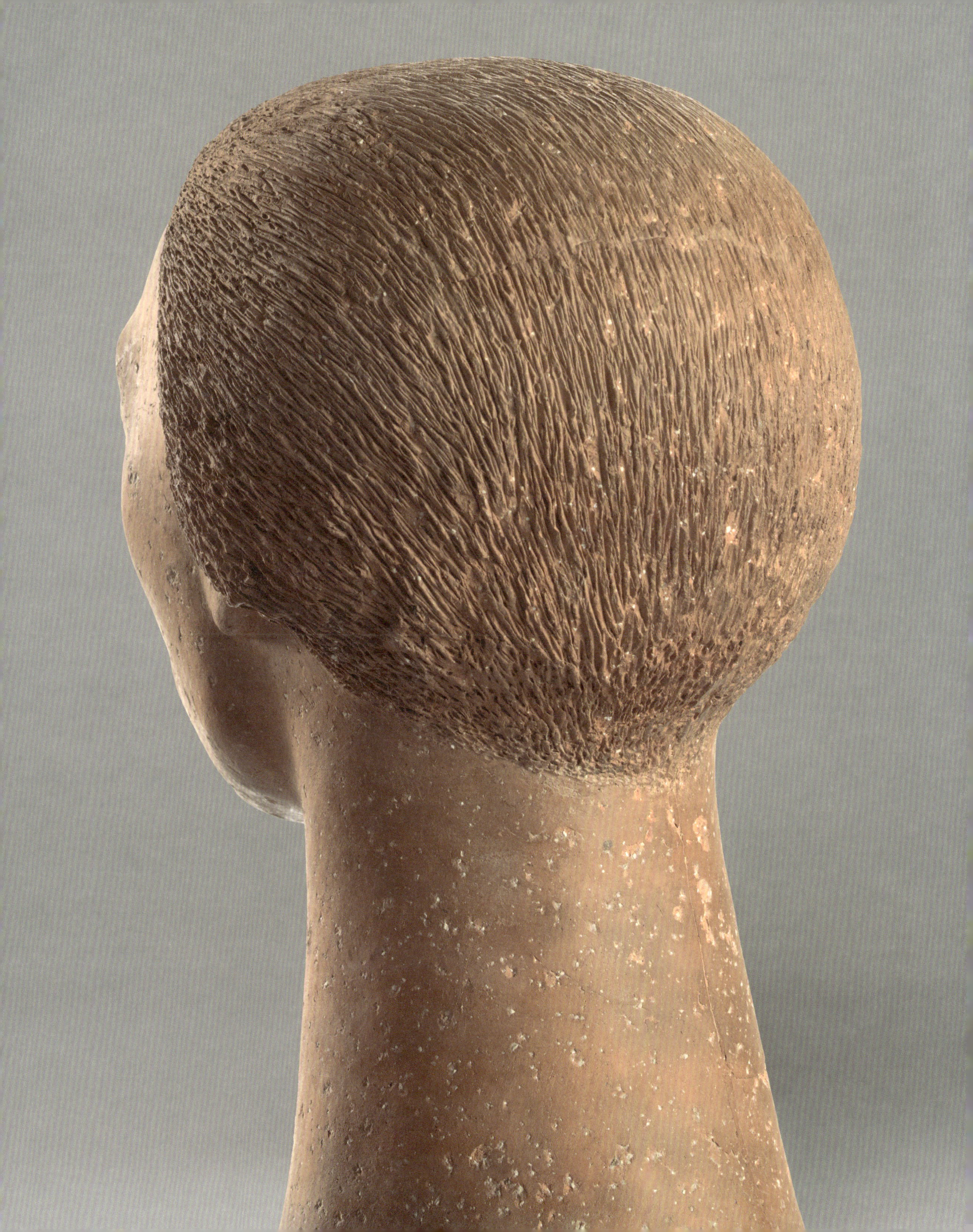

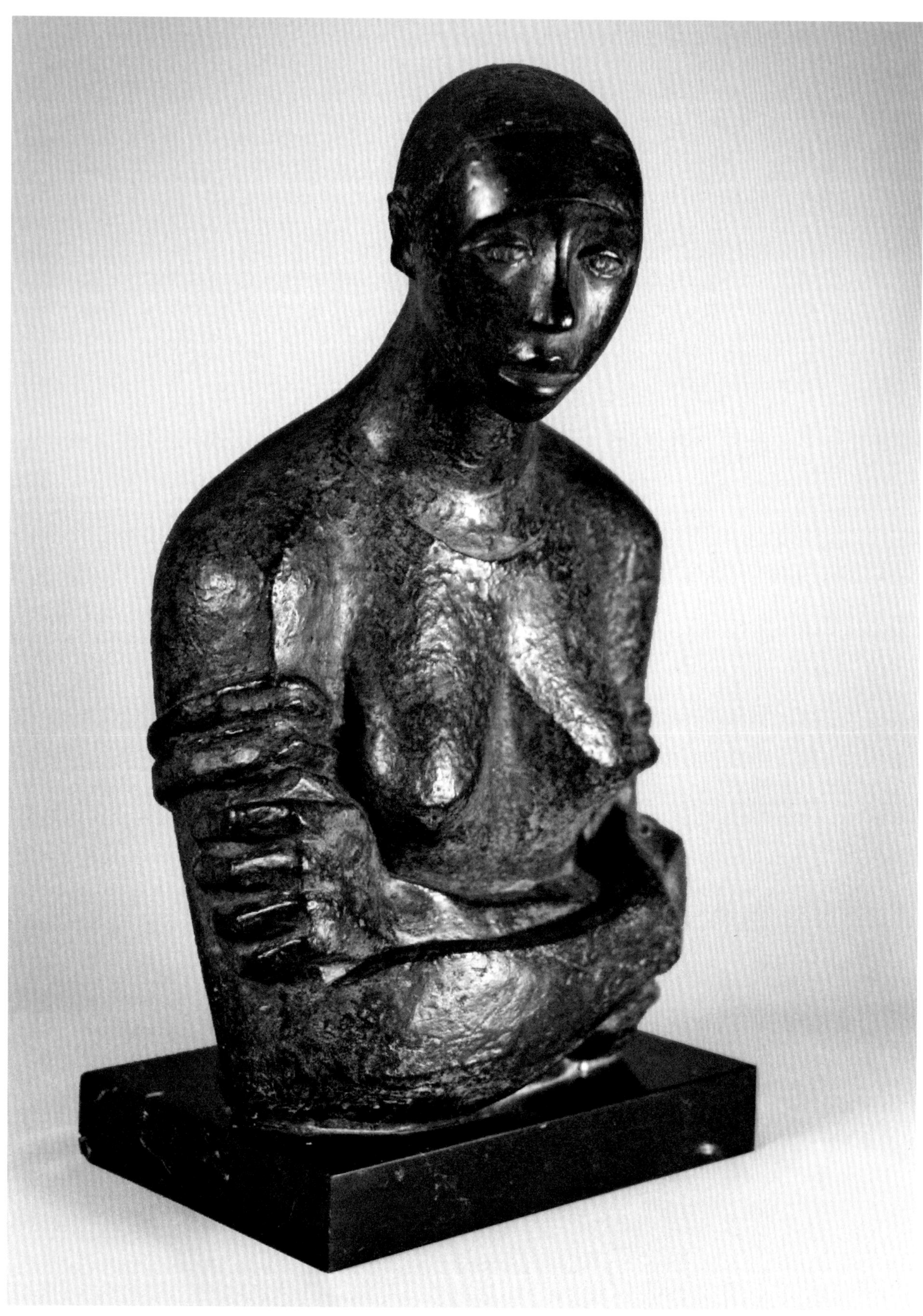

Pensive, 1946, bronze, 18½ × 9 × 7 in., From the Hampton University Museum Collection, Hampton, VA

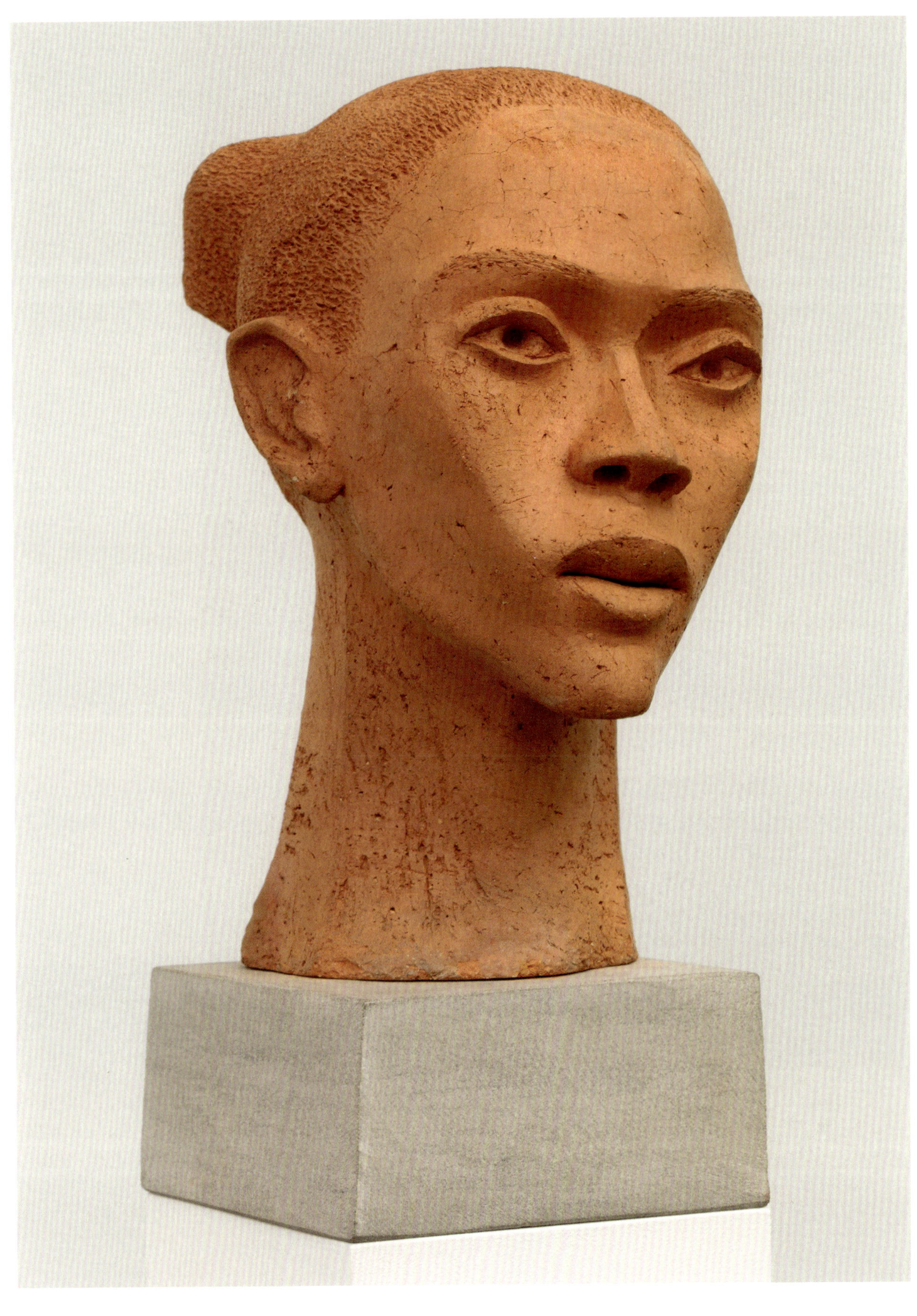

Young Girl, 1946, terracotta, 11½ × 6½ × 9 in.,
Clark Atlanta University Art Museum, Atlanta
Art Annuals: Second Edward B. Alford Purchase
Award, Sculpture, 1946.008

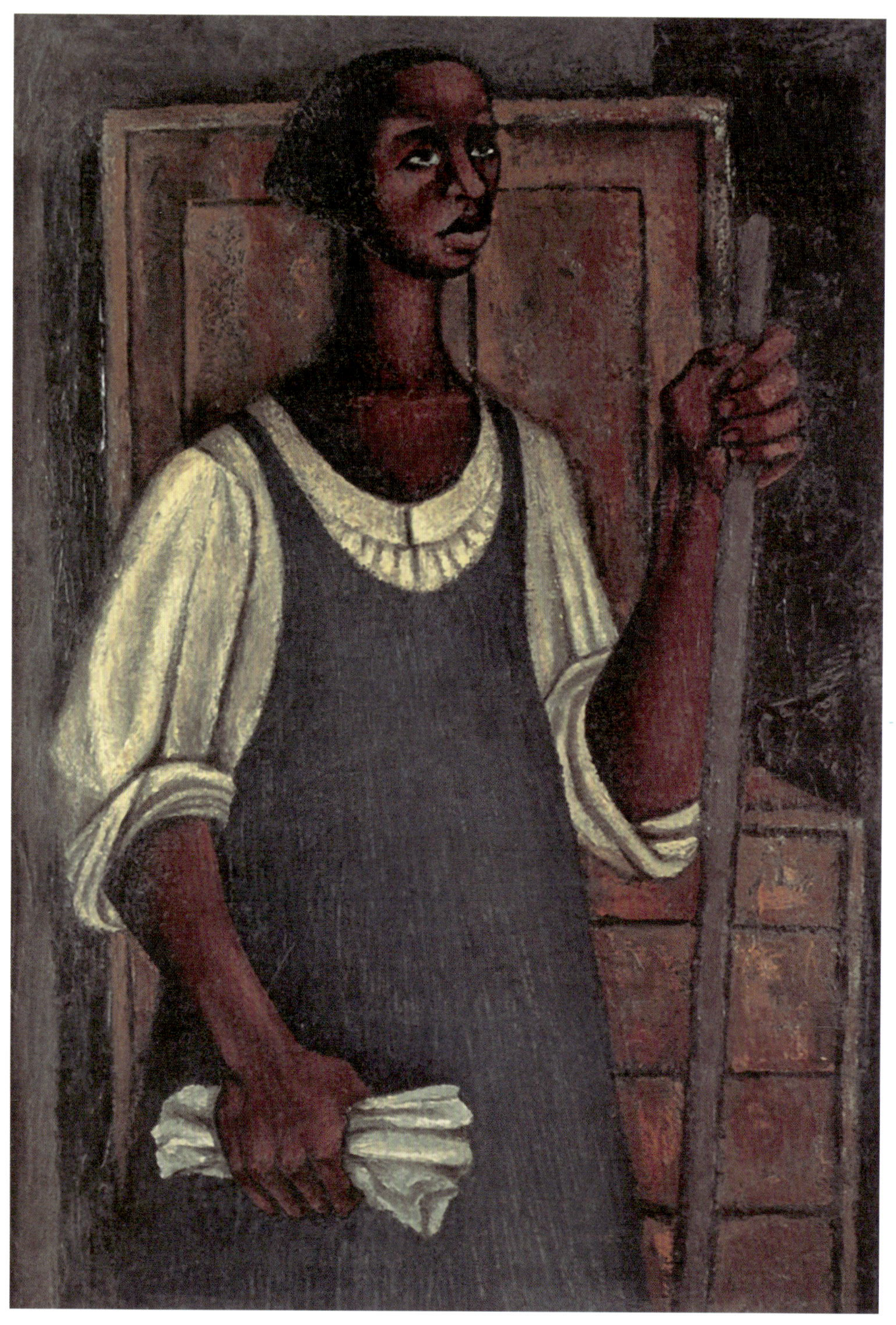

Working Woman, 1947, oil on canvas, 23⅜ × 16⅛ in., Robert L. Johnson, from the Barnett Aden Collection

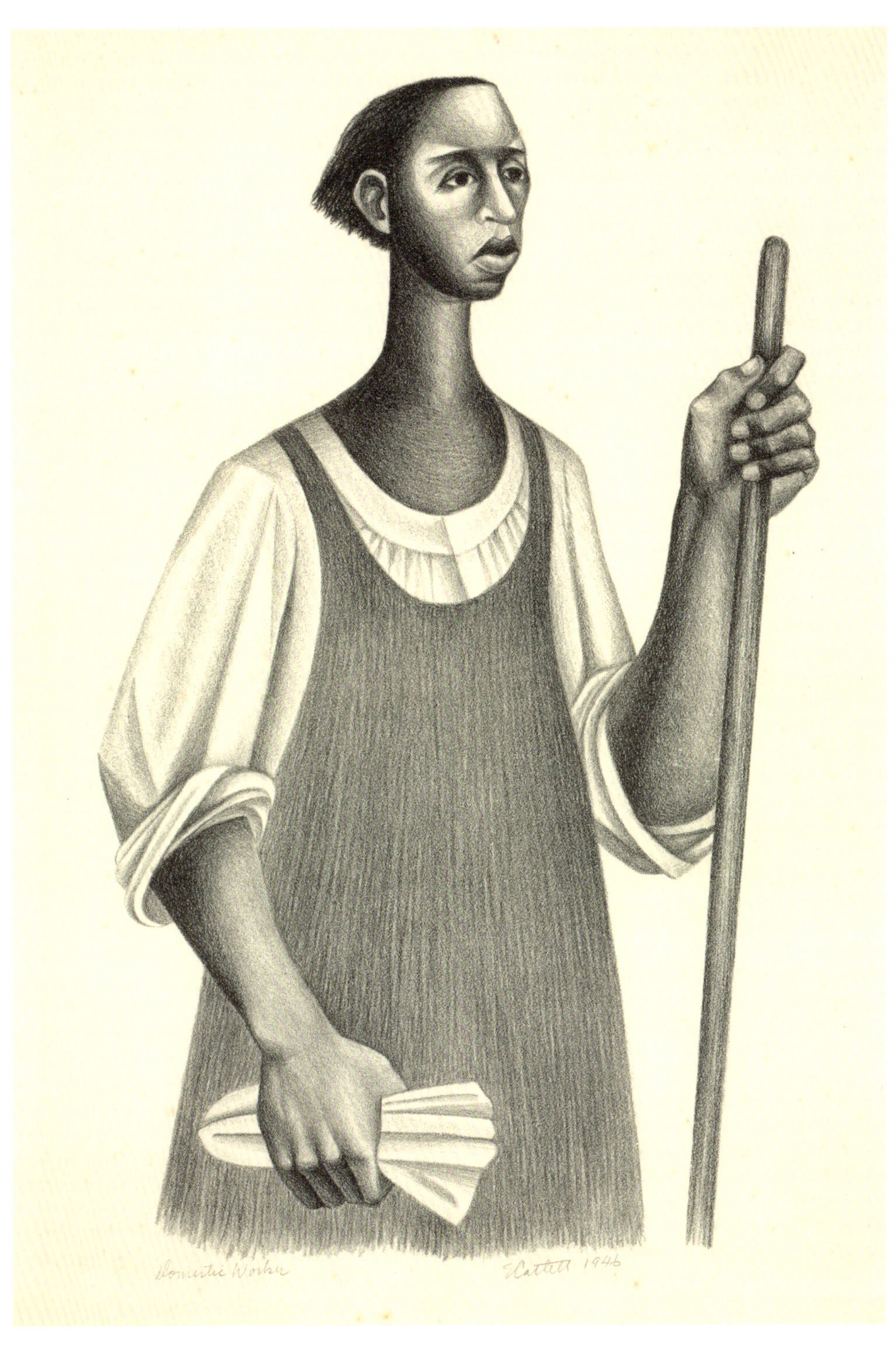

Domestic Worker, 1946, crayon lithograph with scraping, 24⅜ × 19⅝ in., The Baltimore Museum of Art, Purchased as the gift of Lorraine and Mark Schapiro, Baltimore, BMA 1997.20

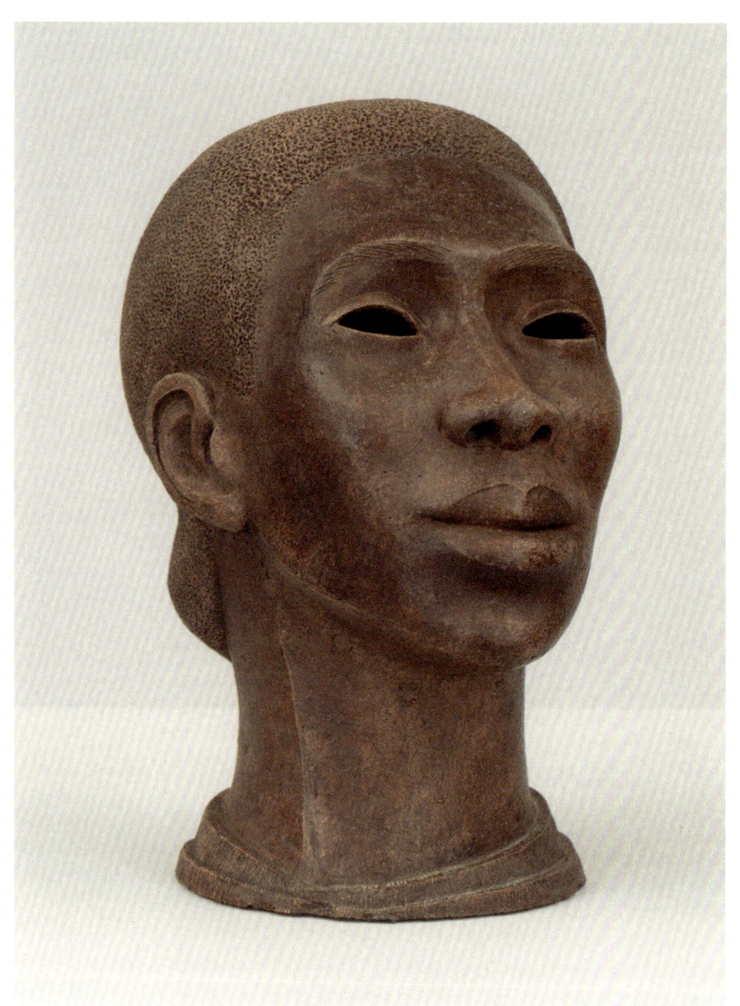

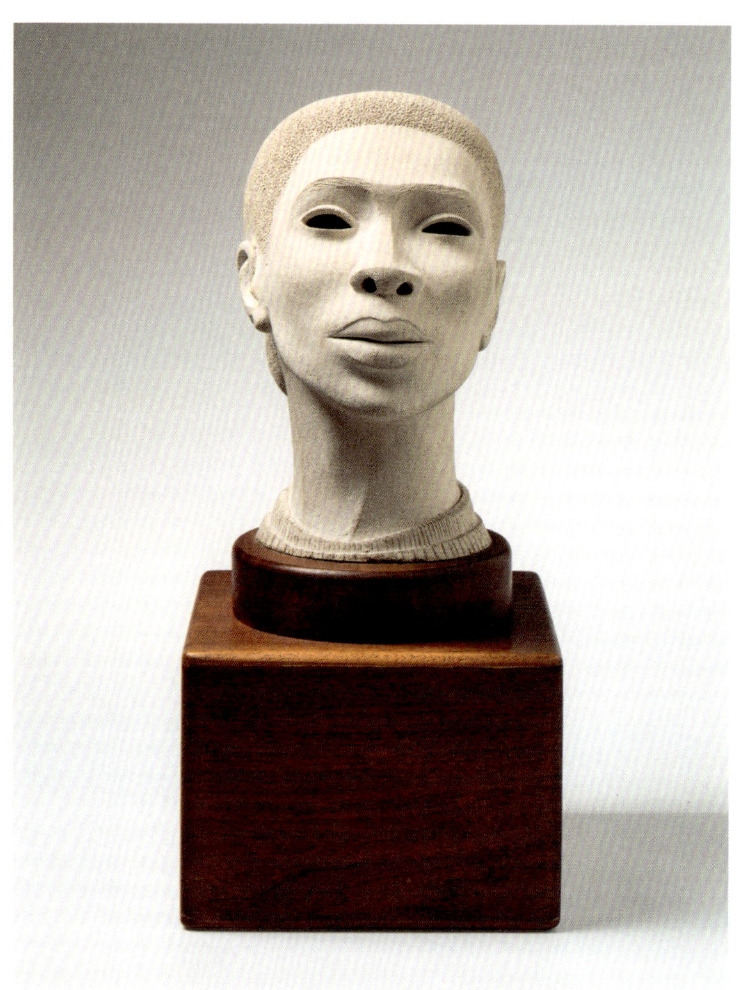

Head, 1947, terracotta, 10¾ × 6½ × 8¾ in., Whitney Museum of American Art, New York, Purchase, with funds from the Jack E. Chachkes Purchase Fund, the +6Schmidt Shubert Purchase Fund, and the Wilfred P. and Rose J. Cohen Purchase Fund in memory of Cecil Joseph Weekes, 2013.103

Head of a Young Woman, c. 1947, grit-tempered clay, 10½ × 8¾ × 6¼ in., Toledo Museum of Art, Gift of Florence Scott Libbey, by exchange, 2006.145

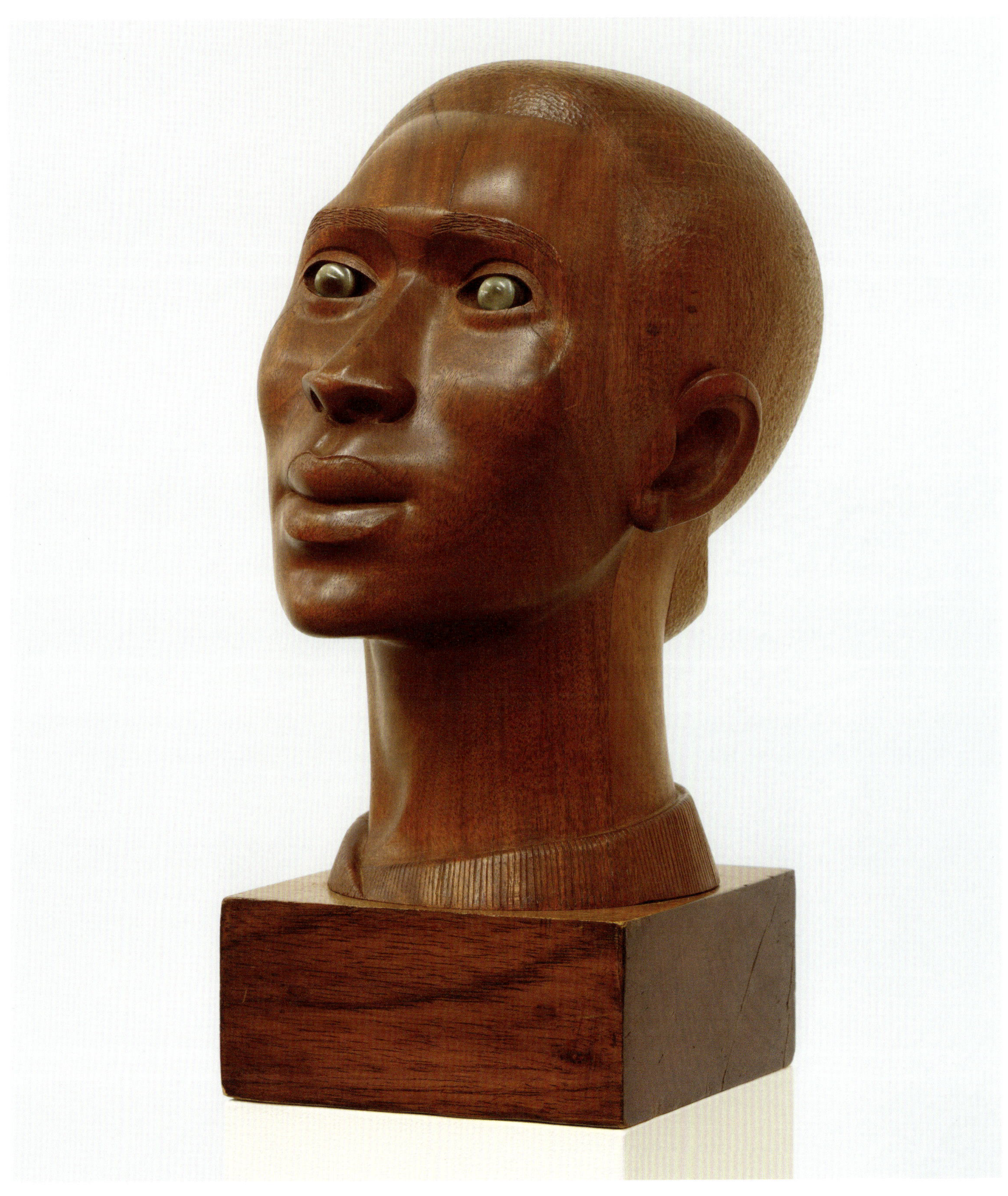

Negro Woman, 1956, wood, 11½ × 6½ × 9 in., Clark Atlanta University Art Museum, Atlanta Art Annuals: Second Atlanta University Purchase Award, Sculpture, 1956.008

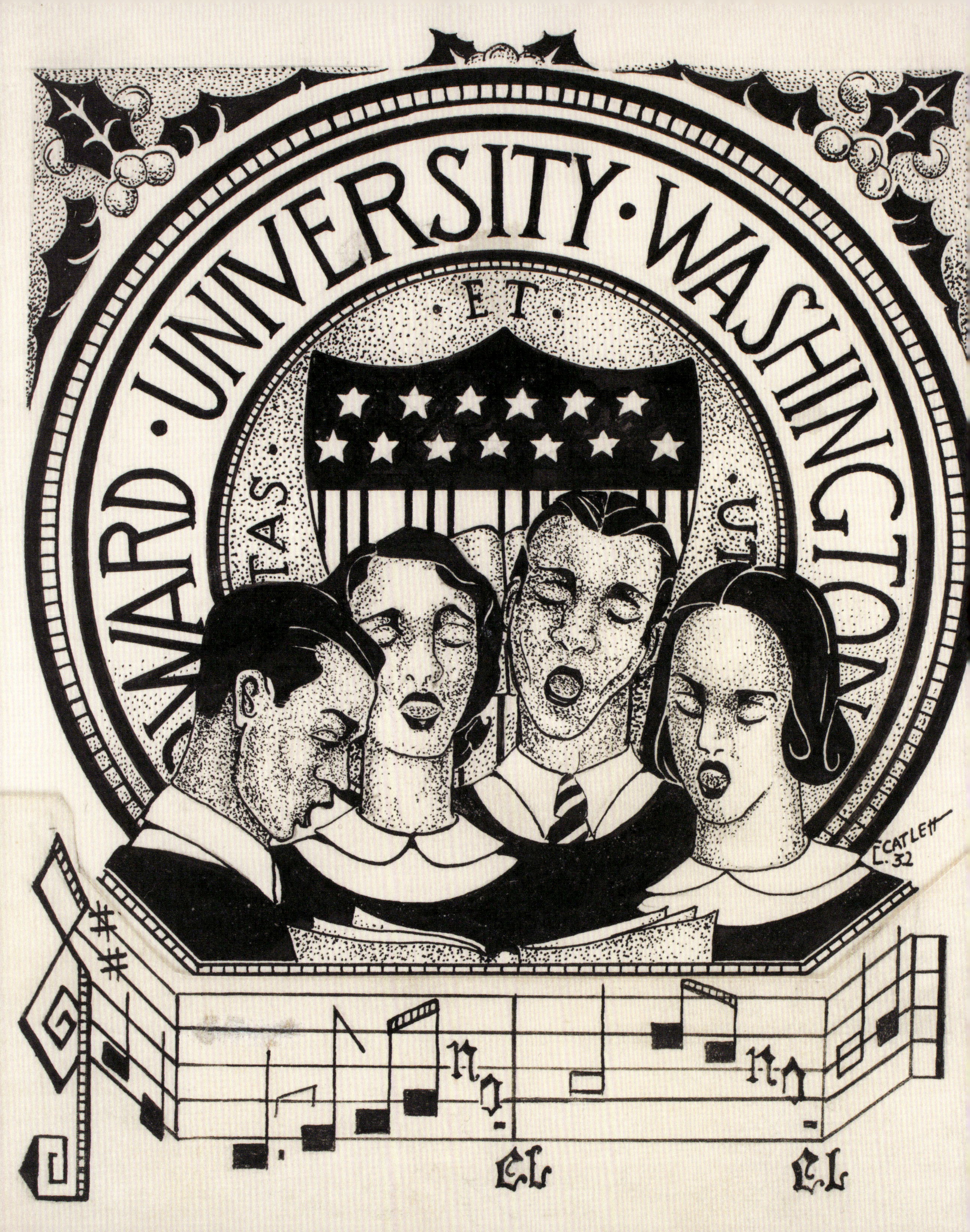
WARD · UNIVERSITY · WASHINGTON
· ET ·
NO
EL
NO
EL

MELANEE C.
HARVEY

BECOMING AN ARTIST-ACTIVIST AT HOWARD UNIVERSITY

Since its founding in 1867, Howard University has instilled in its student body a sense of social responsibility through its motto Veritas et Utilitas (truth and utility). As one of the university's most prestigious art graduates, Elizabeth Catlett actualized the university's motto across her career by creating *useful* art that advances equality, Black empowerment, and global revisionist Black histories. Akin to the first generation of art students educated at Howard University during the 1920s and 1930s, Catlett established a reciprocal relationship with Howard, where she was shaped by this community and in turn impacted it.[1] This art community comprised the foundation upon which Elizabeth Catlett built a practice of aesthetic activism, anchored in a commitment to Black creative legacies and Black women.

Carnegie Institute of Technology's rejection of Catlett's application for admission became a part of her artist biography as a testament to the racism inherent in the American art landscape during the first half of the twentieth century.[2] This encounter with systemic racism was swiftly met with assurance from her mother, Mary (Carson) Catlett, who restored her confidence with these words: "We'll send you to Howard, they have an art department."[3] Far from an inferior, alternative educational path, Howard University was a leader among historically Black educational institutions in establishing degree programs in art. Howard's art department and gallery provided students with access to practicing art professionals as faculty, rigorous art education, and art itself—often inaccessible to African Americans due to segregation policies and practices. Catlett's admission into the art department at Howard placed her in one of the leading art and design programs defining pedagogy and art practice for American art. It also introduced her to Howard's rich art communities—which laid the foundation for her aesthetic activism.

THE CAPSTONE

When Catlett, who went by Alice Elizabeth during her early years at Howard, entered as a first-year student during the fall of 1931, she arrived at a campus rapidly evolving in its curricular constitution, physical character, and national stature as the "Capstone of Negro education."[4] The art department was an integral component of the university's development. During the early 1930s

Howard's art activities were lauded in *The Crisis* (the publication of the NAACP) for the institutional encouragement of artistic "talent among Negro students and...the appreciation of art."[5] Catlett arrived at Howard primed to excel in her social and academic endeavors.

She entered the art department, then housed in the College of Applied Science, to pursue a bachelor of science degree in art with a concentration in design.[6] Howard passed several milestones during her first year in 1931: the ten-year anniversary of the founding of the art department, the first year since James Herring's promotion to associate professor, and the second year of the Gallery of Art, which boasted an increasingly full exhibition and lecture calendar.[7] Catlett's courses included introductory design taught by Loïs Mailou Jones; anatomy studios and sketching with James A. Porter; and drawing free-hand and composition with James Wells.[8] Catlett was also required to take a quarter-long course on mechanical drawings with Darnley Howard, assistant professor of mechanical engineering, and Howard H. Mackey, assistant professor of architecture.[9]

Curricular offerings were augmented by art exhibitions sponsored by the College Art Association of America (CAA) and mounted in Howard's Gallery of Art. For example, Catlett and her peers viewed and engaged a collection of seventeenth-century Dutch artworks as well as an exhibit of high-quality reproductions of modern art during her first semester. The university newspaper's coverage of the exhibition dubbed "The Little Dutch Masters" conveys the enthusiastic response of the campus. Under the subtitle "Exhibition Is First Showing of Masters in the United States," the *Hilltop* emphasized Howard as a premier venue for international art, noting, "The eyes of the art world at large has turned its eyes Washington wise wondering how such a thing happened. It is the signal honor of having in the Art Gallery an exhibition of genuine Masters painted in the time when Holland was coming to the fore in art production."[10] Catlett and her peers had access to Dutch genre paintings and a "smaller room of the gallery" dedicated to prints composed after paintings by Johannes Vermeer. These exhibitions are significant as they brought international prestige to Howard University and shaped the artistic paths of students like Catlett. She identified her experience with the modern art exhibit as a significant moment in her artistic development, recalling:

> *I remember an exhibition by Van Gogh, reproductions in the gallery. But they were so good, that you could see the texture, the thickness of the paint he used. That inspired me as to what a painting should look like. I never had any idea of how you were an artist. How you should be an artist. That inspired me to want to go to New York. Washington was Jim Crow then and we didn't have a chance to go to many things. In New York, I saw plays and went to exhibitions and I remember going to New York especially to see a big Van Gogh exhibition.*[11]

Catlett gained a sense of direction and orientation as a first-year art student through her experience in the gallery. She began critically studying canonical artists and techniques while also identifying specific design elements that captured her attention. Close study of the impasto surfaces of Van Gogh initiated her sustained interest in texture. Although it may seem exceptional for a historically Black college or university to offer an art curriculum steeped in Western aesthetics, HBCUs like Howard University and Wilberforce University have maintained a rich tradition of cultivating such interest among students since the nineteenth century. Howard's art gallery was a portal that encouraged students to explore art centers like New York, significant chapters of global art, and contemporary art trends.

Fig. 1—Alice Elizabeth Catlett, *Untitled (Wynona Wing Seated)*, 1932, On loan from the Howard University Gallery of Art

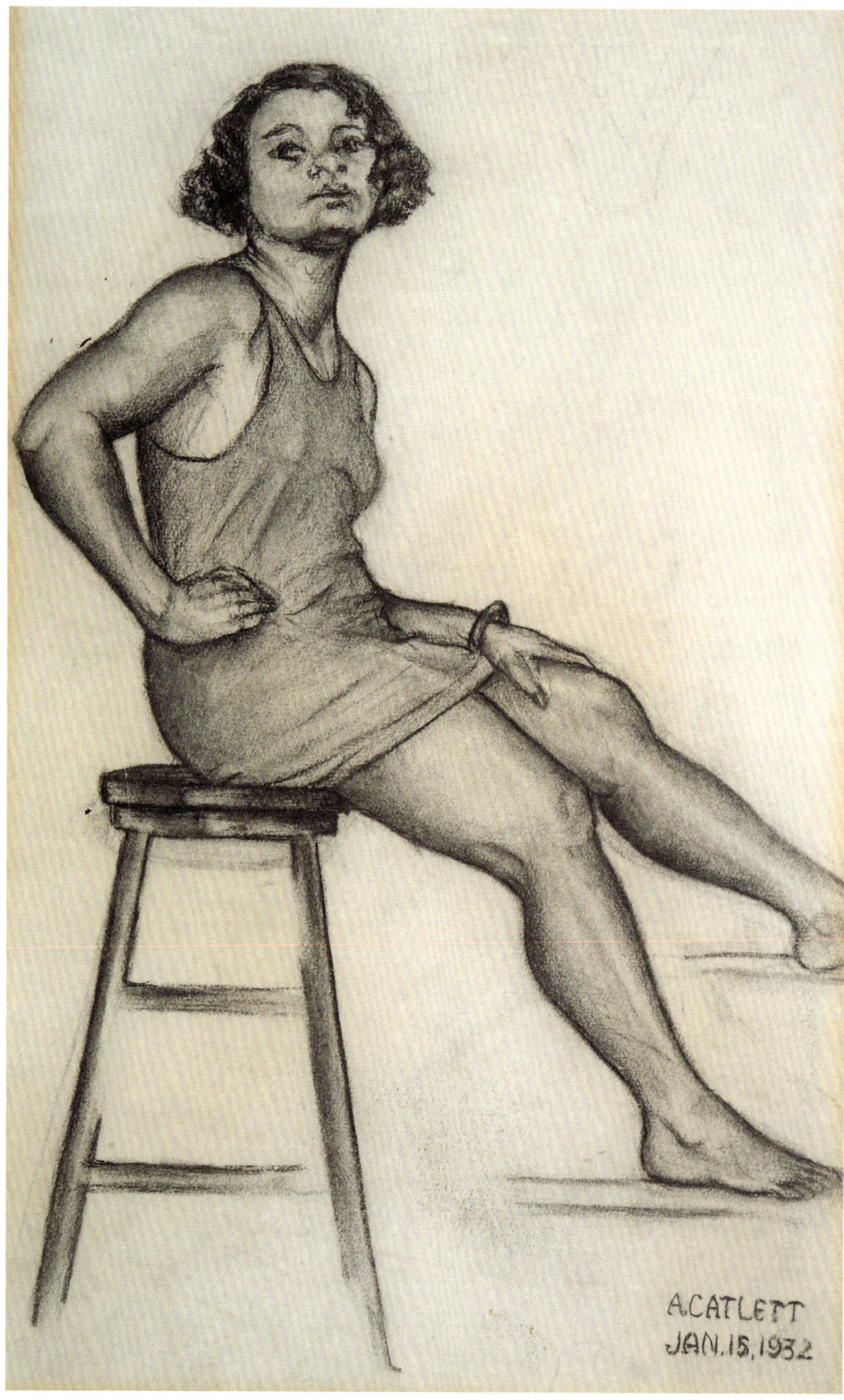

A student artwork by Catlett from her first year indicates her stylistic range in rendering the human figure (fig. 1). This drawing was completed during the winter session of Porter's Sketch and Anatomy course sequence, which required "conceptual and memory drawings," full-length charcoal figurative renderings, and anatomical studies.[12] Catlett demonstrated drafting skills across line, modeling, and textural variety in this composition, conveying tension across the surfaces of the loose T-shirt and projections of the body, most prominent in the shoulders, arms, torso, and legs. Even at this early stage, she renders the human form through sharp, rounded geometric shapes. This drawing also

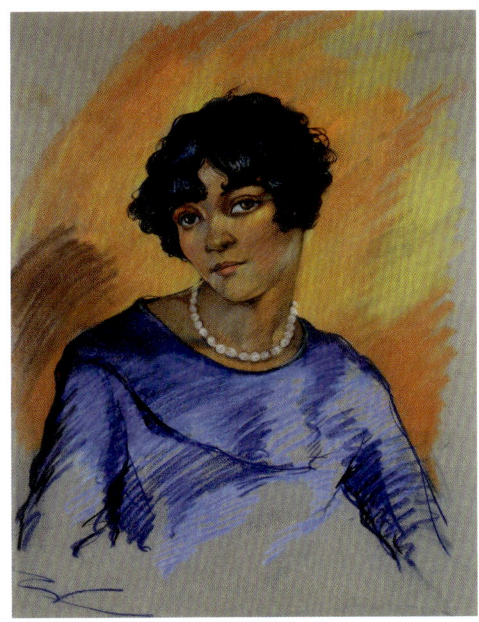

Fig. 2—Herman Rogers, *Wynona Wing*, c. 1929, pastel, Howard University Gallery of Art

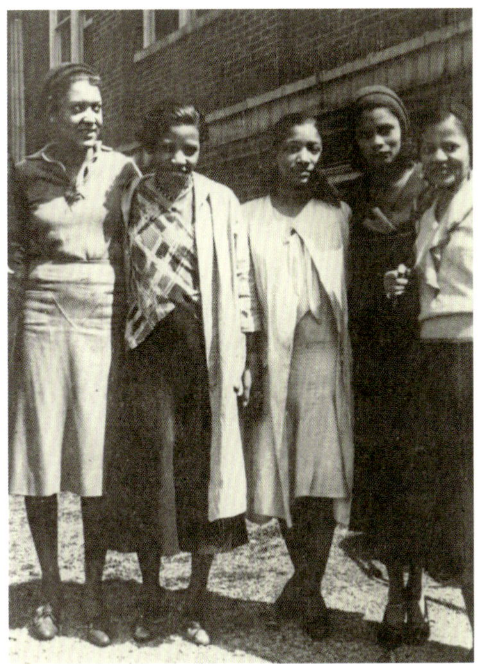

Fig. 3—At Howard, Elizabeth Catlett (far left) standing next to Loïs Mailou Jones, with other students, c. 1933, Loïs Mailou Jones Collection, Moorland-Spingarn Research Center, Howard University

shows Catlett's interaction with her peers. The sitter appears to be Wynona Wing, an advanced art education major. Catlett and her classmates frequently used Wing as a model, as indicated by student art in the Gallery of Art's permanent collection (fig. 2). Catlett represented Wing much differently than her male peers did. Under Catlett's hand, Wing is a modern woman, as evidenced by her hair, attire, and attitude—exuding confidence in her direct gaze and posture.

Catlett also created *Howard University Choir* during the winter quarter of the 1931–1932 academic year (p. 18). This design was submitted to Jones as an assignment in the introduction to design course, which focused on "a study of lettering and construction of design."[13] Her decision to retain Catlett's student work marks Jones's investment in Catlett during her first two years as a design student (fig. 3). For instance, at the close of her first year, Catlett was one of ten art and architecture students selected by Jones to attend a dinner party at a studio owned by playwright, actress, and stage director Gertrude P. McBrown. The gathering was a gesture of appreciation for students who assisted Jones and Catlett's classmate Henry Hudson in painting "Egyptian panels used as decorations for the Alpha Phi Alpha spring prom."[14] Other members of Howard art faculty attended, including Porter and Wells. These events exemplify the aesthetic, academic, and social experiences Howard University art faculty facilitated for students.

Howard's art community accelerated momentum in gallery programming and departmental growth during this period. During the winter quarter the gallery opened another CAA-sponsored exhibition featuring mural painting, organized by New York's Roerich Museum. According to Wells, this exhibit was the first show in the history of Howard's gallery that exclusively featured tempera paint. He explained the significance:

> *This exhibition is very timely because of the great interest manifested in mural painting. Probably the most outstanding exhibition of the season has been that of the Mexican mural painter [Diego] Rivera. Many critics are saying that the future of American art lies close to the Mexican group. They probably take this attitude not only because of the fresh vision the Mexican artist brings to him from his native soil, but because the medium usually employed by the Mexican painter of murals will be more adapted to the buildings of future thought and easel pictures. This view is probably far-fetched but it does indicate that the return of an art form...the fact that the process of [contemporary designers] to employ almost exclusively murals for the interior decoration of its buildings indicates the significance of mural painting as an art form.*[15]

At the time of this exhibition, Catlett was enrolled in Wells's composition courses, where he required students to demonstrate "an understanding of tempera painting, each student having to prepare the board and the ground on which he ultimately placed his decoration."[16] Catlett's interest in mural painting developed during this quarter as a direct result of this exhibition, Wells's instruction, and her personal research.[17]

In addition to exposure to canonical Western art, Catlett and her peers received lessons on the current state of African American art through exhibits at Howard's gallery. One, *Exhibition of Paintings by Negro Artists*, assembled sixty-five paintings from private collections and the Harmon Foundation, with the sponsorship of the Cultural Committee of the Washington Branch of the NAACP.[18] Students observed the stylistic range of Chicago modernist Archibald Motley Jr., from the precise naturalism of the portrait *Uncle Bob* (1928) to the round forms of *Brown Girl after the Bath* (1931). The exhibition promoted African American artists as engaged with global perspectives by featuring Haitian views by William E. Scott and Parisian scenes by Laura Wheeler Waring, William H. Johnson, and Palmer Hayden. The exhibition also provided Catlett with popular approaches to racialized maternal iconography popular during the New Negro Movements across urban centers, best exemplified by Charles C. Dawson's *Quadroon Madonna*. As art historian Rebecca VanDiver has argued, in many ways, Catlett's maternal artworks from the 1940s advance this tradition of maternal imagery, insisting on the recognition of Black mothers' labor.[19]

Catlett and her peers gained more insight into the practice of Howard's core art faculty (Herring, Jones, Porter, and Wells) in the winter quarter of 1932 when Howard's gallery mounted an exhibition of "Rare Negro Paintings" that prominently featured their work—including Jones's tempera painting *Buddha* (1927); Wells's *Plowman* (as well as two other oil paintings); and Porter's *Reflections* (with two more pastels).[20] Herring's research agenda for the summer of 1932 suggests his interest in developing Howard into a global art center specializing in African Diasporic art. Herring joined Fisk University linguistics professor Lorenzo Dow on a research trip to the islands off the coast of South Carolina. Herring investigated "the weaving and pottery found on the islands to discover if the original motifs of the textiles are close to African art and design or influence."[21] Across exhibitions, faculty research, and creative production, Howard's Gallery of Art and art department shaped one of the first spaces dedicated not only to recovering stories of aesthetic African retentions but also to emphasizing contemporary art by African American artists.

One under-recognized aspect of the art activity at Howard during the early 1930s is the trailblazing organizational development that connected Howard students, faculty, local art enthusiasts, and practicing artists in DC. On March 26, 1932, the *Afro-American* reported "110 Organize New Arts Guild," noting that Herring sponsored "the movement."[22] Bringing together visual and performing artists as well as community supporters of the arts, this new organization took up art appreciation as its mission and endeavored "to foster an interloan system with public schools and other colleges, to establish scholarship funds, and to create the taste for art through free Saturday morning classes and through civic recognition." This large group was divided into nine committees and Howard art faculty were prominent, with Porter serving as vice president and Wells chairing the finance committee. The art guild also attracted the support of educators Mary Church Terrell and Nellie M. Quander. This example of active engagement with cultural practitioners and local community provided an important precedent and context for the communities Catlett would shape with her art practice during the second half of the twentieth century.

DEEMED MERITORIOUS

Catlett continued to excel in her academic and social pursuits during her second year at Howard. In watercolor painting classes with Porter, she refined her use of elongated soft lines and developed her eye for the sculptural by adjusting how she articulated the human form through fabric. In one design (fig. 4), Catlett's interest in visual weight and mass remains consistent in her control of value to render volume. While Porter and Wells taught the majority of her courses this year, she enhanced her graphic designs in Jones's design course. She was recognized for her stellar work across her courses at the 1933 university commencement, where she was presented with the Cohen's Inc. Company Prize of "$5 to the student whose work is deemed meritorious by the head of the department of art."[23] Catlett earned a full scholarship for the 1933–1934 academic year, her third at Howard.[24]

Her junior year marked a period of profound personal development in her academic and social life as well as her sense of self-definition. Catlett changed

Fig. 4—Elizabeth Catlett, *Dress Model*, 1932, watercolor, The D. L. Demps Collection

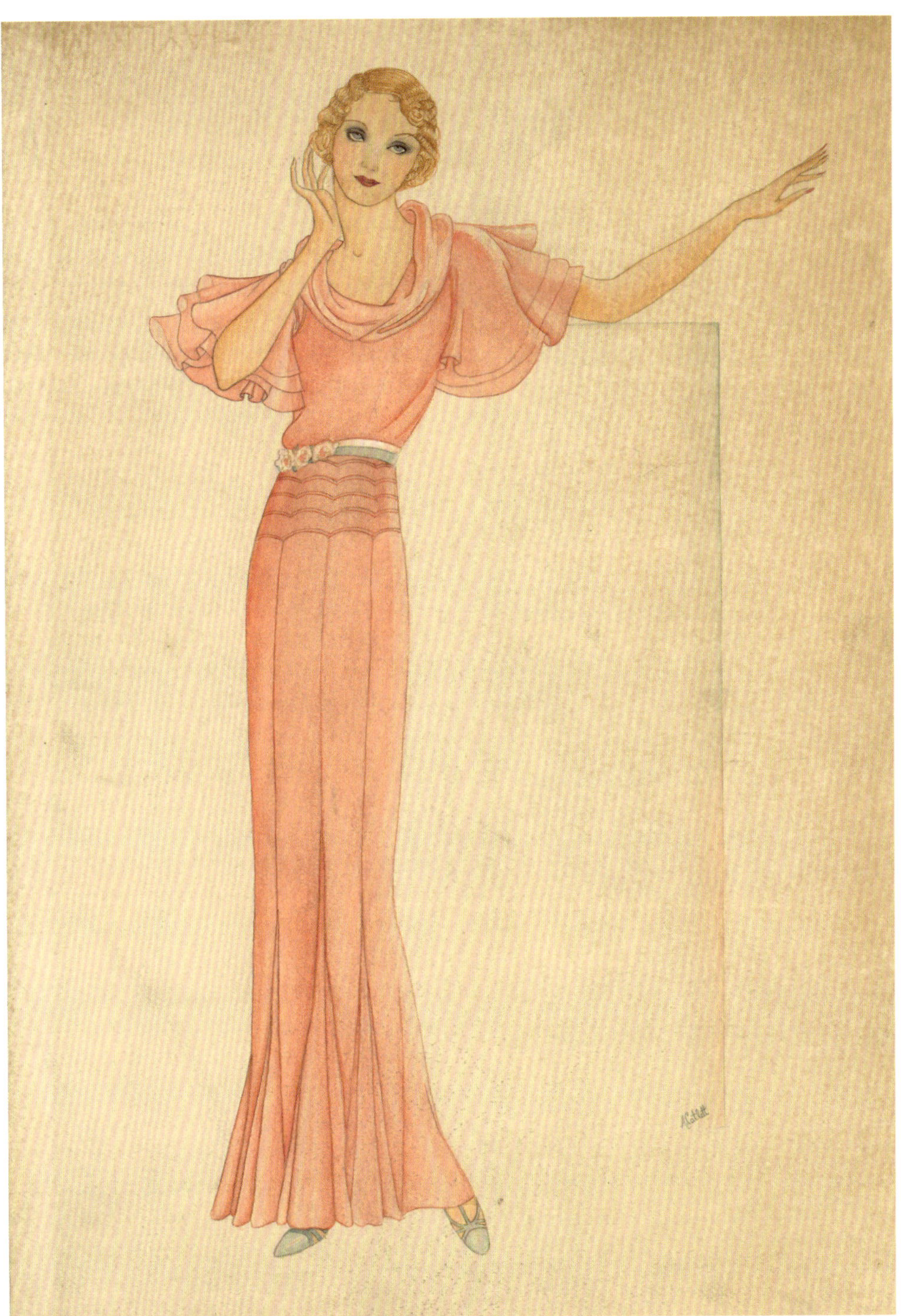

her major from design to painting during the summer of 1933, which allowed her more latitude to enroll in classes taught by Porter and Wells. Art students navigated a fall semester of exhibitions "dominated by African subjects" in Howard's Gallery of Art. Students investigated the formal and cultural possibilities of African art traditions under the tutelage of faculty (including Jones and Wells), who frequently engaged African aesthetics in such modernist compositions as Jones's *Ascent of Ethiopia* (1929) and Wells's *Looking Upward* (1928).[25] Howard art faculty and students were highly visible in the 1933 *Exhibition of Works by Negro Artists*, sponsored as a part of the annual conference of the Association for the Study of Negro Life (now known as the Association for the Study of African American Life and History) and mounted at the Smithsonian Institute's National Gallery of Art.[26] Art historian Tobias Wofford articulates the significance of this exhibition to Howard's art community, noting "the participation of Herring as curator, [Alain] Locke as theorist, and Porter as the artist

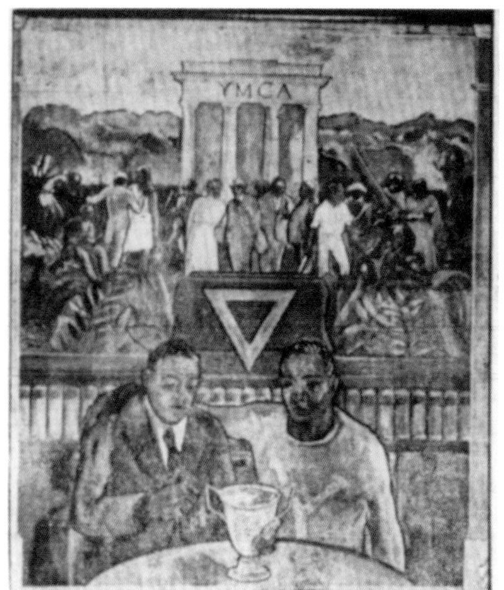

Fig. 5—James A. Porter, *Twelfth Street YMCA Mural*, c. 1933–1934, from *The Hilltop*, February 16, 1934, 4, Moorland-Spingarn Research Center, Howard University

scholar reveal the discourse that emerged to interpret, celebrate, or even resist [race as a frame for exhibiting work by African Americans]."[27] It certainly demonstrates the integral role of visual art in African American public scholarly discourse during the 1930s.

Catlett defined her junior year with her struggle to balance academic responsibilities and extracurricular commitments. During the spring semester, Catlett took courses in composition and life drawing with Porter in addition to taking landscape painting with the departmental chair, Herring.[28] As a promising student on a merit scholarship, Catlett faced pressure to excel in the classroom as well as professional art opportunities extended to her, such as her appointment as a muralist for the Public Works of Art Project (PWAP). Catlett recalled that while a classmate (Hudson) "went about doing his mural very conscientiously...I was taking classes from nine to five and leading a big social life."[29] Although Catlett viewed her experience with the PWAP as a missed opportunity, it facilitated an intensive study of the contemporary Mexican Muralist Movement as well as the mural practice of Porter, who was completing his mural for the Twelfth Street YMCA (fig. 5).[30]

By the middle of her junior year, her social activities centered on her membership with at least three student organizations. Catlett had selected the Daubers' Art Club as one of the first organizations to join at Howard. Under the supervision of the core art faculty, members of this group engaged in art enrichment beyond the classroom "through constant contact with contemporary art and artists and ancient masters and masterpieces...[as well as] frequent visits to museums, art galleries and other centers of interest."[31] By her third year, Catlett was serving as business manager for the club (fig. 6) and was initiated into the Stylus Literary Society, a selective student group dedicated to cultivating "original compositions in art, literature and music."[32] Perhaps revealing her leadership tendency to reform and improve, Catlett immediately went to work on the Stylus committee for revision of initiation rituals.[33] In December 1933 Catlett was elected vice president of the founding chapter of Delta Sigma Theta Sorority, the second oldest historically Black sorority in the US. She was admitted as a member during her sophomore year and quickly emerged as a leading voice in the organization.[34]

Because of her record of academic achievement and leadership, Catlett secured access to the African American Greek community (often referred to as the Divine Nine), akin to her early instructor Jones and mentor Porter, who were members of Alpha Kappa Alpha Sorority and Alpha Phi Alpha Fraternity, respectively. But as Catlett evolved in her activist orientation, she increasingly became critical of exclusionary aspects of sorority culture. In a 1989 interview with artist Camille Billops, Catlett shared this memory of Delta Sigma Theta Sorority: "At Howard University, I joined Delta. As a pledge, one of my first problems with the sorority was that I wanted them to pledge a friend of mine who is brown-skinned. They didn't want to but finally did...the question of color in Alpha chapter annoyed me no end. From then on, I began to see other things within the chapter that turned me off. I went from social life with Delta Sigma Theta and the sororities and frats straight into the Liberal Club."[35] Although she maintained her critical stance, Catlett actively participated in her sorority and continued to serve as an executive officer (p. 257).

VERITAS ET UTILITAS

During her senior year Catlett was an impassioned participant in the Liberal Club's anti-war protest planning—a movement across DC-area universities including Howard and Georgetown.[36] She also continued to mature into a focused, socially conscious artist. Howard's art department was also evolving

Fig. 6—Elizabeth Catlett (second from the left) in Daubers' Club, 1934, from *The Bison* (Howard University yearbook, 64), Digital Howard, Moorland-Spingarn Research Center, Howard University

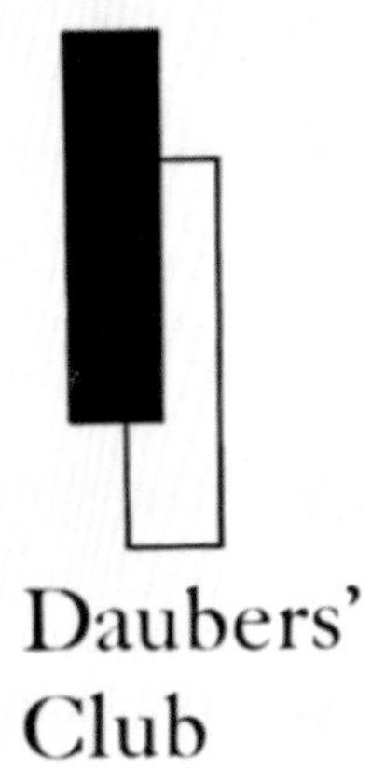

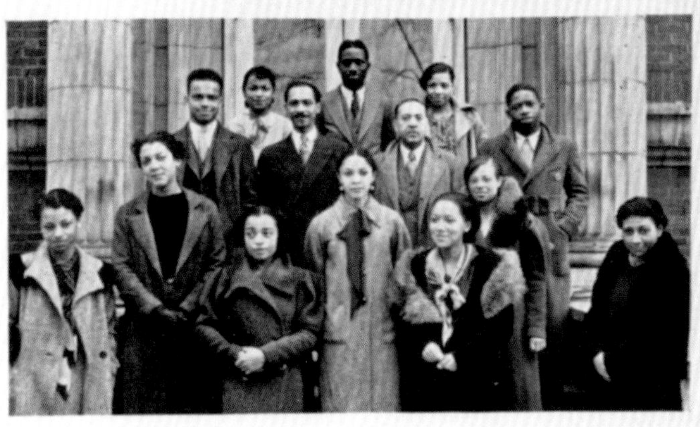

within a rapidly expanding university. In addition to Wells's craft course, which included sculptural instruction, Catlett registered for courses in life drawing, portraiture, and still life, for which she produced the 1935 untitled pastel portrait during her final semester (p. 20). Her senior instruction was rounded out with one semester of both illustration and landscape painting. Other experiences planted seeds that she would tend and investigate as themes during the late 1930s and 1940s. The Gallery of Art hosted in November 1934 the exhibition *Kuan-Yin, an Outstanding Example of Chinese Sculpture,* which introduced Buddhist Kuan-Yin iconography as "an Eastern counterpart of the Madonna and Child."[37] The sustained interaction with a range of sculptural materials and techniques across this exhibition cemented Catlett's interest in sculpture. She created studies as well as an oil painting entitled *Head of Kwan Yin*, thus demonstrating her aesthetic contemplation of this show.[38] Moreover, the mother and child imagery featured in it quite likely resonated with Catlett, considering the social and political issues of the 1930s.

Throughout Catlett's time at Howard, the concerns of African American mothers maintained visibility in the press with events such as the Scottsboro Boys Trial.[39] Catlett confronted the social issues of motherhood in her work with Delta Sigma Theta. Serving as parliamentarian for the sorority chapter during her senior year, Catlett would have been actively engaged in the chapter's responsibilities of "partial guardianship of little two-year-old Delores Sapp."[40] *The Hilltop* provides more insight: "On a visit to a FERA Nursery School, in the poor section of the city, Flaxie Pinkett was attracted to Delores and soon learned her story. Her father died when she was 5 months old; her mother Works in Maryland for a small salary which is barely enough for sustenance... the Delta girls have undertaken to see that the little Miss is well provided with clothes in the future and that she and her 8-year-old sister will have a warm home during the coming months."[41] Catlett would further explore the realities of Black motherhood and the sculptural solidity of religious deities in her graduate studies at the University of Iowa. In 1940 she would arrive at her award-winning sculpture *Negro Mother and Child*—a work whose subject seems akin to her active engagement with social issues as a Delta.

Catlett graduated cum laude with a bachelor of science degree in art and a painting concentration in 1935. Through both her academic pursuits and extracurricular affiliations at Howard, she established the foundation of her artist-activist philosophy. Her years there laid the groundwork for her maturation into a focused, socially conscious artist. Throughout her career, Catlett remained a part of the fabric of Howard University—engaging with its art community and returning to celebrate fellow alums, former instructors, and lifelong mentors. Elizabeth Catlett is an important link in Howard University's aesthetic "proud continuum," which connects generations of visual artists advancing innovative approaches to Veritas et Utilitas.[42]

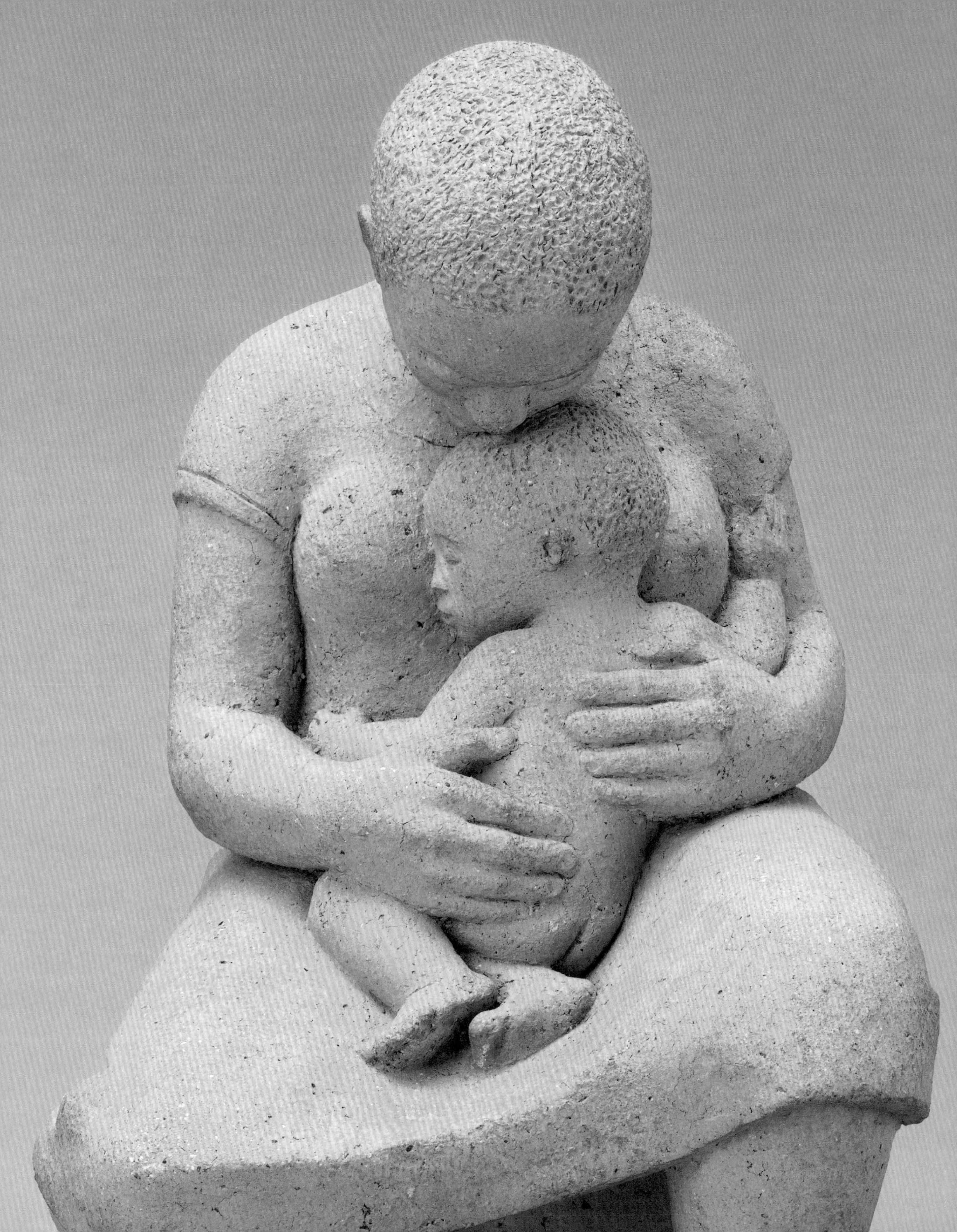

SARAH KELLY OEHLER

SOCIAL(IST) NETWORKS IN CHICAGO AND NEW YORK

On October 25, 1941, Elizabeth Catlett was named queen of the Artists and Models Ball, an annual fundraiser for Chicago's South Side Community Art Center (SSCAC) that was held in the Savoy Ballroom.[1] To satisfy the ball's Pan-American theme, she chose Mexico—evidence of her early interest in the culture of that country—and accessorized with items borrowed from her roommate, fellow artist Margaret Taylor Goss (later Burroughs), and other friends who, unlike Catlett, had visited that country.[2] Catlett herself later recalled that one of those friends was playwright Lorraine Hansberry.[3]

This moment in Catlett's long and dedicated life could be dismissed as a purely social, even frivolous, night of celebration, but it can also be seen as functioning in a much more significant way. By locating Catlett within the milieu of the SSCAC, the event opens the door to an investigation into the brief but impactful period that she spent in Chicago (fig. 1). It hints at the friends she made (such as Burroughs and Hansberry) and the artistic infrastructure she joined. Moreover, this type of involvement did not end with her departure from Chicago; she then sought out a similar community in New York City. In truth, her participation in the Artists and Models Ball attests to her significant engagement with politically Left-wing, interracial artistic communities first in Chicago, and then in New York, in the early 1940s. Coming at a pivotal moment in her career in the years from 1940 to 1946, these social(ist) networks were central to her development as an artist. By understanding her position within the Chicago and New York art scenes, we can explore how these two settings furthered her artistic education, honed her political instincts, offered her important exhibition opportunities, and acted as vital precursors to her later work in Mexico.[4]

CHICAGO: COMMUNITY AS CATALYST

The art scene that Catlett entered in Chicago in the early 1940s was a thriving one, and it had two crucial hubs with which she engaged: the flourishing community of Black artists developing on the South Side, particularly in the Bronzeville neighborhood around the SSCAC, and longtime downtown institutions, especially the museum of the Art Institute of Chicago (AIC) and its related school (SAIC). Although racial discrimination in the city was widespread and persistent—

Fig. 1—Margaret Taylor Goss Burroughs (standing left) and Elizabeth Catlett (seated center) in their Chicago studio with an unidentified visitor, c. August 1941, from Samella Lewis, *The Art of Elizabeth Catlett* (Claremont, CA, Hancraft Studios, 1984), 13

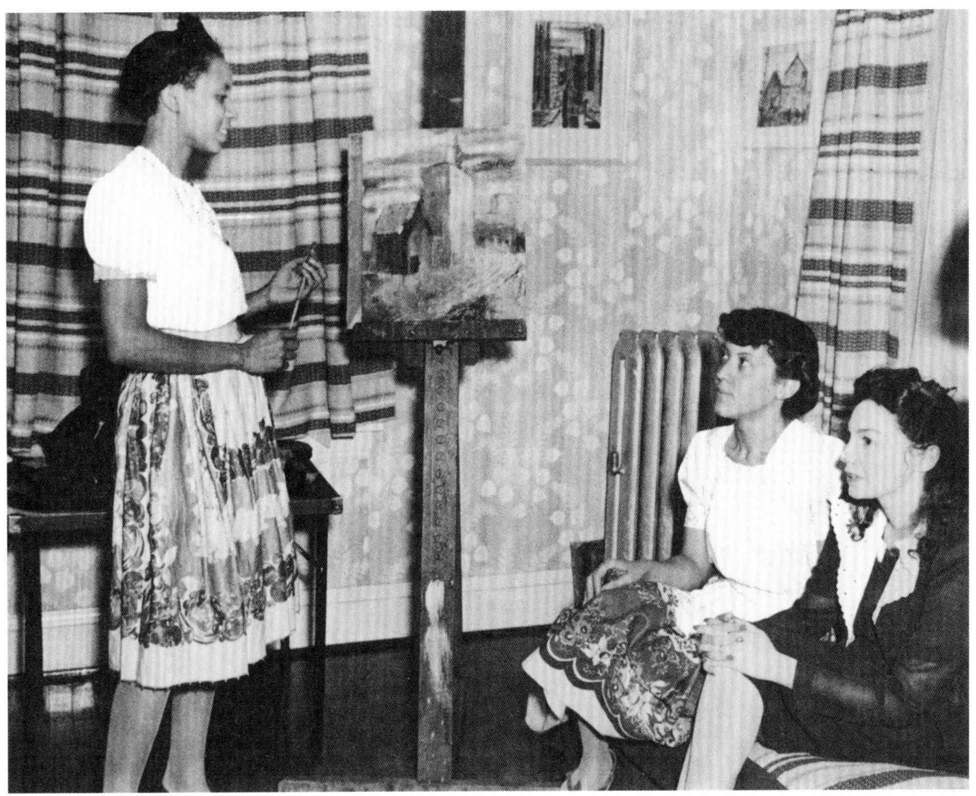

rampant redlining, for instance, forced increasing numbers of southern-born African American migrants into substandard housing in limited neighborhoods—many Black artists navigated successfully between these interconnected creative centers, using both to further their ambitions.[5]

Education was often a key link. The SAIC, for instance, had long accepted African American students—counting William A. Harper and Archibald Motley Jr. as some of its earlier graduates—and by the late 1930s had become an important interracial training ground for the city's growing cohort of Black artists. Attendees included Burroughs, Eldzier Cortor, and Charles White; Burroughs later recalled the school as being relatively, if not entirely, free from racial discrimination: "But going to the Art Institute where we had the racial mix, the ethnic mix—we were all together. The only important thing that people looked at was your work and what it expressed."[6] Aspiring artists also had support from long-standing settlement houses such as Jane Addams's Hull-House, located on the West Side, and the Abraham Lincoln Centre, in Bronzeville; these institutions attracted an interracial cohort of Jewish immigrant and Black teachers, and offered students additional training and opportunities to display their works.

Many members of the city's artistic communities, both Black and white, also shared Leftist political beliefs. This shaded from general progressivism to (more frequently) radical socialist and communist leanings, as a diverse group of artists affiliated themselves with the Chicago Artists Union, the John Reed Club, and the Communist Party, the latter bolstered by the success of the Popular Front during the Great Depression.[7] The Artists Union in particular united a large number of Chicagoans in its efforts to achieve fair treatment for all people; in addition to organizing exhibitions, lectures, and social occasions for its members, the union also was politically active. For example, in 1938 it successfully protested the racist and exclusionary practices of the local director of the Federal Art Project, enabling Black artists such as Cortor, Motley, White, and Charles Dawson to join the federal employment rolls and earn their livings as artists.[8] This political climate encouraged Chicago's Left-leaning artists to advocate for social justice by focusing their art on inhumane conditions experienced daily by the poor and working classes.

Most important, by the early 1930s a strong community of Black artists on the South Side had begun to generate their own groups and institutions to advance their careers, in what has become known as the Black Chicago Renaissance.[9] It encompassed several forms of creative expression: not only literature and dance, but also the visual arts, which centered on a group called the Arts Craft Guild, founded by Burroughs, White, Cortor, and others, in 1932. An important tenet of the group was a shared commitment to education: since not all members could afford the cost of a full-time course at the SAIC, they deputized (and often jointly funded) individual members to study and then return to teach the others. The dedication demonstrated by members of the guild directly influenced the decision by the directors of the Federal Art Project's Community Art Center program (CAC), in 1939, to locate a new center in Bronzeville.[10] They could ensure its successful launch while also advancing their own cause. The SSCAC's charter members, among them Burroughs, Cortor, Motley, and White, raised the funds to open the center, at 3831 South Michigan Avenue, in 1940. They found a ready ally in Peter Pollack, the white head of the local CAC program, who had previously demonstrated his willingness to show works by Black artists in his Chicago Artists' Group Gallery, located downtown on Michigan Avenue. Intentionally located far from the downtown art center of Chicago, the SSCAC became (and still serves as) a crucial neighborhood Black arts organization.

Into this heady mix arrived Catlett, who found in Chicago alignment with her already established political and pedagogical interests. Her encounters with a Black community determined to catalyze change would affirm those interests, giving her educational and exhibition opportunities along with key allies. The Artists and Models Ball of 1941, however, was not the first time that Catlett visited Chicago. Her introduction to the city's two artistic circles came in early 1940, when she made a "Picasso pilgrimage" with a group of students from the University of Iowa to see *Picasso: Forty Years of His Art*, an extensive retrospective organized by the AIC and the Museum of Modern Art, and shown in Chicago from February 1 to March 3, 1940.[11] It was an opportunity to see the breadth of Picasso's oeuvre up to that point, including *Les Demoiselles d'Avignon* (1907, Museum of Modern Art) and *Guernica* (1937, Museo Reina Sofia). Both undoubtedly appealed to Catlett at this moment in her studies: Grant Wood, her instructor and advisor at Iowa, had encouraged her toward stylization and abstracted form, and the mural *Guernica* also gave her a particular model for political engagement. (She would later circumvent segregation to organize a trip for Dillard University students to see the *Picasso* exhibition when it traveled to the Isaac Delgado Museum in New Orleans.) During her pilgrimage to Chicago Catlett recalled, "I went to the exhibition and then someone took me to a party and I met Margaret and Bernard Goss, and Charles Sebree, and...a lot of the artists in Chicago at the time, and Charles White, and others. So then when I went back to Chicago [the following year] I had met them already."[12] This 1940 visit to Chicago, therefore, immediately indicated to the young artist what the city had to offer in terms of artistic and personal growth.

One key opportunity came just a few months later when Catlett's thesis sculpture for the University of Iowa, *Negro Mother and Child* (fig. 2), won the first prize for sculpture at the art exhibition of the American Negro Exposition. This massive display opened on July 4, 1940, in celebration of the seventy-fifth anniversary of the abolition of slavery by the Thirteenth Amendment. As one of many emancipation expositions, it showcased the economic, political, and cultural progress of African Americans through hundreds of exhibits, from historical dioramas to agricultural and other educational displays. However, Chicago's fair in particular reflected the strong Leftist political leanings of the city's Black cultural workers, who played a key role in shaping the display of visual arts. These ranged from individual murals such as *The History of the Negro Press* (created by Catlett's future husband Charles White and

Fig. 2—Elizabeth Catlett, *Negro Mother and Child*, 1940, limestone (location unknown), from *Exhibition of the Art of the American Negro (1851 to 1940)* (catalog, American Negro Exposition and Tanner Art Galleries, Chicago, 1940), 11

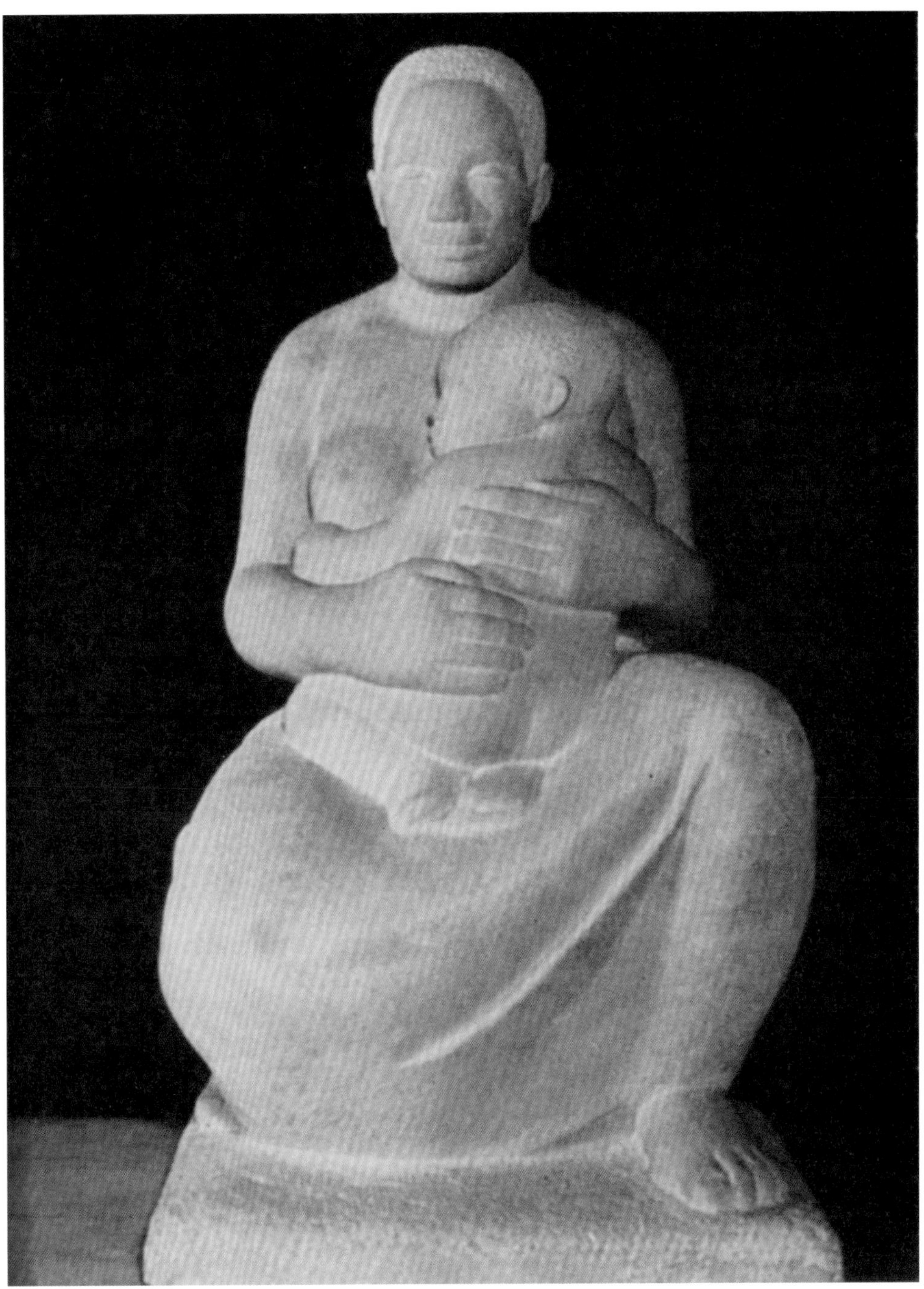

commissioned by fair organizer Claude Barnett, head of the Associated Negro Press) to a sweeping exhibition of historical and contemporary painting, sculpture, and works on paper, along with a small selection of African objects.[13]

Alain Locke, who chaired the art exhibition's national committee, described the display as "the most comprehensive and representative collection of the Negro's art that has ever been presented to public view."[14] Numbering well over three hundred works, it was held in a section of the exposition called the Tanner Art Galleries in honor of artist Henry Ossawa Tanner. The art committee and jurors included familiar faces from Catlett's time at Howard University: in addition to Locke, her mentors James Herring and James A. Porter were involved in various capacities, while the lead curator was Alonzo Aden.[15] The exhibition also introduced her work to numerous Chicagoans who would become part of her extended network of peers and supporters. Burroughs was involved behind the scenes in organizing the Tanner Art Galleries, while the jury included Black artists Dawson and Motley, along with Pollack, AIC director Daniel Catton Rich, and Edwin Embree, president of the Julius Rosenwald Fund.

The jury selected Catlett's sculpture out of a field of over forty works by some of the most significant artists from across the country: for example, Richmond Barthé, Sargent Claude Johnson, and Augusta Savage were well represented, joined by Chicago sculptors Marion Perkins and Joseph Kersey. Catlett's carving exemplified the important aesthetic turn by Black artists in the late 1930s away from a "jazzy, superficial show," as Locke noted, toward an approach grounded in social realism: "And yet, he must somehow reflect what he sees most and knows best, his own folk, and his own feeling of life. In so doing, he can teach us to see ourselves, not necessarily as others see us, but as we should be seen."[16] Despite Locke's gendered terminology, this approach was one Catlett had already adopted in her work. Wood had encouraged her to focus on subjects from her own life, and she remained steadfast in this commitment. *Negro Mother and Child* was her first attempt to represent in stone what would become one of her most important themes: "The implications of motherhood, especially Negro motherhood," she wrote, "are quite important to me, as I am a Negro as well as a woman."[17] It was one that clearly resonated with the jurors of the Chicago exposition. The award brought her significant national recognition at a key early moment in her career, setting the stage for future accolades and publicity, exhibition opportunities, and advancement.

Following her first academic year teaching at Dillard University, Catlett returned to Chicago in the summer of 1941. She roomed with and shared a studio with Burroughs, and quickly became a notable part of Black Chicago's social scene (see fig. 1). The *Chicago Defender* reported on a studio open house held by the two: "Lovely pieces of work done by the young artists were on display and friends contributed to a delightfully impromptu program."[18] Her friendship with Burroughs further opened the door to Chicago's community of Black artists: "We would meet at each other's houses," Catlett recalled, "and we would get together socially and discuss...creative things. People would read and we would look at each other's work."[19] This shared interest in helping their artist friends improve their craft was one that Burroughs would encounter and support several years later at the Taller de Gráfica Popular (TGP, People's Graphic Workshop).

One of the creative people Catlett met was Charles White, whom she would marry in December 1941. Their courtship revolved around artmaking and politics: "All that summer he would come by, he was a friend of Margaret's. They were all in the Communist Party. There was a lot of discussion, they were trying to recruit me into the Communist Party...That was where I drew the line."[20] While Catlett might not have officially joined the Communist Party, she admired socialism as a means of fighting for social justice: "And where rights for Black people were concerned, I was always very active. And whether there were Communists involved or not, I mean, I'm interested in socialism."[21] Her inclusion into this world of South Side artists thrust her for the first time into a community of dedicated Leftist artists who saw their art as a weapon in the political fight for equality. White especially promoted what he called the "social, even the propaganda angle" in art.[22] Dedicated to carrying his message to broad audiences, during this period he was focused on painting murals for the SSCAC, the American Negro Exposition, the Chicago Public Library, and Hampton University. His murals visualized Black history for all to see, reminding his viewers of the everyday Americans, such as Crispus Attucks and Sojourner Truth, who became heroes through their actions. For White, the act of painting was his most important act of resistance: "Paint is the only weapon I have to fight what I resent."[23]

Catlett's determination to succeed as an artist and educator was equally an act of resistance, and she dedicated her summer to perfecting her craft. She later highlighted the importance of obtaining technical proficiency: "I learned technique from traditional, establishment schools, and it took me a long time to realize that technique was the main thing to learn from them. But technique is so important! It's the difference between art and ineptitude. Because our audiences deserve the best, we must equip ourselves to give them the very best."[24] No works by Catlett can be confirmed to be extant from her time in Chicago, but she recalled the summer was a productive one: "It was a very fulfilling summer...I felt like I was progressing."[25] She enrolled in a ceramics course at the SAIC and studied lithography at the SSCAC. She also remembered working on a stone carving.[26] It is plausible that *Head (Head of a Man)* (p. 24) dates to this summer. Carved from Indiana limestone, it displays a naturalistic approach to form and a keen attention to individual subjectivity. It demonstrates the subtle stylization Catlett had learned from Wood, but without the greater embrace of abstraction that occurred through her studies with Ossip Zadkine in New York in 1942. Furthermore, it is possible that Catlett carved *Head* with White as her model. While it cannot be conclusively proven, the head—with its thin, angular face—bears a resemblance to White, and he retained the sculpture after their divorce.[27]

Catlett returned to Dillard in the fall of 1941, but was briefly back in Chicago for her award-winning turn at the Artists and Models Ball in October. She later recounted that some subterfuge was necessary at Dillard to make the trip: "I got a permit to go up to be on the jury at the Art Institute, and I was really going to the Artists and Models Ball."[28] She married White in December, honeymooning in New York. During that time Catlett exhibited at a groundbreaking exhibition at the Downtown Gallery, *American Negro Art, 19th and 20th Centuries*, which had as its goal the creation of a fund to purchase works by Black artists for presentation to museums. An august list of sponsors, headed by Eleanor Roosevelt, pledged their support. Locke led the coordination committee, aided once again by Chicagoans Pollack and Rich.[29] The show featured a significant contingent of Chicago artists, including White, Cortor, Motley, and Sebree. The *Defender* linked Catlett with this group, suggesting how integral she had become.[30] She contributed *Margaret and Gayle* (location unknown), a watercolor tondo portrait of Burroughs and her daughter that was called out as "exciting" in the national press and further demonstrates her close connections with the Chicago community.[31] Although she would never live in Chicago again, the community she joined there came with her in spirit, encouraging her to continue along the path of activism through art as she stepped into the next phase of her life in New York City during World War II.

NEW YORK: A COMMUNITY AT WAR

Catlett and White settled in New York in June 1942 to pursue their careers as artists, after teaching at Dillard in the spring term and then resigning in protest of the university's pay structure. The war, and its impacts, predominated. White had received a grant from the Julius Rosenwald Fund, and hoped to travel to Mexico, but the draft board denied his request to leave the country (he would serve in the army in 1944). They settled first into a building located at 409 Edgecombe Avenue, in the Sugar Hill neighborhood, where their neighbors included the journalist Marvel Cooke and the poet Langston Hughes. There, she quickly developed another network of cultural relationships that echoed those she had built in Chicago: politically active, socially committed, and dedicated to artmaking and education. For example, Marvel Cooke, then employed by the *People's Voice*, later achieved fame for her five-part series "The Bronx Slave Market," which exposed the unjust hiring practices faced by Black women working as domestic laborers. With Ernest Critchlow as her introduction into New York's Black artistic circles, Catlett met, among others, the painters Jacob Lawrence and Norman Lewis, the master printmaker Robert Blackburn, and the poet Gwendolyn Bennett.

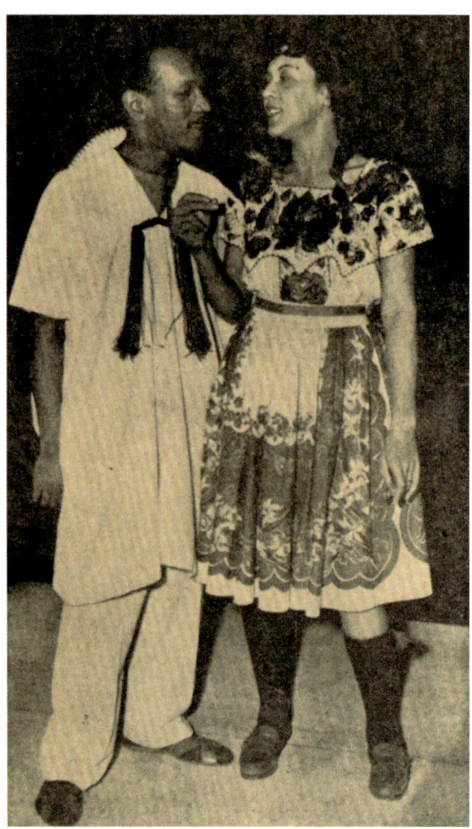

Fig. 3—Elizabeth Catlett and Charles White at a ball to benefit Russian War Relief, *People's Voice*, December 12, 1942, clipping in Charles W. White Papers, Archives of American Art, Smithsonian Institution, box 12, scrapbook 1, folder 45

Many were directly involved in the war effort. Hughes, she recalled, "would come from time to time to tell us about his new songs for the war effort that he was writing…about the new black and white together, unite and fight."[32] Catlett herself was quickly drafted into leading the Russian War Relief effort in Harlem; this national organization raised funds on behalf of Russian citizens and soldiers following Germany's invasion in 1941 (fig. 3). Her sculptures were also displayed alongside those of Barthé, Savage, and Malvina Hoffman in an exhibition benefitting the French Relief Societies, just one example of how her works circulated on behalf of wartime causes.[33]

Education remained central to Catlett's life, and reflected her Leftist politics and long-standing principles of serving others through art. For example, in the summer of 1942 Catlett worked as an arts coordinator at the interracial Workers Children's Camp (Camp Wo-Chi-Ca) in New Jersey, joined by White and Burroughs. Sponsored by the Communist-affiliated International Workers Order, it manifested the belief that advancing the causes of racial rights and of workers' rights went hand in hand. Catlett, aware that the camp was located on the traditional homelands of the Lenape, worked with the campers to research and carve a totem pole.[34]

A similar ethos bolstered her work at the George Washington Carver School, a community school in Harlem. Like the SSCAC—and its New York counterpart, the Harlem Community Art Center (which had closed in 1942)—the Carver School brought education to working-class people in their own neighborhood. It was founded in late 1943 and run by Bennett, her poet-friend. Catlett worked there from January 1944 until her departure for Mexico in 1946, serving as fundraiser and promotion director, and teaching sculpture and dressmaking. Other members of her circle offered their skills as well; White taught drawing while Critchlow and Lewis taught painting. At the Leftist-oriented Carver, even the most innocuous of topics could lead to political discussion. Catlett recalled: "People said, 'How do you teach Marxism making a dress?' And I said, 'Well, while we're sewing, we talk.'"[35] Catlett would seize opportunities to educate her students about politics, events, and the prejudices and injustices of the world.

Catlett's own studies were focused, as they had been in Chicago, on advancing her artistic abilities. She sought out the Russian-born French sculptor Ossip Zadkine for lessons, then worked in his studio during the summer of 1942. With Zadkine's encouragement, she explored expressions of abstraction in African art: "It had never occurred to me that the study of African art could be a way of learning about abstract forms."[36] This enabled her to move from gentle stylization into a greater embrace of abstraction in sculptural form, as she emphasized angularity and geometries, reducing the human figure to essential, expressive lines. This is apparent in a terracotta *Head* that she produced in 1944 (fig. 4), a work that in its planarity recalls the ways cubist sculpture frequently translated three-dimensional forms into simplified geometric shapes shown from varying viewpoints. Catlett deftly carved away the clay to render the proper left eye socket as a severe concavity, its negative space contrasting sharply with the more fully modeled opposing side. Sharp edges along the nose and cheekbones further enhance the planar disparities and create a dramatic play of shadow across the face. Catlett then added incised details that only reinforce her deliberate abstraction: curving grooves define the eyes and lips, short hatch marks denote eyebrows, while on the proper right side, brief overlapping cuts suggest hair even as the angular hollow on the left remains unmarked. Zadkine, however, was a proponent of using abstraction to achieve an "international" or universal style that he unconsciously rooted in whiteness, while Catlett remained determined to portray Black women, children, and men.[37]

This determination was more readily manifested in Catlett's two-dimensional work in painting and printmaking. Such works also demonstrate the ties to her

Fig. 4—Elizabeth Catlett, *Head*, 1944, terracotta (location unknown), from Charles W. White Papers, Archives of American Art, Smithsonian Institution

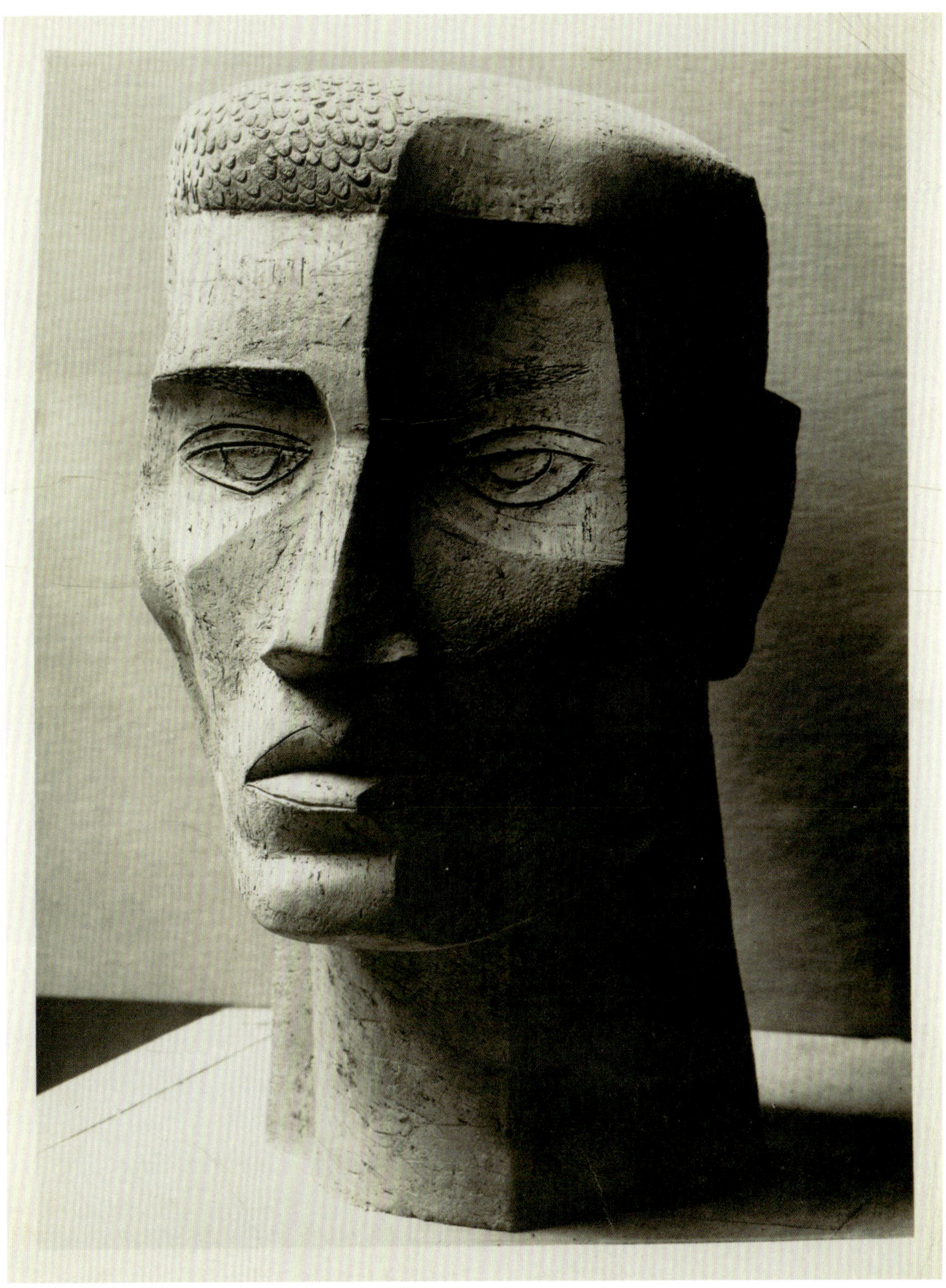

community, as her style can be seen in dialogue with those of her artist friends. In *Untitled (Woman in a Yellow Hat)* (p. 25), for instance, she experimented with the planes of the figure's face, hat, and shirt, expressing them as flat patches of pigment that evoke the work of her friend Lewis in the 1930s and 1940s, including his own *Woman with Yellow Hat* (1936, private collection). In *Friends* (1944, Princeton University Art Museum), the linear quality of the tempera and colored pencil shares similar qualities to contemporaneous paintings by White, among them *Soldier* (1945, Huntington Library, Art Museum, and Botanical Gardens). Indeed, Catlett's painting at this time (when their marriage was already troubled) suggests a complex artistic exchange with White. Certain aspects of her paint application suggest his influence, especially the sweeping volumetric brushstrokes that contrast with the fast-paced crosshatching that then characterized much of his work. But the exchange was in both directions: Catlett recalled suggesting to White that he use collage in *Headlines* (fig. 5), an unusually abstracted treatment of the figure that also evokes her angular sculptures.[38]

Always interested in representing Black Americans in her art, with the outbreak of World War II her subject matter became more politically charged, as

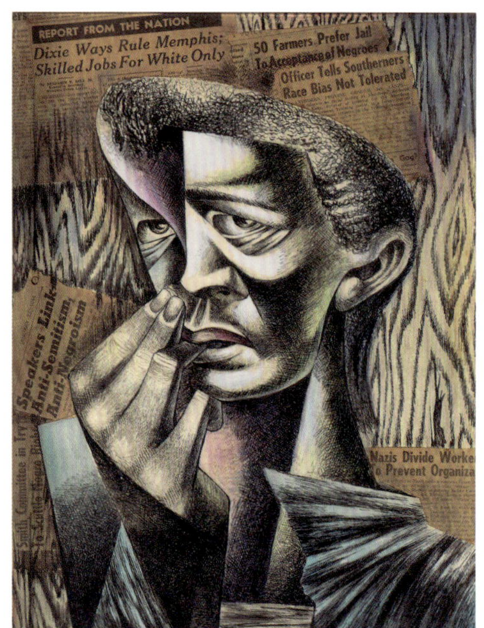

Fig. 5—Charles White, *Headlines*, 1944, ink, gouache, and newspaper on board, Collection of William M. and Elisabeth M. Landes

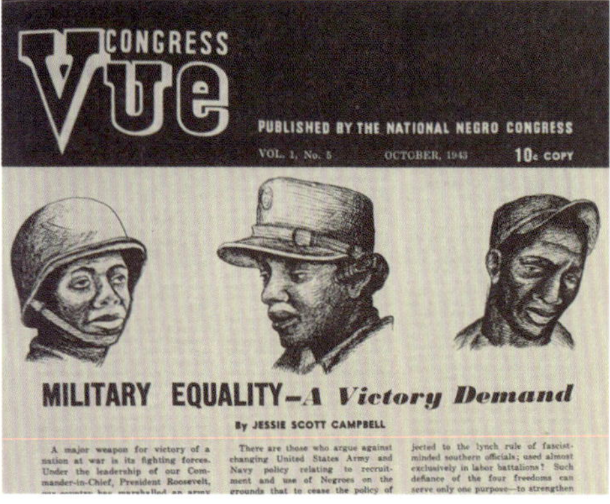

CONGRESS Vue

PUBLISHED BY THE NATIONAL NEGRO CONGRESS

VOL. 1, No. 5 OCTOBER, 1943 10¢ COPY

MILITARY EQUALITY—A Victory Demand

By JESSIE SCOTT CAMPBELL

A major weapon for victory of a nation at war is its fighting forces. Under the leadership of our Commander-in-Chief, President Roosevelt,

There are those who argue against changing United States Army and Navy policy relating to recruitment and use of Negroes on the grounds that to cease the policy of

jected to the lynch rule of fascist-minded southern officials; used almost exclusively in labor battalions? Such defiance of the four freedoms can serve only one purpose—to strengthen

Fig. 6—Elizabeth Catlett, Portrait sketches for "Military Equality—A Victory Demand," *Congress Vue* 1, no. 5 (October 1943), National Negro Congress records, Schomburg Center for Research in Black Culture, The New York Public Library

the inequalities faced by Black men and women during the war effort became even more visible. While soldiers died for their country, war workers faced ongoing discrimination on the home front. Catlett and many of her peers seized the opportunity to address these issues in their artworks, in a communal visual protest bolstered by their shared political beliefs and experience of racial oppression. Illustration became an important avenue for Catlett, as she took direct action through her work for *Congress Vue*, the periodical of the National Negro Congress (NNC). She later contrasted her printmaking with her sculpture: "I'm thinking differently in the two mediums. In the printmaking I'm thinking about something social or political, and in the sculpture I'm thinking about form."[39] In alignment with the NNC's agenda, Catlett's images in published issues of *Congress Vue*, along with unpublished drawings, helped urge Black Americans to vote for Franklin Delano Roosevelt, demand military equality, and argue for workers' rights (fig. 6).

For Catlett, it was also a moment of heightened attention to painting, though it is unknown how many compositions she created in response to war.[40] The medium offered her another vehicle for conveying a message of social justice; while formal considerations were undeniably important, they were in service to her political point. In *War Worker* (p. 22), a subject that White also painted two years later (1945, Montclair Art Museum), Catlett drew on her lessons in abstraction as she emphasized the man's angular facial features, such as the sharp line of the nose. Here Catlett's sweeping brushstrokes create a dynamic rhythm around the face, heightening the focus on his downcast eyes. The composition is expressive and empathetic, evoking the man's humanity despite his working-class origins. Similarly, in *Red Cross Woman (Nurse)* and its related study *Army Nurse* (pp. 27, 26), Catlett accentuated the shadows around the figure's uplifted eyes, calling attention to the woman's determination in the face of weariness and hardship. Black women nurses faced significant racial discrimination during World War II, but here Catlett endowed the subject with heroic notes, positioning the Black woman as vital to the war effort.

FOR A BETTER FUTURE

Catlett's wartime paintings and sculptures directly resulted from her accumulative experience, friendships, and contact with the Chicago art scene and her equally vital participation in New York's socialist artistic community. They brought her increased visibility, building on the recognition she achieved initially at the American Negro Exposition in 1940, and anticipate her later efforts to right political wrongs through printmaking and consistently uplift Black womanhood. In April 1945, Catlett at last received her own Rosenwald Fellowship to produce a series on Black women in painting, prints, and sculpture. Busy in New York with her work at the Carver School, she found it difficult to make progress. When it was renewed the following year, after the end of war had opened up travel again, she and White traveled to Mexico to work at the national art school known as La Esmeralda (Escuela Nacional de Pintura y Escultura) and at the TGP. The couple also initiated divorce proceedings, and Catlett began the next phase of her life. But her experiences in Chicago and New York gave her insight into how a supportive community of politically aligned peers could help her grow as an artist, advance her career, and create art in the service of a better future.

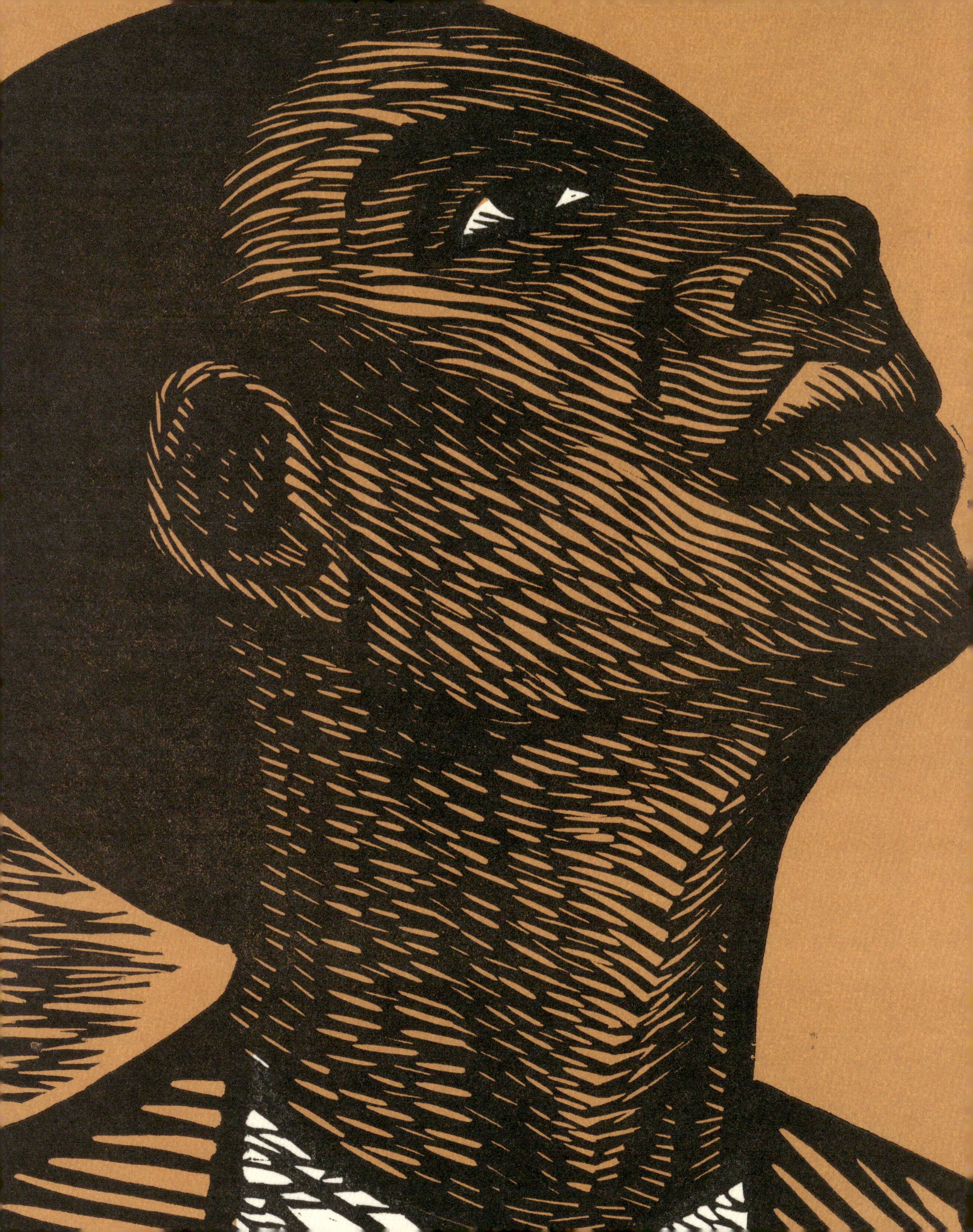

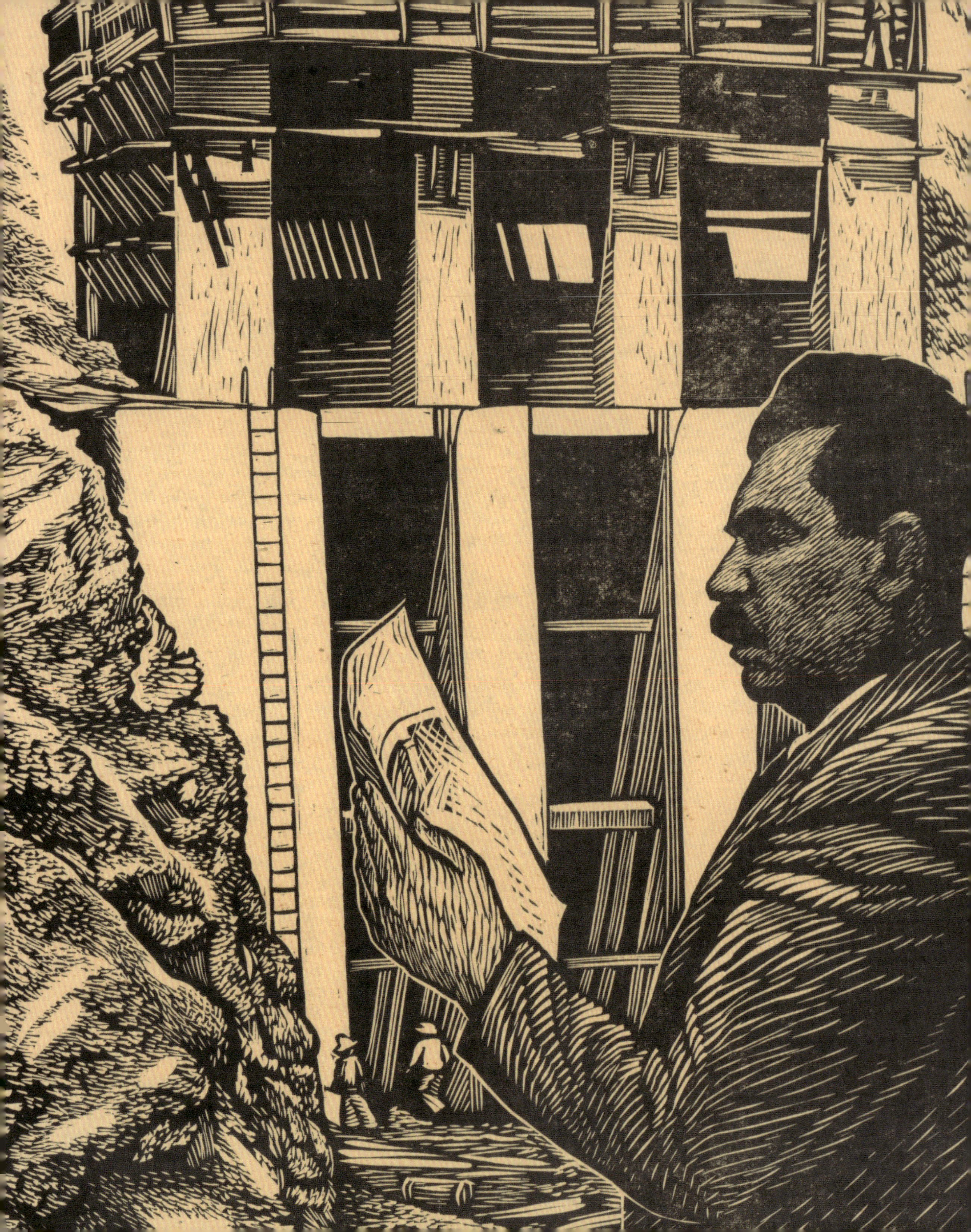

PLATES

1947–1960

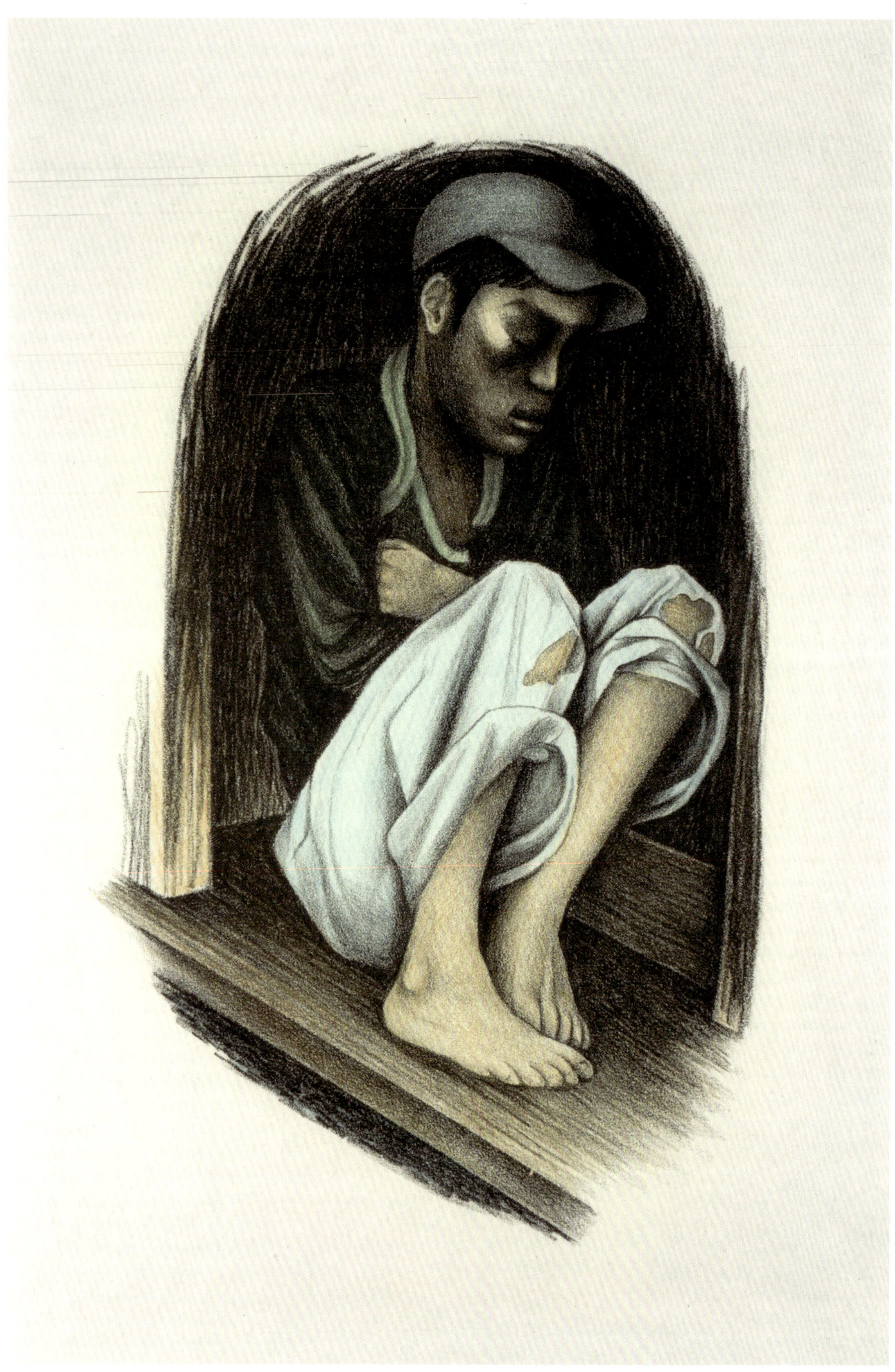

Niño Papelero, 1947, color lithograph, 18⅞ × 12¹³⁄₁₆ in., Colección Academia de Artes, México

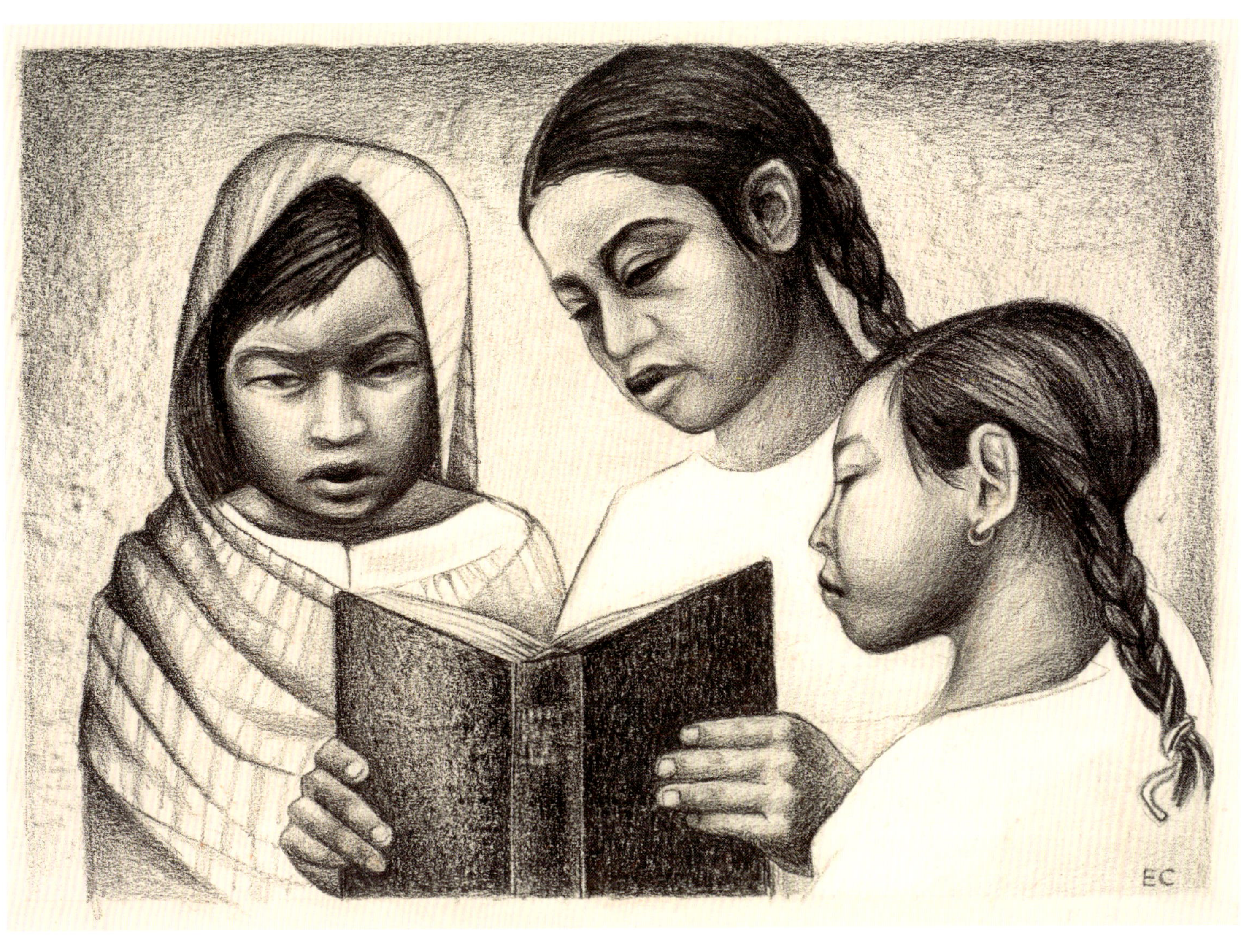

The Lesson, c. 1948, crayon, 17$\frac{3}{8}$ × 22$\frac{15}{16}$ in., Rhode Island School of Design Museum, Providence, RI, Helen M. Danforth Acquisition Fund

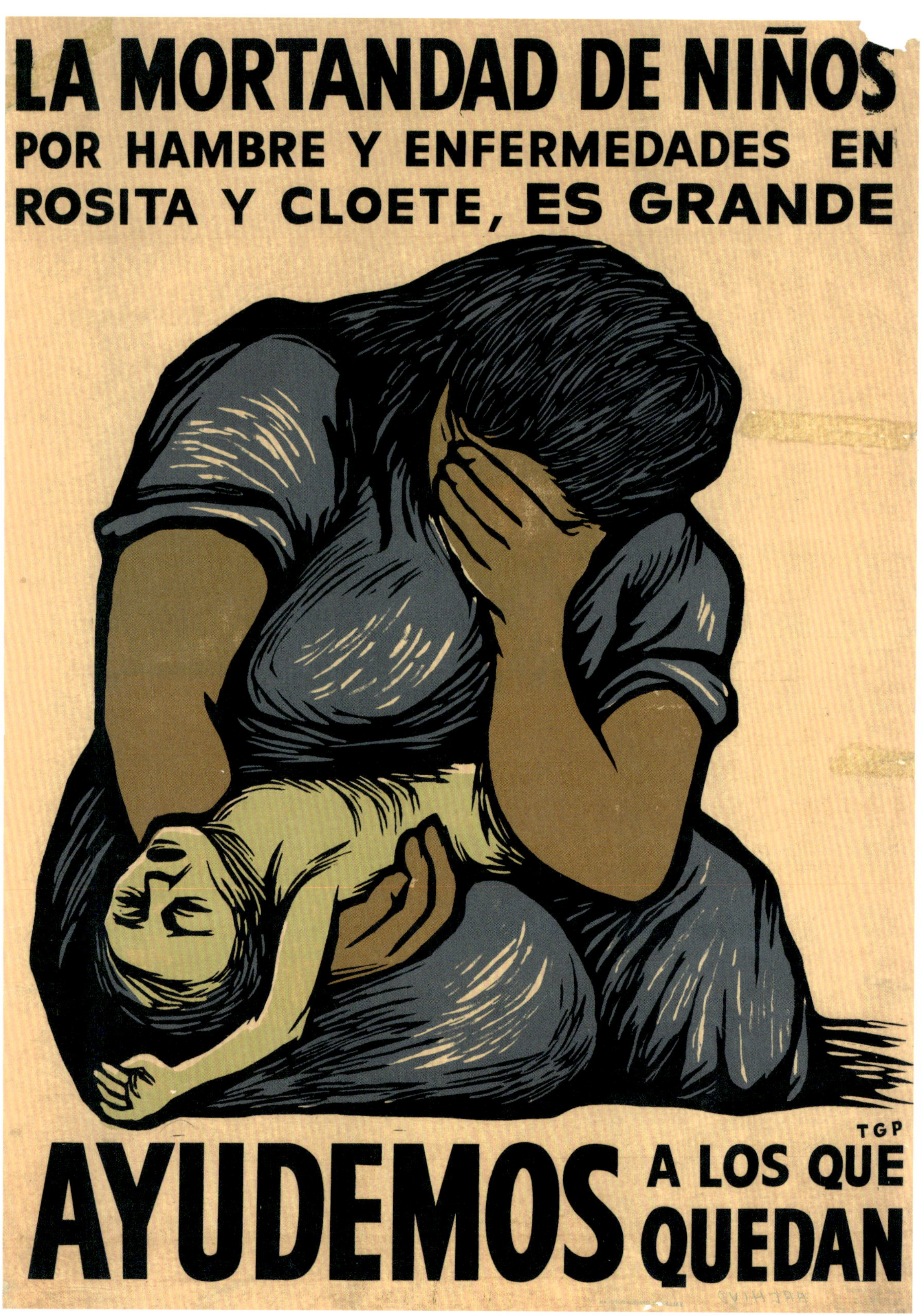

Elizabeth Catlett, Leopoldo Méndez, Pablo O'Higgins, Jesús Escobedo, *La mortandad de niños por hambre y enfermedades en Nueva Rosita y Cloete es grande*, c. 1950, screenprint, 37⅜ × 27¾ in., Center for Southwest Research and Special Collections, University of New Mexico Libraries

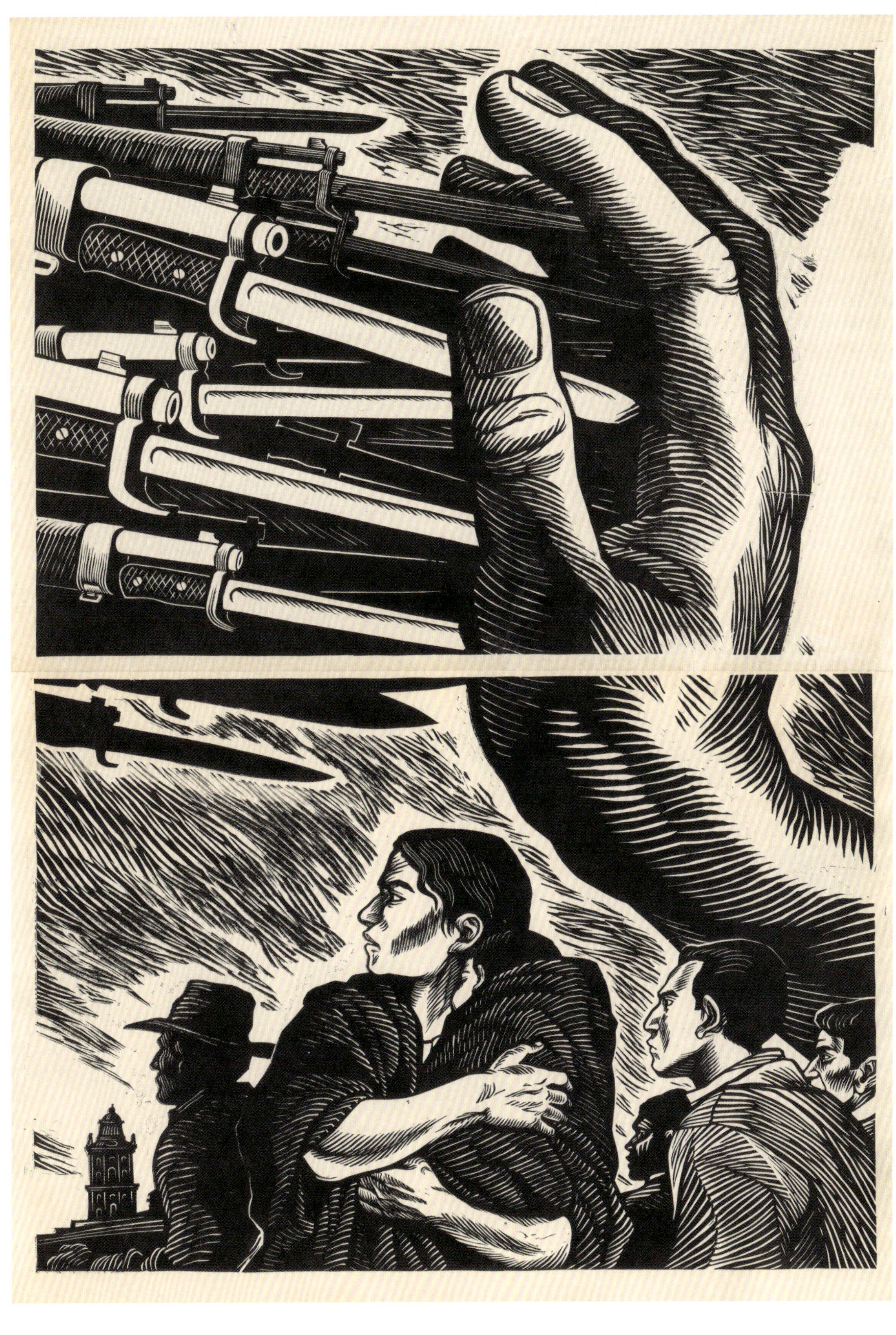

Elizabeth Catlett, Alberto Beltrán, *Untitled (Composition for a Peace Poster)*, c. 1950, linocut on two sheets, 74¾ × 55⅛ in., The Art Institute of Chicago, Prints and Drawings Purchase Fund, 2014.582

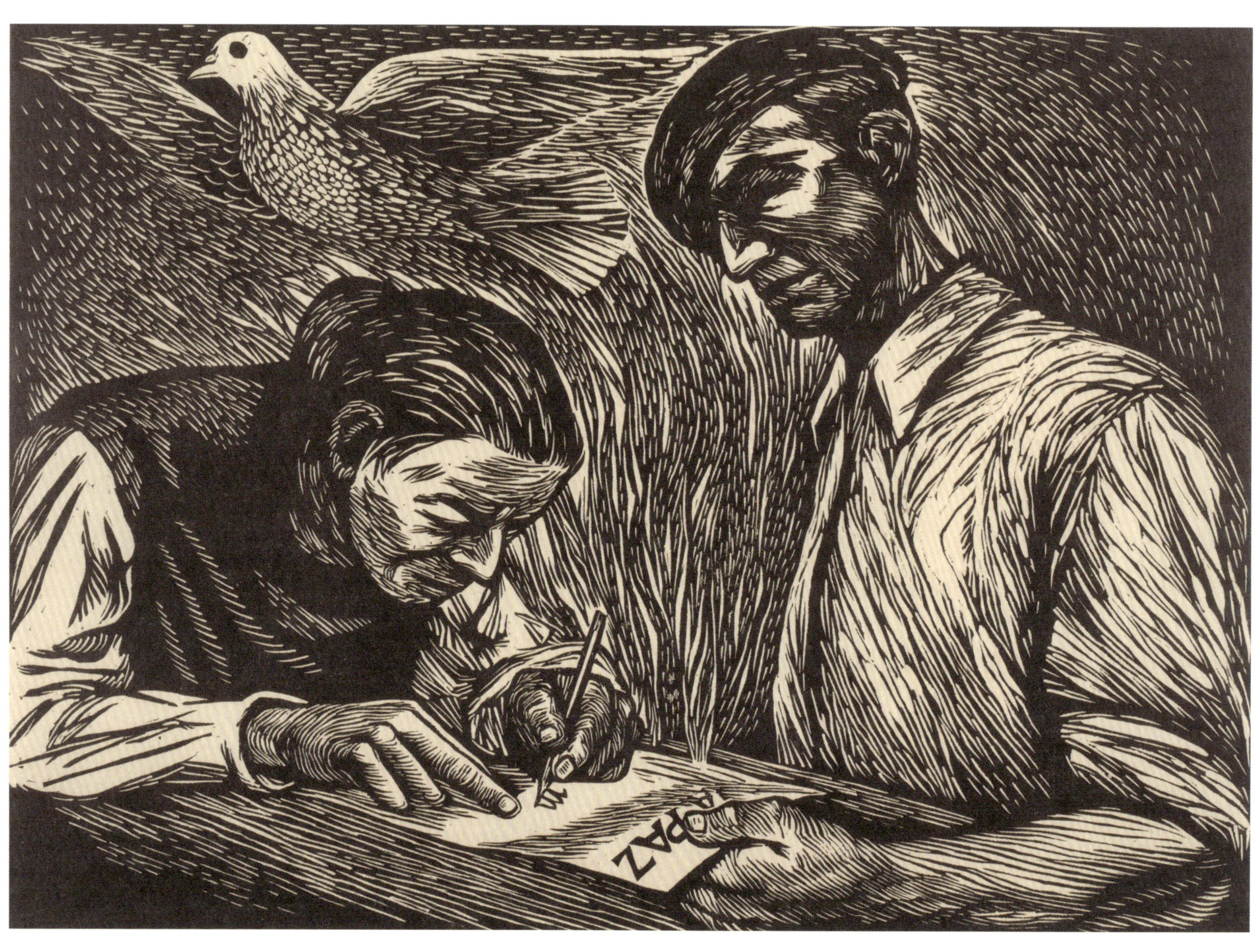

Firmas para la Paz, 1952, linocut, $19\frac{1}{8} \times 25\frac{3}{16}$ in., Peter Schneider and Susan DeJarnatt

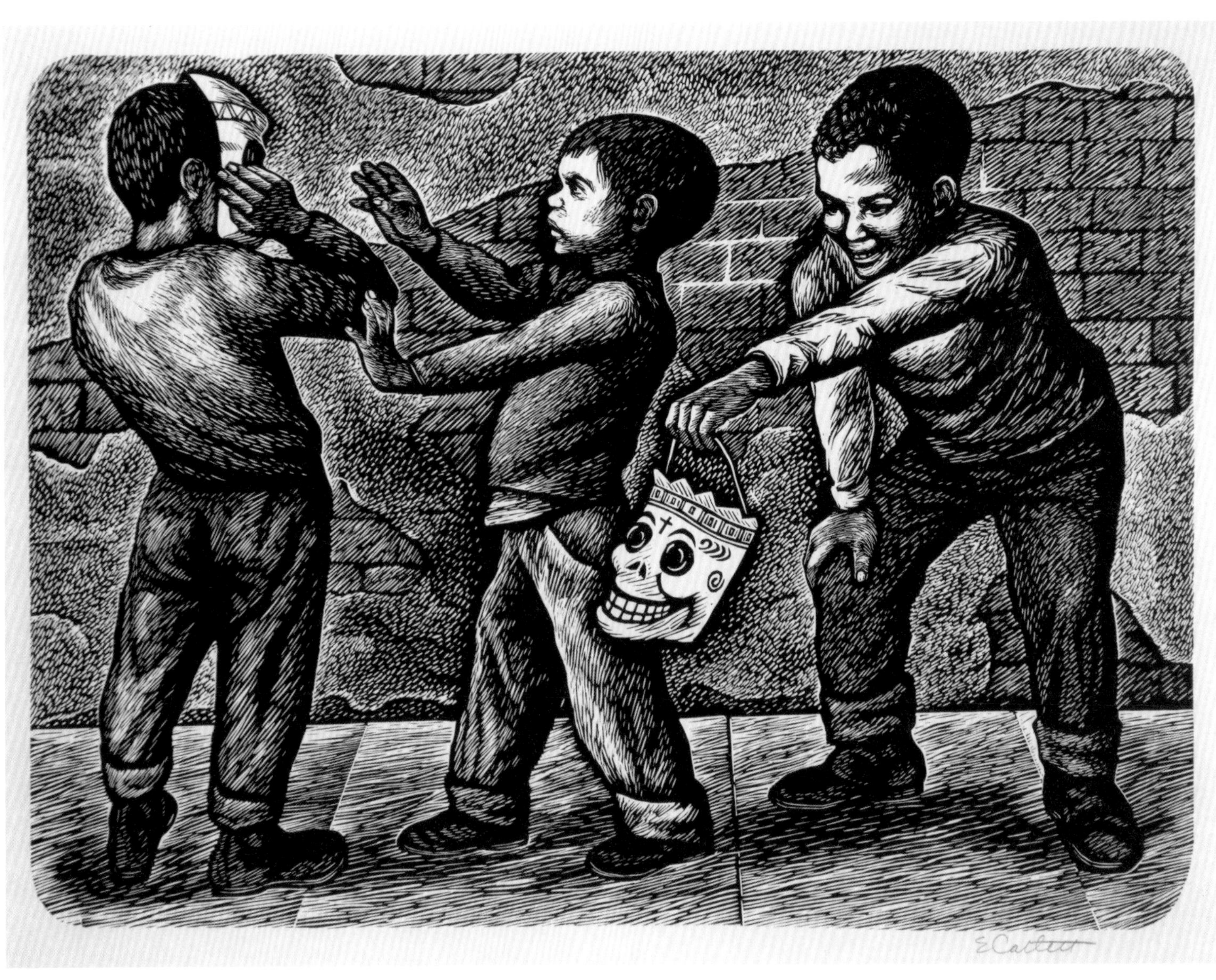

Mis Niños, 1958, linocut, 12$\frac{13}{16}$ × 19$\frac{11}{16}$ in., Colección Academia de Artes, México

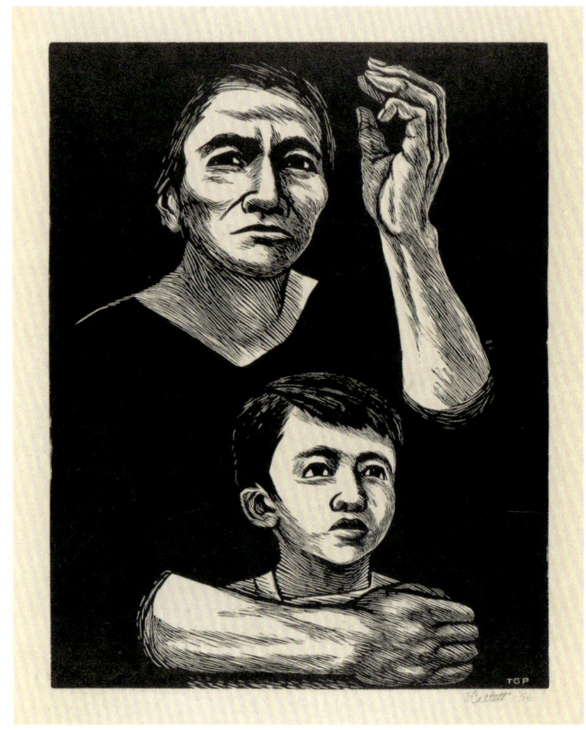

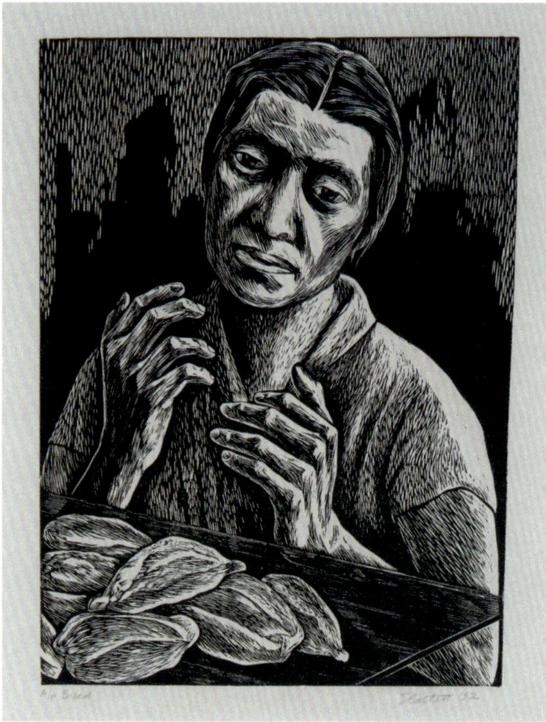

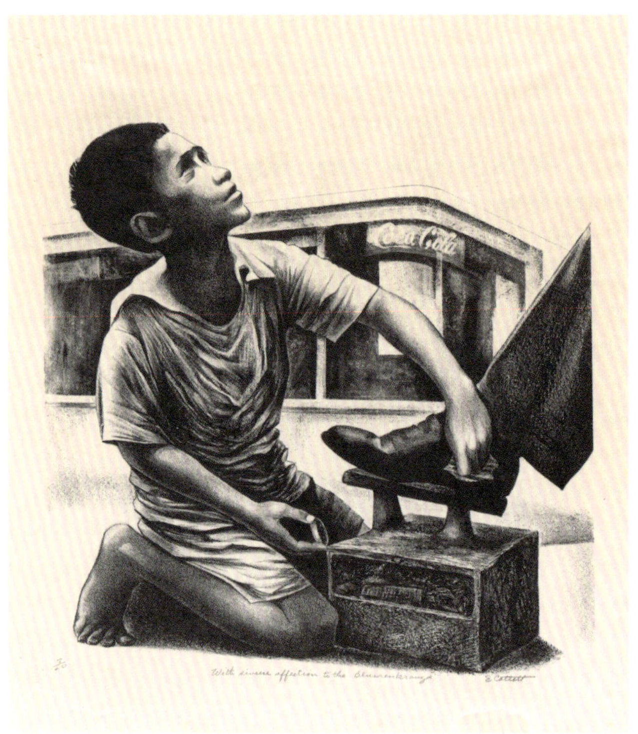

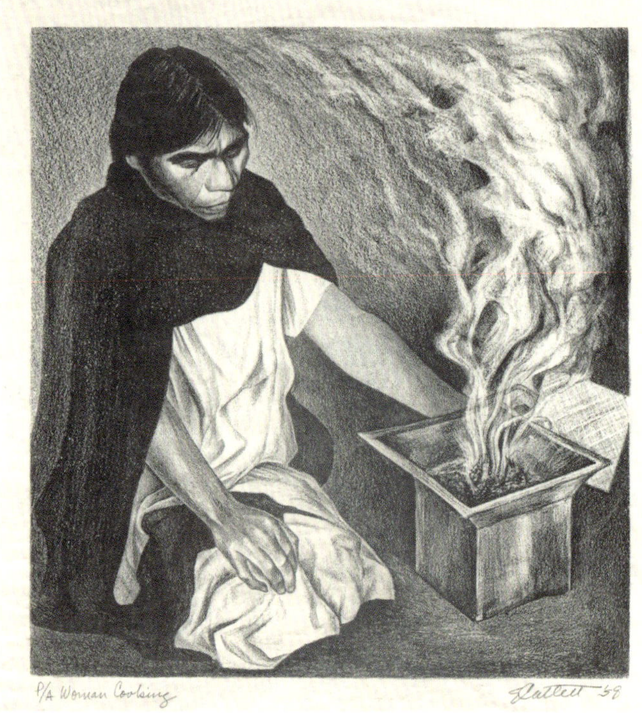

Untitled (Mother and Child), 1956, linocut, 20½ × 15¾ in., From the Collection of the Elizabeth Catlett-Mora Family Living Trust

Shoeshine Boy, 1958, lithograph on wove paper, 22¹³⁄₁₆ × 19¾ in., National Gallery of Art, Ailsa Mellon Bruce Fund

Pan, 1952, linocut, 16 × 11¾ in., From the Collection of the Elizabeth Catlett-Mora Family Living Trust

Mujer Cocinando (Woman Cooking), 1958, lithograph on wove paper, 15³⁄₁₆ × 13⅞ in., Yale University Art Gallery, Leonard C. Hanna, Jr., Class of 1913, Fund

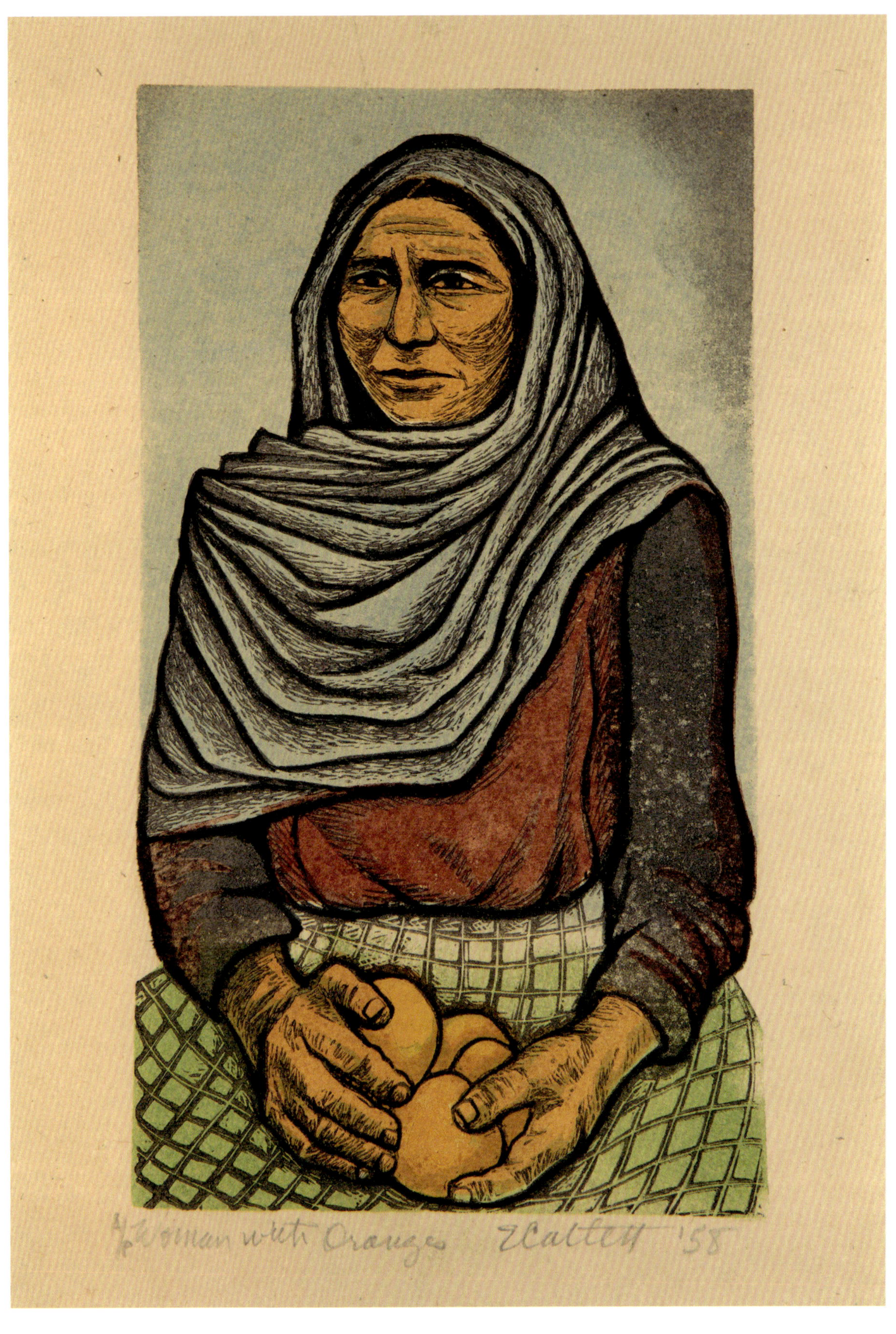

Woman with Oranges, 1958, linocut, 20$\frac{15}{16}$ × 17 × 1$\frac{13}{16}$ in., From the Hampton University Museum Collection, Hampton, VA

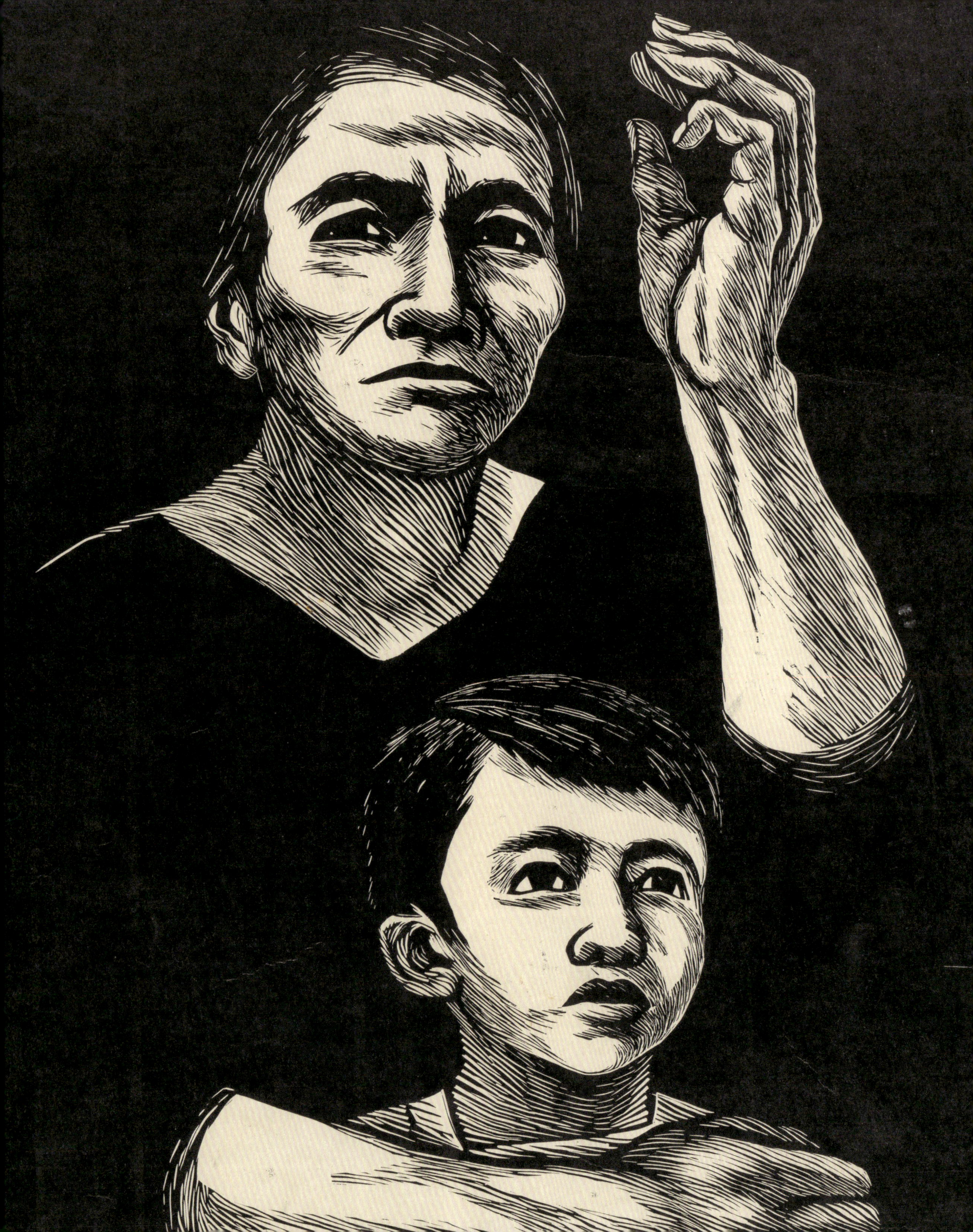

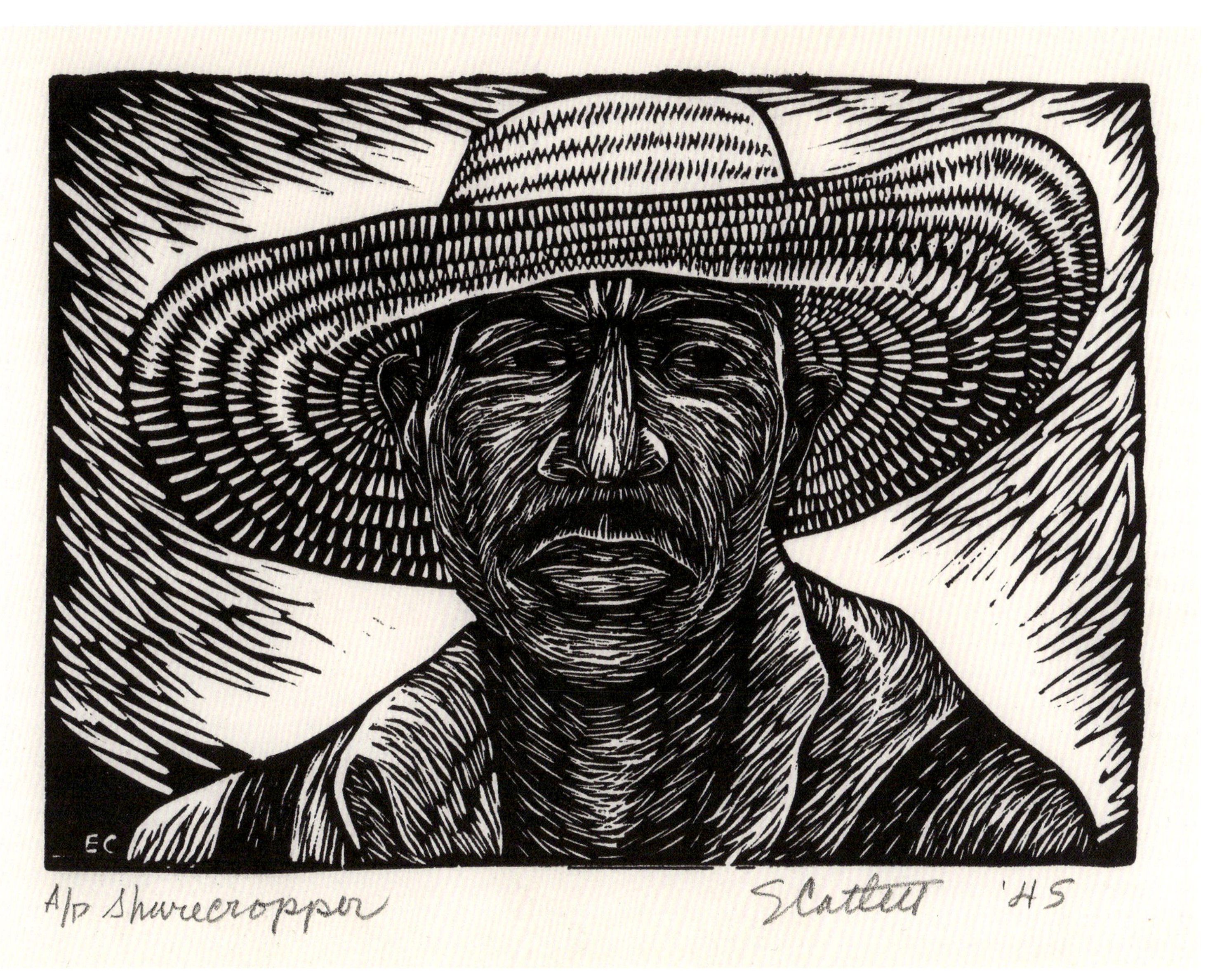

Sharecropper (male), 1945, linocut, 9½ × 12¼ in., Williams College Museum of Art, Museum purchase, Kathryn Hurd Fund

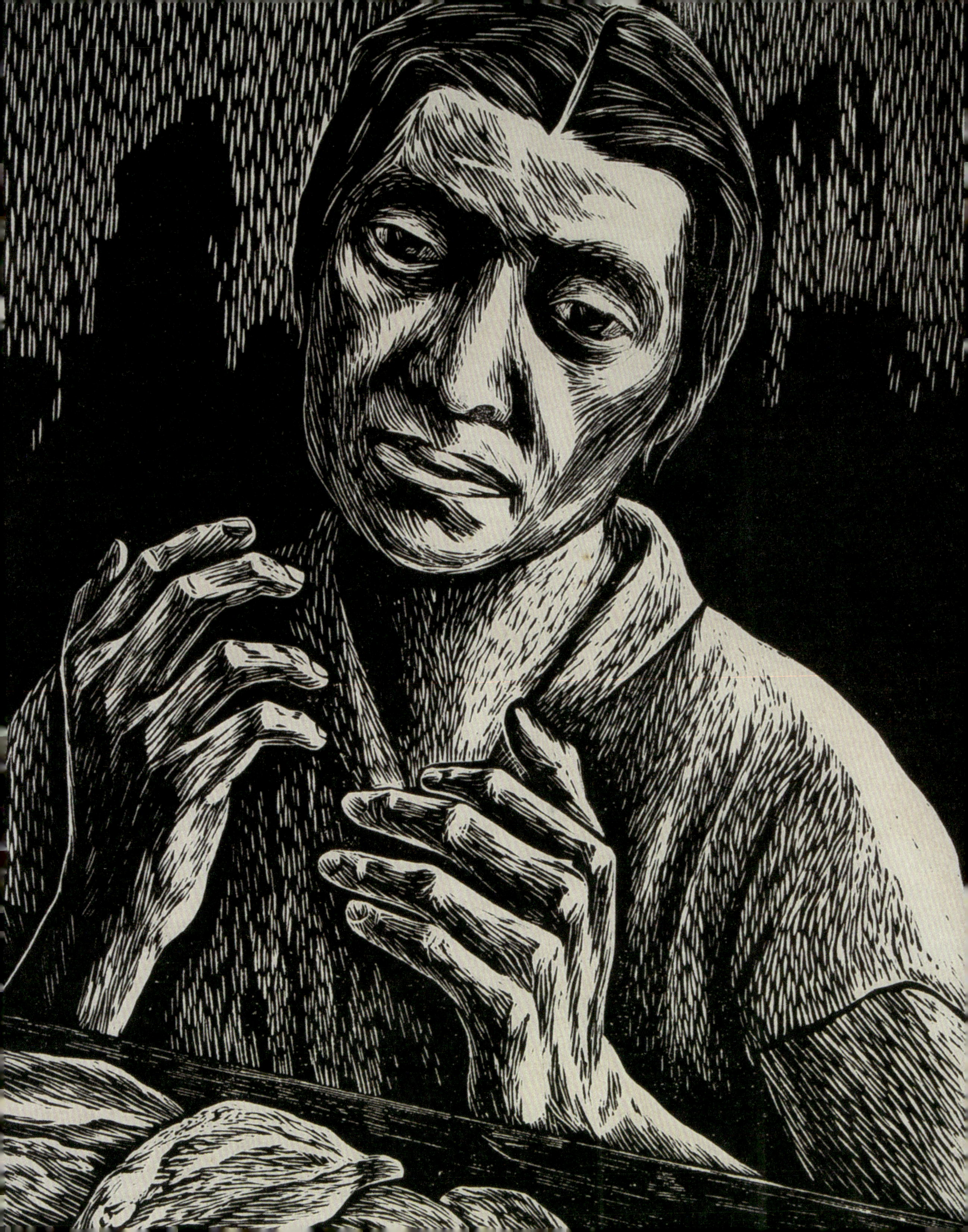

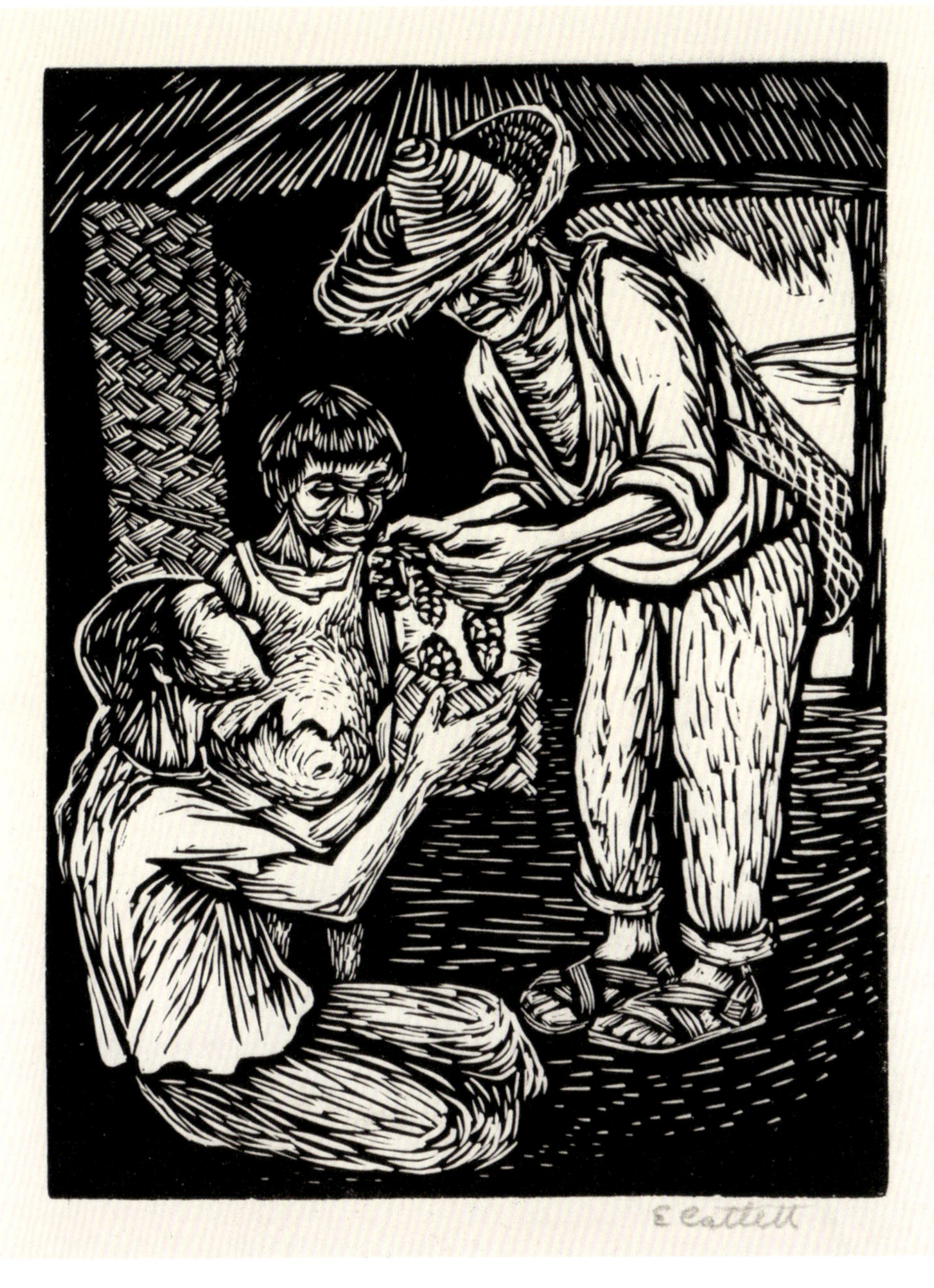

Campesinos Mexicanos, 1947, printed 1958, linocut, 13⅜ × 10¹⁄₁₆ in., Colección Academia de Artes, México

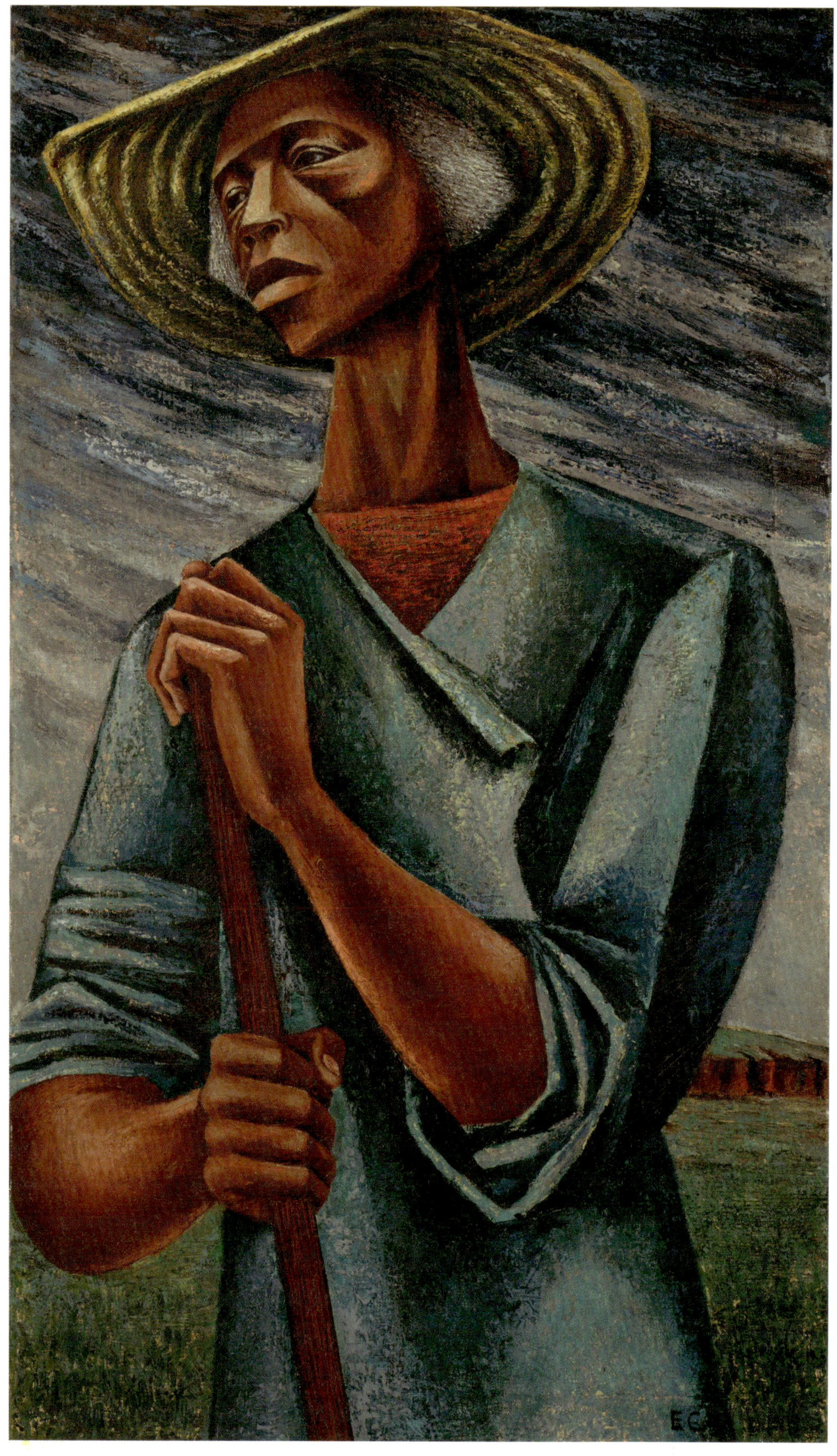

Sharecropper, 1946, oil on canvas, 39½ × 22½ in., Collection of John and Hortense Russell

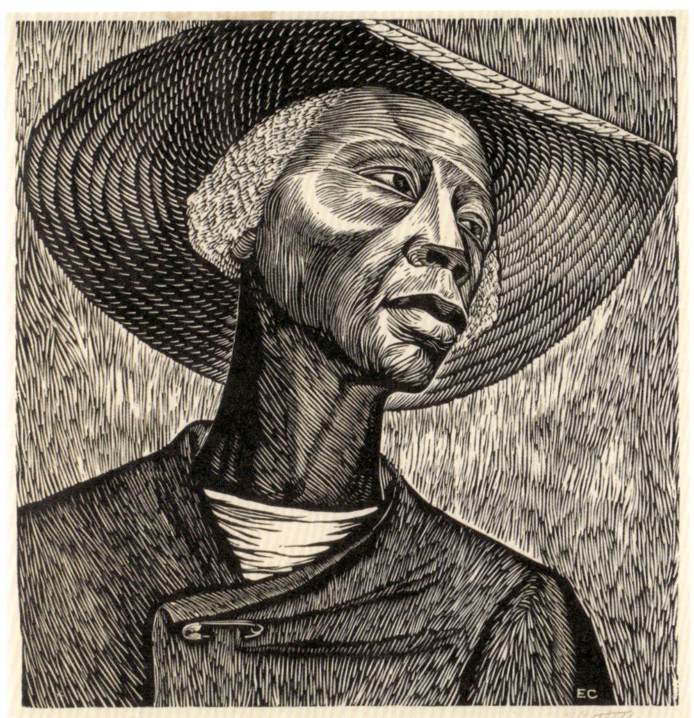

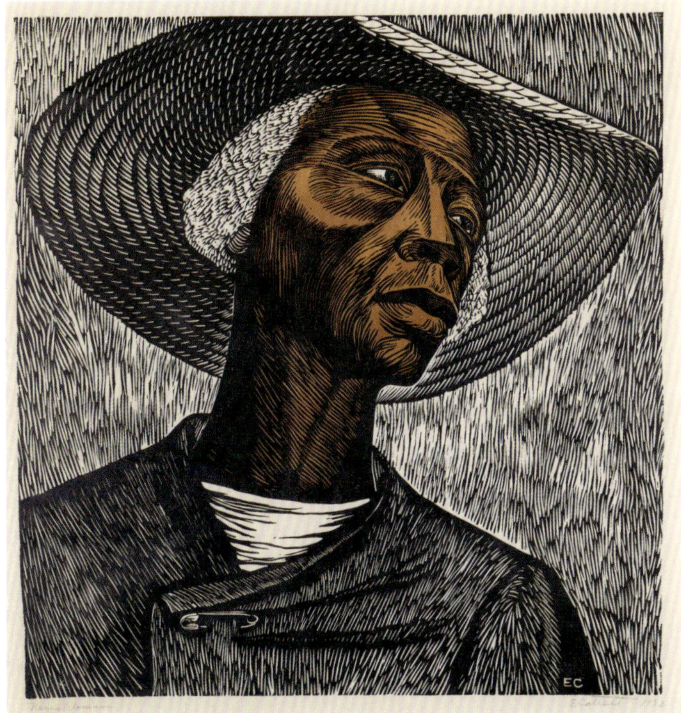

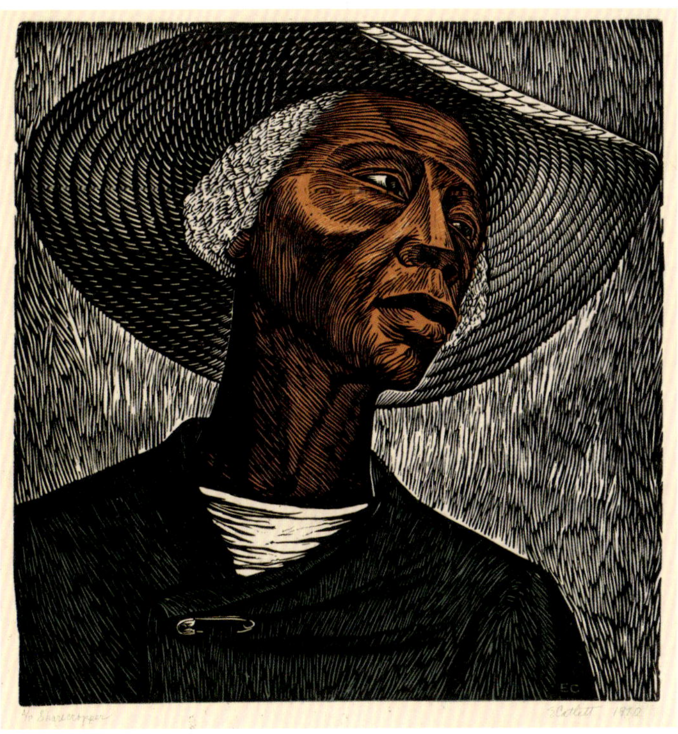

Sharecropper, 1952, linocut, 24 15/16 × 19 11/16 in., Davis Museum at Wellesley College, Wellesley, MA, Gift of Paula Kaplan Hawkins (Class of 1957), 2003.13

Sharecropper, 1952, linocut, 16½ × 17½ in., Clark Atlanta University Art Museum, Atlanta Art Annuals: Second Atlanta University Purchase Award, Print, 1952.008

Sharecropper, 1952, printed 1970, color linocut on cream Japanese paper, 21 15/16 × 20 5/16 in., The Art Institute of Chicago, Purchased with funds provided by Mr. and Mrs. Robert S. Hartman, 1992.182

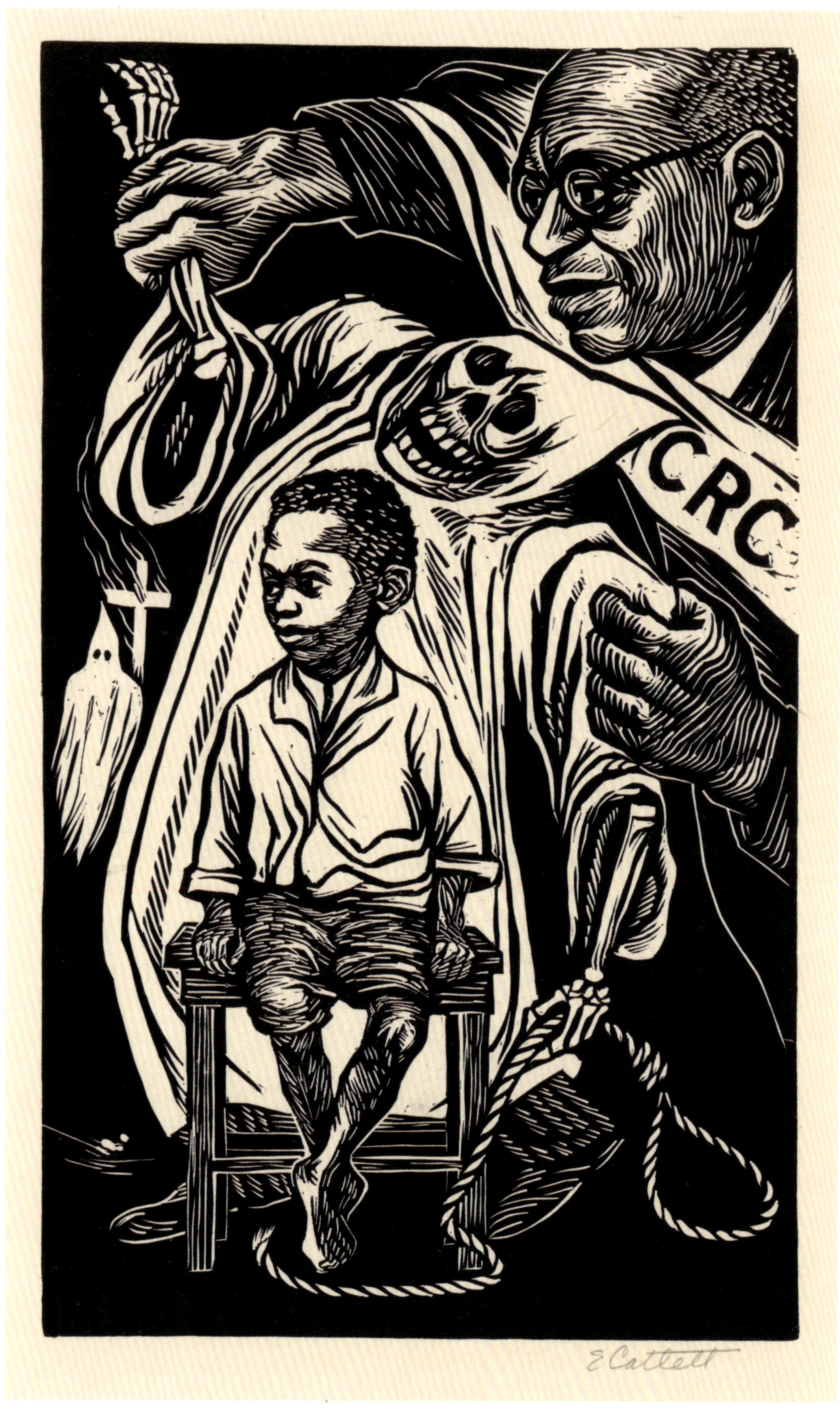

Civil Rights Congress, 1949, linocut, 12¼ × 7⅛ in., Donald Hardy and P. Bruce Marine Collection

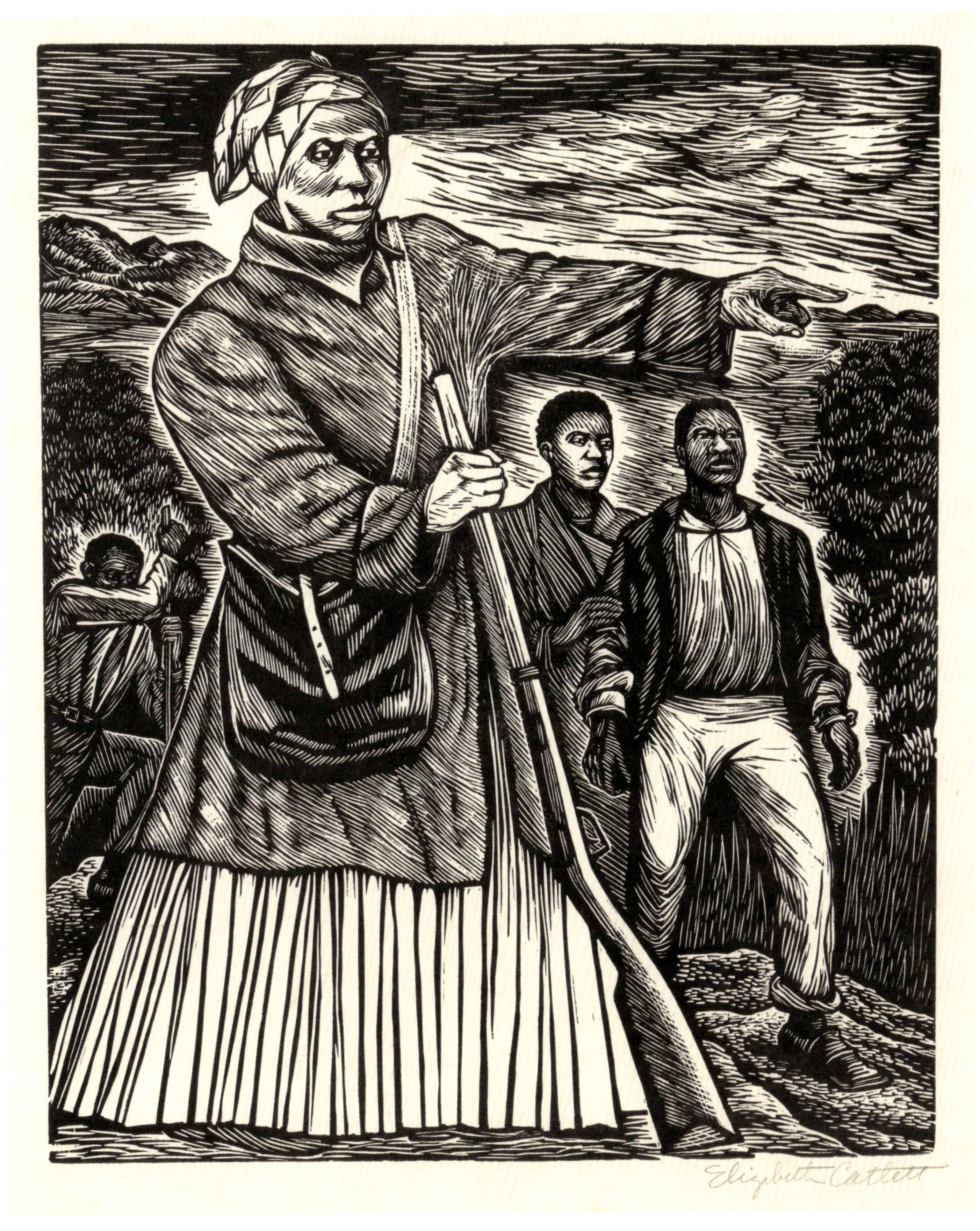

Untitled (Harriet Tubman), from *Against Discrimination in the US* series, 1953, linocut, 16⅛ × 12⅞ in., National Gallery of Art, Reba and Dave Williams Collection, Florian Carr Fund and Gift of the Print Research Foundation

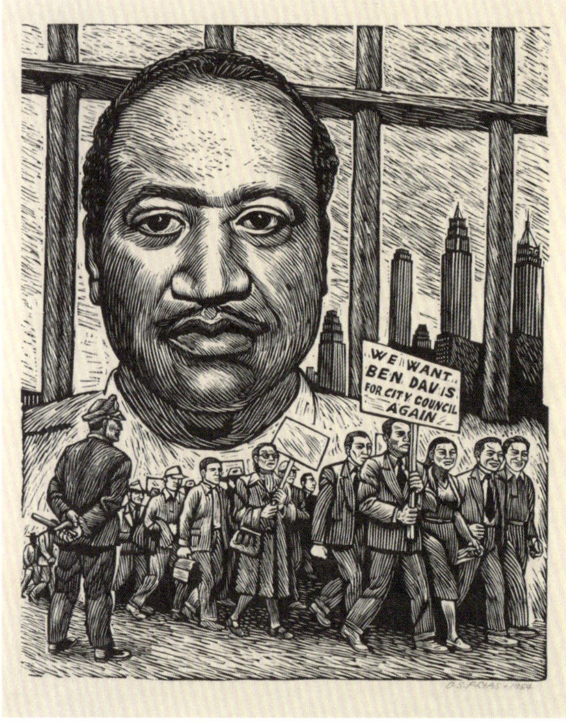

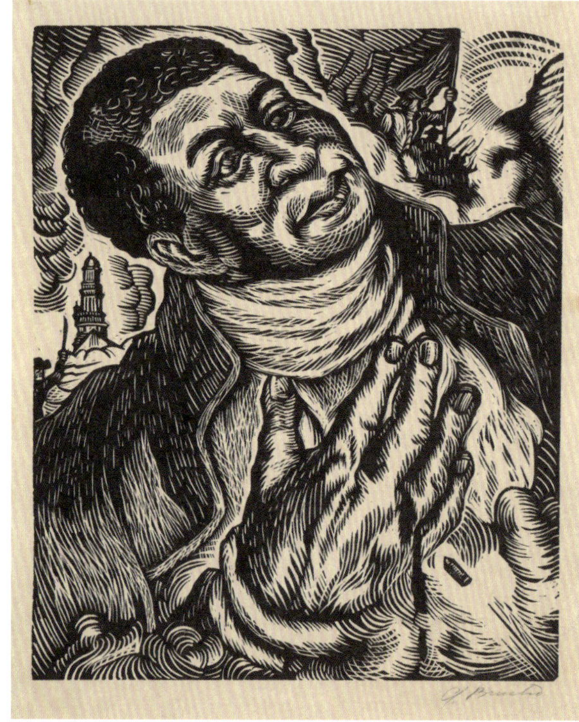

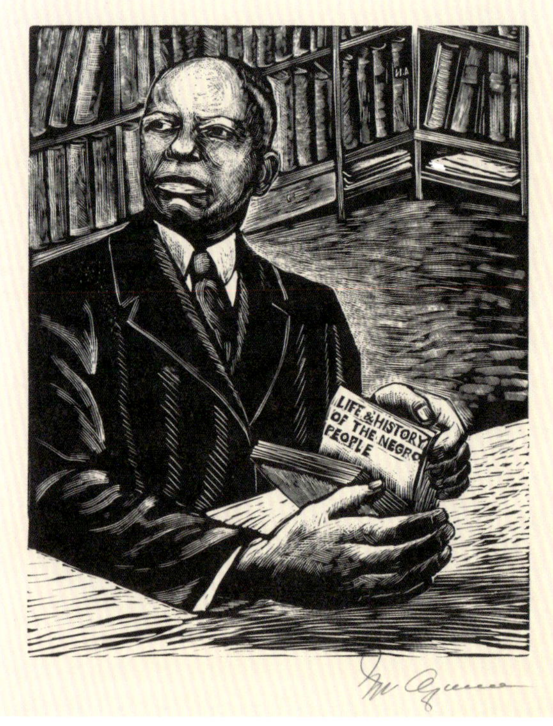

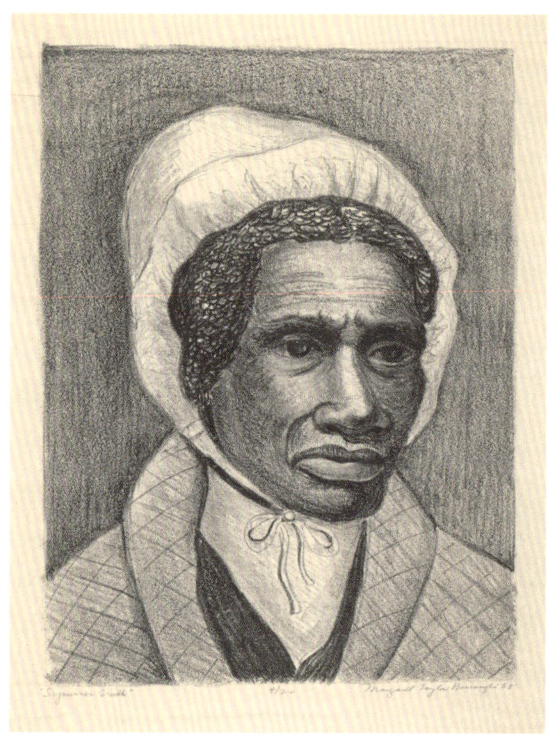

Óscar Frías, *Benjamin Davis*, from *Against Discrimination in the US* series, 1954, linocut, 17 3/16 × 12 13/16 in., Prints and Photographs Division, Library of Congress, Washington, DC

Ignacio Aguirre, *Carter G. Woodson*, from *Against Discrimination in the US* series, c. 1950, linocut, 19 11/16 × 12 13/16 in., Prints and Photographs Division, Library of Congress, Washington, DC

Ángel Bracho, *Heroe negro (Crispus Attucks)*, from *Against Discrimination in the US* series, c. 1970, linocut, 15 13/16 × 11 1/8 in., Prints and Photographs Division, Library of Congress, Washington, DC

Margaret Burroughs, *Sojourner Truth*, from *Against Discrimination in the US* series, 1953, lithograph, 25 5/16 × 17 9/16 in., Prints and Photographs Division, Library of Congress, Washington, DC

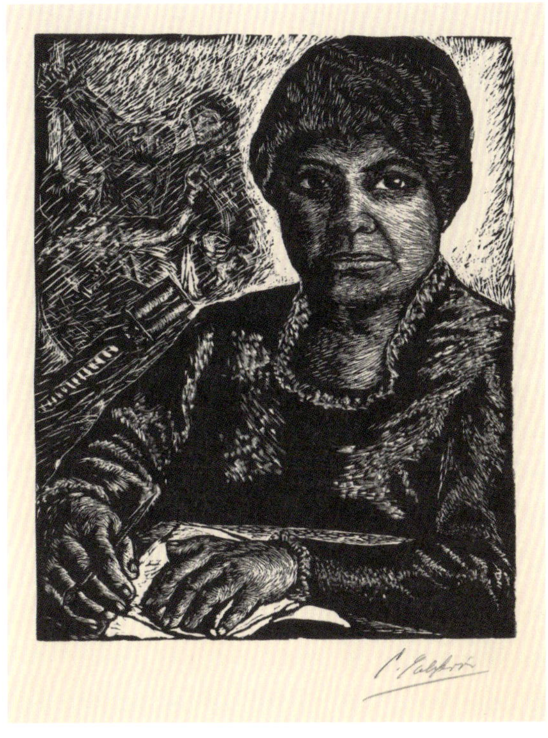

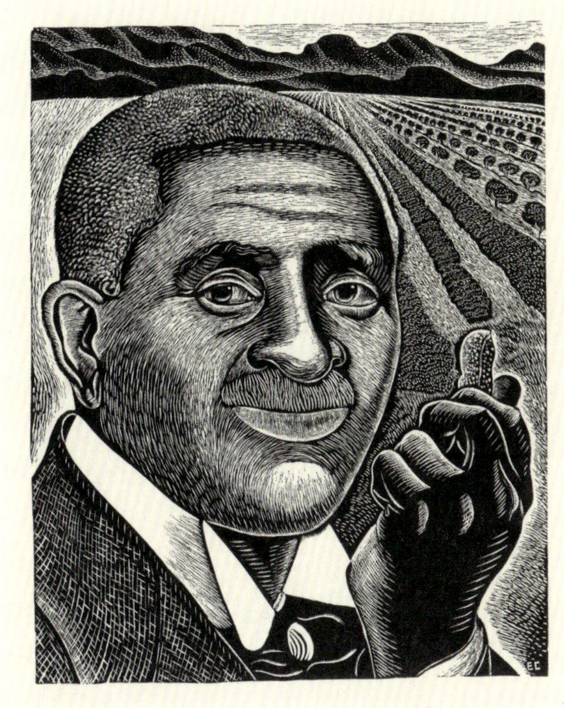

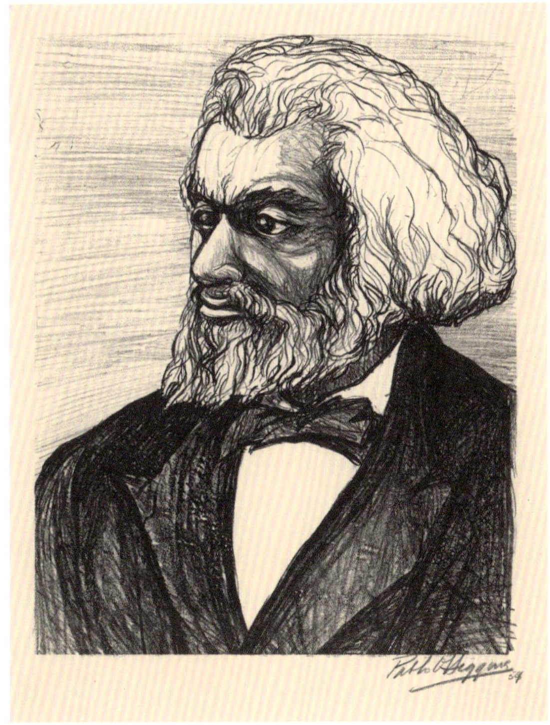

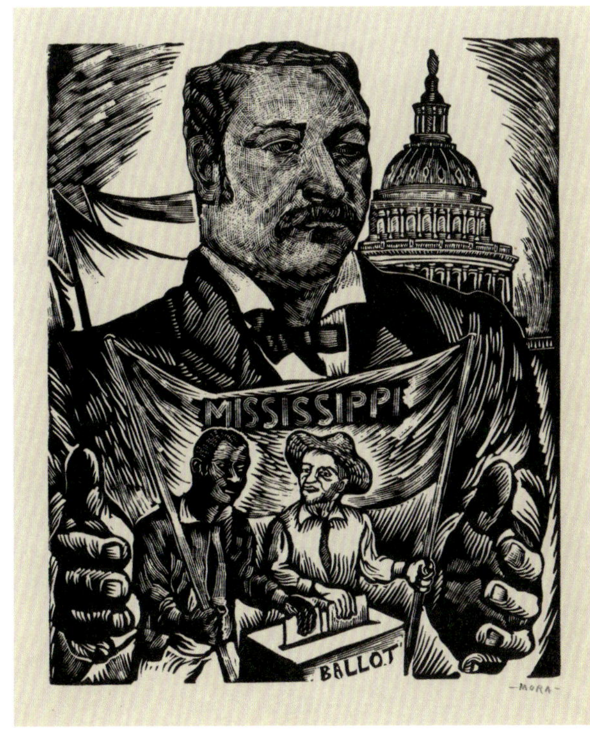

Celia Calderón, *Ida B. Wells-Barnett*, from *Against Discrimination in the US* series, c. 1950, linocut, $19\frac{11}{16} \times 12\frac{13}{16}$ in., Prints and Photographs Division, Library of Congress, Washington, DC

Pablo O'Higgins, *Frederick Douglass*, from *Against Discrimination in the US* series, c. 1953–1954, lithograph, $19\frac{11}{16} \times 13$ in., Prints and Photographs Division, Library of Congress, Washington, DC

Erasto Cortés Juárez, *George Washington Carver*, from *Against Discrimination in the US* series, 1952, linocut, 19¾ × 12¾ in., The New York Public Library, The Miriam and Ira D. Wallach Division of Art, Prints and Photographs

Francisco Mora, *Mississippi/Ballot (Blanche K. Bruce)*, from *Against Discrimination in the US* series, c. 1953–1954, linocut, 17¾ × 12¾ in., Ben Goldstein Poster Collection, Print Collection, Miriam and Ira D. Wallach Division of Art, Prints and Photographs, The New York Public Library, Astor, Lenox and Tilden Foundations

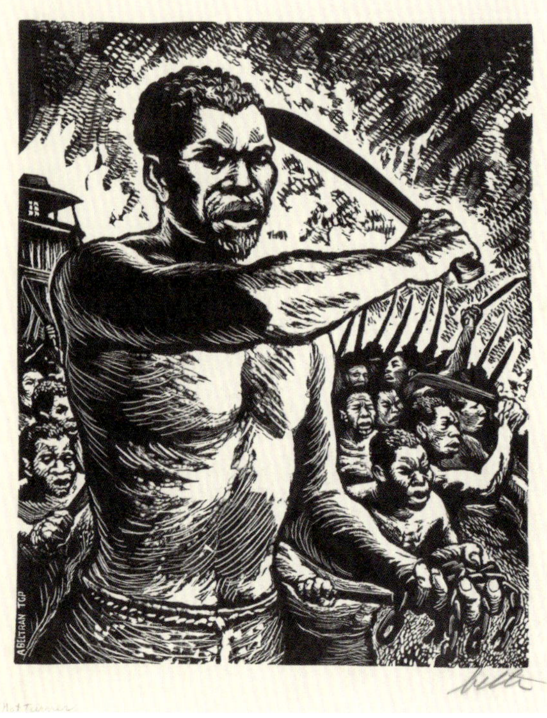

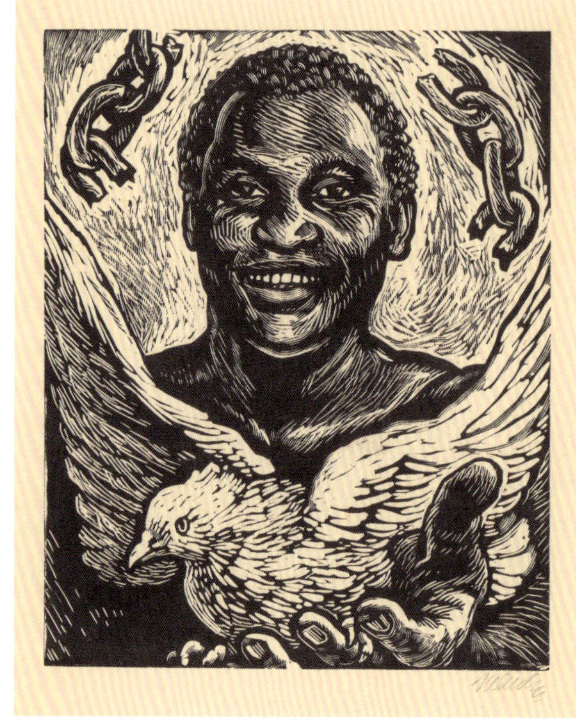

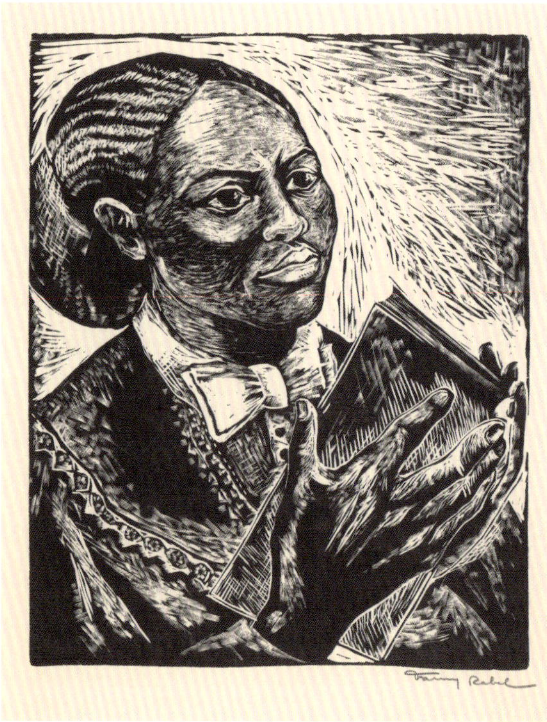

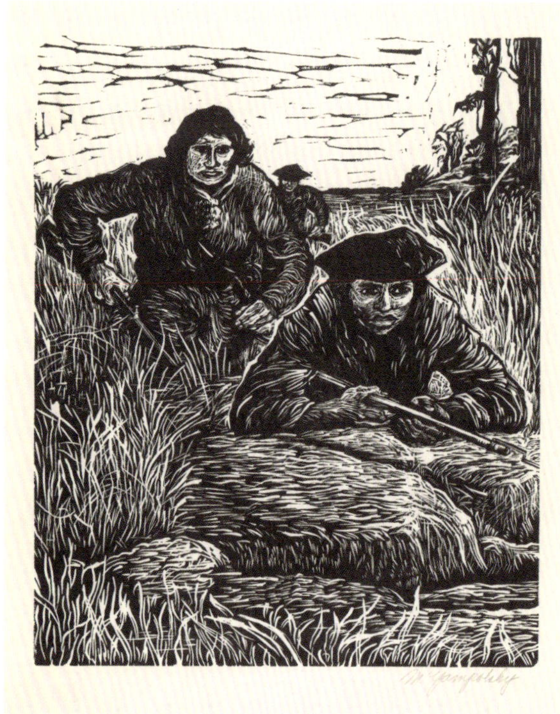

Alberto Beltrán, *Nat Turner*, from *Against Discrimination in the US* series, c. 1953–1954, linocut, 14 × 11 in., Ben Goldstein Poster Collection, Print Collection, Miriam and Ira D. Wallach Division of Art, Prints and Photographs, The New York Public Library, Astor, Lenox and Tilden Foundations

Leopoldo Méndez, *Paul Robeson*, from *Against Discrimination in the US* series, 1960–1970, linocut, $19\frac{11}{16} \times 12\frac{15}{16}$ in., Prints and Photographs Division, Library of Congress, Washington, DC

Fanny Rabel, *Frances Ellen Watkins Harper*, from *Against Discrimination in the US* series, c. 1950–1970, linocut, $19\frac{11}{16} \times 12\frac{13}{16}$ in., Prints and Photographs Division, Library of Congress, Washington, DC

Mariana Yampolsky, *Guerillero negro*, from *Against Discrimination in the US* series, c. 1950–1970, linocut, $19\frac{11}{16} \times 12\frac{13}{16}$ in., Prints and Photographs Division, Library of Congress, Washington, DC

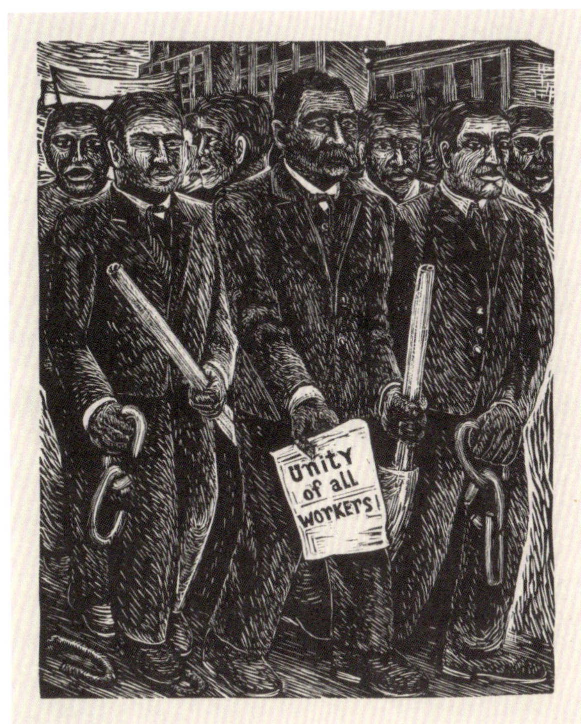

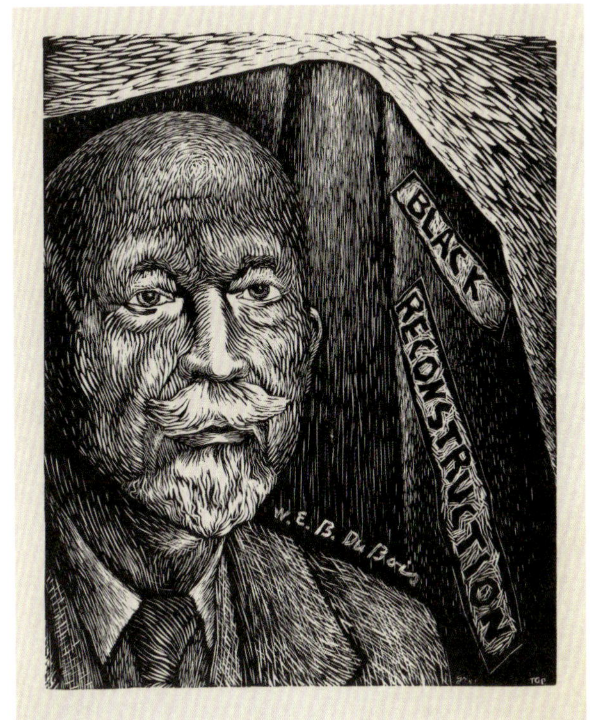

Francisco Luna, *Unity of All Workers (Isaac Myers)*, from *Against Discrimination in the US* series, 1954, linocut, 18½ × 13⅝ in., Prints and Photographs Division, Library of Congress, Washington, DC

Guillermo Rodriguez, *W. E. B. Du Bois (Black Reconstruction)*, from *Against Discrimination in the US* series, c. 1953–1954, linocut, 18¾ × 13¾ in., Ben Goldstein Poster Collection, Print Collection, Miriam and Ira D. Wallach Division of Art, Prints and Photographs, The New York Public Library, Astor, Lenox and Tilden Foundations

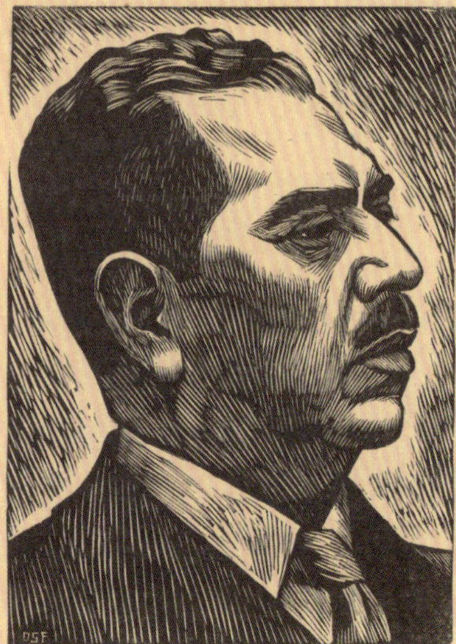

LAZARO CARDENAS, ilustre ex-presidente de México, hombre del pueblo y símbolo de sus mejores luchas. Por sus labios, la patria ha expresado sus más claros y rotundos anhelos de libertad y justicia social, amistad, comprensión y paz para todos los pueblos. El eco internacional de su invariable actitud pacifista ha conquistado, para él y para México simpatía, prestigio y respetabilidad. Este gran mexicano ha sido distinguido con el Premio Stalin de la Paz. Unámonos todos en el justo homenaje que los hombres de cinco continentes le rinden por su ejemplar actitud.

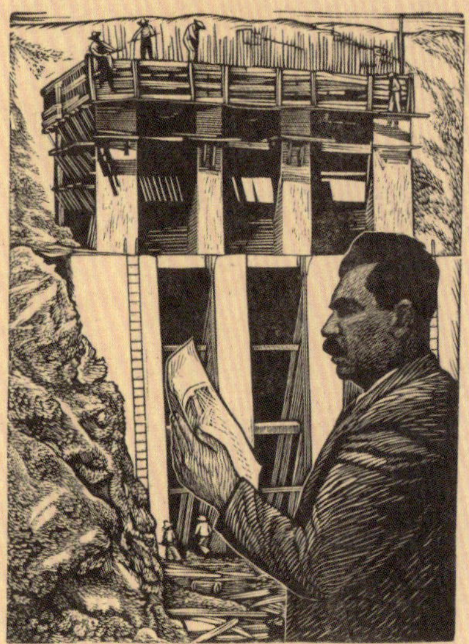

FIEL A LAS MEJORES banderas revolucionarias, LAZARO CARDENAS supo encauzar por canales de beneficio popular los recursos de la nación. En Zacatepec, donde aún se escucha el grito de Zapata, así como en tantos otros rincones del país, sacudido por la heroica lucha de nuestros campesinos, Cárdenas puso el poder al servicio de los sectores mayoritarios de nuestra población. Tierra y libertad, para que el campesino encuentre en el trabajo su liberación y no su esclavitud. ¡Honremos al mexicano ilustre!

HOMENAJE A CARDENAS

DOMINGO 26 DE FEBRERO A LAS 10 HORAS

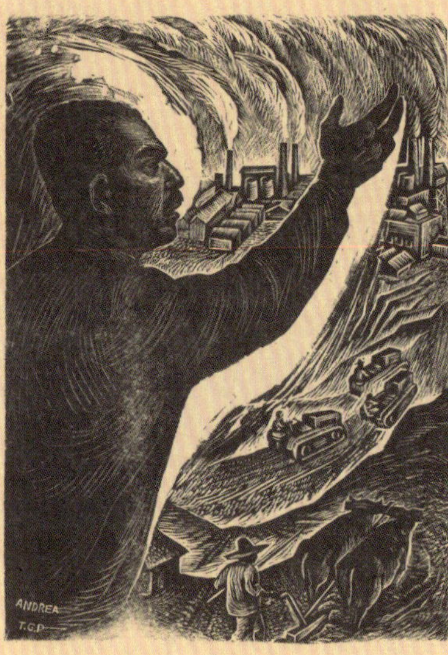

Su reconocida convicción pacifista, que dió jerarquía al nombre de la patria en el mundo entero, lo hace hoy objeto de una distinción mundial: el Premio Stalin de la Paz. Cárdenas representa hoy a los hombres que, en todo el mundo, están luchando por la paz y por el entendimiento entre los pueblos. ¡Unámonos al homenaje del mundo pacifista a Cárdenas.

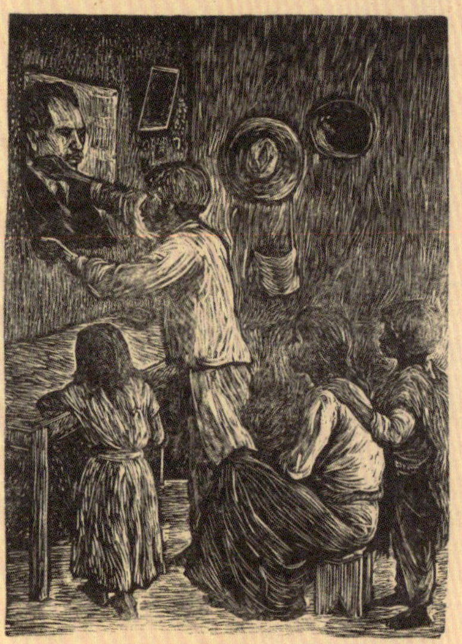

EN LA CHOZA MAS HUMILDE de nuestro país, hay siempre un lugar de veneración para LAZARO CARDENAS. Alejado de las urgencias y responsabilidades de la vida pública, Cárdenas sigue haciendo honor a su historia y su voz es siempre un llamado a la paz, a la concordia, a la tolerancia, en un mundo amenazado por la guerra. Hoy, el nombre de Cárdenas es pronunciado con respeto y simpatía. Su designación como acreedor al Premio Stalin de la Paz, es el reconocimiento de su limpia y leal militancia por la paz para todos, sin tolerancias.

NUEVO TEATRO IDEAL — SERAPIO RENDON 15

Movimiento Mexicano por la Paz

Elizabeth Catlett, Óscar Frías, Andrea Gómez, Mariana Yampolsky, *Homenaje a Cárdenas*, 1956, linocut, 34¹⁄₁₆ × 22¹⁄₁₆ in., Prints and Photographs Division, Library of Congress, Washington, DC

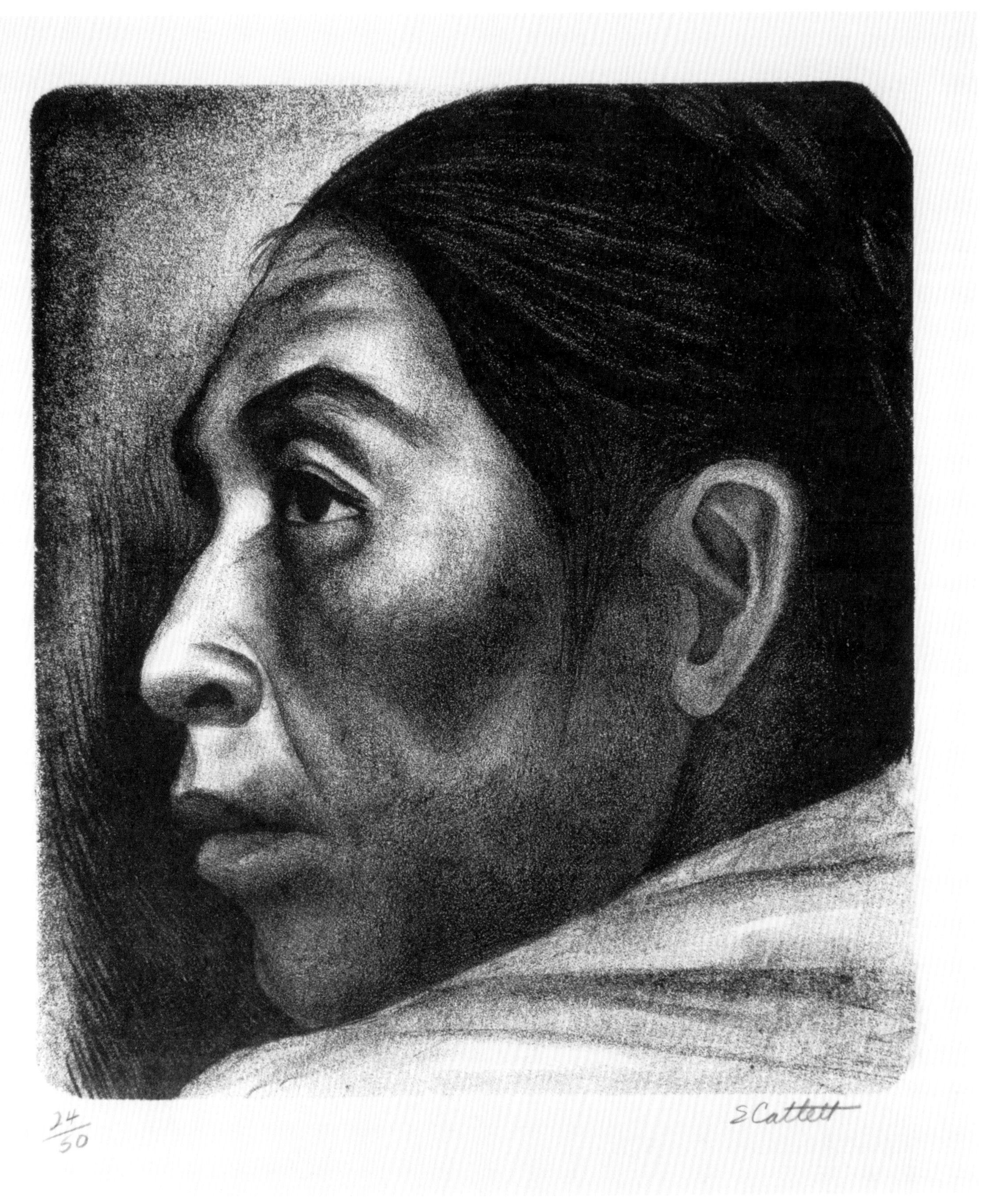

Cabeza Indígena, 1955, lithograph, 22 13/16 × 17 11/16 in., Colección Academia de Artes, México

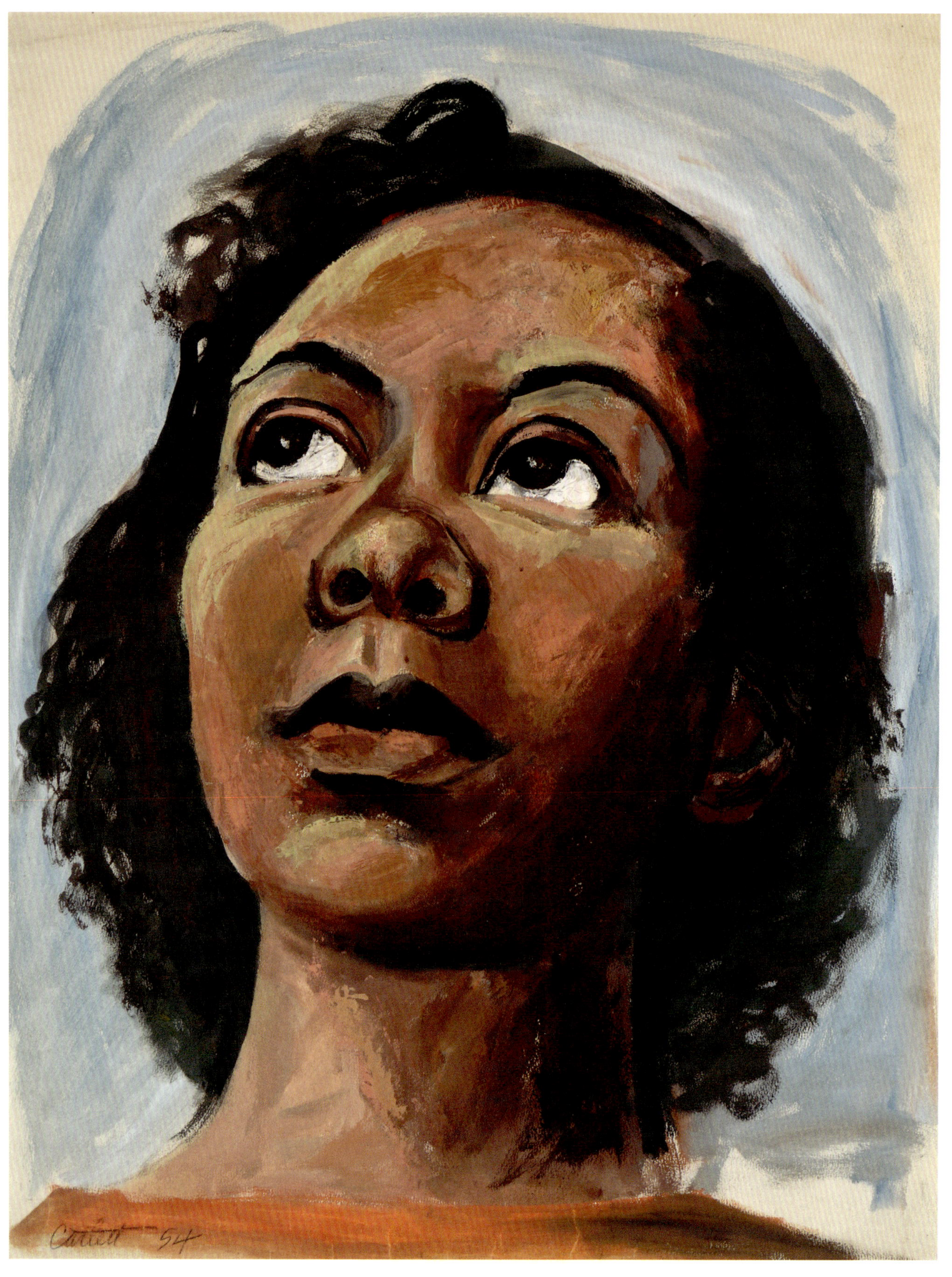

Untitled (Young Woman Looking Up), 1954, tempera on wove paper mounted to board, 28½ × 22 in., Collection of Kyra E. Hicks

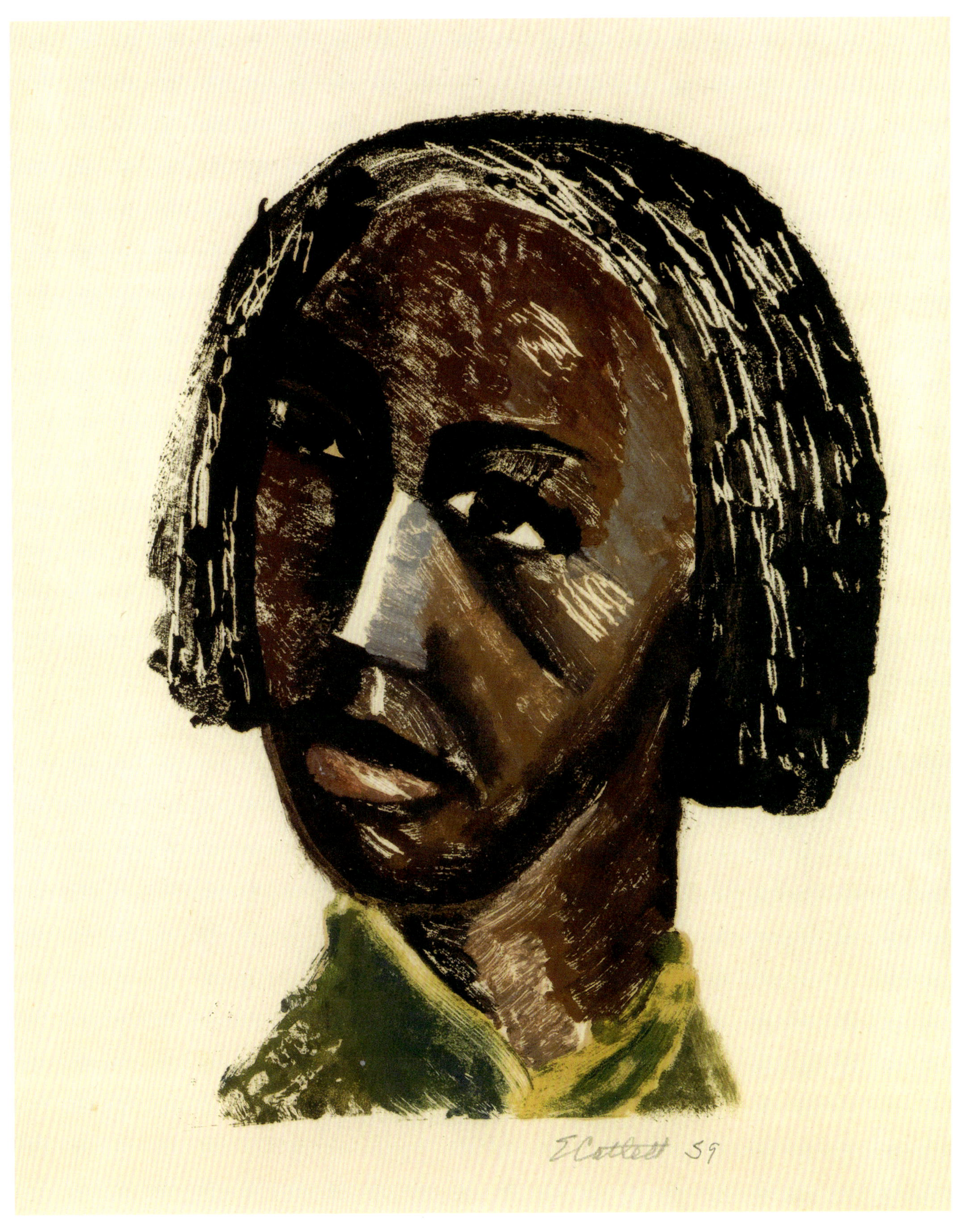

Untitled (Head of Woman), 1959, oil on oil monotype on cream wove paper, 13¾ × 10⁵⁄₁₆ in., Private collection

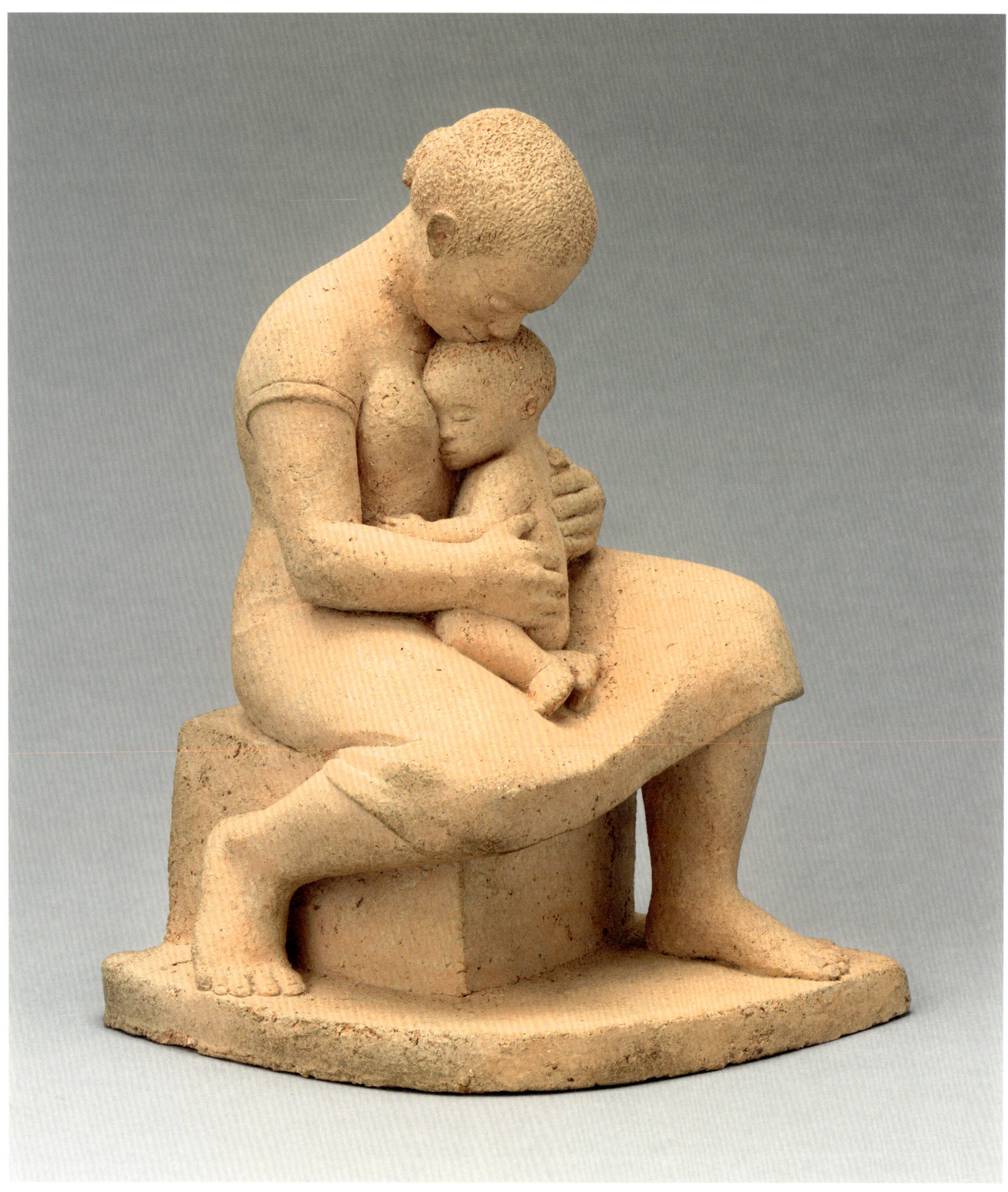

Mother and Child, 1956, terracotta, 11¼ × 7 × 7 in., The Museum of Modern Art, New York, Gift of The Friends of Education of The Museum of Modern Art, The Modern Women's Fund, and Dr. Alfred Gold (by exchange), 2011

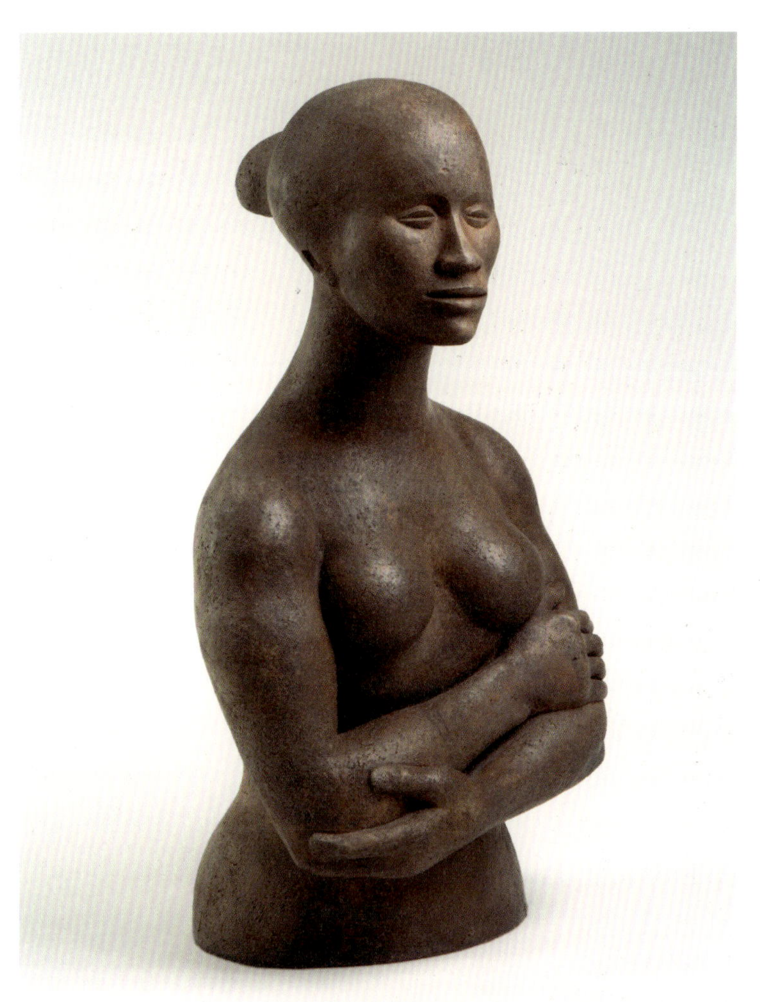

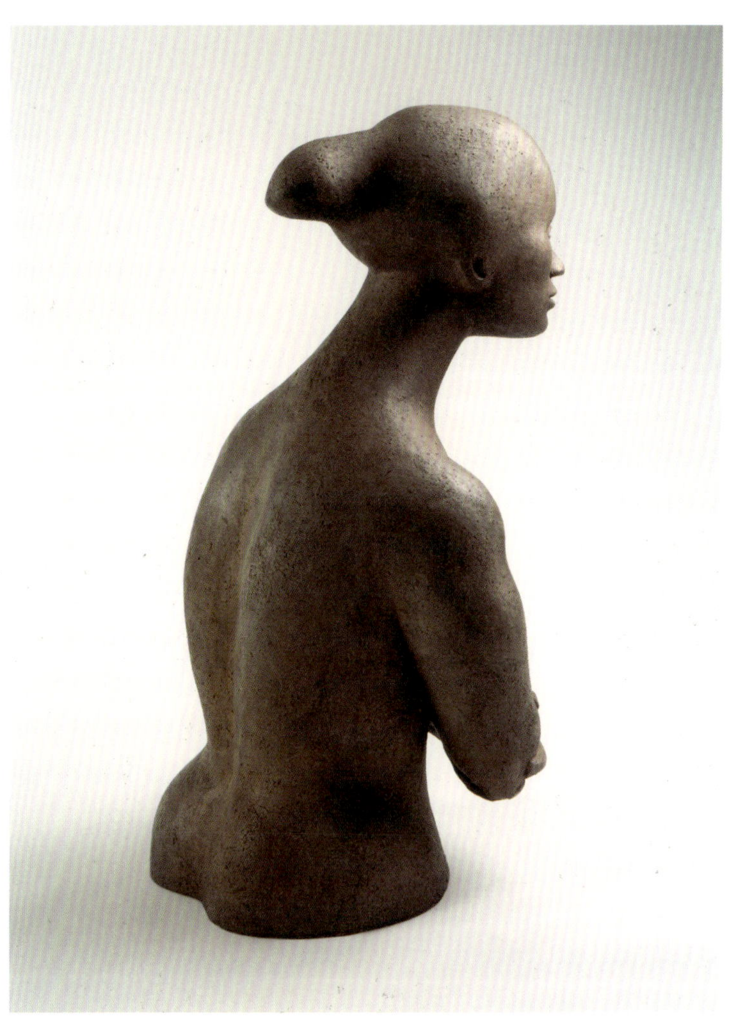

Torso, Portrait of Joan, 1960, fired terracotta, 25¾ × 14½ × 11¾ in., Private collection

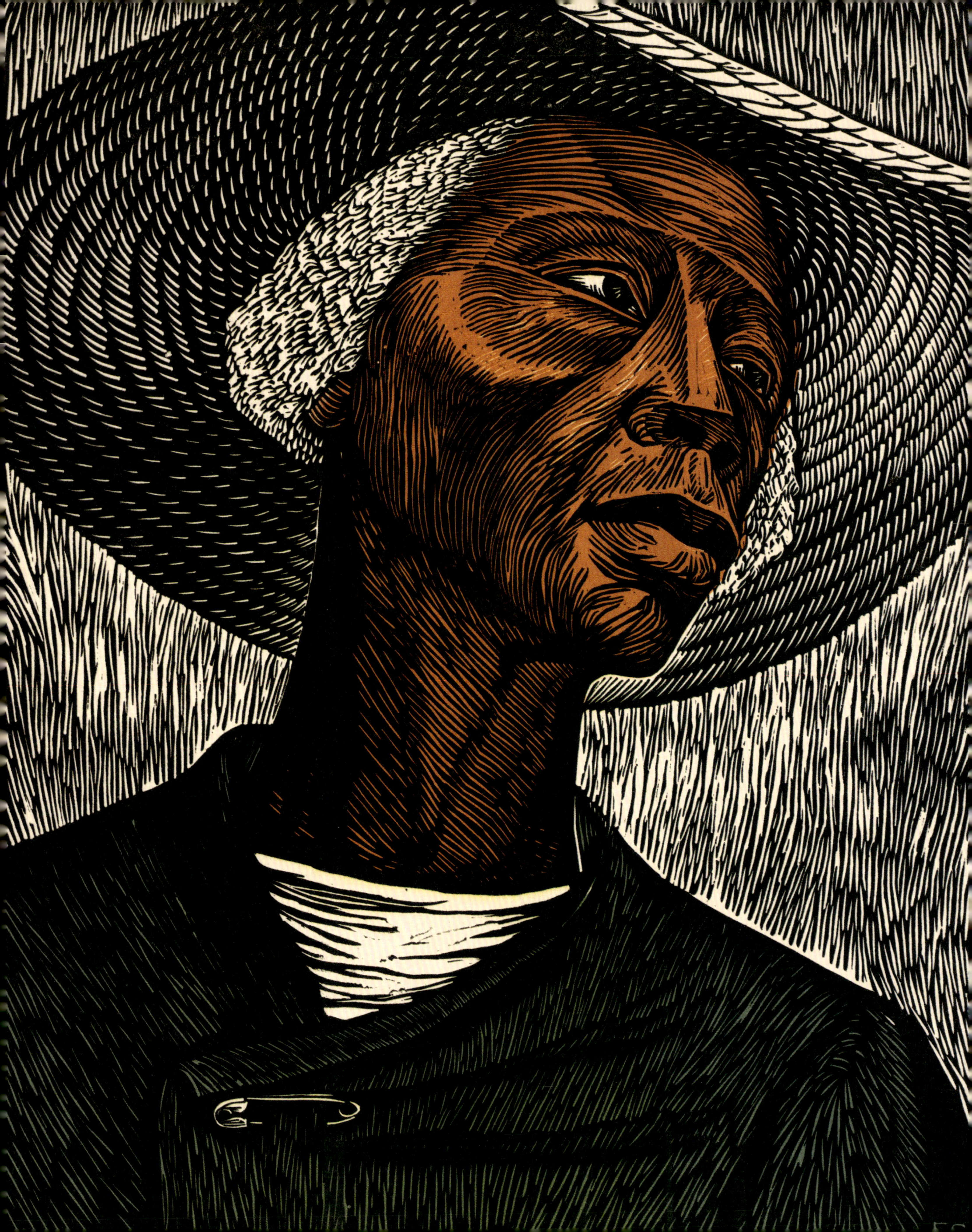

JULIA
FERNANDEZ

SHARECROPPER AND CAMPESINO

In 1946, Elizabeth Catlett traveled to Mexico City on a Julius Rosenwald Fund Fellowship. In her first application to the fellowship in 1943, Catlett had proposed creating public sculptures of "the Negro in Industry and Agriculture" so to inspire "admiration and esteem" for the Black farmer and industrial worker.[1] In 1945, Catlett's plan for the fellowship indicated that she would create a series about Black womanhood that combined the struggles for Black rights and equality for women. The series was to be sent to Black and white colleges and galleries in the United States, particularly in the South.[2] Catlett's second plan would win her the prestigious fellowship and land her among the leading artists in sociopolitical art in Mexico at the time. The encounter would have a lasting influence on Catlett's iconography. In particular, her time with the Taller de Gráfica Popular (TGP) would produce a transnational visual vocabulary that envisioned the common struggles and successes of the sharecropper in the US and the campesino in Mexico.

The TGP was founded in 1937 by Leopoldo Méndez, Luis Arenal, Raúl Anguiano, and US artist Pablo O'Higgins. It was meant to "connect graphic art with the immediate problems of Mexico...but also international affairs, such as the struggles for national liberation in other countries."[3] Such ambitions were clearly signaled in a series released by the TGP in 1947, while Catlett was in residence: *Estampas de la revolución mexicana*. *Estampas* sought to provide "art for the people," celebrating ordinary people as heroes while making visual art accessible to all.[4] The TGP artists believed the series to be timely, since the fight for human rights in the Mexican Revolution resonated with the same struggle during the recently concluded World War II. The series aimed to revisit the principles, causes, results, and heroes of the Mexican Revolution "in order to understand the heroic fight for '*Tierra y Libertad*/Land and Freedom.'"[5]

In a scene from the series about the hacienda system during the Porfiriato (the regime of Mexican dictator Porfirio Díaz), TGP artist Arturo García Bustos focuses on the difficult yet dignified labor of an indentured worker, or campesino.[6] In his linocut of an indentured laborer cutting maize, Bustos foregrounds a stooped, faceless worker against an endless field (fig. 1). In the distance, three figures walk in front of a structure titled "Hacienda" carrying large bales on their backs. A person on horseback monitors their labors as a radiating sun burns behind a mountain range. The image calls for an empathic response from the viewer on the side of the indentured laborer or campesino, while

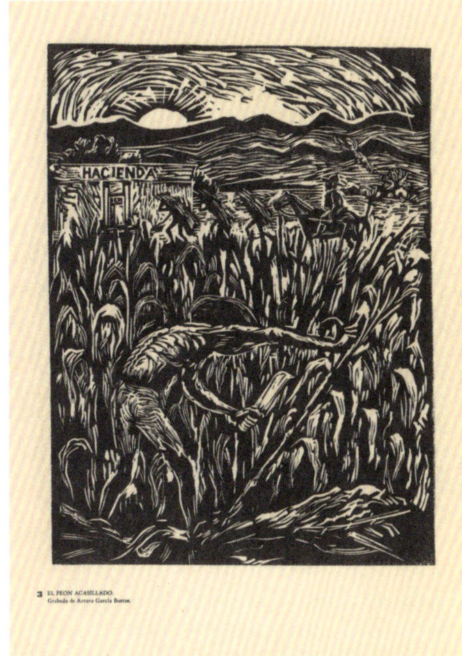

Fig. 1—Arturo García Bustos, *Peon acasillado*, from *Estampas de la revolución mexicana* series, 1947, linocut, The Metropolitan Museum of Art, Gift of Norman S. Rothschild, 1993

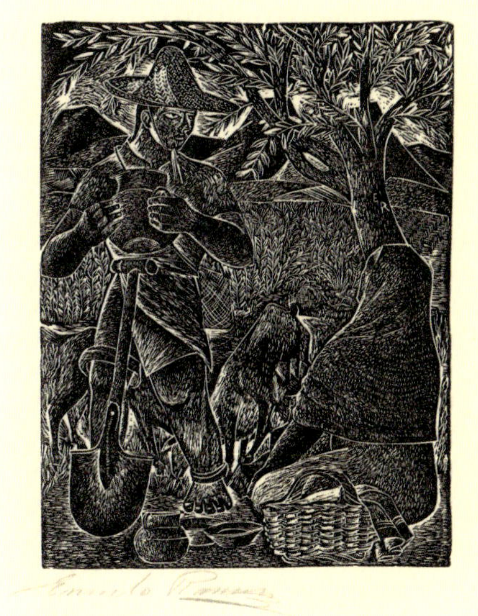

Fig. 2—Everardo Ramírez, *La hora del almuerzo*, from the portfolio *Vida en mi barriada*, 1948, lithograph, Center for Southwest Research and Special Collections, University of New Mexico Libraries

acknowledging the power disparities between them and the hacendado giving orders behind them. Bustos's work exemplifies the hierarchical dynamic between the powerful hacendado and the campesino forced to work under the hacienda system. During the Porfiriato, about 90 percent of the rural population lost their lands to the wealthy haciendas. Therefore, to continue their subsistence farming, campesinos were required to work for meager wages on the lands of the hacendados. Such social disparities were one of the leading causes of the Mexican Revolution.

Bustos's *Peon acasillado* depicts visual vocabulary that was used to highlight the causes and the primary benefactors of the revolution. The image of the campesino was symbolic of the revolution itself and a constant reminder of the fight for Indigenous and working-class rights. The iconography after the revolution played an important role in representing the ideals of Mexican modernism that sought to reintegrate an Indigenous historical and visual narrative. As evidenced in Bustos's image, the campesinos were represented at work or in relation to their labors. Therefore, they were often depicted with the tools of labor, as seen here in Bustos's image with a machete, or in an image by Everardo Ramírez, *La hora del almuerzo*, with a shovel (fig. 2). Noticeably, in both works by Bustos and Ramírez, the campesinos are in a rural setting with visible hills or mountains and agriculture or animals, again connecting them to their labors. Although the surroundings of the campesinos may change, they were typically represented barefoot with modest clothing and a straw hat. These features served to distinguish the campesino from the wealthier hacendado. In Ramírez's image, the campesino is placed alongside an Indigenous woman seated on the ground wrapped in a traditional rebozo. At the TGP, Catlett combined the visual vocabulary of Bustos and Ramírez, depicting a barefoot campesino with a straw hat and a seated woman in a rebozo with their backs toward the viewer, as they face an hacendado on horseback possibly yelling orders at the two figures in the foreground (*Campesinos*, c. 1940s). The iconography during this time served to tell the stories of Indigenous and working-class populations that had been erased during the Díaz regime. Catlett would utilize the same campesino iconography in her depictions of sharecroppers to argue for the similar marginalization that occurred against Black working-class populations in the US.

As evidenced with the relationship perceived between *Estampas de la revolución mexicana* and World War II, artists within the TGP continuously connected national concerns with broader struggles over human rights. During a 1939 trip sponsored by the Guggenheim Foundation, Méndez witnessed firsthand the racial and class injustices against the Black population in the US. As he traveled from Mexico to New York, Méndez passed through the South, and he was particularly marked by an encounter in Texas with Black prisoners working and singing while being guarded by police on horseback. Méndez compared this visually resonant experience with the pre-revolutionary Porfirian era in Mexico.[7] The police on horseback watching over the Black prisoners were no different than the hacendados ordering around the campesinos. The TGP artists' sympathy for the ideals of the revolution, and its calls for land reform for the campesinos, aligned with the struggle abroad against discrimination in the post-Reconstruction South.

CATLETT'S TRANSNATIONAL VOCABULARY

Catlett plays a key role in the TGP by advancing a transnational visual vocabulary and highlighting parallel histories around common struggles of marginalized populations in the US and Mexico, as evidenced with her images of the

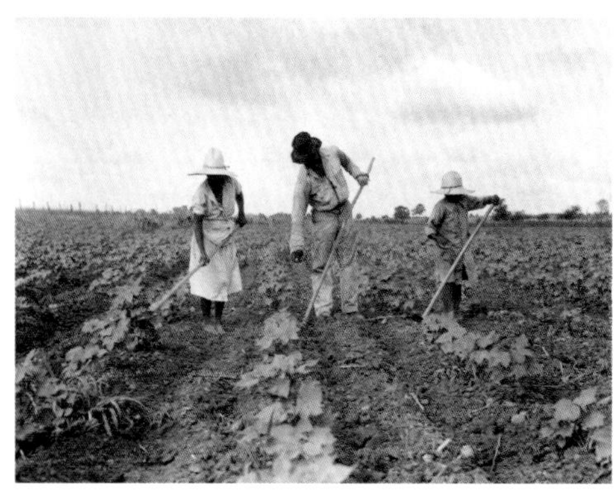

Fig. 3—Dorothea Lange, *Hoeing Cotton (A Negro tenant farmer and several members of his family hoeing cotton on their farm in Alabama)*, 1936, digital file from negative, Prints and Photographs Division, Library of Congress, FSA/OWI Collection

sharecropper and campesino. She was invested in uplifting underrepresented narratives, especially those of Black agricultural workers, domestic workers, and everyday heroic women. Her proposals for the Rosenwald Fellowship explained that her goal was to have these figures respected and redeemed in history, as their histories were often ignored or erased.

Before arriving in Mexico, Catlett had already been experimenting with the image of the sharecropper (p. 100). In her 1945 linocut, Catlett depicts a male sharecropper with a straw hat and an open-collared shirt. The straw hat recalls campesino iconography. The image is tightly framed to expose a tired yet determined expression on the subject's face and points to strategies that Catlett would advance during her time in Mexico. She would increasingly focus on portraits of the subjects to highlight their dignity.

While completing *The Black Woman* series, she was inspired by the TGP's *Estampas de la revolución mexicana*. *Estampas* told an underrepresented narrative of the Mexican Revolution that valorized both ordinary and now-mythic figures. Like *Estampas*, Catlett's series included prints of ordinary and heroic figures, including domestic workers, farm workers, musicians, organizers, and students alongside Sojourner Truth, Harriet Tubman, and Phillis Wheatley. The series was created to be viewed and read in order, as the titles of the prints narrate the trials and triumphs of Black women (p. 32).

Catlett drew inspiration for her prints of everyday women from personal experiences as well as photographs from the Farm Security Administration (FSA). We can see one specific reference in the third print of the series, ...*In the Fields* (p. 36). The print is a reference to Dorothea Lange's *Hoeing Cotton (A Negro tenant farmer and several members of his family hoeing cotton on their farm in Alabama)* from 1936 (fig. 3). The photograph was taken for the FSA, a US government photography project headed by economist Roy E. Stryker that included photographs by artists such as Jack Delano, Walker Evans, Russell Lee, Carl Mydans, Gordon Parks, Arthur Rothstein, Ben Shahn, Marion Post Wolcott, and John Vachon.[8] A portion of the project "focused on the lives of sharecroppers in the South and migratory agricultural workers in the midwestern and western states."[9] The image by Lange depicts a Black tenant farmer, or a farmer working on land owned by a landlord. Like the Mexican campesino's reliance on the hacendado for subsistence, in the US the tenant farmer was able to live and work off the land only if they shared a portion of their harvest and profits with the landlord—a practice known as sharecropping.

Lange's image of the tenant farmer and his family, including his wife and child, depicts the generational impact of sharecropping. In Catlett's print, she focuses on the female figure on the left in Lange's photograph. Several similarities between the female figures in Lange's photograph and Catlett's print suggest that Catlett was likely inspired by the photograph. Both figures are wearing a collared white button-down dress with rolled-up sleeves. Both are hoeing cotton barefoot in a straw hat. However, though the figures are off in the distance in the photograph, Catlett brings her figure to the foreground of the print. While the subject of Lange's work is tenant farming, the subject of Catlett's work is the heroic Black (female) farm worker. Like Bustos, Catlett not only humanizes the image, but moves the figure of the worker to the front and center. Inspired by the TGP's *Estampas*, Catlett heroicizes the worker in the same manner that Harriet Tubman or Emiliano Zapata would be idealized in an image. Like the artists of *Estampas*, Catlett wanted to show the contributions and dignity of everyday, working-class people. And though in Lange's photograph the woman's face is not visible under the shadow of her sunhat, hiding any emotions, Catlett uncovers the unwavering strength in her face. Catlett's *Black Woman* series provided the perfect transition to her creative production in Mexico, allowing her to highlight the very similar experiences of Black and Indigenous working-class populations in the US and Mexico.

Catlett's early work in the TGP resonates with Alain Locke's ideas in *The New Negro* from 1925, which declared that visual art should not be aimed at erasing histories of struggle in an attempt to assimilate into US society, but should rather focus on these struggles with pride and strength, and that as a result, newfound commonalities and connections would emerge with other racial and ethnic communities in the US and abroad.[10] This new pride in Black cultural struggles compared to the newfound focus on often-ignored Indigenous histories in post-revolutionary Mexican modern art. Catlett's work bridges the gap between Black and Mexican subject matter, while aligning with the International Left. It creates a transnational visual vocabulary that critiques racist, classist, and sexist hegemonic structures while uplifting Black and Indigenous working-class, heroic yet ordinary figures. Catlett's work highlights the colonial violence still impacting marginalized populations in the twentieth century in the US and Mexico. However, her dignified portrayal of the sharecropper and the campesino acts as a countervisual and decolonial alternative to hundreds of years of social and visual denigration.

Soon after completing the *Black Woman* series, Catlett printed *Campesinos Mexicanos*, a linocut depicting three figures in a humble domestic interior (p. 101). Wearing rolled-up pants and a straw hat that covers his eyes, a campesino shares his meager harvest with two other figures—a young girl with braids who is seated on the ground, and a male child with a torn shirt. The image recalls Lange's photograph of the family of tenant farmers braving a lifecycle of subsistence farming. Catlett's use of differing ages and genders reiterates this generational cycle. She also highlights the communal support that fellow campesinos offered each other to survive. Though provided only the leftover harvest of the hacendado, the campesino in Catlett's print is willing to share, while the hacendado withholds.

EMERGING WITH STRENGTH

In "On the Coloniality of Being," Nelson Maldonado-Torres discusses ontology as it intersects with legacies of colonialism. He argues that colonialism has created a system where people are othered and seen as neither human nor worthy of Being. He explains that this is why we get "non ethics of war" and people are just seen as disposable. To combat this, he advocates for what he calls the decoloniality of Being. Here, it is "necessary for the you to emerge."[11] Inspired by her experiences and time with the TGP, Catlett's depictions of the sharecropper and campesino are dedicated to the emergence of the state of Being of the indentured farm worker in the US and Mexico. Catlett's iconography combats histories of colonization and the othering of the farm worker, and especially the othering of Black and Indigenous farm workers that stems from histories of enslavement and the encomienda system. Catlett's time in the TGP was an important moment for her development of a radical internationalism rooted in decolonial thought. This period would prove pivotal for her during her exile from the US, laying the groundwork for her deep understanding of coloniality and solidarity movements that emerges with strength in the 1960s and '70s.

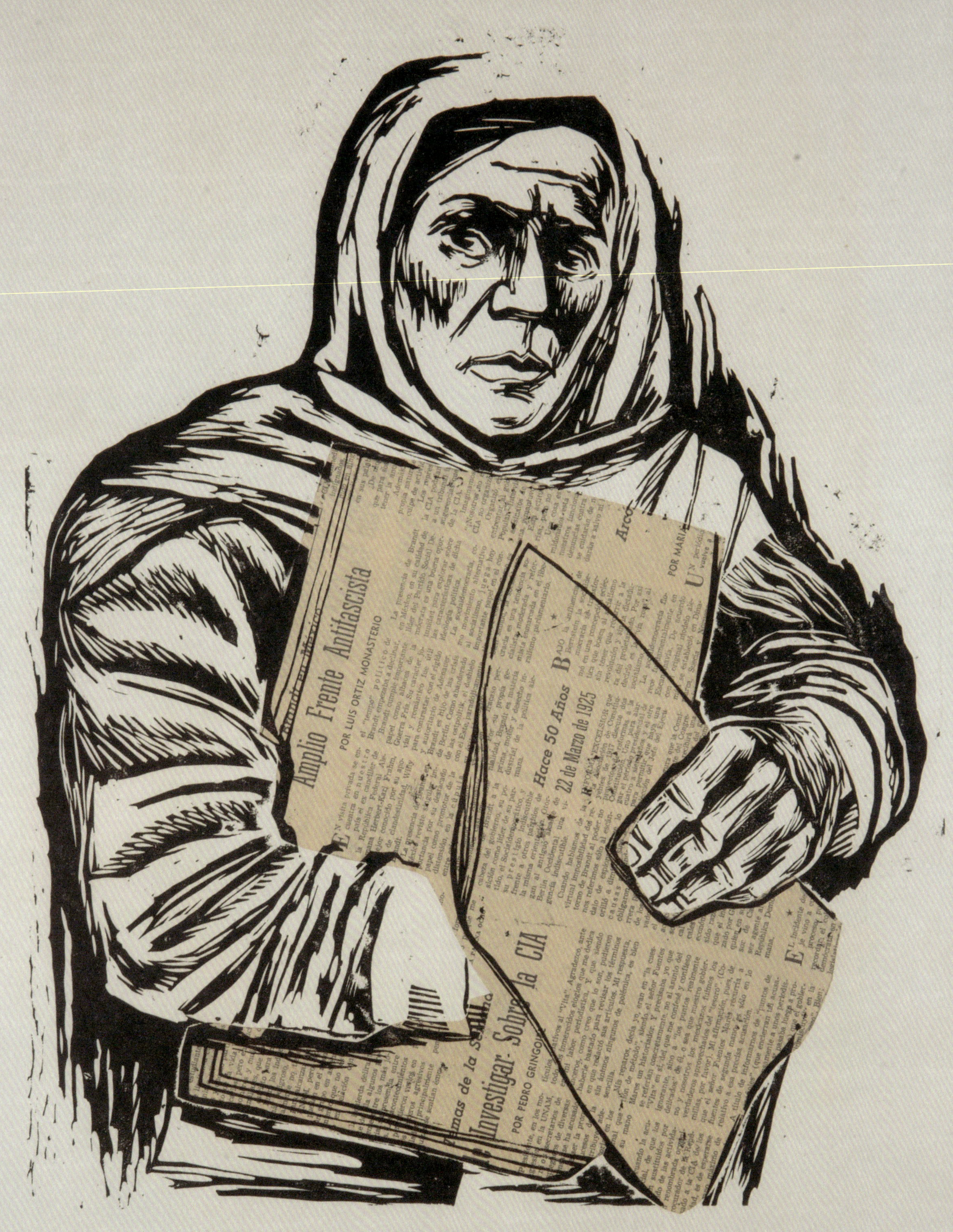
Amplio Frente Antifascista
POR LUIS ORTIZ MONASTERIO
Hace 50 Años
22 de Marzo de 1925
Investigar Sobre la CIA
POR PEDRO GRINGOIRE

DALILA SCRUGGS

AN ARTIST-ACTIVIST AT THE CENTER OF THE GLOBAL SIXTIES

Eight years into her new life as an American expat in Mexico, Elizabeth Catlett recarved an image she had originally included in her *Black Woman* series.[1] And she was calling the stand-alone print *Separation* (fig. 1). Barbed wire stretches across the page, nearly flush with the picture plane. The figure, standing perilously close to the twisted steel spikes along the fence, looks forlorn but not cowed. Striated lines appear like sunrays anointing the figure's presence, suggesting life beyond her physical constraints. The print itself is structured so that we (as viewers) are estranged from the subject within the work. In this way, the composition visualizes the conditions of the print's reception.

Catlett labored over this print hundreds of miles away from the Black communities in the United States that she privileged in her work and regarded as her primary audience. In the years following its production, Catlett's immigration status would shift from that of an émigré to political exile barred from entering the US for nearly ten years. Not until 1971 would she regain entry, when the Studio Museum in Harlem successfully lobbied for a visa.

How did Catlett's years of exile affect her artistic practice? Scholars widely recognize the 1960s and '70s as a period Catlett devoted to participating in the Black Power and Black Arts Movements from afar. While scholars uphold *Negro es Bello II* (p. 157) and *Malcolm X Speaks for Us* (p. 156) as exemplars of Catlett's participation, few attend to the ways that her physical remove from the US materially affected her work.[2] Instead, the literature on Catlett presumes a relatively unmediated relationship to the political activism unfolding in the States.

Rather than framing Catlett through the rigid boundaries of the nation state that rejected her, I explore how the conditions of her exile shaped both the production and reception of her work during this period. Even as she turned toward the Black Arts Movement in the 1960s and '70s, her feet remained firmly planted in Mexico. Indeed, her commitment to Black Power was reinforced and echoed by her investment in Leftist protest in Mexico. Remarkably, she remained steadfast in her activism despite being subjected to both US and Mexican state surveillance that hampered access to information about current events in Black America, impeded the exchange of political ideals, and disrupted the flow of artworks across the US-Mexico border. Catlett deployed a remarkable arsenal of aesthetic and practical strategies to overcome her geopolitical estrangement from the US as she responded to the social unrest of the global sixties, a transnational age of dissent spanning 1956 to 1973.

Fig. 1—Elizabeth Catlett, *Separation*, 1954, linocut, The Studio Museum in Harlem, Gift of the artist, 1972.9.5

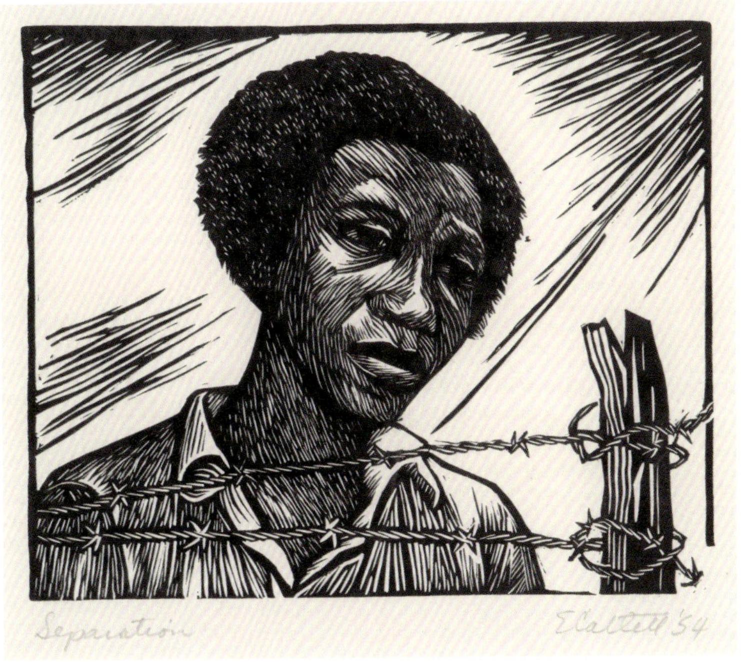

FROM COLD WAR EXILE TO GLOBAL SIXTIES ACTIVIST

Exile, as scholar and activist Edward Said writes, is a distinctly modern phenomenon, born of the mass death and displacement resulting from modern warfare, imperialism, and totalitarianism. Said distinguishes between exiles, refugees, expatriates, and émigrés. Unlike expatriates and émigrés, exiles do not leave by choice but are banished. Their "condition," Said continues, is "legislated to deny dignity—to deny an identity to people."[3] Yet amid such loss and alienation, he notes, exile also offers redemptive possibility: banishment yields a "contrapuntal" vision. Just as in music where the term "contrapuntal" describes the relationship between two independent lines of music that combine to form one harmonious sound, the exile sustains a plurality of perspectives simultaneously, merging memories of old and new environments as well as cultural knowledge from the homeland and adopted country. In sum, "Exiles cross borders, break barriers of thought and experience."[4]

Elizabeth Catlett's contrapuntal vision was enabled by what scholar Rebecca Schreiber has called her critical transnational perspective.[5] As Schreiber cogently describes, Catlett was one of many Leftist cultural producers—artists, writers, filmmakers—who moved to Mexico to escape the rise of McCarthyism in the US. Before arriving in Mexico in 1946, Catlett was a member of a vibrant community of artists and intellectuals with formal and informal ties to the Communist Party USA (CPUSA; see Sarah Kelly Oehler's essay in this book) and once she settled in Mexico, she continued to create art to support socialist causes as a member of the Taller de Gráfica Popular (TGP, People's Graphic Workshop). After she became a Mexican citizen, she was able to participate even more actively in Mexican politics.

Mexico was a significant Cold War actor whose influence extended far beyond its bilateral relationship with the US. As with countries across Latin America, Mexico embraced relations with the Soviet Union, Cuba, and China, and in the process gained greater leverage in the face of US political dominance. Positioned in Mexico, Catlett was immersed in cultural networks that reflected its nonaligned status and traveled to several countries with diplomatic ties to the USSR, including East Germany (Berlin), China, and Cuba. From her vantage point outside the US, Catlett decried the hypocrisy of American exceptionalism, denounced the US's racist treatment of African Americans, and advocated for solidarity with others struggling against colonialism and US imperialism worldwide.[6]

Building on Schreiber's study of Catlett as a Cold War exile in Mexico during the 1940s and '50s, I turn to the 1960s and '70s when the repressive politics of the Cold War clashed with the resistance tactics of the global sixties. This term is used both to describe a transnational framework that accounts for broad "geopolitical, ideological, cultural and economic forces" and to indicate a period (c. 1956–1973) characterized by a surge in public protest, most notably in 1968, by activists demanding democratic and revolutionary change.[7] Liberation was the watchword of the day. Leftist activists around the world shared "'an international language of dissent' linked to the transnational circulation (and appropriation) of common written texts, film, graphic arts, music and individuals."[8] They sought international solidarity against colonialism and imperialism. This postwar generation, many of them students, were regarded as a New Left that extended and critiqued the work of Old Left activists and intellectuals who espoused communist ideals in the 1930s and '40s. The global sixties—as both framework and period—is useful in understanding Elizabeth Catlett because it helps us grasp not only how the artist tapped into international protest and Third World resistance,[9] but also how her formative years in New York and as a member of the TGP in the 1940s and '50s prompted her to remain attuned to the younger generation of Black and Mexican artists and activists in the 1960s and '70s.

Catlett was at the fulcrum of the global sixties—as her role in the Free Angela Davis campaign shows—but first we must examine how the conditions of exile shaped Catlett's ability to connect with and respond to the Black Power Movement from afar, and then attend to the local Mexican context that informed her work.[10]

PROFESSING BLACK POWER FROM AFAR

Fashioned of mahogany, Catlett's life-size sculpture *Homage to My Young Black Sisters* (1968, pp. 153–155) punctuates voluptuous curves with a jutting arm. The upraised arm is an unmistakable reference to the Black Power salute. Catlett had originally intended to fill the void with a heart, according to art historian Nicole Gilpin Hood, but ultimately decided to forgo that compositional detail. Hood sees the void as "a comment on the unfulfilled promises of American liberty" and a symbol of the sacrifices made by the young women activists of the civil rights movement.[11] Catlett drew a direct connection between this activism and her geopolitical displacement. As she later recalled, "I did that piece because I was living in Mexico City. If I'd been [in the US], I would have been in Mississippi. But since I was in Mexico, I had to express my support through my work."[12]

To overcome her distance from Black America, Catlett employed a simple but impactful strategy: she provided a home away from home for friends and acquaintances visiting Mexico, who in turn brought with them fresh insight from the States and, occasionally, took Catlett's artwork back with them across the border.[13] This is made palpably clear by comparing *Homage* and Barbara Jones-Hogu's *Unite* (1971, fig. 2). A member of the Chicago-based African Commune of Bad Relevant Artists (AfriCOBRA), Jones-Hogu traveled to Mexico, saw *Homage* in Catlett's studio, and later fashioned a rejoinder to Catlett's work.[14] Subsequently, Catlett gave Jones-Hogu an artist's proof of *Negro es*

Fig. 2—Barbara Jones-Hogu, *Unite*, 1971, screenprint, Brooklyn Museum, Dick S. Ramsay Fund, 2012.46

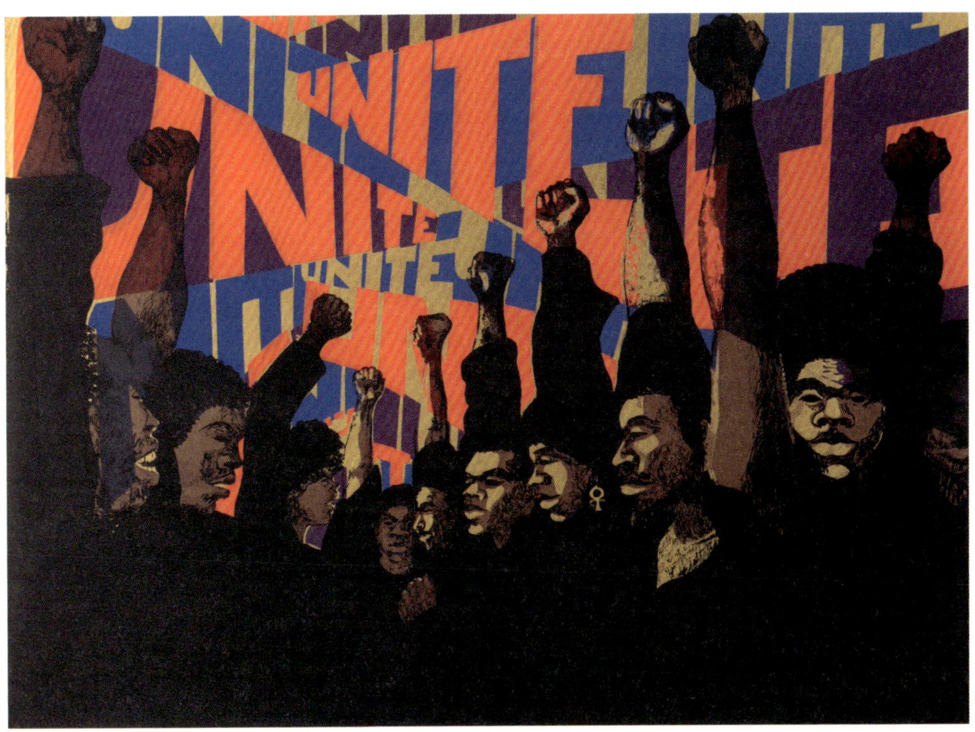

Bello II.[15] And many young people wrote to Catlett in search of guidance, no doubt reassuring the artist of her connection to the Black liberation struggle in the US.[16] Unfortunately, this mode of vicarious border crossing was intensively monitored by US intelligence agencies, which closely documented visitors they suspected of maintaining Communist ties.[17] Informants even reported when Catlett made art that responded to Black activism in the States.[18]

Though Catlett cited her desire to protest in Mississippi as the impetus for *Homage*, both she and Jones-Hogu understood that the work responded to political events unfolding right in Mexico City. *Homage* echoes the widely circulated photograph of track athletes John Carlos and Tommie Smith, who bravely raised their fists in protest while they stood on the winners podium at the 1968 Summer Olympics in Mexico City. "My raised right hand stood for the power within black America," Smith told a reporter on ABC television the day after the protest. "Carlos's left hand stood for the unity of black America. Together, they formed an arch of unity and power."[19] Later Catlett recalled feeling a sense of pride when watching Carlos and Smith's protest on TV.[20] Ironically, she may have watched the same news coverage as people in the US because the Mexican TV channel Telesistema (now Televisa) used ABC's feed.[21] Within this circuit of mediated influence, Catlett was both recipient and relay of Black Power ideals.

While *Homage* emerged from a moment when the Black Power Movement unfolded on her doorstep in Mexico City, Catlett typically had to work much harder to get information about the state of Black liberation in the US. *Mask* (p. 160) is, as I have argued elsewhere, a physical manifestation of the artist's efforts to overcome her geographic remove by tapping into an "imagined community."[22] The collaged interior of *Mask* (p. 160) features clippings from the pages of the *Black Panther Black Community News Service*, the official newspaper of the Black Panther Party.[23] Catlett's experiments in collage were a kind of brainstorm, a messy reckoning with a political milieu that was out of reach, knowable only through the missives of others.

The Panthers understood that print culture could foster national identity. As the *Black Panther* explained, "Millions and millions of oppressed people might not know members of the vanguard party personally or directly, but they will gain through indirect acquaintance the proper strategy for liberation via the mass media and the physical activities of the party."[24] Subscriptions were at their highest from 1970 to 1971, circulating nationally and internationally. In reading the *Black Panther*, Catlett joined a group of at least 139,000.

When it came time to send *Mask* to her art dealer Alonzo Davis in the US, Catlett was again confronted by the geopolitical constraints of her exile. Davis would often drive from Los Angeles into Mexico, sometimes meeting her at a halfway point and putting her work in his truck. He, in turn, would have to navigate the customs office in Tijuana to bring the work into the US.[25] In a letter to Davis on February 1, 1971, Catlett included this warning about the container holding *Mask*: "Don't take plastic cover off for customs. It has political message inside."[26] The sculpture's Janus construction offered an additional safeguard, as the mask exterior marked it as a "primitive" objet d'art that obscured the ardent politics held within. Catlett understood well that her political messaging made the sculpture as much an "undesirable alien" as she was.

GODMOTHER TO THE MOVIMIENTO ESTUDIANTIL

Whether cutting newspaper clippings from California, watching TV broadcasts produced in New York, welcoming visitors from Chicago, or reading letters mailed from Boston, Catlett honed her contrapuntal vision with an interpretive lens sharpened in local communities in Mexico City. Her Black Power period—her artistic production during the 1960s and '70s—must be understood within the context of the ongoing unrest of the Movimiento Estudiantil (Student Protest Movement) of 1968, which stemmed from significant demographic and economic shifts that had produced social change and political discontent in Mexico. From the 1940s to the 1960s, the country experienced an economic boom accompanied by exponential population growth, substantial migration from the countryside to urban centers, and growing numbers of students enrolling in higher education. While the government celebrated these changes as a "Mexican miracle" of stable development, income inequality had in fact worsened. Students in Mexico galvanized around a New Left, which they saw as a revival of the socialist and egalitarian values of the Mexican Revolution, to advocate for a democratic nation with more equitable distribution of wealth. They also looked for international models and inspiration for their own protest, including Black liberation movements in the US. In the face of social protest, the Mexican government grew increasingly authoritarian, leveraging soft power and outright violence. It claimed that the unrest was the result of foreign (read, Soviet) Communist interlopers, rather than homegrown discontent—a claim that pointed to Mexico's complicated Cold War position as a country with diplomatic and cultural ties to both the US and the Soviet bloc. Conflict between the Movimiento Estudiantil and the Mexican government came to a head in Mexico City—just ahead of the Olympic Games—when government soldiers shot and killed hundreds of peaceful demonstrators on October 2, 1968, in the historical plaza of Tlatelolco, an event remembered as the Massacre of Tlatelolco. Still more student organizers were arrested and jailed as political prisoners.[27]

Elizabeth Catlett's stake in the Movimiento Estudiantil was both personal and political. She had close relationships with young people participating in the protests, both as a professor at Mexico's premier university, Universidad Nacional Autónoma de México, and as the mother of college-aged sons. Her youngest, painter David Mora Catlett, recalls the days leading up to the massacre, including the day when his mother had to evacuate the university as the protests reached a fever pitch. David himself participated in those protests, but decided not to attend on the fateful day of the massacre.[28]

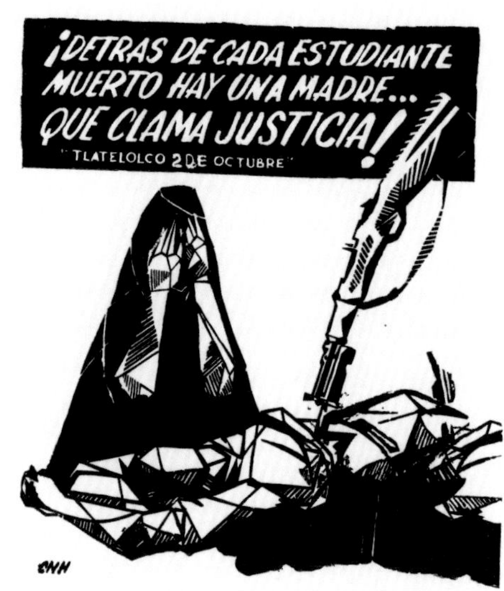

Fig. 3—Movimiento Estudiantil C.N.H., *¡Detrás de cada estudiante muerto, hay una madre... que clama justicia!* poster, 1968, Miscellaneous Print Collection, Kislak Center for Special Collections, Rare Books and Manuscripts, University of Pennsylvania

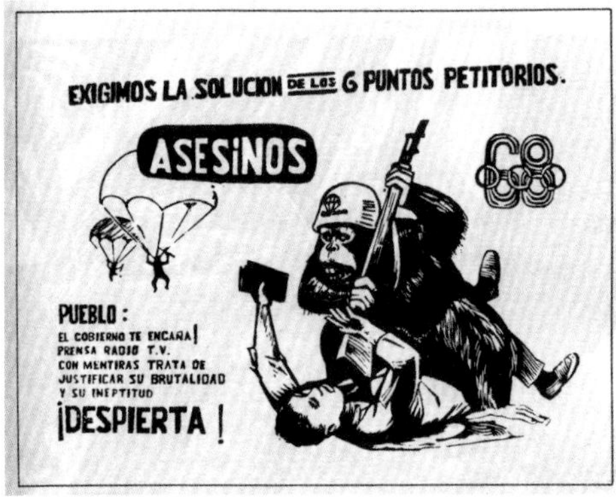

Fig. 4—Adolfo Mexiac, Movimiento Estudiantil protest poster, 1968

If this deeply personal connection were not enough, Catlett also showed her support as an active member of the protofeminist Unión Nacional de Mujeres Mexicanas (UNMM, National Union of Mexican Women), which framed its allegiance to the student movement through the lens of womanhood and as the mothers, sisters, and wives of the students jailed and killed in such protests.[29] Feminist artist, and one of the organization's primary historians, Ana Victoria Jimenez regarded the older generation of women in the union like Catlett as madrinas (godmothers) of the student movement—a designation that paralleled the "foremother" title bestowed upon Catlett by the young Black artists who gathered at the Conference on the Functional Aspects of Black Art (CONFABA) in 1970. The women of the union passed out flyers, like the anonymously designed National Strike Council poster (fig. 3) emblazoned with the words "¡Detrás de cada estudiante muerto, hay una madre...que clama justicia! (Behind Every Dead Student There's a Mother...Who Cries Out for Justice!)."[30]

These events and Catlett's involvement in them require us to rethink her signature Black Power work *Torture of Mothers* (p. 162). It represents, as Melanie Anne Herzog notes, a slain African American boy and likely held double meaning for Catlett, who was as concerned with the riots in the US as she was with the massacre at Tlatelolco.[31] The lifeless body of a young Black child splayed across the cover of the July 28, 1967, issue of *Life* magazine provided Catlett with inspiration for this work, as we learned from Rebecca VanDiver.[32] Sadly, Catlett had a surfeit of photographs of dead Mexican youth to choose from as well. Mexican activists published scores of graphic photographs spotlighting the state-led violence against protestors. Catlett's fellow UNMM member and journalist Elena Poniatowska was developing her landmark exposé *La noche de Tlatelolco* (1971) around the same time that Catlett was making this print. Thus, the two were engaged in parallel projects of truth-telling.

Not only was Catlett metabolizing the Leftist news coverage of the Movimiento Estudiantil, she was also in tune with the movement's aesthetics. Its artists discovered that the visual language codified by the TGP was a useful model for their posters, flyers, and banners critiquing state oppression. Invoking the TGP's social realist approach had the added benefit of being undeniably homegrown, countering the Mexican government's claims that post-1968 uprisings were part of a foreign Communist plot to undermine the government rather than genuine political outcry.[33] Police in helmets, rifles with bayonets, splayed bodies, and the vigorous hatching of relief printing are all compositional elements that link *Watts/Detroit/Washington/Harlem/Newark* (p. 162) with the poster Adolfo Mexiac created in support of the student protests (fig. 4). By taking seriously Catlett's groundedness in a Mexican geopolitical context, we can see more clearly how her Black Power imagery was a product of a transnational perspective that was both Black and Mexican.

ANGELA LIBRE

In banning Catlett for the better part of a decade, the US government had intended to diminish her impact on the political activism unfolding in the country. The outcome of this act of diplomatic ostracization was quite the opposite. Her involvement in the Free Angela Davis campaign is an instructive case study that invites us to see Catlett's exile not as a period spent on the periphery of cultural and political events unfolding in the US, but rather as a moment when she was fully immersed in the art and activism at the center of the global sixties.

The movement to free Angela Davis took shape in late 1970, after she was accused of aiding an armed hostage confrontation at the Marin County courthouse in the San Francisco Bay area led by seventeen-year-old Jonathan Jackson. Davis was linked to this incident because of her work on the defense campaign for the Soledad Brothers, three Black inmates at Soledad State Prison who had been accused of murdering a white guard. Jonathan's older brother George Jackson was one of the Soledad Brothers and investigators found that Jonathan had used guns registered to Davis. Linked by this circumstantial evidence, Davis was charged as a principal in the crime, which meant that she would be tried for kidnapping, murder, and conspiracy. Davis went into hiding and the FBI placed her on its Ten Most Wanted Fugitives list. After a nationwide hunt, Davis was arrested in New York City on October 13, 1970. She was initially denied bail and remained in jail for nearly fifteen months.

When Angela Davis was apprehended by the FBI, her family, friends, and colleagues quickly rallied to organize the National United Committee to Free Angela Davis (NUCFAD). It sought to raise funds for Davis's legal defense, advocate for her release on bail, and shape her public image by countering the mainstream portrayal of the activist as a criminal Black Power monster.[34] NUCFAD coordinated protests and circulated literature to oppose what they saw as a racially motivated conspiracy to imprison, and potentially execute, Davis for her political activism. Harnessing their connection to the CPUSA and a network of progressive organizations, NUCFAD galvanized global support for their cause. As a result, Davis became an icon of the New Left protest movement in the 1970s alongside Ernesto "Che" Guevara and Mao Zedong.[35]

Catlett played an instrumental role in raising public awareness of Davis's case in Mexico. Though her artworks depicting Davis are well known, long before Catlett sketched, sculpted, or printed anything, she engaged in grassroots activism. She authored a pamphlet, spoke at a rally, and helped forge an alliance between UNMM and NUCFAD.[36] In this way, her activism reached beyond protest imagery toward direct action.

Indeed, this activism brought the artist into contact with Davis's friend, and a leader of NUCFAD, Bettina Aptheker. Catlett had been part of her father's (renowned historian Herbert Aptheker's) circle of Leftist artists and intellectuals in New York in the 1940s.[37] In Mexico, Catlett was reintroduced to Bettina through a mutual friend, who told her of Catlett's displeasure with the Mexican media: "Betty writes that the reactionary press is giving the case a big display, publishing [Davis's] picture and stating she herself took the guns into the courtroom."[38]

Following up on this initial introduction, Aptheker wrote to Catlett directly: "I am absolutely delighted to hear that you want to do some publicity on Angela. Will you do a sketch from the photos [you requested]? Could you send us a copy? Do you think it might be serviceable for a poster? This is something we really need to do—we don't yet have a really good poster with a well-done portrait of Angela."[39]

After months of correspondence spanning February to April 1971, swapping updates about their respective organizing efforts and discussing potential poster designs, Catlett sent Aptheker two different versions of *Freedom for Angela Davis and All Political Prisoners*. The finalized design features the upturned face of Angela Davis (fig. 5).[40] The shading suggests a ray of light shining down on her, while her signature Afro encircles her face like a halo and anchors the upper half of the composition. Compared to the more iconic depictions of Davis as a "charismatic radical," Catlett's composition reflects the activist's soft-spoken personality more closely. Moreover, by showing Davis's smile, this particular portrayal offers the individuating detail of the gaps in her smile to counter the fixation on the Afro hairdo that linked Davis with countless other light-skinned Black women at the time.[41]

Below Davis's radiant portrait, the words "freedom for Angela" unfurl in staggered lines variegated by a heterogenous mix of font styles, sizes, and languages. Though it was Aptheker's suggestion to include many different

Fig. 5—Elizabeth Catlett, *Freedom for Angela Davis and All Political Prisoners* poster, 1971, Elizabeth Catlett Papers, Amistad Research Center, New Orleans (addendum II), box 1, folder 3

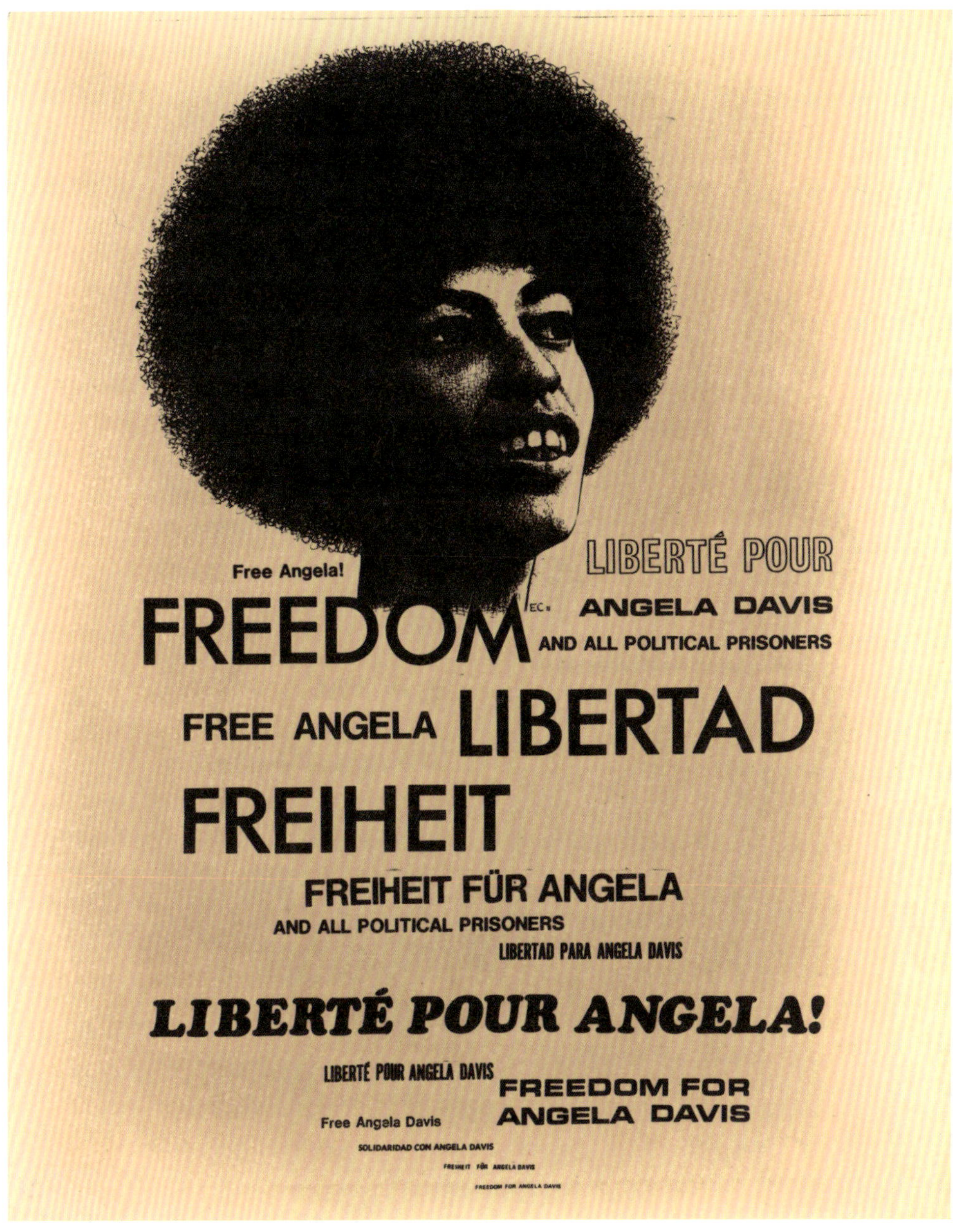

languages, Catlett's graphic design draws out the ideological import.[42] As English, French, German, and Spanish iterations of the refrain vie for attention, the composition evinces a kind of visual glossolalia, producing what Bettina Aptheker described as the "unity-effect" of sharing a common international statement.[43] In essence, Catlett created a graphic designed to circulate internationally.

After months of correspondence with Aptheker about the ideation and production of a poster, Catlett struggled to find a way to get her fresh pile of *Freedom for Angela Davis and All Political Prisoners* posters out of the country. As she explained in late May 1971: "You should have the posters by the end of this week. They will be mailed from N.Y.C. The problem has been finding someone to take them. All the 'liberal' white folks have been afraid to cross the border with them—but I found someone with a little more guts."[44] Yet, in November, Aptheker would write to the New York office, proclaiming, "I still haven't received Elizabeth's poster!!!"[45] The posters were stalled in New York City en route to NUCFAD's primary headquarters in California.

All of Catlett's grassroots organizing on behalf of the movement to free Angela Davis ultimately led her back to the studio, where she would metabolize the international crosscurrents of the movement. In a contemporaneous interview with Frederick Lewis of the Studio Museum in Harlem, she mused:

> *I have had a big piece of wood sitting there (in studio) for I guess almost a year now and I wanted to do whatever I felt strongest about during that period before I started working on it. For example, what I feel strongest about now are the Black people in prisons because I have been doing a lot of reading. Not just Angela Davis, but all the political prisoners. And we have a lot here in Mexico too. Students and teachers who have been in prison ever since 1968 who really should never have been and other people, trade unionists, who have been in prisons since 1958...And I have been thinking about how I could express it, but at the same time I have to think about expressing it in sculptural form, so that it hits people, so that they understand or so that they feel.*[46]

This quote is a lucid example of what Said describes as the simultaneity of contrapuntal vision. Catlett swiftly links Mexican student protestors to Angela Davis in a framing made possible by her critical transnational perspective.

Furthermore, the quote underscores the ways that *Political Prisoner* (p. 168) enacts a visual manifestation of the synecdochic operations at play in radical prison activist rhetoric. For example, Soledad Brother George Jackson argued that racial oppression meant that all Black people lived under conditions of imprisonment. For him, the Black prisoner was a symbol for the Black condition more broadly.[47] Angela Davis and her defenders likewise cast her predicament as merely one facet of a larger imprisonment of Black America to racism and white supremacy. As scholar Dan Berger notes, James Baldwin makes this rhetorical turn in his open letter to Angela Davis, in a stroke of devastating poetics: "We must fight for your life as though it were our own...For, if they take you in the morning, they will be coming for us that night."[48] Catlett was able to see how this synecdoche extended to both her peoples.[49]

This articulation of Black imprisonment with white supremacy also helps explain a key difference between the photographic representation of Davis's arrest and Catlett's symbolic portrayal of the political prisoner. In the photograph, Davis's hands are in front of her. By contrast, Catlett's political prisoner is not so much locked into handcuffs as bound by manacles. Prison radicalism posited that incarceration was the contemporary manifestation of a long history of slavery that linked Blackness with criminality.[50]

If the presence of manacles was too subtle a symbol of Black liberation politics, Catlett made her message explicit in her bold use of red, black, and green. Against the restrained asymmetry of the arms, the figure's strong bilateral symmetry is anchored by a wedge of negative space that runs down the vertical axis of the sculpture. Catlett deftly used negative space to afford her sculptures both compositional and symbolic dynamism, as Michael Brenson has observed of *Political Prisoner* and other works: "[Catlett's] respect for the integrity and personality of the void is essential to their ability to communicate the importance of trust and freedom."[51] Painted in the colors of the Black nationalist flag, this is *core imagery* of a different kind that, nonetheless, provides a cross section of what the woman is made of.

After Angela Davis was vindicated by a jury that declared her not guilty in June 1972, Catlett made one final artwork dedicated to the woman who by then had become a global icon of the Left. In *Angela Libre* (p. 169) the repeating visage of Angela Davis floats above a reflective surface. Each face is a silk-screen copy of the Angela Davis portrait Catlett first created for the NUCFAD poster in 1971. Although its serialized composition and silk-screen medium call to mind Andy Warhol's *Gold Marilyn Monroe* and *Marilyn Diptych* (both 1962), it is unlikely that Catlett would have intended to invoke Warhol as a direct art-historical precedent for her work. By the 1970s, Warhol was known for his society portraits and Pop as a movement was largely out of vogue in the mainstream

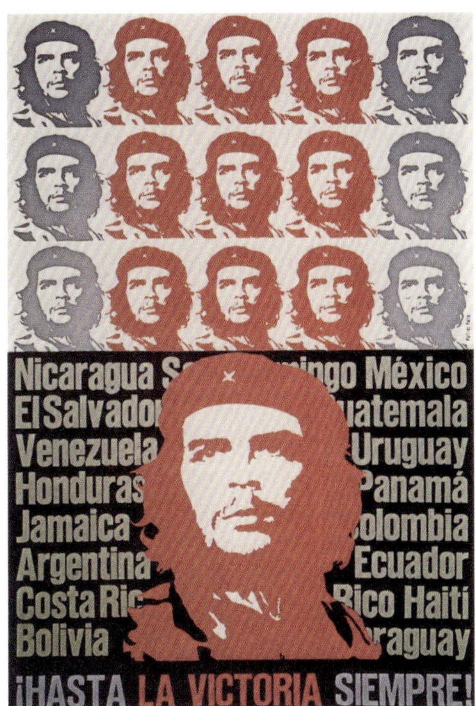

Fig. 6—Alfredo Rostgaard, *Che* poster, 1967

American art world. Moreover, Catlett—informed by the socialist ideals of the Popular Front and the broad Marxism of revolutionary Black nationalism—would have likely critiqued Warhol's commodity fetishism as a symptom of unequal access to the economy and damaging effects of capitalism, rather than a celebration of communal American identification. Her embrace of Pop art was influenced by New Left protest art in Mexico, which was in turn associated with an international array of New Left revolutionary movements.

Pop art was a shared visual language that linked the Cuban Revolution, the student movement in Mexico, and the Black Power and Chicano Movements in the US. Although the political and cultural connection between these social movements is, as Jennifer Josten points out, well known as Third World solidarity, the connection was "arguably never more apparent than in the Pop-derived designs that circulated widely among these areas in the late 1960s and early 1970s."[52] Catlett, of course, was positioned to engage with each of these movements on their own and understood well the political solidarity that drew them together.

Understood within the context of New Left protest art, Catlett's choice to render Angela Davis with a Pop art aesthetic may have been indebted, in part, to the omnipresence of Che Guevara posters. For example, *Angela Libre* has much in common with Alfredo Rostgaard's *Che* (1967) (fig. 6), which mobilizes the serialized portrait of Warhol to celebrate Guevara as a hero of the Cuban Revolution. Davis's upturned face resembles Che's faraway gaze, a pose Josten describes as evoking "the internationally inclined 'new man' he called forth in his writings."[53] Likewise, the sharp contours of Davis's face in *Angela Libre* suggest that the activist is bathed in the light of moral right. Rostgaard was a leading graphic designer of the Cuban Revolution whose impact was felt internationally. His work was published in the Mexico City–based poetry journal associated with the New Left *El Corneo Emplumado (The Plumed Horn)*. Catlett might also have encountered his work in the Organization of Solidarity of the People of Asia, Africa & Latin America journal *Tricontinental*, which was the locus of stylistic exchange between Rostgaard and the Black Panthers' Emory Douglas, another artist whose work she knew well.[54]

In addition to encountering Cuban graphic design in Mexico, Catlett would have had direct experience during her travels to Cuba.[55] In 1971 she traveled there as a delegate representing the UNMM at celebrations for International Women's Day. Taking advantage of the fact that she was in the company of Left-leaning women from around the world, Catlett circulated a Free Angela Davis petition and collected signatures from women representing North Korea, Vietnam, Algeria, France, Guinea, East Germany, and more. Writing to NUCFAD's Aptheker from Havana, Catlett proclaimed: "Angela Davis's name and solidarity with her and the Black liberation cause are expressed on every occasion. There were no women here who had not heard of her struggle. Her picture is seen in remote places which we have visited."[56] Linking *Angela Libre* to the lineage of the Cuban poster situates Catlett as both a producer of and a subject shaped by a global phenomenon where Pop aesthetics were a visual idiom for the New Left and Third World movements.[57]

GLOBAL ARTIST-ACTIVIST

Catlett was an activist-artist whose exile provided her with a unique vision. Attending to the local realities of her position in Mexico City opens up new ways of seeing her Black Power work as reverberating in an international arena racked by utopian protest and state terrorism. This activist-in-exile framing also requires us to recalibrate which works we center as canonical to this period of her career. We need to think of Catlett's travels to Cuba, East Germany (Berlin), and China as integral to her participation in the global sixties, as they mirror the journeys of scores of Mexicans who regarded these Soviet-aligned countries as centers of revolutionary activism.[58] As a result we should consider shifting our characterization here from Black Power to global sixties, so that works like *Women of America* and *Worldwide Congress of Women, Moscow* (both 1963, p. 149) are understood as being of a piece with *Malcolm X Speaks for Us* and *Angela Libre*.

While we celebrate Catlett as an activist in exile, we must resist romanticizing or ignoring the conditions of her geographical and political ostracization. Following Said's observation that "exile is strangely compelling to think about but terrible to experience," we cannot lose sight of the perilousness of Catlett's position. She was subjected to intensive state surveillance throughout the sixties and seventies. Not only did the US CIA locate one of its largest offices in the world in Mexico City, but Mexican bureaus of secret intelligence infiltrated Leftist activist groups, including the UNMM.[59] Indeed, US intelligence attempted to link her both to Lee Harvey Oswald, who was in Mexico just before he assassinated John F. Kennedy, and to an unrealized plot to kill another US president, Richard Nixon.[60]

Despite the risks, Catlett persisted in using her artwork as an extension of her activism. She found ways to push back against the geopolitical barbed wire that constrained her. She nurtured long-distance friendships, participated in networks of Old and New Left activists, gathered evidence from newspapers and photographs, and wrote letters and speeches, willing her voice to be heard. Buffeted by Cold War politics, invested in Third World coalition-building, inspired by the Movimiento Estudiantil, and buoyed by the international reach of Black Power, Catlett was positioned at the fulcrum of the global sixties.

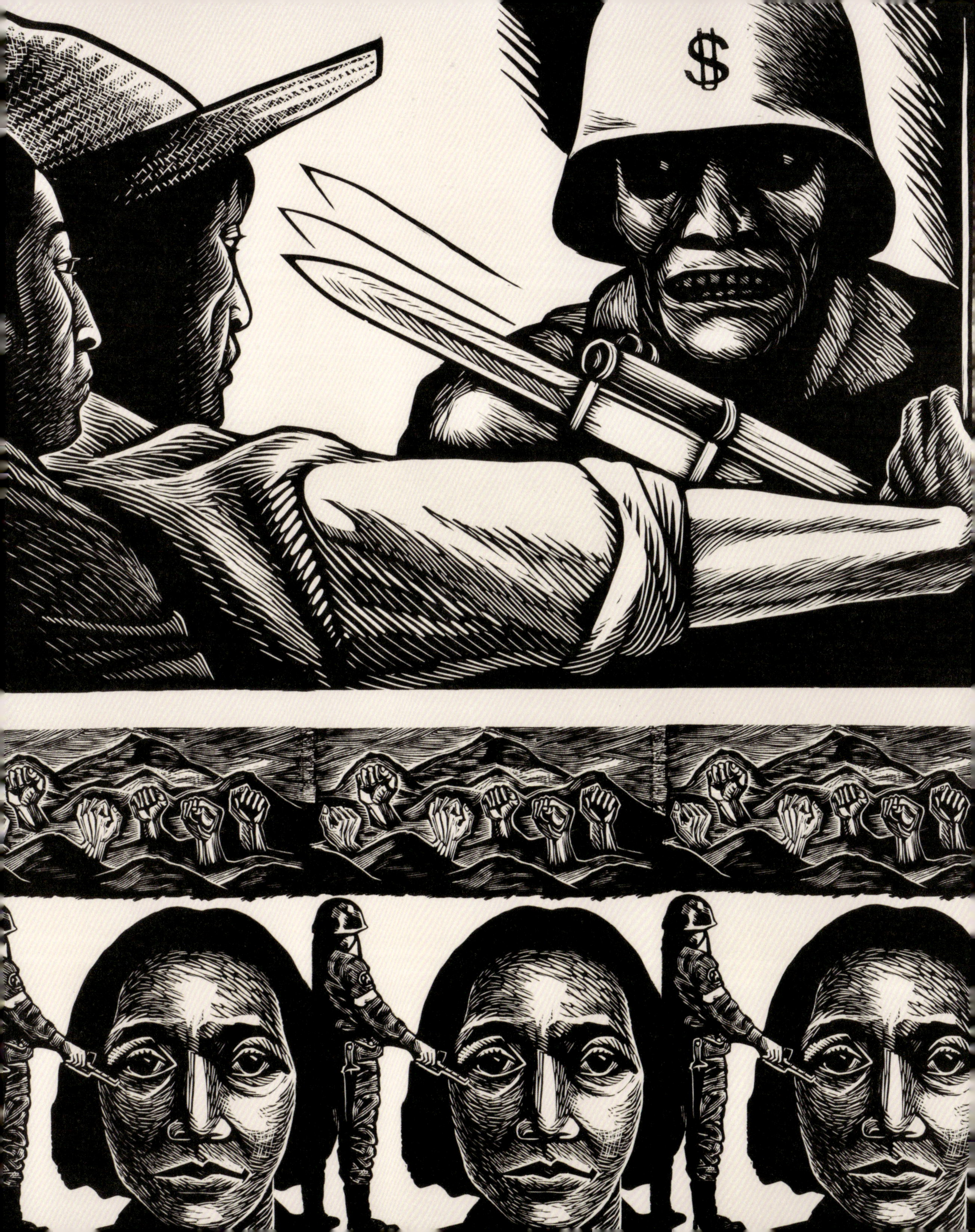

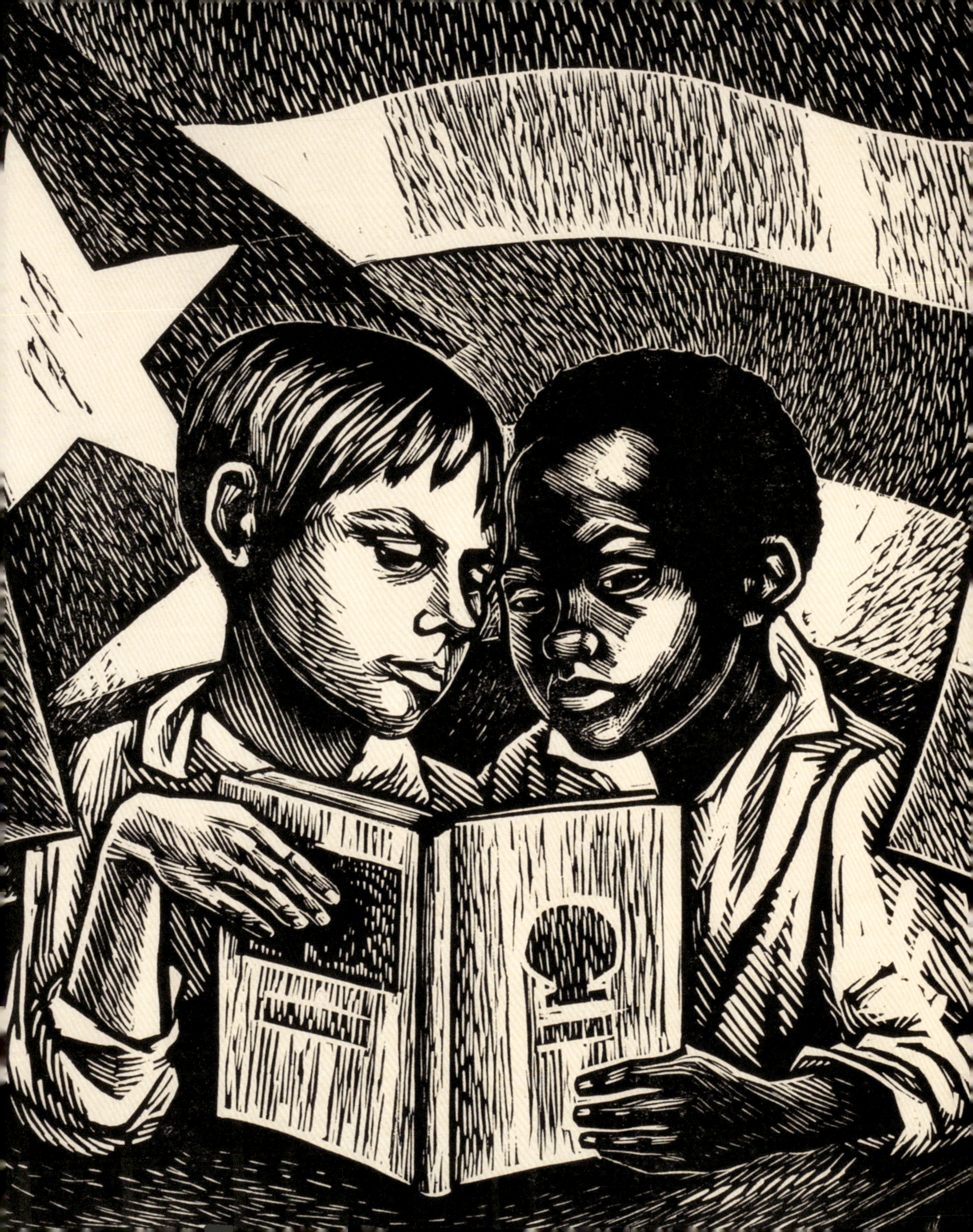

J.V.
DECEMVIRALE

LA MAESTRA'S FUGITIVE PEDAGOGY IN MEXICO

Maestras, women teachers, are among the most depicted personages in the canon of twentieth-century Mexican art history. Pictured in the artworks of some of the greatest Mexican artists, education was as central to the revolutionary aesthetic project as land, liberty, and the people. Not often thought of as rugged outdoor professionals, maestras were known to travel long distances to reach their rural students and even had to teach outdoors when there was no school building available.[1] Artworks like Diego Rivera's *La maestra rural* panel in his seminal fresco series in the Secretaría de Educación Pública of 1923, Leopoldo Méndez's *Pequeña maestra, ¡Que inmensa es tu voluntad!* (1947, fig. 1), and Elizabeth Catlett's *Alfabetización* (1953, fig. 2) all document this reality. Maestras repeatedly bore the hardships of Mexico's politically turbulent twentieth century and almost always worked without resources to create alternative learning spaces—creating learning communities with their voices, bodies, books, and the textiles they wore. Learning under the sun meant that their bodies and their will became the infrastructure that held these learning circles together.

The Mexican tradition of teaching as a revolutionary practice overlaps with the radical Black American educational tradition and Elizabeth Catlett brought both together in the alchemy of her life. Borrowing Jarvis R. Givens's definition of *fugitive pedagogy* as a form of activism in opposition to the white racial terrorism that consistently prohibited educational opportunities to Black Americans, I trace Catlett's teaching in Mexico as form of fugitivity.[2] As guide, professor, and mentor, Catlett not only encouraged and historicized transgression of boundaries for her students, she demonstrated through the example of her life how a politically engaged artist could live her cultural politics and therein offer a space for others to feel and see what artistic freedom looked like beyond racial and gendered logics.

Her expanded pedagogy in Mexico is an archive of strategies in transgression that far exceeded the expectations of a professor of sculpture. Teaching by example meant Catlett's body and actions outside the classroom became sites of instruction through a public pedagogy. Furthermore, such teaching offered students sanctuary, stability, and reconnection with imaginaries beyond the imperatives of domination on which most classroom-based curricula are based. This practice of connecting students to alternative reference points and narratives made Catlett a resource to those artists making their way beyond the Euro-American imaginary.

Fig. 1—Leopoldo Méndez, *Pequeña maestra, ¡Que inmensa es tu voluntad!*, 1947, linocut, Los Angeles County Museum of Art

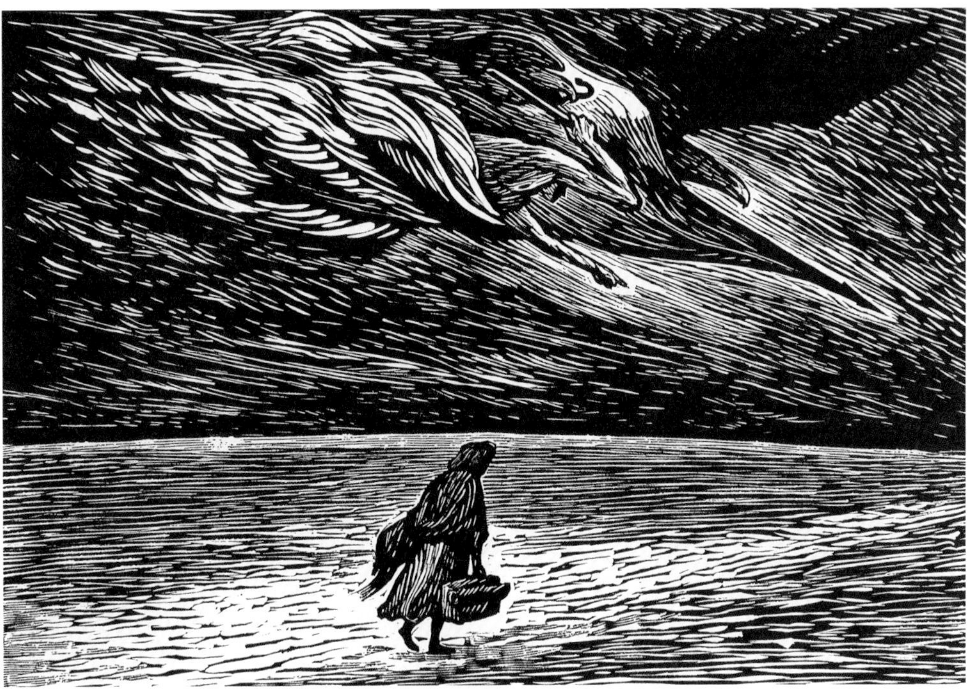

This fugitive pedagogy, however, is not entirely legible or linear, as it required repeated evasion from both a white and mestizo male-dominated Mexican art world obstinate to Catlett's Black feminist mandate. As she always had to make her place by hand, I review her pedagogy as a series of stitches.[3] Tracing the visible work she did within the university, I equally offer testimony from artists who all testify to the under stitch of her work as mentor and role model beyond the university. Important to consider together, they encompass a tension between her roles as touchstone and disrupter that made her cultural activism impactful and lifelong.

LA MAESTRA IN THE CLASSROOM

Catlett encountered multiple fronts of opposition as a foreign-born Black woman teaching in Mexico City.[4] In her first years as an instructor she was confronted by anti-Black, xenophobic, and anti-woman fears from students, faculty, and directors. Her entry into the Mexican workforce meant outmaneuvering hostile obstruction and suspicion of her pedagogy, a common experience shared across the United States and Mexico for Black women in the arts.[5] As her prestige grew, and she introduced students to her dear friends (all legendary figures in the Mexican art scene), opinions shifted into a collegiality that she came to enjoy.[6] The struggle, however, to make a place for herself meant she had to build her authority strategically, letting the force of her example counter the prejudices that preceded her in the minds of faculty and students.

From 1959 to 1975, Catlett was a professor of sculpture in the Escuela Nacional de Artes Plásticas at the Universidad Nacional Autónoma de México (UNAM). Tiburcio Ortiz and Armando Ortega both studied with Catlett at UNAM and recall the incredible range of Catlett's technical and art-historical knowledge.[7] She was known to lecture on abstract European and US sculpture, Harlem as a world cultural center, African sculpture, ancient Greek sculpture, Mesoamerican sculpture, Chicano and Black American muralism, as well as close-looking exercises exploring the philosophical dimensions of form and voids so central to her sculpture.[8]

In keeping with her role as expander of the typically nationalistic art history taught within Mexican art schools, Catlett denounced white supremacy in

Fig. 2—Elizabeth Catlett, *Alfabetización*, 1953, lithograph, Ben and Beatrice Goldstein Foundation Collection, Library of Congress, Washington, DC

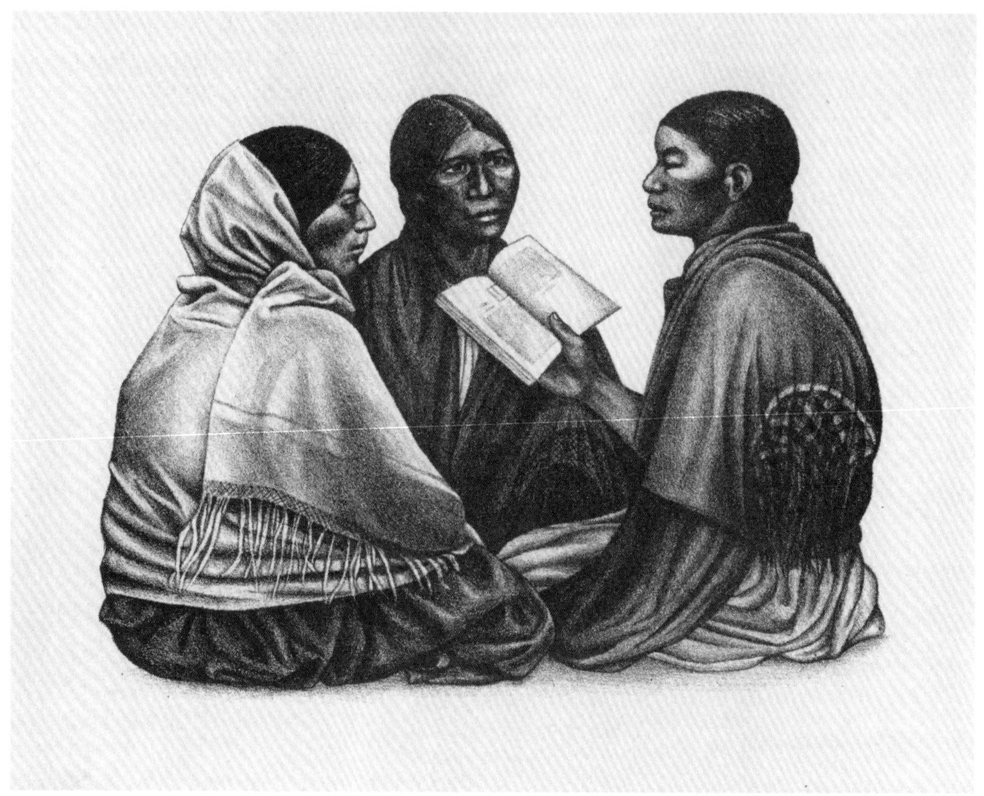

the US when she shared a photograph of a lynched Black man in class.[9] With most Mexicans knowing little of the US's racialized realities, and even less of Mexico's African history, Catlett broadened the imaginaries her students could access by acting as conduit to a wider world of struggle that she personally witnessed and researched. It also testified to her ability to bring multiple currents of cultural and political movements into a classroom setting that did not traditionally reach beyond Mexico and Europe. Rendering the classroom into a "site of convergence," in the words of scholar Christina Heatherton, Catlett made high modernist sculpture collide with the racial realities of Black folk in the US.[10] It was a pedagogical maneuver that resituated Mexican students into a broader decolonial worldview wherein the struggles of Black Americans were understood as part of the Third World's anti-imperialist and anti-racist struggles.[11] As Ortega remembers fondly of his maestra: "No era normal. Era activa. Muy politica. Sumamente politica y muy consciente." (She was not normal. She was active. Very political. Summarily political and very conscious.)[12]

Catlett did not see her pedagogy as strictly limited to the sharing of technical craft, as was common among faculty at UNAM.[13] As she stated in her notes for a class lecture: "Lo unico que puede hacer el maestro es, apuntar el camino que conduce a la realizacion y tratar de persuadir sus estudiantes a tomar este camino. Esto no puede ser un asunto de pura formula." (The only thing that a teacher can do is indicate the way that leads to realization and to try to persuade their students to take this path. This cannot be a purely formulaic affair.)[14] Having herself gone through the motions of building a socially engaged artistic practice, Catlett believed that a younger generation of politically engaged artists were "confused" by the capitalist art market's demands to be salesmen.[15] Speaking of the politically engaged artists' marginalization in the art world, she lamented that they were "thrice damned: first for realism, second for social and political content, third for attempted communication with a non-existent public. For in the US as in the international art world oppressed people do not exist."[16] Explicitly unwilling to train students to be apolitical commodity-makers for the wealthy, she understood that she had chosen a path that meant marginalization from the mainstream art market.

As Ortega recalls in conversations following his studies, the violent political repression of the Mexican government in 1968 chilled the "freedom of classes" across the art schools in Mexico City.[17] And, "disillusioned" with university leadership's implementation of a more conservative arts pedagogy, which she named "Mexican Bauhaus," Catlett did not want to teach technique without historical or political awareness.[18] Working within the institution meant not an unstrategized recalcitrance but a strategic maneuverability where the classroom could become a liberated space for thinking. When that was no longer an option, she opted to continue her teaching in another form beyond the university.

EXPANDED PEDAGOGY: ¿POR QUÉ CARAMBAS NO COSES?

At the Taller de Gráfica Popular (TGP) Catlett and her colleagues Celia Calderón and Mercedes Quevedo developed feminist aesthetics during their leadership tenure from 1963 to 1966, as art historians Dina Comisarenco Mirkin and Helga Prignitz have detailed. In her classic study of the graphic workshop, Prignitz describes this feminist turn as the group opening "a new field of activities."[19] Catlett's retirement from the organization in 1966 did not signal the end of this initiative, however.[20] The international feminism that developed in the TGP, with Catlett at the center, would be passed down in the unofficial fugitive school Catlett ran adjacent to her artistic practice.

These pro-woman values would be adopted by her unofficial students Silvia Tinoco and Ana Iturbe, two younger Mexican artists who embraced Catlett's project of solidarity and the importance of the artist-pueblo bond to creative work. Catlett's circle was guarded, but Tinoco was able to gain access through her husband, Armando Ortega, a friend and mentee of Catlett and her husband Francisco "Pancho" Mora. Iturbe and her husband, artist Raul Cabello, began making fine art prints for Catlett in 1978 and would remain her trusted printmakers until her death.

The impact of Catlett in motion was inspiration for Tinoco, who was herself a mother and wife. As she explains: "Betty llego con un otro feminismo. Pancho, toma, cuida al niño!" (Betty arrived with another feminism. Pancho, here, hold the child!)[21] Understanding that like Catlett she too would have to "make her own place" in a male-dominated art world, she felt empowered by Catlett's example.[22] Wanting to take the next step in the life of a professional artist, Tinoco asked Catlett to support her induction into the Salón de la Plástica Mexicana in 1983, a critical recognition for an emerging artist in Mexico. Even though she had never officially studied under Catlett in the university, Catlett supported Tinoco's successful application.[23]

Confronting what she described as a nearly insurmountable misogynistic Mexican art world, Tinoco worked diligently on her own craft for decades, simultaneously creating "spaces for women."[24] Her projects include sojourns as artist and teacher with Zapatista revolutionary women in Chiapas in the 1990s; founding workshops and collectives for women artists to learn techniques and art history in Mexico City; and curating exhibitions in support of women's rights throughout the 2000s.

Tinoco centered the questions "Where do I come from? Where am I going?" as guiding principles in her own aesthetic projects, which she defined as aligned with the broader currents of liberation theology.[25] Concluding that her own identity was made of the three main currents of Mexican identity—Indigenous, Spanish, and African—elicited a profound shift in her understanding of herself. She has explored the interlacing of these roots for eighteen years in her series *Torres de Babel* (2005–2023, fig. 3). The raku and ceramic towers speak to the

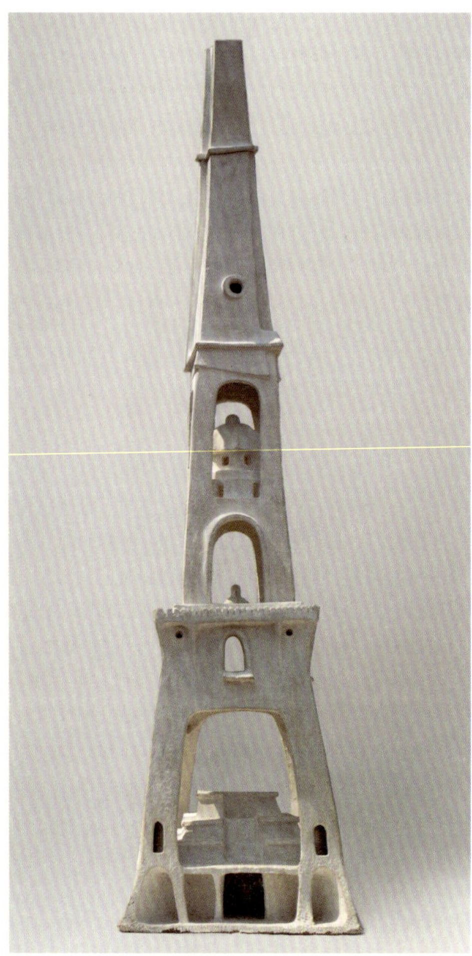

Fig. 3—Silvia Tinoco, *Tres Culturas*, 2012, from the series *Torres de Babel*, 2005–2023, ceramic sculpture, Silvia Tinoco Collection, Mexico City

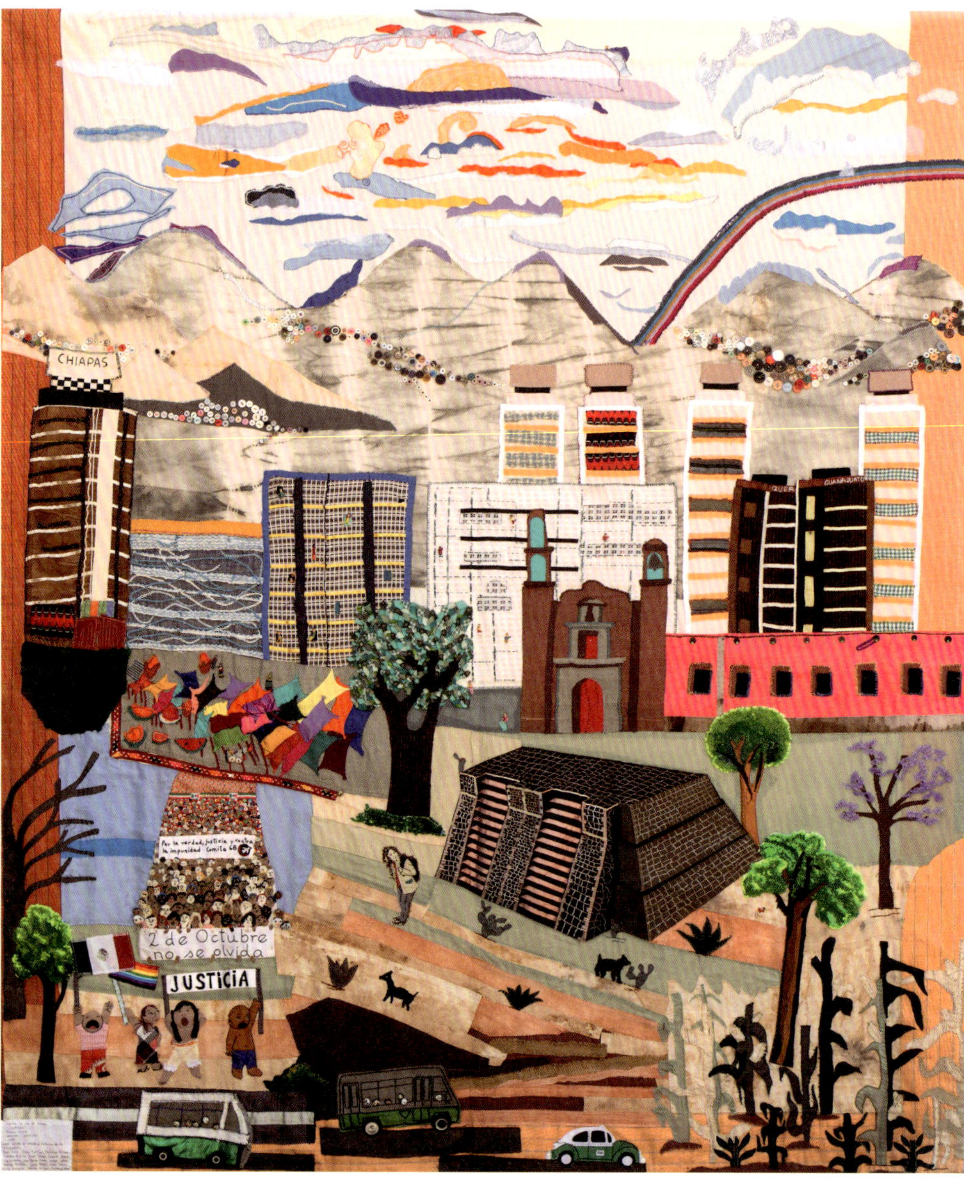

Fig. 4—Colectiva Ira del Silencio, *Lienzo de Tlatelolco*, 2008, cloth-collaged quilt, Colección Ana María Iturbe; the artists are Rocío Pérez, Elvia Martinez, Frederique Drilhon, Lisandra Aparicio, Teresa Solano, Zenaida Abascal, Lilia Valencia, Ana María Iturbe, Carmen Gómez, Patricia Medellín, Lucero Robles, Silvia Tinoco, Odilia Mezquita, Patricia Quijano, and Pastora del Moral.

beauty of pluriculturalism, as well as the destabilizations it creates when misunderstandings and untranslatability are part of the collective work of building another world.

Iturbe also learned from Catlett as role model both in the print studio and the more intimate spaces of the living room. She recounts an important lesson learned in the 1970s: "Un día la maestra me dijo: 'Ana, puedes venir aqui? Sientate. Sabes coser?' Respondi si. Y me pregunto: ¿'Y por qué carambas no coses?'" (One day la maestra said to me: "Ana, can you come here? Sit down. Do you know how to sew?" I responded yes. And she asked: "So why the hell don't you sew?")[26] Charmed and surprised, Iturbe would take this advice and collaborate with Tinoco in 2008 on their own series of collaboratively made multimedia textile works. Sewing with forty younger women artists—known as the Colectiva Ira del Silencio (Ire of Silence Collective)—they walked their hand-stitched visual proclamations through the streets of Mexico City calling for women's rights and an end to femicide throughout Mexico.[27] One example of the collective's work is *Lienzo de Tlatelolco* (2008, fig. 4), a quilt depicting a march demanding justice for the students massacred by the Mexican government at Tlatelolco square during the student-led protests of 1968. Political in both content and by the collective women's hands that produced it, the textile demonstrates how Catlett pushed her students to explore new directions in their artmaking by tapping into the commonly held creative practices of women.

Cuernavaca, Morelos, a 10 de Septiembre de 2007.

A Jesús Álvarez Amaya:
Como tengo 92 años es para mi imposible asistir a esta reunión.
Le escribo esta carta por no tener otra manera de expresar mis pensamientos sobre sus arrogantes declaraciones sobre el Taller de Grafica Popular.
Yo nunca lo vi en una reunión del TGP y fui miembro de este equipo de 1946 a 1967. Tampoco observé ninguna participación de usted en los trabajos colectivos.
Parece que usted no sabe que nuestro Archivo -que usted descaradamente admite vender por pedazos y pocos pesos- es el resultado de más de 60 grabadores ¿Y quién de ellos le ha dado permiso de vender su obra? Ni usted mismo sabe quiénes son Moshe Gal, Roberto Verdeció, Jesús Escobedo, Galo Galecio o Jules Heller.
¿Qué derecho tiene usted de vender nuestra obra colectiva y personal? Estoy escribiendo por todos aquellos que están muertos y no están aquí para proteger sus grabados y litografias.
Debe usted leer la declaración de principios del TGP antes de usar nuestro nombre. Yo fui parte de la denuncia legal en su contra hace muchos años, que fue aplastada por influencia de algún político.
Pero usted no tiene derecho a pedir dinero en nuestro nombre porque usted no tiene nada suyo en el Archivo del TGP en el periodo que abarca de 1937 a 1969. Yo no le digo nada del Archivo que se hizo de 1979 a la fecha.

Su posesión y venta de la obra del TGP ES UN ROBO NO SOLO A NOSOTROS, QUE LO HICIMOS. ES UN ROBO AL PUEBLO DE MEXICO PARA QUIEN FUE HECHO.

ATTE
Elizabeth Catlett Mora.

Fig. 5—Letter from Elizabeth Catlett to Jesús Álvarez Amaya, 2007, Ana Iturbe and Raul Cabello Collection, Mexico City

In September 2007, the ninety-two-year-old Catlett sent the younger Iturbe to an opening for an exhibition of the TGP with a letter, one of the last pieces she wrote before her death. Iturbe arrived at the gallery, but the intended recipient refused the letter (fig. 5). After some back and forth, a concession was reached: Iturbe could read it out loud at the opening.[28] Unknown to her, she carried a fiery denunciation of the TGP's management since Catlett's departure. The letter accused the newest director of selling off and compromising the legacy of her beloved taller.[29] As Iturbe read out the letter, she found herself a conduit for disruption, her voice and la maestra's becoming one, giving an entirely new dimension to artistic inspiration.

WHY DON'T WE MEND?

Unguarded and vulnerable—the state of the TGP by 2007 speaks volumes about a philosophy of aesthetic solidarity that Catlett had devoted so much of her life to but had increasingly come to worry over among a younger generation.[30] Iturbe and Tinoco had been inducted into this tradition and have faithfully preserved their teacher's legacy in their practices and in their collections. While Catlett indeed lives in the hearts of her students, she is regrettably in danger of being forgotten in Mexico, as she continues to be a "thrice damned" artist—foreign-born, Black, and a woman. All three characteristics continue to make her appear, to a Mexican curatoriate, as an outsider. In haunting and prophetic words, Catlett once explained that she made "work for my people. Not for an elite, and I've paid a price for my commitment."[31]

As the generation that followed Catlett enters retirement, what mending must be done to keep the broad avenues of her liberatory world building project alive? It is a pressing question and the response will require a radically inclusive range of cultural and political workers, something comparable to the Catlett described in Sonia Sanchez's "6 haiku (for Elizabeth Catlett in Cuernavaca)." Respectfully referring to her mentor as "La Señora," the inhale of the poem centers on Catlett's practice of solidarity—"O how you / help us catch / each other's breath"—and it exhales with her diving into a pool, her hands "humming hurricanes / of beauty."[32] As the poem attests, these *habits of being*, to borrow a phrase from bell hooks, as centering touchstone and tempestuous disrupter, were some of her most important lessons.[33]

What indeed will be lost when we can no longer catch Catlett's breath from those who caught it directly from her? With no center in Mexico or the US devoted to the work of Catlett and with no substantial collection in the hands of the Mexican state, one of the cornerstones of socially engaged artistry in the Americas continues to pay the price for her cultural political transgression even in death.

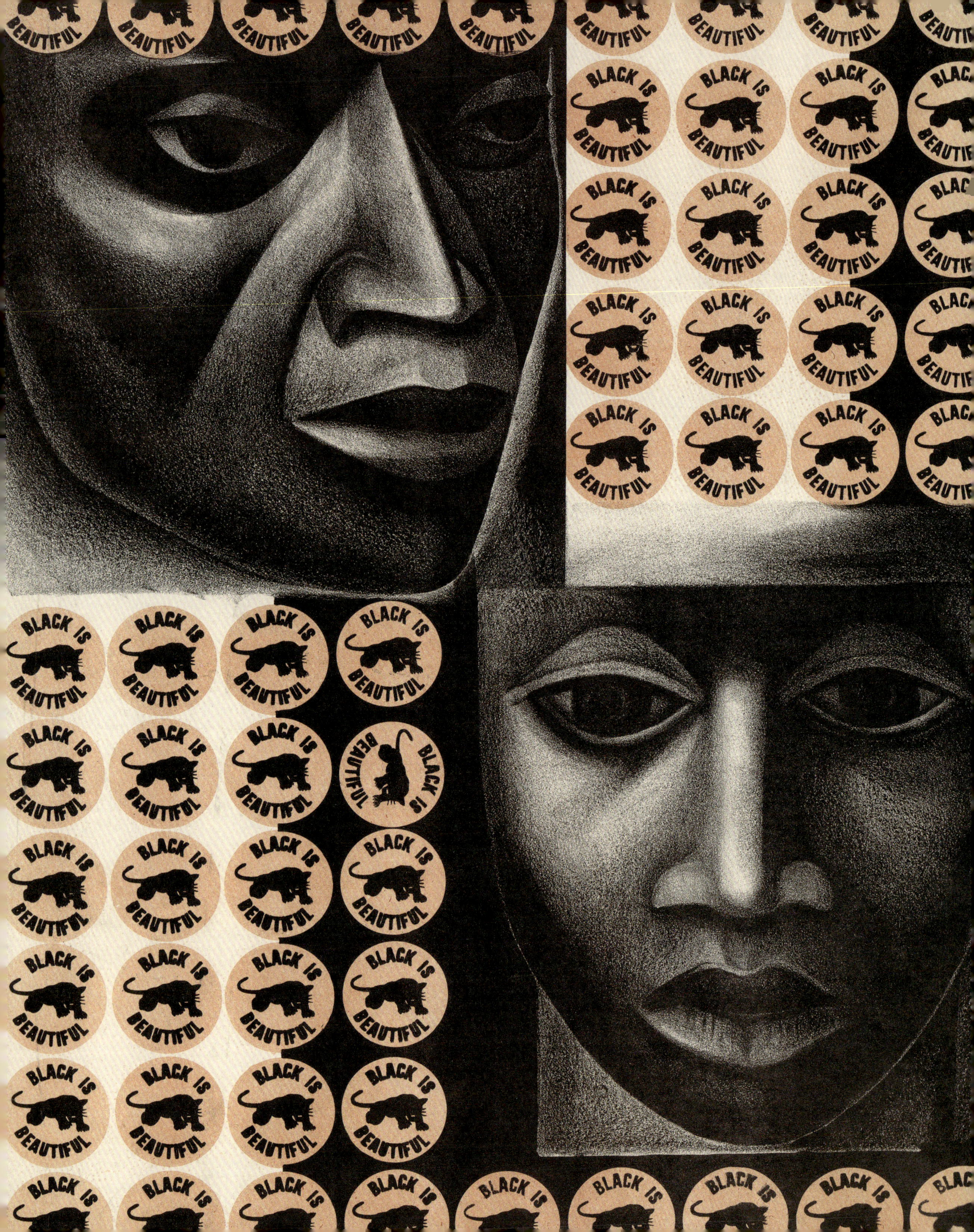
BLACK IS BEAUTIFUL

PLATES

1960–1975

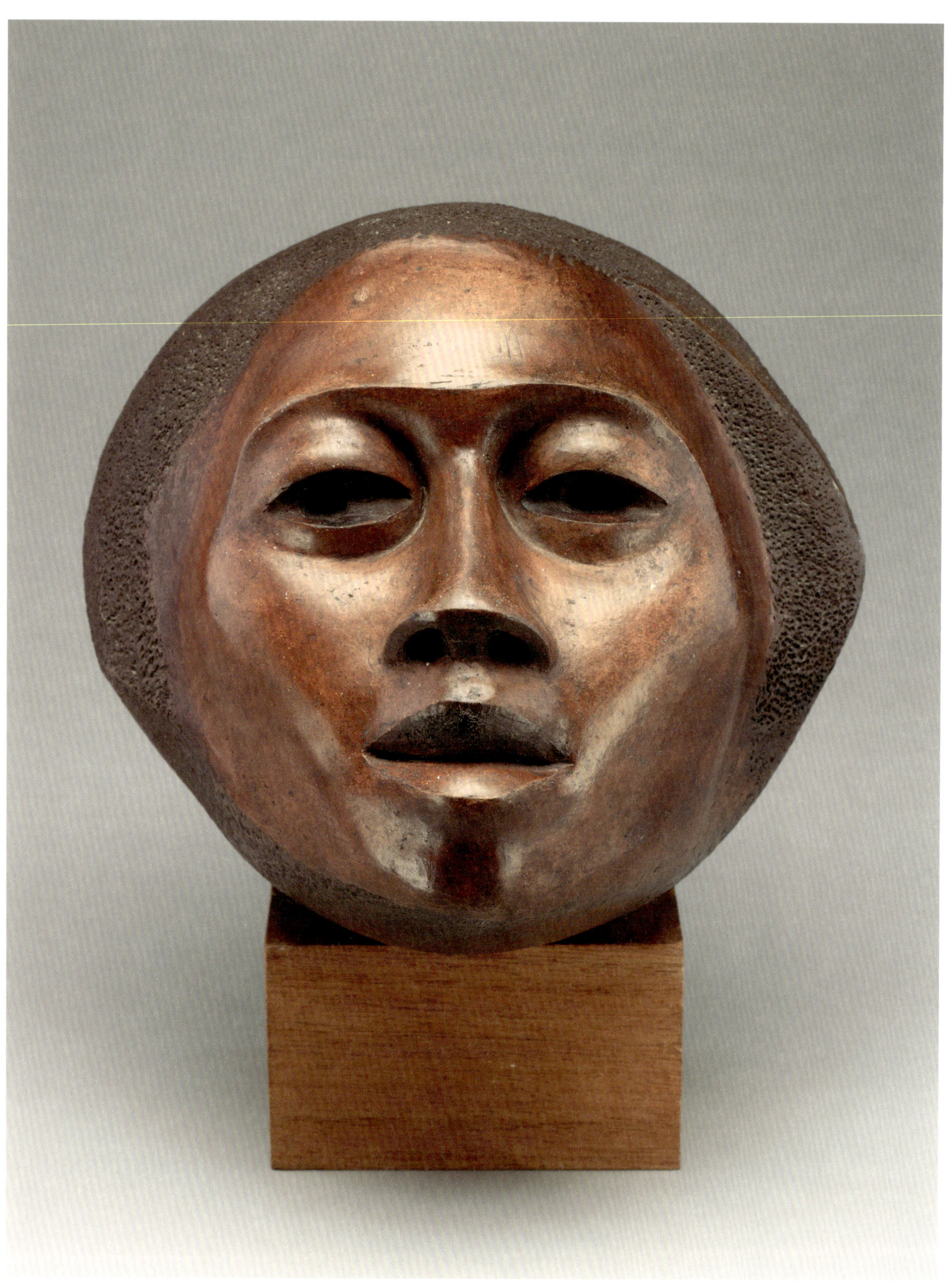

Terra-Cotta Head, c. 1960, terracotta, 8¼ × 9¼ × 11 in., Detroit Institute of Arts, Museum Purchase, Friends of African and African American Art

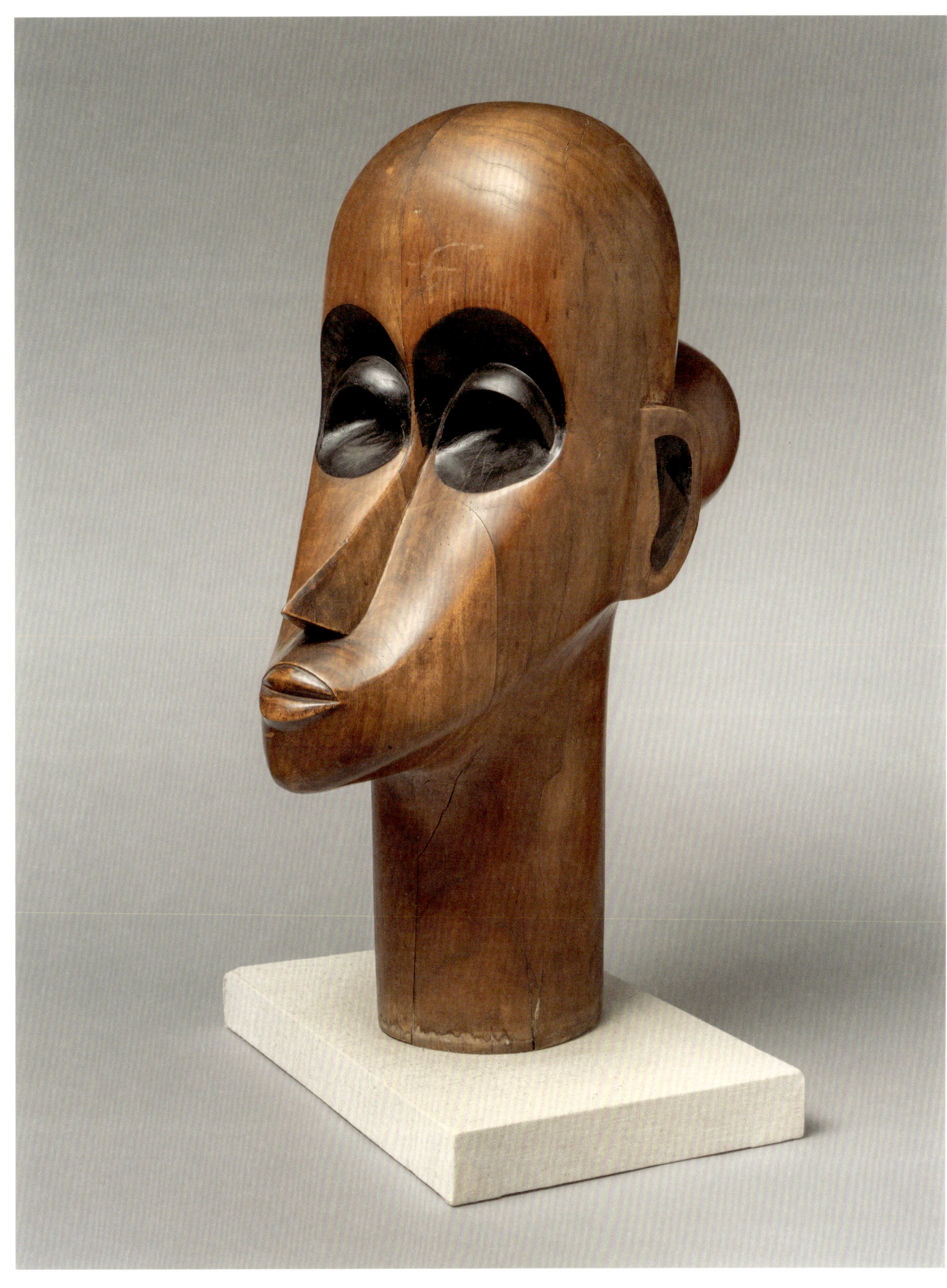

Head, 1960s, polychromed mahogany, 29½ × 12 × 17½ in., Collection of The DuSable Black History Museum and Education Center

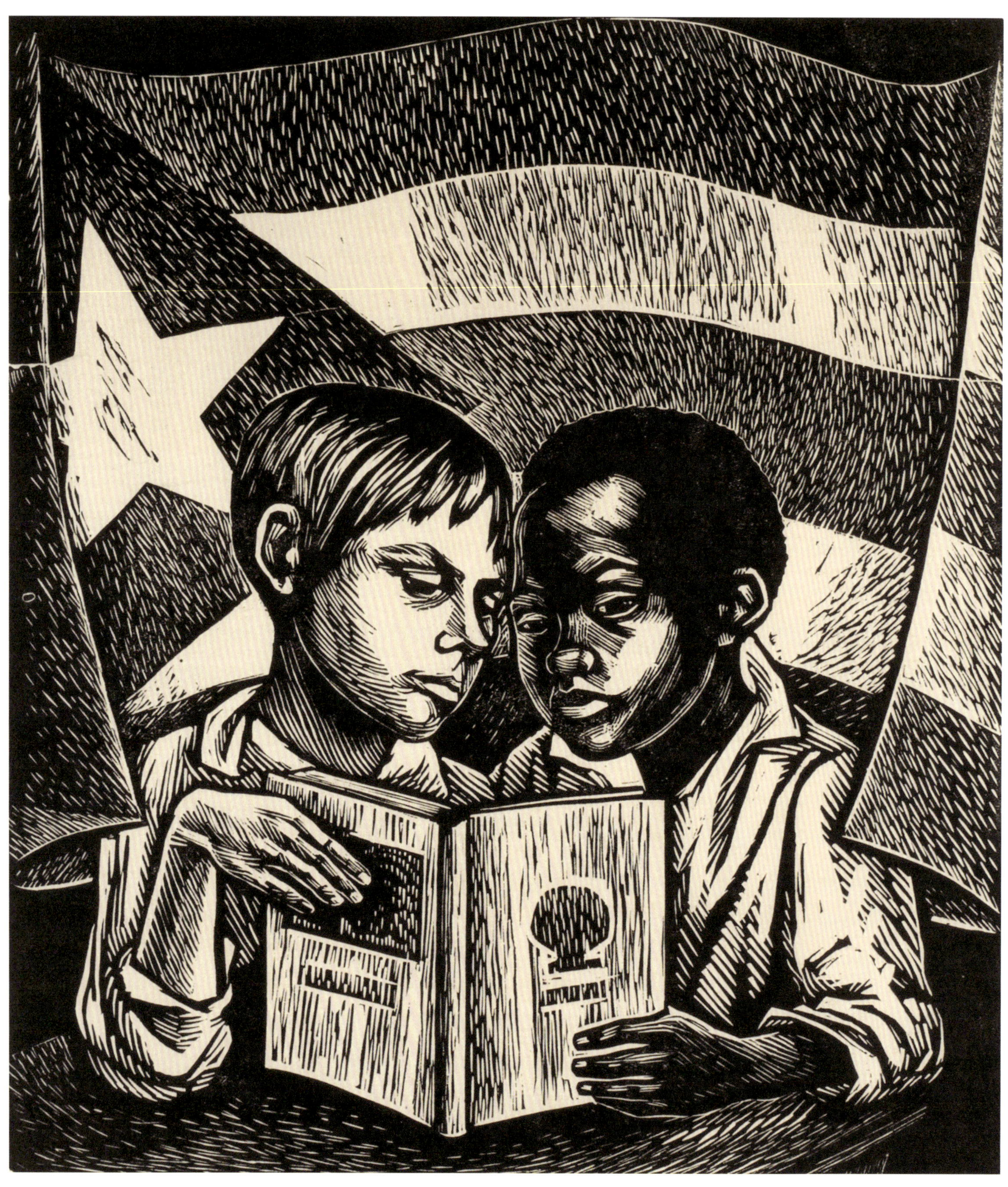

La Integración Racial en Cuba, c. 1962–1964, linocut, 10¼ × 8$^{11}/_{16}$ in., Peter Schneider and Susan DeJarnatt

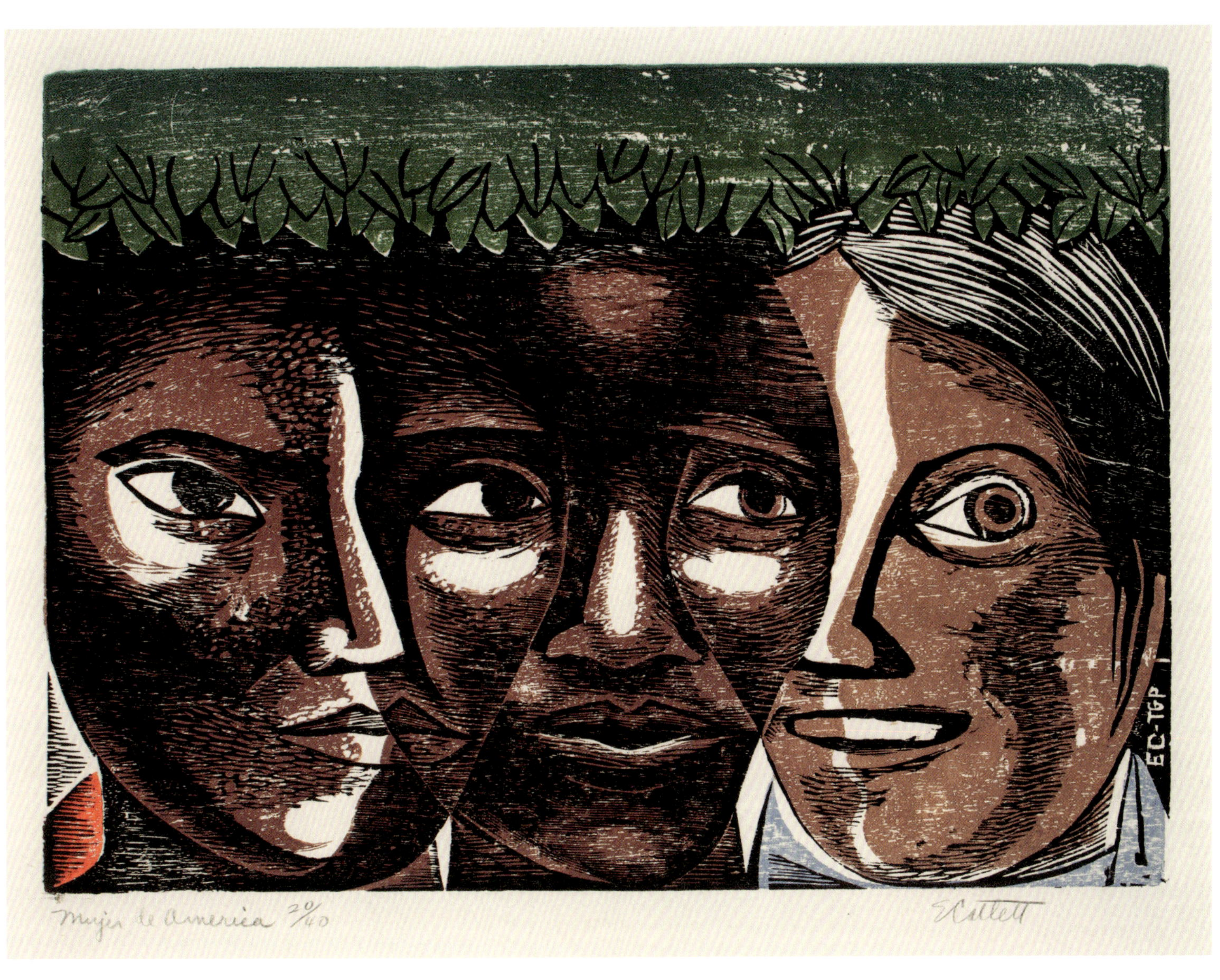

Women of America, 1963, linoleum cut printed in color on off-white wove paper, 14 × 18¾ in., Detroit Institute of Arts, Museum Purchase, Elizabeth P. Kirby Fund, Associates of the American Wing Special Projects Fund, et al.

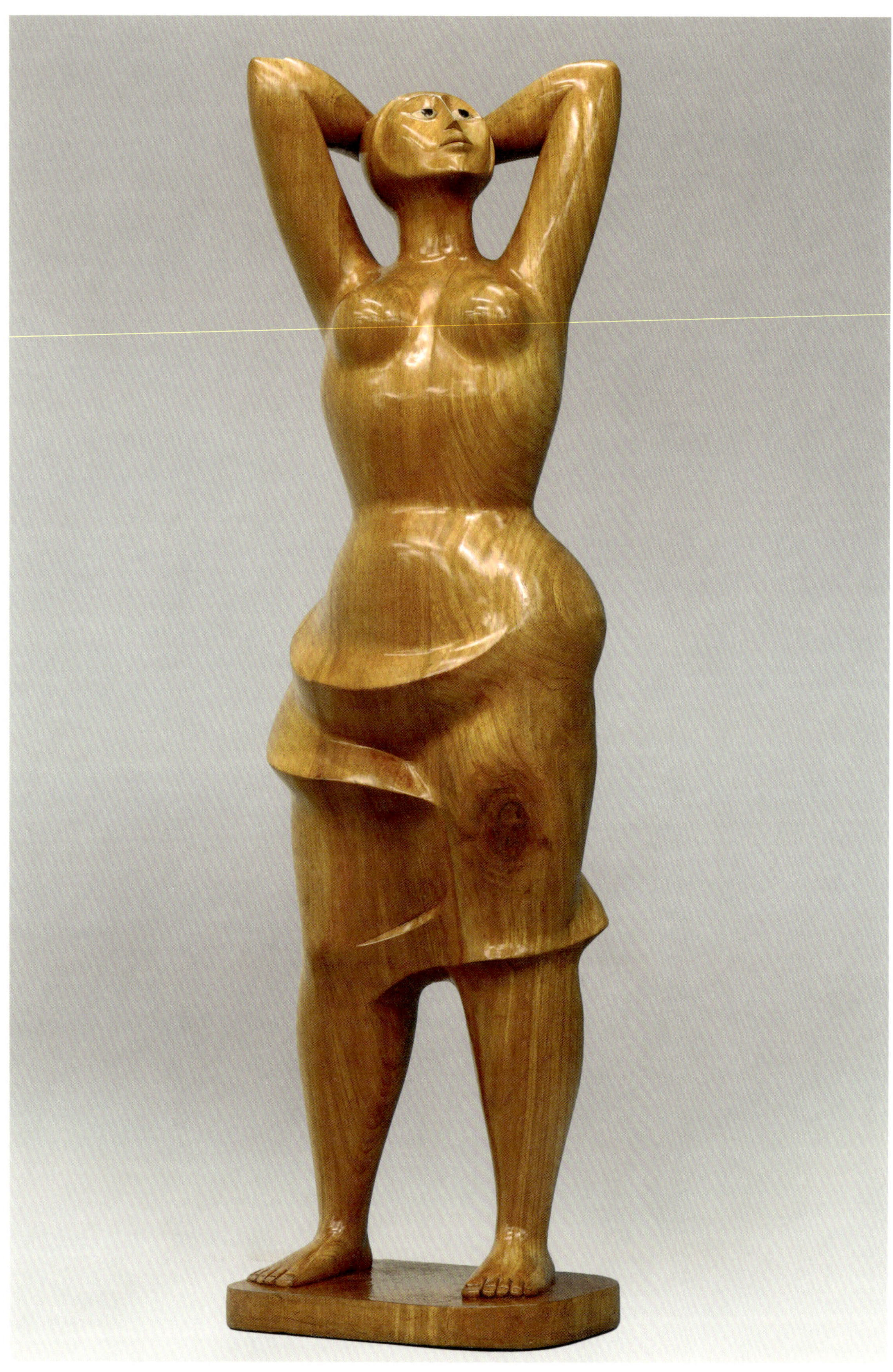

Mujer, 1964, cedar, 62⅝ × 14³⁄₁₆ × 17¹¹⁄₁₆ in., Acervo Museo de Arte Moderno, INBAL / Secretaría de Cultura

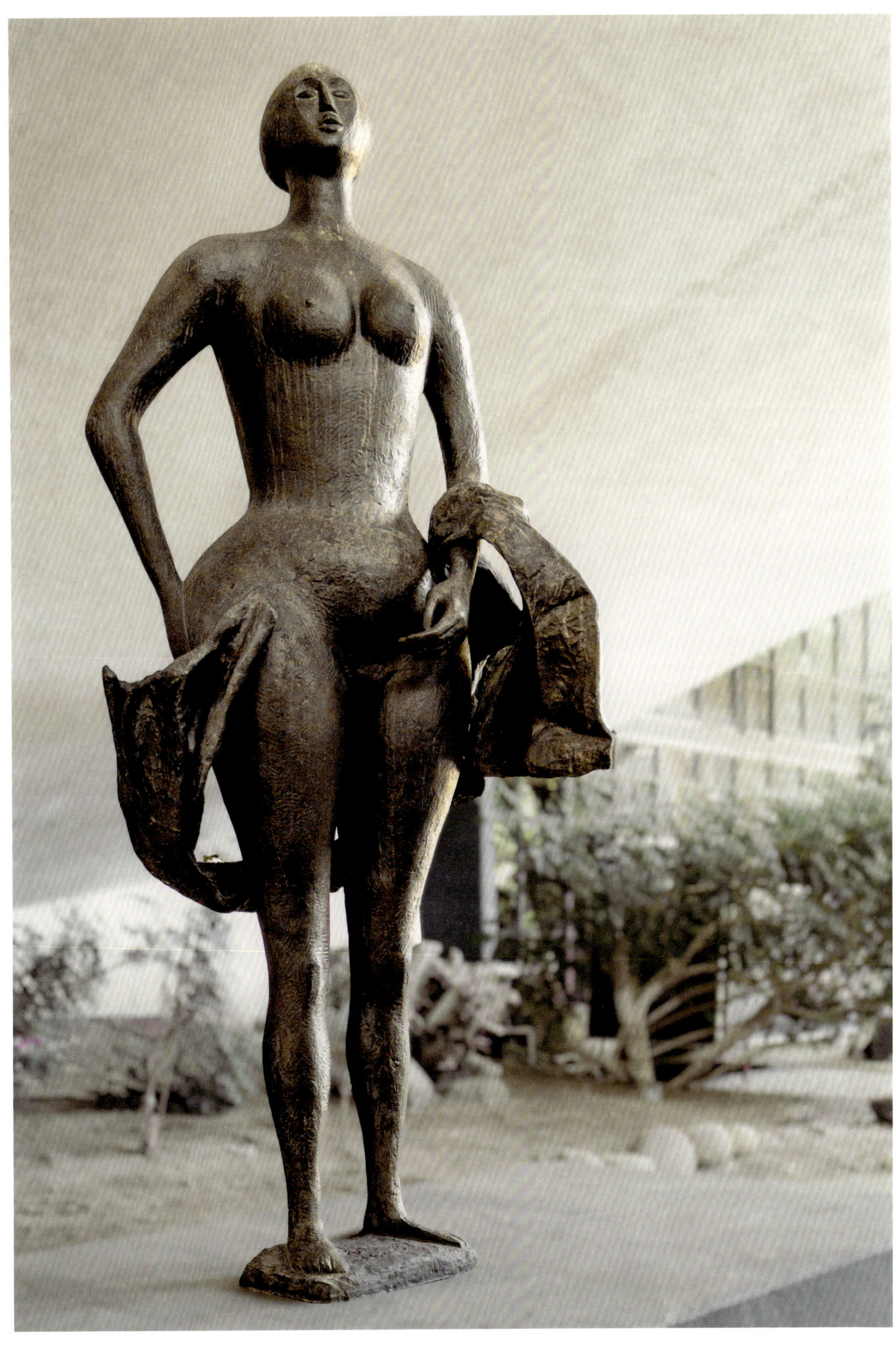

Bañista Olmeca (Olmec Bather), 1966, bronze, 120 × 43 in., in situ photograph, Instituto Politécnico Nacional de México, Centro Cultural Jaime Torres Bodet, Unidad Profesional Adolfo López Mateos, Mexico City

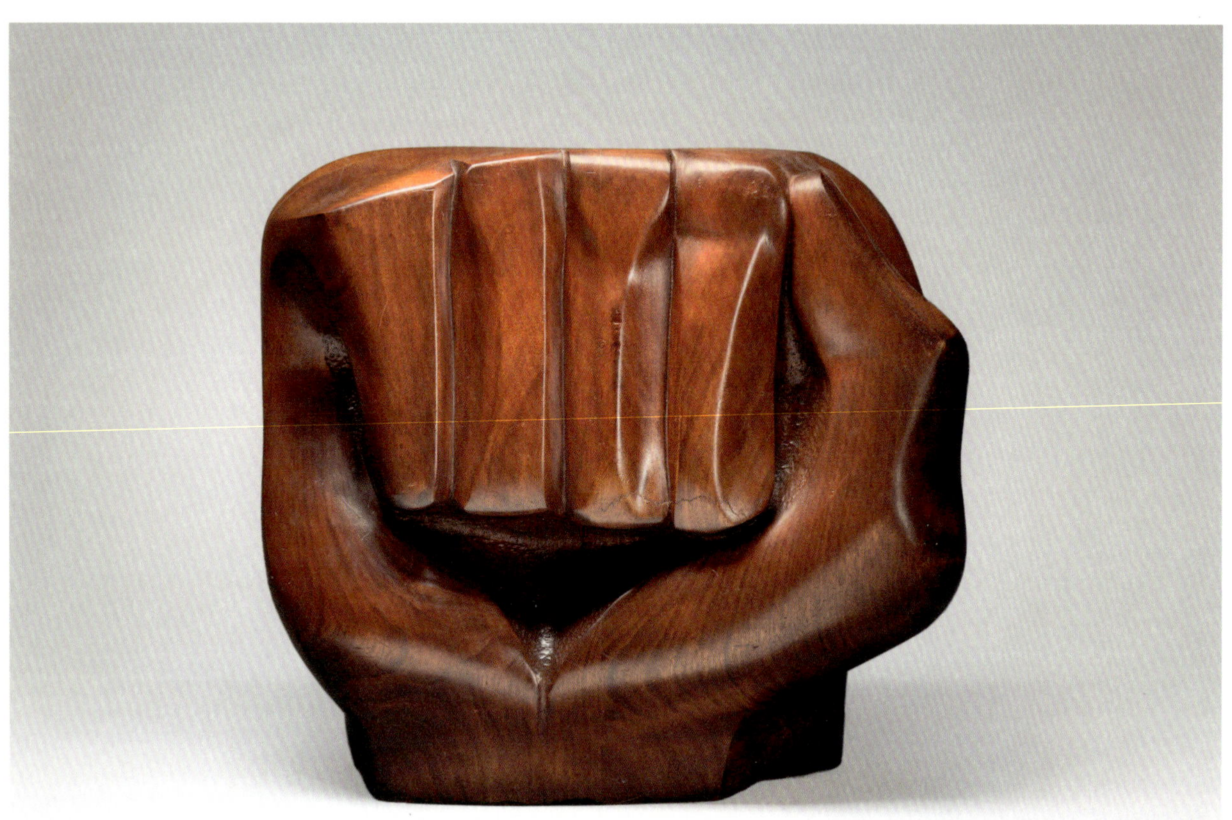

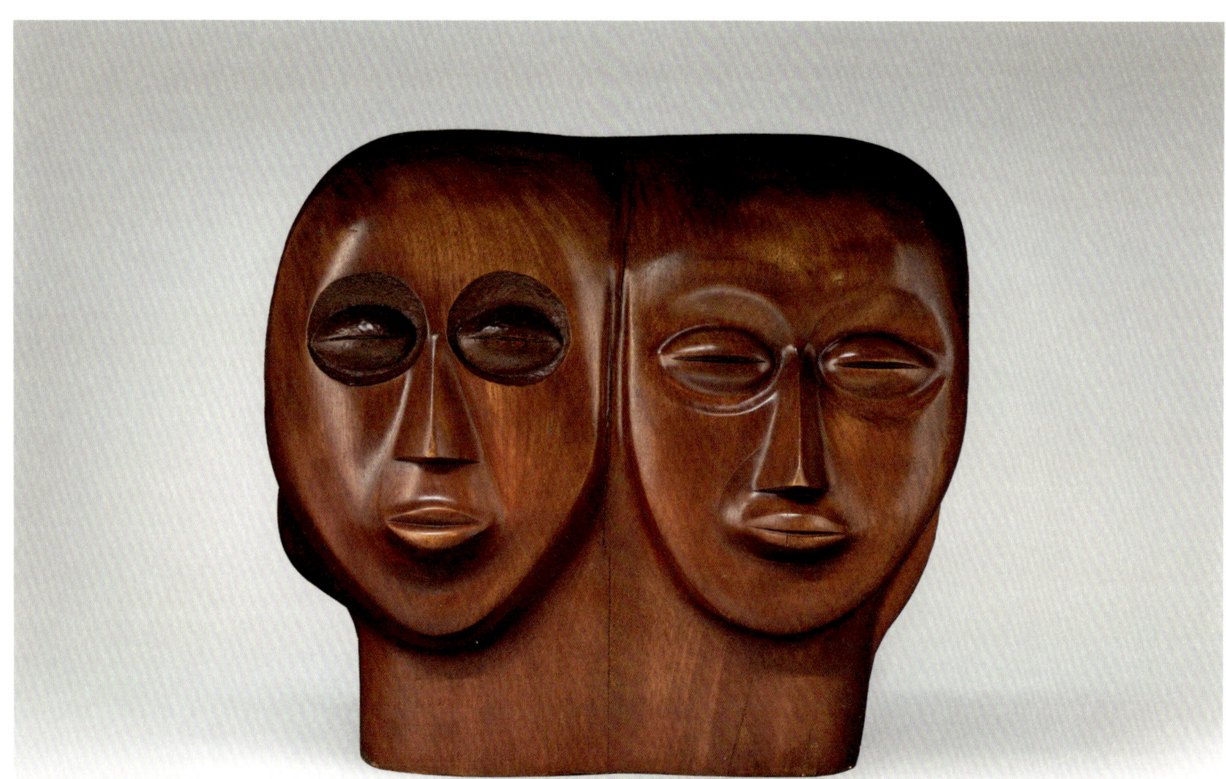

Black Unity, 1968, cedar, 21 × 12½ × 23 in., Crystal Bridges Museum of American Art, Bentonville, AR, 2014.11

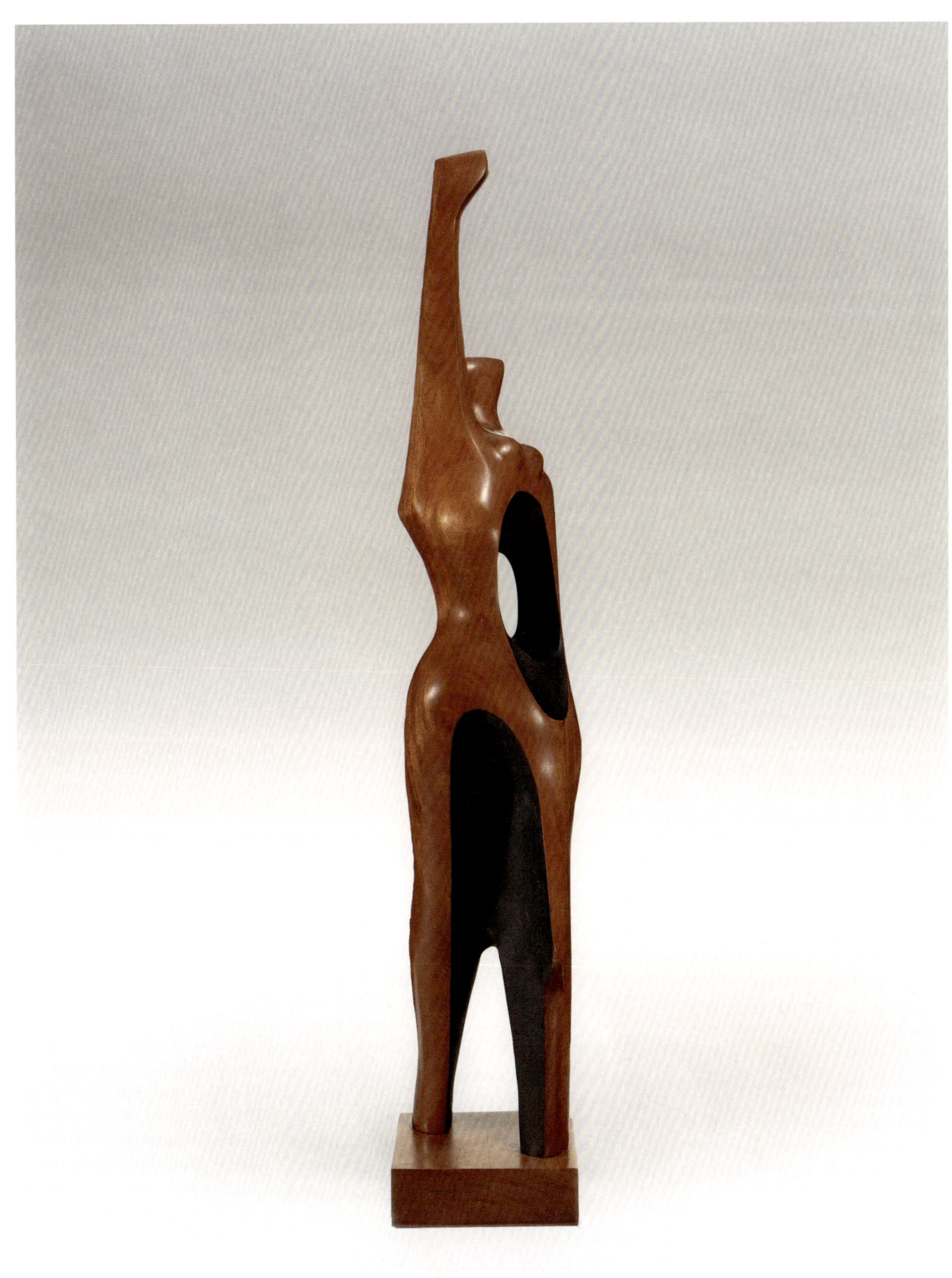

Homage to My Young Black Sisters, 1968, red cedar, 71½ × 13 × 12½ in., Art Bridges

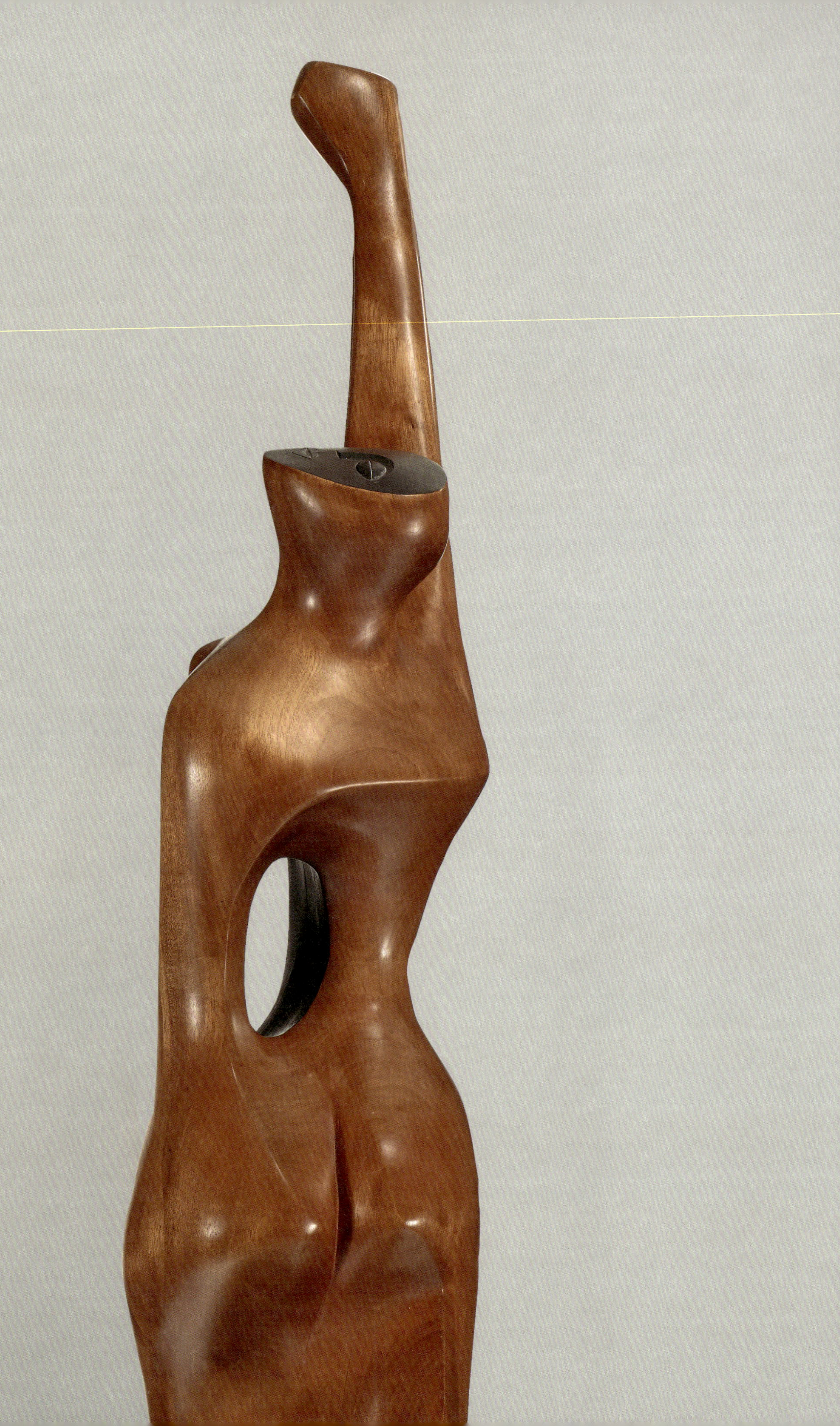

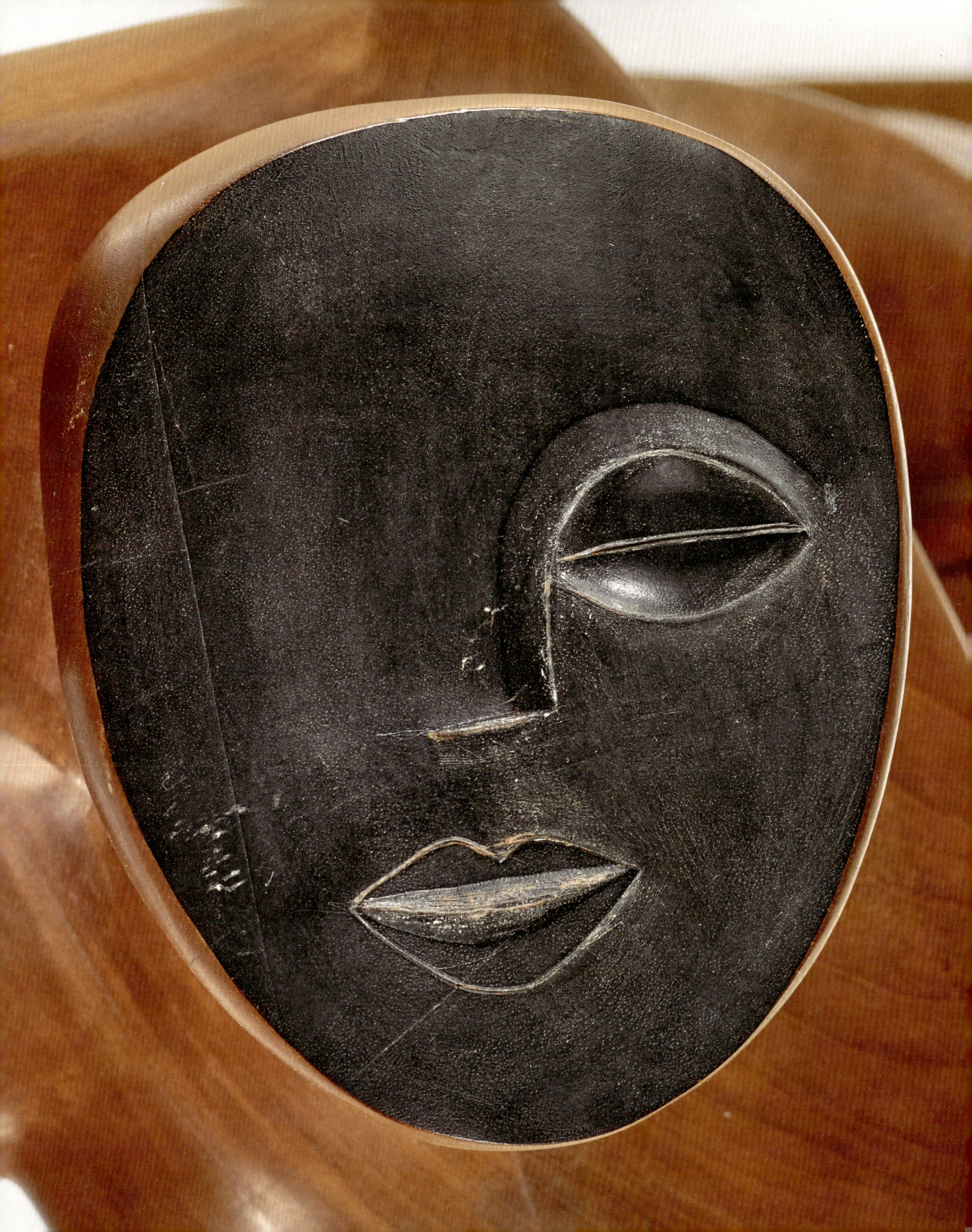

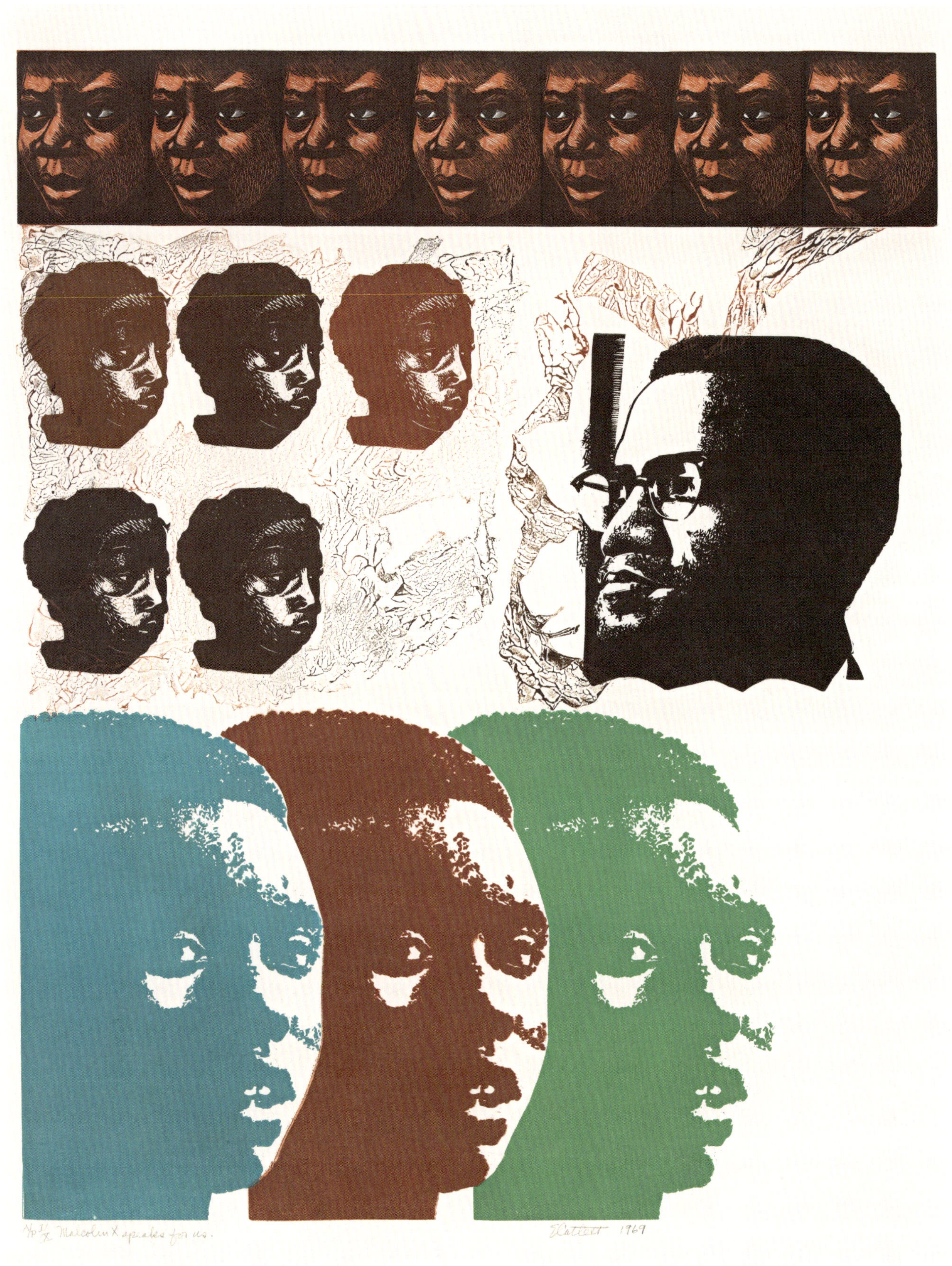

Malcolm X Speaks for Us, 1969, linocut [ed. 40], $41\frac{5}{16} \times 30\frac{11}{16}$ in., The Museum of Modern Art, New York, Gift of the artist, 1988

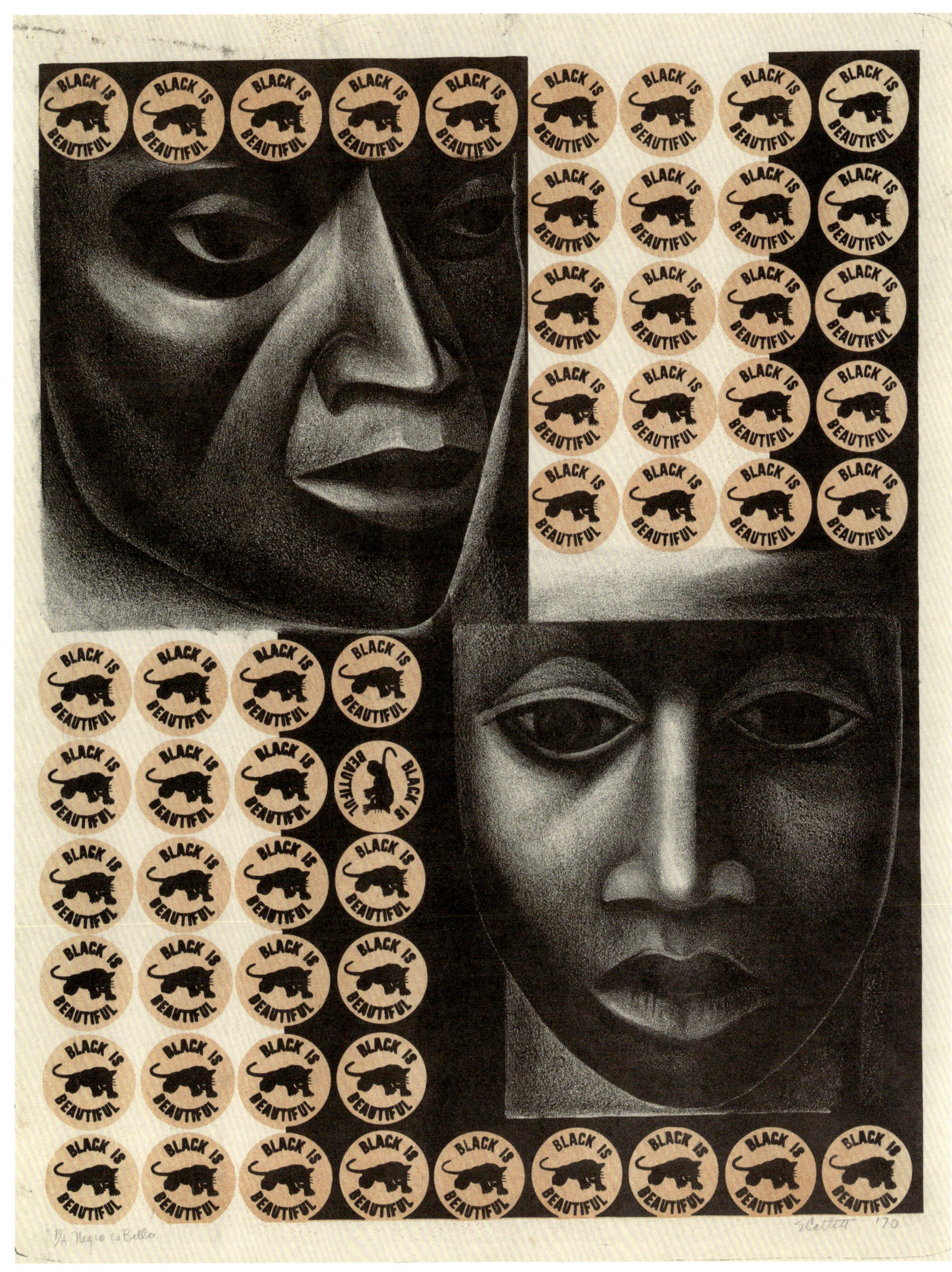

Negro es Bello (Negro es Bello II), 1969/1970, color lithograph, 29 13/16 × 23 9/16 in., National Gallery of Art, Ailsa Mellon Bruce Fund

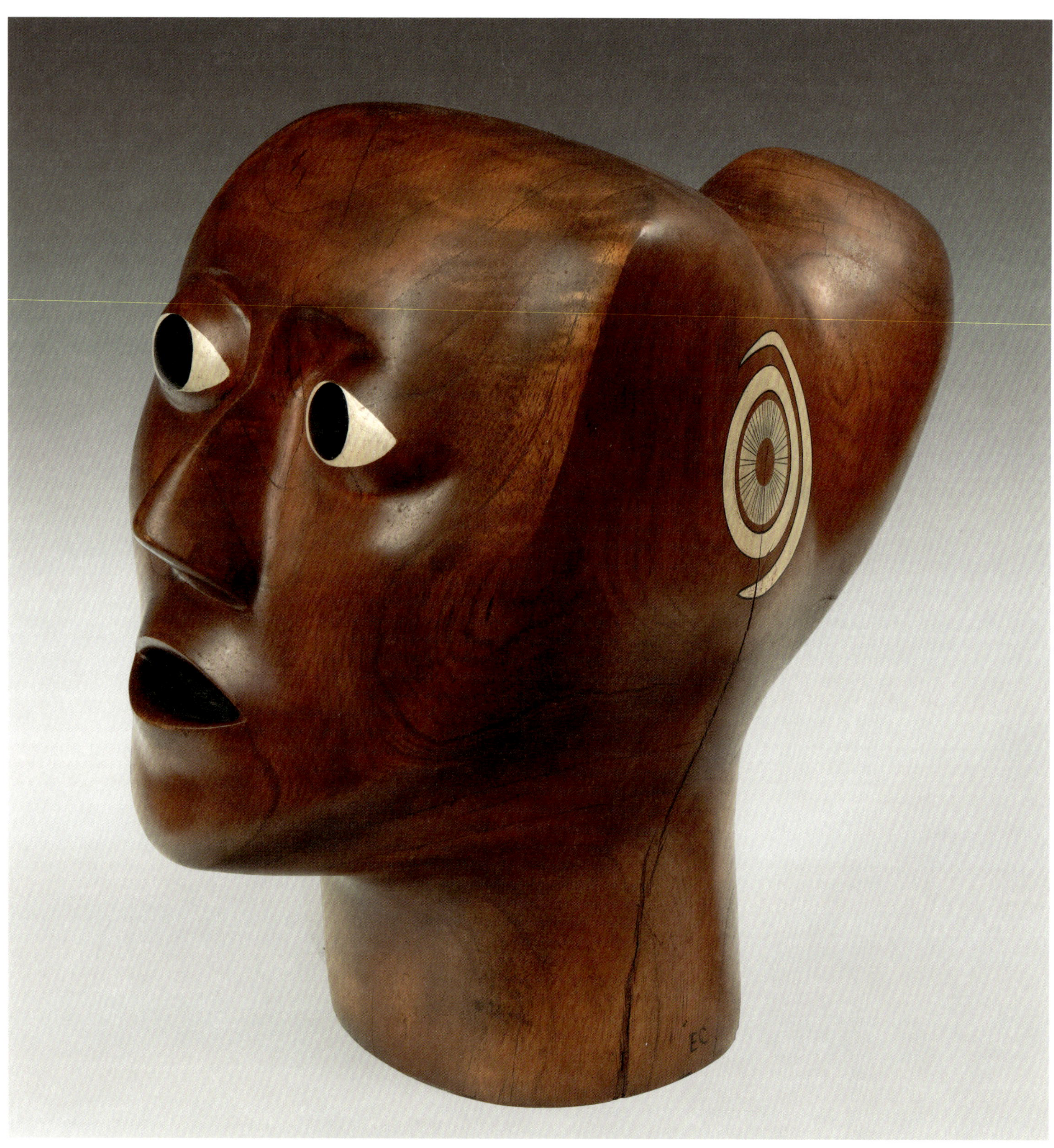

Black Woman Speaks, 1970, Spanish cedar, 15½ × 7½ × 15¼ in., Mrs. Thelma Driskell

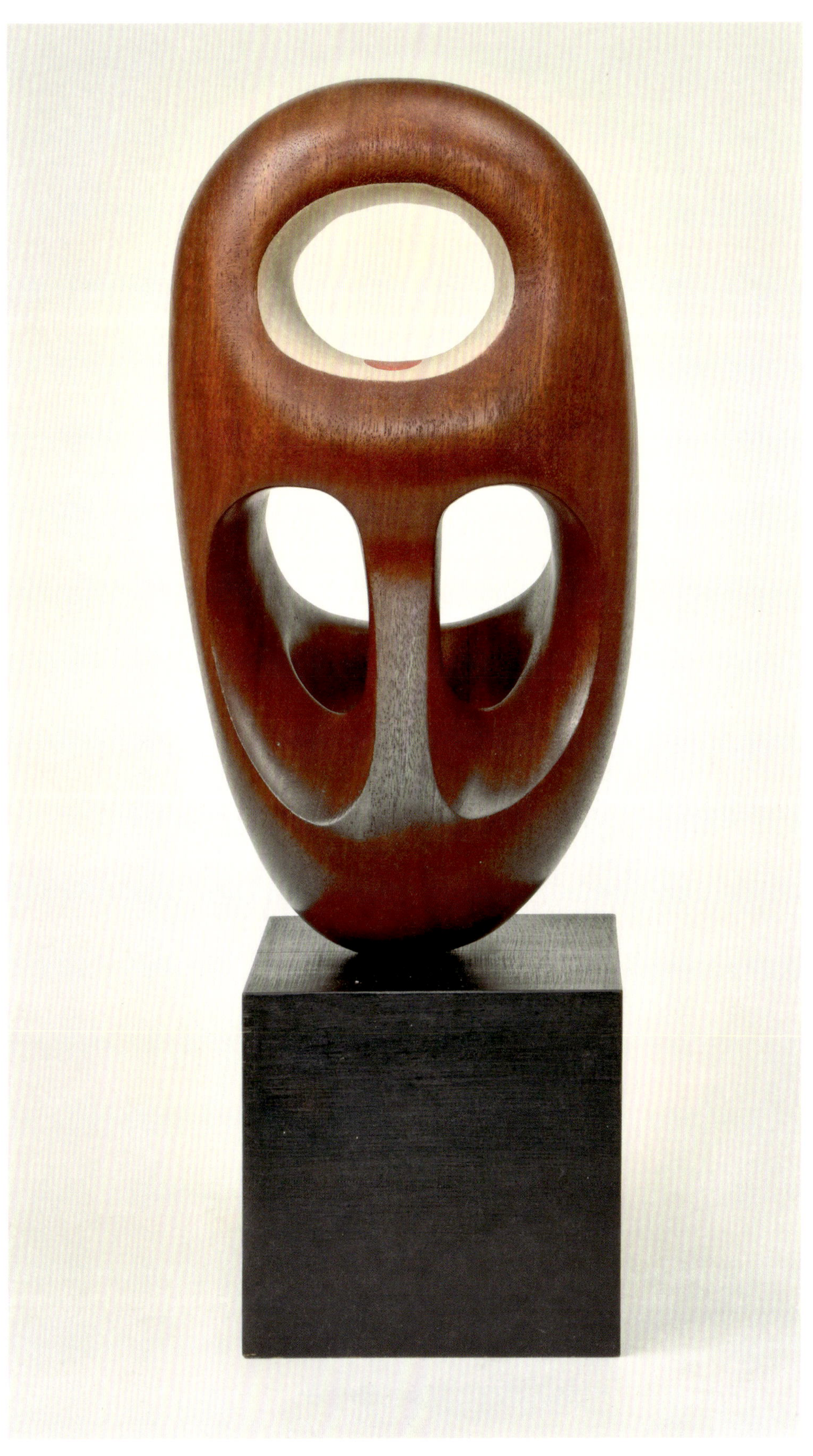

Magic Mask, 1971, mahogany, 11⅜ × 6 × 5½ in., Courtesy of the Estate of Samella Lewis

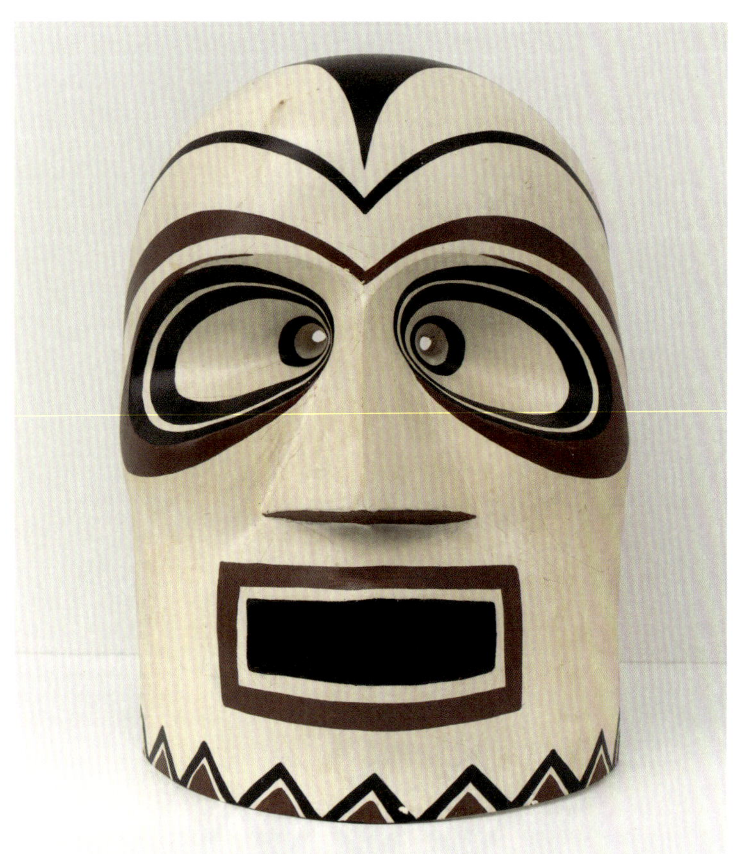

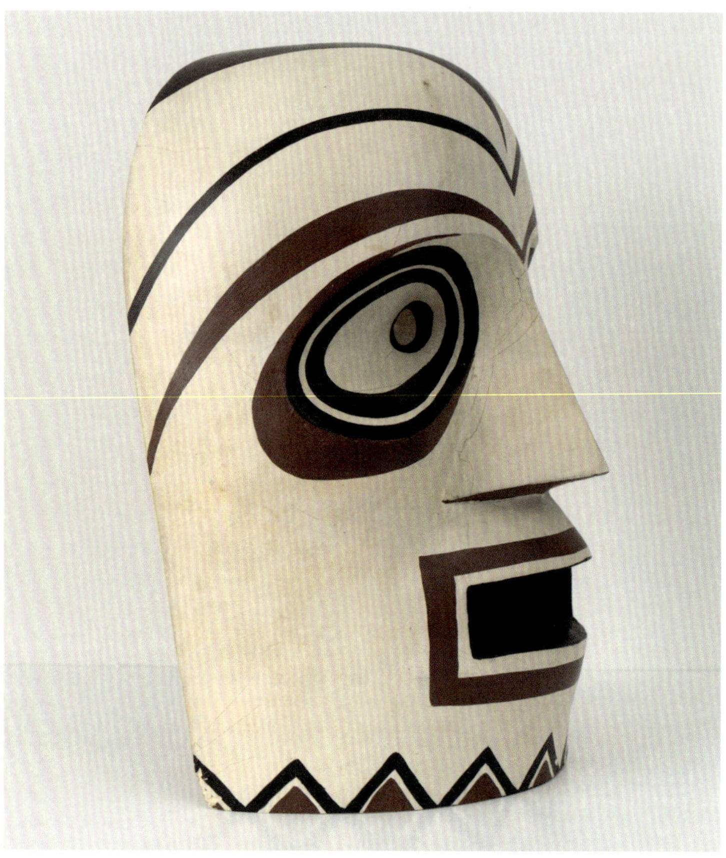

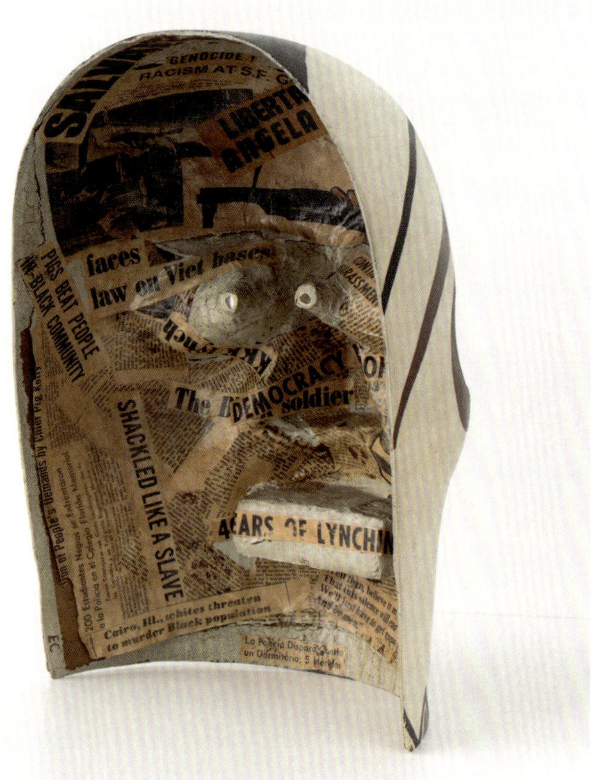

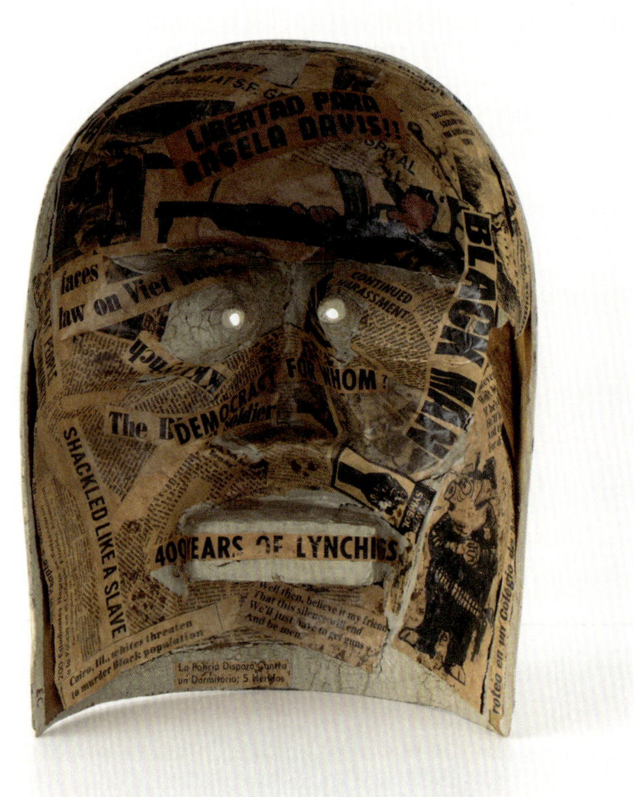

Mask, c. 1970, fiberglass and paper collage, 17¾ × 12¾ × 10 in., The Studio Museum in Harlem, Gift of the artist

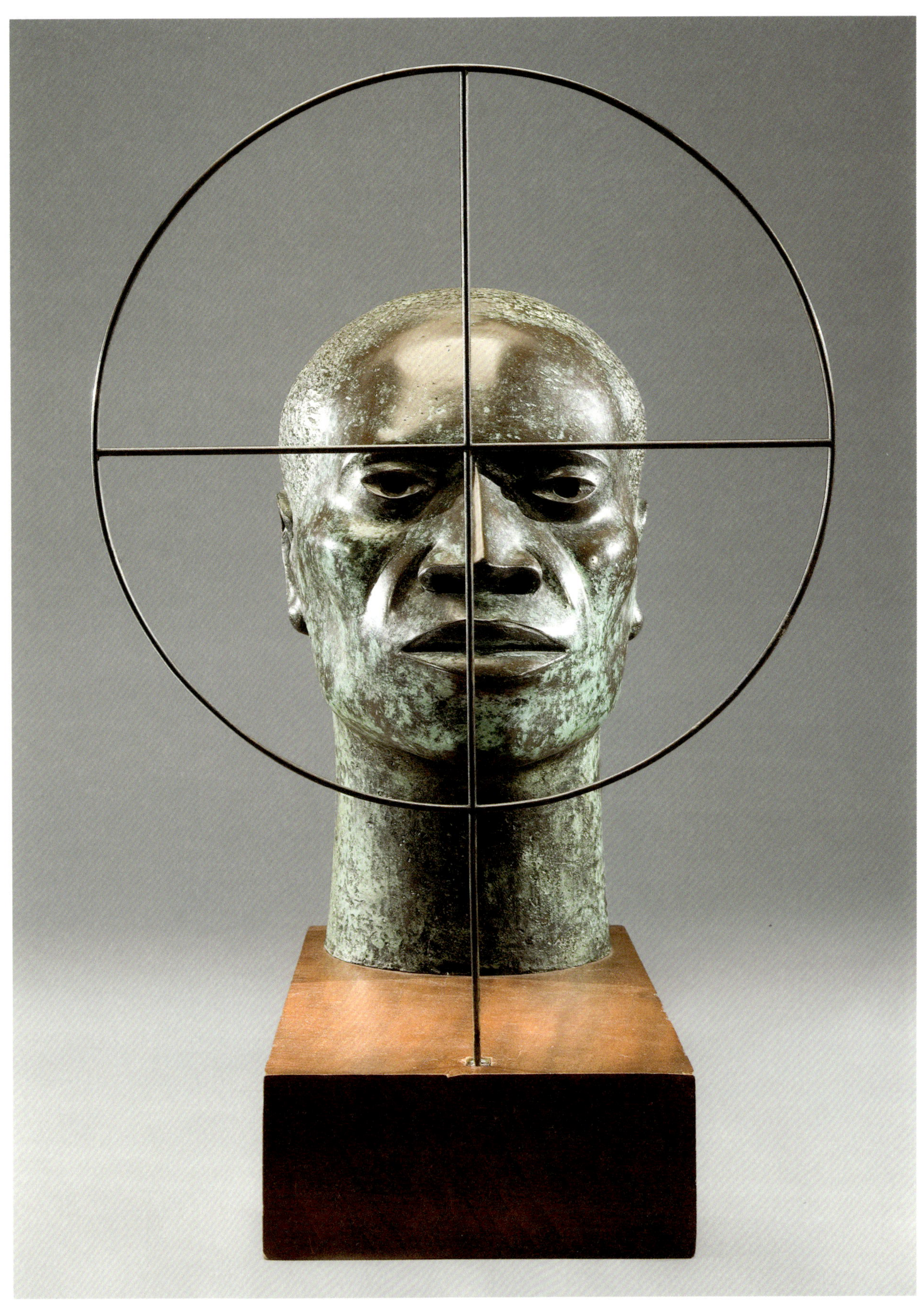

Target Practice, 1970, bronze, 19 × 15½ × 12¼ in., Courtesy of the Amistad Research Center, Tulane University, New Orleans, LA

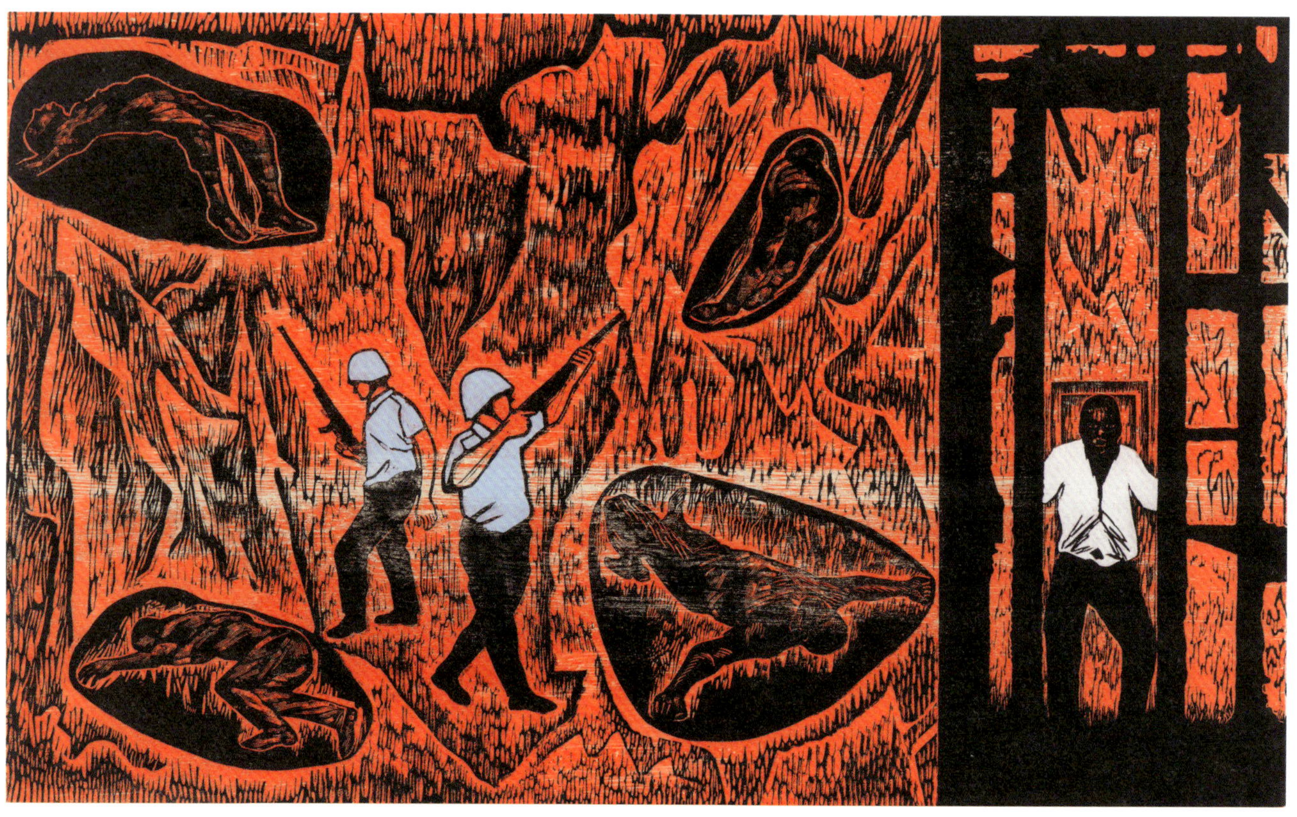

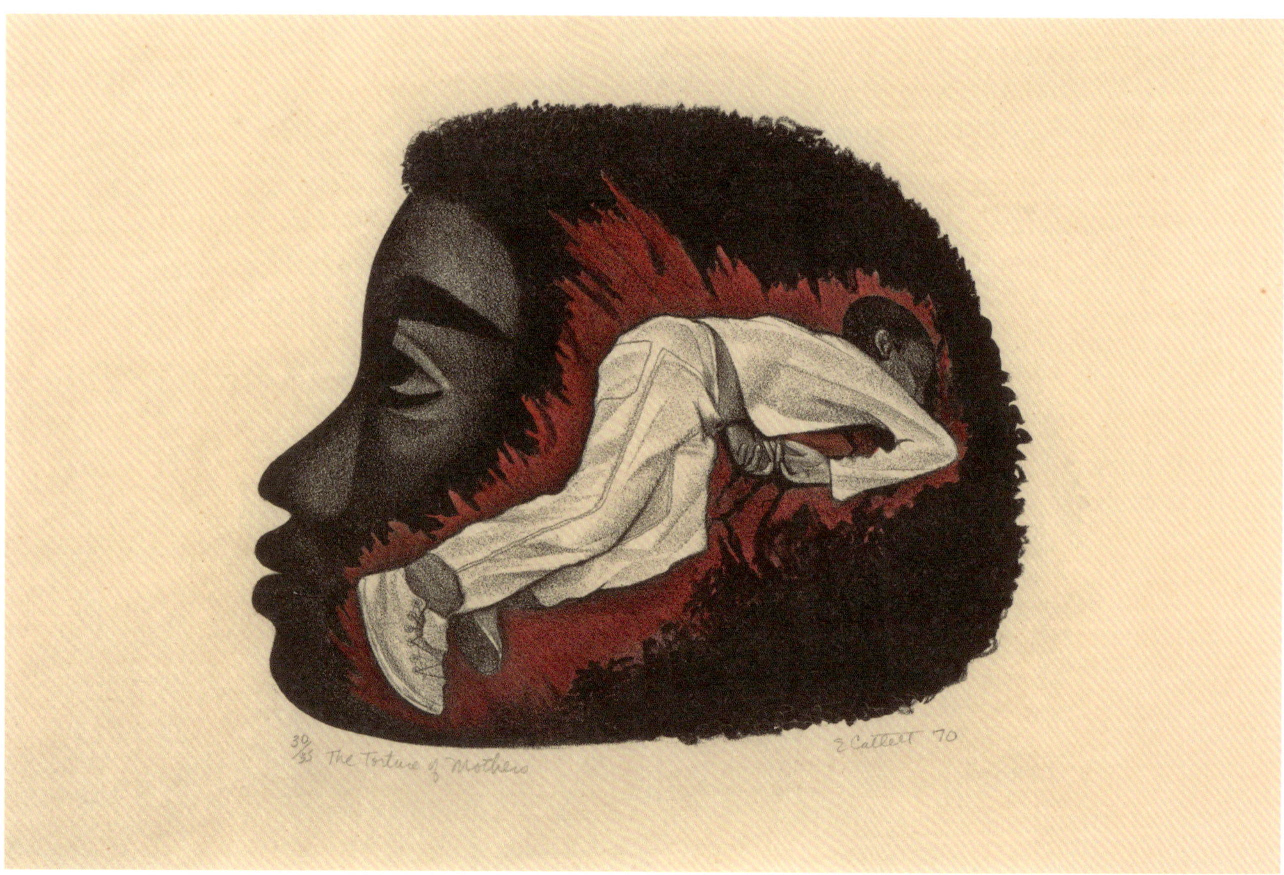

Watts/Detroit/Washington/Harlem/Newark, 1970, linocut, 26½ × 37½ in., The Studio Museum in Harlem, Gift of the artist

Torture of Mothers, 1970, hand-colored lithograph, 15 × 22¼ in., Collection of Juanita and Melvin Hardy

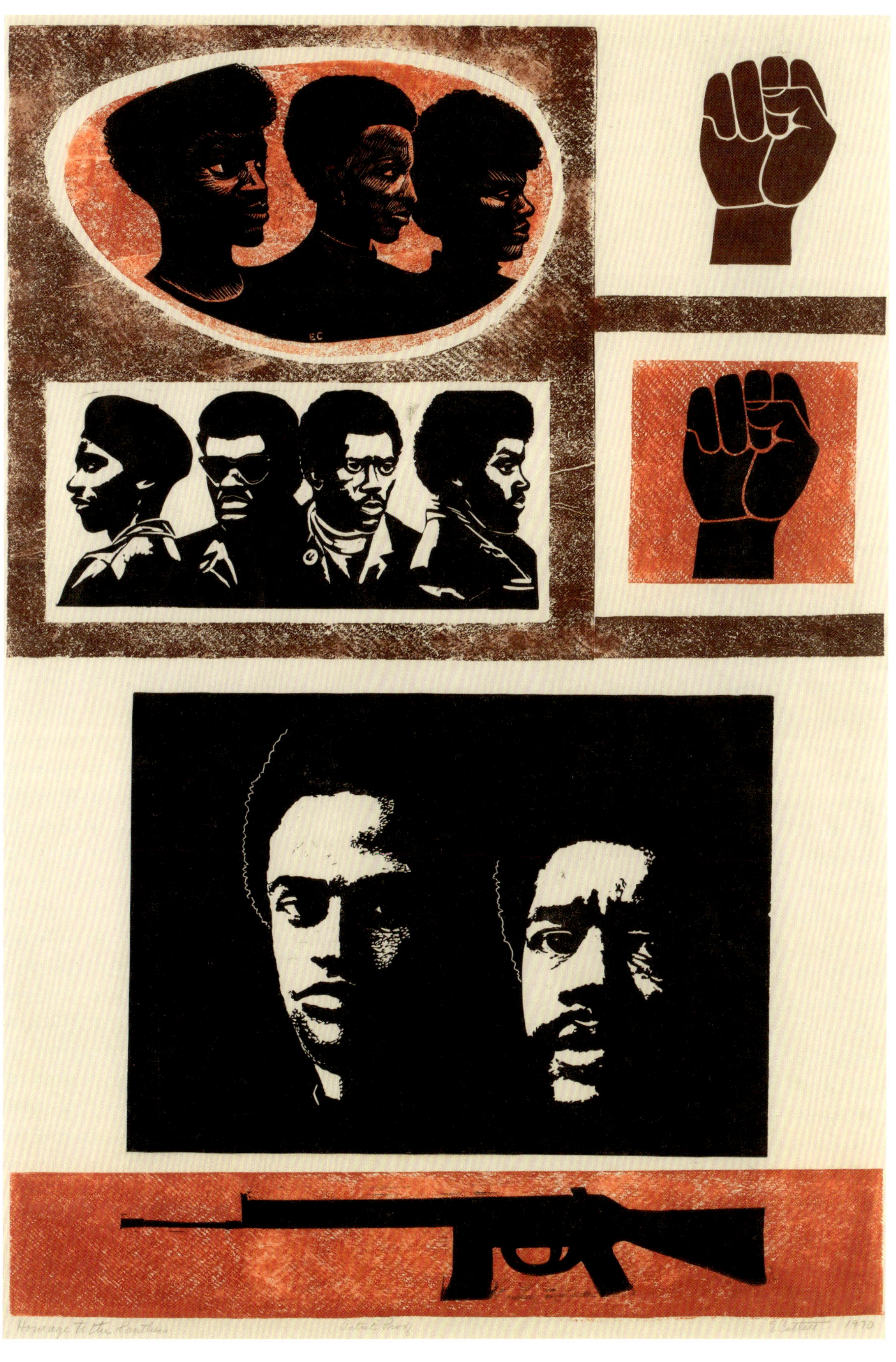

Homage to the Panthers, 1970, linocut,
37¼ × 27½ in., The Studio Museum in Harlem,
Gift of the artist

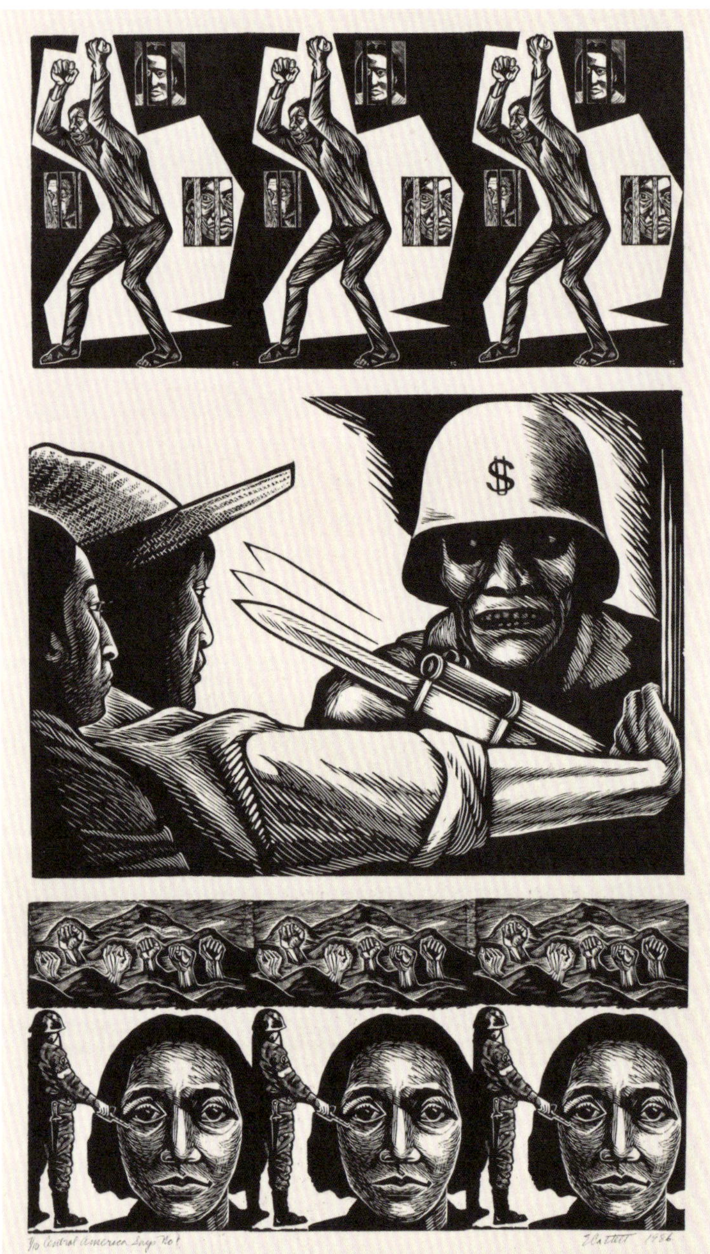

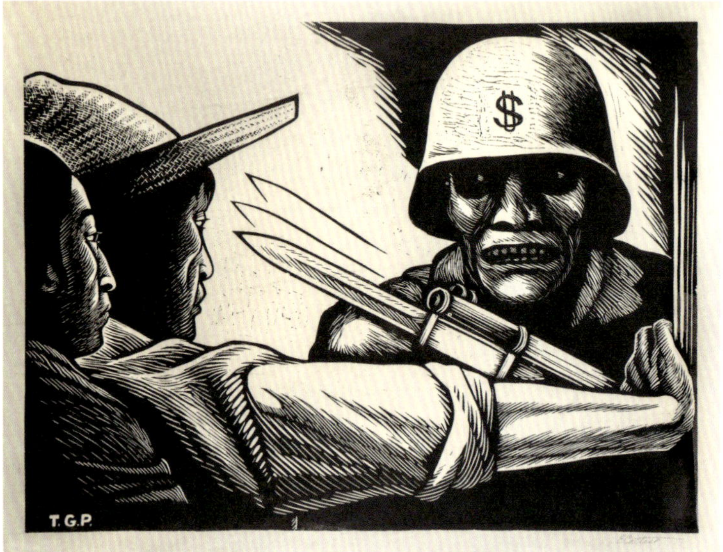

Central America Says No!, 1986, linocut [ed. 10], 47$\frac{9}{16}$ × 31$\frac{9}{16}$ in., The Museum of Modern Art, New York, The Ralph E. Shikes Fund, 1995

Alto a la agresión, 1954, linocut, 18$\frac{9}{16}$ × 24$\frac{7}{16}$ in., Colección Academia de Artes, México (also reprinted as *Latina America Says No!*, 1963, and *Latin America Says No!*, 1968)

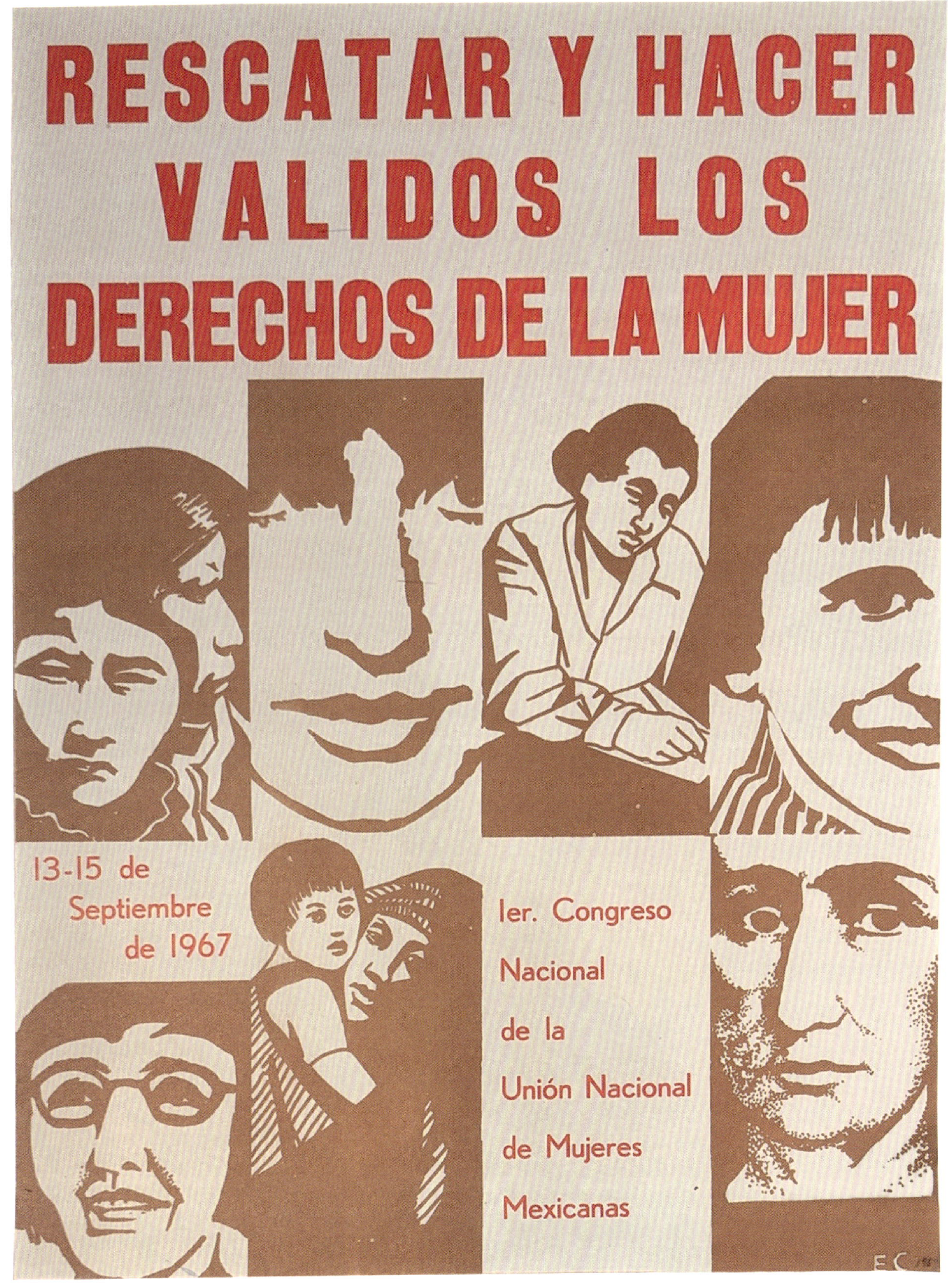

Rescatar y hacer validos los derechos de la mujer, 1967, photomechanical and letter press, 21 × 17 in., The New York Public Library, The Miriam and Ira D. Wallach Division of Art, Prints and Photographs

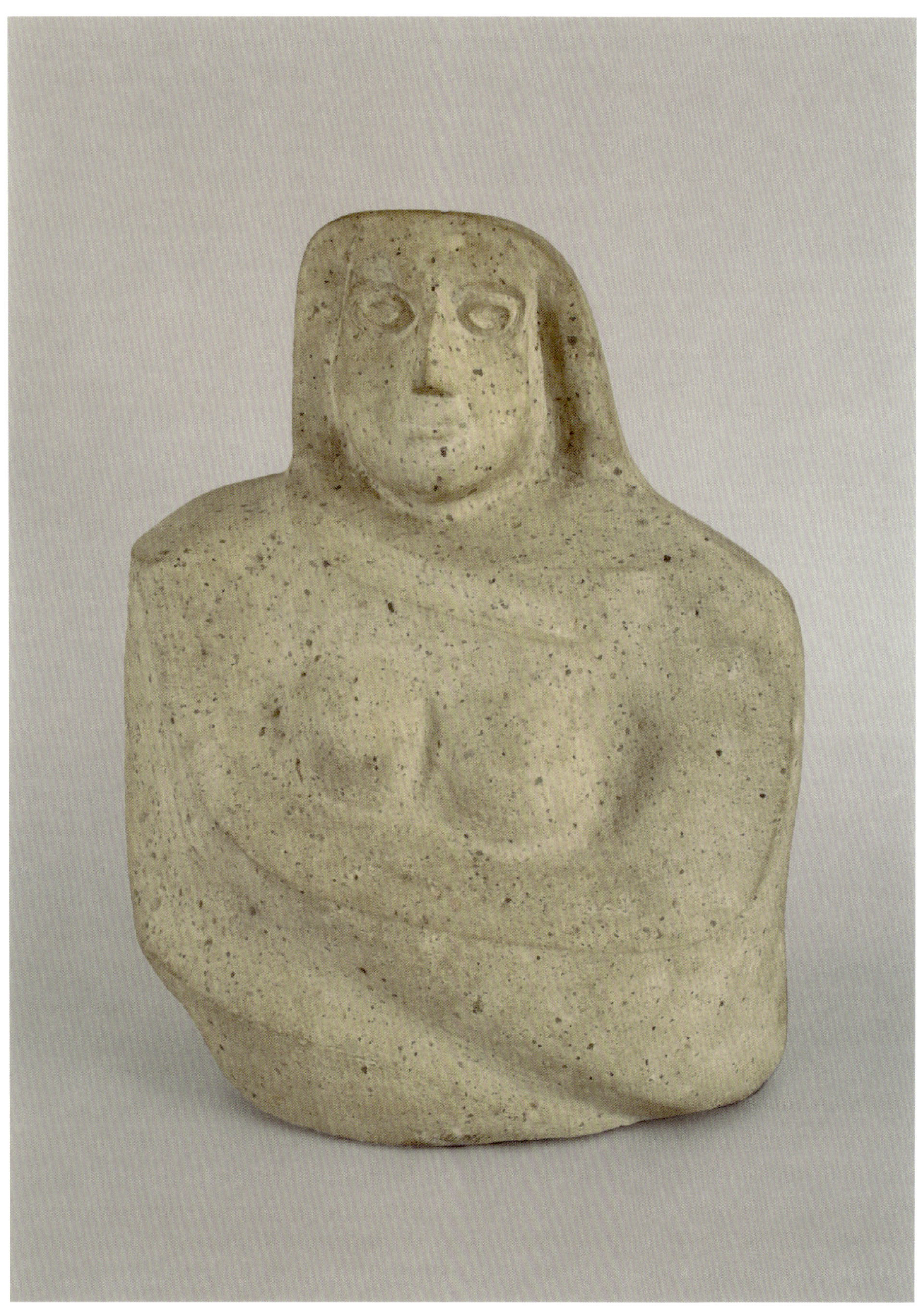

Rebozo, 1968, limestone, 16¼ × 12 × 10 in.,
Collection of Shahara Ahmad-Llewellyn

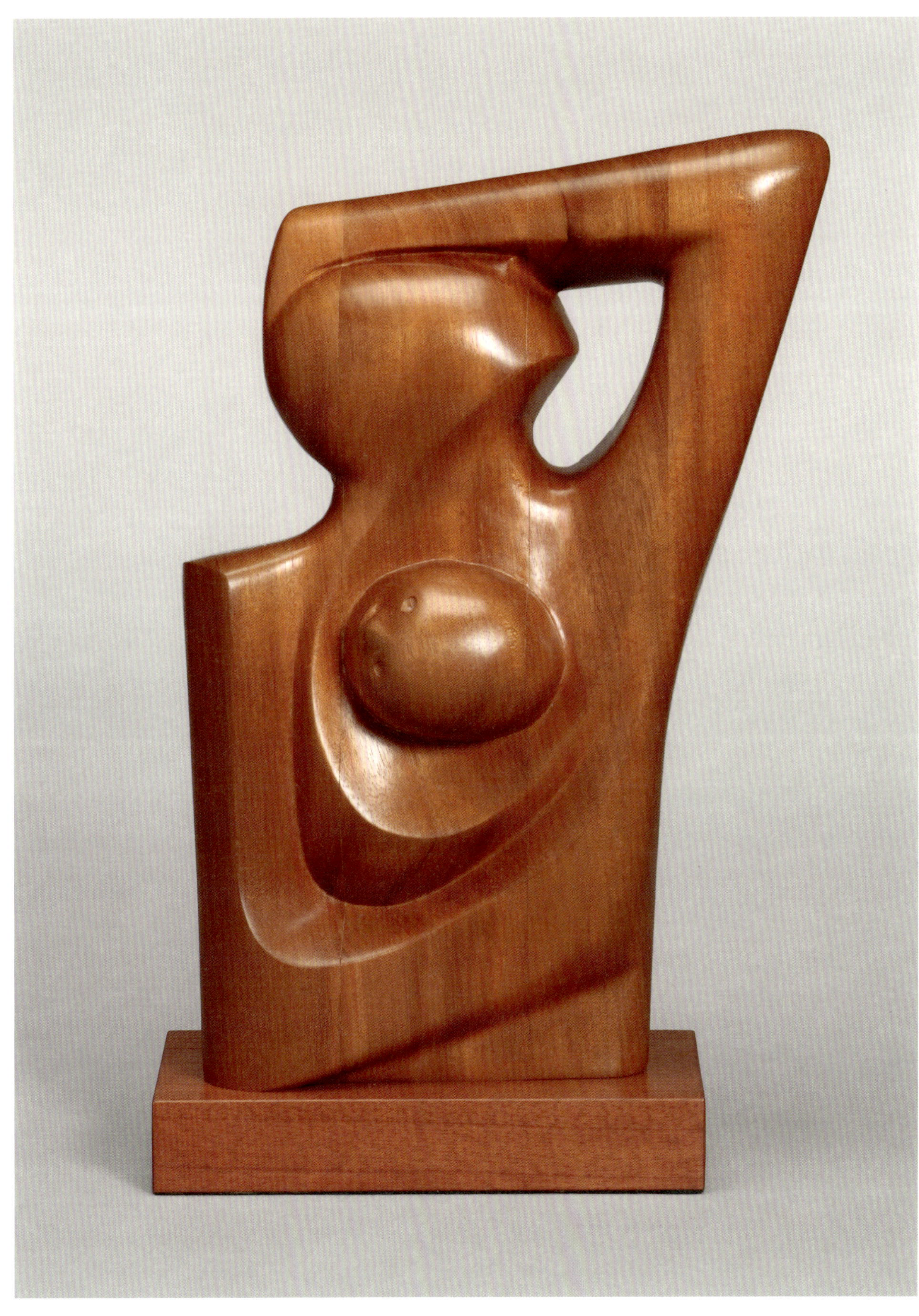

Mother and Child, 1970, wood, 19⅛ × 13 × 8¼ in., Currier Museum of Art, Manchester, NH, Kimon S. Zachos Fund and Henry Melville Fuller Fund

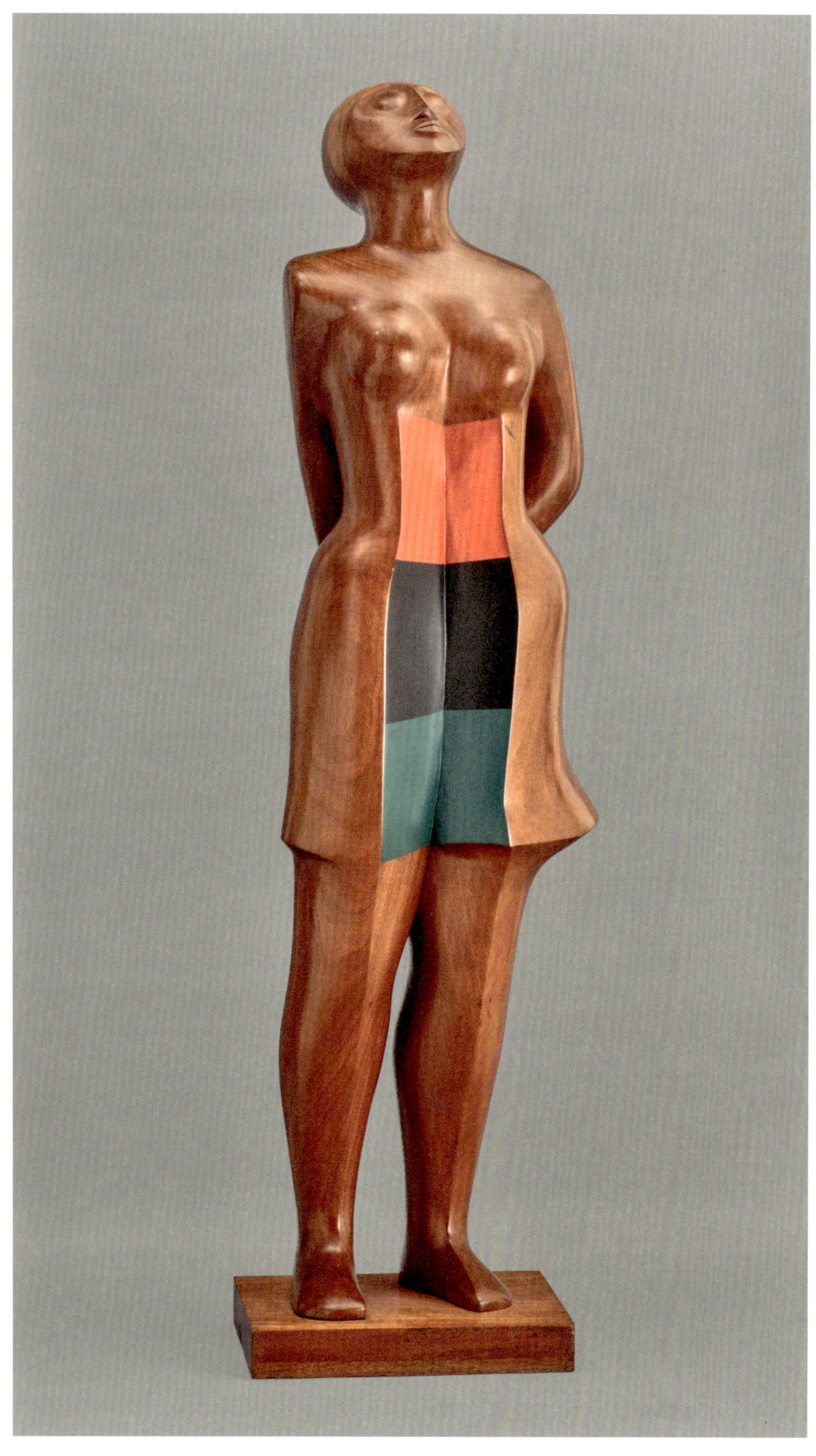

Political Prisoner, 1971, polychromed cedar, 70 × 20 × 14 in., Art and Artifacts Division, Schomburg Center for Research in Black Culture, The New York Public Library, Astor, Lenox and Tilden Foundations

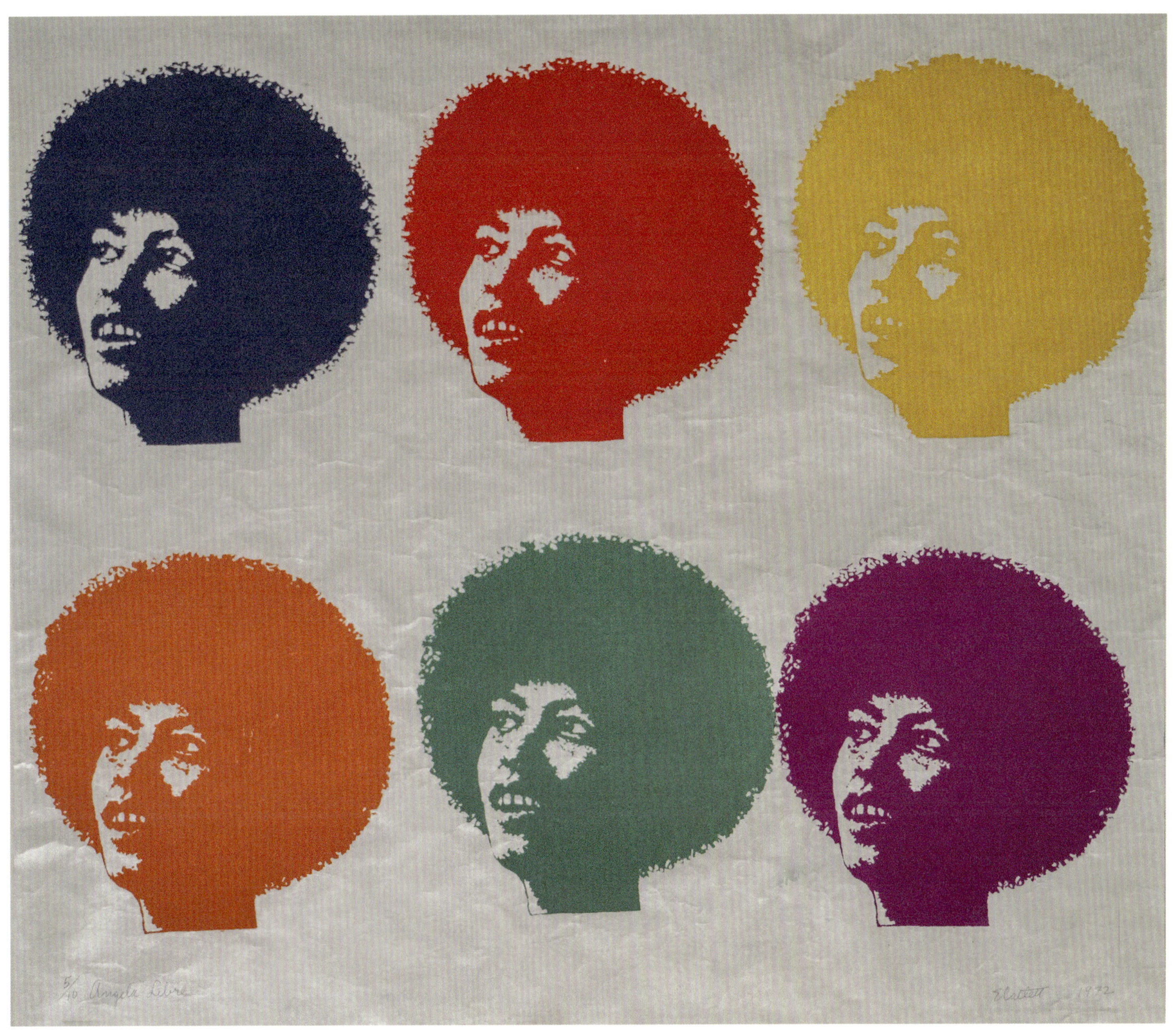

Angela Libre, 1972, lithograph in color on silver foil, 22 × 25½ in., Private collection

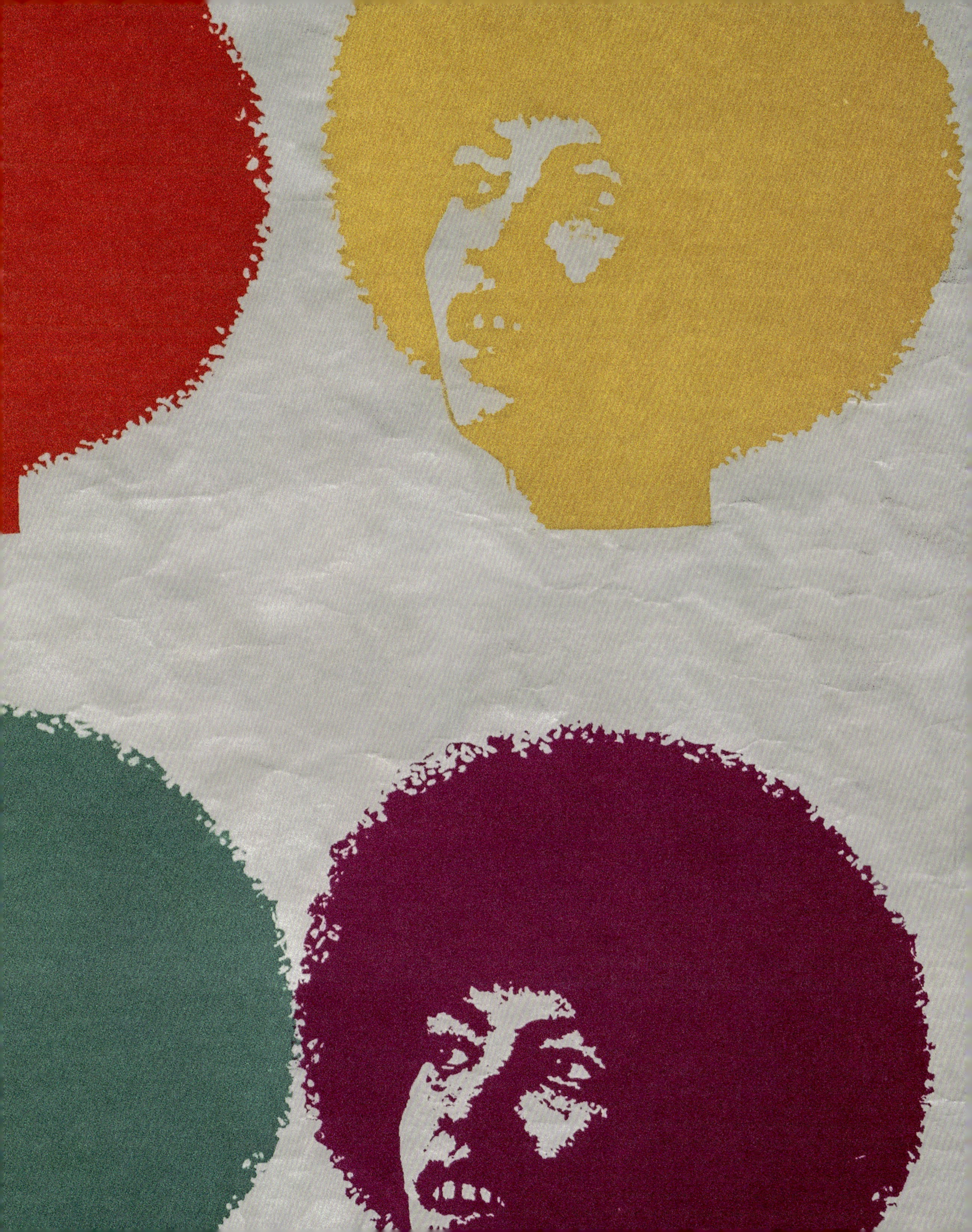

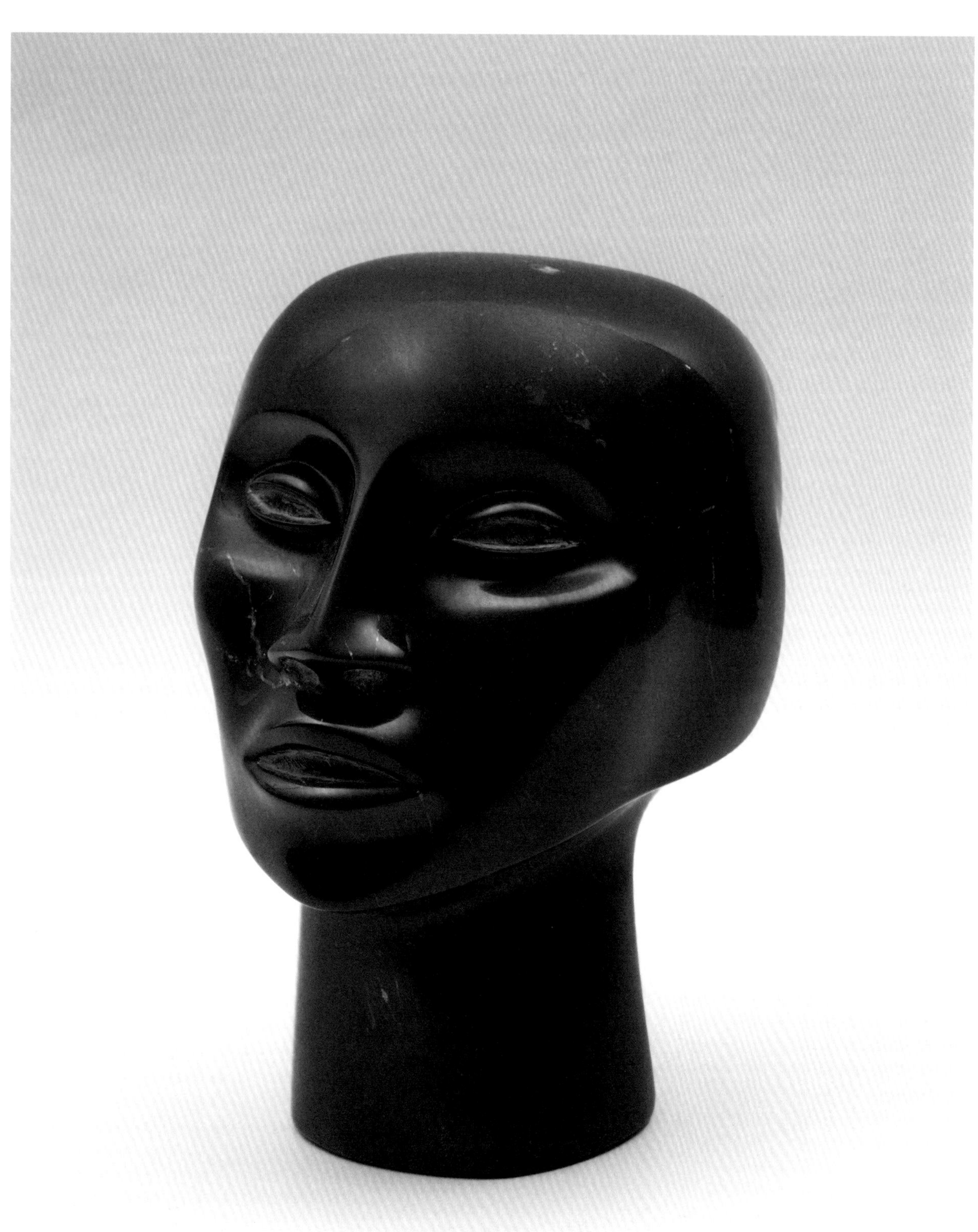

Indian Woman, 1973, black marble, 9 × 6 × 7 in., Courtesy of Laura and Richard Parsons

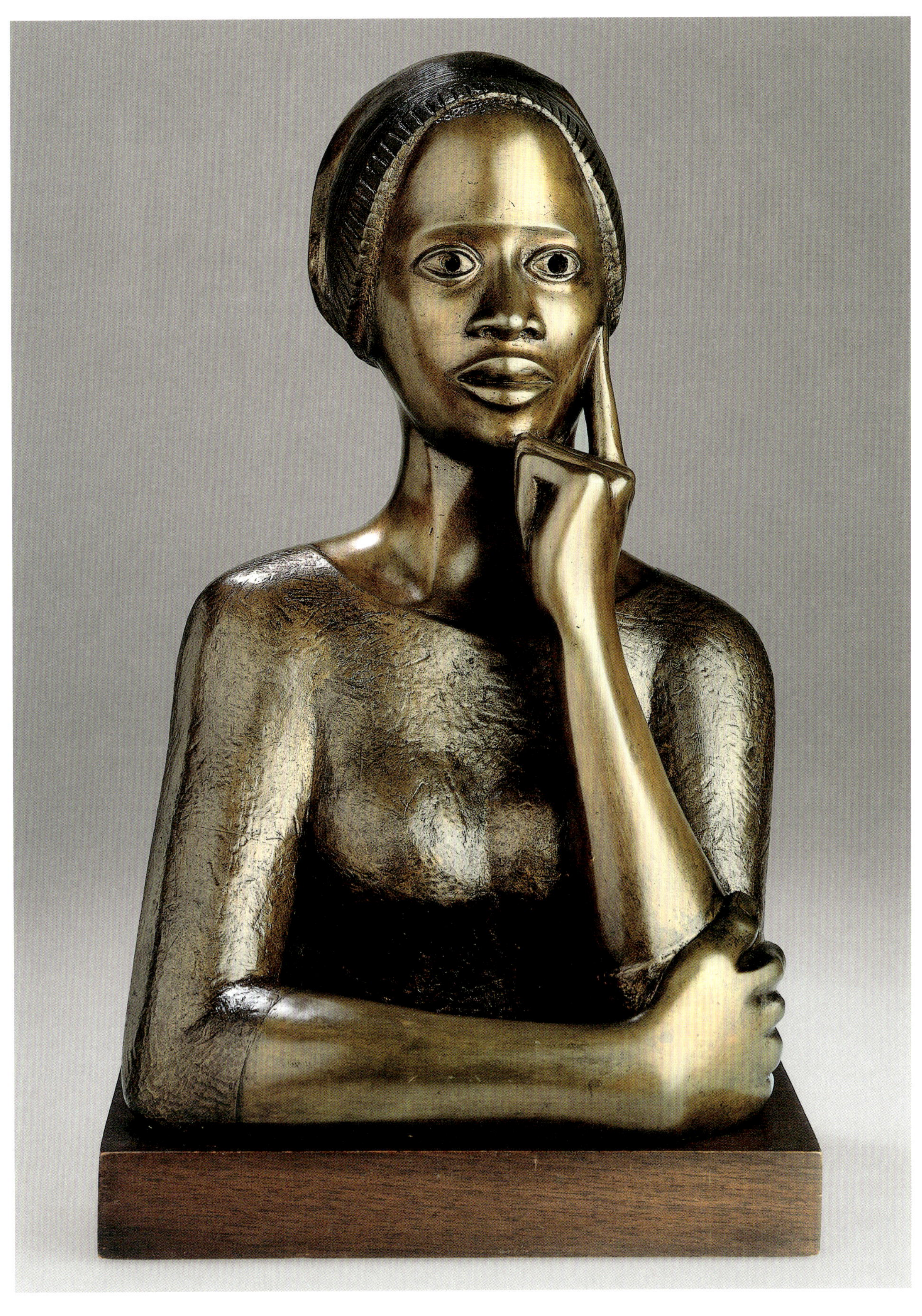

Phillis Wheatley, 1973, bronze, 19½ × 11¾ × 13¹¹⁄₁₆ in., Cincinnati Art Museum, Museum Purchase: Dr. Sandy Courter Memorial Fund, Lawrence Archer Wachs Trust, A. J. Howe Endowment, Henry Meis Endowment, Phyllis H. Thayer Purchase Fund, Israel and Caroline Wilson Fund, On to the Second Century Endowment

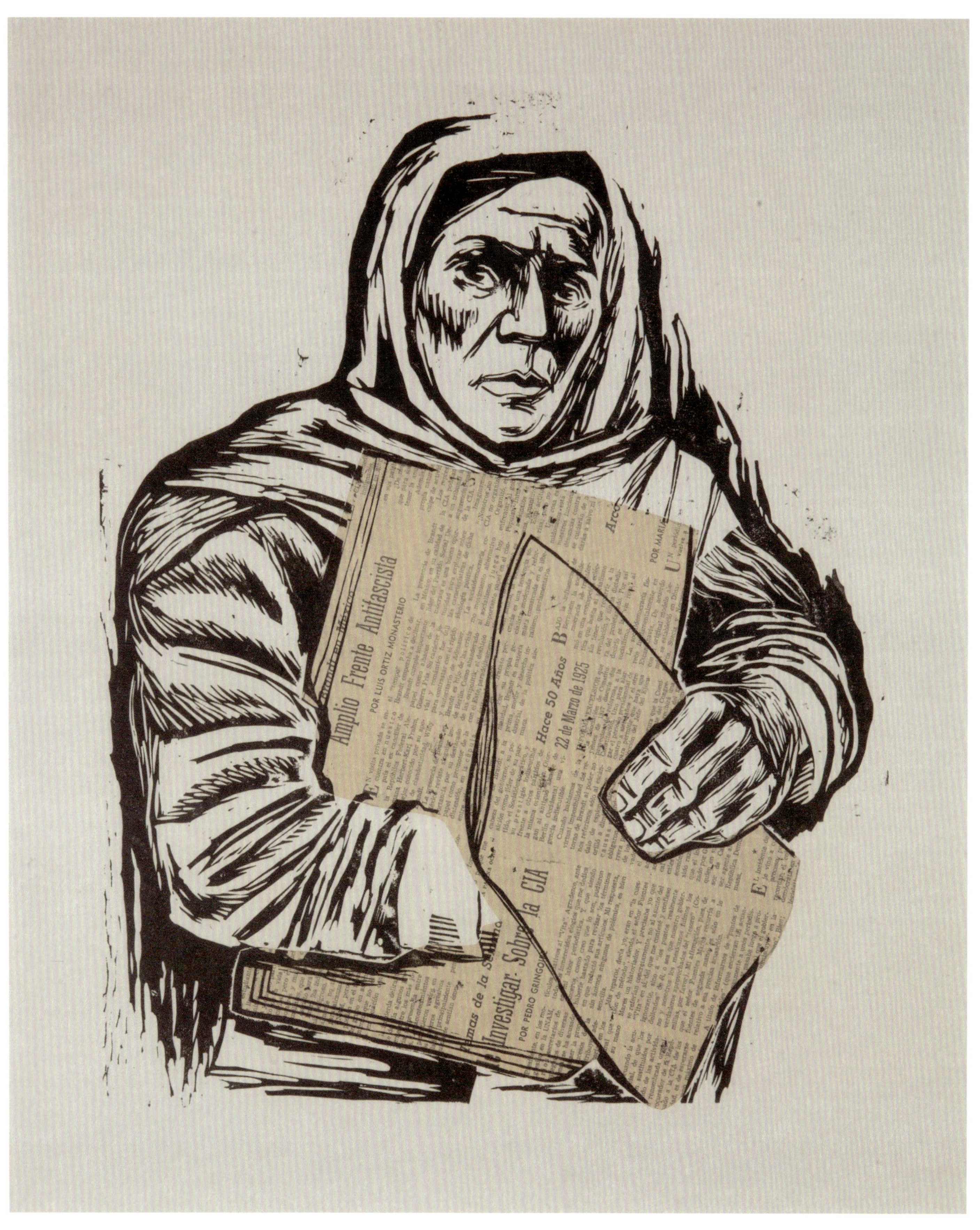

Collage Study for Vendedora de periódicos, c. 1975, linocut proof with collage from Mexican newspapers, 27½ × 18¾ in., From the Collection of the Elizabeth Catlett-Mora Family Living Trust

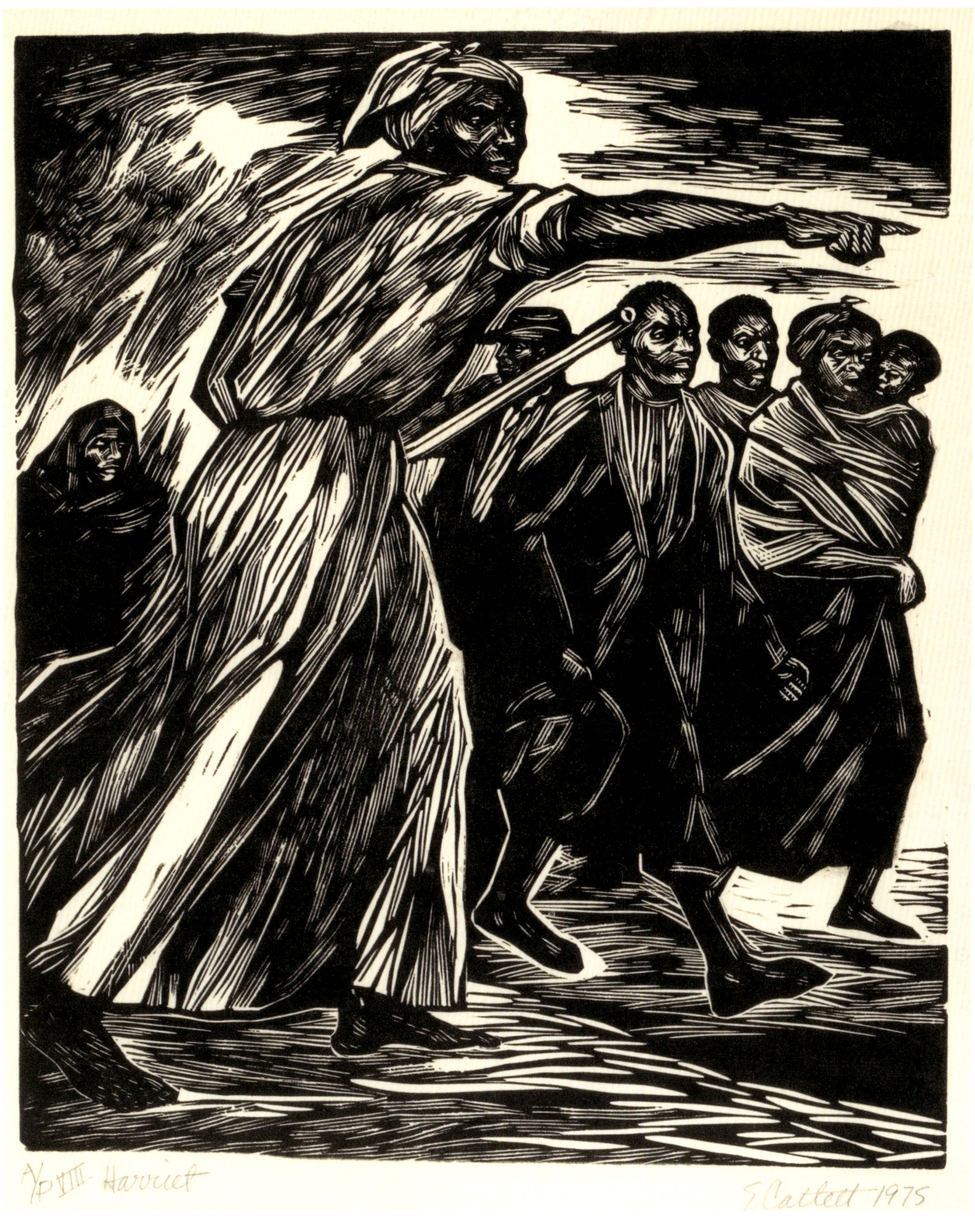

Harriet, 1975, linocut artist proof, 18 × 15 in., Larry D. and Brenda A. Thompson

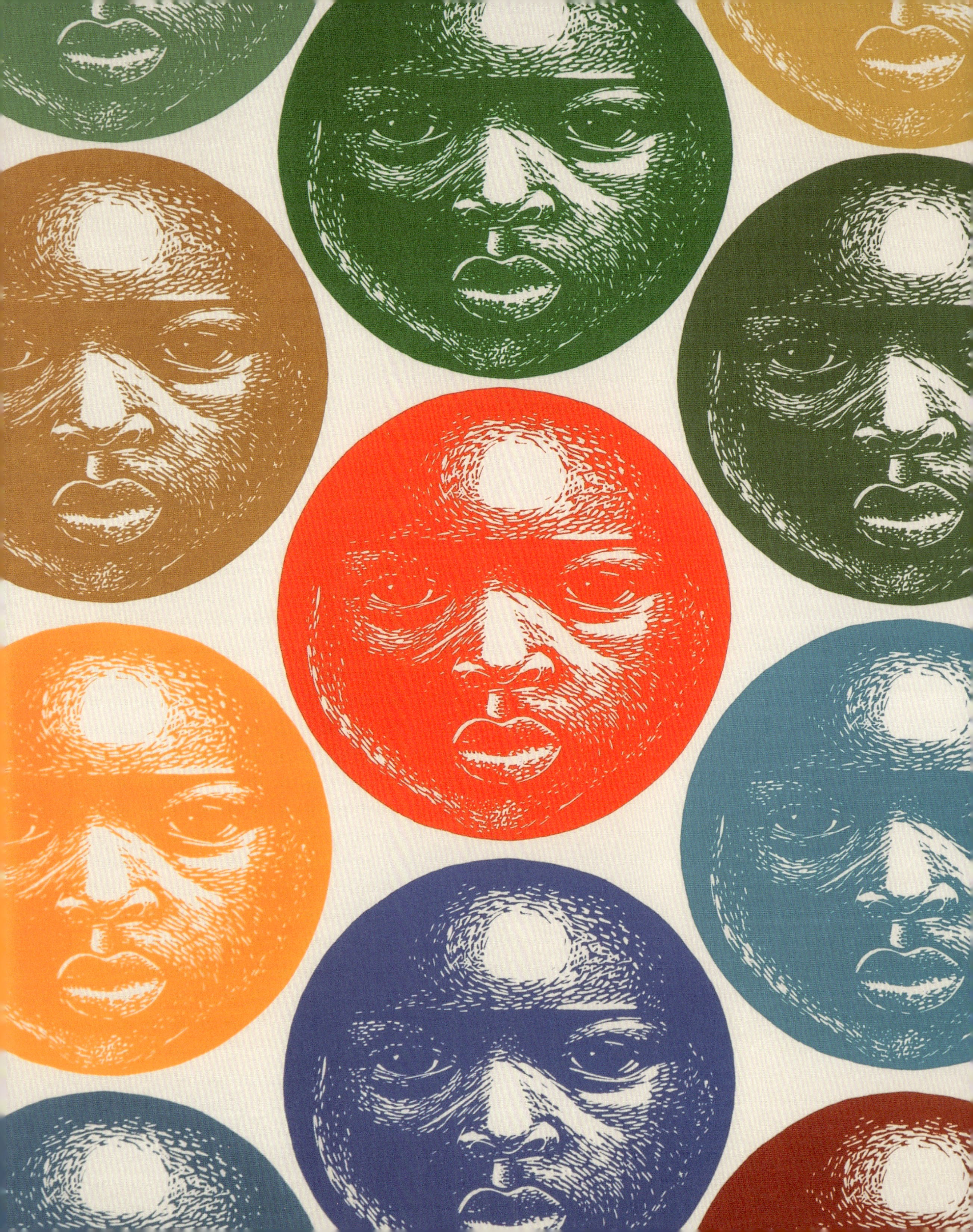

MARY LEE CORLETT

PRESSING NARRATIVES

"I am here to tell you about my work and about myself," Elizabeth Catlett began, in her draft address for students at the University of Mississippi in 1984. "I am Black, a woman, a sculptor and a printmaker. I am also married, the mother of three sons and the grandmother of five little girls. I am a teacher and a student. I was born in the United States and am now a citizen of Mexico, having lived there since 1946. I believe that these states of being have influenced my work and made it what you see today."[1]

Rather than an artist whose practice merely included printmaking, Catlett made being a *printmaker* an essential part of her artistic identity, as her own statements repeatedly indicate. Throughout her career, she used printmaking techniques to create exceptional and compelling images infused with both artistry and activism. For her, printmaking was the "real public art," and her belief in the print as a democratic art form—one easily made available to all—never wavered.[2]

From the beginning of her career in the United States, Catlett had valued the power of the print, and this appreciation flourished in Mexico. She traveled there as part of her Rosenwald Fellowship and became one of the few women members of the legendary printmaking collective Taller de Gráfica Popular (TGP) in Mexico City, whose art was committed to social purpose and political expression in service to the Mexican people. There she learned what she described as the "true value of printmaking...that with one print it is possible to reach thousands of people" and that "needed education, a desired message or unseen beauty can be visualized for so many more people with a print than with any other art form."[3] The variety of printmaking techniques and collaborations practiced at the TGP inspired Catlett to new ways of thinking and working in print and set the course for her career as a printmaker.

ROSENWALD FELLOWSHIP

As the means by which Catlett first studied and worked in Mexico—and as the true beginning of her printmaking journey, nurtured through the creative and collaborative spirit of the TGP—the Rosenwald Fellowship was critical to Catlett's actualization as an artist. Perhaps no prints in this artist-activist's decades-long career as a printmaker are more fundamental than the fifteen linocuts of *The Black Woman* series, produced in 1946 and 1947 at the TGP as part of her Rosenwald project (pp. 33–48).[4] *The Black Woman* series, celebrated both for the creative impulse behind it and for its skillful execution in linocut, stands at the heart of Catlett's Rosenwald project and firmly established her printmaking credentials.

Before embarking on the project, Catlett had minimal printmaking experience. She had done rudimentary linoleum block printing at Howard University but "wouldn't say it was really printmaking...We did only "very simple designs, and we rolled the roller on them, and we rubbed the paper. We didn't have a press."[5] In Iowa City, Catlett pursued a master of fine arts degree—the first ever awarded, by the University of Iowa—with painter Grant Wood's support, and despite not having taken a printmaking course, as thought necessary for the MFA degree by the art department chairperson.[6]

Catlett's first application to the Rosenwald Fund in 1943, a proposal for a sculpture project, was rejected.[7] By the time she reapplied in 1945 her vision for the project had expanded, with a new focus on Black women and with prints as an essential component: "It is my earnest desire to portray this history of Negro womanhood in lithography, painting and sculpture, and to send these portrayals to Negro and white colleges so that young men and women, especially in the south, can get some idea of the contributions of Negro American women."[8]

Likely in service of her Rosenwald project, Catlett took a class in lithography with Harry Sternberg at the Art Students League,[9] where she made two prints, *Mother and Child* (p. 28) and *Negro Woman* (p. 29), perhaps the two unnamed prints she mentioned in her grant progress report.[10] In conversation with Ellen Sragow, Catlett's friend and longtime New York gallerist, Catlett described her introduction to lithography with Sternberg: "He told me to start out with fine hard crayons, and work up to soft ones and I did. And I always work like that now."[11] In the same interview Catlett suggested that the actual printing of these first lithographs was likely done by now-legendary printer and artist Robert Blackburn. Catlett also revealed that she based the *Mother and Child* print on an earlier watercolor: "I went to stay with [artist and poet] Margaret Burroughs one summer, in Chicago. She had a little baby and I did a sketch and then a watercolor of it. The watercolor was in the first African American Artists show at the Downtown Gallery, with [dealer] Edith Halpert."[12] Thus, Catlett most likely painted this watercolor in 1941, some years before the *Mother and Child* print—following a methodology typical for Catlett, whose process included "working with an image over and over until she is satisfied that she has grasped its essence."[13]

She expected that her Rosenwald project prints would be lithographs. In her grant renewal application, she restated her goal "to do painting, sculpture and lithography in [my] own studio," adding her wish "to visit Mexico for a[t] least one month, spending the time in field work."[14] Her first year's work in New York led to some rethinking, indicating her increasing desire to reach a wide audience:

> *In addition to circulating one exhibition of sculpture, painting, and lithographs, I would like to do a complete unit of lithographs alone. In this way I could reach people in many places where there are not facilities for handling the original exhibit. Churches, libraries, YW and YMCA's could hang a show of prints that would be seen by many more average Americans. These are the people that are so often denied the art of contemporary America. Some sets of the litho series could be allocated to Negro institutions by the Rosenwald Fund.*[15]

She did not mention linocut or the TGP, but wrote, "I would like to strengthen my clarity of approach to art through a visit to Mexico. There I could get at first hand an understanding of the new techniques developed by the Mexican artists in painting for and about the people of their country. This would help me, I feel, in developing art techniques to reach my own people and others in America."[16]

Not until after Catlett had arrived in Mexico did she reference the TGP in her communications with the Rosenwald Fund. In October 1946 she wrote to William C. Haygood, director of the Rosenwald Fellowship program, describing her work there and noting her nascent association with the TGP and its artists, and indicating that she and artist Charles White (her husband at the time) "worked as special students in the government school of painting and sculpture, in the mornings. In the evenings we worked at the [TGP]. We were honored here by being made life members and were very fortunate to be a part of a cooperative group of artists containing such people as Pablo O'Higgins, Alfredo Zalce and Leopoldo Mendez."[17] She noted that she had produced three lithographs, but again made no mention of any interest in linocut.[18] Catlett's adoption of the technique, however—in tandem with the philosophy and methodologies she encountered at the TGP—would soon transform her art and practice, beginning with *The Black Woman* series, and in the decades to follow would distinguish her as a consummate artist-printmaker.[19]

TGP

At the TGP Catlett worked side by side with virtuoso Mexican printmakers including its cofounder Méndez, whose work was a stylistic guiding force for her.[20] As a collective of artist-printmakers who prized both technical excellence and the visual power of prints to inspire and educate, the TGP workshop provided space for Catlett to develop the technical virtuosity and elegance of her linocuts, along with a deft handling of lithographic techniques, while at the same time illuminating the path on which artistry and social purpose would no longer seem to be opposing forces. "The whole problem of art as a social force and propaganda vs aesthetics is no longer a problem for me," she resolutely stated.[21]

For a decade after she made Mexico her home, married the painter and printmaker Francisco "Pancho" Mora (with whom she had three sons), and began raising their young family, Catlett's artmaking centered on prints and, in particular, her work at the TGP—a supportive space where artists regularly and constructively critiqued each other's work. "Working collectively was a completely new experience for me, as an artist who had always created alone," Catlett remembered. "Working collectively provoked new methods of creating, as well as intense discussions on what graphic symbols, what images best expressed the social or political problems confronting us."[22]

Prized for its expressive potential, the linocut was a preferred medium of TGP artists—also because, as Hannes Meyer noted, linoleum was substantially cheaper and easier to procure than quality wood blocks, and the sizable lithographic stones necessary for large-scale posters were scarce.[23] The advantage of using linoleum block matrices to create a work of art includes the ease with which they can be reused and maintain their integrity through multiple reprintings—from print to poster, flyer, and more. Linocuts made by TGP printmakers, including Catlett, found repeated use in the workshop environment through multiple interconnected projects, increasing both the visibility and availability of images, serving the TGP mission.

Collective projects included exhibitions and a variety of publication strategies, such as books, filmstrips produced in collaboration with the Bryant Foundation in Los Angeles (p. 91 and fig. 1), the calaveras newspapers, and portfolios.[24] Both the prints and the matrices produced for collective projects remained available at the workshop for reprinting, repurposing, exhibition, and sales.[25]

Fig. 1—Elizabeth Catlett, *Learning*, 1948, hand-colored lithograph, University of Iowa Stanley Museum of Art, Museum purchase, 2006-55

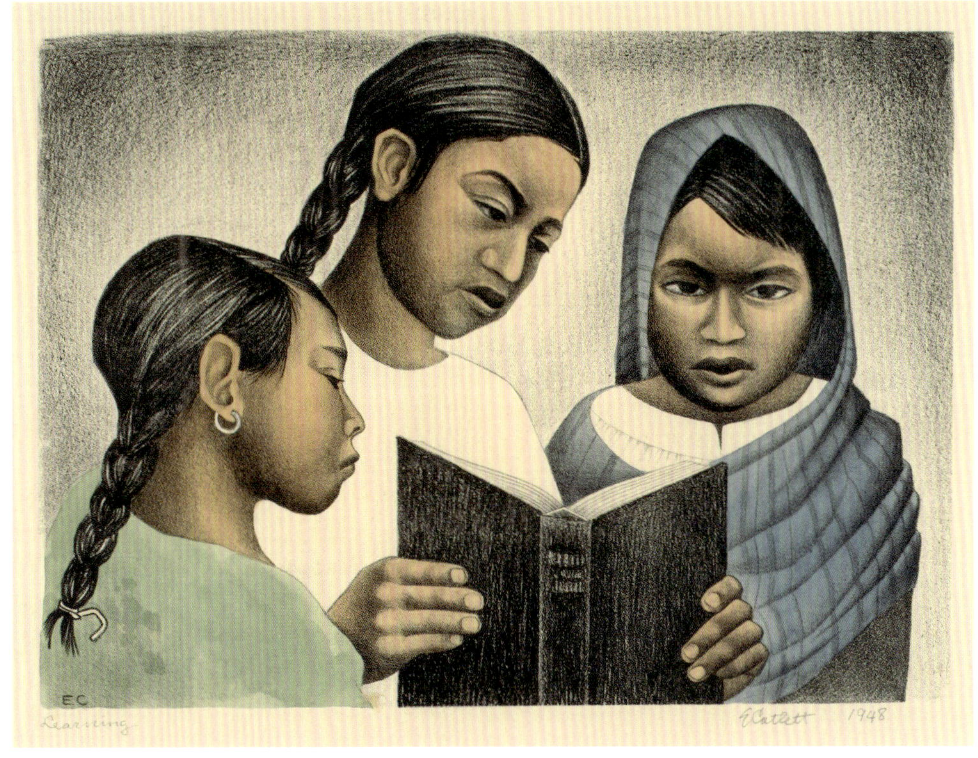

During her years of TGP membership Catlett participated in a variety of collective projects. In 1953 she initiated a project involving a series of prints of African American heroes, known now as *Against Discrimination in the US*.[26] Adopting a distribution methodology previously employed by the TGP, Catlett met with *Freedom* magazine's managing editor, Louis E. Burnham, in New York in November of that year and an agreement was made for the submission of twelve graphics depicting the contributions and heroes of Black history in the US, to be published one per month for the next year.[27] Catlett "researched the lives and obtained photographic material on twenty Black Americans from different times and occupations,"[28] choosing Harriet Tubman as the subject for her own print.

Sixteen prints, produced in December 1953 and January 1954, are associated with the project (see pp. 105–109).[29] When the lithograph of Frederick Douglass was rejected by the magazine, however, the entire series—as a product of a collective—remained unpublished, although four prints were illustrated in *Artes de Mexico* in 1957 and the series was shown in Guinea in 1960.[30] TGP scholar Helga Prignitz credited Catlett and this project for restoring a unity of purpose to what was becoming an increasingly factionalized TGP.[31]

The *Against Discrimination in the US* series represented one in a variety of approaches for TGP collective work. Another was collaboration on design and carving, as for the large-scale, two-part linocut poster Catlett created with Alberto Beltrán to promote the Primer Congreso Nacional por la Paz, held in Mexico in May 1951 (p. 93). Catlett created the composition and the blocks were carved by Beltrán.[32] *Homenaje a Cárdenas* (p. 110) was the collective effort of four artists, including Catlett, each contributing a block that was then incorporated into a unified poster design.[33] Catlett's *Cárdenas* was also printed separately in an unspecified edition and reproduced as a book illustration.[34]

Even after her association with the TGP ended, Catlett continued to employ the techniques and strategies of the collective in her individual practice, including remaking or repurposing previously printed linocut matrices and creating compositions by combining multiple matrices. Furthermore, she embraced TGP practices that fundamentally challenged the narrow definition of the "multiple original," the orthodoxy of printing only a prescribed number

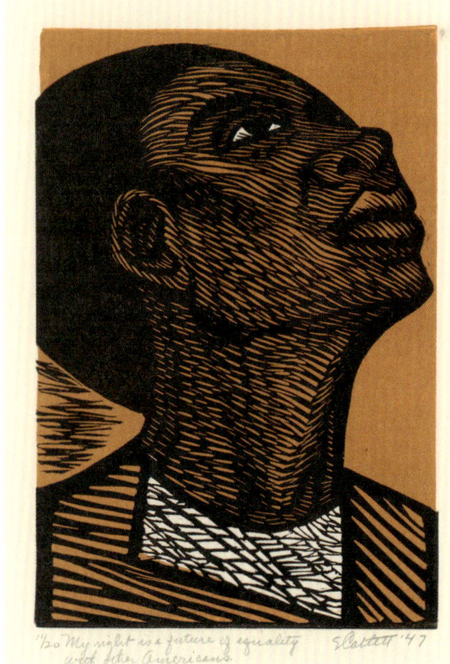

Fig. 2—Elizabeth Catlett, *My right is a future of equality with other Americans*, from *The Black Woman* series, recarved and reprinted 1989, ink and graphite, Collection of the Smithsonian National Museum of African American History and Culture, Gift of Winifred Hervey, 2017.21.14

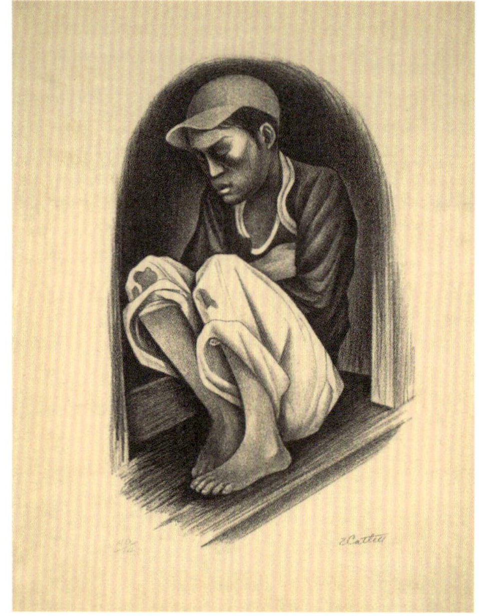

Fig. 3—Elizabeth Catlett, *Niño Papelero*, 1947, lithograph on wove paper, National Gallery of Art, Reba and Dave Williams Collection, Gift of the Print Research Foundation, 2008.115.346

of impressions in a single, finite edition. She did not hesitate to print a matrix repeatedly over time, perhaps using different-quality papers, while also using reprinting as a springboard to explore color variation—her iconic *Sharecropper* being only one, classic, example (p. 103); many of her editions were similarly open-ended.[35] When *The Black Woman* series was reprinted in 1989,[36] she carved a second matrix for *My right is a future of equality with other Americans* (fig. 2), likely because the first matrix had, by that time, gone missing.[37]

Catlett sometimes redrew lithographic matrices, too, effectively extending an edition—*Niño Papelero* (fig. 3, and p. 90) is one example—thereby forgoing finite multiplicity and costly rarity in exchange for affordability and availability, reaffirming the TGP philosophy of prints as a democratic art form with a place in the lives of everyday people. Both reprinting from an existing matrix and remaking a matrix to extend the life of a previously printed image whose first matrix is no longer available are forms of serial editioning.

Conversely, Catlett also printed compositions that apparently exist only as a single impression, but with which she was satisfied enough to title, sign, and date: for instance, *Portrait* (fig. 4).[38] She also printed very small, unspecified editions, such as *Civil Rights Congress* (p. 104), a compelling early linocut. It was carved in conjunction with an appeal to the United Nations in 1951 by the Civil Rights Congress, which under the leadership of William L. Patterson (whose portrait appears in the print) demanded international accountability for the human rights violations perpetrated in the US. The print was never formally editioned and very few were printed.[39]

Other of Catlett's print practices, including her inconsistent titling and dating, also challenged conventional American print market expectations. During the TGP years especially, the date on Catlett's prints (when she dated them at all) might be based on the date the matrix was made, or it could signify the printing date—possibly years later, as in the case of *Sharecropper*. Variant titles are common and not always inscribed on impressions themselves; when prints were pulled they were not necessarily simultaneously signed, titled, or dated.[40] Some title variants are due to translation—*Sharecropper*, for example, is also titled *Cosechadora de algodón*—but at other times a new title added nuance or extended meaning, as with *Cabeza de Negra* (fig. 5). In 1973 Catlett chose to include *Cabeza de Negra* in the folio of photomechanical reproductions of five of her lithographs.[41] There, titled *The Black Woman Speaks* and dated 1960, it serves as the cover image. Significantly, in 1970 she used the title for a work of sculpture (p. 158). In both cases, the title *Black Woman Speaks* is surely a deliberate eponymic reference to a landmark and epic poem by Catlett's friend Beah Richards.[42]

An inventive and resourceful printmaker, Catlett expertly leveraged distinct characteristics of individual processes to serve an overall image, an approach exemplified in *Women of America* (p. 149; revisited and retitled in fig. 6)—a small-scale exploration of line, color, and texture achieved through the combination of linocut and woodcut.[43] Developed from a sketch Catlett made while attending the women's congress in Cuba in the spring of 1963, this print was produced during her late TGP years, at a moment when women had taken the helm of the collective.[44] In August of 1963, in response to internal conflicts, mounting resentments, and increased factionalism among the members, TGP leadership changed hands: Celia Calderón became president, Mercedes Quevedo treasurer, and Catlett herself secretary-general. The result was an improved working atmosphere and better financial management, with the women's movement becoming a uniting cause for the workshop.[45] Art historian Helga Prignitz described the poster Catlett created for the World Congress of Women in Moscow, held in June of 1963, as "the most beautiful in its simplicity" of any work to leave the workshop that year.[46] In the fall of 1964 the TGP received an enthusiastic thank-you letter from the Unión Nacional de

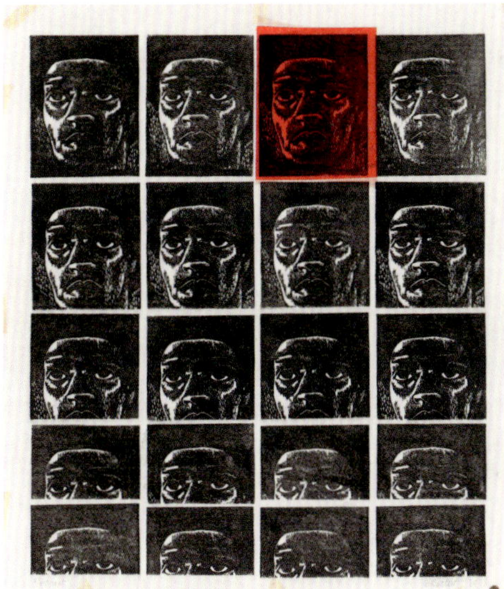

Fig. 4—Elizabeth Catlett, *Portrait*, 1973, linocut with red plastic film overlay, MUSEUM MMK FÜR MODERNE KUNST

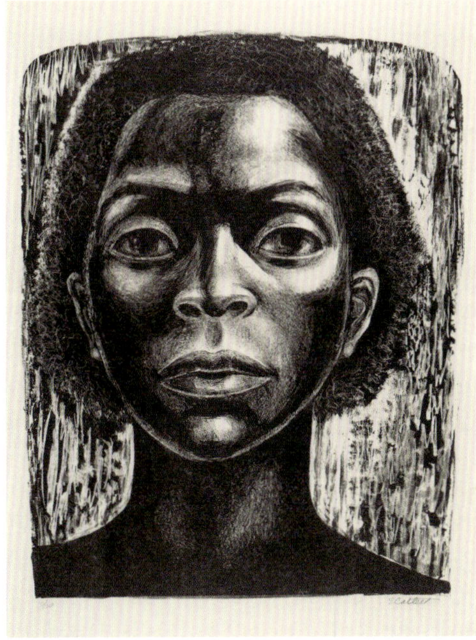

Fig. 5—Elizabeth Catlett, *Cabeza de Negra*, c. 1948, lithograph, Harvard Art Museums/Fogg Museum, Margaret Fisher Fund, 2006.76

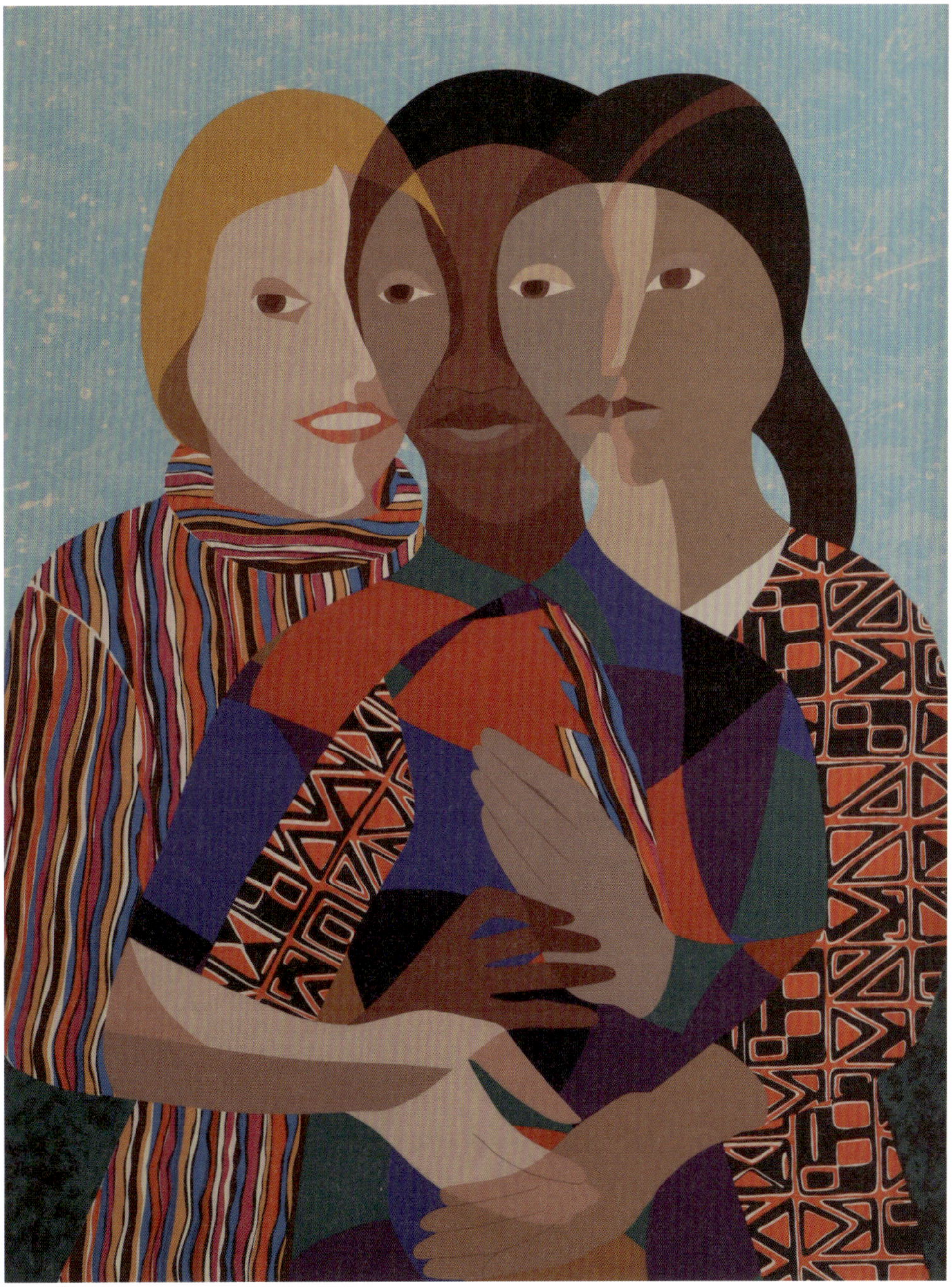

Fig. 6—Elizabeth Catlett, *Three Women of America*, 1990, screenprint, Dr. Sheila D. Wright

Mujeres Mexicanas for the poster and podium decoration that TGP members, including Catlett, had produced for their inaugural meeting; previously commonplace, this was the first such letter the TGP had received in many years.[47]

AN IDEAL MEANS

The art of the linocut remained at the center of Catlett's printmaking even after her time at the TGP. She sometimes used linocuts as a starting point for prints she ultimately produced in other print mediums, such as *Fiesta* (fig. 7) or *Girls* (fig. 8)—both are screenprints, both originate from linocut matrices, combined and repeated.[48] And because Catlett regularly repurposed linocut matrices in multiple compositions (sometimes many years after the initial carving), it was largely through linocut that she leaned into printmaking as a repeatable process that supported modernist strategies such as iteration, engagement with pattern and line, texture, color play, the interaction of positive and negative space, and reversals—all of which she used to great effect. Catlett took advantage of the ways in which printmaking offered the potential to revisit themes and create resonances, interweaving past and present through the inherited and associative meaning of repurposed matrices. In Catlett's prints repetition is a metaphor for connection, strength, and resilience, and provides an ideal means for communicating urgent social and political perspectives.

There are many instances of this in Catlett's body of work, but *Malcolm X Speaks for Us* (1969, p. 156) and *Central America Says No!* (1986, p. 164) are two important examples. Both combine multiple linocut blocks from previous print projects in new compositional arrangements that build upon those histories. Both were produced in very small editions and are among Catlett's most complex and innovative prints.

Malcolm X Speaks for Us was printed by Catlett on the large press at La Esmeralda (as the Escuela Nacional de Pintura, Escultura y Grabado is known)—a process so time consuming that she only printed a small number.[49] The print combines linocut and collagraph. "The techniques are linocut and acrylic," Catlett explained. "Each image was cut separately in one or more clichés and later assembled. I worked out this plan of work myself...I feel it was an important print in my production."[50]

"'Malcolm X Speaks for Us,'" she wrote, "means also for women and children."[51] All the subjects depicted in the composition are female.[52] Catlett repurposed *I am the Black Woman* (p. 34), the first linocut print of *The Black Woman* series, repeating it seven times across the top to create an insistent rhythm, a measured beat through repeated form that, when combined with the set of five heads in the middle frieze and the three heads below, suggests a poetic meter. "I experimented with the heads in different ways—repeated one that I had already printed someplace else," Catlett said. "And I used repetition to strengthen the idea."[53]

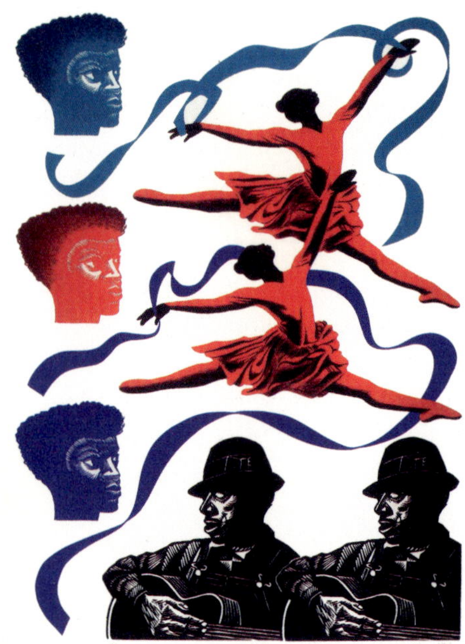

Fig. 7—Elizabeth Catlett, *Fiesta*, 1988, screenprint, Gift of the Jean and Robert E. Steele Collection, Courtesy of The Driskell Center at the University of Maryland, College Park

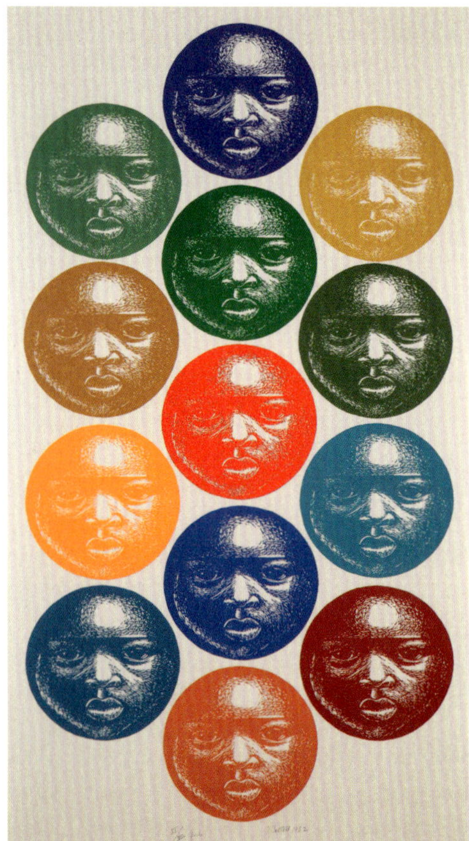

Fig. 8—Elizabeth Catlett, *Girls*, 1982, screenprint, Collection of the Hampton University Museum, Hampton, VA

Central America Says No! repurposes linocut blocks created in the early 1980s to protest US intervention in Chile, combining them with a linocut first printed in 1954 in opposition to US intervention in Guatemala.[54] Amplified through association and strengthened through repetition, *Central America Says No!* is one of Catlett's exceptionally powerful anti-imperialist statements. The problems she set out to solve in this and other of her most ambitious prints often resulted in an arduous printing process and, by extension, small editions. An early proof of *Central America Says No!*—printed on paper just wide enough to accommodate the image and yet still fit the dimensions of Catlett's studio press—is one example of the challenges she met in her practice.[55] The edition, printed on paper with proper margins, was by necessity printed on a larger press by José Sánchez.[56]

Catlett approached lithography with her characteristic inventive mastery, adroitly manipulating tusche and crayon to create lush textures in prints such as the 1956 special edition lithograph she made after a painting by David Alfaro Siqueiros.[57] She extended and amplified her engagement with textures in later works by incorporating fabric or fabric-like materials in appliqué form.[58] This may be seen in *Virginia* (1984, p. 227),[59] where the delicate lace pattern of the Japanese paper appliqué of the sitter's collar is echoed in the richly textured background. Catlett reprised this lacelike patterning in 1992 with the bridal veil in *For My People: To Marry*.[60] Printed patterns reappear in dresses of figures in successive prints as well, linking them through association. The lithograph *Harlem Woman* (1992, p. 225)[61] incorporates a fabric appliqué collar, the pattern reappearing in printed form in the dress of the kneeling figure in the upper right of *For My People: Singing Their Songs* (1992), and again in the dress of the figure on the right in *Gossip* (2005; p. 203, fig. 3).

Among Catlett's final prints, *Gossip* was published by the Print Club of New York and printed at the Rutgers Center for Innovative Print and Paper.[62] At ninety, the artist was still exploring new methods; she worked with Anne McKeown in

Cuernavaca to make the key drawing in ink and lithographic crayon on Mylar, then with Randy Hemminghaus in New Jersey to construct the background and dress patterns by creating a digital collage from scans of fabrics she brought with her.[63] The result was a combination of photolithography (using Catlett's drawing on Mylar) and digital printing, Catlett's first experience working with a computer. Artist Robin Holder, former assistant director of the Blackburn Printmaking Workshop,[64] noted:

> *Elizabeth was genuinely interested in new, innovative, and unfamiliar techniques. She was also very dedicated to connecting with younger artists. Printmakers by nature are probably more collaborative than painters but I think that her experience as an African American woman and her experiences in Mexico emphasized her communal spirit of sharing, learning and exchanging.*[65]

In *Gossip*, fabrics are digitally "stitched" together and become a sewing metaphor, foregrounding the role of textiles as a creative, economic, and political practice in Black women's lives.[66] Catlett adds layers of meaning by repeating fabric patterns used in previous prints, suggesting further connected narratives. Finally, her metaphorical stitching celebrates Black women's empowerment through community, conversation, and resistance—especially resistance, signified by the raised fist. Art, in Catlett's words, "does not need revolution as its subject in order to be revolutionary."[67]

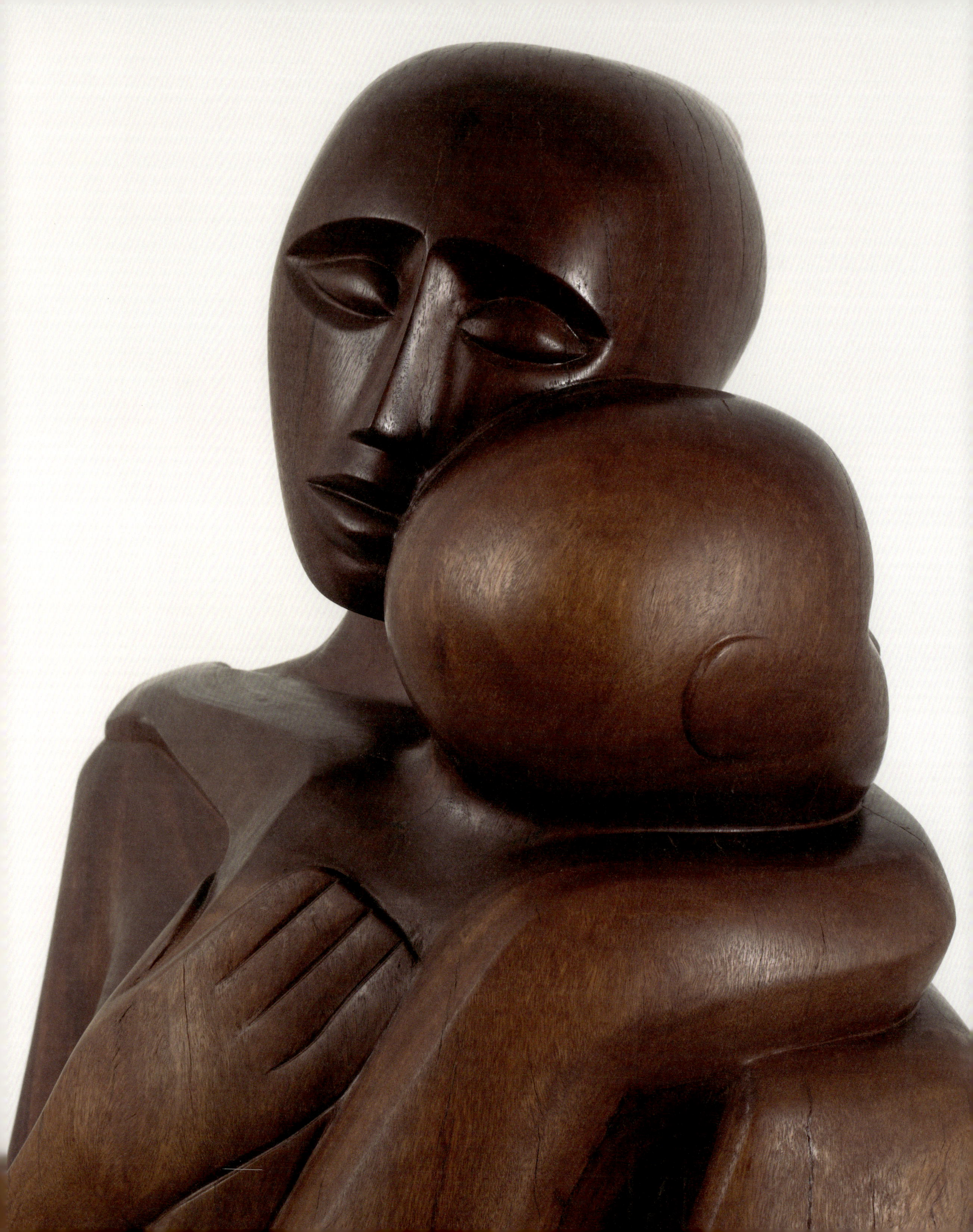

MELANIE ANNE HERZOG

"THINKING ABOUT WOMEN" THROUGH FORM, SUBSTANCE, AND RADICAL POLITICS

Elizabeth Catlett's sculptures are revelatory expressions of her radical politics, profound empathy, and abiding aesthetic of care. When sculpting, she said, "I'm thinking about form. But I'm also thinking about women, Black women."[1] Grounded in her representations of these women, Catlett's sculptural practice fused form and politics through her choice and handling of materials and her sculptures' formal elegance, organic vitality, and commanding presence. Whether intimate in scale, life-size, or larger than life, these figures are effectively monumental; visually and materially, they take up space.

The root sources for the visual and material language of Catlett's sculpture were, she said, "not the female nudes of the European artists, but the women of the African wood carvers and the pre-Hispanic stone carvers."[2] Of African figurative sculpture, Catlett wrote, "I am impressed by the use of form to express emotion...by the life and vitality achieved through form relations. All African art interests me. I see such force, such life!"[3] Particularly resonant for her was African sculptors' use of form to communicate feeling through angular turns and subtle curves, the juxtaposition of concave and convex shapes, and the abstraction of anatomical or physiognomic structures to their essential components. "I look for the relationship between African art which I cannot live without and the relation of that to Black people, and I see in their faces and bodies African sculpture," she said. "It's something I've been living with all my life."[4] She was also drawn to the stylized naturalism of Pre-Encounter Mexican figurative sculpture in stone and clay. These sources grounded and enriched the modernist sculptural vocabulary of simplified abstraction that she developed during her early years in the United States. Important, too, was her own bodily awareness. "I am a Black woman," she said. "I use my own body in working. When I am bathing or dressing, I see and feel how my body looks and moves. I never do sculpture from a nude model...Mostly I watch women."[5]

MATERIAL AS MEANING

As she explored the expressive potential of form, Catlett's handling of her sculptural mediums demonstrates her engagement with their tactile materiality along with their inherent visual qualities. She exploited the malleability of clay as she modeled ceramic figures that appear to swell and breathe from

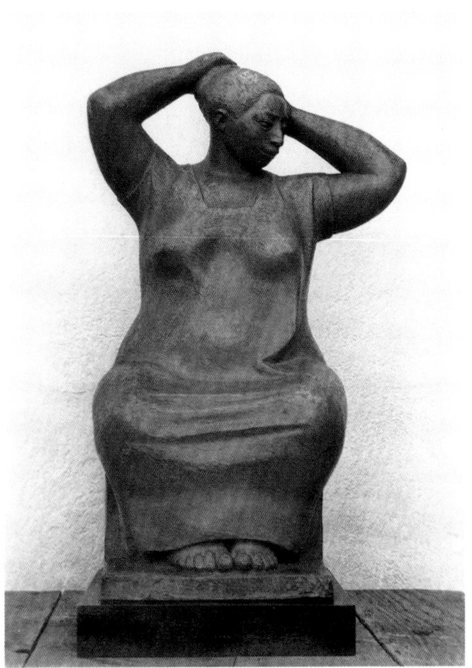

Fig. 1—Francisco Zúñiga, *Mujer sentada con las manos en el pelo*, 1950, terracotta, Private collection

within, and highlighted the grain of various woods and the granularity, sheen, and translucency of different types of stone as she carved rounded volumes, precisely delineated planes, and nested concave forms that enfold interior openings within her more abstract pieces. She then sanded and polished her wood and fine-grained stone carvings to a smooth, often radiant finish. "When I carve, I am guided by the beauty and the configuration of the material," she said. "When I use wood, for example, I might exaggerate the form to bring out a little more of the grain of the wood. I like to finish sculpture to the maximum beauty attainable from the material from which it is created."[6] Hers is the work of the human hand; the carefully wrought details and textures of her clay figures and lustrous surfaces of her stone and wood sculptures suggest—and invite—caress.

Continually curious about how forms translate differently in additive and subtractive mediums, Catlett created and re-created nearly identical sculptural forms and compositions in varying materials. Smaller figures in clay were a means to work out a composition or explore an idea before committing herself to the more arduous work of carving and finishing larger pieces in wood and stone or creating models to be cast in bronze. Materials and processes of making sometimes resulted in variously nuanced meanings; the intimacy of an embrace or the interiority of a figure engaged in self-reflection reads differently when modeled or carved, and changes, too, when fashioned in wood and different types of stone.

ARTISTIC LINEAGES

Catlett's return to sculpture in the mid-1950s followed a pause while her children were small and printmaking became her exclusive artistic focus. Resuming her work in clay, she built upon her study ten years earlier with Francisco Zúñiga, whose weighty ceramic figures fused elements of Mexico's long-standing Indigenous ceramics and stone-carving traditions with modernist abstraction (fig. 1). She also studied figurative wood carving with José L. Ruiz. Her clay, wood, and stone figures from these years resemble those of her teachers, but their poses and facial expressions convey active awareness. Their sturdy legs and firmly planted feet ground them in the world and imply potential movement.

Mother and Child (1956, p. 114) is one of Catlett's many sculptural representations of maternity from this time, constructed from coils of clay as one would build a hollow vessel, the method she learned from Zúñiga. In its simplified naturalism and the mother's protective embrace of the child that nestles its body into hers, this terracotta sculpture echoes Catlett's thesis carving for her master of fine arts, *Negro Mother and Child* (1940, see p. 81, fig. 2), described in her written thesis as "two figures, one smaller than the other, so interlaced as to be expressive of maternity, and so compact as to be suitable to stone."[7] Perhaps due to the pliability of clay compared to stone, or her ongoing quest for "form that achieves sympathy," or her own embodied experience of motherhood, the later *Mother and Child* depicts maternity as a more profound emotional and corporeal bond.[8]

She also sculpted distinctly Mexican subjects. Carved in Mexican limestone, *Rebozo* of 1957 (fig. 2) is a slightly stylized representation of a seated woman with broad shoulders, ample hips, and large, generalized hands. The shawl referred to in the title is suggested by the curved line, carved in subtle relief, that arcs across the figure's left shoulder and encircles her head. In its modernist reduction of form to its essentials, *Rebozo* recalls the work of British sculptor Henry Moore, which Catlett admired, and the Pre-Encounter Mexican figures that inspired both artists. Exemplifying Moore's simplified, blocky treatment and attention to both solids and voids in sculptural compositions, his alabaster

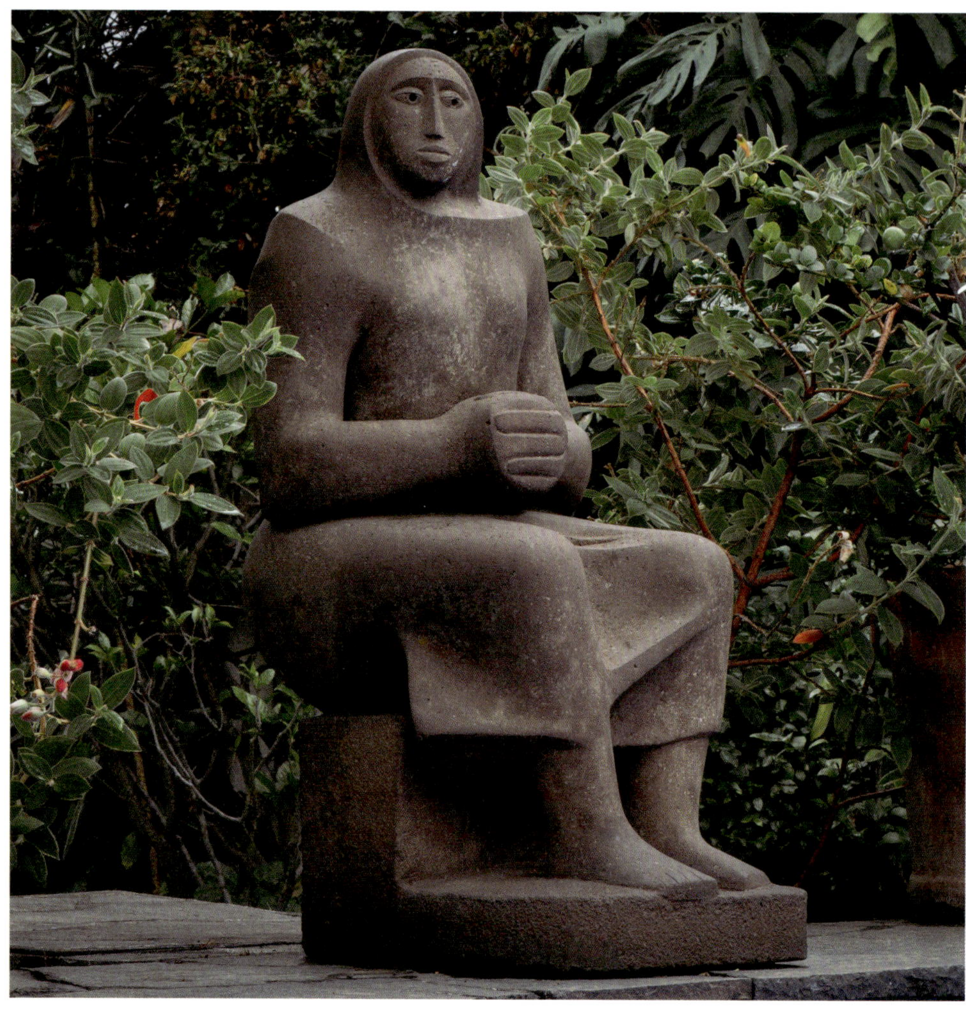

Fig. 2—Elizabeth Catlett, *Rebozo*, 1957, Mexican limestone, Elizabeth Catlett Studio, Cuernavaca, Mexico, From the Collection of the Elizabeth Catlett-Mora Family Living Trust

Seated Figure (fig. 3) also resembles *Rebozo* in pose. Catlett clearly prized this limestone work—it was a touchstone from her early years as a sculptor in Mexico that she kept throughout her life.

Sourced in Mexico, Catlett's sculptural mediums—clay, limestone, marble, and onyx, and wood such as primavera, Spanish cedar, and mahogany—materially signify the social, cultural, political, and geographic terrain that shaped her sculptural practice for over half a century in her adopted homeland.[9] While her choice of materials was, in part, determined by their availability—trees cut down in her neighborhood, limestone left over from building projects—she also valued the rich variety of mediums available to sculptors in Mexico and continued to use them even when she had the resources to import materials from elsewhere. The geological and organic origins of these materials in Mexican earth reinforce the grounding in the world of the women she depicted, and she understood as signifiers of race the rich, warm hues of her woods and stones such as orange onyx and black marble. Of her highly abstracted *Singing Head* (1980, p. 216), acquired by the Smithsonian American Art Museum in 1989, Catlett said, amidst all the white marble at this institution, "Now they have one black marble."[10] The long-standing utilization of these materials by object makers in Mexico also places Catlett's figures within an artistic lineage that she claimed as inspiration, marking her Black subjects, as well as those that appear ethnically ambiguous, as indelibly Mexican.

Catlett's "thinking about women, Black women" thus grew in Mexican ground, and she acknowledged that her images of Black women often look Mexican.[11] Figures she designated as Mexican also echo African stylistic sources. While the Spanish title *Mujer* (1964, p. 150) gives primacy to a Mexican identity, the subtly curved planes of the upturned face that evoke skin stretched over

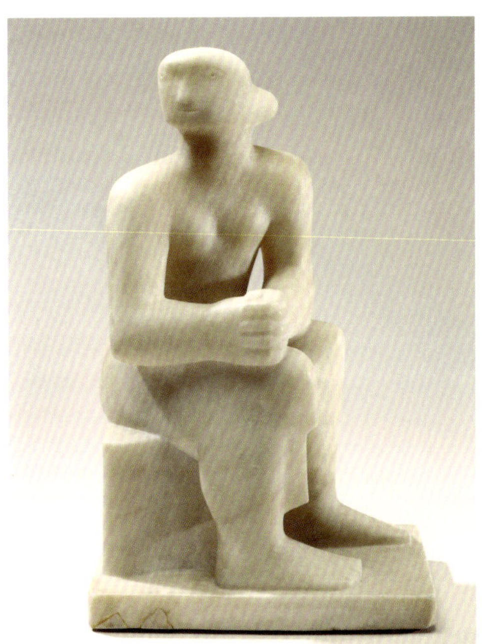

Fig. 3—Henry Moore, *Seated Figure*, 1930, alabaster, Art Gallery of Ontario, Purchase, 1976, 76/164

bone, counterpoised with the more sharply delineated nose and mouth, summon African as well as Mexican visual references. The life-size figure's satiny sheen highlights swirls of wood grain and the sculpture's robust curves. The skirt of her close-fitted dress spirals dynamically around her lower body as *Mujer* commands the space she occupies.

TRANSNATIONAL RADICALITY

Catlett became a Mexican citizen in 1962 and was immediately declared an "undesirable alien" by the US State Department due to her political affiliations and activities, and barred from her country of origin.[12] In Mexico, she expressed her embrace of the revolutionary promise of Black nationalism and the Black Power ethos of self-determination and pride in works such as *Homage to My Young Black Sisters* (1968, pp. 153–155). The face of this highly abstracted figure, carved in low relief, looks skyward, while the unequivocal gesture of her upthrust arm and clenched fist activates the energy contained within the concavity at the core of her body. Catlett intended to carve a heart for this space but changed her mind, perhaps recognizing that the formal correspondence between this void and the figure's raised fist most powerfully conveyed her message. It matters that Catlett carved this figure in Mexico, of Mexican wood, for her transnational sensibility and radicality took root there. While *Homage* foregrounds Black Power, this sculpture also signals Catlett's solidarity with women whom she joined in protests for justice in Mexico and women engaged in struggles against injustice throughout the world.

Similarly, Catlett's sculptural representations of motherhood affirm what she regarded as experiences shared transnationally by working-class women and women living in economic precarity. She conveyed the intimate physicality of maternity, the stoic endurance of mothers, and, in *Mother and Child* (1970, p. 167), their anguish when they cannot protect their children against the social forces arrayed against them. In this abstracted, visceral representation of maternity, the child is nearly subsumed into the mother's body, enfolded by the sweep of the mother's arm. Catlett carved two versions of a larger-scale *Mother and Child*: in 1983 and in 1993 (p. 219, and fig. 4) as a stately standing figure who gently cradles her child. Other pairings of mothers and children are playful, joyful, tender, and resolute.

Catlett's later sculptural representations of Black women demonstrate the prowess of an artist who spent a lifetime honing her visual language and her consummate handling of her sculptural mediums. An organic warmth infuses figures that Catlett carved from wood and sanded to a glossy sheen, while the reflective surfaces of those she carved from stone convey their visual and metaphorical shine. *Seated Woman* (1993, p. 240) is regal in bearing, sculpted from Mexican yellow onyx in a pose reminiscent of ancient Egyptian royalty. Catlett carved every curve and sharply delineated angular turn of this figure with the utmost precision. Polished smooth, it seems to glow from within. Her black marble *Stargazer* (1997, p. 241) reclines comfortably, holding space for herself as she gazes skyward. Etched on her skirt are lines that not only emphasize the repeated triangles formed by the spaces between her arms and torso and between her legs and the hem of her skirt, but also evoke charts of the night sky. Uniting physical and celestial bodies, *Stargazer* simultaneously conveys repose, aspiration, and hope. Other figures such as *Stepping Out* (2000) stride confidently forward; a six-foot-tall bronze iteration of this high-heeled, ample-bodied woman is now located in the Memorial Union at the University of Iowa, one of the artist's alma maters.

Larger-scale public commissions that Catlett completed in the last decades of her life center ordinary and extraordinary Black women. Installed in

Fig. 4—Elizabeth Catlett, *Mother and Child* in process in the artist's studio, Cuernavaca, Mexico, 1991, From the Collection of the Elizabeth Catlett-Mora Family Living Trust

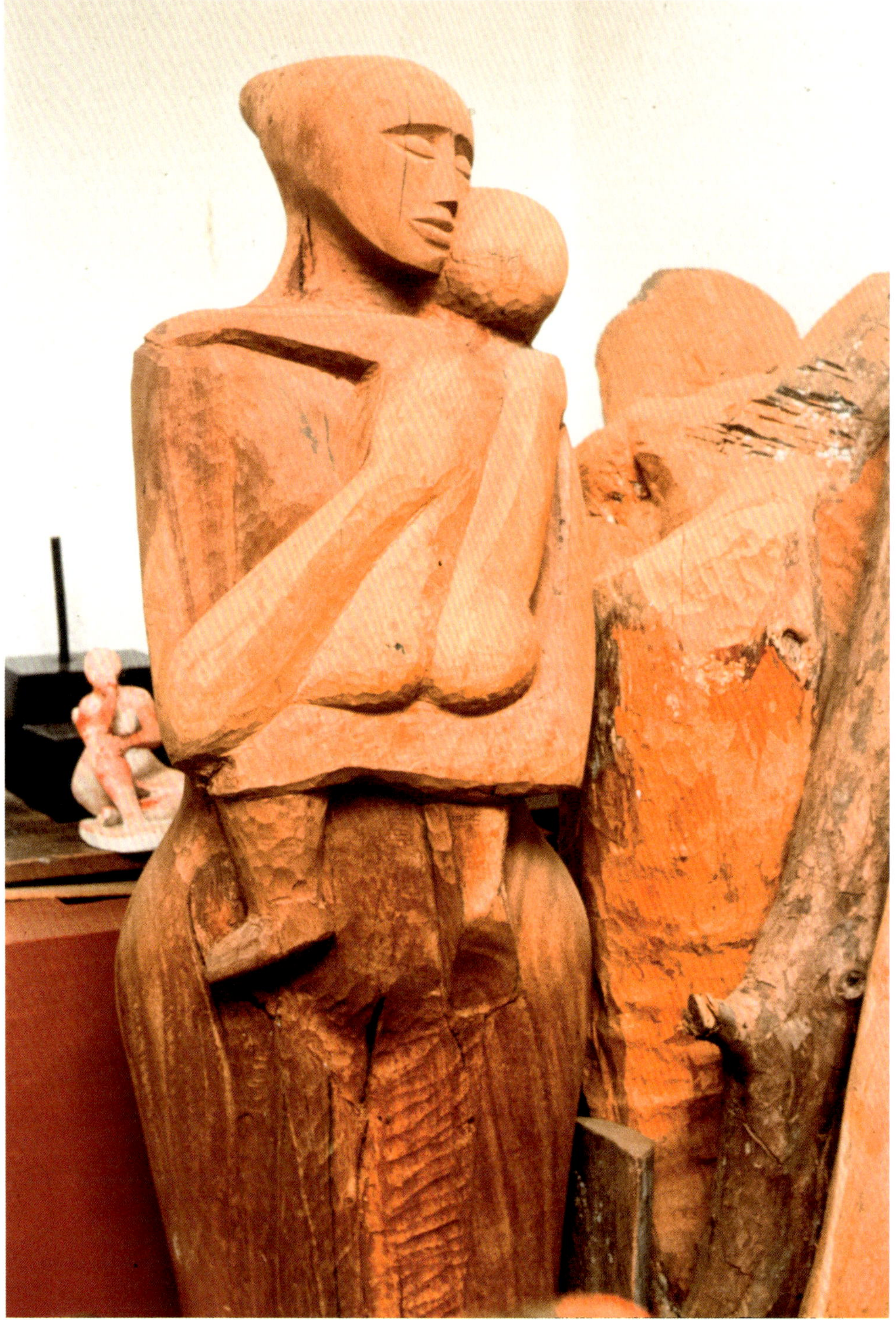

the Henry E. Legler Regional Branch of the Chicago Public Library on the city's West Side, *Floating Family* (1995, pp. 232–233) comprises two horizontally suspended figures—presumably a mother and daughter—reaching toward each other with outstretched arms and joined by their interlocked hands. Carved from Mexican primavera wood, they are strikingly reminiscent of Ernst Barlach's bronze *Floating Angel* (fig. 5), a memorial to those who perished in World War I that bears the face of Barlach's fellow German expressionist sculptor and printmaker Käthe Kollwitz; Catlett esteemed the work of both artists. In this space devoted to the acquisition of knowledge, *Floating Family* refuses the historical denial of access to education for Black people in the US and the sundering of family ties under enslavement, and claims intergenerational continuity and literacy as rights for African Americans and other peoples from whom these rights have been withheld.

Fig. 5—Ernst Barlach, *Floating Angel*, 1952, bronze, cast from the 1939 re-creation of the artist's original working model (1927), Dom zu Güstrow

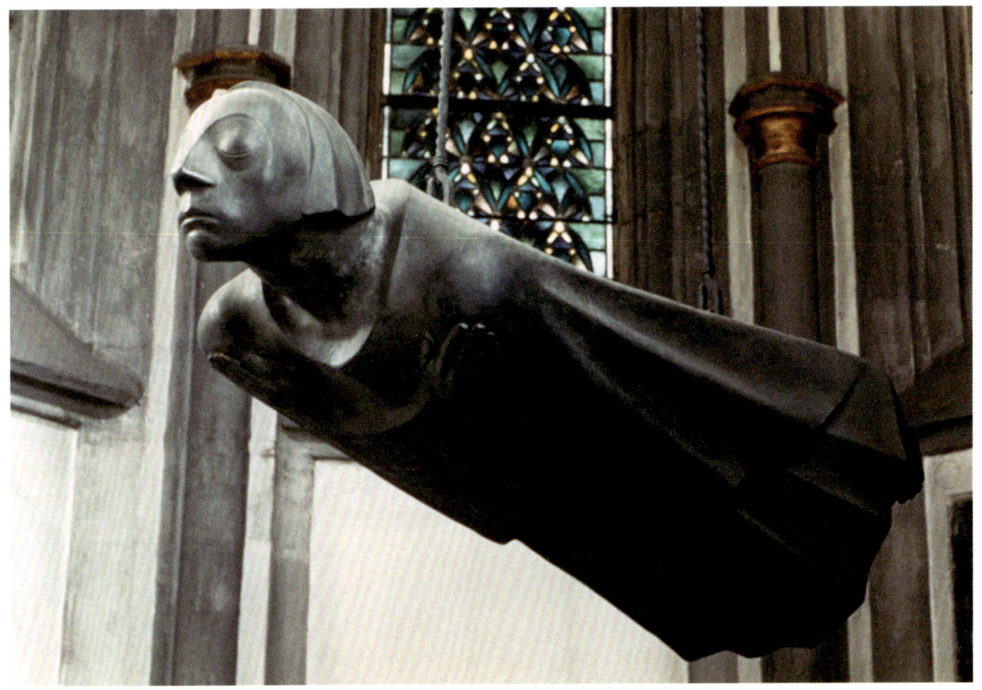

The imposing *Sojourner* (1999, p. 235), commissioned by the City of Sacramento, California, represents the abolitionist orator and activist Sojourner Truth in the elegantly geometricized manner of art deco modernism. With eyes closed, head turned toward the sky, and arms crossed in a pose of self-containment, the seven-foot-tall *Sojourner* appears to be marshaling the energy necessary to persevere in her pursuit of civil rights for African Americans and women. Emphasized by the flare of her dress, her stance implies motion, counterbalancing the weighty solidity of the dark gray Mexican limestone from which Catlett carved this figure.[13]

On April 28, 2010, two weeks after her ninety-fifth birthday, Catlett celebrated the unveiling of her ten-foot-high bronze *Mahalia Jackson* (2010, fig. 6) in Louis Armstrong Park in New Orleans, the culmination of her long-standing desire to create a sculpture of the legendary gospel singer and staunch civil rights activist.[14] One of the last sculptures Catlett completed, *Mahalia Jackson* stands adjacent to the theater that bears her name and not far from Catlett's *Louis Armstrong* (1971–1976, p. 208). With raised arms and radiant face upturned, skirt billowing and voluptuous body swaying with the rhythm of her songs of sorrow and praise, *Mahalia Jackson* embodies the power of voice.

MONUMENTAL AFFIRMATION

At the heart of Catlett's sculptural practice is her aesthetic of care—for her subjects and for the visual and material language she developed to represent them. Her skilled and sensitive handling of rounded and planar elements, subtle and decisive transitions, and the interplay of solids and spaces reveals her attention to form in works produced at any scale. She rendered sculptural detail with an exquisite precision that is evident when closely observed. Formally imbued with the potential to be scaled up as larger figures, even her small sculptures of women can appear monumental. Conceptually, formally, and materially, their presence holds.

Catlett's sculptures become—under her sure hand—radical affirmations embodying these women's subjectivity and existence in the world. Sensuous and elegant, these figural representations illumine the lived experiences of women who have borne the weight of exclusion, abuse, economic privation, and fear

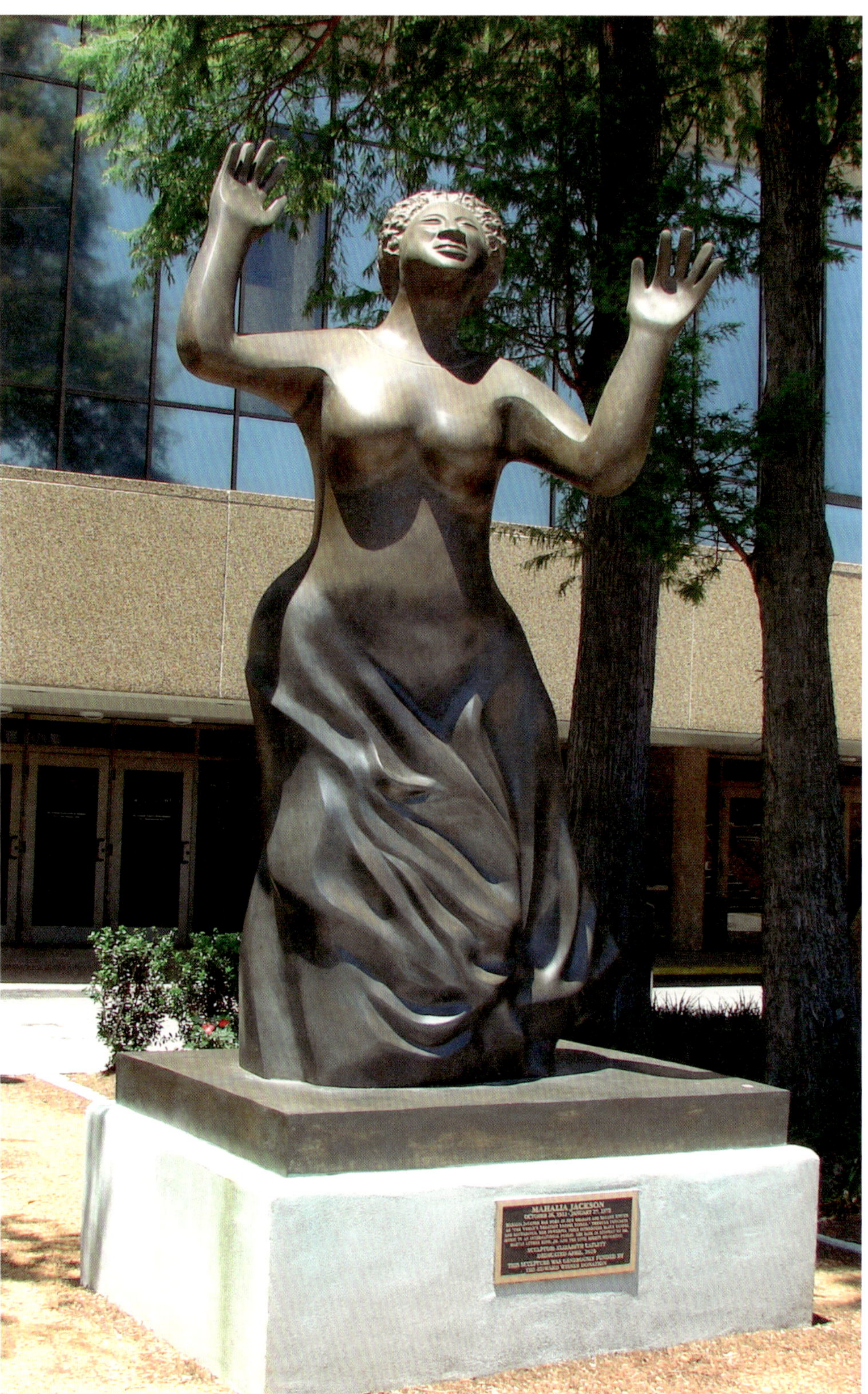

Fig. 6—Elizabeth Catlett, *Mahalia Jackson*, 2010, bronze, Louis Armstrong Park, New Orleans

for their loved ones. Some represent women who have put their bodies on the line in the struggles for justice that were central to Catlett's uncompromising politics. Yet Catlett chose not to inscribe trauma on the bodies of her female sculptural subjects. Instead, she portrayed them with compassion and attentive care, signified by their expressive forms, luminous finishes, and substantial bodily presence. Self-possessed and whole, they embody what art historian and curator Mora J. Beauchamp-Byrd terms "an aesthetic of survival."[15] With profound empathy, Elizabeth Catlett's sculptures serve not only as witness to this survival, but eloquently and insistently demand that we join her in "thinking about women."

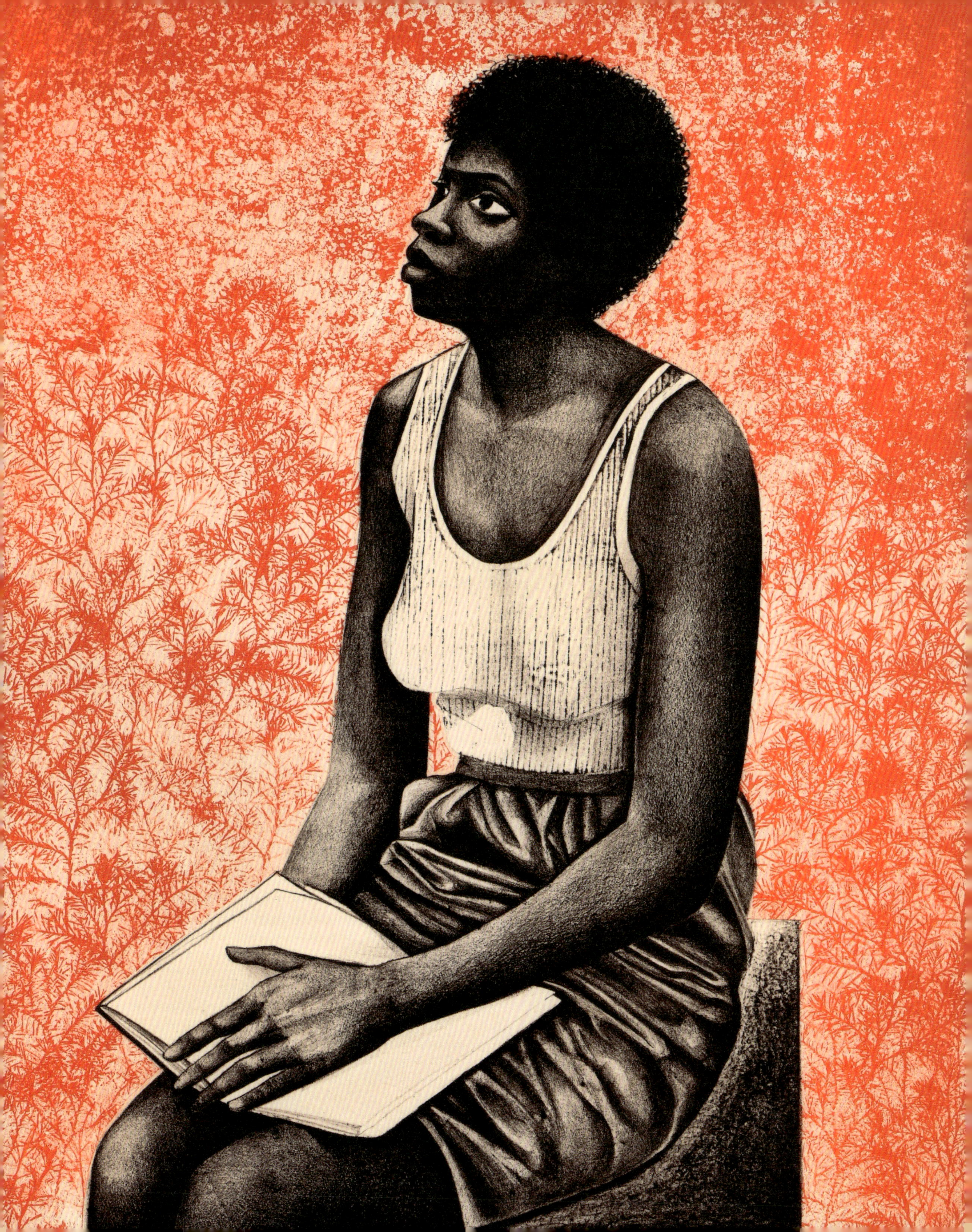

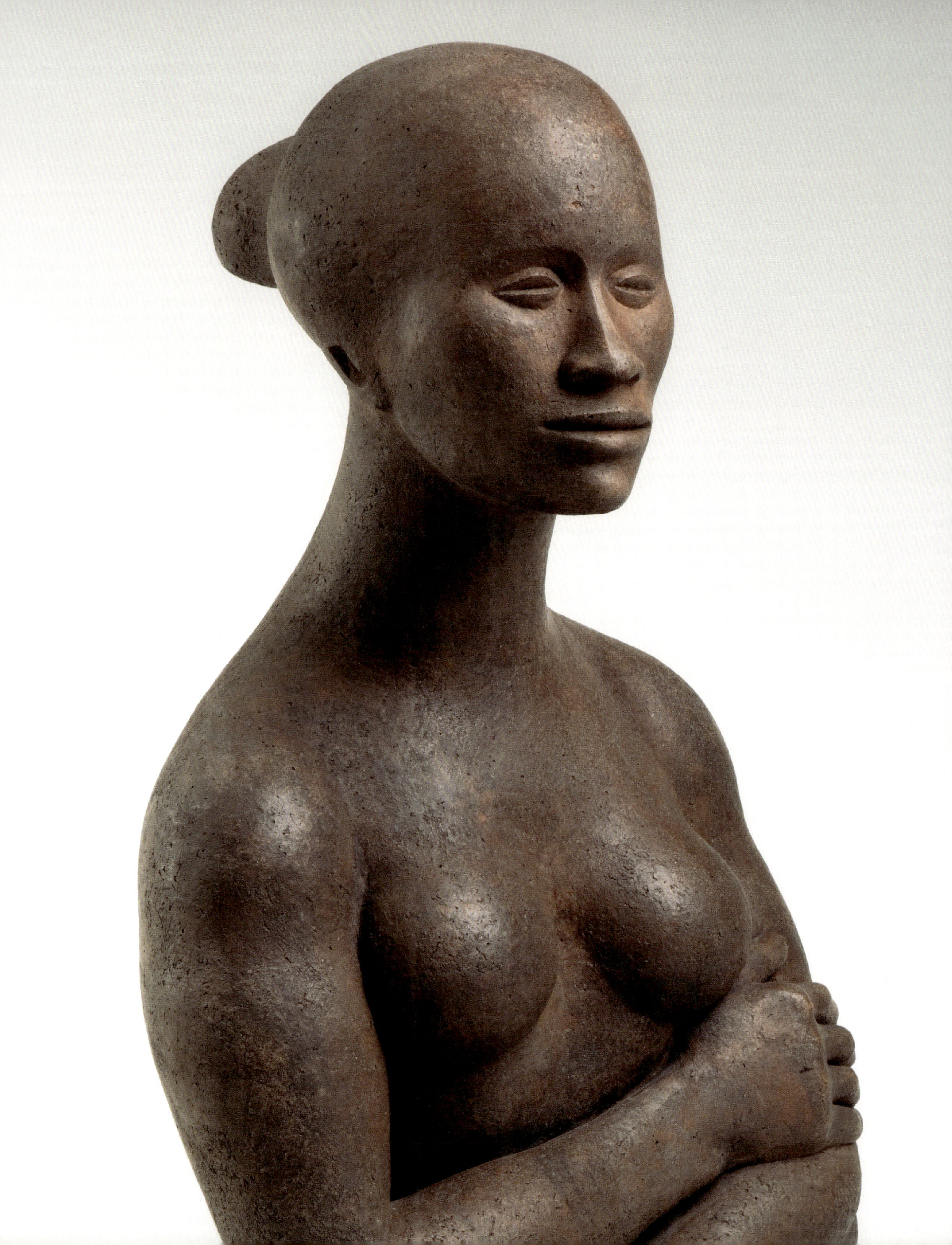

CATHERINE MORRIS

GIVING FEMINISM A SHOVE IN THE RIGHT DIRECTION

To trace Elizabeth Catlett's feminism is to write her biography. Hers was a feminism that prioritized the autonomy of Black women, the power of Black and Mexican families, the nurturing and safety of children, and a class consciousness that placed social and economic equity at the heart of her belief system. For Catlett, art "must develop from a necessity within my people. It must answer a question, or wake somebody up, or give a shove in the right direction—our liberation."[1] Feminism was central to both her activism and her creative vision. As a Black woman artist, Catlett deeply valued the lessons history offered and saw herself and the work she made as inextricably connected to the people who came before her and the generations that would follow. Throughout the entire body of her work, Catlett built a narrative of the twentieth century that centers the experiences of women within the historical and contemporary movements for Black and Mexican liberation.

In the conventional telling, feminism in the West emerged in the twentieth century in several significant waves.[2] In a teleologically inclined structure, the first wave appeared as the suffrage movement gained strength in the early decades of the century. Driven primarily by the priorities of financially and socially advantaged white women, activist efforts focused on overturning legal restrictions to voting and property rights. In the 1960s and 1970s, the second wave of the feminist movement brought a wider range of political critiques to bear on issues including reproductive rights, sexuality, family, and the workplace. Emerging alongside anti-war, civil rights, gay rights, and disability justice movements, the voices of women of color nonetheless struggled to be heard on their own terms. Within the mainstream, second wave feminism largely operated on what artist Lorraine O'Grady has characterized as "the hostess and guest" model of inclusion.[3] A third wave of feminist activism arrived in the 1990s. With a growing awareness of the political necessity of understanding how political agendas overlap, women born in the 1960s and '70s were compelled to public action by diverse cultural factors including the riot grrrl punk subculture, the testimony of Anita Hill against the appointment of judge Clarence Thomas to the United States Supreme Court, and the publication of *Gender Trouble: Feminism and the Subversion of Identity*, Judith Butler's treatise theorizing against a normative and homogenizing definition of "woman."[4]

The neatness of the waves model belies its significant inadequacies.[5] Primary among them is that the framing largely overlooks the ongoing contributions of generations of women, particularly women of color and poor women, whose voices, actions, and lived experiences fall outside the neat temporal staging of the waves narrative. Recent intersectional scholarship revises it, developing a more expansive understanding of radical feminist practices on the Left. In his book *Sojourning for Freedom: Black Women, American Communism, and the Making of Black Left Feminism*, Erik S. McDuffie states:

> *Black left feminism is useful for critically and broadly examining the gender, race, class and sexual politics within black radicalism, American Communism, and U.S. women's and transnational women's movements from the 1920s through the 1950s and beyond. Black left feminism also provides a lens for appreciating the contours of twentieth-century black feminism and inter-generational linkages between black women of the Old Left and black feminism of the 1960s and 1970s.*[6]

Particularly pertinent in the case of Elizabeth Catlett are the largely unexplored contributions her feminism—and her creative commitment to creating images of it—makes as a meaningful generational bridge in art history. Catlett's life experience offers an unwavering intersectional vision across eighty years of making feminist art for social change within Black and Mexican communities.

Drawing on a group of examples stretching across a century, the brief vignettes that follow establish Catlett's feminism as part of a multigenerational movement defined not by waves, but by a remarkable constancy of purpose: to document the long history of Black feminism by supporting and making visible the radical vision of Black women whose contributions continue to shape global movements for gender equity.

MARCH 3, 1913, WASHINGTON, DC

Born April 15, 1915, Elizabeth Catlett came of age at the height of the anti-lynching movement, an organized political effort to stamp out racialized terror that included effective public awareness campaigns overseen by the NAACP.[7] In multiple interviews Catlett described her participation in anti-lynching protests while still in high school.[8] She also noted that she was aware of her own radical inclinations from an early age, adding that her two siblings were not so politically inclined. Raised as she was by a single mother in a relatively affluent household that prioritized middle-class values, the rights of women were arguably also part of the artist's early exposure to social politics.

Looking for the roots of what art historian Rebecca VanDiver has termed the artist's later charting of "the matriarchal lineage of Black liberation"[9] brings to the fore a significant historical event in Washington that occurred two years before Catlett was born. The story of the 1913 Woman's Suffrage Procession, and the organizers' grievous decision to prioritize a politically expeditious alignment with white women from southern states at the expense of Black women participants, has been well documented.[10] In short, the social forces of Jim Crow prevailed when the largely northern women organizers led by Quaker Alice Paul requested that Black women participants march at the back of the parade.[11] While some Black suffragists challenged the decision, with attendance estimates ranging from 5,000 to 10,000 women, the event marked a decisive turning point away from the earlier alignment of white suffrage activists with the abolitionist movement and toward an acquiescence to de facto segregation.[12]

Journalist and anti-lynching crusader Ida B. Wells remains the best known of those who refused to comply with the order. In her own form of protest, Wells waited on Pennsylvania Avenue for her Illinois Delegation to pass before stepping in to join them along the rest of the route. The story of Wells's bravery

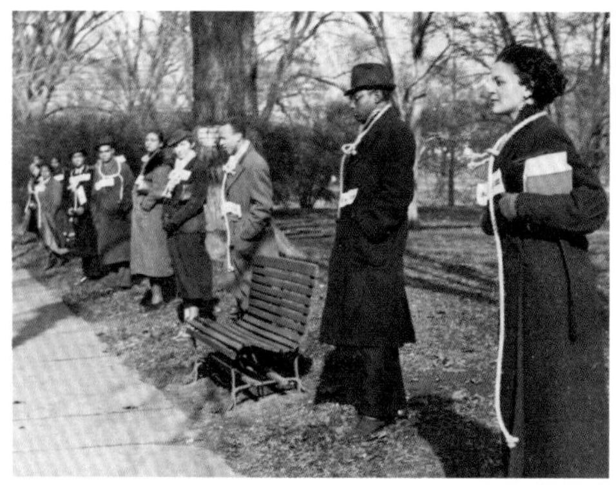

Fig. 1—Howard University students picket the National Crime Conference in Washington, DC, when its leaders refused to discuss lynching as a national crime, 1934, gelatin silver print, Library of Congress, Washington, DC

was closely chronicled in Black newspapers, particularly in Chicago where her reputation loomed large, and where she had founded the first Black women's suffrage club just two months before the Washington parade.[13]

Wells's historic work encompassing both anti-lynching and women's rights made her part of the pantheon of foremothers to Catlett. She would later include a portrait of Wells by artist Celia Calderón (p. 107) in the print series *Against Discrimination in the US*, whose creation Catlett oversaw at the Taller de Gráfica Popular.[14]

Another significant group of marchers included twenty-two founding members of the newly formed Delta Sigma Theta Sorority at Howard University. Their participation marked the incorporated sorority's first public appearance.[15] Catlett joined the sorority when she was an undergraduate, though she also sought out more radical groups, saying, "I went from social life with Delta Sigma Theta and the sororities and frats straight into the Liberal Club" (fig. 1).[16]

1942–1946, HARLEM

In Chicago and New York Catlett had formative encounters with what cultural historian Michael Denning has called "social modernism"—artists and cultural producers who sought to combine modern experimentation with social content fostering community education and calls to action.[17] Her experiences in these cities made clear to her that the nexus of class was the fundamental aspect of social justice, first at the South Side Community Center in Chicago, and then at the George Washington Carver School in Harlem, where, among other duties, she taught dressmaking. Working there, she noted, was a major influence "because I grew up in a kind of middle class situation...the Carver School gave me a reason for producing or let me know for whom I was producing."[18] In New York, she also taught ceramics at the Jefferson School of Social Science, an adult learning institute established by the US Communist Party, and volunteered for Russian War Relief. The active experience of class struggle established Catlett's priorities as an artist—working people became both the subject and audience of her work. Her goal was "to put art in service of people."[19]

In numerous contexts Catlett declared that she made her work for "my people," or often, "my two peoples." In writing on Catlett's peer Alice Childress, an actress and writer committed to "Black centered left radicalism," scholar Mary Helen Washington describes how "'the people' was radicalized to 'my people,' a phrase that, in the more doctrinaire period of the 1930s, might have earned her a reprimand for putting race before class solidarity."[20] Catlett's pointed and continued use of this seemingly straightforward phrase throughout her life becomes a poignantly—and subtly—radical acknowledgment of the roots of her political awakening in the pre–World War II era.

Catlett's time at the Carver School was dominated by women. As she noted, "Gwen [Gwendolyn Bennett] was the director and Mamie Brown came over to us from another organization. Hermie Dumont, also. We were a small group of women who ran that school and we did a very good job."[21] In an era before the term "feminism"—let alone "intersectional"—came into use, Catlett's experience enacted a "triple consciousness," a keen awareness that, in order to be successful, multiple forms of social and political oppressions must be dismantled simultaneously.[22]

Some labor scholars have proposed a reframing of the "long civil rights movement," a paradigm that links movements for racial equity from the 1930s to the 1970s. Catlett functions as such a link.[23] Critics of the model point to the destructive impact of the Cold War on Black radicalism, though Catlett's transnational experience in Mexico both attests to that rupture and points to her strategies to continue and expand their work into the transnational arena.[24]

1962–1977, FEMINISM IN MEXICO

The active period of Catlett's transnational feminism aligns with her gaining of Mexican citizenship in 1962. Her engagement with multiple communities of women in the context of Third World activism decentralizes the history of feminism during the Cold War. As art critic Aruna D'Souza has described it, Third World feminism is "a set of theorizations that aligned the political goals of Black feminists in the United States with a worldwide struggle for decolonization that cut through lines of class, gender and race."[25] Catlett's transnational experience in Mexico points to the strategic choices a wider world view offered as a means to continue her work. As the period of the Cold War gave way to the era of decolonization in the 1960s, Catlett's increasing work with international women's organizations was one of her strategies.

In 1963 Catlett attended the Congress of Women of the Americas in Cuba. Fidel Castro closed the event, stating in his remarks: "The fact is that in the world in which the American woman lives, the woman must necessarily be revolutionary...Because woman, who constitutes an essential part of every people, is, in the first place, exploited as a worker and discriminated against as a woman."[26] As a member of the Mexican delegation, and a recent citizen, Catlett must have heard the reports on American women that were presented from a unique position.

The Cuba delegation came back to Mexico inspired to form the Unión Nacional de Mujeres Mexicanas (UNMM), which Catlett remained a part of until 1977. Catlett was instrumental in the group's taking up reproductive justice as a cause. As VanDiver writes regarding her 1970 work *Torture of Mothers*, "Catlett levied her critique of anti-Black violence and state power through the maternal—connecting the conditions of Black life with those of Black maternity."[27]

Catlett surely felt an affinity with the feminism she encountered in Mexico. As historian Manuel Ramirez Chicharro describes, "Mexican women's emancipation was inextricably connected to deeper social reforms. It is no coincidence that the letters and reports sent to both the federal government of Mexico and the Women's International Democratic Federation (WIDF) by the National Bloc of Revolutionary Women (BNMR) were signed with the slogan 'For the liberation of women and for the progress of Mexico.'"[28]

Catlett's engagement with Black nationalism, Black art, and feminist movements in the US also continued.

NOVEMBER 19, 1974, JUST ABOVE MIDTOWN GALLERY

There were direct intellectual, political, and personal linkages between Black Left feminists who came of age before World War II and younger Black women whose feminism emerged in tandem with the civil rights movement. Acknowledging intergenerational connections of Black women is important because rather than establishing lineages of support, many histories of the period focus on either integrating Black feminist activists with the mainstream second wave feminism movement, or differentiating the two.[29]

Before the first exhibition opened November 19, 1974, at Just Above Midtown (JAM), the legendary Black owned and run gallery, and later, alternative art space, in New York City, a group of young artists and supporters joined JAM's founder, Linda Goode Bryant, in a jubilant snapshot (fig. 2). Crowded around Catlett's sculpture *Homage to My Young Black Sisters* (pp. 153–155) are Andy Owens, Goode Bryant, David Hammons, curator Lowery Stokes Sims, Cheryl

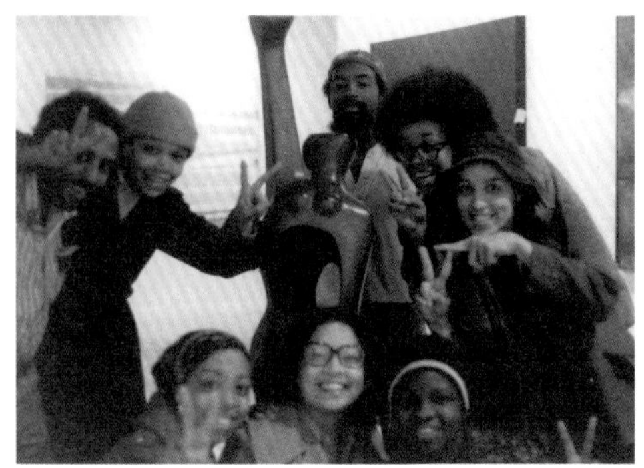

Fig. 2—Jubilant group at the *Synthesis* exhibition opening with *Homage to My Young Black Sisters* (pp. 153–155), JAM, Fifty-Seventh Street, 1974

Mason Dorman, Faythe Weaver, Florence Harding, and Roberta Wolfe Bryant. The celebration that evening was for a show Goode Bryant curated called *Synthesis: A combination of parts of elements into a complex whole*, which announced JAM's unique mission to support avant-garde Black artists and to offer them a meaningful context in which to present their work. Goode Bryant understood the uniquely multivalent conversations within which Black artists made their work. Since the early 1960s Black artists had debated the value of abstraction vs. representation and positioned avant-garde conceptualism as antithetical to making work that spoke to people who did not see themselves in contemporary art. *Synthesis* brought together these disparate parts of the art world. As Kellie Jones has written, "Goode Bryant's synthesizing vision made space for an expansive coalition and revealed a broader history of African American Art practice."[30]

At the heart of the show, which traversed geography, generations, and formal approaches, was Catlett's monument to a new generation of Black feminist women. Made in her Cuernavaca studio in 1968 when the artist was fifty-three-years old, *Homage to My Young Black Sisters* marks multiple links in the artist's political, cultural, and stylistic concerns across decades. An organically abstracted figure with gentle curves aligning to a beautifully burnished wood grain, the form fits in the lineage of modern sculpture while its overt political content of a Black Power fist and a Black feminist solidarity speaks to the necessity of narrative as an effective means of communicating to communities beyond the art world.

The title also communicates that, generationally, Catlett places herself in a position of elder who not only offers the activists emerging in the late 1960s decades of lived experience with political engagement but also elegantly acknowledges her admiration for the approaches she sees the new generation developing. Finally, this brilliant work functions across space—Catlett produced it in Mexico while in exile from the US. There is an added poignancy in knowing the artist made the work as a contribution to and in solidarity with a movement in which she couldn't directly participate. "Through this celebration of 'young black sister,' Catlett again charted a genealogy of Black political kinship through the achievements of Black women."[31]

1981, SECOND WAVE FEMINISM AND THE WHITE ART WORLD

In the 1970s Catlett paid enough attention to the mainstream art world and the predominantly white second wave feminist movement to keep abreast of their work and activities. From her vantage point in Mexico City and Cuernavaca, she took a dim view of the pertinence of either to her life or the lives of the people she sought to engage through her own work and activism. As she notes in a 1984 essay called "The Focus on Women," "I'm a feminist but I get the same feeling about the feminist movement that I get when I hear the very sad problems that middle-class women in the U.S. have in their need to express themselves. When I put it beside what is going on in the Black ghetto and the Chicano ghetto and in countries in Latin America and Africa—especially South Africa—and the Far East, middle-class feminism doesn't get to be that important to me."[32]

Catlett continues, "I want my children to grow up in a world where mathematics and sculpture are more important than comic books and fashionable clothes, where art is not judged by monetary values."[33] Catlett's suspicions about the art world included her belief that a focus on acceptance by the market-driven New York scene was misguided. In a 1981 interview with Glory Van Scott, Catlett mentions a recent catalog essay on the feminist artist Miriam

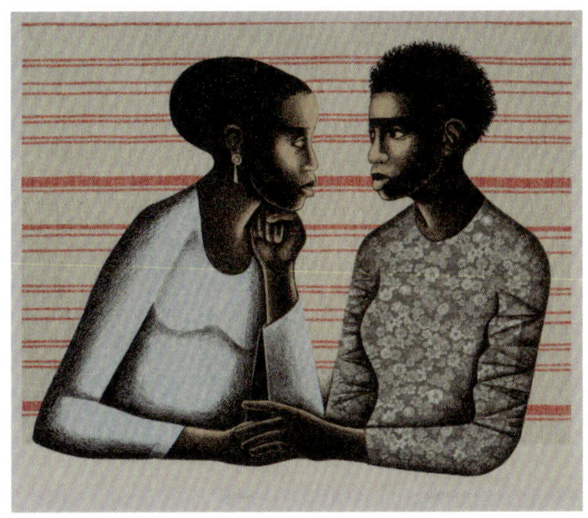

Fig. 3—Elizabeth Catlett, *Gossip*, 2005, digital print and photo lithograph, Brooklyn Museum, Gift of Ruth Bowman in honor of Marilyn Kushner, 2006.60

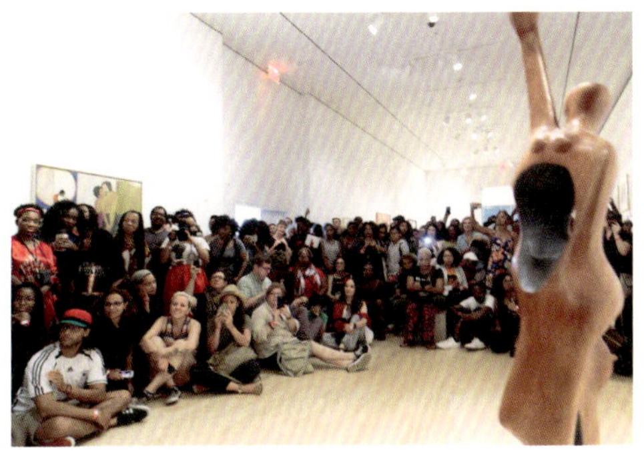

Fig. 4—Closing ceremony of the exhibition *We Wanted a Revolution*, 2017, Performance by Black Women Artists for Black Lives Matter, Brooklyn Museum

Schapiro, in which she describes coming into her own as an artist alongside her growing feminist awareness. In Catlett's telling, Schapiro links her recent creative breakthroughs to her experience with feminist consciousness raising, which empowered her to incorporate domestic subjects into her work. However, Schapiro then gives "herself away" by linking her new success to making a splash at a prestigious New York gallery. As Catlett notes, "Even though she is expressing her feelings as a woman, this is her audience, the New York art circles."[34] For Catlett, there is disappointment in the way Schapiro chooses to measure her own success, particularly given that her creative advance grew from a feminist awakening.

Later in the same interview, Catlett observes that while her own work is included in many prestigious collections, "it is put away somewhere"—meaning that once acquired, work by Black artists was rarely shown in galleries and tended instead to languish unseen in storage. For Catlett, then, the acknowledgment of being in large museums is solely meaningful in terms of "carrying on your career as a professional artist." Her focus is decidedly different. As she says, "In the States, we really have to get to the people."[35] The people, in other words, who don't have access to the world of art museums and galleries (fig. 3).

Particularly as Catlett entered the later period of her career in the 1980s, her minimal engagement with mainstream feminism can be characterized as having a related set of goals but fundamentally different priorities. Her social justice roots and formal strategies remain ever present, but the focus of her radicality is now driven by her desire to share her work directly with working and marginalized communities.

SEPTEMBER 16, 2017, SIMONE LEIGH AND BLACK WOMEN ARTISTS FOR BLACK LIVES MATTER

"Women," Catlett tells us, "will have to look back at the history of women in art in order to base the future on that history."[36] The exhibition *We Wanted a Revolution: Black Radical Women, 1965–1985*, organized by the Brooklyn Museum in 2017, presented a history of Black feminism in a twenty-year period of significant civil and political upheaval in the US. The artists included crossed generational divides, from Loïs Mailou Jones and Elizabeth Catlett to Lorna Simpson and Carrie Mae Weems—to show Black feminist artists "conversing" and working in support of one another as well as the emancipatory goals they shared over decades.[37] A total of six works by Catlett were shown,[38] with *Homage to My Young Black Sisters* anchoring a gallery devoted to the Black Arts Movement. In one of the events, which marked the closing of the show, members of a recently formed coalition called Black Women Artists for Black Lives Matter (BWAforBLM) created an extended responsive performance that moved throughout the exhibition and engaged with multiple works, including *Homage to My Young Black Sisters* (fig. 4).

The event was initiated by artist Simone Leigh, who has always envisioned Black women as the primary audience for her archetypal and monumental sculptural representations of the female form.[39] Offering a real-time engagement with legacies the participating artists wished to honor, uplift, and be in conversation with, the group simultaneously made space for the viewing audience to understand how art objects can continue to live in the present and be in conversation with living artists. Member Nomaduma Rosa Masilela said of the formation of the group: "This collaboration was only possible because of Simone Leigh, who belongs to a long line of black women who are not thwarted and silenced by the (art) world's overwhelming inequalities, but who decide to leverage their abilities into a wealth of potential for others. Rather than remain part of the trickle, she made space for a flood."[40]

And so, more than forty years after *Homage to My Young Black Sisters* was celebrated at JAM, a new generation of Black feminists celebrated Elizabeth Catlett's vision and legacy, making clear the radical creative lineage in which they place themselves.

A COMPANY OF VOICES

Black feminism provides a necessary throughline to the larger history of feminism in the twentieth century, ousting preoccupations with notions of exceptionalism and the mainstream penchant for discovery models that prioritize firsts over an acknowledgment of structures of support and the foundational communities upon which later radicalism is built. Elizabeth Catlett understood that history offers living artists a company of voices from which to gain strength in one's convictions and to build a platform for those who come after. She also understood that her feminism was intended to support entire communities and better the lives of all people. "I have been criticized for being old fashioned, for not contributing anything new to art, and for exhibiting in places where there are no galleries. To me, such criticism is absurd. I continue to bring art to my people and to bring my people to art as I recognize my debt and our need. There has to be something for us outside of the mainstream, and something of our lives we can offer to others."[41] In that way, the example of Elizabeth Catlett's career gives the feminist movement a shove in the right direction.

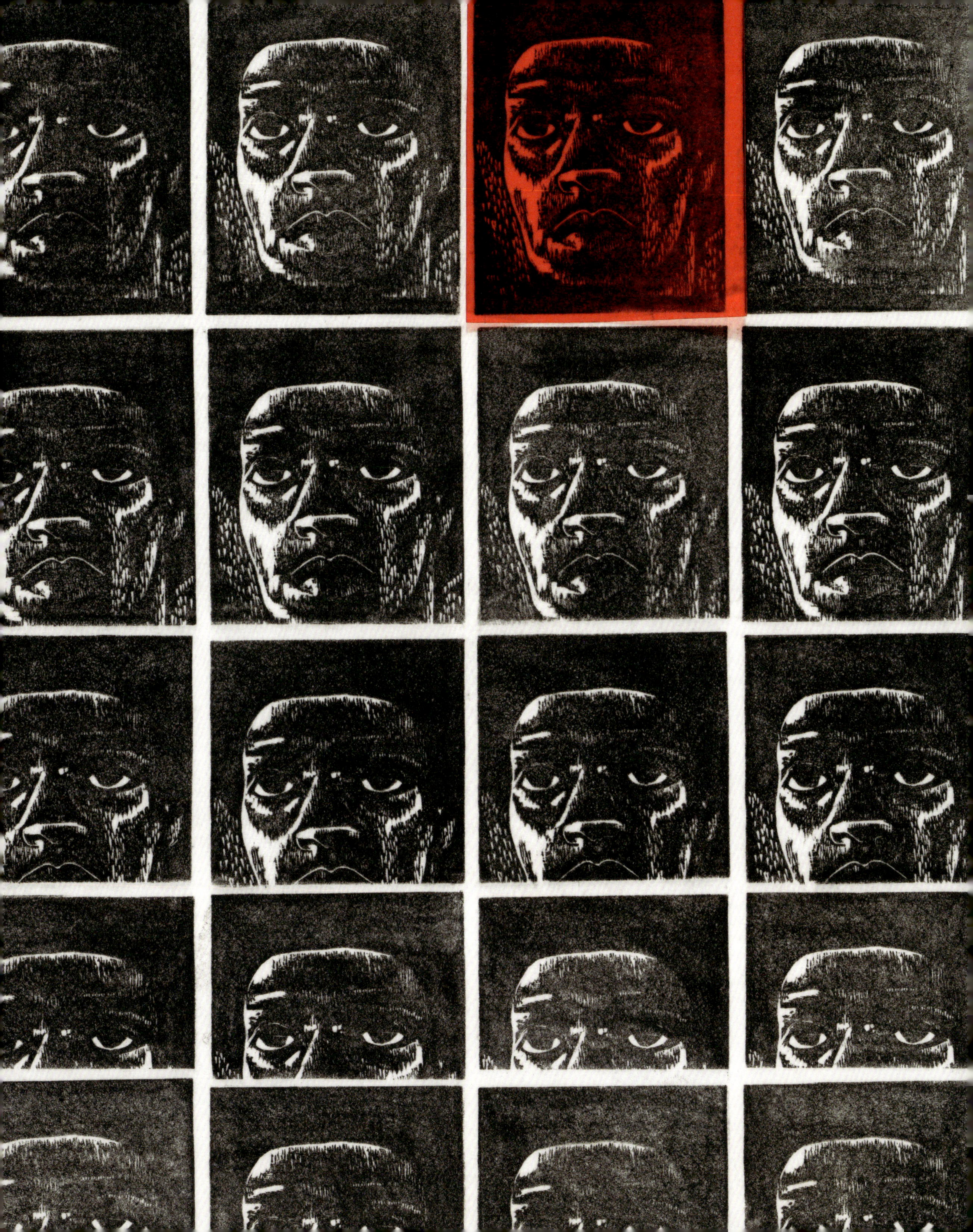

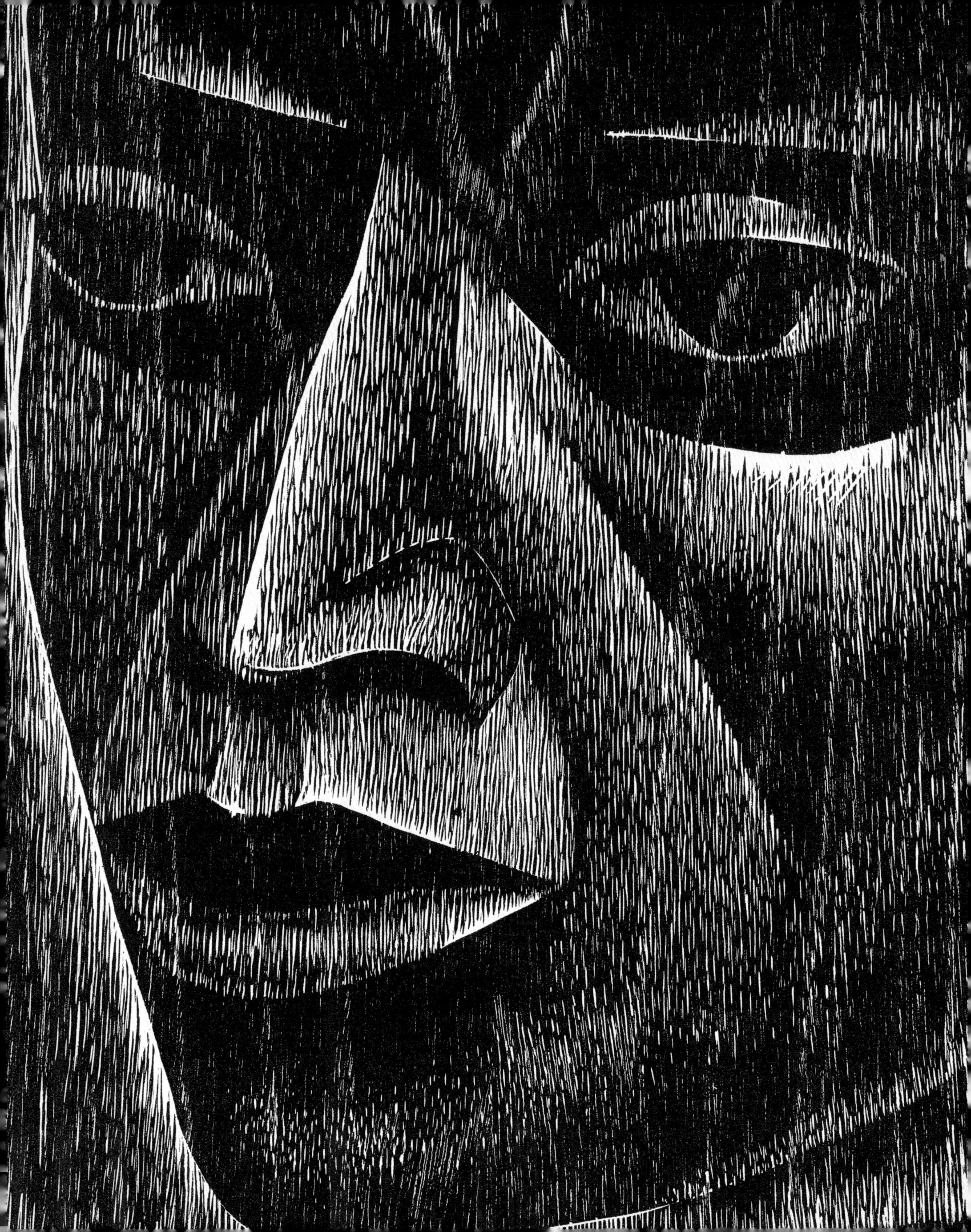

PLATES

1975–2012

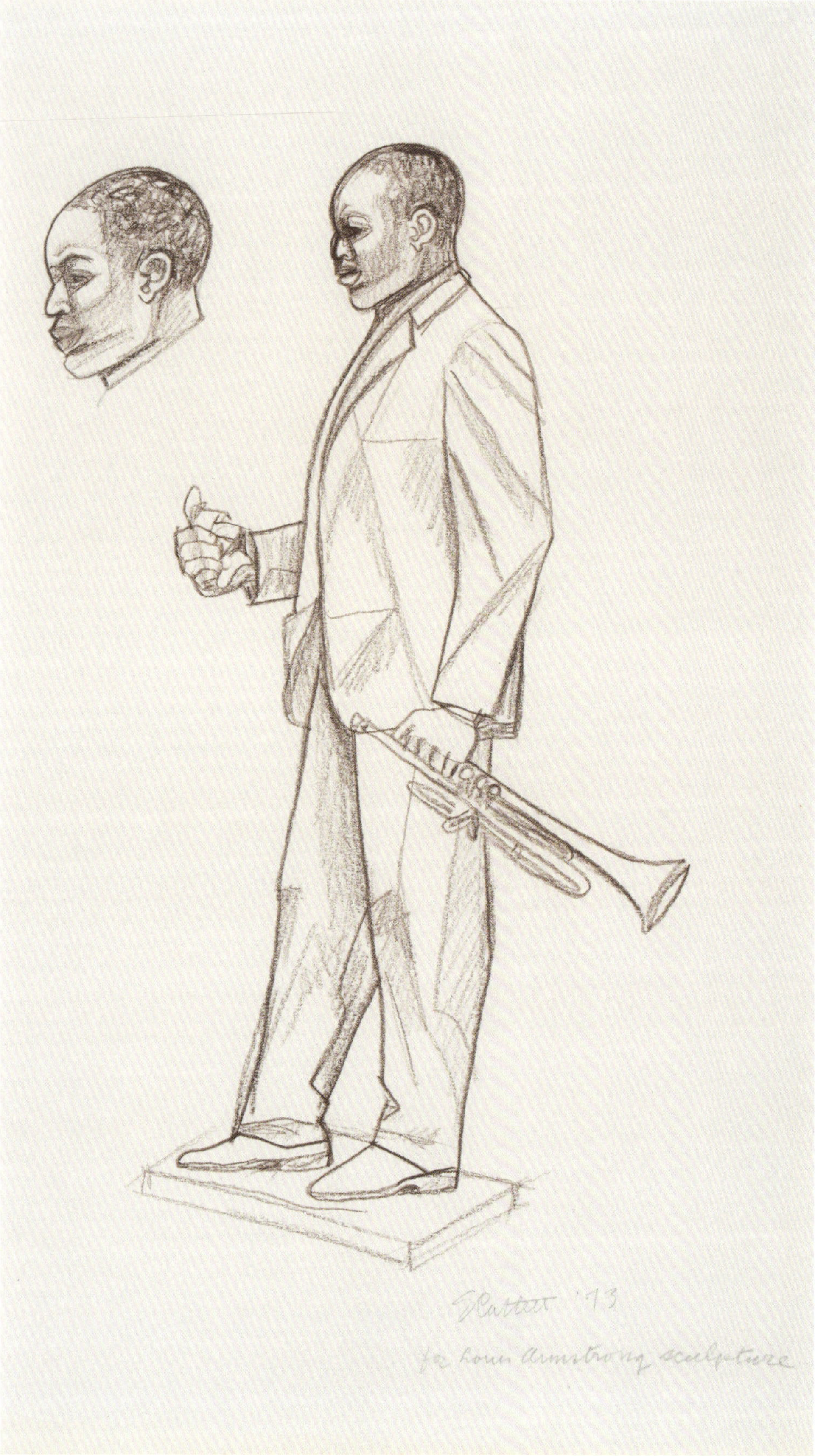

Sketch for Louis Armstrong, 1973, Stella Jones Gallery

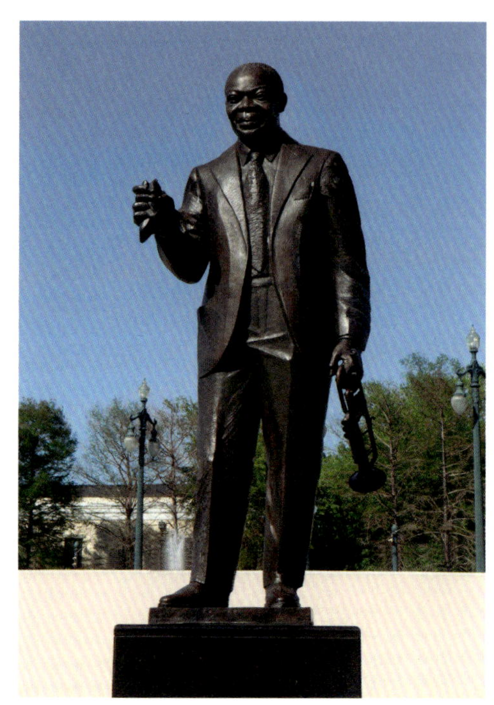

Louis Armstrong, 1971–1976, bronze, 120 in., in situ photograph, Louis Armstrong Park, New Orleans

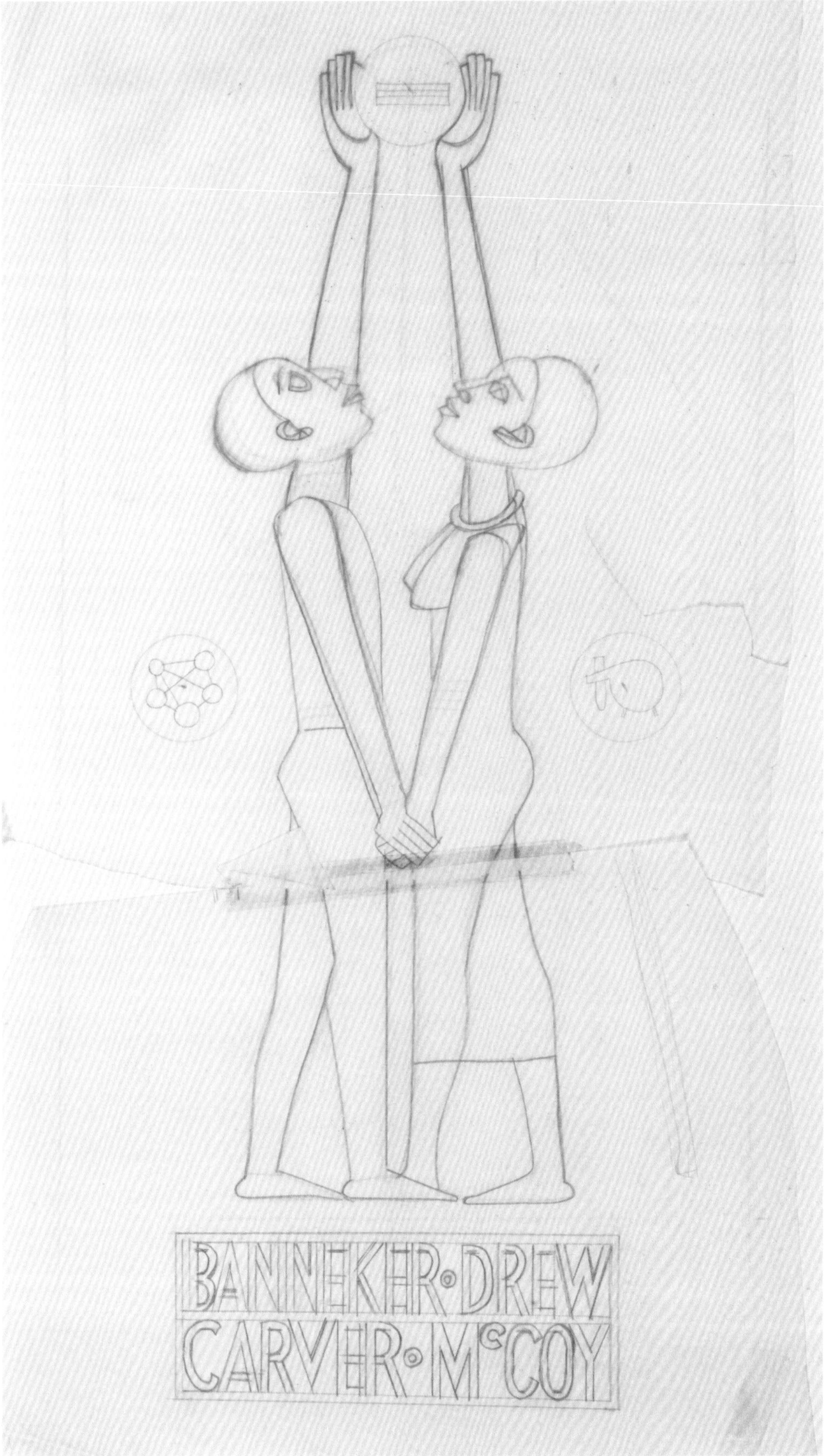

Early Sketch for Students Aspire, 1975–1977, 21¾ × 12 in., From the Collection of the Elizabeth Catlett-Mora Family Living Trust

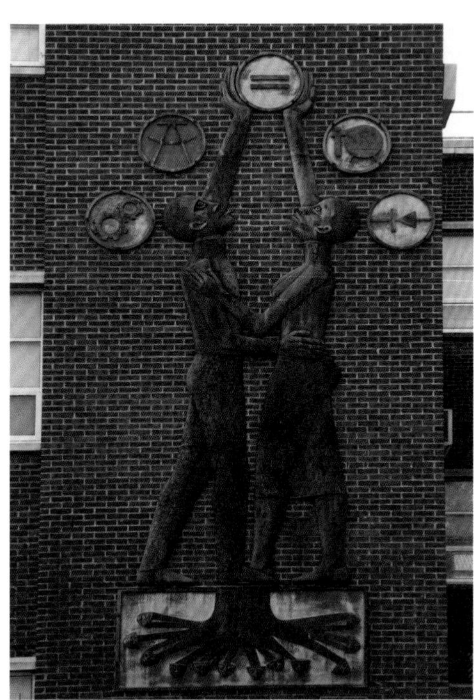

Students Aspire, 1975–1977, bronze, 168 × 55⅕ in., in situ photograph, Howard University, College of Engineering Building, Prints and Photographs Division, Library of Congress, Washington, DC

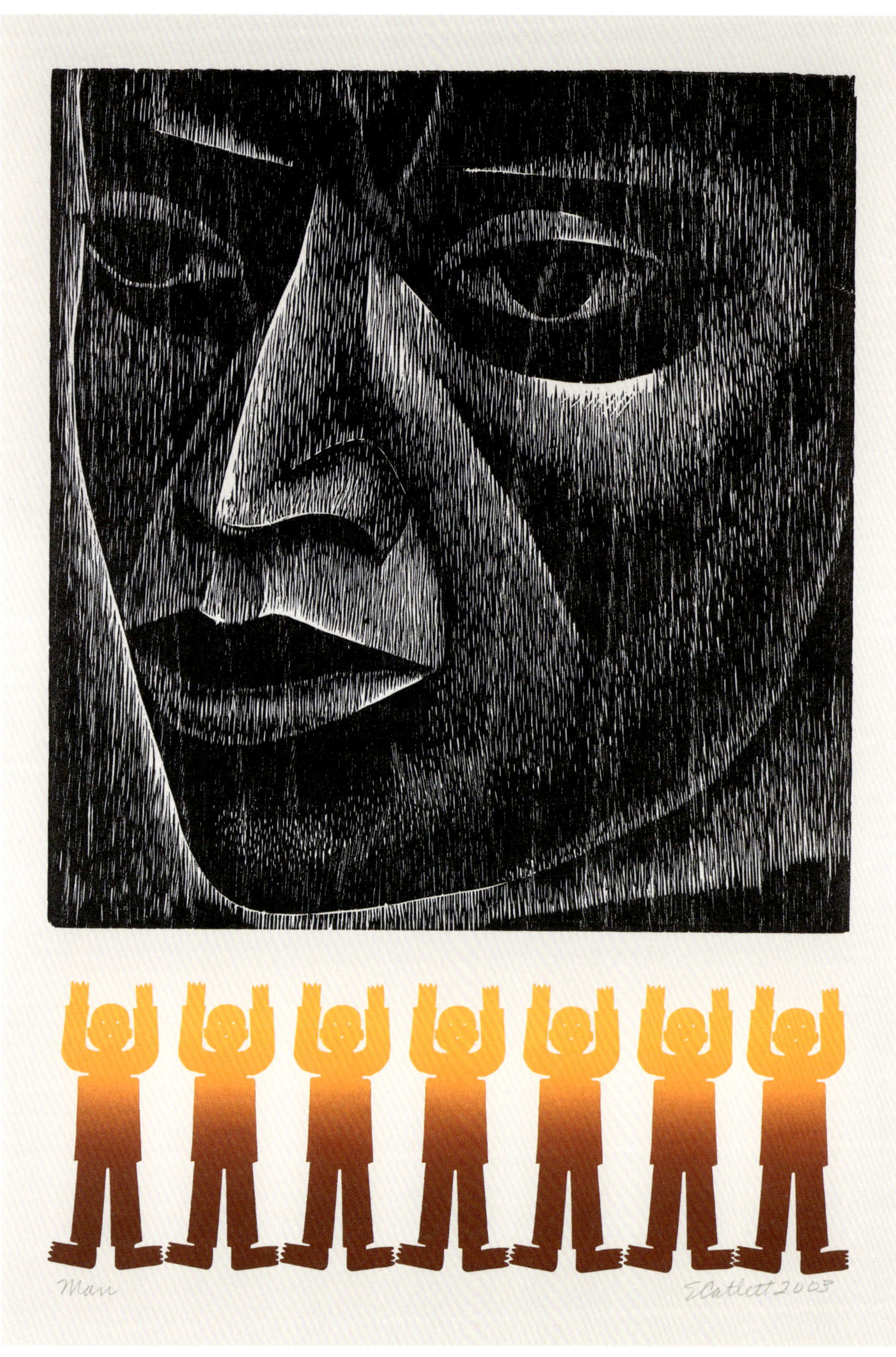

Man, 1975, reprinted 2003, woodcut and color linocut, 26 × 17¹³⁄₁₆ in., The Cleveland Museum of Art, Gift of The Print Club of Cleveland, 2005.36

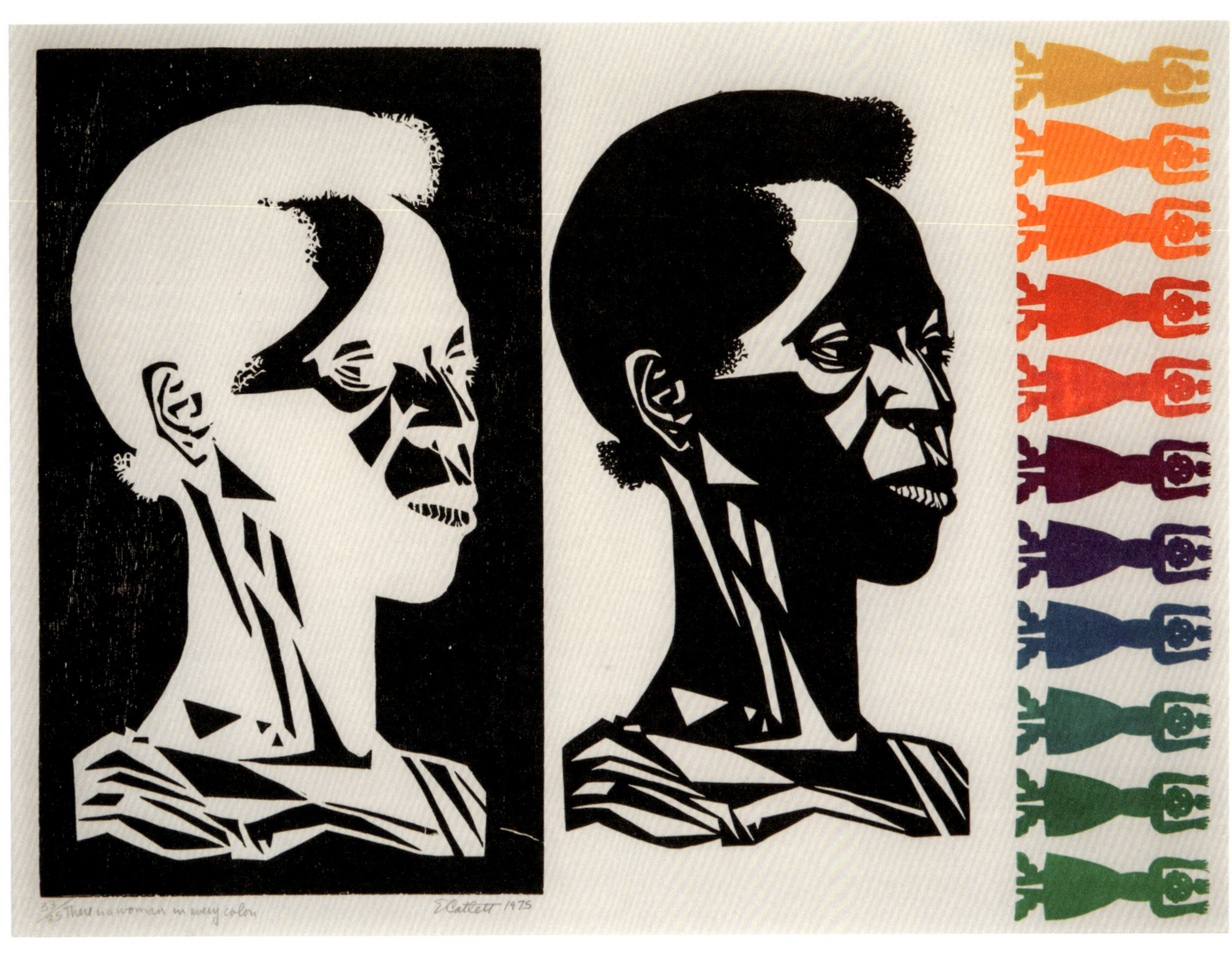

There Is a Woman in Every Color, 1975, woodcut and linocut, 22 × 30 in., From the Hampton University Museum Collection, Hampton, VA

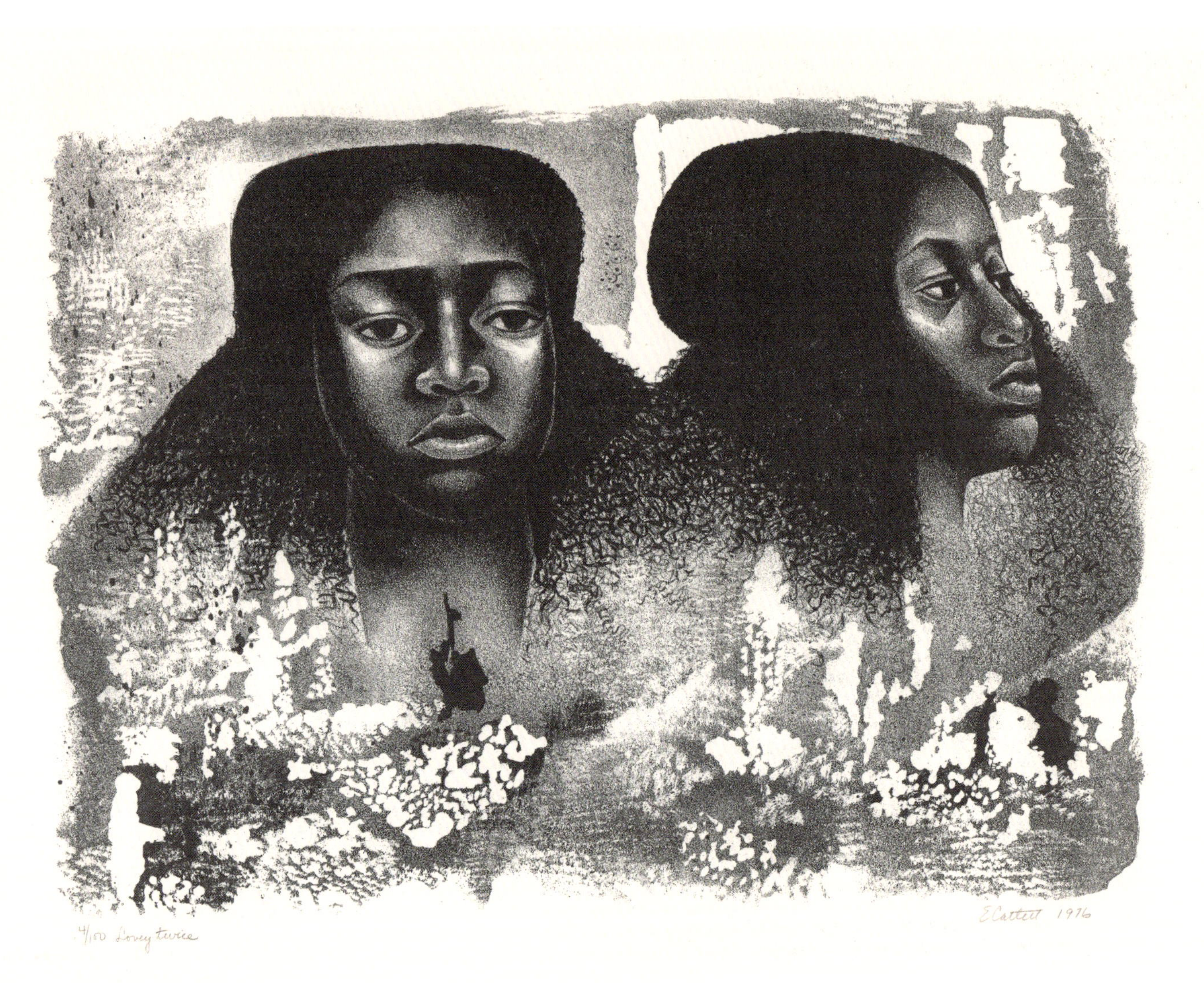

Lovey Twice, 1976, lithograph in black on wove paper, 22¼ × 30 in., National Gallery of Art, Corcoran Collection (Gift of Dr. Charles Warfield and Mrs. Savanna Clark)

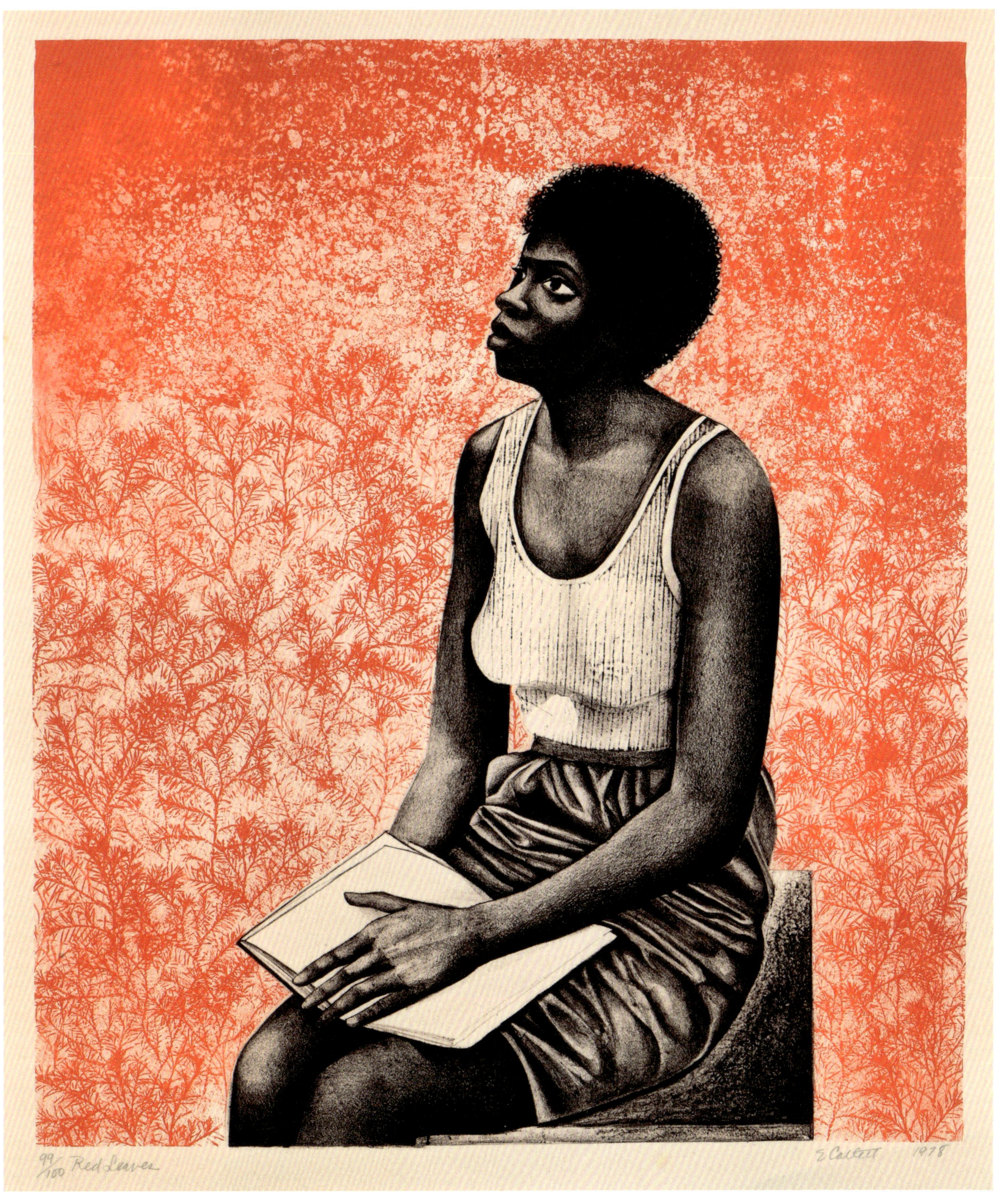

Red Leaves, 1978, lithograph, 22½ × 18¾ in., University of Iowa Stanley Museum of Art, Museum purchase, 2006.59

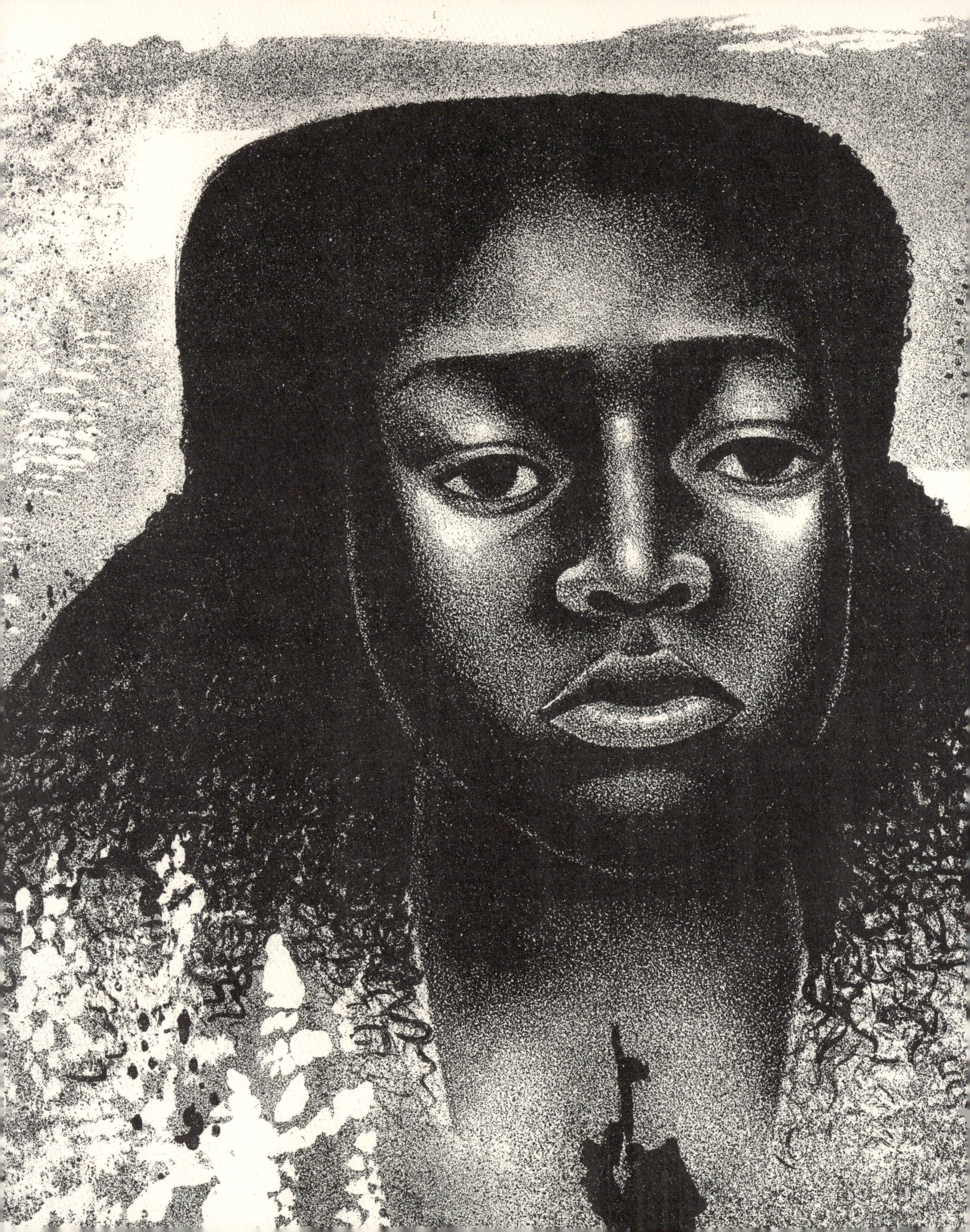

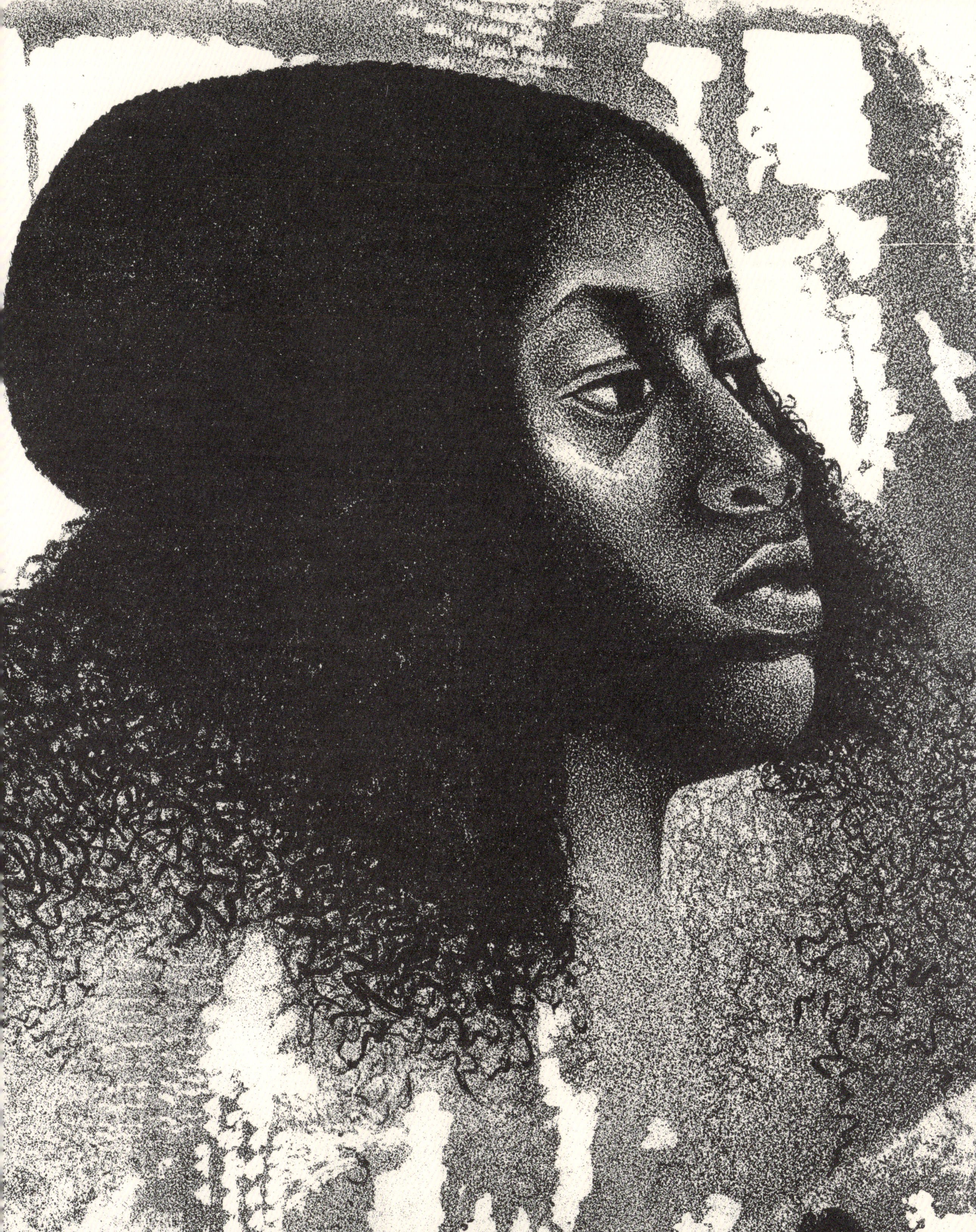

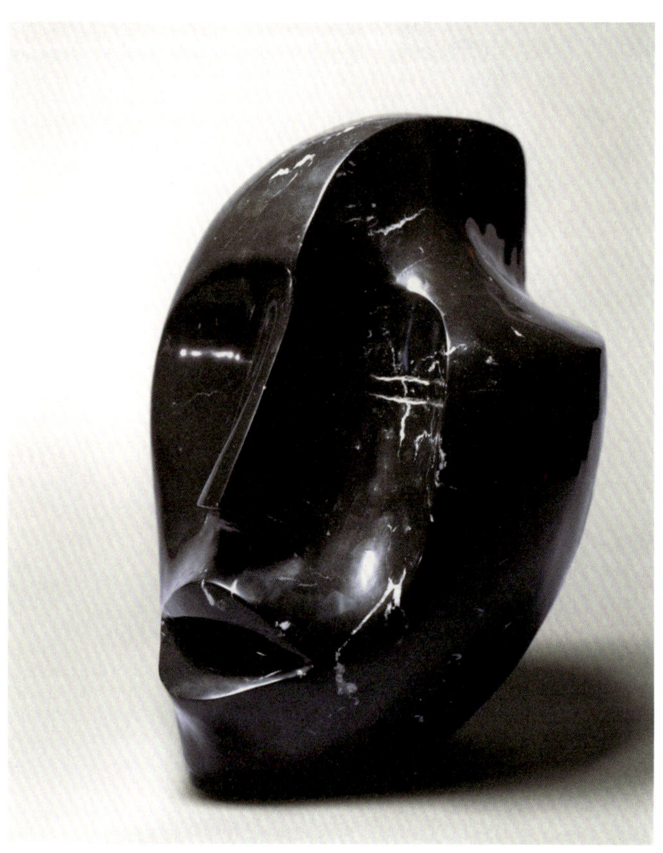

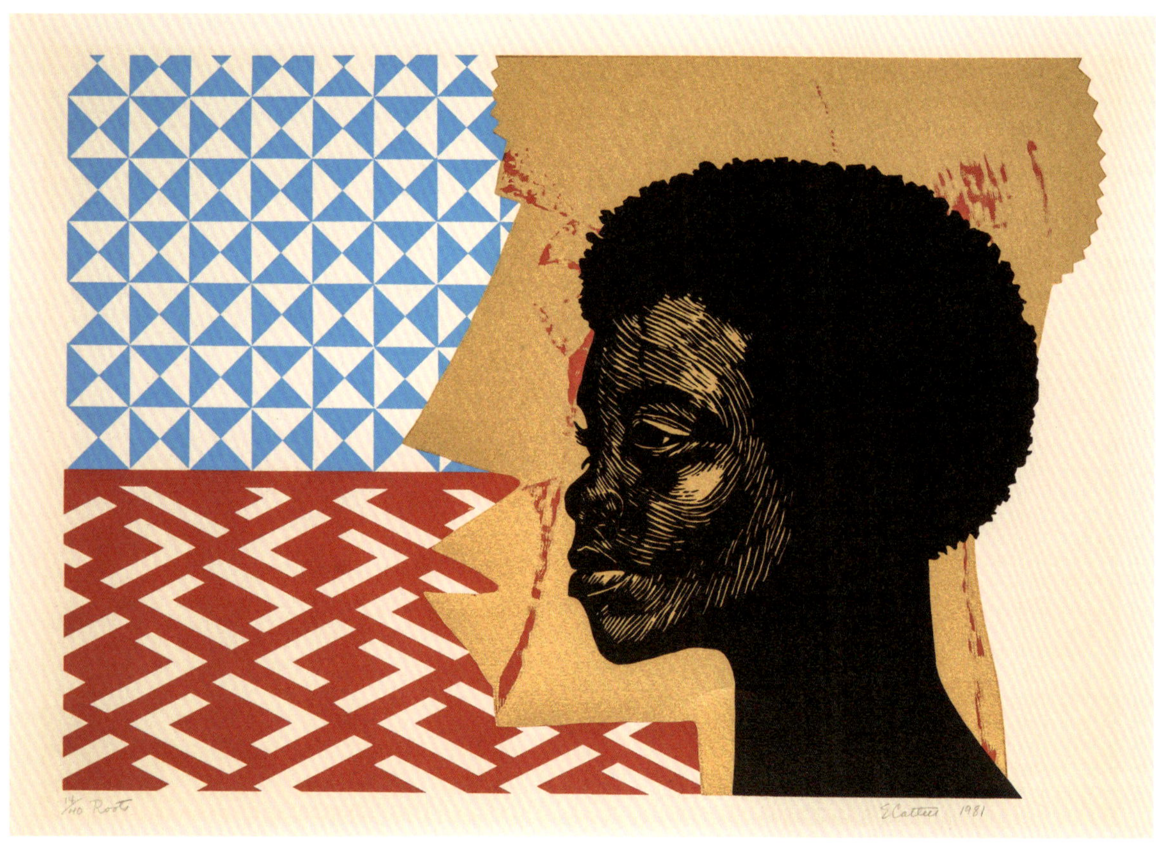

Singing Head, 1980, black Mexican marble, 16 × 9½ × 12 in., Smithsonian American Art Museum, Museum purchase

Roots, 1981, screenprint, 14 × 19¾ in., From the Hampton University Museum Collection, Hampton, VA

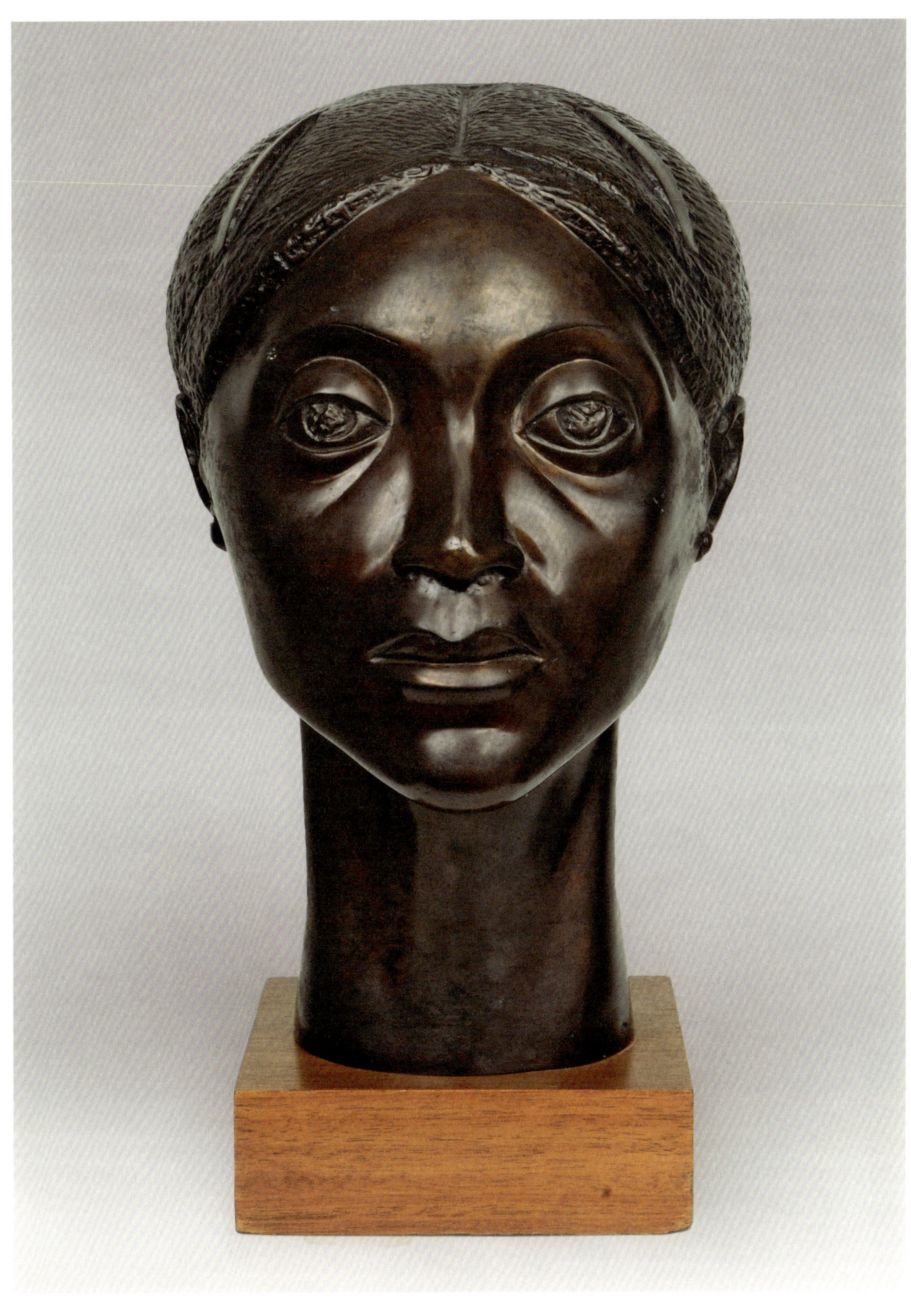

Glory, 1981, cast bronze with a black patina on a wooden base, 14 × 9½ × 10 in., The Ronald W. and Patricia Turner Walters Collection, On loan from the Howard University Gallery of Art

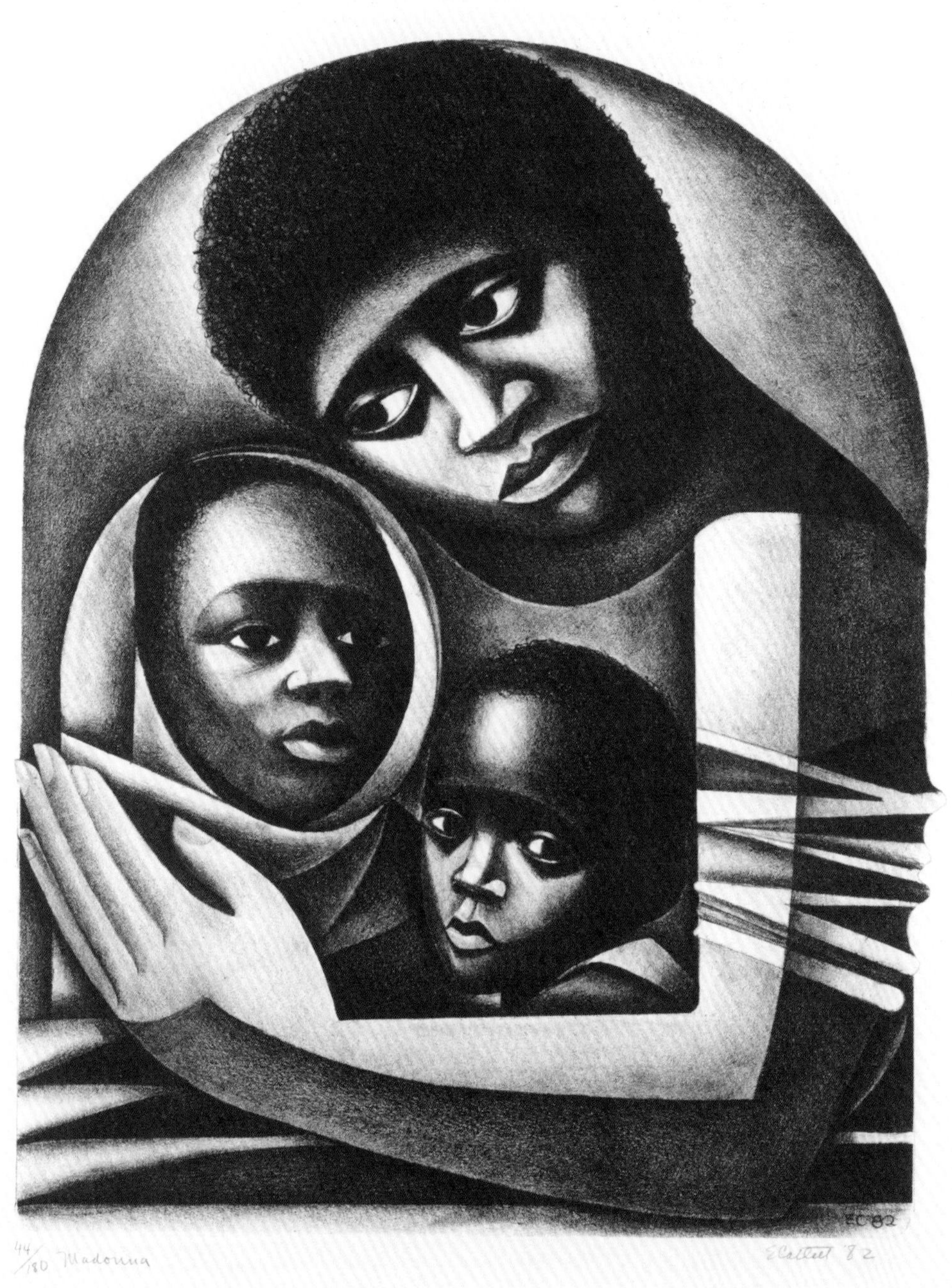

Madonna, 1982, lithograph, 30 × 22¼ in., University of Iowa Stanley Museum of Art, Museum purchase, 2006.66

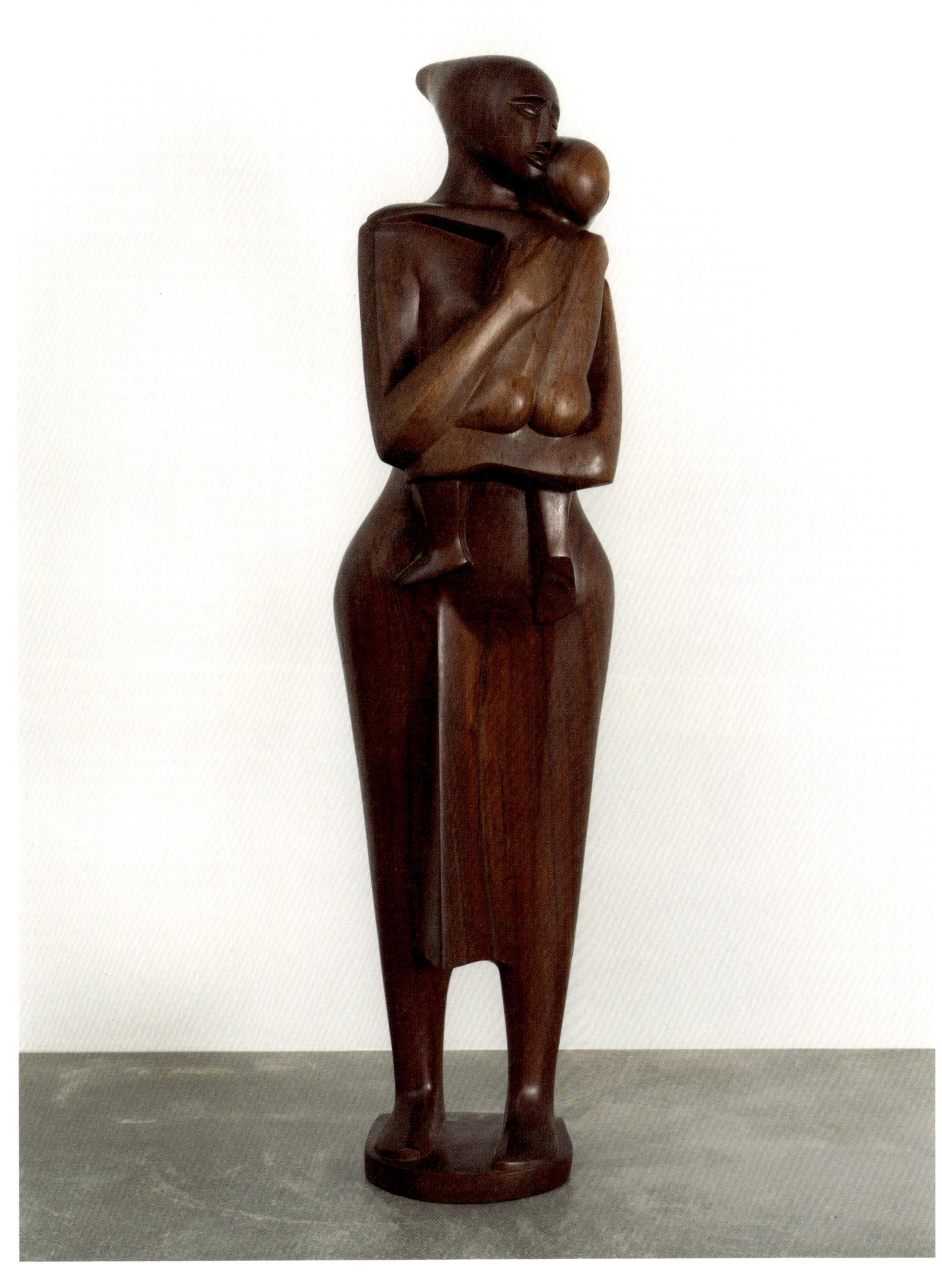

Mother and Child, 1993, mahogany, 67½ × 16½ × 15½ in., The Studio Museum in Harlem, Museum purchase, 1996.13

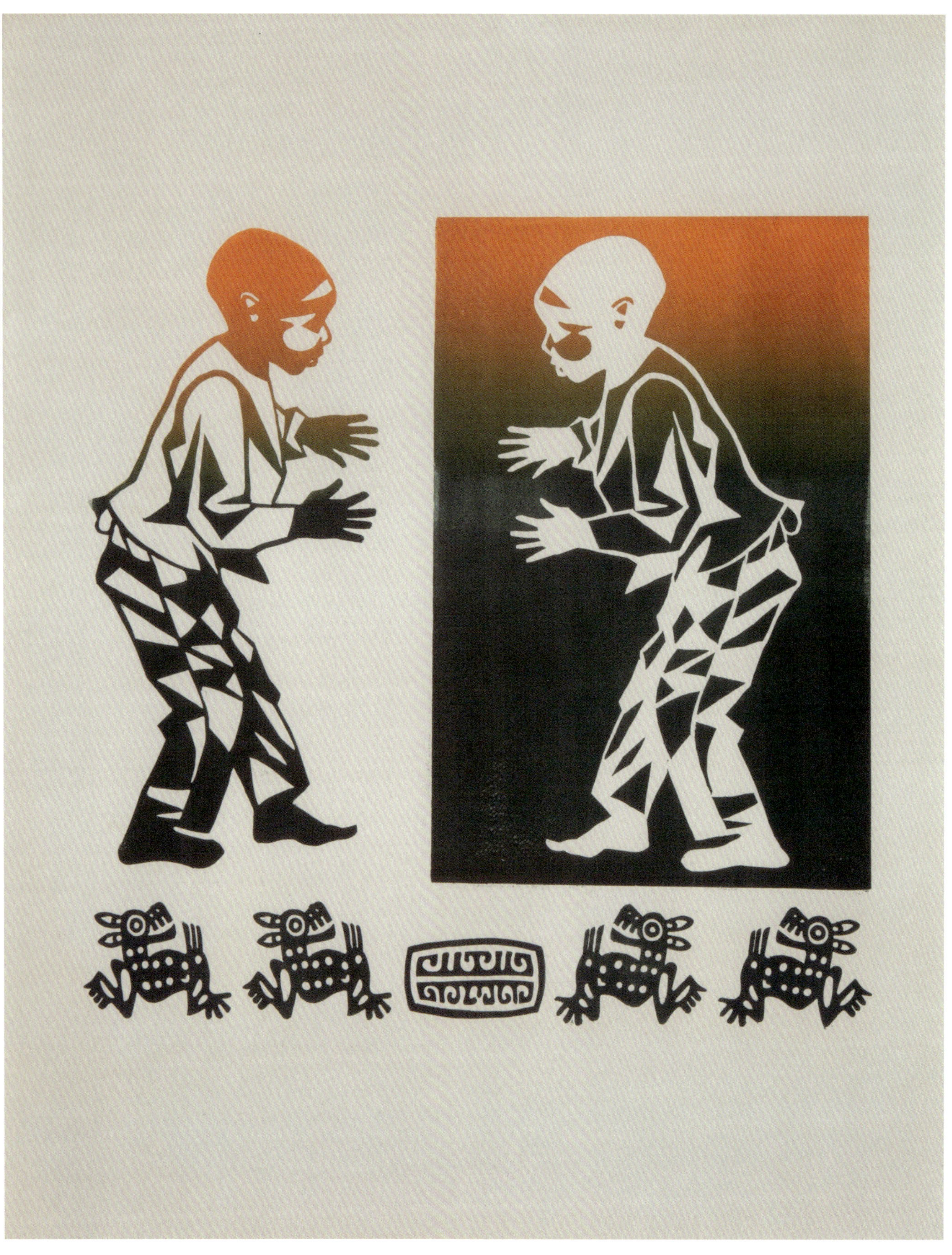

Playing, c. 1983, lithograph, 17 × 16 in., From the Collection of the Elizabeth Catlett-Mora Family Living Trust

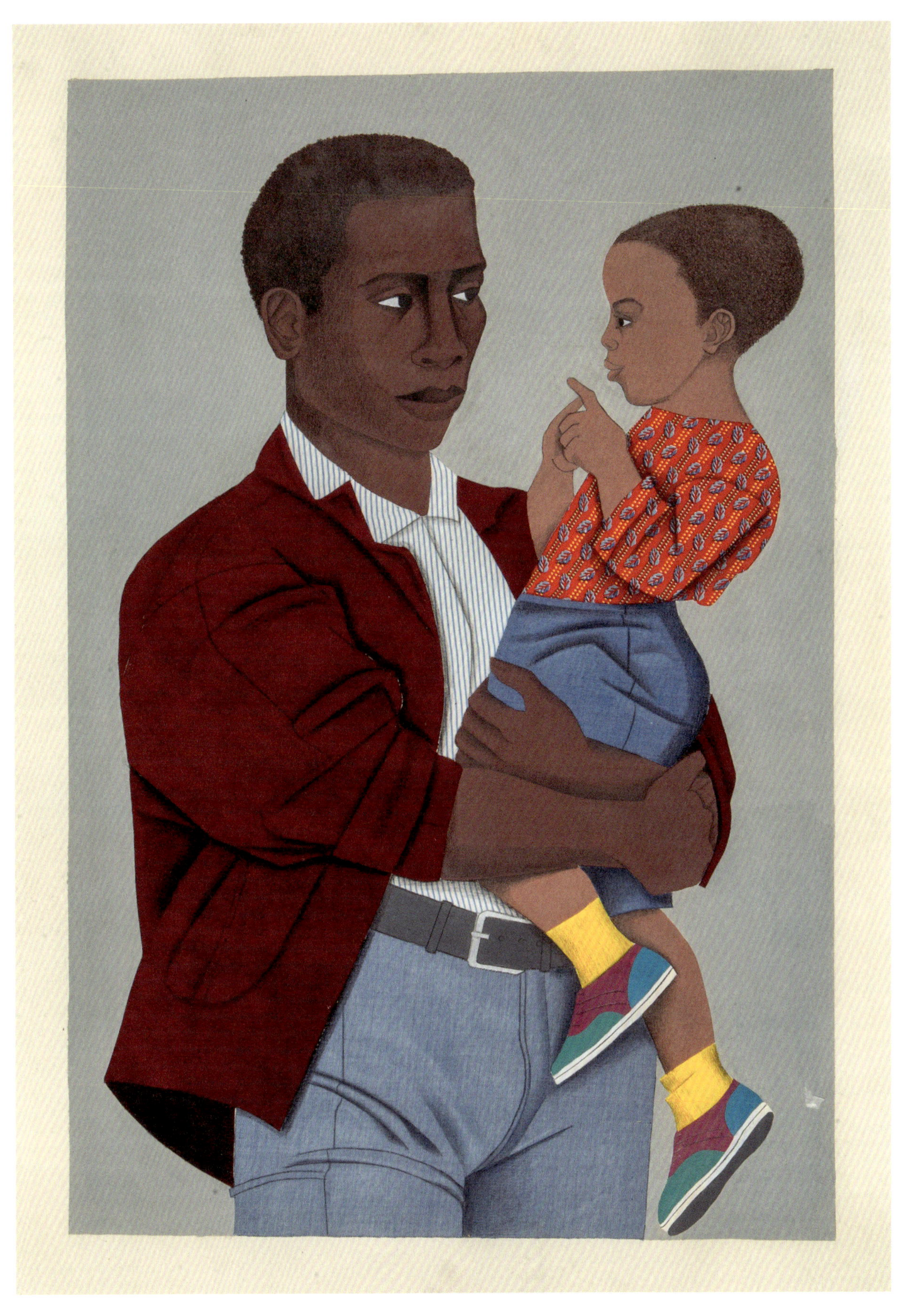

Collage Maquette for Father and Son, c. 1992, paint or ink (?) and fabric collage, 35 × 24 in., From the Collection of the Elizabeth Catlett-Mora Family Living Trust

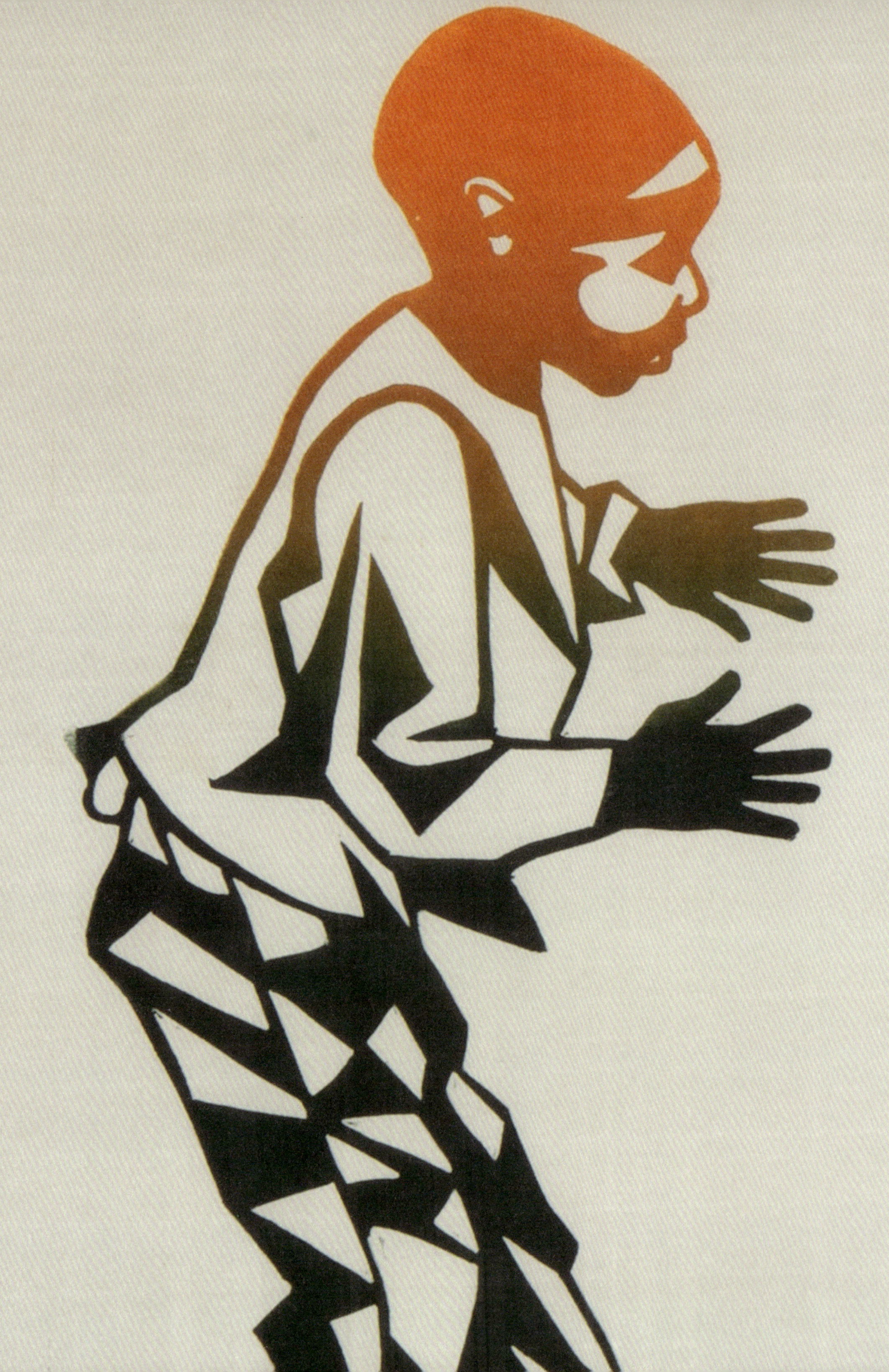

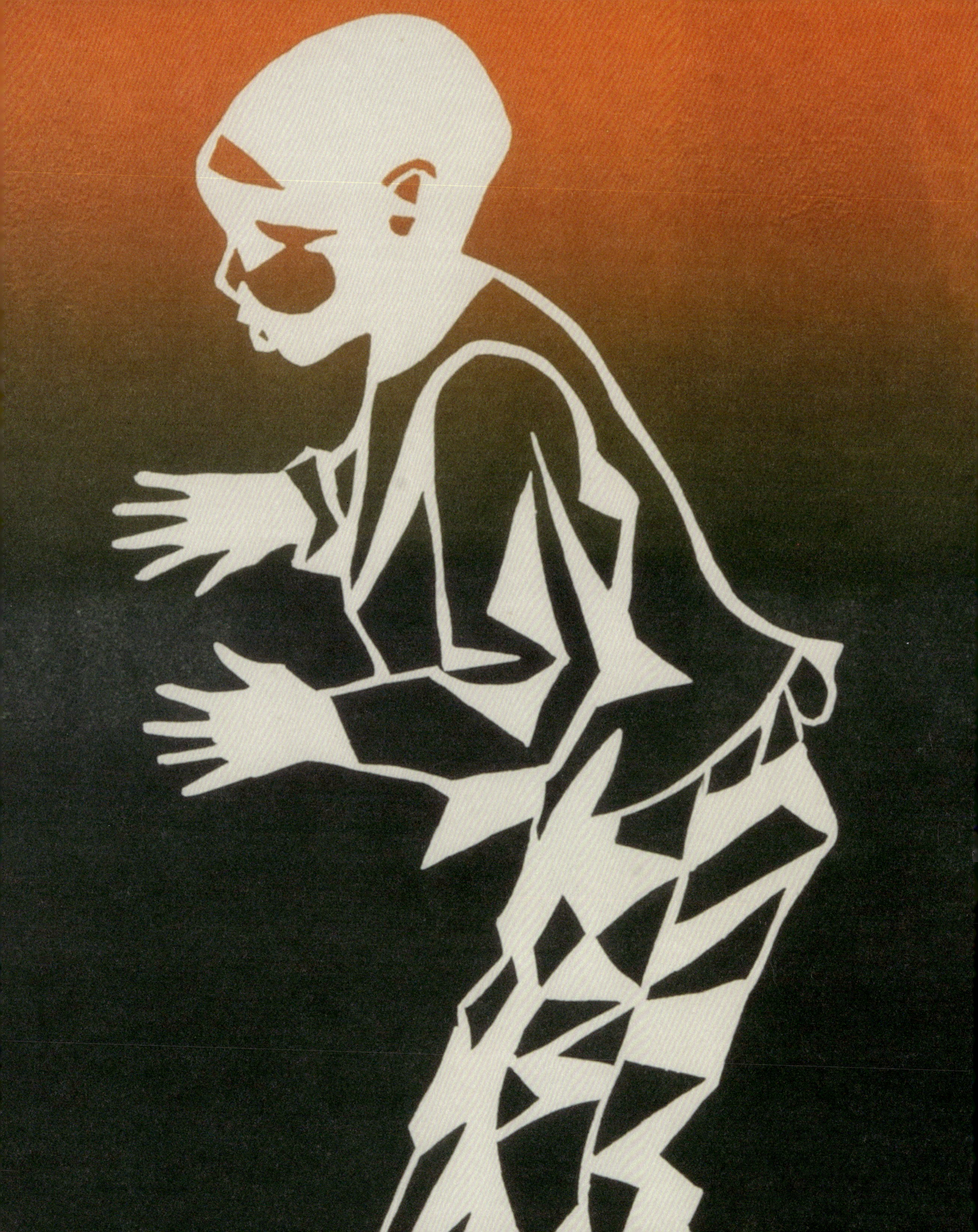

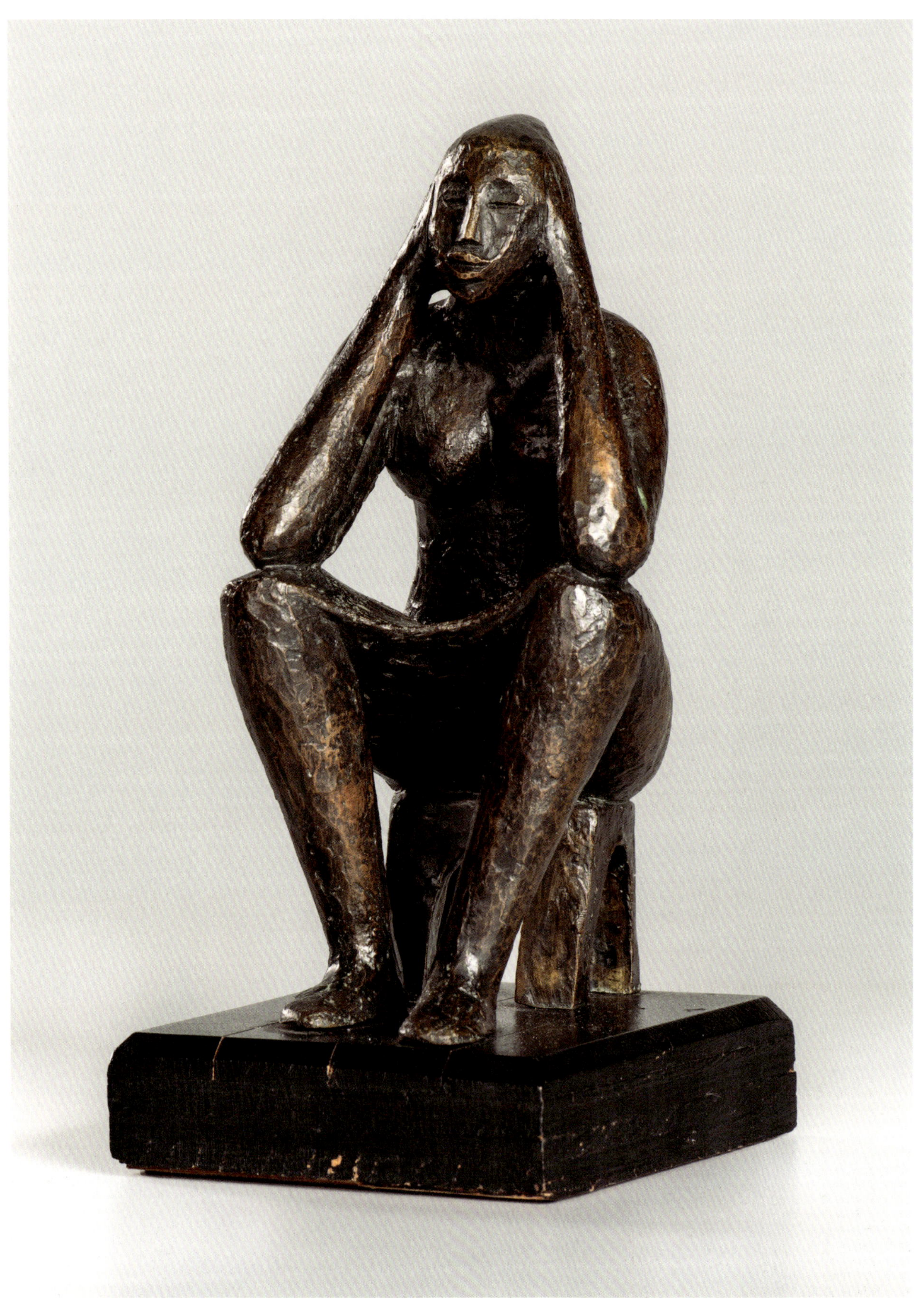

Seated Figure with Hands to Head, c. 1984, bronze, 8⁵⁄₁₆ × 3⅝ × 4½ in., Sidney and Lois Eskenazi Museum of Art

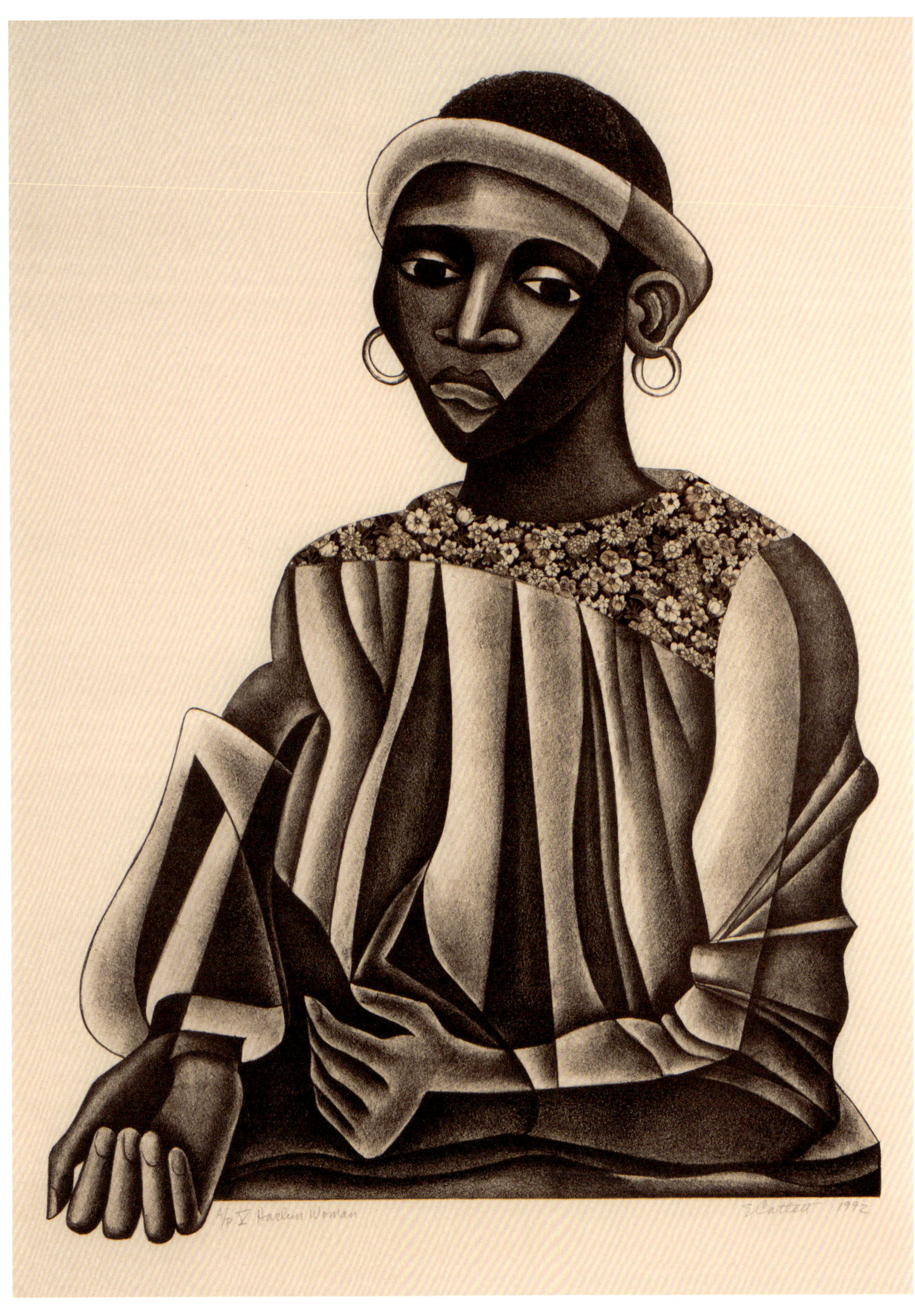

Harlem Woman, 1992, color lithograph with fabric collage, 28 × 21 in., Gabriel Tenabe and Monilola Tenabe

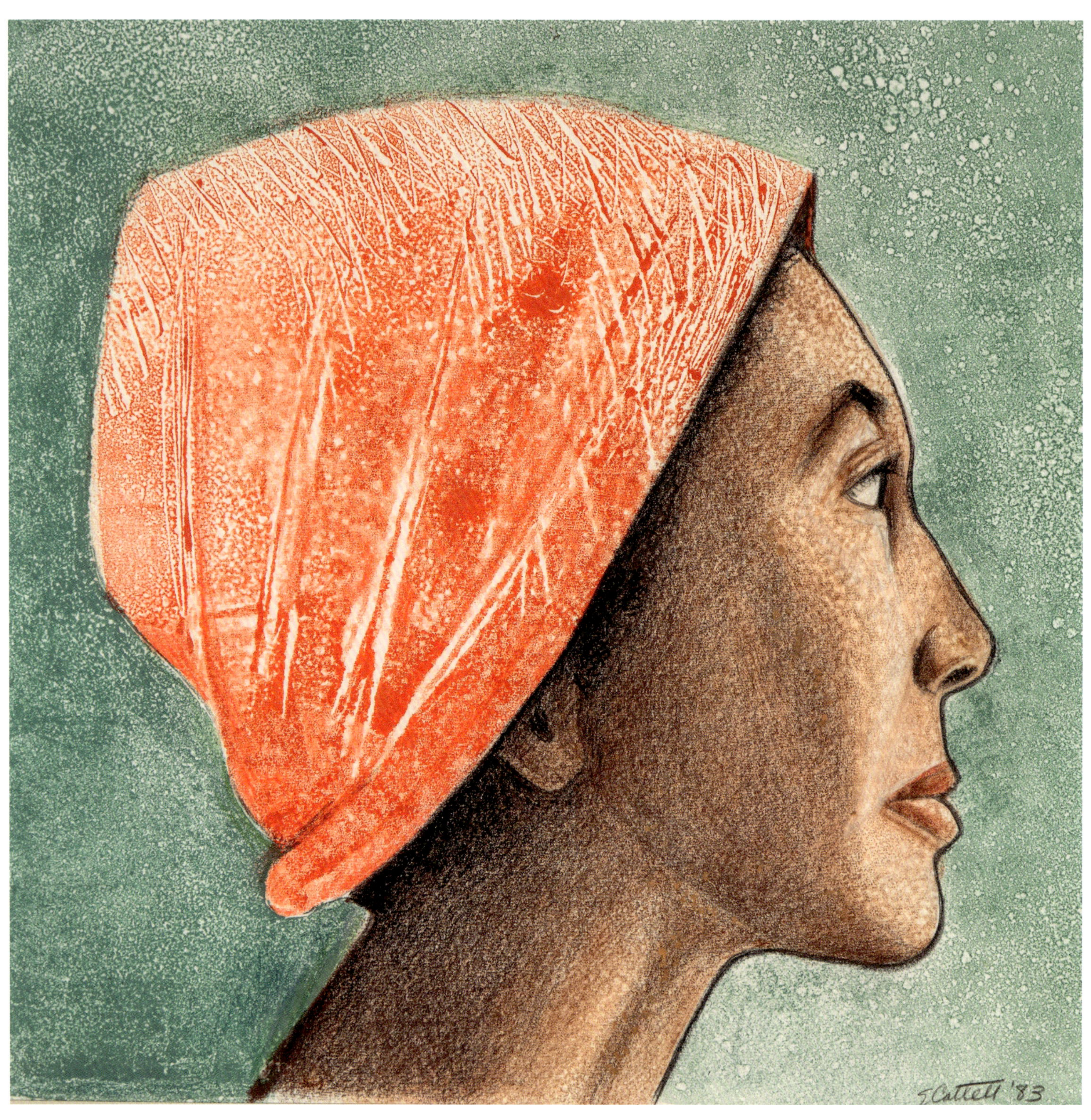

Terry, 1983, monoprint, 29⅞ × 27⅞ in., From the Hampton University Museum Collection, Hampton, VA

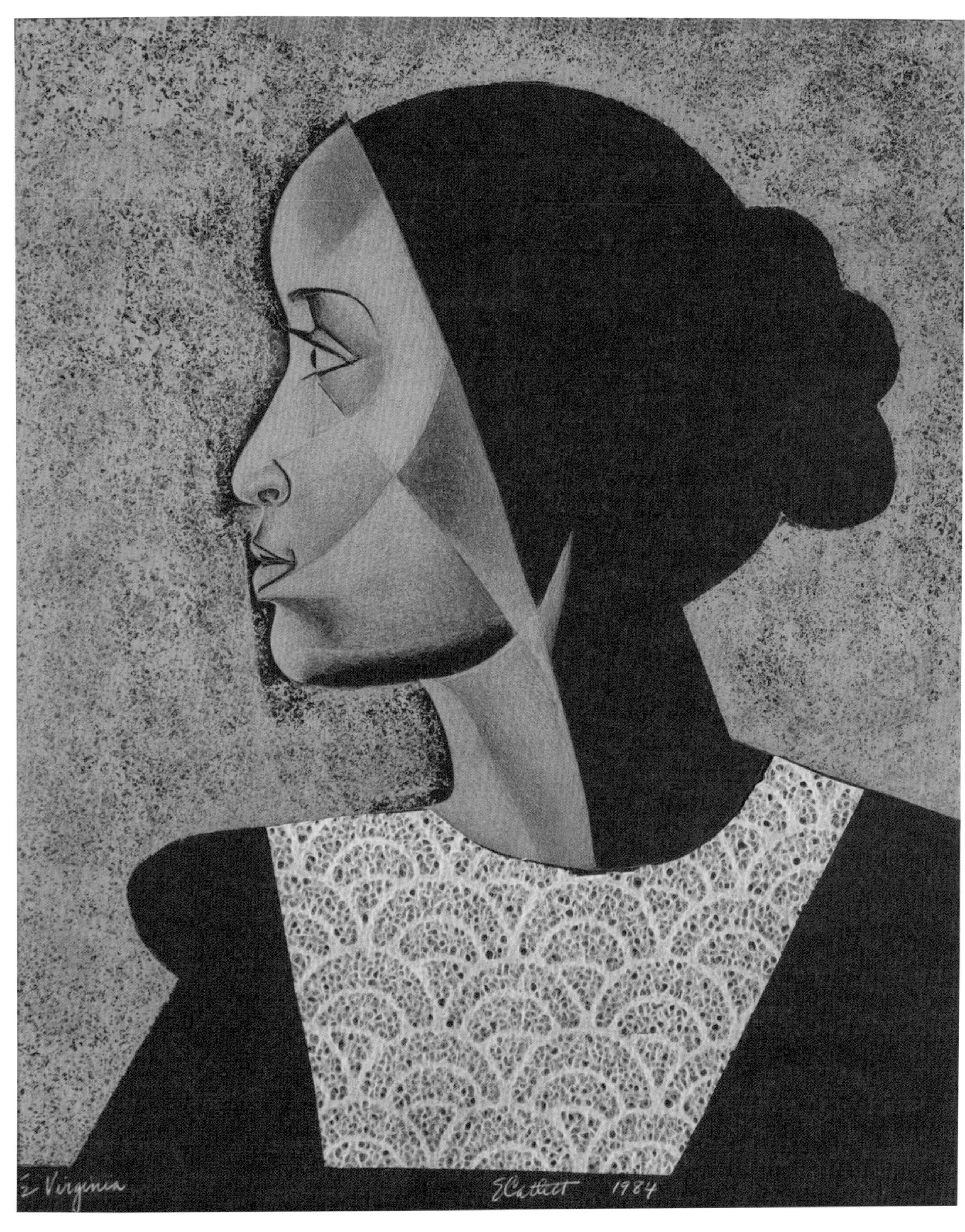

Virginia, 1984, lithograph printed in blue and collage on black wove paper, 22 × 15 in., From the Hampton University Museum Collection, Hampton, VA

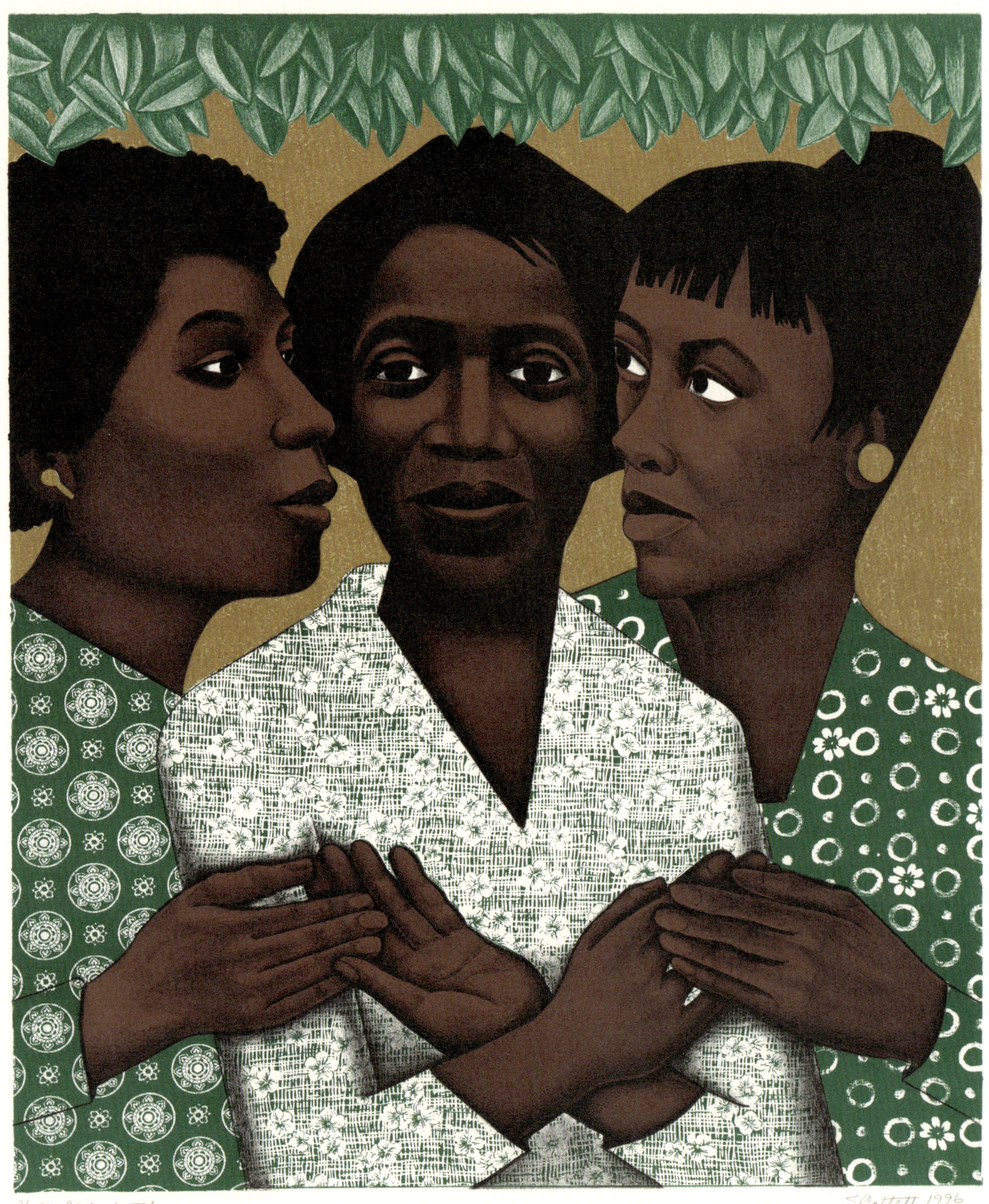

Links Together, 1996, lithograph on wove Arches paper, $29\frac{5}{16} \times 22\frac{15}{16}$ in., National Gallery of Art, Purchased as the Gift of Art Information Volunteers in Honor of Dianne Stephens

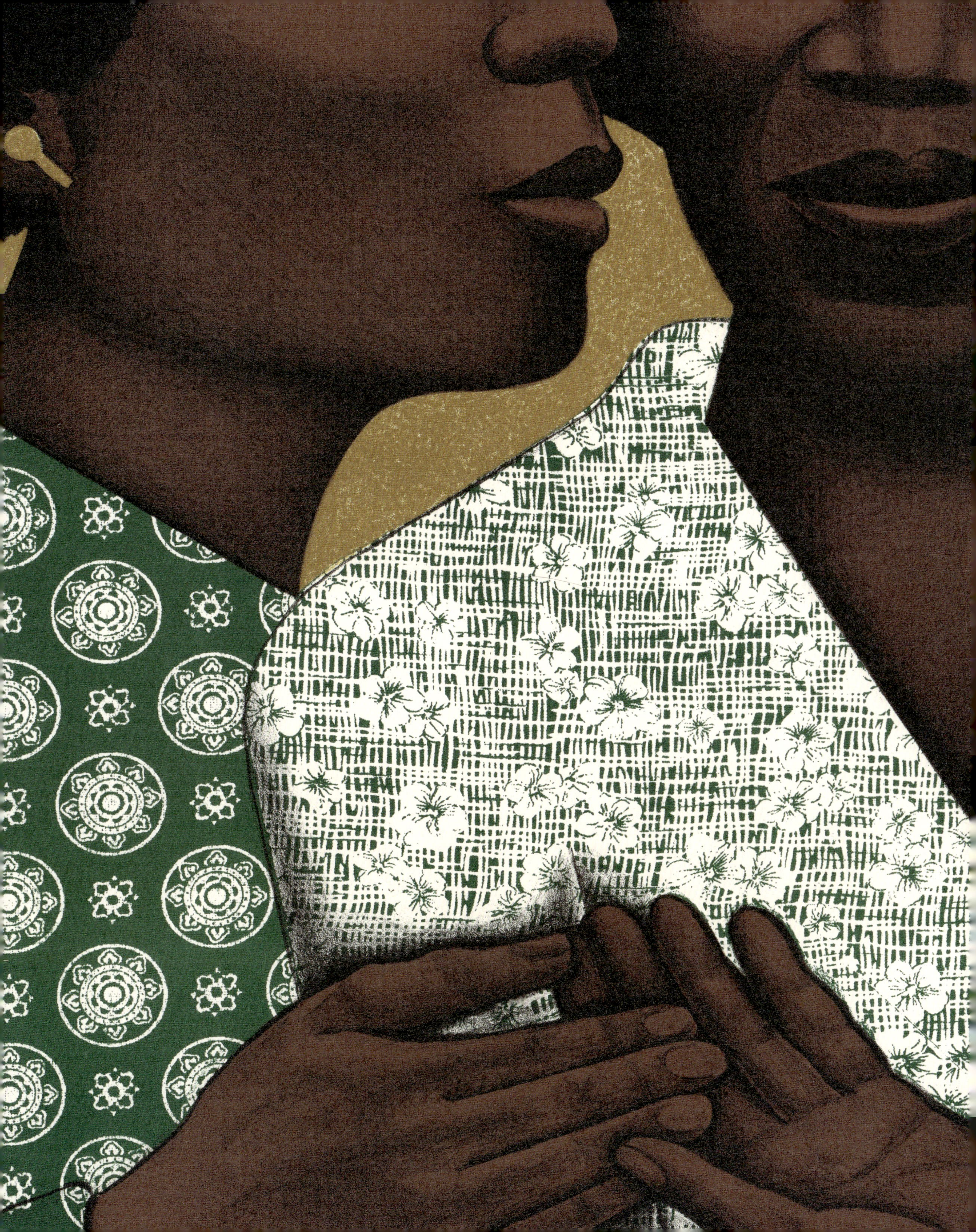

Jaime Torres Bodet and José Vasconcelos, 1981, in situ photograph, Secretaria de Educación Pública, Mexico City

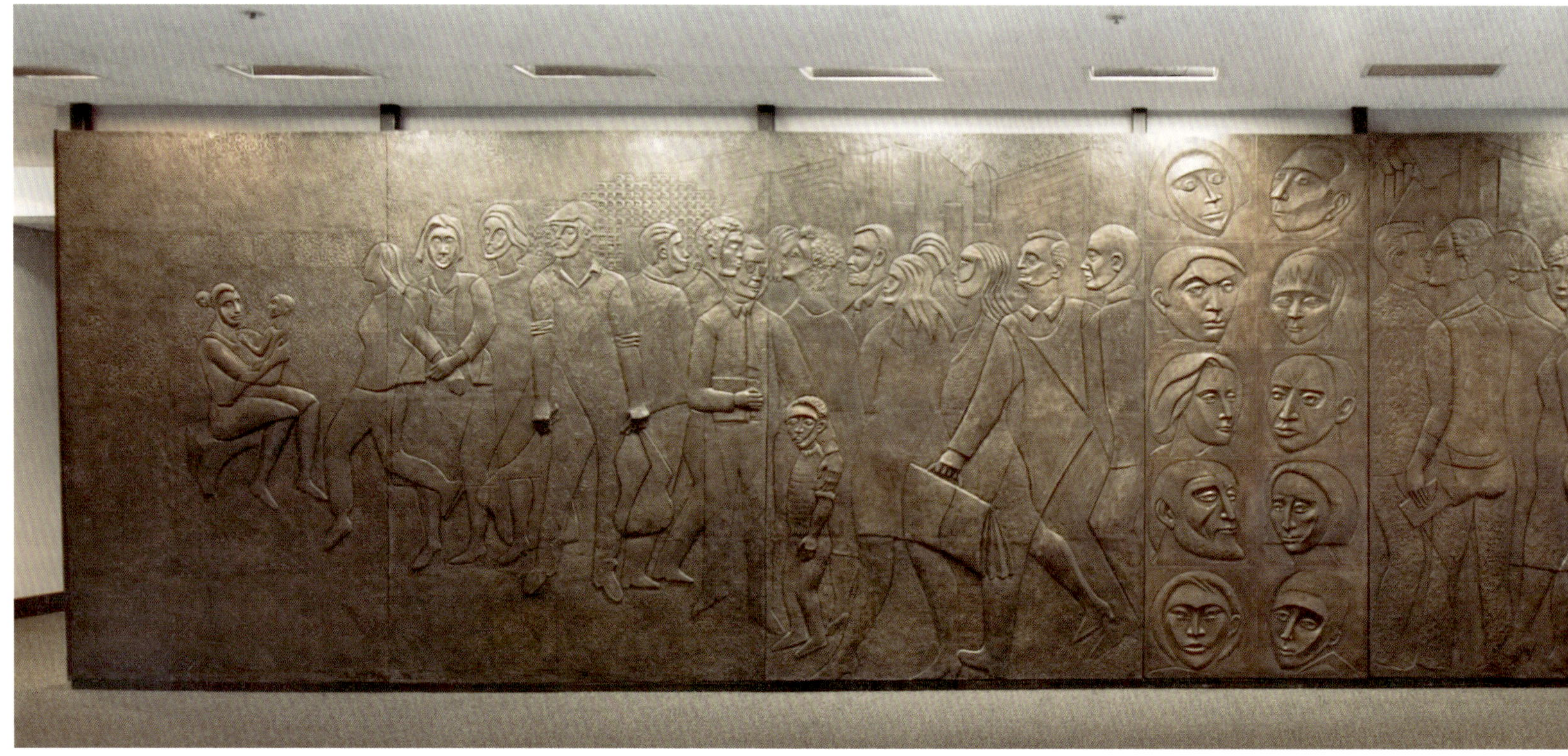

People of Atlanta, 1989–1991, bronze relief, in situ photograph at Atlanta City Hall, 55 Trinity Avenue, City of Atlanta, Mayor's Office of Cultural Affairs

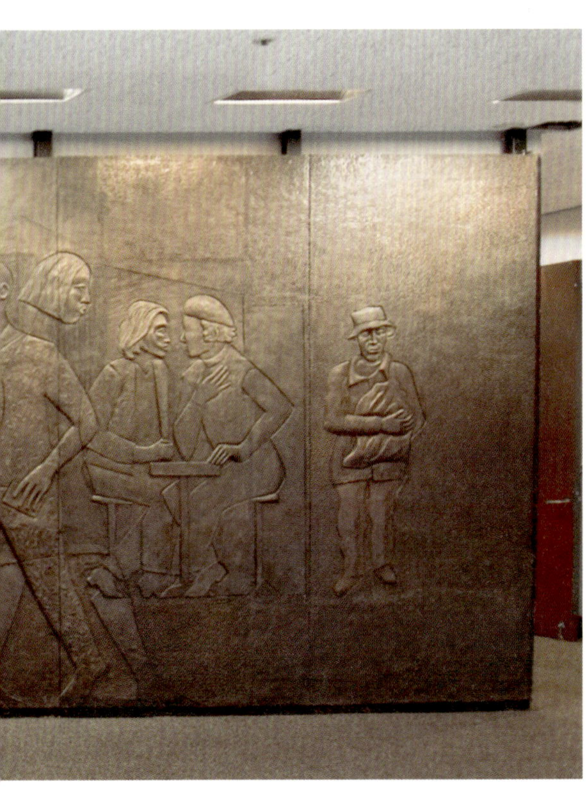

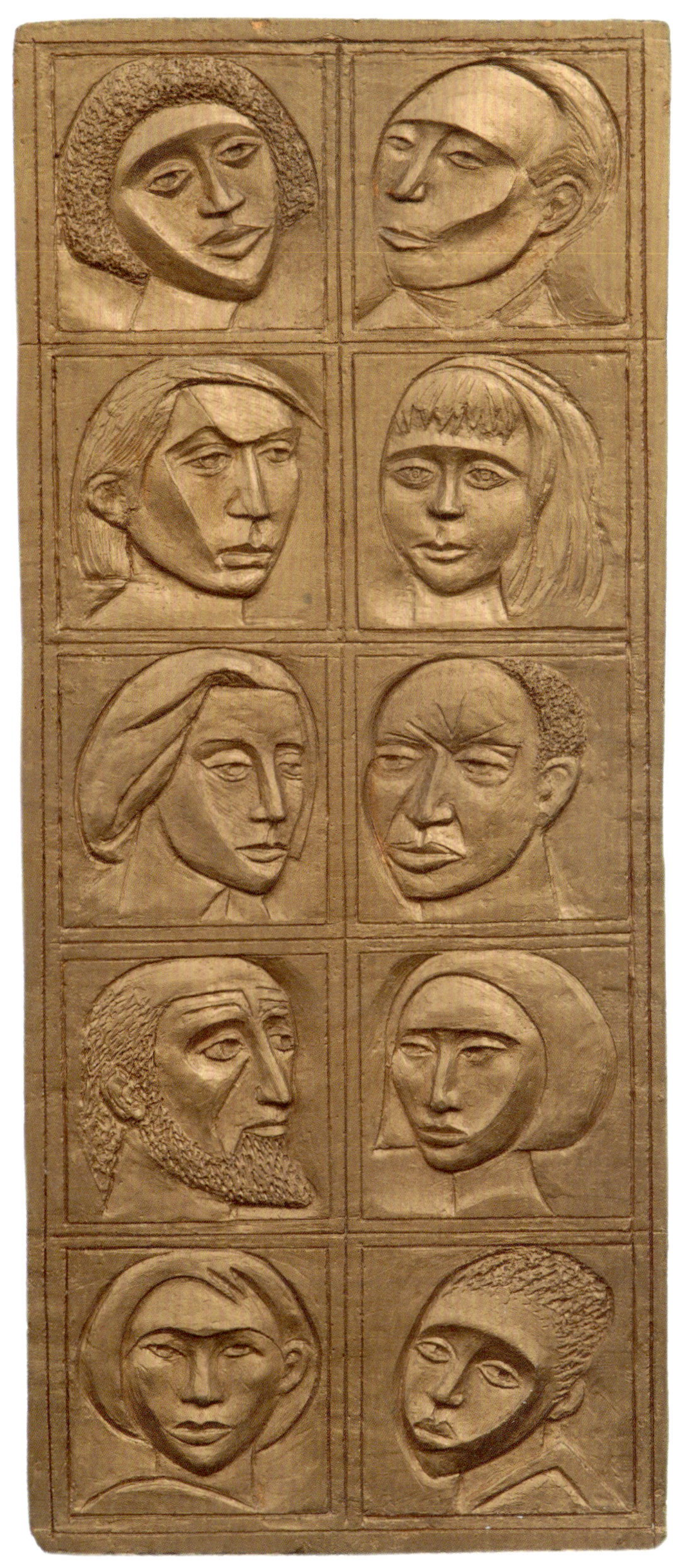

Relief Study (Sculptural Sketch of *People of Atlanta*), 1989–1990, plaster, 20¾ × 8¾ in., City of Atlanta, Mayor's Office of Cultural Affairs

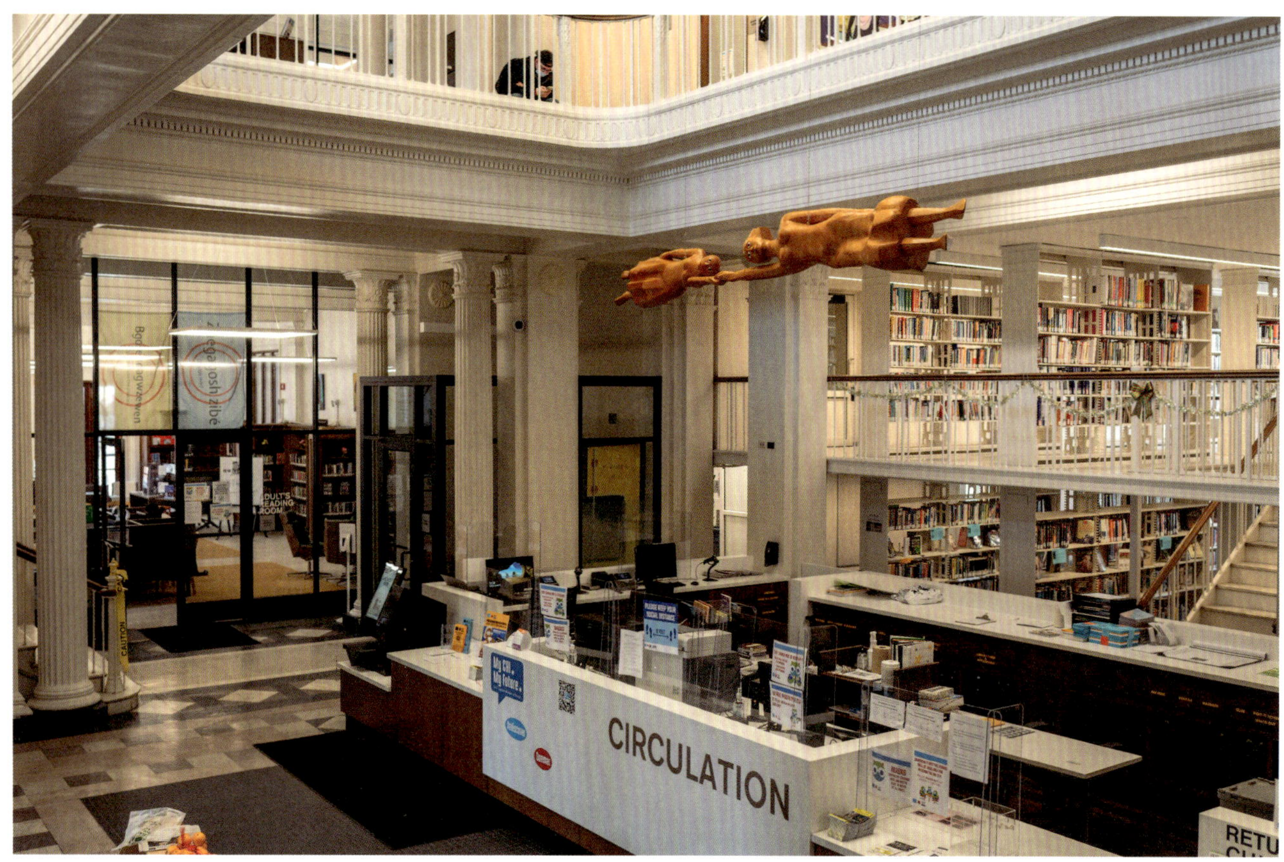
CIRCULATION

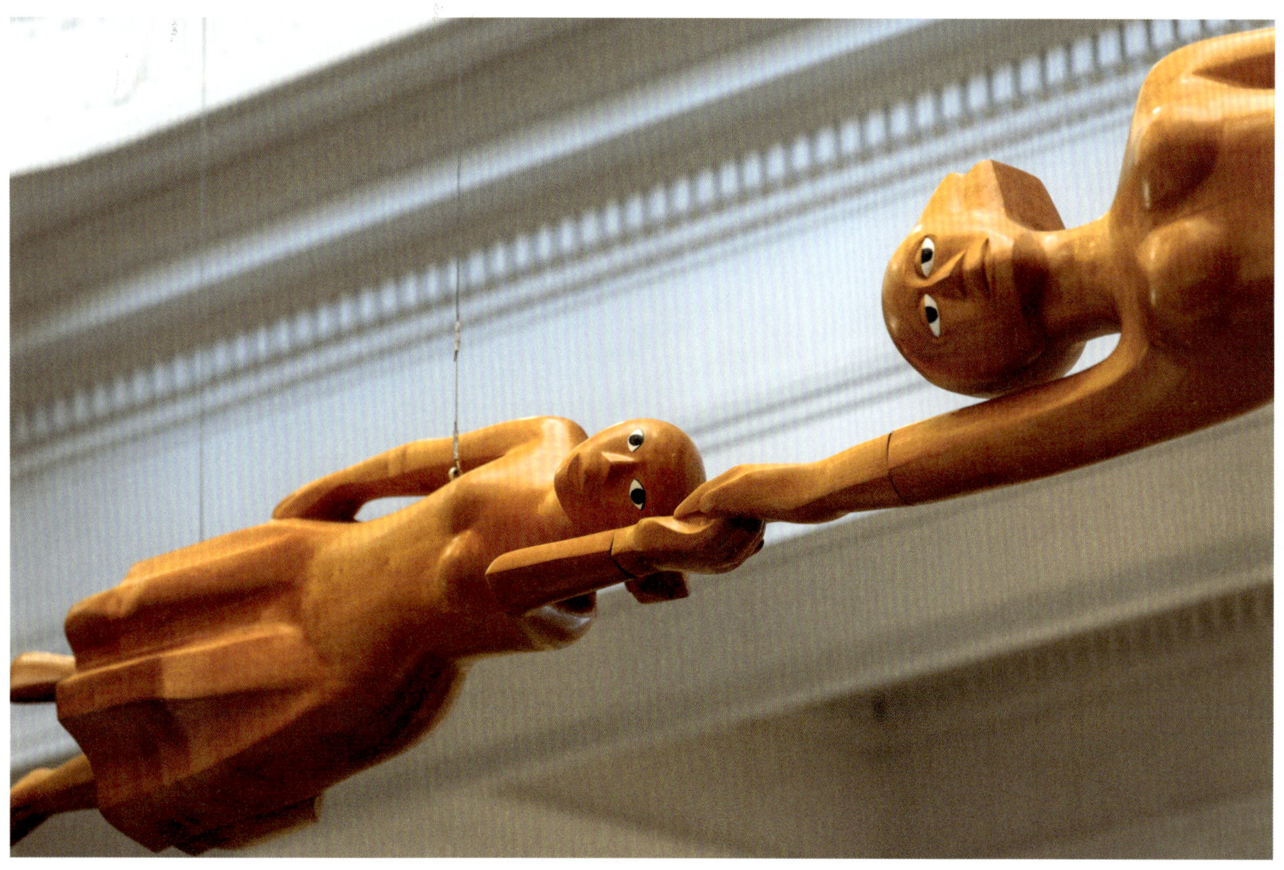

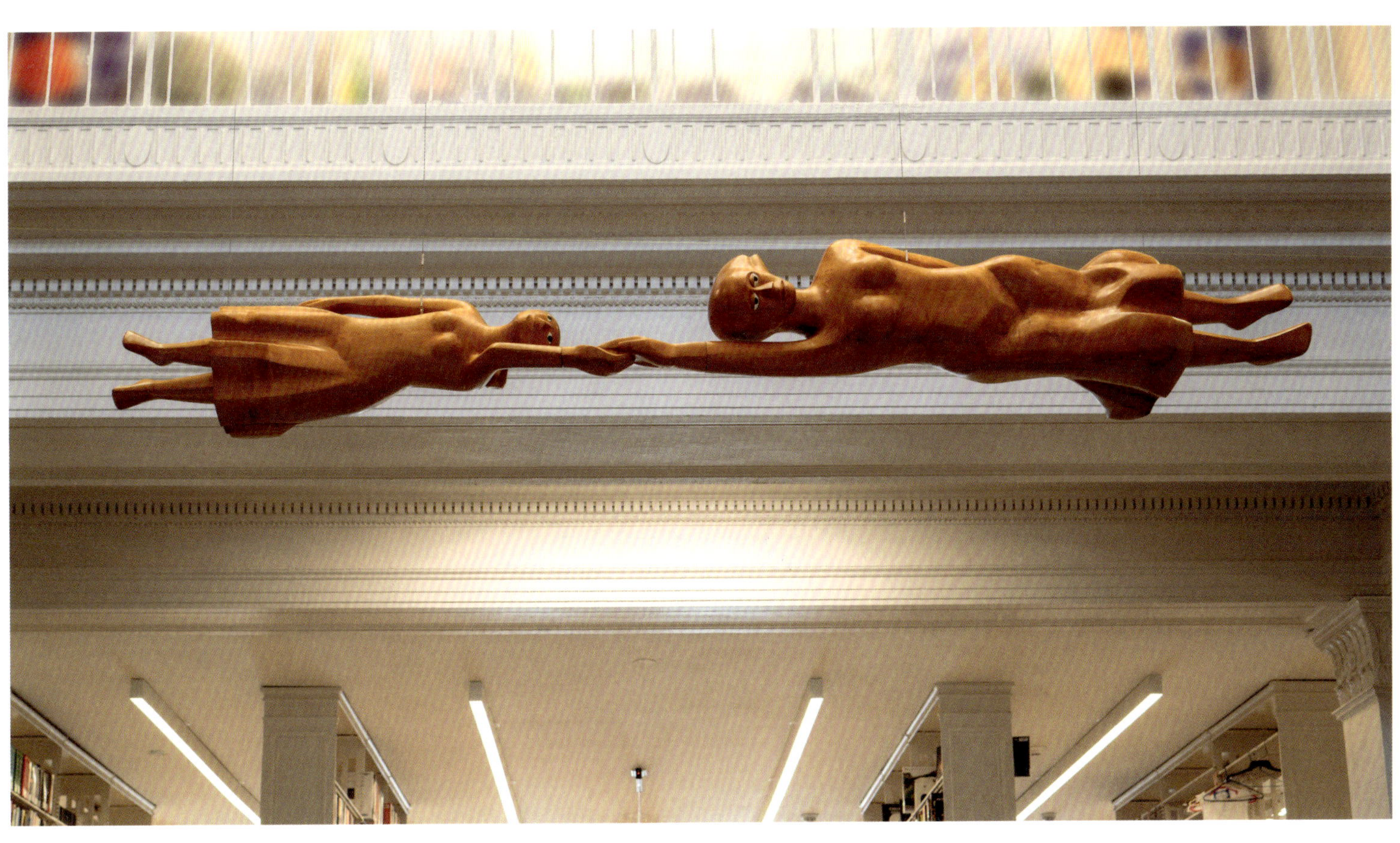

Floating Family, 1995, primavera wood, in situ photograph, Legler Regional Library, Chicago Public Library

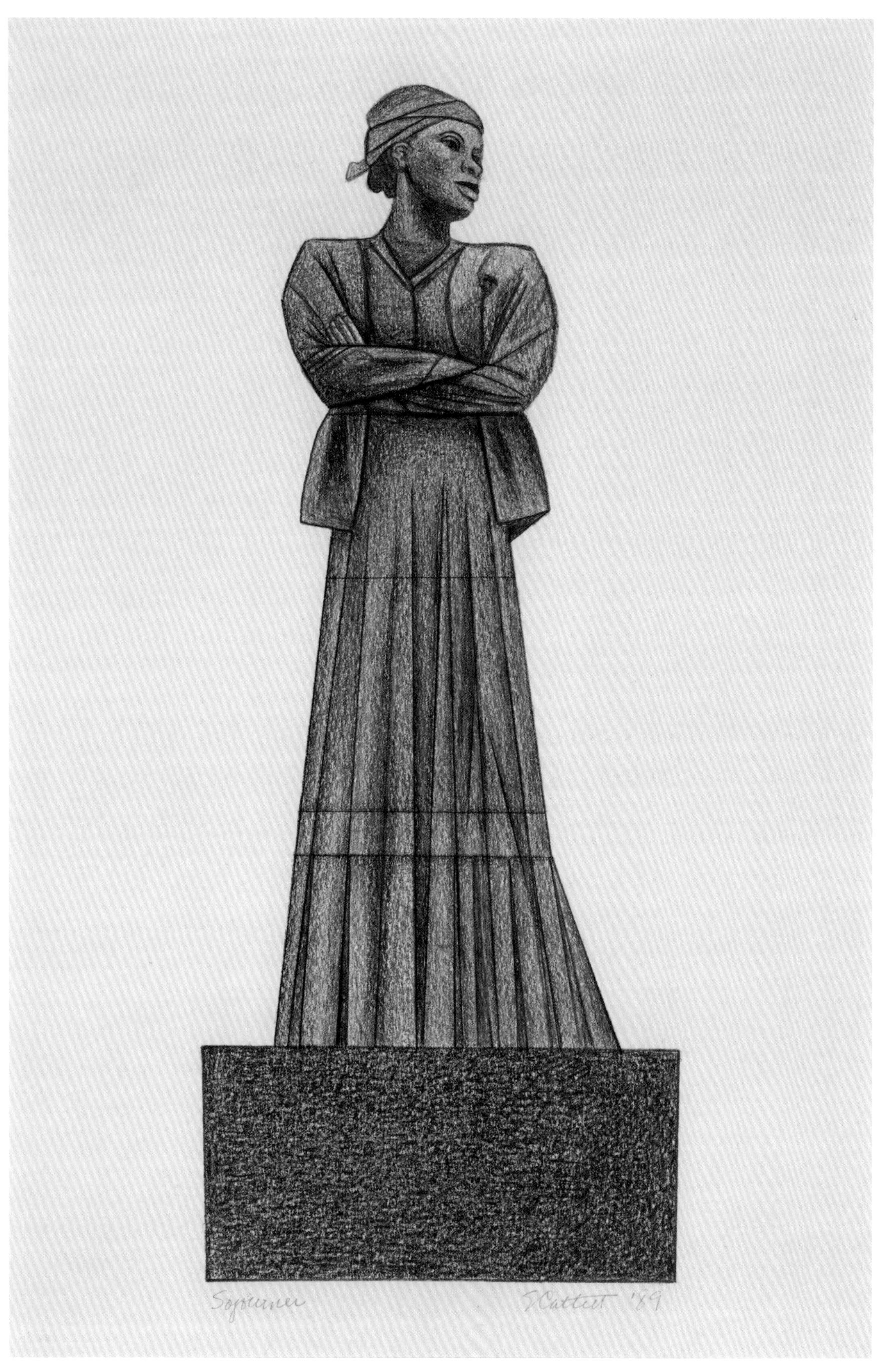

Sketch for Sojourner, 1989, graphite, 11½ × 7 in., Geryll Robinson and Deanna Downes

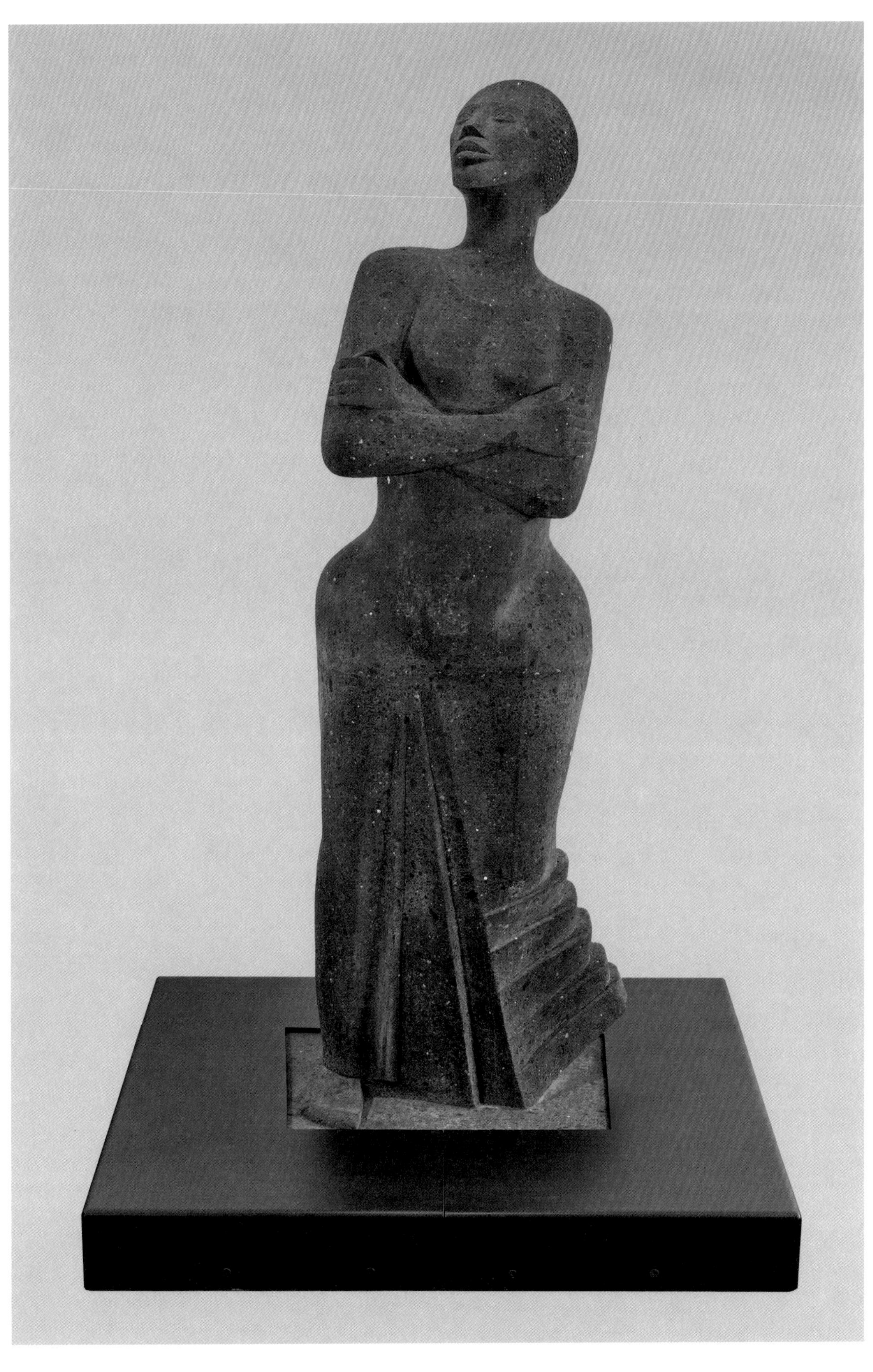

Sojourner, 1999, porous volcanic stone (possibly basalt), Crocker Art Museum, Gift of the Sacramento Metropolitan Arts Commission, 2017.68

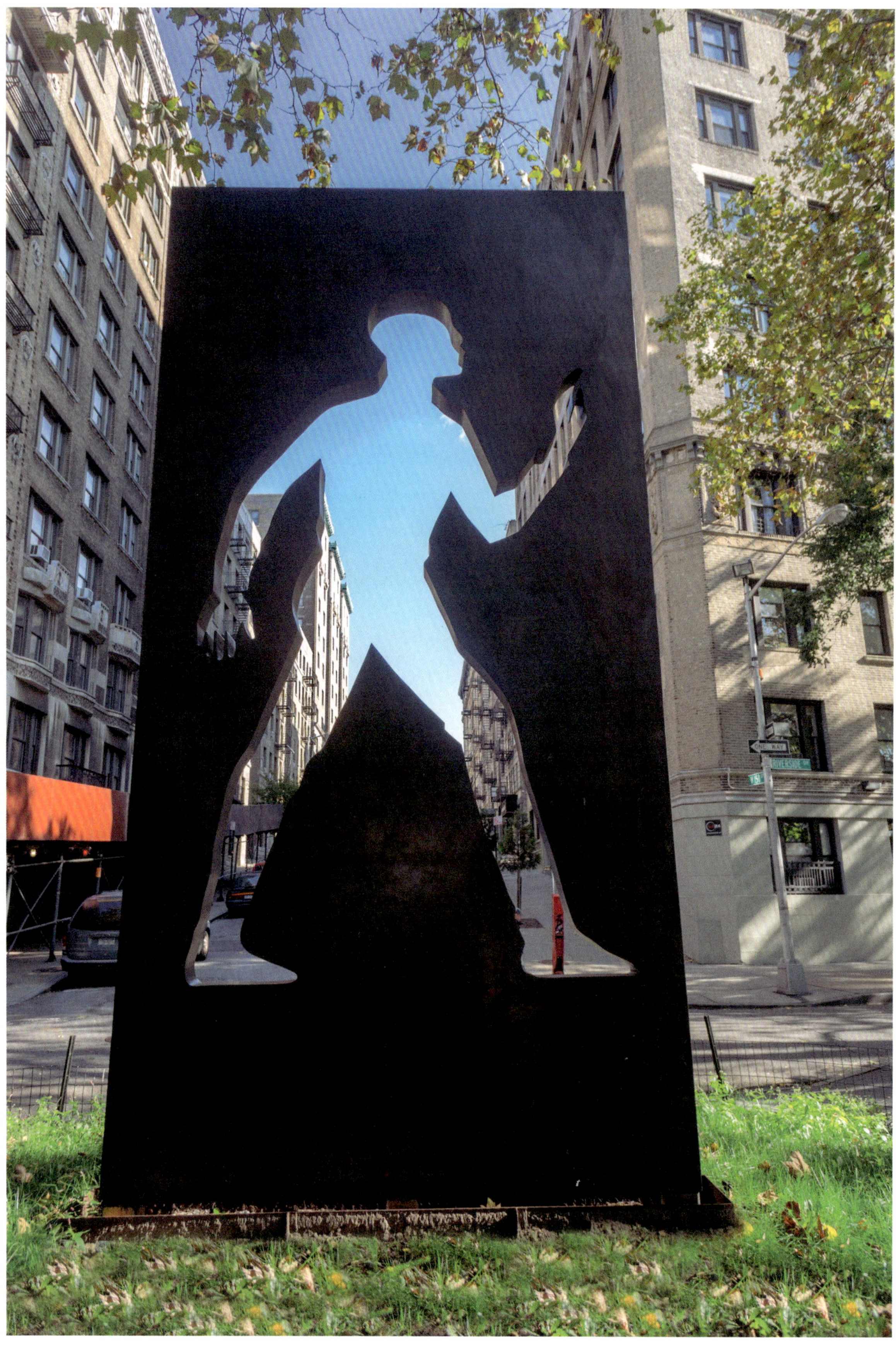

Ralph Ellison Memorial, 2001–2003, bronze, 180 in., in situ photograph taken in 2013, Riverside Drive, Harlem, NY

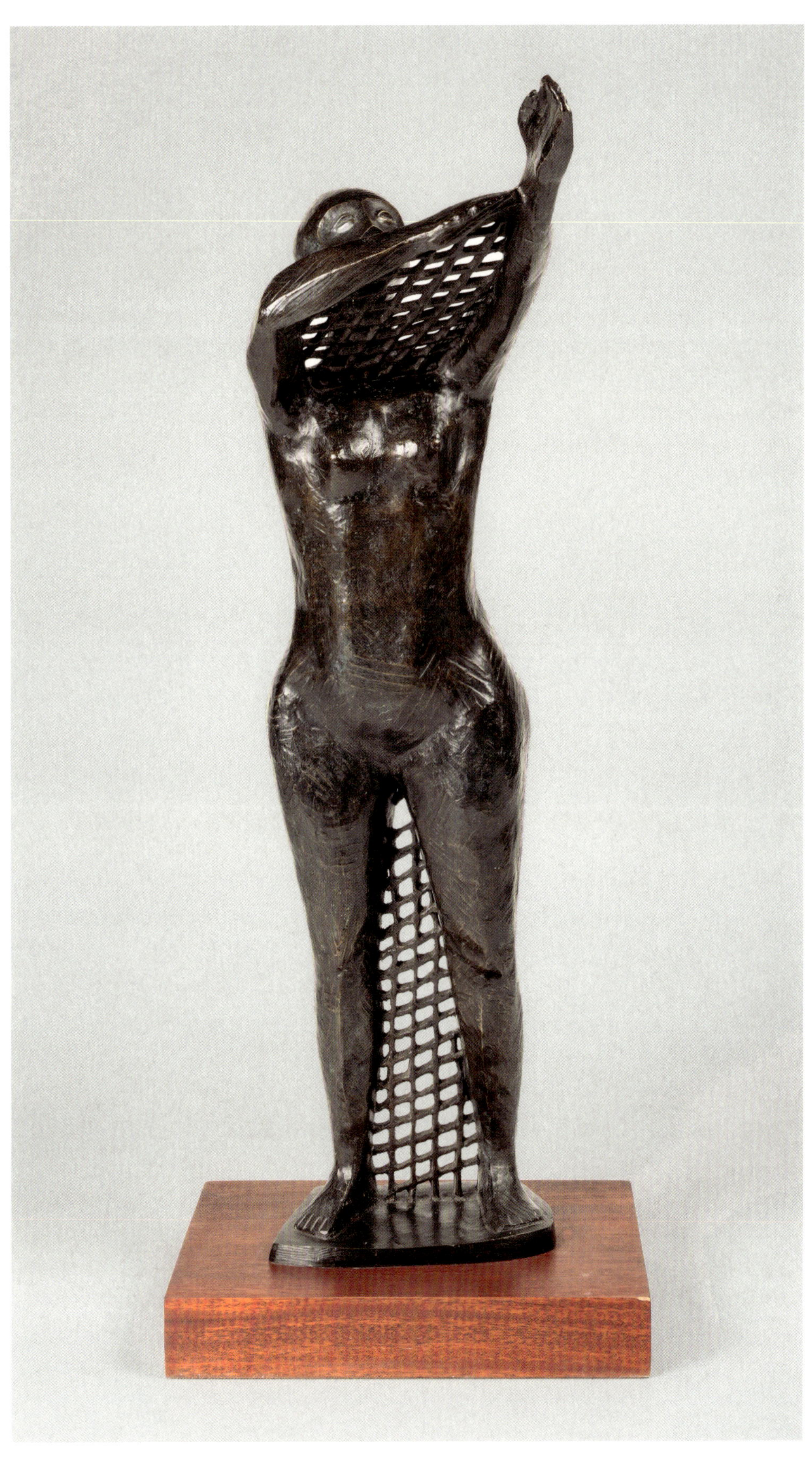

Webbed Woman, 1995, bronze, 39½ × 12 × 16 in., Courtesy of The Elizabeth Catlett Mora Family Living Trust and June Kelly Gallery, New York

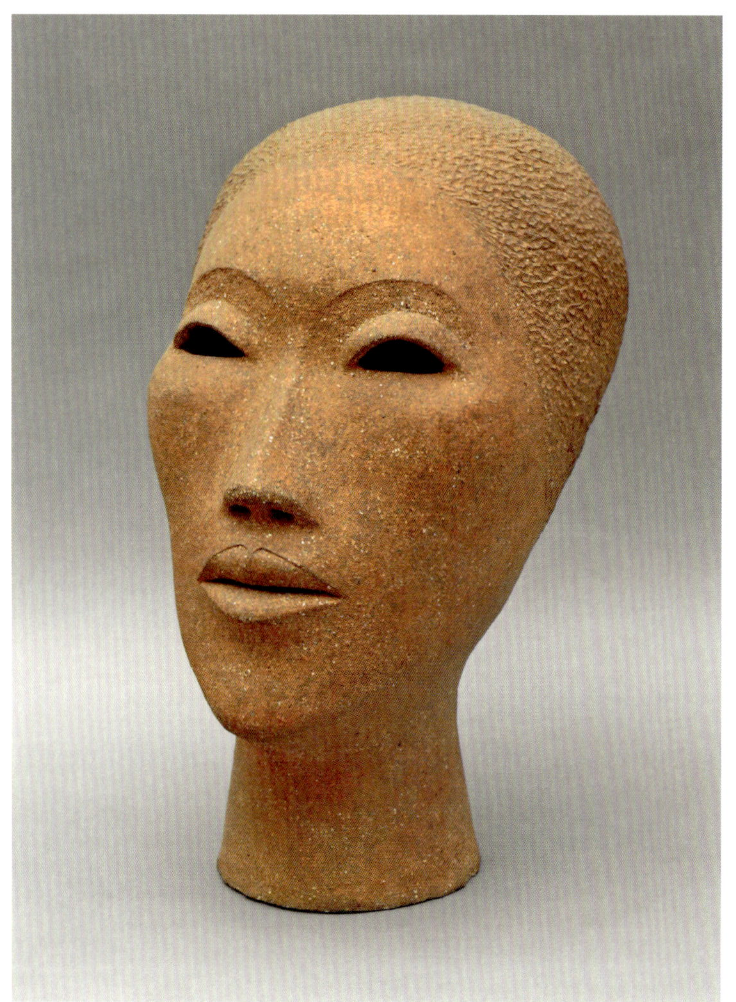

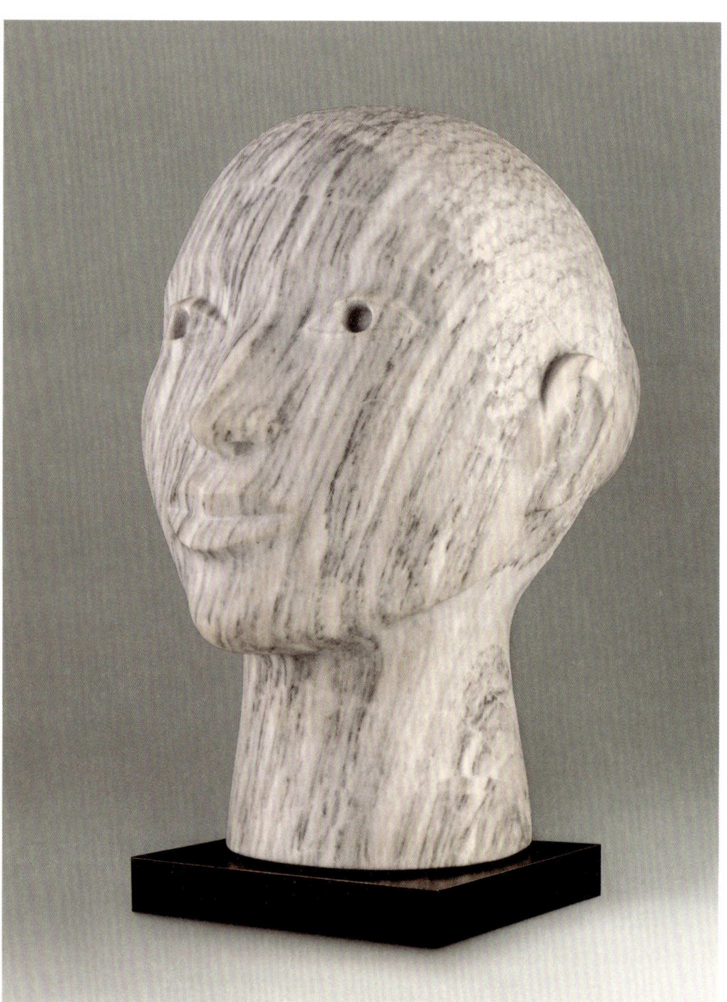

Elvira, 1997, terracotta, 15¾ × 8¼ × 11½ in., The Bronx Museum of the Arts Collection, Purchased with funds from the Ford Foundation, 2013.19

Naima: My Granddaughter, 1998, marble, 13 × 7 × 12 in., Collection of David and Susan Goode

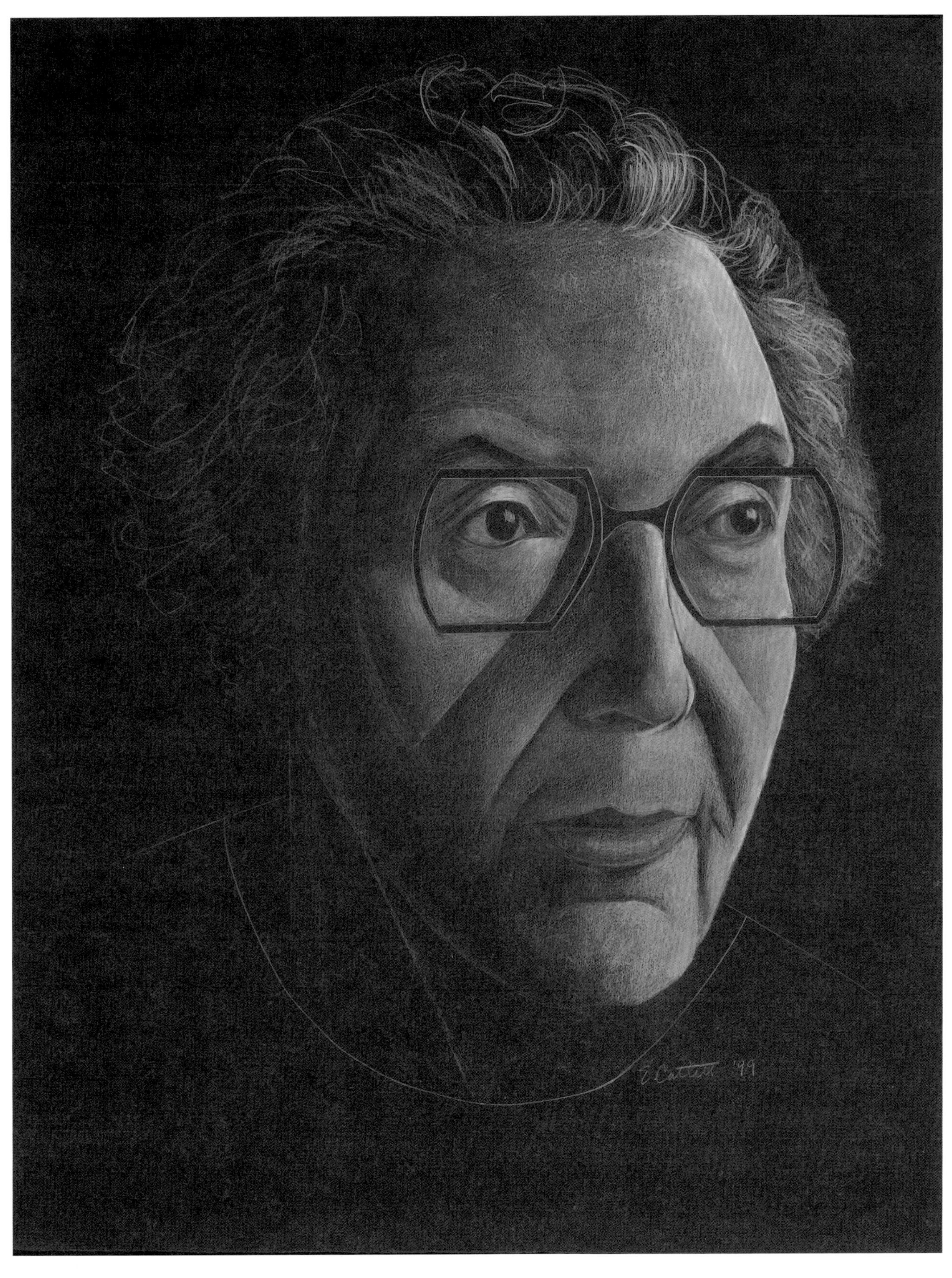

Self-Portrait, 1999, silver pencil on black paper, 24 × 17⅞ in., Courtesy of the Pennsylvania Academy of the Fine Arts, Art by Women Collection, Gift of Linda Lee Alter, 2010.27.5

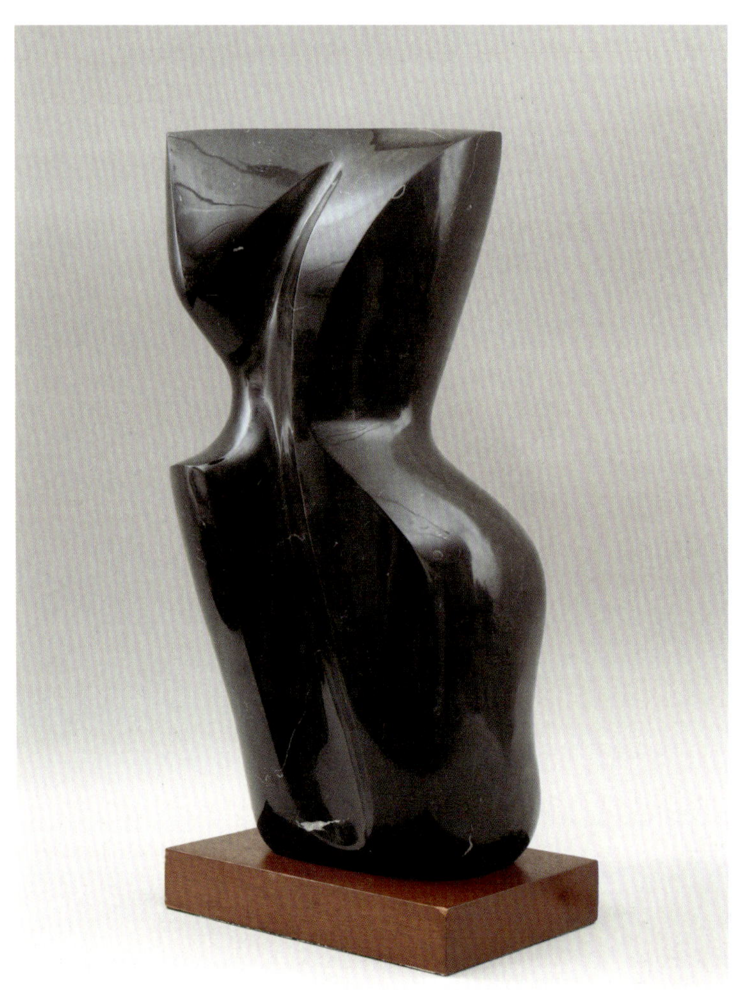

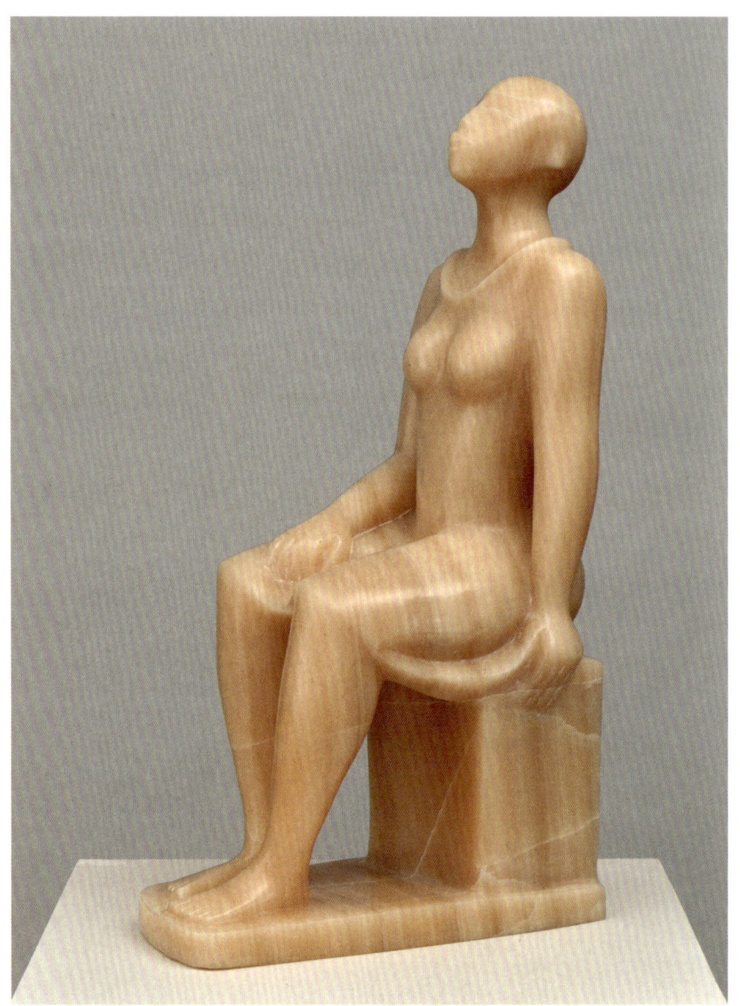

Torso, 2008, black marble, 23½ × 11½ × 8 in., Courtesy of The Elizabeth Catlett Mora Family Living Trust and June Kelly Gallery, New York

Seated Woman, 1993, yellow onyx, 26¾ × 8 × 14⅛ in., Wadsworth Atheneum Museum of Art, Hartford, CT, The Henry D. Miller Fund

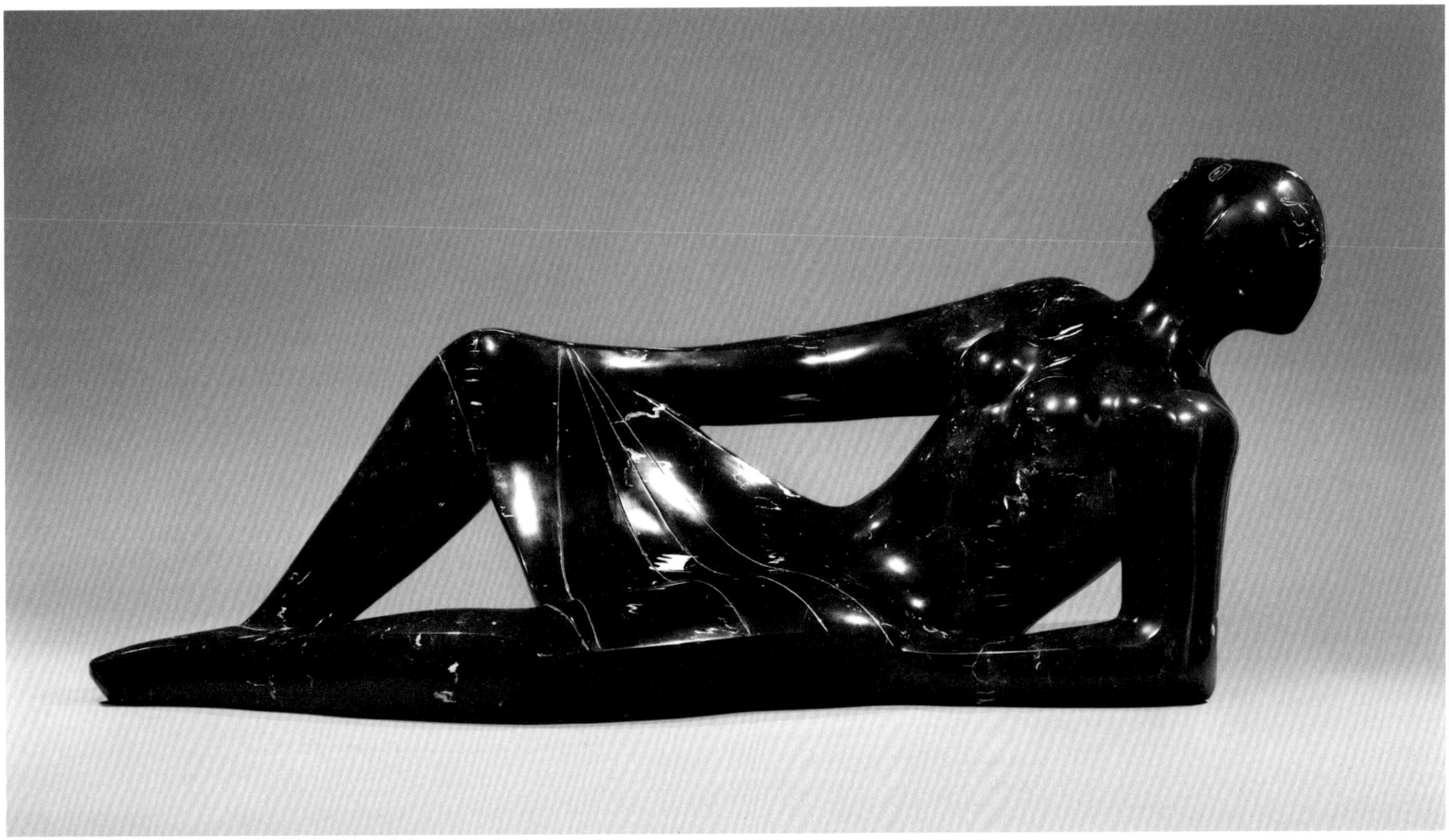

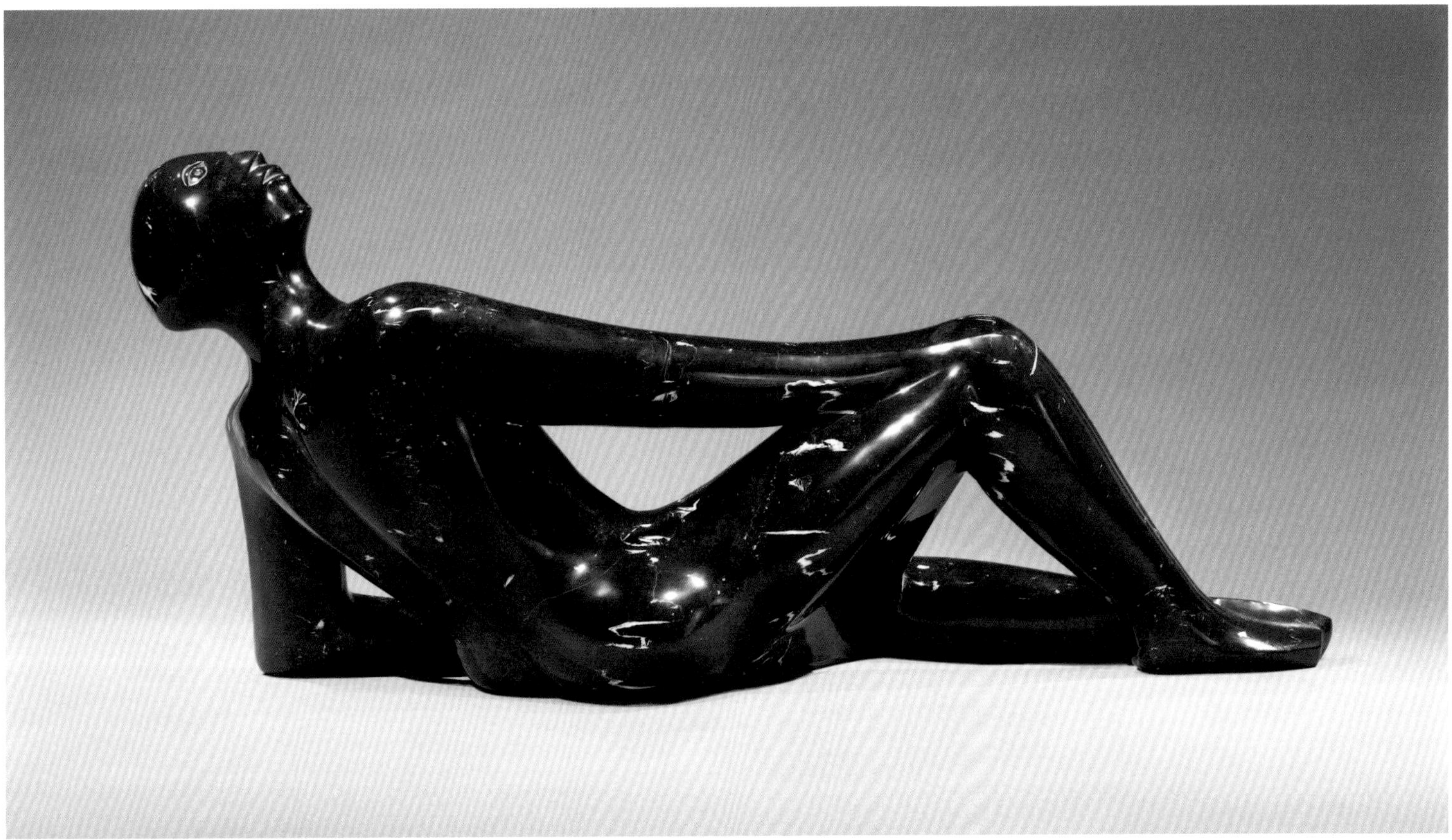

Stargazer, 1997, black marble, 14½ × 32 × 11 in., Collection of Reginald and Aliya Browne

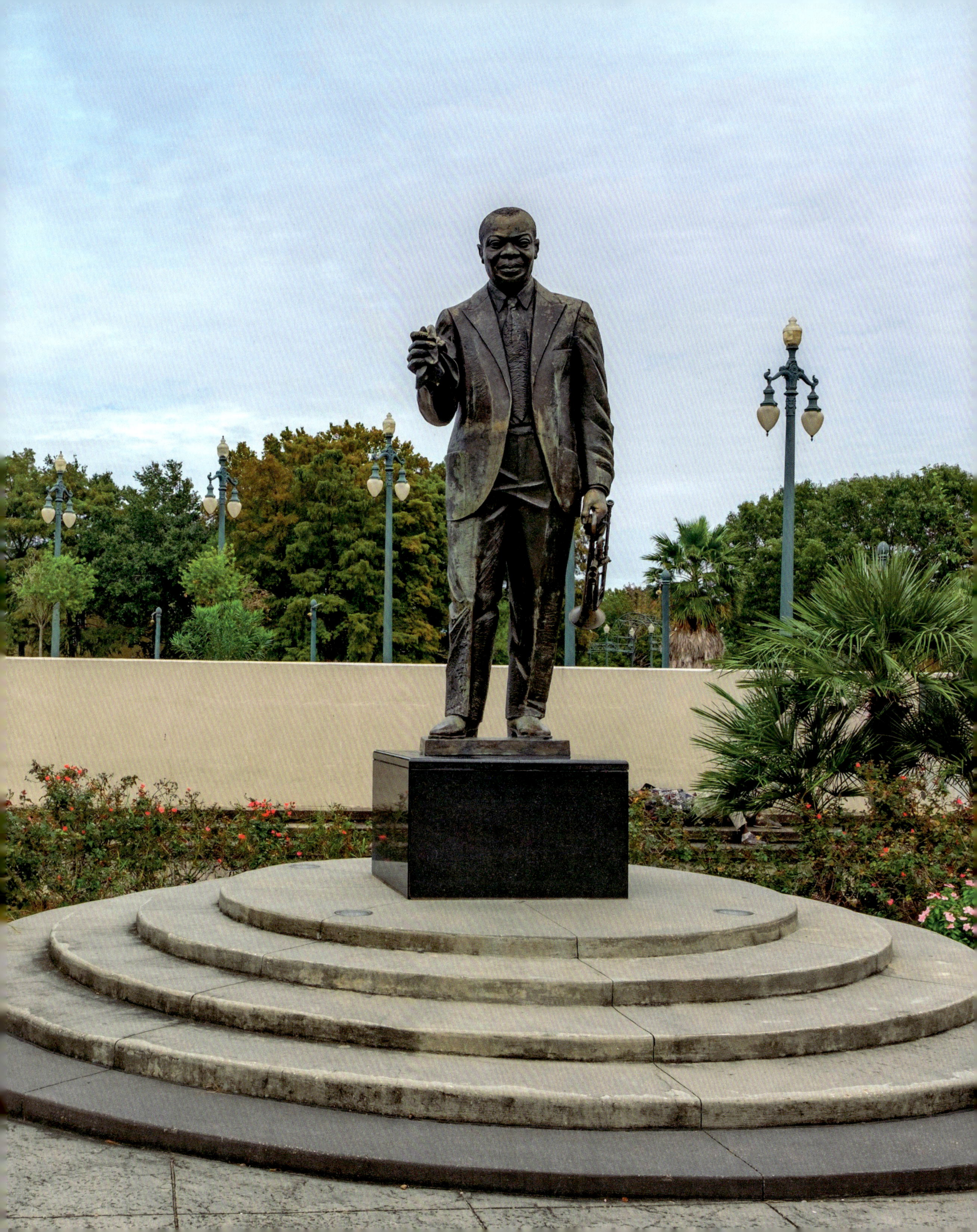

DALILA SCRUGGS

SHAPING PUBLIC SPACE

From her earliest engagement with mural painting as a student at Howard University, Elizabeth Catlett had an abiding commitment to public art. For most of her life that impulse was satisfied through printmaking. By the end of her career, however, she had leveraged her position in the art world so that she could pursue public commissions.[1] She was making art for the people, but now she executed her work on the scale of landscape. "Art in public places is only valid when it has some relationship to the community," she asserted. "It is not good enough to be merely functional or even beautiful. We must also meet the psychological and social needs of our people."[2] For Catlett, shaping public sculpture was an invitation to shape the public space as well.

Her philosophy first emerged in the 1970s, as she contemplated two new trends in public art. On the one hand, she considered *La Ruta de Amistad*, a series of abstract sculptures commissioned for the 1968 Olympics and lining the southern section of the beltway around Mexico City. On the other hand, she looked to Chicano and Black Arts Movement murals in Los Angeles and Chicago. While she held both approaches in high esteem—lauding the deeply intellectual and formal process apparent in *La Ruta*—she ultimately found the work self-serving.[3] By contrast, Catlett was drawn to community murals: "[This muralism movement] tries to change the urban environment, focusing on the desires and objectives of the community...The phenomenon of murals painted in the streets has brought art back to the people...The evidence to date shows that many artists have found a new source to reinforce their creativity and at the same time their responsibility towards their brothers."[4]

Public commissions, however, were not without their challenges. Didactic accessibility and formal rigor—she was committed to each, equally—could, she found, become opposing imperatives. The strains of this conundrum were in full effect as she embarked on the long process of creating the Louis Armstrong memorial now installed in Armstrong Park in New Orleans (p. 208). "The maquette that I did in plaster stands in my studio and glares at me daily, inert and lifeless," she confessed.[5] The commissioning body for the memorial wanted academic portraiture, and yet Catlett saw shades of minstrelsy in their desire for a smiling Black performer. Catlett wanted dignity and rigorous design. "My aim is to create a good portrait and a good sculpture at the same time so that those who know a lot about Louis and a little about sculpture—or

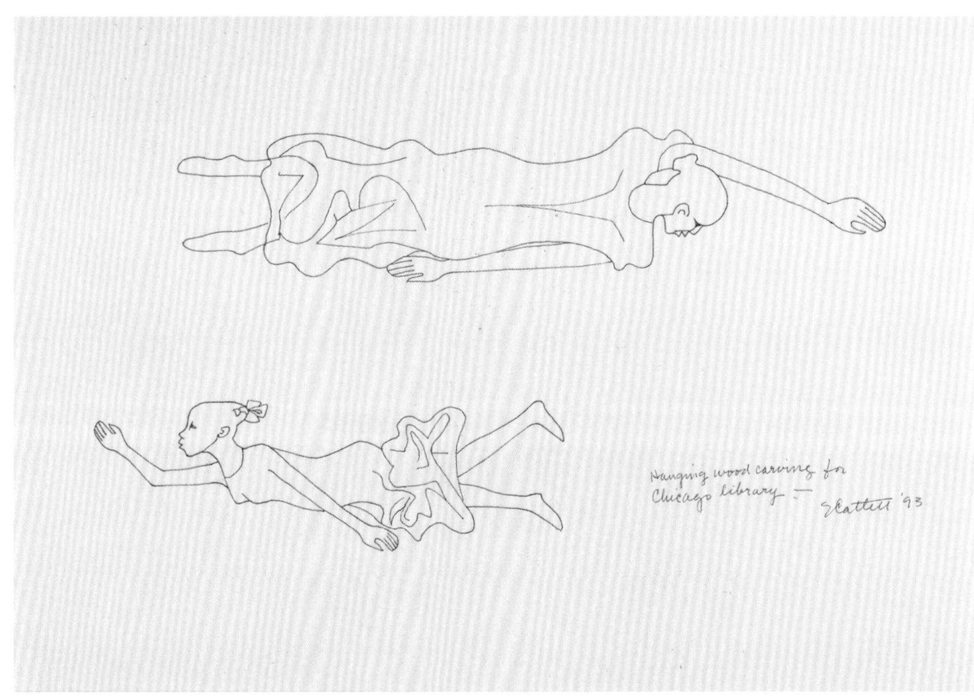

Fig. 1—*Drawing of Floating Family for Chicago Library*, 1993, Stella Jones Gallery

vice versa—will be able to appreciate both," she explained.[6] For years after the fact, Catlett bemoaned her struggles with this project.

But she remained constant in her approach to monumental public art: viewing it as an opportunity to make work that is site specific, relatable, and responsive. Before beginning *Students Aspire* (p. 209), Catlett met with students and faculty at Howard University. "I listened to what they had in mind and then I incorporated that in my own way."[7] When small production budgets proved to be a financial burden, she all but renounced public commissions. In the 1990s she came back to make the monumental sculpture *Floating Family* (pp. 232–233 and fig. 1) for the Legler branch of the Chicago Public Library: "I was excited just about the prospect of people sitting there, black people sitting in that building, reading."[8] She also produced the *People of Atlanta* (p. 230), which powerfully underscores government's civic responsibility to speak for and be accountable to the people. With a multicultural cast of denizens—including a figure on the far right, whose marginalized position and large duffel bag suggest he lacks housing—the frieze is located at the entrance of the executive offices in Atlanta's City Hall and often serves as a backdrop for mayoral press conferences. The artist's public sculptures continue to activate communal spaces, even years after her death. The *Ralph Ellison Memorial* (p. 236) proved particularly essential during the COVID-19 pandemic, drawing locals together for jazz concerts—impromptu and socially distanced—at the foot of the sculpture.[9]

The public art competitions that Catlett lost are every bit as informative as those she won. Making bids for the Harriet Tubman monument and a Schomburg Center commission (both in Harlem), she lost to Alison Saar and Houston Conwill, respectively—a younger generation of Black artists who embraced experimental and conceptual strategies, treading the line between experimentation and didacticism that Catlett had hoped to explore herself.[10]

Catlett's public sculptures are unabashedly beautiful and unironically dedicated to uplifting her audiences. She strove for lyricism, and the core tensions between abstraction and realism that run throughout her career surface through them in new and complex ways. As with her printmaking practice, Catlett's public commissions allowed her to transport her art out of the realm of bourgeois collecting and into streets, parks, and plazas.

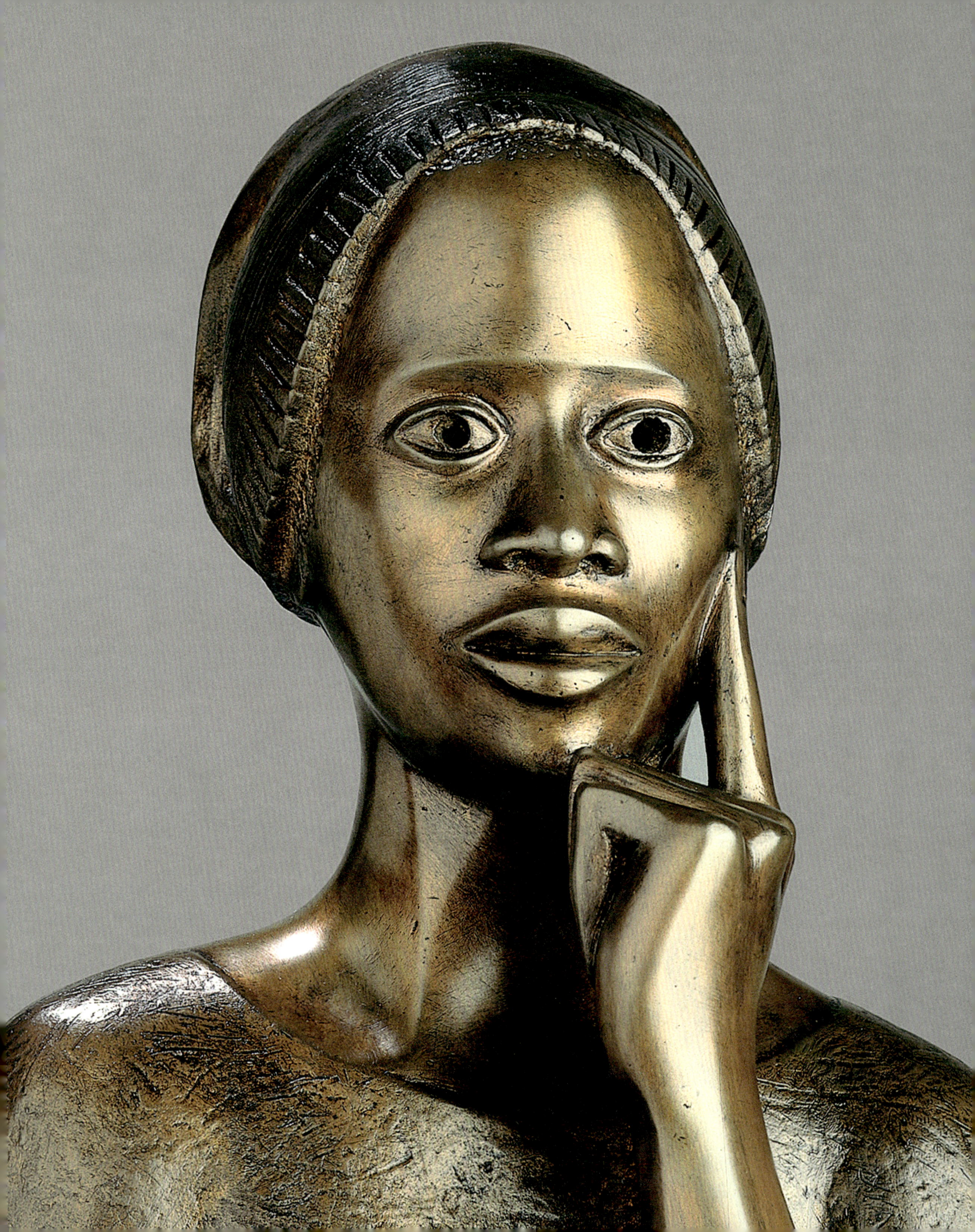

LOWERY
STOKES SIMS

A WOMAN OF GREAT INTEGRITY, AND BRAVERY

To tell the truth, before I met her, I was slightly intimidated by Elizabeth Catlett. In 1971 when I was in graduate school, the Studio Museum in Harlem organized *Elizabeth Catlett: Prints and Sculpture*, one of the first surveys of her work in the United States since she had relocated to Mexico in the mid-1940s. The occasion of the exhibition generated tales of Catlett's political travails: how she lost her US citizenship due to her own Leftist politics and her association with the Mexican organization Taller de Gráfica Popular. As an expatriate, forging a new life in a new country, she demonstrated the same courage and determination she had showed during her studies at the University of Iowa—despite not being allowed to room on campus. What I came away with from all this information was a perception of Elizabeth Catlett that I described in a note to her in 1987:

> *I've grown up with near apocryphal stories of your integrity and no-nonsense life, as a woman of great integrity, uncompromising values, and bravery.*

I can't remember when I actually met Elizabeth, probably in the early 1980s: I received a telephone call from her, inviting me to a visit at her residence in Battery Park City. And a friendship was formed. When I was featured in "Blacks at the Top," an article published in *New York* magazine in January 1987, reactions to the piece ranged from mild ridicule to exasperation to awe.[1] So it was a thrill to receive a note from Elizabeth, bluntly declaring that of all the individuals quoted in the article I made the most sense. Infatuated, I responded in the same note just quoted:

> *How the hell are you? How's Pancho? What's doing?...Hope to see you when you're next in New York. Come see our new 20th Century Wing. Maybe I'll get to Mexico, even. Stay well, and again. Thanks for the words.*

Over the next decade I worked with and encountered Elizabeth for a number of projects. I wrote the essay for her 1990 exhibition at the June Kelly Gallery, and then did visit her and her family in Cuernavaca in 1994 after participating on a panel in Mexico City giving grants for US/Mexico joint art projects. I got to experience firsthand Elizabeth's extended multicultural family, as well as the creative dynamics between her and her husband, the painter and printmaker Francisco Mora—which were featured in the 1991 exhibition *A Courtyard Apart: The Art of Elizabeth Catlett and Francisco Mora*, organized by the Mississippi Museum of Art and explored in Floyd Coleman's illuminating essay for the catalog. I also learned of the special collaboration between Catlett and her son, sculptor David Mora Catlett, who worked as her apprentice and assistant. These familial ties were a special aspect of Catlett's creativity and approach to life.

Our conversations during that 1994 visit amplified my sense of Elizabeth's life events and perspectives. I listened with vicarious delight of her strategy to bypass the segregation laws of New Orleans, when in 1941 she arranged for the bus carrying students she was teaching at Dillard University to drive up to the stairs of the New Orleans Museum of Art (then the Isaac Delgado Museum of Art)—which was not segregated—on a day the museum was closed, to see a Picasso exhibition. They thus avoided setting foot in the segregated public park in which the museum was located. She also regaled me with recollections of teaching at the extremely Leftist George Washington Carver School in Harlem, and her own realizations about her students that countered her own perceptions. Hers was a firsthand account of the attraction that Leftist ideas held for Black Americans during the 1930s and '40s—including my own mother, who was growing up and living in Harlem.

One event that stands out in my memory is our participation on a panel—which may very well have coincided with Elizabeth's 1998 retrospective exhibition at the Neuberger Museum of Art, curated by then-director Lucinda H. Gedeon, with essays by me and critic Michael Brenson. During the panel discussion the issue of Kara Walker's work came up—controversy was then crackling around Walker's work with members of the Black community, with some protesting the awarding of a MacArthur Genius Grant to her. In response Harvard University had organized the symposium *Change the Joke and Slip the Yoke: A Series of Conversations on the Use of Black Stereotypes in Contemporary Visual Practice* and I had participated. Later, the subject of figuration and content came up at the Neuberger discussion and another panelist there—a younger artist whose name escapes me—locked horns with Elizabeth over Walker's work. In that moment I realized the generational rift in the reception of Walker's art. Specifically for Elizabeth—whose work is replete with her strong commitment to celebrating Black people and their lives—I could understand her consternation about work that was based on satire and parody, and dangerously flirted with stereotypical imagery.

Elizabeth's imagery, throughout her work, invariably captures the fierceness and the pride of Blacks and Mexicans: Figures reaching clenched fists into the air, or sitting meditatively (predicting the current modality of rest as resistance among Black people[2]), using a minimalist vocabulary that is informed by African and Pre-Encounter Mesoamerican art. They project what Brenson describes as "a deeply human image of African-Americans while appealing to values and virtues that encourage a sense of common humanity."[3] Along with the strong planes in her work, there are nuances that are breathtaking. This was revealed to me as I looked at the sculptures in the Neuberger retrospective. In one, a reclining woman leaning on her hip, I could see how Elizabeth had captured the gentle curve and pressure on the figure's leg. It was indicative of the sensuousness with which Elizabeth approached her work in terracotta, wood, or stone—where she had a particular predilection for translucent alabasters and veined marbles.

I also remember that we sparred over the details of her life—specifically any references to her first husband, the painter Charles White. While I wanted to discuss their respective approaches to the planar lessons of cubism at that moment (in my essay for the Neuberger catalog), Elizabeth was concerned that any mention of White would be perceived as disrespecting her second husband,

Francisco "Pancho" Mora (they were married for a much longer time, over fifty years). So I had to put on my art-historian's hat, intone the imperatives of history and aesthetic analysis, and assert that—truthfully—her husbands were beside the point as we endeavored to establish *her* unique place in the history of art.

Throughout the 1990s and into the early 2000s, I was privileged to be part of huge gatherings of Elizabeth's friends and family at Moran's, a restaurant on Manhattan's Tenth Avenue. In 2002 we did a dialogue at June Kelly Gallery, as part of "Inside / Out Private Gallery Tour," organized by the Studio Museum in Harlem. As I continued in my tenures there and at the Museum of Arts and Design, I saw less of Elizabeth and her visits to New York City were fewer and far between. After her death in 2012, I had the opportunity to give a lecture for the exhibition *Elizabeth Catlett: Artist as Activist*, organized in 2020 by the Reginald F. Lewis Museum of Maryland African American History & Culture in Baltimore (my new home).

Elizabeth Catlett's legacy endures for me to this day. This book, which accompanies a new exhibition organized by the Brooklyn Museum and the National Gallery of Art, not only explores her role as a revolutionary Black artist but also indicates that her legacy will abide for us all into the future.

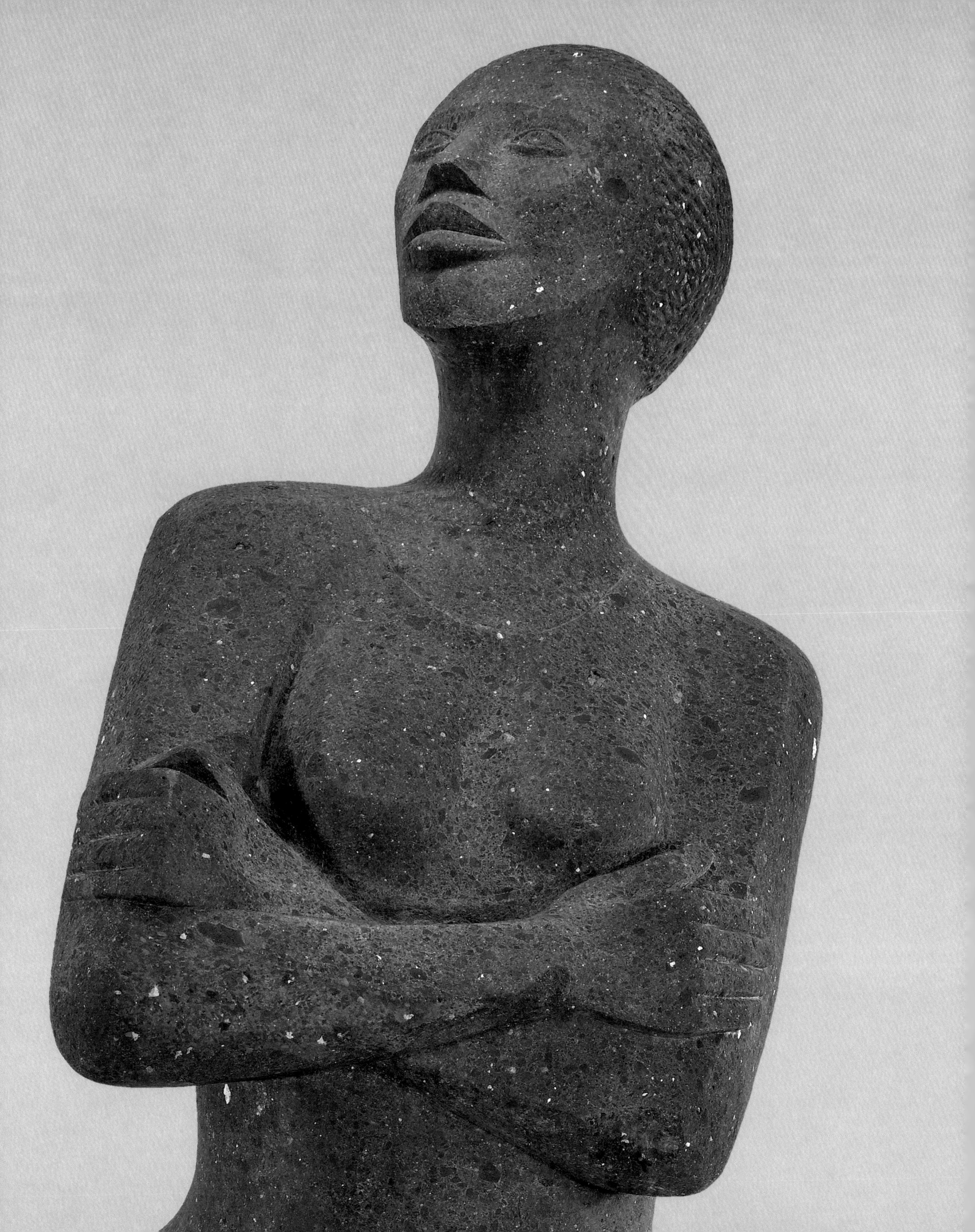

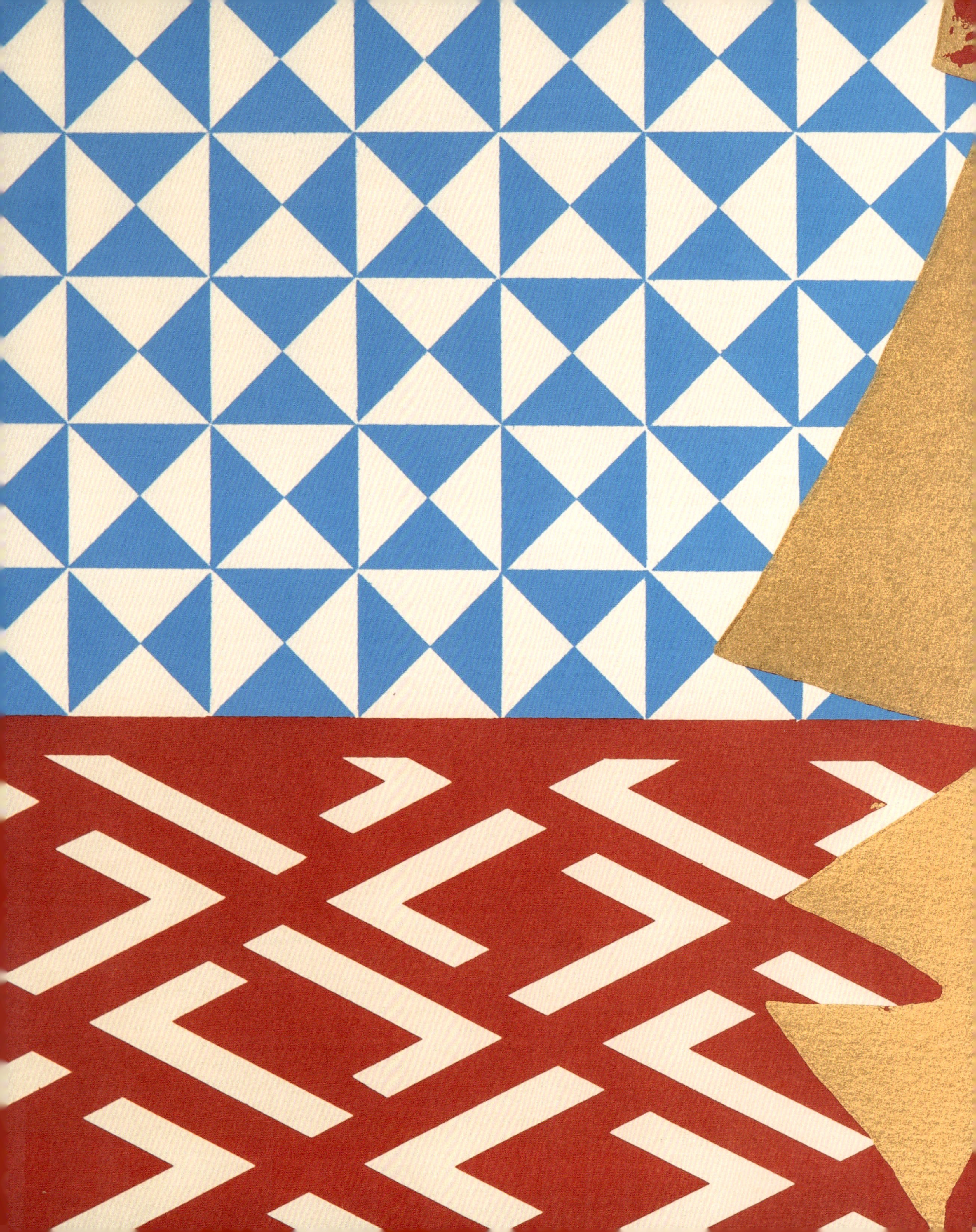

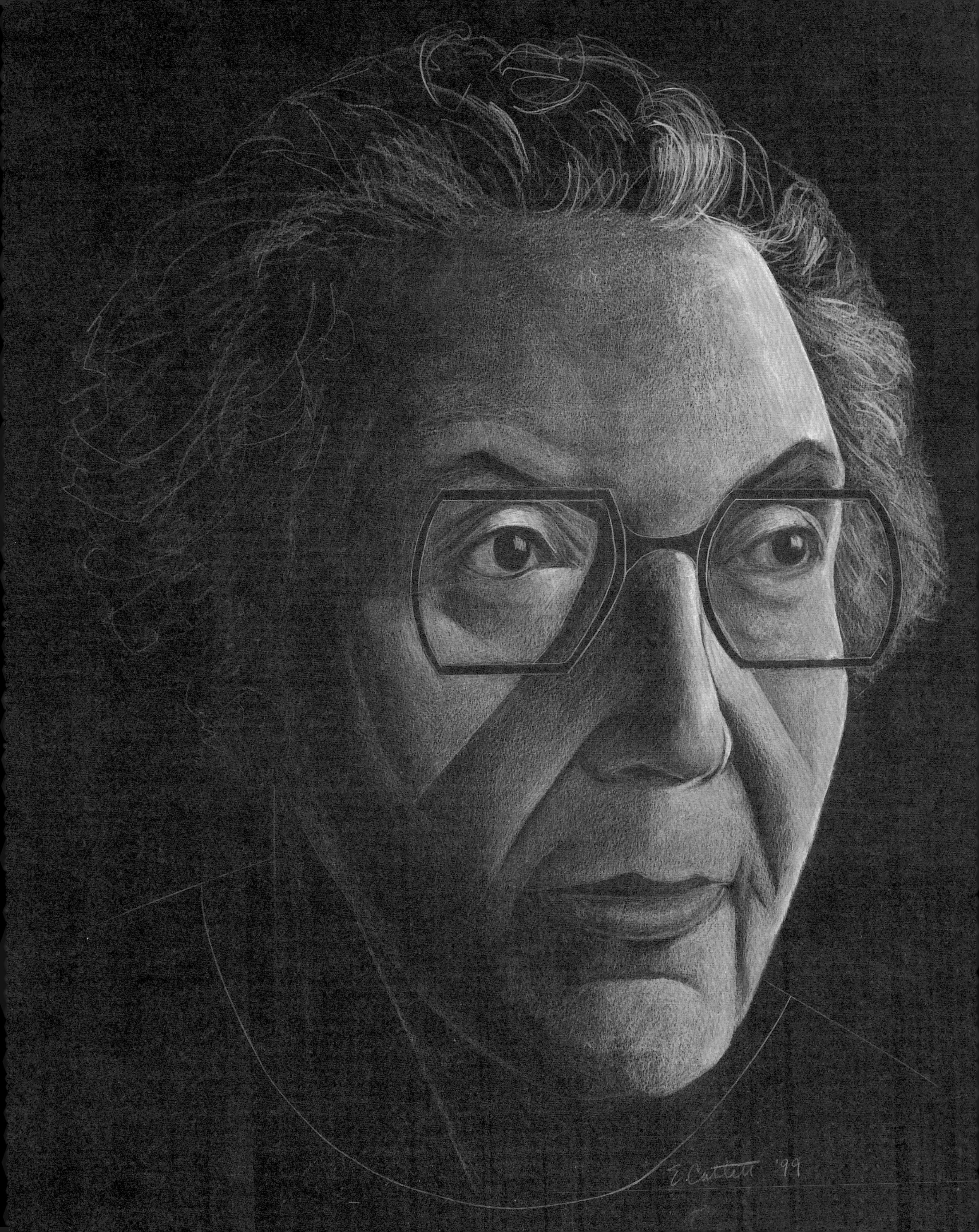

RASHIEDA
WITTER

CHRONOLOGY

1915

April 15: Alice Elizabeth Catlett (EC) is born at Freedmen's Hospital in Washington, DC, to John H. Catlett (1878–1914) and Mary S. (Carson) Catlett (1883–1970).[1]

1916–1920S

EC is raised in Northwest DC along with two older siblings—John H. Catlett Jr. (1910–1940) and Cera L. Catlett (1911–2004)—and her paternal grandmother, Louisa (Jamison) Catlett (1853–1934).[2]

EC spends summers visiting her maternal grandparents, Charles H. Carson (1845–1927) and Cera Carson (1843–1934), on their farm in Lincolnton, North Carolina.[3]

The Red Summer of 1919: Racist attacks, mob violence, and riots against Black veterans and civilians occur across cities in the wake of World War I and the Great Migration.[4]

1928–1930

EC attends Paul Laurence Dunbar High School in DC, America's first public high school for Black students.[5]

Haley Douglass—EC's first art teacher and a descendant of Frederick Douglass—encourages her artistic ambitions.[6]

EC makes her first carving—an elephant from a bar of Ivory soap—and decides on a career as an artist.[7]

Participates in a protest against lynching, standing in front of the US Supreme Court with a noose around her neck, and is detained by police.[8]

1931

June: EC graduates from Dunbar.

August: Spends a week in Pittsburgh, Pennsylvania, taking the entrance exams at Carnegie Institute of Technology. Although praised for her artistry, she is denied admission because of her race.[9]

October: Enrolls at Howard University in DC and declares a major in design; its art department is the first to be established at any HBCU (historically Black colleges and universities).[10]

Takes courses in Design with Loïs Mailou Jones, Freehand Drawing with James Wells, and Sketch and Anatomy with James A. Porter.[11]

1932

Encounters African sculpture for the first time when works from the Barnes Collection of Merion, Pennsylvania, are exhibited at Howard Gallery of Art.[12]

1933

Works at the Corcoran Gallery of Art in DC on Friday nights.[13]

Inspired by her courses with James A. Porter, EC changes her major from design to painting.[14]

May: Pledges to be a member of Delta Sigma Theta Sorority.[15]

Learns about socialism and communism through E. Pauline Myers, a graduate student at Howard who rents a room from EC's mother. Myers goes on to become a lifelong activist and stalwart in the civil rights movement.[16]

1934

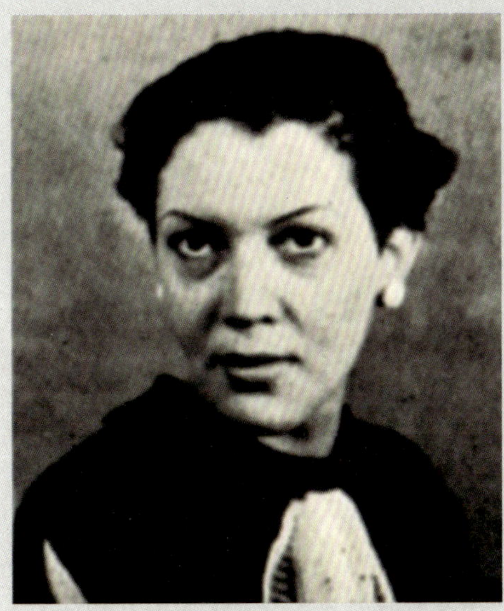

Alice Elizabeth Catlett, vice president of Delta Sigma Theta Sorority, 1934, from *The Bison* (yearbook, 75), Digital Howard, Moorland-Spingarn Research Center, Howard University

January: Public Works of Art Project commissions EC to paint a mural on the importance of Black educators at Miner Teachers College in DC.[17]

March: EC is fired from the mural project for not completing it on time, but her research leads her to the work of Mexican muralists and printmakers, including caricatures of the Harlem Renaissance by Miguel Covarrubias and murals by Diego Rivera.[18]

Member of the Stylus Literary Society, an organization and publication dedicated to literature, art, and music, founded by Alain Locke and Montgomery Gregory.[19]

Member of Liberal Club, an anti-war, anti-fascism organization dedicated to discussing and finding solutions to the social, political, and economic issues of the time. Participates in a strike against war and fascism.[20]

Is business manager of the Daubers' Art Club, which seeks to develop the appreciation of art on campus.[21]

Becomes vice president of the Alpha Chapter of Delta Sigma Theta Sorority.[22]

December: Howard students participate in National Crime Conference demonstrations, protesting lynching by wearing nooses.[23]

1935

EC visits New York and sees two influential exhibitions at the Museum of Modern Art (MoMA): *African Negro Art* (March 18–May 19, 1935) and *Vincent van Gogh* (November 4, 1935–January 5, 1936).[24]

May: Shows two charcoal drawings in the 13th Annual Student's Exhibition of Paintings, Drawings, and Designs, at the Howard Gallery of Art.[25]

June: Graduates cum laude with bachelor of science degree in art.[26]

1936–1937

Moves to Durham, North Carolina, to teach art at Hillside High School, while supervising art programs in eight elementary schools.[27]

As a member of the YWCA'S Business and Professional's Girls Club, EC meets Thurgood Marshall, who shares a plan on how to advocate to equalize teachers' salaries. EC joins the North Carolina Teachers Association and becomes an activist for the movement.[28]

June 1937: Taller de Gráfica Popular (TGP, People's Graphic Workshop) is founded in Mexico City by Raúl Anguiano, Luis Arenal, Leopoldo Méndez, and Pablo O'Higgins.[29]

1938–1939

Summer 1938: Begins graduate school at the University of Iowa. Meets writer and lifelong friend Margaret Walker, her second year (first semester) roommate.[30]

Studies painting with Grant Wood, art history with H. W. Janson, and sculpture with Henry Stinson.[31]

An avid Red Cross–certified swimmer since childhood, EC integrates the pools at the University of Iowa.[32]

November 1939: Jean Charlot, a French American painter and illustrator known for his murals and close relationships with the Mexican muralists, exhibits paintings with primarily Mexican themes in the Iowa Memorial Union. His work and presence at the university—as visiting artist during the summers of 1939 and 1940—nurture EC's growing interest in Mexico and printmaking.[33]

November 30: The Soviet Union invades Finland, and the Winter War begins. EC invests in updates, following the war and advocating for Finland, the considered underdog, to win.[34]

Influenced by Wood's advice to make works about what she knows best, EC creates a marble bust entitled *Negro Girl*.[35]

1940

EC pilgrimages to Chicago with Iowa classmates to view *Picasso: Forty Years of His Art* at the Art Institute of Chicago (February 1–March 3). Meets Margaret Taylor Goss (later Burroughs) during this trip.[36]

Completes her thesis sculpture *Negro Mother and Child* (p. 81, fig. 2), which is influenced by William Zorach's *Mother and Child* (c. 1927–1930).[37]

June: Becomes the first student in the United States to graduate with a master of fine arts degree.[38]

Submits *Negro Mother and Child* to the American Negro Exposition in Chicago (July 4–September 2) and wins the first award in sculpture.[39]

Takes summer job teaching classes on design and color at Prairie View College in Texas.[40]

August: Begins teaching drawing, painting, printmaking, and art history as the chair of the art department, Dillard University, New Orleans. One of her students, Samella Lewis, becomes her lifelong friend and eventual biographer.[41]

1941

Summer: During the height of the Black Chicago Renaissance, EC lives in the city with Burroughs, one of the founders of the recently opened South Side Community Art Center (SSCAC). There, she meets literary and visual artists such as Gwendolyn Brooks, Charles Sebree, William McBride, Frank Neil, and Charles White, whom she begins to date.[42]

Studies ceramics at the Art Institute of Chicago and lithography at the SSCAC.[43]

Fall: Returns to Dillard. Campaigns against segregation by throwing "For Colored Only" signs into the aisles on buses, advocates for wrongfully arrested Dillard students, and crafts a successful plan to take 160 students to the Picasso exhibition at the Isaac Delgado Museum of Art (now the New Orleans Museum of Art), which is in a park that bars African Americans.[44]

Goes to a segregated movie theater on Canal Street in New Orleans, pretending to be a white person for the first and only time in her life. Leaves in shame when the person next to her uses a racial slur.[45]

December 8: Exhibits work alongside Charles Alston, Romare Bearden, Eldzier Cortor, Charles White, and others in Downtown Gallery's influential exhibition *American Negro Art, 19th and 20th Centuries*, in New York.[46]

December 24: EC marries Charles White (CW) at her mother's home in DC, and they honeymoon in New York.[47]

1942

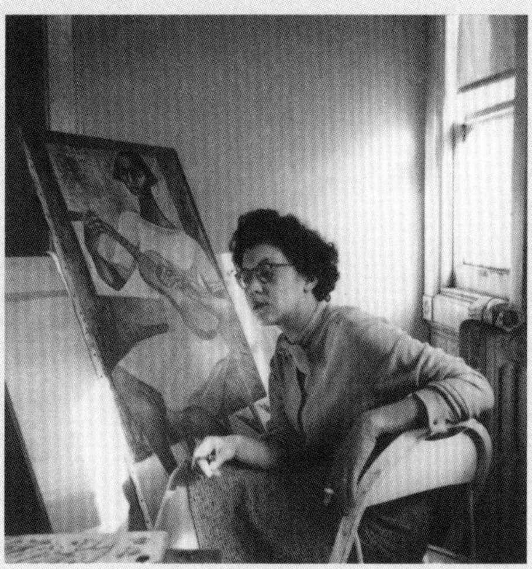

Charles White, *Elizabeth Catlett in Her Studio*, 1942, Courtesy of The Charles White Archives

EC returns to Dillard, where CW eventually joins her. Resigns from her teaching position at the end of the semester after an unfair decision regarding teachers' salaries is made against the union.[48]

Summer: EC and CW move to Harlem, New York, and join a community of artistic luminaries, including Robert (Bob) Blackburn, Marvel Cooke, Ernest Critchlow, Langston Hughes, Duke Ellington, Ralph Ellison, Jacob and Gwendolyn Lawrence, Norman Lewis, and Paul Robeson.[49]

EC is appointed chair of Russian War Relief in Harlem, where she manages fundraising.[50]

EC and CW spend part of the summer as arts coordinators at the Workers Children's Camp (Wo-Chi-Ca) in Hunterdon County, New Jersey.[51]

EC studies sculpture with Ossip Zadkine, a Russian-born French artist who came to New York as a refugee fleeing the Nazis. He inspires EC to experiment with abstraction while looking to African art as a guide.[52]

September: The couple embark on a trip through the South, visiting Louisiana, Mississippi, Virginia, and Georgia to conduct research for CW's mural at Hampton Institute (now Hampton University) in Virginia.[53]

1943

January: EC and CW temporarily relocate to Hampton, Virginia, where CW completes the mural—entitled *The Contribution of the Negro to Democracy in America*—for the institute.[54]

EC teaches sculpture for the semester at Hampton and studies pedagogy in fine arts with Viktor Lowenfeld.[55]

Applies for a grant from the Julius Rosenwald Fund to study stone and wood carvings, and to create a sculpture "dedicated to the Negro in agriculture and industry, to be placed in a Negro Agricultural and Technical school in the south." Her application is denied.[56]

July: EC and CW return to New York and live at 34 Bedford Street in Greenwich Village with Margaret Walker.[57]

1944

January: EC begins working at the Marxist-inspired George Washington Carver School in Harlem. She teaches (sculpture, pottery, block printing, stenciling, clay modeling, and dressmaking) and fundraises as the promotion director. This experience of connecting with working-class communities heavily influences her work going forward.[58]

April: EC's essay "The Negro Artist in America" is published in *American Contemporary Art*.[59]

Teaches ceramics at the Communist Party–affiliated Jefferson School.[60]

Serves on the Arts Committee of the National Negro Congress (NNC), an organization advocating for Black liberation. As staff artist for its periodical *Congress Vue*, she publishes political cartoons on themes such as trade unions and voter registration.[61]

September 3: Recy Taylor, an African American woman from Abbeville, Alabama, is kidnapped while leaving church and sexually assaulted by six white men. EC advocates for Taylor—publishing a drawing in *Congress Vue* and citing her story as an impetus for the iconic *Black Woman* series (pp. 33–48).[62]

1945

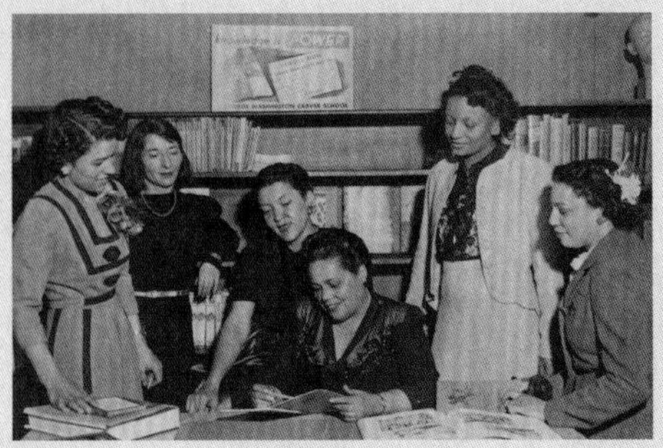

Elizabeth Catlett (third from left) with other teachers at the George Washington Carver School, 1945, from Samella Lewis, *The Art of Elizabeth Catlett* (Claremont, CA, Hancraft Studios, 1984), 18

January–February: EC participates in the exhibition *The Negro Artist Comes of Age* at the Albany Institute of History and Art alongside CW, Lewis, Romare Bearden, Aaron Douglas, Jacob Lawrence, and Hale Woodruff.[63]

Spring: EC teaches Publicity Techniques, Sculpture and Pottery, and How to Master Mimeographing courses at the Carver School.[64]

Reapplies for a Rosenwald Fellowship to do a "series of lithographs, paintings, and sculptures on the role of the Negro woman in the fight for democratic rights in the history of America." Her application is approved in April.[65]

Summer: EC and CW return to Wo-Chi-Ca to oversee the art program.[66]

October: EC enrolls in Harry Sternberg's Graphics class at the Art Students League to learn lithography, etching, and silkscreen printing.[67]

1946

January: EC's essay "Negro Artists" is published in *New Masses* (1926–1948).[68]

EC serves as executive secretary of the Committee for the Detroit Art Exhibit, leading plans for *Tribute to the Negro People*, an exhibition sponsored by the NNC and *New Masses*, which opened in May at the Urban League there.[69]

Speaks at the *Art Is a Weapon* symposium alongside William Z. Foster, a radical American labor organizer and Communist politician, and general secretary of the Communist Party USA from 1945 to 1957.[70]

Applies for and is granted a renewal of her Rosenwald Fellowship. Decides to complete the project in Mexico.[71]

June: EC and CW depart for Mexico and live with artist David Alfaro Siqueiros's mother-in-law in Mexico City. They work and attend classes at Escuela de Pintura y Escultura (La Esmeralda, National School of Painting, Sculpture, and Printmaking), and meet artists such as the painter and printmaker Francisco "Pancho" Mora and TGP cofounders Arenal, Méndez, and O'Higgins. The couple are permitted to work at the TGP.[72]

EC assists Méndez and O'Higgins on a mural entitled *Motherhood* at the Instituto Mexicano del Seguro Social (IMSS) in Mexico City.[73]

September: EC and CW return to New York to initiate divorce proceedings.[74]

October: EC returns to Mexico and begins a romance with Mora. Continues to work with and learn from TGP members. Learns the TGP method of making linocuts from Mora and Ignacio Aguirre and implements it for her *Black Woman* series.

Gonzalo Aguirre Beltrán releases his book *La poblacion negra de México, 1510–1810: Estudio etnohistorico* (The black population of Mexico, 1519–1810: Ethnohistorical study).[75]

Winter: EC's article "Tribute to the Negro People" is published in *American Contemporary Art*.[76]

The administration of Mexican president Miguel Alemán Valdez (1946–1952) passes laws that reverse land reform, privatize education, limit free expression, and undermine existing labor organizations, opposing many of the rights fought for during the Mexican Revolution. During his term, the Institutional Revolutionary Party (PRI) is founded, and the Federal Security Directorate (DFS) and the granaderos (riot police) become key tools of surveillance and repression.[77]

1947

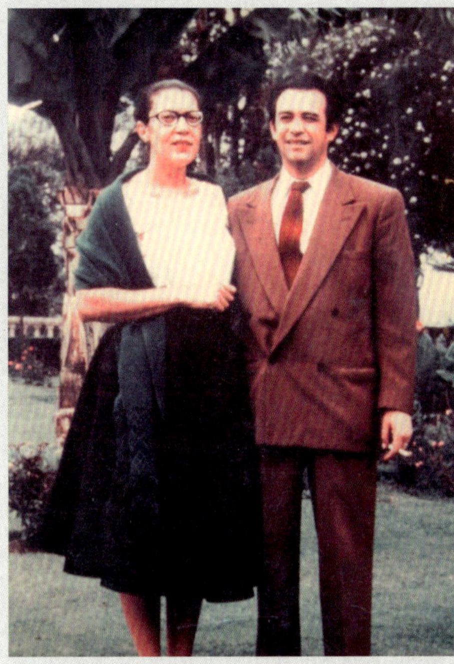

Elizabeth Catlett and Francisco Mora, creative and romantic partners, From the Collection of the Elizabeth Catlett-Mora Family Living Trust

The TGP issues the portfolio *Estampas de la revolución mexicana*. The eighty-five original linoleum cuts depict events from the Mexican Revolution and following years.[78]

EC marries Mora. They remain creative collaborators and romantic partners until Mora's death in 2002.

Studies terracotta sculpture with Francisco Zúñiga, learning the Mexican method—in use since Pre-Encounter times—of building hollow ceramic sculpture. Also studies wood carving with well-known sculptor José L. Ruiz at La Esmeralda.[79]

August 31: Gives birth to her son Francisco Mora Jr. at Freedmen's Hospital in DC.

Remains in the US until the opening of her debut solo exhibition *Paintings, Sculptures, and Prints of the Negro Woman* at Barnett-Aden Gallery in DC.[80]

1949–1950

March 3, 1949: Gives birth to her second son, Juan, in Mexico.

La Estampa Mexicana publishes *El Taller de Gráfica Popular: Doce años de obra artistica colectiva* (The Workshop for Popular Graphic Art: Twelve years of collective artistic work), a promotional tool and summary of the TGP's achievements. EC contributed work to the publication.[81]

Salón de la Plástica Mexicana opens in Mexico City. EC becomes a founding member of this cooperative gallery dedicated to the promotion of Mexican art.[82]

1950: The TGP engages in an extended series of international exhibitions. The workshop's domestic production focuses on human rights, workers' rights, and antinuclear protests.[83]

1951

World powers take opposing sides in the Korean War: China and the Soviet Union support North Korea, while the US and the United Nations support South Korea.[84]

May: Primer Congreso Nacional por la Paz (First National Peace Congress) is held in Mexico.[85]

June 22: EC gives birth to her third son, David.

Participates in international exhibition *Mexikansk grafik, i samverkan med Mexikanska Legationen, Stockholm* (Mexican graphics, in collaboration with the Mexican Legation, Stockholm) at the Götesborg Konstmuseum, Sweden.[86]

September: Burroughs, a longtime friend, visits EC in Mexico and publishes a profile on her.[87]

1953

EC spearheads and contributes to TGP's print series *Against Discrimination in the US* (1953–1954), which celebrates African American heroes such as Paul Robeson, Sojourner Truth, Harriet Tubman, Nat Turner, and Ida B. Wells (pp. 105–109).[88]

The Cuban Revolution begins.[89]

October 17: Mexican women gain suffrage rights.[90]

1954

EC advocates for peace and extends solidarity to the citizens of Latin American countries through *Por la Paz y Evitan los Pactos Militares,* denouncing US imperialism, including the CIA's role in the 1954 Guatemalan coup d'etat.

Rigorous FBI and CIA surveillance and harassment of EC and her affiliates begins, a result of anti-communist fears intensified by the Cold War.[91]

1955

EC resumes her sculpture-making practice once her youngest son David goes to kindergarten. Returns to La Esmeralda to study wood carving with Ruiz.[92]

1956–1957

Arranges for visitors to take her work into the US, as she believes that showing it to African Americans there is imperative. Her sculpture *Negro Woman* wins a purchase prize at the Atlanta University Annual Exhibition.[93]

EC's work is shown in several international exhibitions, including *Mexican Contemporary Art* in Brno, Czechoslovakia, and a Mexican print show at the National Museum, Poznań, Poland.[94]

1958

Members of the Mexican Railroad Workers' Union (STFRM), teachers, and university students stage a series of strikes (1958–1959) that constitute the most powerful grassroots movement and the largest labor strikes since the Mexican Revolution. The government violently suppresses the final strike by enforcing the Law of Social Dissolution and involving the army and police.[95]

September 10: EC is among several American citizens with previous records of communist affiliations arrested by Mexican authorities. She is detained for three days and—because she is married to a Mexican national—permitted to stay in Mexico.[96]

1959

April: Wins a competitive examination and becomes the first woman hired to teach sculpture in the Escuela Nacional de Artes Plásticas (ENAP, National Fine Arts School) at the Universidad Nacional Autónoma de México (UNAM).[97]

EC is appointed head of the sculpture department at the ENAP. She experiences prejudice from her all-male colleagues due to her gender and nationality.[98]

1960

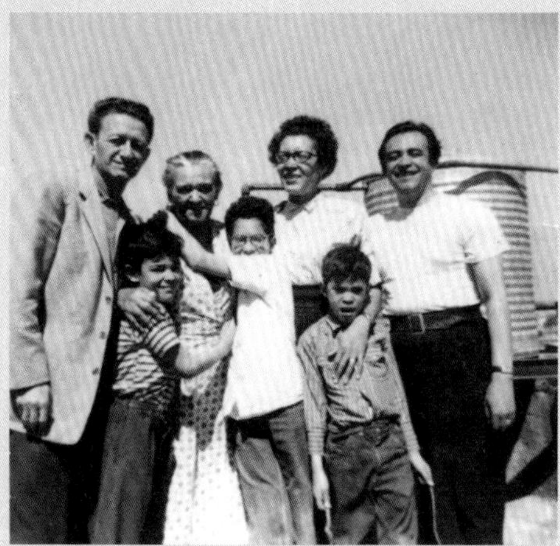

Elizabeth Catlett and her husband, the artist Francisco Mora, with their children, architect Hannes Meyer, and Mary (Carson) Catlett in Mexico, c. 1960s

Applies for Mexican citizenship due to repeated US harassment and increasing complicity of Mexican government.[99]

Contributes work to *450 años de lucha: Homenaje al pueblo mexicano* (*450 Years of Struggle: Tribute to the Mexican People*), a TGP portfolio of reproductions about the history of Mexico. This publication marks the end of the primary phase of the workshop.[100]

1961

Returns to the US to give the keynote address "The Negro People and American Art" at Howard University for the National Conference of Negro Artists. The speech is published in the inaugural issue of *Freedomways*.[101]

1962

June: Has first solo exhibition in Mexico, *Grabados y Esculturas de Elizabeth Catlett* (Prints and Sculptures of Elizabeth Catlett), at the Escuela Nacional de Artes Plásticas.

EC's sculpture *Figura* wins the Tlatilco prize at the First Mexican Sculpture Biennial.[102]

Granted Mexican citizenship and deemed an "undesirable alien" by the US. Subject to harassment due to her political perspectives and affiliations, she is barred from returning to the US and denied travel visas several times.[103]

1963

Visits Cuba for the first time to attend the 1963 Congress of Women of the Americas. It coincides with celebrations of the fourth anniversary of the Cuban Revolution in Havana. She is granted a courtesy visa by the Instituto Cubano de Amistad con los Pueblos (Cuban Institute of Friendship with the Peoples).[104]

Elected secretary-general of the TGP, one of the first women to be appointed to a directorial position in the organization.[105]

On behalf of Mexico City's Comite Unificador Nacional de Mujeres (National Women's Unification Committee), EC creates a poster (*Congreso Mundial de Mujeres*) for the Fifth World Congress of Women in Moscow.[106]

1964

Receives the Xipe Totec prize for *Mujer*, at the Second National Sculpture Biennial in Mexico City.[107]

October: EC and other women of the TGP are involved in establishing the Unión Nacional de Mujeres Mexicanas (UNMM, National Union of Mexican Women), an organization that supports the rights of working-class women and efforts such as strikes (for teachers, railroad workers, and doctors) and the anti-colonial movements of the 1970s.[108]

1965

February 15: Malcolm X is assassinated in New York. His death catalyzes the Black Power and Black Arts Movements, which EC later captures in her 1969 *Malcolm X Speaks for Us* (p. 156).

April–August: Students protest in Mexico City against US invasions in the Dominican Republic and Vietnam.[109]

EC receives first prize in sculpture for *Bather* at the Atlanta University Annual, one of the premier exhibitions that consistently supports EC during her exile.[110]

After several years of internal struggles at the TGP, EC, Mora, and others write an open letter to members expressing their dissatisfaction with the workshop's deterioration.[111]

1966

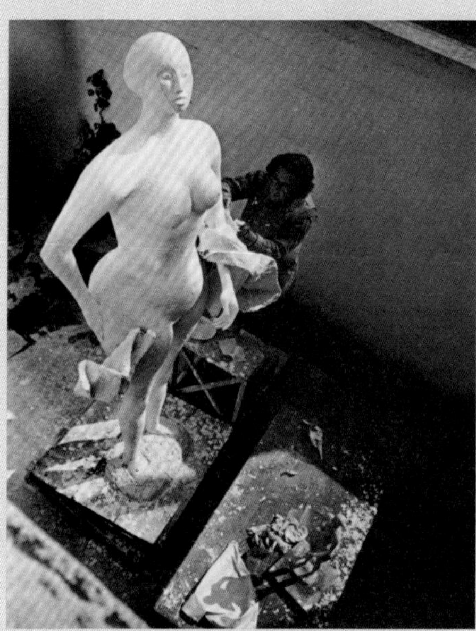

Elizabeth Catlett working on *Bañista Olmeca (Olmec Bather)*, c. 1966, from the *International Review of African American Art* 6, no. 1 (1984)

The Instituto Politécnico Nacional (National Polytechnic Institute) in Mexico City commissions EC to create *Bañista Olmeca* (*Olmec Bather*), a ten-foot bronze sculpture that celebrates ancient Mexican civilization.

EC officially resigns from the TGP.[112]

1968

April 4: Civil rights activist Dr. Martin Luther King Jr. is assassinated in Memphis, Tennessee, prompting the Holy Week Uprising in 196 US cities—this wave of social unrest is America's most extreme since the Civil War.[113]

October 2: Police and military forces open fire on peaceful demonstrators in Tlatelolco plaza, killing hundreds. The massacre culminates months of protests in Mexico City led by the Movimiento Estudiantil (Student Protest Movement). EC supports the students, and her sons are active participants in the movement.[114]

October 12: The Summer Olympics begin in Mexico City. EC shows work in the Stone Carving, Solar, and Olympic Villa Exhibitions.[115]

Barbara Jones-Hogu of AfriCOBRA (African Commune of Bad Relevant Artists) visits EC in Mexico while she is working on *Homage to My Young Black Sisters*. The figure's raised fist inspires Jones-Hogu to create her iconic print *Unite* (1969).[116]

1969

A drawing by EC is featured on the January cover of *Freedomways*; the issue highlights Native Americans and Mexican Americans.[117]

Malcolm X Speaks for Us wins a purchase prize at the annual Sálon de Grabado in Mexico (p. 156).[118]

1970

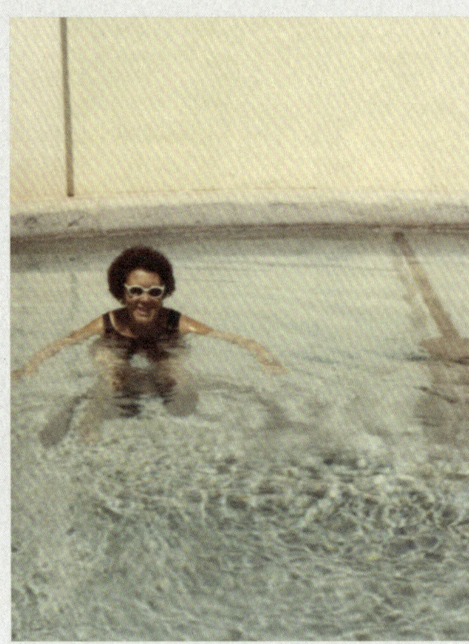

Elizabeth Catlett in swimming pool, 1970, Elizabeth Catlett Papers, Amistad Research Center, New Orleans (addendum II), box 4, folder 8

January: *Ebony* magazine publishes "My Art Speaks for Both My Peoples," a profile on EC providing insights into her life and work in Mexico and expanding her visibility in the US.[119]

May: Delivers her keynote address via phone from Mexico after her visa to attend the Conference on the Functional Aspects of Black Art (CONFABA) at Northwestern University in Evanston, Illinois, as advisor and elder of distinction, was denied by the US Embassy.[120]

July: Critically acclaimed solo exhibition *Experienca Negra: Escultura y grabado de Elizabeth Catlett* (Black Experience: Sculpture and engravings by Elizabeth Catlett) opens at the Museo de Arte Moderno in Mexico City.[121]

October 13: Political activist Angela Y. Davis is apprehended by the FBI, galvanizing global support for her release. EC organizes the Comité Mexicano Provisional de Solidaridad con Angela Davis (Provisional Mexican Committee of Solidarity with Angela Davis) with her sister Cera and other Black women in Mexico.[122]

EC is awarded a prize to travel and study in East Germany.[123]

1971

February: EC's first solo show in the US in over two decades opens at Brockman Gallery in Los Angeles.[124]

March: EC travels to Cuba as a delegate representing the UNMM at celebrations for International Women's Day.[125]

August: Mary Ann Pollar opens Rainbow Sign in Berkeley, California. A Black arts and culture hub, the venue presents visionary Black leaders, including Betye Saar, Nina Simone, James Baldwin, Maya Angelou, Shirley Chisholm, and (in the following year with a solo exhibition) EC.[126]

September: A decade after her last visit, the US Embassy grants EC a visa to return to the US for the opening of her solo exhibition *Elizabeth Catlett: Prints and Sculpture* at the Studio Museum in Harlem. The show travels for several years (through 1975) to ten or so predominately Black institutions.[127]

EC is awarded a grant from the British Council to study teaching methods at art schools in Great Britain. Also visits Wales, Czechoslovakia, Germany, Paris, Brussels, and Amsterdam.[128]

1973

June: Gives a presentation at Mexico's ENAP entitled *Murales en las calle de Chicago* (Chicago's Street Murals), which makes connections between public art by Black artists, such as the Wall of Respect, and the Chicano Mural Movement.[129]

November: Commissioned by Margaret Walker to create a life-size bust of the poet for the Phillis Wheatley Poetry Festival at Jackson State University, Mississippi (p. 173).[130]

1974

Donates 3,300 portfolios of offset prints to raise money for *Freedomways* magazine, the Studio Museum in Harlem, the Chile Defense Committee, and other organizations.[131]

1975

March: Attends the National Conference of Artists in Pomona, California, where she recites her speech "The Role of the Black Artist." It is published that summer in the journal *The Black Scholar*.[132]

EC is named Rainbow Sign's art honoree of the year, and Elizabeth Catlett Week (beginning March 29) is declared by the City of Berkeley, California, as part of International Women's Year.[133]

Retires from her teaching position at UNAM, leaves Mexico City, and relocates to Cuernavaca, Mexico.[134]

November: Defends the revolutionary aspects of art-making and Mexican muralism in an essay published in the Mexican newspaper *El Día*.[135]

1976

July: Completes a commission to create a ten-foot bronze sculpture of Louis Armstrong for the City of New Orleans (1971–1976).[136]

September: Participates in the groundbreaking exhibition *Two Centuries of Black American Art*, curated by David C. Driskell.[137]

1977

March: Conducts workshops in sculpture and printmaking at Howard University.[138]

1978

Unveils the bronze relief *Students Aspire* at the Chemical Engineering Building, Howard University.

Tours Alabama, visiting and lecturing at eight HBCUs.[139]

Visits China and the Soviet Union. In China, discusses the work of Black artists in America and answers inquiries about Pop art and abstract expressionism.[140]

Ana Iturbe and her husband, artist and master printmaker Raul Cabello, begin printing fine art prints for EC.[141]

1979

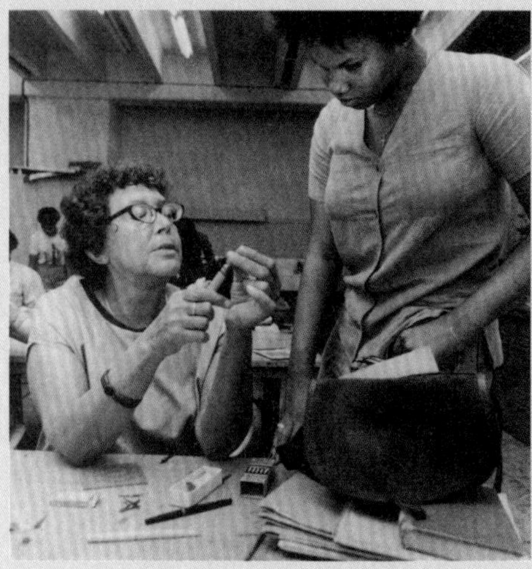

Elizabeth Catlett and a student at a sculpture workshop hosted by Your Heritage House, Detroit, 1979, Elizabeth Catlett Papers, Amistad Research Center, New Orleans (addendum II), box 4, folder 6

EC is an artist in residence at Your Heritage House in Detroit, where she hosts studio classes in sculpture and printmaking for adults and youth.[142]

October: EC and Mora present the lecture "African Influences in Mexican Art" at Trotter House (named for William Monroe Trotter), University of Michigan, Ann Arbor.[143]

1981

EC is commissioned to create two life-size bronzes of Jaime Torres Bodet and José Vasconcelos for Secretaría de Educación Pública (Secretariat of Public Education), Mexico City.[144]

December: Dancer and civil rights activist Glory Van Scott visits EC in Cuernavaca, and she works on the clay model for the bronze sculpture *Glory*.[145]

1982

EC and Mora purchase an apartment in New York to split their time between the US and Mexico.[146]

EC makes prints at Robert Blackburn's Printmaking Workshop in New York.[147]

1983

October: Solo exhibition *Elizabeth Catlett: Sculpture and Graphics* opens at the New Orleans Museum of Art; in conjunction with it, EC presents a series of lectures at three nearby HBCUs: Xavier University, Southern University, and Dillard University.

EC at Brandywine Workshop as visiting artist.[148]

1984

First monograph on EC, *The Art of Elizabeth Catlett* by Samella Lewis, is published by Hancraft Studios, in collaboration with the Museum of African American Art, Los Angeles.

1985

Receives commission for bronze sculpture for National Council of Negro Women, New York.[149]

1986

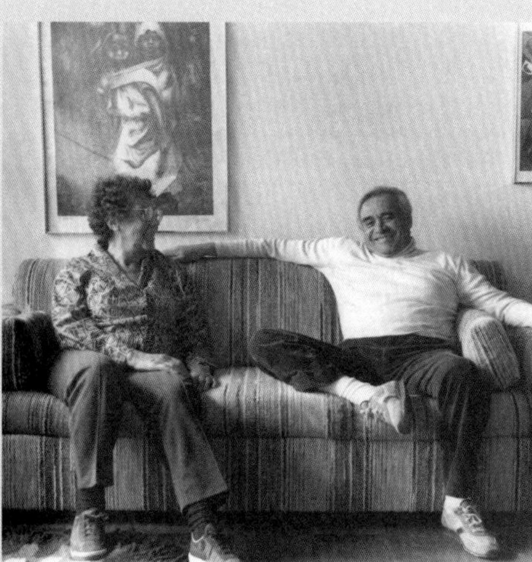

Fern Logan, *Betty + Pancho '86*, 1986, From the Collection of the Elizabeth Catlett-Mora Family Living Trust

Participates in Sculpture Salón, Museo de Moderno, Mexico City.[150]

1987–1988

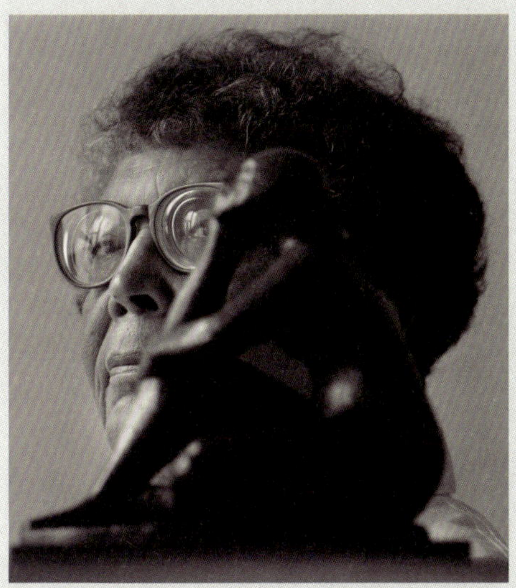

Brian Lanker, *Elizabeth Catlett*, 1988, gelatin silver print, National Portrait Gallery, Smithsonian Institution, Partial gift of Lynda Lanker and a museum purchase made possible with generous support from Robert E. Meyerhoff and Rheda Becker, Agnes Gund, Kate Kelly and George Schweitzer, Lyndon J. Barrois Sr. and Janine Sherman Barrois, and Mark and Cindy Aron

Participates in a family exhibition alongside her husband and son: *Elizabeth Catlett, Francisco Mora, & David Mora*, New Visions Gallery, National Black Arts Festival, Atlanta.

Participates in a panel discussion about the exhibition *Flashpoints: The Art of Social Upheaval*.[151]

1989

September: *Elizabeth Catlett: Print Retrospective* opens at the Jamaica Arts Center, New York.

The Negro Woman series (1946–1947) is reprinted at the Robert Blackburn Printmaking Workshop and officially retitled *The Black Woman* to reflect then-preferred usage.

1992

Commissioned by the Limited Editions Club to create six lithographs for a republishing of *For My People* (1937) by Margaret Walker.[152]

1993

Joins the June Kelly Gallery, New York, and presents a solo exhibition.

Begins a multiyear relationship making prints with Joseph Kleinman and Maureen Turci in New Brunswick, New Jersey.[153]

1994

Receives Civil Rights Award, "Women Making a Difference," from Delta Sigma Theta Sorority, Inc., St. Louis, Missouri.[154]

1996

Receives an honorary doctorate from Howard University.

Receives Distinguished Alumni Award for Achievement, University of Iowa.

Solo exhibition *Struggle and Serenity: The Visionary Art of Elizabeth Catlett* opens at the Caribbean Cultural Center / African Diaspora Institute, New York.

1998

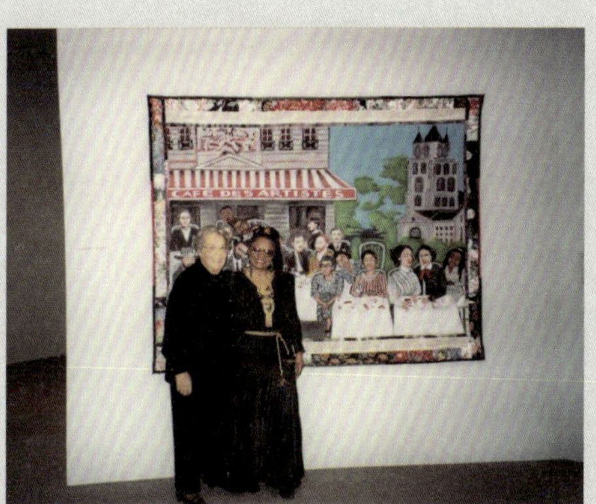

Elizabeth Catlett and Faith Ringgold in front of *Le Cafe des Artistes* at the Baltimore Museum of Art, 1999, Elizabeth Catlett Papers, Amistad Research Center, New Orleans (addendum II), box 4, folder 6

Solo exhibition *Elizabeth Catlett Sculpture: A Fifty-Year Retrospective* is organized by the Neuberger Museum of Art, Purchase, New York.

EC's son Juan Mora Catlett releases *Betty y Pancho*, his documentary about his parents.

2002

February 22: EC's husband Francisco "Pancho" Mora dies.

The US reinstates EC's citizenship.[155]

2003

May: EC's sculpture *Invisible Man: A Memorial to Ralph Ellison* is unveiled at Riverside Park in New York.[156]

2006

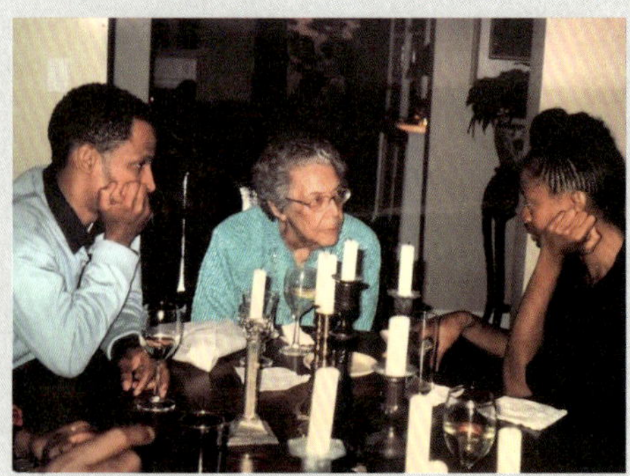

Artists Radcliffe Bailey (left) and Kara Walker (right) in conversation with Elizabeth Catlett, 2006, Photo courtesy of the Kara Walker Archives

University of Iowa's Stanley Museum of Art acquires 28 prints directly from EC. She donates the money to the University of Iowa Foundation to invest in the Elizabeth Catlett Mora Scholarship Fund, which supports African American and Latinx students studying printmaking.[157]

2007

September: EC writes an open letter to the director of the TGP denouncing the handling of its legacy since her departure.[158]

2008

Awarded an honorary doctorate by Carnegie Mellon University, Pittsburgh.[159]

April: EC films a conversation with Maya Angelou in conjunction with the exhibition *Solitude and Solidarity: The Art of Elizabeth Catlett* at Delta Arts Center in Winston-Salem, North Carolina.[160]

2010

EC's sculpture honoring Mahalia Jackson is erected in Louis Armstrong Park, New Orleans.

2011

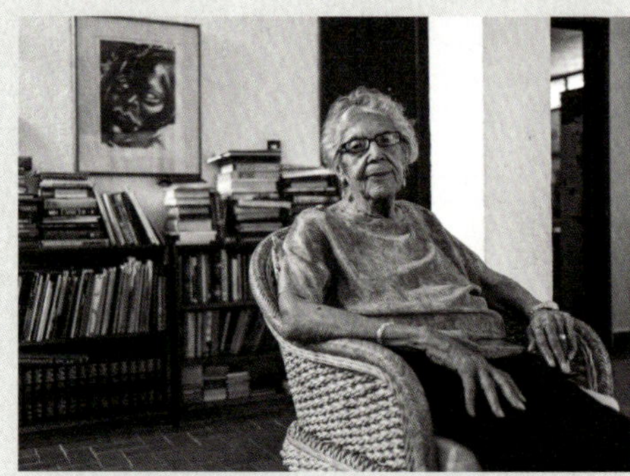

Adriana Zehbrauskas, Catlett at her home in Cuernavaca, Mexico, April 8, 2011

January: *Stargazers: Elizabeth Catlett in Conversation with 21 Contemporary Artists* exhibition opens at the Bronx Museum of Art in New York.[161]

March 10: *DIGAME: Elizabeth Catlett's Forever Love* opens at the W. E. B. Du Bois Research Institute, Harvard University, Cambridge; a conversation with EC and Henry Louis Gates Jr. is presented in conjunction with the exhibition.[162]

2012

April 2: Alice Elizabeth Catlett Mora dies at her studio home in Cuernavaca at the age of ninety-six. She is survived by three sons, ten grandchildren, and six great-grandchildren.

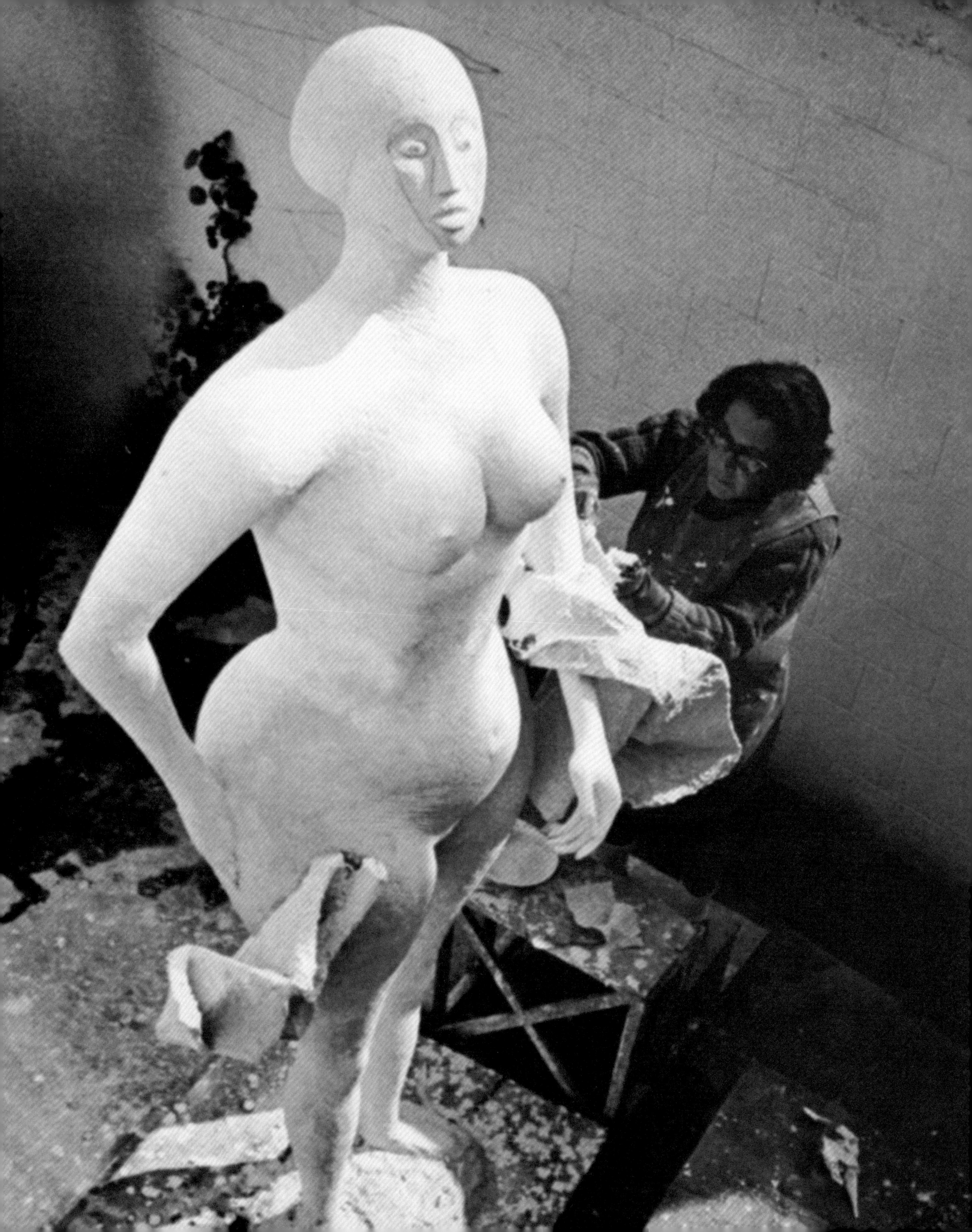

NOTES

A NOTE ON ART TITLES

If known, art titles reflect the artist's (or the lender's) intent, including styling or use of English glosses for Spanish titles. Some art titles in the book's plate sections reflect updated usage—for instance, "Black" replaces "Negro" in some English titles. We follow Catlett's lead, as she reprinted *The Negro Woman* series (1946–1947) in 1989 and officially retitled it *The Black Woman*. Catlett often revisited prints—reprinting, revising, and retitling them. At times, she signed and dated her prints well after they were printed; details that rely on memory may contradict other elements in her biography.

TO THAT DEGREE AND MORE

1 Elizabeth Catlett Mora's speech, by phone, to CONFABA at Northwestern University, May 6, 1970, transcript with handwritten additions and corrections, box 6, folder 8, Elizabeth Catlett Papers (addendum), Amistad Research Center, Tulane University.

2 Our task was made infinitely easier thanks to the impeccable research of Melanie Anne Herzog, the leading scholar on the artist and author of the foundational monograph *Elizabeth Catlett: An American Artist in Mexico* (Seattle, 2000), and the extraordinary scholarship of many, many others, including Anita Bateman, Samella Lewis, Rebecca Schreiber, Freida High Tesfagiorgis, Rebecca VanDiver, and Lowery Stokes Sims, who contributed with Michael Brenson to *Elizabeth Catlett Sculpture: A Fifty-Year Retrospective* (Purchase, NY, 1998).

3 Elizabeth Catlett, quoted in Herzog, *Elizabeth Catlett*, 19.

4 See the chronology, p. 258.

5 Kellie Jones, "Swimming with E. C.," in *We Wanted a Revolution: Black Radical Women, 1965–85: New Perspectives*, ed. Catherine Morris and Rujeko Hockley (Brooklyn, 2018), 64; Erik S. McDuffie, *Sojourning for Freedom: Black Women, American Communism, and the Making of Black Left Feminism* (Durham, 2011), 145.

6 Elizabeth Catlett, "Elizabeth Catlett, 1945 Plan of Work," box 400, folder 7, Special Collections, Rosenwald Collection, John Hope and Aurelia E. Franklin Library, Fisk University.

7 Alice Walker's definition of "womanism," from *In Search of Our Mothers' Gardens* (San Diego, 1983), xi.

8 See Christina Heatherton, *Arise! Global Radicalism in the Era of the Mexican Revolution* (Oakland, CA, 2022), especially 145–174.

9 Elizabeth Catlett, quoted in Marc Crawford, "My Art Speaks for Both My Peoples," *Ebony* 25, no. 3 (January 1970): 94.

10 See the chronology, p. 258.

11 Michael C. FitzGerald and Julia May Boddewyn, *Picasso and American Art* (Whitney Museum of American Art, New York, 2006), 169.

12 Isabel Cooper, "Picasso," Sights and Sounds, *New Masses* 33, no. 10 (November 28, 1939): 28.

13 Elizabeth Catlett Mora's phoned CONFABA speech, May 6, 1970, box 6, folder 8, Elizabeth Catlett Papers (addendum).

14 My thanks to Julia Fernandez for this insight.

THE BLACK WOMAN SERIES

1 The language in some print titles has altered slightly over time, to reflect styling choices or updated usage. See the note on art titles.

BECOMING AN ARTIST-ACTIVIST AT HOWARD UNIVERSITY

1 For examples of Catlett's contributions to Howard, see the chronology: 1961 (speech); 1977 (workshops); 1978 (*Students Aspire*); and 1996 (honorary doctorate). Rebecca VanDiver, "Art Matters: Howard University's Department of Art from 1921 to 1971," *Callaloo* 39, no. 5 (2016): 1,202, identifies 1921 to 1936 as the founding phase of the art department. For this essay, I would like to thank Dalila Scruggs, Catherine Morris, Mary Lee Corlett, and Nancy Eickel for the groundbreaking research at the foundation of this exhibition and publication; Jade Flint, who was integral to the archival research; the staff and student assistants at the Howard University Gallery of Art, including Kathryn Coney Ali, Scott Baker, Abby Eron, and Jada Brooks; at Howard's Moorland-Spingarn Research Center, Sonja Woods, Lela Sewell Johnson, and Charice Thompson for providing access to archival materials; and staff at the Clark Atlanta University Art Museum, the Spelman College Archives, the archives at the Robert W. Woodruff Library at the Atlanta University Center, and the Stuart A. Rose Manuscript, Archives and Rare Books at Emory University.

2 "DC Society," *Afro-American*, August 8, 1931, 2; "Elizabeth Catlett, Glory Van Scott, Interviewer, Cuernavaca, Mexico, December 8, 1981," in James V. Hatch and Leo Hamalian, eds., *Art and Influence* (New York, 1991), 5. Building on the creative foundation cultivated at the historic Dunbar Public High School, she had carved her first sculpture there.

3 Van Scott, interview, 5.

4 Walter Dyson, *Howard University, the Capstone of Negro Education: A History, 1867–1940* (Washington, DC, 1941), 440.

5 Ruby Moyse Kendrick, "Art at Howard University: An Appreciation," *The Crisis* 39, no. 11 (November 1932): 348.

6 *Howard University Bulletin, Annual Catalogue, 1931–1932* (Washington, DC, 1932), 137. In addition to the art department, the College of Applied Science included three other departments: engineering, architecture, and music.

7 "Howard Began 6th Session Thursday," *Afro-American*, October 10, 1931, 13.

8 *Howard University Bulletin, 1931–1932*, 145, 179–180. Loïs Mailou Jones was a graduate of the School of the Museum of Fine Arts, Boston, and brought to Howard experience in design. Her art practice blossomed during the Harlem Renaissance and her exploration of African themes extended through the late twentieth century. James A. Porter was a graduate of Howard University's art department program. He was known as an artist-scholar, as he produced a body of modernist two-dimensional work throughout his career and published the first academic survey of African American art, *Modern Negro Art* (1943). An artist of the Harlem Renaissance era, James Wells was educated at Columbia University's Teachers' College. He worked across painting and printmaking. He is widely recognized for his aesthetic innovations in printmaking.

9 *Howard University Bulletin, 1931–1932*, 29–30.

10 "Howard U. Art Gallery Exhibits Little Dutch Masters," *The Hilltop*, October 29, 1931, 1.

11 Van Scott, interview, 2.

12 *Howard University Bulletin, 1931–1932*, 179.

13 *Howard University Bulletin, 1931–1932*, 179.

14 "Society in the Nation's Capital: Give Chinese Supper," *Afro-American*, June 4, 1932, 4. Alpha Phi Alpha Fraternity is the African American collegiate fraternity founded in 1906 on the campus of Cornell University. Howard University was home to the Beta Chapter of the organization, founded in 1907.

15 "First Exhibit of Mural Art Comes to HU," *The Hilltop*, February 4, 1932, 1.

16 "First Exhibit of Mural Art Comes to HU," 1.

17 Van Scott, interview, 2.

18 Information in this paragraph on the *Exhibition of Paintings by Negro Artists* is drawn from its brochure in the Loïs Mailou Jones Collection, box 215-17, folder 9, pp. 1–3, Moorland-Spingarn Research Center, Howard University, Washington, DC.

19 Rebecca VanDiver, "The Torture of Mothers: Elizabeth Catlett's Prints as a Call for Reproductive Justice," *Art Journal* 80, no. 2 (2021): 18.

20 Mary Wade, "History Week Brings Exhibit of Rare Negro Paintings," *The Hilltop*, February 11, 1932, 1. The art practices and accomplishments of Howard's art faculty were particularly visible during the winter and spring quarters of Elizabeth Catlett's first year at Howard. Jones, Porter, and Wells were all recognized by the Harmon Foundation during the early 1930s. Charcoal drawings by Dorothy Gibson, a Boston-based African American artist, were also included in the show.

21 "Seeking Origins of Gullah Art Motifs," *Philadelphia Tribune*, July 7, 1932, 6.

22 "110 Organize New Arts Guild," *Afro-American*, March 26, 1932, 5, for this and other details on the guild cited in this paragraph.

23 "Prizes Awarded at Howard University," *Afro-American*, June 24, 1933, 8.

24 "50 Awarded HU Scholarships," *Afro-American*, September 9, 1933, 15.
25 "Six Art Exhibits Scheduled at HU," *Afro-American*, October 7, 1933, 24.
26 Tobias Wofford," Perspectives on the 1933 Exhibition: Herring, Locke and Porter," *American Art* 33 (Summer 2019): 11; "Howard Prominent in Negro Life Meet," *The Hilltop*, November 10, 1933, 1.
27 Wofford, "Herring, Locke and Porter," 16.
28 *Howard University Bulletin, 1932–1933*, 115.
29 "Elizabeth Catlett, Camille Billops, Interviewer, October 1, 1989," in Hatch and Hamalian, *Art and Influence*, 16.
30 "Howard Artist's Mural of 'YMCA,'" *The Hilltop*, February 16, 1934, 4.
31 "The Bison: 1934," Howard University Yearbooks, Digital Howard, Moorland-Spingarn Research Center, Howard University, 64.
32 "The Bison: 1934," 64, 54.
33 "Stylus in First Meet of Year," *The Hilltop*, October 10, 1934, 1, Digital Howard, Moorland-Spingarn Research Center, Howard University.
34 "The Bison: 1934," 76.
35 Billops, interview, 17.
36 "Antiwar Group Plans Meeting," *The Hilltop*, November 9, 1934, 1; "Liberal Club Hears Reports from Delegates," *The Hilltop*, January 16, 1935, 4; "Liberal Club Movies of Anti-Lynching Scenes," *The Hilltop*, March 6, 1935, 4.
37 "Kuan-Yin, Goddess of Mercy, in Art Gallery," *The Hilltop*, November 9, 1934, 1.
38 *Exhibition for the Ten Year Anniversary of the Howard University Gallery of Art*, brochure, Loïs Mailou Jones Collection, box 215-16, folder 56, Moorland-Spingarn Research Center, Howard University.
39 "Davis Speaker at Scottsboro Defense Meet," *The Hilltop*, March 6, 1935, 1. In 1931, nine African American young men were accused and convicted of raping two white women in Alabama, resulting in the Scottsboro Boys Trial. This is one of the events that gave birth to the modern civil rights movement of the mid-twentieth century.
40 "Delta Girls Care for Two Year Old Nursery School Tot," *The Hilltop*, November 9, 1934, 1.
41 "Delta Girls Care," 1.
42 Carolyn Elizabeth Shuttlesworth-Davidson, ed., *A Proud Continuum: Eight Decades of Art at Howard University* (Howard University, Gallery of Art, Washington, DC, 2005).

SOCIAL(IST) NETWORKS IN CHICAGO AND NEW YORK

1 "Beauty Reigns at Artists and Models 1941 Ball," *Chicago Defender*, November 1, 1941.
2 See Diana Briggs, "Glamour Is Keynote of Artists, Models Ball," *Chicago Defender*, November 1, 1941; Margaret Goss Burroughs, "Chicago's South Side Community Art Center: A Personal Recollection," in *Art in Action: American Art Centers and the New Deal*, ed. John Franklin White (Metuchen, NJ, 1987), 141.
3 Elizabeth Catlett, interview by Clifton Johnson, January 5, 1983, Elizabeth Catlett Papers, Amistad Research Center, Tulane University.
4 This essay is indebted to the research presented in two key publications: Melanie Anne Herzog, *Elizabeth Catlett: An American Artist in Mexico* (Seattle, 2000); and Samella Lewis, *The Art of Elizabeth Catlett* (Claremont, CA, 1984). See also Lucinda H. Gedeon, ed., with Michael Brenson and Lowery Stokes Sims, *Elizabeth Catlett Sculpture: A Fifty-Year Retrospective* (Purchase, NY, 1998), and Christina Heatherton, *Arise! Global Radicalism in the Era of the Mexican Revolution* (Oakland, CA, 2022), 145–174, for her discussion of Catlett's immersion in radical political networks in Harlem and Chicago, where the SSCAC's ball provides a romanticized cover for Black artists to draw inspiration from Mexico as a site of anti-racist, anti-fascist internationalist culture.
5 The history of institutionalized racism in Chicago continues to have an impact to the present day. The growth, successes, and challenges faced by the city's Black populations became the subject of intense sociological study by researchers at the University of Chicago in the first decades of the twentieth century, including the magisterial *Black Metropolis*, first published in 1945 and featuring an introduction by the novelist Richard Wright; see St. Clair Drake and Horace R. Cayton, *Black Metropolis: A Study of Life in a Northern City*, rev. ed. (Chicago, 1993). For a discussion of the Great Migration, Chicago's immigrant communities, and the intersections of sociology and artmaking in the city, see Sarah Kelly Oehler, *They Seek a City: Chicago and the Art of Migration, 1910–1950* (Chicago, 2013).
6 Margaret Taylor Burroughs, oral history interview by Anna Tyler, December 11, 1988, transcript, 51, Archives of American Art, Smithsonian Institution.
7 See Bill Mullen, *Popular Fronts: Chicago and African-American Cultural Politics, 1935–46* (Urbana, IL, 1999).
8 George J. Mavigliano and Richard A. Lawson, *The Federal Art Project in Illinois, 1935–1943* (Carbondale, IL, 1990), 30–45.
9 For discussions of the Black Chicago Renaissance, see Robert Bone and Richard A. Courage, *The Muse in Bronzeville: African American Creative Expression in Chicago, 1932–1950* (New Brunswick, NJ, 2011); Steven C. Tracy, ed., *Writers of the Black Chicago Renaissance* (Urbana, IL, 2011); Darlene Clark Hine and John McCluskey Jr., eds., *The Black Chicago Renaissance* (Urbana, IL, 2012). More generally, see also Stacy I. Morgan, *Rethinking Social Realism: African American Art and Literature, 1930–1953* (Athens, GA, 2004).
10 The history of the founding has been told in Margaret T. Burroughs, "Saga of Chicago's South Side Community Art Center (1938–1943)," in *The South Side Community Art Center: 50th Anniversary, 1941–1991* (Chicago, 1992), 1–16. See also Anna M. Tyler, "Planting and Maintaining a 'Perennial Garden': Chicago's South Side Community Art Center," *International Review of African American Art* 11, no. 4 (1994): 31–37. It is the only Works Progress Administration art center still in operation.
11 Catlett, interview.
12 Catlett, interview. Although Lewis, *Art of Elizabeth Catlett*, 12, stated that Catlett and Burroughs were roommates at the University of Iowa along with Margaret Walker, this was not the case.
13 Mabel O. Wilson makes the connection between the Left's Cultural Front and the American Negro Exposition; see Mabel O. Wilson, *Negro Building: Black Americans in the World of Fairs and Museums* (Berkeley, 2012), 193–196, 211–233.
14 Alain Locke, "The American Negro Exposition's Showing of the Works of Negro Artists," in *Exhibition of the Art of the American Negro (1851 to 1940)* (Chicago, 1940), n.p.
15 As Melanie Anne Herzog notes, Catlett denied being influenced by Locke, who had an adversarial relationship with James Herring and James A. Porter. Nevertheless, Locke was clearly willing to support Catlett's career by including her in exhibitions and publications, including *The Negro in Art*, in which he published Catlett's *Negro Mother and Child* and *Negro Girl*. Herzog, *Elizabeth Catlett*, 17–18; Alain Locke, ed., *The Negro in Art: A Pictorial Record of the Negro Artist and of the Negro Theme in Art* (Washington, DC, 1940), 115.
16 Locke, "American Negro Exposition's Showing," n.p.
17 Alice Elizabeth Catlett, "Sculpture in Stone: Negro Mother and Child" (MFA thesis, State University of Iowa, 1940), 1.
18 Elizabeth Galbreath, "Typovision," *Chicago Defender*, August 23, 1941. Galbreath also reminded her readers that Catlett had won the sculpture award at the American Negro Exposition the year prior.
19 Catlett, quoted in Herzog, *Elizabeth Catlett*, 29.
20 Catlett, quoted in Herzog, *Elizabeth Catlett*, 26.
21 Catlett, interview.
22 Charles White, quoted in Willard F. Motley, "Negro Art in Chicago," *Opportunity: Journal of Negro Life* 18, no. 1 (January 1940): 22.
23 White, quoted in Motley, "Negro Art in Chicago," 22. For more on White's four murals, see Sarah Kelly Oehler, "Yesterday, Today, Tomorrow: Charles White's Murals and History as Art," in *Charles White: A Retrospective*, ed. Sarah Kelly Oehler and Esther Adler (Chicago, 2018), 21–37.
24 Catlett, quoted in Lewis, *Art of Elizabeth Catlett*, 148.
25 Catlett, interview.
26 Catlett, interview.
27 Lewis, *Art of Elizabeth Catlett*, 188, cataloged only one stone head during this period, dating it to 1943, based on Catlett's recollections decades later. However, period sources indicate that

she carved other stone heads, including one illustrated in 1942 while in progress; see *People's Voice*, July 18, 1942; clipping in box 31, folder 1, James A. Porter Papers, Emory University.

28 Catlett, interview. Such a permit, required by Dillard for Catlett to make the trip, would likely have been obtained through members of the SSCAC. It has not been confirmed through the AIC's records that Catlett served on a jury.

29 Pollack also served as advisor to the show *Paintings, Sculpture by American Negro Artists*, organized by Smith College Museum of Art and the Institute of Modern Art, Boston, which was held February 18 to March 7, 1943, and included a watercolor by Catlett titled *Freyer* (location unknown).

30 "Local Artists Exhibit Works in New York," *Chicago Defender*, December 13, 1941.

31 The catalog lists the sponsors and advisors; see *American Negro Art, 19th and 20th Centuries*, December 9, 1941–January 3, 1942, Downtown Gallery pamphlet file, Institutional Archives, Ryerson and Burnham Libraries, Art Institute of Chicago. For "exciting," see J. W. L., "Negro in Art," *Art News*, December 15–31, 1941, 24.

32 Catlett, interview.

33 The show was *Sculpture: Hoffman, Barthé, Savage, Catlett-White*, organized by the Coordinating Council of French Relief Societies, and held at the Whitelaw Reid Mansion, September 18, 1942, no catalog. See "Artist at New York Exhibit," *Baltimore Afro-American*, September 12, 1942.

34 June Levine and Gene Gordon, *Tales of Wo-Chi-Ca: Blacks, Whites and Reds at Camp* (San Rafael, CA, 2002), 17–18.

35 Catlett, quoted in Herzog, *Elizabeth Catlett*, 37.

36 Catlett, quoted in Herzog, *Elizabeth Catlett*, 31.

37 Herzog, *Elizabeth Catlett*, 32–33, discusses Catlett's recollection of her debates with Zadkine about universality versus particularity.

38 Catlett, interview. She does not refer to *Headlines* by title, but it seems plausible she might have been referring to it when she said, "I would give him an idea, why don't you put something like little pieces of paper, newspaper or something, in the background." *Headlines* is the only known collage by White.

39 Quoted in Herzog, *Elizabeth Catlett*, 115.

40 For instance, she showed two unlocated works, *Air Raid* and *Protection*, in the exhibition *New Names in American Art*, held at the G Place Gallery in Washington, DC, in 1944.

SHARECROPPER AND CAMPESINO

1 Elizabeth Catlett's Plan of Work for Rosenwald application, 1943, Rosenwald Collection, box 400, folder 7, John Hope and Aurelia E. Franklin Library Special Collections, Fisk University-1943, Julius Rosenwald Fund.

2 Elizabeth Catlett's Plan of Work for Rosenwald application, 1945, Rosenwald Collection, box 400, folder 7.

3 Pablo O'Higgins, quoted in Deborah Caplow, *Leopoldo Méndez: Revolutionary Art and the Mexican Print* (Austin, TX, 2007), 124.

4 Melanie Anne Herzog, *Elizabeth Catlett: An American Artist in Mexico* (Seattle, 2005), 57.

5 "Prologue," *Estampas de la revolución mexicana: 85 Grabados de los artistas del Taller de Gráfica Popular*, 1947. Marta Adams Papers, c. 1914–c. 1991, Archives of American Art, Smithsonian Institution.

6 The term "campesino" has varied definitions, including someone who comes from a rural part of Latin America, a peasant, or a farmer. However, in the context of this essay and the period following the Mexican Revolution, "campesino" specifically referred to peasants who worked the land but did not own the land and therefore worked for a landowner. (During the revolution campesinos would work for an hacendado, or hacienda/plantation owner.)

7 Caplow, *Leopoldo Méndez*, 153; Elena Poniatowska, "Los 60 años de Leopoldo Méndez," *Artes de México*, no. 45 (July 1963): 12.

8 "About This Collection," Farm Security Administration/Office of War Information Black-and-White Negatives, Library of Congress, https://www.loc.gov/collections/fsa-owi-black-and-white-negatives/about-this-collection.

9 "About This Collection," Farm Security Administration, Library of Congress.

10 Alain Locke, ed., *The New Negro* (New York, 1997).

11 Nelson Maldonado-Torres, "On the Coloniality of Being," *Cultural Studies* 21, nos. 2–3 (March/May 2007): 260, https://doi.org/10.1080/09502380601162548.

AN ARTIST-ACTIVIST AT THE CENTER OF THE GLOBAL SIXTIES

1 This observation is owed to Mary Lee Corlett, National Gallery of Art. See also p. 44.

2 For instance, the exhibition catalog *Artists in Exile: Expressions of Loss and Hope* (Yale University Art Gallery, New Haven, 2017) primarily featured works made within a year of Catlett's departure from the US (then conceived of as a temporary visit made possible by a travel grant), rather than from the nearly decade-long span (1962–1971) when she was forbidden to enter the US. See Dalila Scruggs, "Activism in Exile: Elizabeth Catlett's *Mask for Whites*," *American Art* 32, no. 3 (Fall 2018), for a brief summary of several scholars' work, including Melanie Anne Herzog, Lowery Stokes Sims, Rosalyn Story, and Rebecca Schreiber.

3 Edward Said, *Reflections on Exile and Other Essays* (Cambridge, MA, 2000), 176.

4 Said, *Reflections on Exile*, 185.

5 Rebecca M. Schreiber, *Cold War Exiles in Mexico: U.S. Dissidents and the Culture of Critical Resistance* (Minneapolis, 2008), xiii.

6 This is Schreiber's key point. See *Cold War Exiles in Mexico*, ix–xxv.

7 Eric Zolov, "Introduction: Latin America in the Global Sixties," *The Americas* 70, no. 3 (January 2014): 354.

8 Zolov, "Latin America in the Global Sixties," 357. The exact dates of the global sixties are debated. See also Eric Zolov, "Integrating Mexico into the Global Sixties," in *México beyond 1968: Revolutionaries, Radicals, and Repression during the Global Sixties and Subversive Seventies*, ed. Jaime M. Pensado and Enrique C. Ochoa (Tucson, 2018), 7, 19–32.

9 "Third World" is a term that emerged during the Cold War to refer to the nonaligned countries in Africa, Asia, and Latin America that were bound by a common struggle against imperialism. Within the US, Asian, Black, and Latinx Americans committed to anti-colonialism and racial liberation also embraced the term to articulate their commitment to this global framework of political solidarity. See "What Is the Third World?," editorial, *Triple Jeopardy* 1, no. 2 (November 1971): 15.

10 My research methodology is grounded largely in archival research, mining the historical record for evidence of how Catlett's artworks traveled between Mexico and the US, paper trails that evidence the transmission (or disruptions in transfer) of information over time and space, correspondence that illuminates Catlett's social networks, and Catlett's own statements about (dis)location and constraints of movement. This attention to distance and geographic remove is indebted to the work of historian of American art Jennifer L. Roberts, whose *Transporting Visions: The Movement of Images in Early America* (Berkeley, 2014) attends to the conditions of distance and travel that inhere in works of art. "These separations had formative effects on cultural production. Distances and delays, that is to say, were not merely passive intermissions or negative spaces between active sites of production," maintains Roberts. Though her study focuses on eighteenth- and nineteenth-century American art, she argues for the broader implications of her approach on visual and material culture studies. Catlett had the benefit of twentieth-century technologies, but the conditions of exile exacerbated the distance between her and the communities in the US with which she dearly wished to connect.

11 Nicole Gilpin Hood, "Theme and Form: The Image of Woman in the Art of Elizabeth Catlett" (PhD diss., University of Michigan, 2001), 49.

12 Dena Mirriam, "All History's Children: The Art of Elizabeth Catlett," *Sculpture Review* 42, no. 3 (1993): 11.

13 Pat and Harry Rambach to Betty [Catlett], c. 1970, box 6, folder 6, Elizabeth Catlett

Papers (addendum), Amistad Research Center, Tulane University.

14 Barbara Jones-Hogu, interview by Hudson Street Productions, 2010, Archives of American Art, Smithsonian Institution; Rebecca Zorach, "Interview with Barbara Jones-Hogu," *Never the Same*, https://never-the-same.org/interviews/barbara-jones-hogu/

15 Art dealer David Lusenhop has established this provenance. Although Barbara Jones-Hogu distinctly links her visit with Catlett to the 1968 Olympics, the date written in Catlett's hand on this print raises questions about the timing of Jones-Hogu's trip to Mexico. Alternatively, the print may offer evidence that Jones-Hogu went to Mexico for a second time in 1970. Additional evidence further substantiates this inquiry. An acquaintance of Catlett's wrote to her in early 1970, referencing someone who may have been Jones-Hogu: "Forgive me for taking so long to acknowledge the beautiful sweater you sent Ami [sp?] via Barbara Jones." David Lusenhop, email message to author, October 1, 2021. See "Anna" to Betty [Catlett], January 27, 1970, box 1, folder 1, Elizabeth Catlett Papers (addendum).

16 See, for example, Dana Chandler to Catlett, March 2, 1972, series 1, box 1, folder 3 correspondence, Elizabeth Catlett Papers; Barbara Perkins to Catlett, April 5, 1970, box 6, folder 8, Elizabeth Catlett Papers (addendum). See also "Correspondence—Artist, Art Scholars, and Admirers, 1959–1976," box 1, folder 3, Elizabeth Catlett Papers.

17 A 1970 FBI "Correlation Summary" listing Catlett's activities, including her visitors from abroad, reads like a who's who of Catlett's collectors, including Richard Long, Asa Zatz, Margaret Burroughs (see p. 106), and George and Ethelene Crockett. FBI, "Correlation Summary," October 20, 1970, NARA record number 124-10313-10012, https://www.maryferrell.org/showDoc.html?docId=232046.

18 "MEX-18 and MEX-19 advised on 8/13/63, that Mora [Catlett, who used Francisco Mora's last name socially] had been collecting money in Mexico to send telegrams of support for the march on Washington, 8/28/63. Mora cast three bronze statuettes to sell for that purpose. The collection was being made in the name of 'League for Defense of Negroes,' a defunct organization of which Mora had been a vice-president. Mora was reportedly to draft telegrams to be sent in the English Language." FBI, "Correlation Summary," October 20, 1970, 31.

19 Harry Blutstein, *Games of Discontent: Protests, Boycotts, and Politics at the 1968 Mexico Olympics* (Montreal, 2021), 112.

20 "I was very interested to see when we had the Olympics in Mexico. Those two gloved fists come up on the television screen." "Elizabeth Catlett Interview 12-18-1986/Latino in Los Angeles," 1983, VHS videotape, Elizabeth Catlett Papers (addendum).

21 Blutstein, *Games of Discontent*, 113.

22 As scholar of nationalism Benedict Anderson explains, newspapers encourage readers to imagine themselves as engaged in "this extraordinary mass ceremony," simultaneously reading the same papers as every other member of the community even though individual members will never meet or know one another. Benedict Anderson, *Imagined Communities: Reflections on the Origin and Spread of Nationalism* (London, 1983), 35.

23 Scruggs, "Activism in Exile," 2–21.

24 Colette Gaiter, "What Revolution Looks Like: The Work of Black Panther Artist Emory Douglas," in *Black Panther: The Revolutionary Art of Emory Douglas*, ed. Sam Durant (New York, 2007), 96.

25 Kellie Jones, "Swimming with E. C.," in *We Wanted a Revolution: Black Radical Women, 1965–85: New Perspectives*, ed. Catherine Morris and Rujeko Hockley (Brooklyn, 2018), 50. There are also numerous letters and shipping receipts that illustrate this point in box 4—Catlett, Elizabeth—Correspondence, 60–70s, Brockman Gallery Archives, Los Angeles Public Library.

26 Catlett to Alonzo Davis, box 4—Catlett, Elizabeth—Correspondence, 60–70s, Brockman Gallery Archives.

27 I publicly presented this argument, including the National Union of Mexican Women's involvement, in my paper "*Angela Libre*: Elizabeth Catlett, Pop Art and the Campaign to Free Angela Davis during the Global Sixties," at the University of Delaware's *My Art Speaks for Both My Peoples: A Symposium on Elizabeth Catlett* in 2019. At that time, these threads were not explored beyond Melanie Herzog's foundational outline of these connections. The Massacre of Tlatelolco has become a seminal moment in historical accounts of Mexico in the 1960s; scholars Jaime M. Pensado and Enrique C. Ochoa argue that the traditional narrative of 1968 homogenizes the protests of the 1960s and overlooks the long history of resistance that preceded and followed this massacre. Nevertheless, for this particular study, highlighting 1968 (the year that Martin Luther King's death set off a wave of urban uprisings) helps point to the ways that Mexico and the US were experiencing similar political unrest at the same time. The literature on the Movimiento Estudiantil, and the broader Dirty War of violent government repression, is too vast to survey here. For a foundational study, see Renata Keller's *Mexico's Cold War: Cuba, the United States, and the Legacy of the Mexican Revolution* (New York, 2015) as well as Pensado and Ochoa's extremely enlightening revision of this history, *México beyond 1968*.

28 David Mora, personal communication with author, June 2022.

29 The UNMM was affiliated with the Women's International Democratic Federation (WIDF; FDIM in Spanish). The union's membership included working- and middle-class women committed to fighting for women's rights. In addition to focusing on local and national issues, they also called for an end to colonialism, apartheid, and racial discrimination in the US. The literature on the UNMM is still relatively small. Verónica Oikión Solano has argued that the overwhelming focus on male students has obscured the significant role that the women of all ages, and especially the UNMM, played in the Movimiento Estudiantil. Ironically, within this overlooked history, Catlett's leadership in the organization is equally ignored in extant literature. In the UNMM's self-authored history, *Sembradoras del futuro*, the authors mention the TGP member Elizabeth Catlett and the UNMM member Betty Mora, but do not seem to understand that they are the same person. Nor do the authors acknowledge Betty Mora's leadership role within the institution. See Verónica Oikión Solano, "Resistencia y luchas femeniles. La Unión Nacional de Mujeres Mexicanas en el verano del 68: Una historia desconocida," *Legajos. Boletín del Archivo General de la Nación* 17 (September–December 2018): 55–84. See also Oikión Solano's conference presentation, "Resistencia y luchas. La Unión Nacional de Mujeres Mexicanas en el verano del 68" (El Historiador frente a la Historia, April 4, 2018), https://youtu.be/rFCgbT841q8; *Sembradoras del futuro: Memoria de la Unión Nacional de Mujeres Mexicanas* (Mexico City, 2000); Ana Lau Jaiven, "La Unión Nacional de Mujeres Mexicanas entre el comunismo y el feminismo: Una difícil relación," *Revista de estudios de género* 5, no. 40 (Summer 2014): 165–185; Gloria Tirado Villegas, *La otra historia: Voces de mujeres del 68 en Puebla* (Puebla, Mexico, 2004), 85.

30 This poster is published in *Sembradoras del futuro* (p. 203), suggesting that UNMM members were familiar with the image at the time.

31 Melanie Anne Herzog, *Elizabeth Catlett: An American Artist in Mexico* (Seattle, 2000), 140.

32 Rebecca VanDiver, "The Torture of Mothers: Elizabeth Catlett's Prints as a Call for Reproductive Justice," *Art Journal* 80, no. 2 (2021): 14–29.

33 Edward J. McCaughan, *Art and Social Movements: Cultural Politics in Mexico and Aztlán* (Durham, NC, 2012), 105.

34 Kenneth Mostern quoted in Yvonne Gutenberger, "I Am Remembered as a Hairdo: Angela Davis's *Autobiography* as a Revision of the Public Persona and Self-Reconstruction as Political Activist," in *Western Fictions, Black Realities: Meanings of Blackness and Modernities*, ed. Isabel Soto and Violet Showers Johnson (East Lansing, 2012), 306.

35 Sophie Lorenz, "Heroine of the Other America: The East German Solidarity Movement in Support of Angela Davis, 1970–73," in *The Routledge Handbook of the Global Sixties*, ed. Chen Jian et al. (London, 2018), 548–563. Significant attention has been paid to German solidarity with

the Free Angela Davis campaign, but I have been unable to find any extended discussion of the Davis campaign in Mexico.

36 UNMM's leadership encouraged its members to begin "comités de luchar" to "resolve the most urgent problems there may be in every locality." Perhaps, this hospitable environment encouraged Catlett to start her own Free Angela committee. Oikión Solano, "Resistencia y luchas femeniles," 68. See also Herzog, *Elizabeth Catlett*, 136; letters from UNMM, Ana Victoria Jimenez Archive, box 4, folder 14, Biblioteca Francisco Xavier Clavigero, Universidad Iberoamericana, Mexico City.

37 Bettina Aptheker reminded her father of the acquaintance: "I wrote to John Henrik Clarke as you proposed...Additionally, I am in communication with the black artist in Mexico Elizabeth Catlett—you must remember her very well. She is helping to organize an Angela Davis Committee there, and seemed interested also in circulating the Lukacs statement there is [*sic*] we do use it as the international statement." See Aptheker to Pop, February 12, 1971, Bettina Aptheker Papers, Special Collections and Archives, University Library, University of California, Santa Cruz.

38 Grace Granich [sp?] to Aptheker, n.d. (c. January 1971), Bettina Aptheker Papers.

39 Carbon copy of letter from Aptheker to Catlett, January 19, 1971, MS 157, Bettina Aptheker Papers. (Original now in Elizabeth Catlett Papers.)

40 Correspondence does not make it perfectly clear which version was selected. I assume that this version is the official poster because it best corresponds to Aptheker's description, "one with all the letters," and has been codified by its inclusion in Herzog's monograph. It should be noted that Herzog dates the poster to 1969, which does not conform to the historical timeline.

41 Indeed, Davis's teeth as identifying feature arise in key testimony during her trial. See Bettina Aptheker, *Intimate Politics: How I Grew Up Red, Fought for Free Speech, and Became a Feminist Rebel* (Emeryville, CA, 2006), 271.

42 Carbon copy of letter from Aptheker to Catlett, February 28, 1971, Bettina Aptheker Papers. (Original now in Elizabeth Catlett Papers.)

43 Aptheker to Catlett, February 18, 1971, Bettina Aptheker Papers.

44 Catlett to Aptheker, May 31, 1971, Bettina Aptheker Papers.

45 Aptheker to Louise Patterson, NUCFAD Office in New York, November 1, 1971, Bettina Aptheker Papers.

46 "Interview between Frederick Lewis of the Studio Museum and Elizabeth Catlett-Mora," August 7, 1971, Hayes-Benjamin Papers on African American Art and Artists, David C. Driskell Center Archives, University of Maryland.

47 Catlett created a print dedicated to George Jackson, suggesting she would have known about his prison abolition rhetoric.

48 Dan Berger, "'We Are the Revolutionaries': Visibility, Protest, and Racial Formation in 1970s Prison Radicalism" (PhD diss., University of Pennsylvania, 2010), 145; James Baldwin, "An Open Letter to My Sister, Miss Angela Davis," *New York Review of Books*, January 7, 1971.

49 Elizabeth Catlett, quoted in Marc Crawford, "My Art Speaks for Both My Peoples," *Ebony*, January 1970, 94.

50 Berger, "'We are the Revolutionaries,'" 148.

51 Michael Brenson, "Elizabeth Catlett's Sculptural Aesthetics," in *Elizabeth Catlett Sculpture: A Fifty-Year Retrospective*, ed. Lucinda H. Gedeon (Purchase, NY, 1998), 29.

52 Jennifer Josten, "Revolutionary Currents: Pop Design between Cuba, Mexico, and California," in *Pop América, 1965–1975*, ed. Esther Gabara (Durham, NC, 2018), 73.

53 Josten, "Revolutionary Currents," 79.

54 Josten, "Revolutionary Currents," 78.

55 Catlett has said that she traveled to Cuba twice. See Camille Billops, "Interview with Elizabeth Catlett," *Artists and Influence* (1991): 24.

56 Catlett to Aptheker, March 12, 1971, Bettina Aptheker Papers. Emphasis in original.

57 Thomas E. Crow, *The Long March of Pop: Art, Music, and Design, 1930–1995* (New Haven, 2014), 342–343.

58 Eric Zolov argues for this framing in his essay "Integrating Mexico into the Global Sixties."

59 Gabriela Aceves Sepúlveda, *Women Made Visible: Feminist Art and Media in Post-1968 Mexico City*, The Mexican Experience (Lincoln, NE, 2019), 152.

60 *Fair Play Magazine*, January–February 1998, 80.

LA MAESTRA'S FUGITIVE PEDAGOGY IN MEXICO

1 Engracia Loyo, "La educación del pueblo," in *La educación en México*, ed. Escalante Gonzalbo (Mexico City, 2010). I thank Dalila Scruggs for her generosity of research spirit in sharing archival photographs from the Amistad Research Center as well as Jill Moniz for her revisions and wisdom.

2 "Fugitive pedagogy names the educational acts of escape constituting the pre-condition of black freedom implied by the very notion of 'education as freedom.' Fugitive pedagogy, then, might be thought of as what it means to put this philosophical ideal into practice." Jarvis R. Givens, *Fugitive Pedagogy: Carter G. Woodson and the Art of Black Teaching* (Cambridge, MA, 2021), 13.

3 Sewing is mentioned repeatedly in Catlett's interviews and her students' memories. See Christina Heatherton's discussion of Catlett's sewing class, "How to Make a Dress," at the George Washington Carver School in Christina Heatherton, *Arise! Global Radicalism in the Era of the Mexican Revolution* (Oakland, CA, 2022); Raquel Tibol, "La obra de Elizabeth Catlett," *Los universitarios* 60–61 (November 15–30, 1975): 16; Ana Iturbe, interview by the author, June 2023.

4 Fourteen male faculty members wrote an open letter denouncing Catlett for being foreign-born, too concerned with African art, a woman, and inept. Elizabeth Catlett, interview by Clifton Johnson, January 5, 1983, Elizabeth Catlett Papers, Amistad Research Center, Tulane University.

5 See art historian, artist, and Catlett student Samella Lewis's account of her resignation from the Los Angeles County Museum of Art in 1970. Samella Lewis and Richard Candida Smith, *Image and Belief: Samella Lewis* (Los Angeles, 2013).

6 Catlett, interview.

7 Armando Ortega, interview by the author, November 2022; Tiburcio Ortiz, interview by the author, November 2022.

8 See "Los Muros en Las Calles de Chicago" and "Rupert Garcia" in Elizabeth Catlett Papers.

9 Ortega, interview.

10 Heatherton, *Arise!*, 17.

11 For a definition of "Third World" within the context of this period, see "An Artist-Activist at the Center of the Global Sixties," note 9.

12 Ortega, interview. Unless otherwise noted all translations are my own.

13 For more on Catlett's disconnection from the Mexican art world, see Melanie Herzog's indispensable study: *Elizabeth Catlett: An American Artist in Mexico* (Seattle, 2000).

14 "Lecture notes #1," Elizabeth Catlett Papers.

15 "Rupert Garcia," Elizabeth Catlett Papers.

16 "Rupert Garcia," Elizabeth Catlett Papers.

17 Ortega, interview.

18 Ortega, interview.

19 Helga Prignitz-Poda, *El Taller de Gráfica Popular en México, 1937–1977* (Mexico City, 1992), 195.

20 Dina Comisarenco Mirkin, "A Collective Roar from the Taller de Gráfica Popular: Mariana Yampolsky, Elizabeth Catlett, Fanny Rabel and Celia Calderón," *Artelogie: Recherche sur les arts, le patrimoine et la littérature de l'Amérique latine*, no. 17 (October 5, 2021).

21 Silvia Tinoco, interview by the author, November 2022.

22 Tinoco, interview.

23 Tinoco, interview.

24 Tinoco, interview.

25 Tinoco, interview.

26 Iturbe, interview.

27 Iturbe, interview.

28 Iturbe, interview.

29 Catlett to Jesús Álvarez Amaya, Ana Iturbe and Raul Cabello Collection, Mexico City.

30 "Los cambios políticos han cambiado al arte. Cada vez son menos los artistas interesados en servir al pueblo; lo que les interesa es la fama y el dinero, y producen un arte que llaman internacional, aunque en verdad hay que calificarlo de comercial europeo o estadunidense." (The changes in politics have changed art. Increasingly there are fewer artists interested in serving the people: what they are interested in is fame and money, and they make an art they call international, even though in truth it should be qualified as European and US

commerce.) Tibol, "La obra de Elizabeth Catlett," 16.

31 Valerie Gladstone, "An Artist for Her People," *American Legacy*, Winter 2003, 64.

32 Sonia Sanchez, *Collected Poems* (Boston, 2021), 382–383.

33 bell hooks, *Teaching to Transgress: Education as the Practice of Freedom* (New York, 1994), 26.

PRESSING NARRATIVES

1 Catlett, draft of speech written for delivery at the University of Mississippi, October 1984, Elizabeth Catlett Papers (addendum), 078-1, box 12, folder 7, Amistad Research Center, Tulane University.

2 "Artist's Statement," in *The Black Woman in America: Prints by Elizabeth Catlett* (Krannert Art Museum, Urbana-Champaign, IL, 1993).

3 Catlett, "Artist's Statement."

4 Initially titled *The Negro Woman*, the series was renamed by Catlett to reflect updated terminology.

5 Melanie Anne Herzog, *Elizabeth Catlett: An American Artist in Mexico* (Seattle, 2000), 16. Catlett's Howard University transcripts (Rosenwald Collection, box 400, folder 7, John Hope and Aurelia E. Franklin Library Special Collections, Fisk University) show that in her first semester of 1933, Catlett enrolled in Art 116, taught by James Wells: "Wood-cut, linoleum-cut, and air brush processes are taught through the creation of patterns for decorative silks, dress fabrics, and wall paper. Introduction to the etchers' craft." The transcripts also reveal that she was likely introduced to Japanese woodblock prints in Wells's composition class during her first semester at Howard, in 1931 (Catalog of the Officers and Students of Howard University, 1931–1932 and 1932–1933, https://dh.howard.edu/hucatalogs/53 and https://dh.howard.edu/hucatalogs/54, respectively). See also Camille Billops, "Elizabeth Catlett: Sculptor, Printmaker. Interview #2," *Artist and Influence* 10 (1991): 17.

6 Herzog, *Elizabeth Catlett*, 20.

7 Rosenwald application, 1943, Rosenwald Collection, box 400, folder 7.

8 Rosenwald application, 1945, Rosenwald Collection, box 400, folder 7. Her reapplication in 1946 maintained the same desired outcome.

9 Art Students League records show that Catlett enrolled in a graphics course with Harry Sternberg in October 1945 (Catlett's 1945 Registration Form, Archives of the Art Students League of New York) that, according to the course catalog, included the study of lithography, etching, and silkscreen.

10 Sternberg was a noted admirer of Orozco prints and sent his students to study them. See James M. Wechsler, "Propaganda Gráfica: Printmaking and the Radical Left in Mexico, 1920–50," in *Mexico and Modern Printmaking: A Revolution in the Graphic Arts, 1920 to 1950* (Philadelphia Museum of Art and McNay Art Museum, San Antonio, TX, 2006), 264n25.

11 Ellen Sragow, "An Interview with Elizabeth Catlett," *Journal of the Print World* 17, no. 4 (Fall 1994): 30.

12 Sragow, "An Interview with Elizabeth Catlett," 30. See Edward Alden Jewell, "Negro Art Display Put on Exhibition," *New York Times*, December 10, 1941.

13 Herzog, *Elizabeth Catlett*, 21.

14 Rosenwald reapplication, 1946, Rosenwald Collection, box 400, folder 7.

15 "Report of Progress and Plan of Work for a Renewal Under a Julius Rosenwald Fellowship," submitted with Rosenwald reapplication, 1946, Rosenwald Collection, box 400, folder 7.

16 "Report of Progress and Plan of Work for a Renewal Under a Julius Rosenwald Fellowship," submitted with Rosenwald reapplication, 1946, Rosenwald Collection, box 400, folder 7.

17 Catlett to William C. Haygood, October 4, 1946, Rosenwald Collection, box 400, folder 7.

18 In an interview with Michael Brenson, Catlett mentions that she learned how to work in linocut at the TGP, implying that it was after arriving in Mexico that she became interested in the technique. "Form That Achieves Sympathy: A Conversation with Elizabeth Catlett," *Sculpture*, April 1, 2003, https://sculpturemagazine.art/form-that-achieves-sympathy-a-conversation-with-elizabeth-catlett/.

19 Catlett's early prints at the TGP included lithographs, but she identified the small linocut of a male sharecropper as her first (p. 100); see Sragow, "An Interview with Elizabeth Catlett," 30. Some known impressions of the print are dated to 1945, but this would have been the year prior to her engagement with the TGP workshop. This *Sharecropper*, similar to the *Mother and Child* lithograph based on an earlier watercolor, may have been based on an earlier rendering of the subject—perhaps drawn originally in 1945 or even earlier, when she was exploring possibilities for her first (rejected) Rosenwald proposal to represent the Black worker in agriculture. Inconsistent dating was not unusual for Catlett.

20 See Herzog, *Elizabeth Catlett*, 86–87. In addition, Catlett credited Ignacio Aguirre with teaching her about various linocut tools and techniques (see Billops, Interview, October 1, 1989, *Artist and Influence*, 22), and also Francisco Mora, as confirmed by David Mora Catlett, April 28, 2024.

21 Catlett to Haygood, October 4, 1946, Rosenwald Collection, box 400, folder 7.

22 Catlett, "Responding to Cultural Hunger," in *Reimaging America: The Arts of Social Change* (Philadelphia, 1990), 246–247.

23 Hannes Meyer, ed., *TGP México: El Taller de Gráfica Popular, doce años de obra artística colectiva* (Mexico City, 1949), xi. Meyer (1889–1954) was a Swiss architect, Bauhaus director (1928–1930), and director of La Estampa Mexicana from 1942 to 1949.

24 *Firmas para la Paz* (1952, p. 94), for example, was one of twelve graphics for the exhibition *Primera exposición conjunta de artistas plásticos mexicanos y españoles residentes en México*. See Helga Prignitz, *TGP Ein Grafiker-Kollektiv in Mexico von 1937–1977* (Berlin, 1981), 411, no. 1262. See the 1949 TGP filmstrip production organized by Pablo O'Higgins, *Who Wants War Who Wants Peace*, which featured drawings by TGP artists. See Prignitz, *TGP Ein Grafiker-Kollektiv in Mexico*, 397–401, nos. 1084–1142 (Catlett is no. 1132). See also Herzog, *Elizabeth Catlett*, 90, and related notes, 201–202. A group of drawings related to the project is in the holdings of the Library of Congress: https://www.loc.gov/pictures/item/2010647089/. In the filmstrip Catlett's drawing (now in the collection of Rhode Island School of Design; p. 91) depicted three Mexican girls studying a book. The drawing was also the source for a lithograph (fig. 1). A copy of the filmstrip is included in the Seema Weatherwax photographs, M0868, Department of Special Collections and University Archives, Stanford University, along with a draft copy of the script. For a TGP calaveras newspaper to which Catlett was a contributor, see https://lccn.loc.gov/2023641148. Finally, books illustrating Catlett's linocuts include Guillermo Contreras, *Silvestre Revueltas: Genio Atormentado* (Mexico, 1954); *Seleccion de Poemas de Adam Mickiewicz* (Mexico, 1957); Mario Gill, ed., *La Huelga de Nueva Rosita* (Mexico, 1959); William Cameron Townsend, *Lázaro Cárdenas: Demócrata Mexicano*, 2nd ed., rev. Lic. Luis García Carrillo, trans. Avelino Ramírez A. (Mexico, 1954). See Prignitz, *TGP Ein Grafiker-Kollektiv in Mexico*, nos. 1438, 1951–1954, and 1683, respectively. Also, *TGP Mexico: El Taller de Gráfica Popular* is a spiral-bound volume that included five original linocuts as a sales incentive.

25 This was clearly demonstrated in the early 1960s, when the internal disagreements between factions resulted in a significant exodus of members aligned with Méndez, who took prints and matrices with them. See Prignitz, *TGP Ein Grafiker-Kollektiv in Mexico*, 202.

26 See Catlett, "Responding to Cultural Hunger," 247, and Herzog, *Elizabeth Catlett*, 101–103, for full description.

27 Prints from the *Estampas de la Revolución Mexicana* were published in the government-backed newspaper *El Nacional* on a daily basis for three months in 1949; see Meyer, *TGP México*, xvii. In addition, Herzog (*Elizabeth Catlett*, 102) describes a similar large-scale TGP project to teach Mexican heroes to rural schoolchildren through the monthly publication *El Maestro Mexicano*.

28 Catlett, "Responding to Cultural Hunger," 247.

29 Prignitz, *TGP Ein Grafiker-Kollektiv in Mexico*, 164–166. Prignitz consulted TGP archive notes and offers some description of the collaboration sessions of the participating

artists. Prignitz, *TGP Ein Grafiker-Kollektiv in Mexico*, 444–445, nos. 1782–1796, recorded sixteen prints that included an attribution of *Sojourner Truth* to John Wilson, who lived and worked in Mexico for five years, 1950–1956. Prignitz, 309, mistakenly recorded his tenure at the workshop as in the 1940s, and this is the only work by Wilson she indexed. She deemed it lost, along with Roberto Berdecio's *Denmark Vesey* and Erasto Cortés Juárez's *George Washington Carver*; it is likely that Margaret Burroughs's Sojourner prints of this period were connected to this project, including the lithograph dated 1953 that is clearly based on a carte de visite (https://www.loc.gov/item/98501256/). See also Herzog, *Elizabeth Catlett*, 101–103. A full examination of Catlett's subject choices as connected to her lived experience has yet to be undertaken: Blanche K. Bruce was the first African American to serve a full term in the US Senate (Mississippi, 1874–1880); afterward he lived in Washington, DC, and served as recorder of deeds and on the DC Board of Trustees of Public Schools (1892–1895). Benjamin Davis had served on the Carver School's board. Rebecca M. Schreiber broaches this question in *Cold War Exiles in Mexico* (Minneapolis, 2008), 48–50, 56–57. Catlett's own *Harriet Tubman* was her second depiction of this formidable Black female leader; she executed a third in 1975, also in linocut, during the period of the Black Arts Movement. That she once again chose linocut—instead of screenprint or other techniques popular at the time—certainly connects the last *Harriet* to her previous two, while also leveraging the linocut's historic place in the printmaking traditions of Mexico and the art of resistance.

30 Leopoldo Méndez, *Paul Robeson*; Ángel Bracho, *Crispus Attucks*; Elizabeth Catlett, *Harriet Tubman*; and Alberto Beltrán, *Nat Turner*, were reproduced in *Artes de Mexico* 18 (July–August 1957), n.p. See Section II: La obra collectiva, Contra La Discriminación en los Estaados Unidos, a–d. Also, see Catlett, "The Negro People and American Art," *Freedomways* 1, no. 1 (Spring 1961): 78.

31 Prignitz, *TGP Ein Grafiker-Kollektiv in Mexico*, 204–205. For more on the series, see Theodore W. Cohen, *Finding Afro-Mexico* (New York, 2020), 247–249.

32 Prignitz, *TGP Ein Grafiker-Kollektiv in Mexico*, 329, no. 124.

33 Prignitz, *TGP Ein Grafiker-Kollektiv in Mexico*, 336, no. 189. Along with Catlett, the artists are Andrea Gómez, Óscar Frias, and Mariana Yampolsky.

34 Townsend, *Lázaro Cárdenas*, 1, 372 (see Prignitz nos. 1554–1583).

35 In consultation with Catlett, Ellen Sragow charted the printing of this serial edition: *Sharecropper* was first carved in 1952 and an unknown number of impressions were printed during the 1950s. Most of the proofs from this period are black and white, but Catlett also experimented with color. The impression exhibited at Atlanta University (now Clark Atlanta) in 1952, where it was awarded a purchase prize, has some color. Most impressions of this period were printed by José Sánchez, but some were printed by Catlett. A very small *x* in the block, visible inside the lower left corner, filled in during later printings. *Sharecropper* was reproduced in *Artes de México*, no. 18 (July–August 1957). Between 1968 and 1970 a full-color, numbered edition of sixty—printed primarily by José Sánchez, with a few by Catlett—was produced from the original block. Some undocumented black-and-white proofs were printed at this time, but there was no black-and-white edition. In 1993 a black-and-white edition of twenty was produced, with a few undocumented artist proofs, printed by Pedro Ascencio in Mexico City. See Ellen Sragow, "Elizabeth Catlett, 'Sharecropper,' 1952–93, Editions, Linoleum Cut," *Artsy*, May 27, 2014, https://www.artsy.net/article/sragow-gallery-elizabeth-catlett-sharecropper-1952-93-editions-linoleum-cut. In addition to those accounted for in Sragow's timeline, there were sixty impressions, which included two versions—black only and black with color—dated 1970 that were printed around 1997 by Joseph Kleineman and Maureen Turci, J. K. Fine Art Editions Co., New Jersey. Because the original blocks for the color areas were by this time lost or destroyed, lithography was used in combination with the original linocut key block. These impressions bear the J. K. Fine Art chop mark. After this printing, the linocut block was defaced, as confirmed by Maureen Turci in an email to author, July 31, 2023.

36 See *The Black Woman in America: Prints by Elizabeth Catlett*. Consistent with TGP practice, the series was likely printed in an ad hoc manner over the years until 1989, when fourteen of the fifteen blocks were printed in an edition of twenty at the Robert Blackburn Printmaking Workshop in New York. Receipts kept by Catlett, now preserved in the Elizabeth Catlett Papers, Amistad Research Center, Tulane University, identify Gloria Escobar as the Blackburn workshop printer of the series.

37 One of the prints in the series, *I Have Studied in Ever Increasing Numbers*, was not reprinted in 1989. The linocut matrix for it may have been damaged or lost, as perhaps also for *My right is a future of equality with other Americans*. The second linocut matrix used for adding color for the original 1946–1947 printing of *My right*... is in the holdings of the Catlett estate, along with the key (black) block and the color block for the 1989 edition. As the final print and the coda of the series, *My right*...was clearly essential and thus Catlett recarved it. The print sometimes titled *Separation* (Studio Museum) or *Barbed Wire* (1954) is a recarving of *My reward has been bars between me and the rest of the land* (p. 44), the eleventh print of *The Black Woman* series. An alternate version of *I am the Black Woman* (p. 33) exists: see Heather Nickels, *Persevere and Resist: The Strong Black Women of Elizabeth Catlett* (Memphis Brooks Museum of Art, 2021), 24n2. Although Catlett's reasons for using variant images are unclear, to have done so is not inconsistent with her practice. The lithographs *Lovey Twice* (1976), *Jackie* (1985), *Pensive* (1985), *Cartas* (1986), *On the Subway* (1986), and *These Two Generations* (1987) were also printed at the Blackburn workshop. Elizabeth Catlett Papers, Printmaking Workshop, New York, 1977–1980, box 3, folder 8, and Elizabeth Catlett Papers (addendum), 1942–2003, box 1, folder 12, Amistad Research Center.

38 Catlett produced variant editions using the same linocut block she used for the singular *Portrait*, including *Portrait in Cuatro* (1976, color), signed edition of twenty (Elizabeth Catlett Estate), and *Portrait in Cuatro* (1978, brown/black), signed edition of twenty (repr. in Jeanne Zeidler, ed., *Elizabeth Catlett: Works on Paper, 1944–1992* [Hampton University Museum, VA, 1993], 26).

39 Per Sragow, from notes based on her conversation with the artist. Sragow Gallery files, shared with the author October 2022. See also Herzog, *Elizabeth Catlett*, 100. Catlett's editioning practices occasionally included small "special editions" inscribed *E/E* [Edición Especial], such as Catlett's lithograph after Siqueiros discussed later in this essay; see note 57. She produced special editions even after the TGP years, exemplified in *There's a Woman in Every Color* (1975, repr. Swann, February 19, 2008, sale 2136, lot 250).

40 It should be noted that inconsistent inscriptions, including titles, dates, and edition sizes, are not unique to Catlett and appear in the work of many printmakers during this period.

41 Printed in Mexico City by Litografos Unidos, S.A. See https://hindmanauctions.com/items/10641440-art-catlett-elizabeth-1915-2012-portfolio-containing-5-lithographs-mexico-city-litografos-unidos-s-a-ca-1973.

42 For a further discussion, see Cynthia Fabrizio Pelak, "Remembering and Reclaiming the Genius of Beah Richards' *A Black Woman Speaks*...of White Womanhood, of White Supremacy, of Peace," *Race, Gender & Class* 21, no. 3/4 (2014): 189–209; Ashawnta Jackson, "The Poem That Inspired Radical Black Women to Organize," *JSTOR Daily*, November 5, 2020, https://daily.jstor.org/the-poem-that-inspired-radical-black-women-to-organize/. For the full poem, see https://www.jstor.org/stable/community.28045786. Longtime friends, Richards and Catlett participated in a program at the California African American Museum when Catlett's 1998 sculpture retrospective, organized by the Neuberger Museum of Art, traveled there. See Rosalyn M. Story, "Elizabeth Catlett," *Emerge* 11, no. 5 (March 2000): 51. A copy of Richards's book, *Black Woman Speaks*, is included in Catlett's personal library in Cuernavaca, Mexico.

43 This print is most often described as a woodcut but is likely also linocut, as noted

by Clare Rogan, curator of prints and drawings at the Detroit Institute of Arts, following her examination of the impression in DIA's holdings. Email message to author, May 31, 2023.

44 The print was exhibited in Havana in 1963 and received an award, as annotated on a photograph in the artist files of the Brandywine Workshop and Archives, Philadelphia. (Catlett created one print, an offset lithograph titled *Blues*, 1983, at the Brandywine Workshop; see https://artura.org/Detail/title/16450). Catlett revisited *Women of America* in a later screenprint, *Three Women of America* (fig. 6), printed in 1990 by Lou Stovall in Washington, DC; Stovall's workshop documentation references the early drawing.

45 Prignitz, *TGP Ein Grafiker-Kollektiv in Mexico*, 202–205.

46 Prignitz, *TGP Ein Grafiker-Kollektiv in Mexico*, 205.

47 See Prignitz, *TGP Ein Grafiker-Kollektiv in Mexico*, 205, n328, 343 (no. 229b, poster), and 406 (no. 1214, podium decoration).

48 In each case individual linocut matrices are in the holdings of the Catlett estate; Mexican printer Raul Cabello created the screens. Cabello and Ana Iturbe, interview by J. V. Decemvirale in Mexico City, June 19, 2023. For more on Cabello, see Decemvirale's essay in this volume. Cabello was the printer for a number of Catlett's lithographs: *Red Leaves* (1978, p. 213), *Double Profile* (1978), *Girl and the City* (1979), *Two Generations* (1979), *Prissy* (1979), *Madonna* (1982, p. 218), *Virginia* (1984, p. 227), *Celie* (1986), *Waving* (1989), *Dancing* (1990), and *Harlem Woman* (1992, p. 225), as well as screenprints: *Roots* (1981, p. 216), *Girls* (1982, fig. 8), *Latch Key Child* (1988), and *Fiesta* (1988).

49 Per Sragow, notes from conversations with the artist. Sragow Gallery files, shared with author October 2022.

50 Catlett, artist questionnaire, signed and dated January 31, 1990, object file for accession no. 1989.11, Pennsylvania Academy of the Fine Arts (PAFA), Philadelphia. The term "cliché" as used by Catlett here refers to the matrix. It is possible that the reference to acrylic is to gesso, used to create the collagraphed texture surrounding Malcolm X. Catlett may have used gesso or modeling paste applied to a board, manipulating it while wet to create texture then allowing it to dry to produce a printable matrix, such as is illustrated in John Ross, Clare Romano, *The Complete Printmaker* (New York, 1990), 137. I thank Maureen Turci and Joseph Kleineman, printers of the 2004 edition, for our discussions of process.

51 Catlett, artist questionnaire, PAFA.

52 Samella Lewis, *The Art of Elizabeth Catlett* (Claremont, CA, 1984), 91.

53 Catlett, quoted in Lewis, *The Art of Elizabeth Catlett*, 91. *Malcolm X Speaks for Us* was awarded a purchase prize at the Salón de Grabado in Mexico City in 1969.

54 In 1954 Catlett protested imperialism in Guatemala with *Defendiendo la soberanía de Guatemala defendémos la soberanía de México*, published in the journal *Polémica sobre el arte y la cultura* (July 1954). Prignitz, *TGP Ein Grafiker-Kollektiv in Mexico*, 335, no. 169 (p. 164). The linocut matrix in the holdings of the Catlett estate does not include the TGP initials as would have been carved into the lower left corner of the 1954 matrix. The estate may hold the original 1954 matrix, which Catlett trimmed to remove the TGP designation; it is also possible that Catlett recarved the image for reprinting in 1986. The Studio Museum in Harlem holds a version dated 1963 and inscribed with the title *Latina America Says No!*, which does not show the TGP initials, but the impression is heavily inked. The Catlett estate has an impression dated 1968 and inscribed with the title *Latin America Says No!* that does show the TGP initials. *Chile I* and *Chile II*, printed in 1980, call out the horrors of Pinochet rule. Among the "disappeared" in Guatemala was Alaíde Foppa, whom Catlett mentioned without identifying her by name, in a 1981 Black Women's Conference interview. Black Academy of Arts and Letters Records, UNT Libraries Special Collections, Portal to Texas History, https://texashistory.unt.edu/ark:/67531/metadc1913231/.

55 Catlett and Mora kept a small press in their studio for proofing and printing linocuts. For some linocut editions, larger-scale prints, or lithography, Catlett sought out larger presses, such as the one at La Esmeralda, and she relied on trusted printers in both New York and Mexico, including Robert Blackburn, José Sánchez and his wife, Maria Louisa Plata, Raul Cabello and Ana Iturbe, and Joseph Kleineman and Maureen Turci of J. K. Fine Art Editions. Catlett's son David pointed out the correlation between the width of the proof and the dimensions of the studio press in conversation with author, June 12, 2022.

56 Catlett identified Sánchez as the printer of this edition of ten, per Sragow, from notes from conversations with the artist. Sragow Gallery files, shared with author October 2022. Catlett maintained a close working relationship with this legendary TGP printer. See Herzog, *Elizabeth Catlett*, 89. Linocuts and lithographs printed by Sánchez include *Mujer Cocinando (Woman Cooking)* (p. 96), *Shoeshine Boy* (p. 96), some of *Sharecropper* (printed 1968–1970, p. 103), *Black is Beautiful* (1968, see https://collection.artbma.org/objects/107704/black-is-beautiful?ctx=b553cccf8c91e8bf21b344d0f531d7062a0a1768&idx=4), *Negro es Bello* (1969, see p. 157), *Torture of Mothers* (1970, p. 162), *Which Way?* (1973, repr. in Zeidler, *Catlett*, 55), and *Central America Says No!* (1986, p. 164). For more on Sánchez, see Masha Zepeda, "José Sánchez: El impresor popular," part 1, *El Alcaraván* 1, no. 3 (October 1990): 18–19; part 2, *El Alcaraván* 1, no. 4 (January 1991): 22–24.

57 For a description of the origination of this special edition and an indication of the respect within the TGP for Catlett's mastery of the process, see Zepeda, "José Sánchez: El impresor popular," 23. For an image, see https://collections.lacma.org/node/193887.

58 Catlett also used fabric to make collage maquettes for prints such as *New Generation* and *Links Together* (p. 228); both lithographs were printed at J. K. Fine Art Editions. Documentation for *Three Women of America* (1990), printed by Lou Stovall, indicates that the maquette for that screenprint, too, was a collage of paper and fabric, with added paint, ink, and graphite.

59 Printed in Mexico City by Raul Cabello.

60 *To Marry* is one of six lithographs produced as a portfolio and in bound volume to honor the anniversary of Margaret Walker's epic poem *For My People*, first published in 1937 and recipient of the Yale Series of Younger Poets Award in 1942. Published by the Limited Editions Club, New York, in 1992, and printed by J. K. Fine Art Editions, the titles of the prints are *Singing Their Songs*, *Play Mates*, *To Marry*, *Walking Blindly*, *All the People*, and *A Second Generation*. See https://www.moma.org/collection/works/22108.

61 Printed by Cabello.

62 Gillian Greenhill Hannum, Print Club of New York newsletter (Fall 2005): 1–2.

63 Catlett was known to be a seamstress and made many of her own clothes; see Brenson, "Form That Achieves Sympathy: A Conversation with Elizabeth Catlett." Robin Holder also mentioned this in an email message to author, July 21, 2023.

64 Holder's role as assistant director at the workshop included directing community programs and developing strategies for scholarships, fellowships, exhibits, and guest artists. She noted the "very powerful impact Betty's presence at the shop had on PMW printmakers and BIPOC artists." Email message to author, July 14, 2023.

65 Email messages to author, July 20–21, 2023. A note from Holder to Catlett dated August 19, 1987, describing in detail a technique that Holder had developed for her own work but which also caught the interest of both Blackburn and Catlett, can be found in Elizabeth Catlett Papers (addendum), 1942–2003, box 1, folder 10, Amistad Research Center. As Holder explained in her email message to the author: "The notes indicate a process I was using that I don't think anyone else was using at the time: cutting plastic shapes, inking them and placing them on top of inked linoleum blocks or inked plexi to print. In addition, around 1987 Bob [Blackburn] and Betty came into etching room 4 one evening to see what I was doing. They both looked at my print and exclaimed, 'How did you get that effect!'"

66 Catlett taught a class, "How to Make a Dress," at the Carver School in New York in 1945. For more on the radicality of dressmaking as related to Catlett's art and politics, see Christina Heatherton, "How to

Make a Dress," in *Arise! Global Radicalism in the Era of the Mexican Revolution* (Oakland, CA, 2022), 145–174. For a broader discussion of fiber arts in African American history and culture, see Carolyn L. Mazloomi, "And Still We Rise: Race, Culture, and Visual Conversations," in *And Still We Rise: Race, Culture, and Visual Conversations* (Atglen, PA, 2015), 6–11.

67 Quoted in Valerie Gladstone, "Elizabeth Catlett: Role Modeler," *ARTnews* 97, no. 1 (January 1998): 54.

"THINKING ABOUT WOMEN" THROUGH FORM, SUBSTANCE, AND RADICAL POLITICS

1 Elizabeth Catlett, interview by Mary Gibbons, 1989, audiocassette recording, Elizabeth Catlett Estate, Cuernavaca, Mexico; copy in author's collection.

2 Elizabeth Catlett, untitled and undated handwritten manuscript for a presentation about her work, artist's files, Cuernavaca, Mexico; copy in author's collection.

3 Catlett to Timothy D. Brown, April 23, 1987, box 1, folder 10, Elizabeth Catlett Papers (addendum), Amistad Research Center, Tulane University, New Orleans.

4 Elizabeth Catlett, quoted in Martha Kearns, "Elizabeth Catlett," in *Gumbo Ya Ya: Anthology of Contemporary African American Women Artists*, ed. Leslie King-Hammond (New York, 1995), 46.

5 Catlett, untitled manuscript.

6 Elizabeth Catlett, quoted in Samella Lewis, *The Art of Elizabeth Catlett* (Claremont, CA, 1984), 90.

7 Alice Elizabeth Catlett, "Sculpture in Stone: Negro Mother and Child" (MFA thesis, State University of Iowa, 1940), 1.

8 See Michael Brenson, "Form That Achieves Sympathy: A Conversation with Elizabeth Catlett," *Sculpture* 22, no. 3 (April 2003): 33.

9 Primavera (*Roseodendron donnell-smithii*), also known as white mahogany, grows in Mexico and Central America. Contrary to what its name suggests, Spanish cedar (*Cedrela odorata*) grows in Mexico, Central America, and the northern part of South America, and is in the mahogany family (Meliaceae). Because of their visual similarity and the confusion presented by their common names, the identification of woods Catlett used in her sculptures has been inconsistent and at times incorrect. My thanks to research botanist Alex Wiedenhoeft at the USDA Forest Products Laboratory in Madison, WI, for helping me understand these discrepancies.

10 Elizabeth Catlett, slide presentation, DuSable Museum of African American History, Chicago, May 7, 1994.

11 Elizabeth Catlett, interview by the author, December 10, 1991.

12 Catlett spoke of her "undesirable alien" status and her experience of being barred from entering the US in numerous interviews, including with the author in Cuernavaca, Mexico, July 6, 1991, on audiotape, and in a speech, by phone, to the Conference on the Functional Aspects of Black Art (CONFABA) at Northwestern University, May 6, 1970, transcript with handwritten additions and corrections, box 6, folder 8, Elizabeth Catlett Papers (addendum)—excerpted in the author's book *Elizabeth Catlett: An American Artist in Mexico* (Seattle, 2000), 147–148.

13 *Sojourner* was vandalized in 2013 and broken into multiple pieces. Following its restoration, it has been housed at Sacramento's Crocker Art Museum.

14 Elizabeth Catlett, conversation with the author, April 25, 2010; Elizabeth Catlett, statement at the unveiling of *Mahalia Jackson*, New Orleans, April 28, 2010.

15 Mora J. Beauchamp-Byrd, "An Aesthetic of Survival: The Visionary Art of Elizabeth Catlett," in *Struggle and Serenity: The Visionary Art of Elizabeth Catlett* (New York, 1996), 9–19.

GIVING FEMINISM A SHOVE IN THE RIGHT DIRECTION

1 Samella Lewis and Ruth G. Waddy, eds., *Black Artists on Art* (Los Angeles, 1971), 2:107.

2 For a concise overview from the perspective of third wave feminists, see chapter 2, "What Is Feminism?," in Jennifer Baumgardner and Amy Richards, *Manifesta: Young Women, Feminism, and the Future* (New York, 2000), 50–86.

3 Lorraine O'Grady, conversation with the author, June 2, 2020.

4 See Toni Morrison, ed., *Race-ing Justice, En-Gendering Power: Essays on Anita Hill, Clarence Thomas, and the Construction of Social Reality* (New York, 1992); and Judith Butler, *Gender Trouble: Feminism and the Subversion of Identity* (New York, 1990).

5 See, for example, "Is It Time to Jump Ship? Historians Rethink the Waves Metaphor," by Kathleen A. Laughlin, Julie Gallagher, Dorothy Sue Cobble, Eileen Boris, Premilla Nadasen, Stephanie Gilmore, and Leandra Zarnow, in the journal *Feminist Formations* 22, no. 1 (Spring 2010): 76–135.

6 Erik S. McDuffie, *Sojourning for Freedom: Black Women, American Communism, and the Making of Black Left Feminism* (Durham, NC, 2011), 3–4; and Mary Helen Washington, *The Other Blacklist: The African American Literary and Cultural Left of the 1950s* (New York, 2014), 4.

7 Jacqueline Jones Royster, ed., *Southern Horrors and Other Writings: The Anti-Lynching Campaign of Ida B. Wells, 1892–1900*, 2nd ed. (New York, 2016).

8 See "Elizabeth Catlett, Sculptor, Printmaker, Glory Van Scott, Interviewer, Cuernavaca, Mexico, December 8, 1981," in James V. Hatch and Leo Hamalian, eds., *Art and Influence 1991* (New York, 1991), 10:5.

9 Rebecca VanDiver, "The Torture of Mothers: Elizabeth Catlett's Prints as a Call for Reproductive Justice," *Art Journal* 80, no. 2 (2021): 21, https://doi.org/10.1080/00043249.2021.1872295.

10 Martha S. Jones, *Vanguard: How Black Women Broke Barriers, Won the Vote, and Insisted on Equality for All* (New York, 2020). See also "1913 Woman Suffrage Procession," National Park Service, last modified November 5, 2021, nps.gov/articles/woman-suffrage-procession1913.htm.

11 For information countering this telling of the story, see "Q and A: Alice Paul, Racism, and the 1913 First National Suffrage March," by J. D. Zahniser, Alice Paul Institute, https://www.alicepaul.org/resources-researchers. See also Zahniser and Amelia R. Fry, *Alice Paul: Claiming Power* (Oxford, 2019).

12 While the Nineteenth Amendment was ratified in 1920, Black women would have to wait until the passage of the Voting Rights Act of 1965 to secure federal legal access to exercising their right to vote.

13 Paula J. Giddings, *Ida: A Sword Among Lions, Ida B. Wells and the Campaign against Lynching* (New York, 2008), see chapter 20.

14 As Catlett oversaw the making of the series *Against Discrimination in the US*, she asked the contributing artists to identify the subjects they wished to depict. See Melanie Anne Herzog, *Elizabeth Catlett: An American Artist in Mexico* (Seattle, 2000), 102.

15 See "A Black Sorority that Faced Racism in the Suffrage Movement but Refused to Walk Away," and Sydney Trent, "Battle for the Ballot," *Washington Post*, August 8, 2020; Brent Staples, "How the Suffrage Movement Betrayed Black Women," *New York Times*, July 28, 2018; and "Timeline: Marching toward progress," Black Women's Suffrage, https://blackwomenssuffrage.dp.la.

16 "Elizabeth Catlett, Sculptor, Printmaker, Camille Billops, Interviewer, October 1, 1989," in Hatch and Hamalian, *Art and Influence 1991*, 10:17.

17 Michael Denning, *The Cultural Front: The Laboring of American Culture in the Twentieth Century* (Brooklyn, 1996). See also Washington, *The Other Black List*, 164.

18 Van Scott, interview, 3.

19 Catlett used this phrase and variations on it in multiple interviews and statements. See, for example, "In Her Own Words: Purpose," in Samella Lewis, *The Art of Elizabeth Catlett* (Claremont, CA, 1984), 21, and 95–96 for further explanation.

20 Washington, *The Other Black List*, 130.

21 Billops, interview, 21.

22 McDuffie, *Sojourning for Freedom*, 4.

23 Perhaps in the aftermath of the civil unrest instigated in the summer of 2020 with the murders of George Floyd and Breonna Taylor, an argument should be made for the civil rights century.

24 See, for example, McDuffie, *Sojourning for Freedom*, 164–166; Rebecca M. Schreiber, *Cold War Exiles in Mexico: U.S. Dissidents and the Culture of Critical Resistance* (Minneapolis, 2008), 169, 214; and Washington, *The Other Black List*, 131, 148.

25 Aruna D'Souza, "Early Intersections: The Work of Third World Feminism," in *We Wanted a Revolution: Black Radical Women, 1965–85, New Perspectives*, ed. Catherine Morris and Rujeko Hockley (Brooklyn, 2018), 74.

26 See Fidel Castro History Archive, "At the Closing of the Congress of Women of the Americans," January 16, 1963, https://marxists.org/history/cuba/archive/castro/index.htm.
27 VanDiver, "The Torture of Mothers," 15.
28 Manuel Ramirez Chicharro, "Radicalizing Feminism: The Mexican and Cuban Associations within the Women's International Democratic Federation in the Early Cold War," in "Women's Rights and Global Socialism," special issue S30, *International Review of Social History* 67 (April 2022): 75–102; published online by Cambridge University Press, March 10, 2022.
29 McDuffie, *Sojourning for Freedom*, 13, also notes: "This scholarship also locates the emergence of black feminist groups such as the Third World Women's Alliance and the Combahee River Collective, primarily as a response to the infamous Moynihan Report of 1965 and the 'resurgent masculinism of Black Liberation.'"
30 Kellie Jones, "The World According to Linda Goode Bryant," in Thomas (T.) Jean Lax and Lilia Rocio Taboada, eds., *Just Above Midtown: Changing Spaces* (Museum of Modern Art, New York, 2022), 138. The artists in the exhibition included Camille Billops, Vivian Browne, Elizabeth Catlett, Dan Concholar, Alonzo David, David Hammons, Suzanne Jackson, Norman Lewis, Valerie Maynard, RoHo, Russ Thompson, and Randy Williams.
31 VanDiver, "The Torture of Mothers," 25.
32 Elizabeth Catlett, "In Her Own Words: Purpose, The Focus on Women," in Lewis, *Art of Elizabeth Catlett*, 102.
33 Elizabeth Catlett, "In Her Own Words: Serving One's Public," in Lewis, *Art of Elizabeth Catlett*, 99.
34 Van Scott, interview, 3–4.
35 Van Scott, interview, 12–13.
36 Van Scott, interview, 13.
37 The catalog for the exhibition opened with a significant overview essay on the artist, "Swimming with E. C.," by Kellie Jones; see note 25.
38 Other works by Catlett in the exhibition included the sculpture *Target Practice*, 1970 (p. 161) and the prints *Malcolm X Speaks for Us*, 1969 (p. 156); *Harriet*, 1975 (p. 175); *There Is a Woman in Every Color*, 1975 (p. 211); and *Madonna*, 1982 (p. 218).
39 Robin Pogrebin and Hilarie M. Sheets, "An Artist Ascendant: Simone Leigh Moves into the Mainstream," *New York Times*, August 29, 2018.
40 Jillian Steinhauer, "Reflections from Black Women Artists for Black Lives Matter," *Hyperallergic*, September 16, 2016, https://hyperallergic.com/322742/reflections-from-black-women-artists-for-black-lives-matter/.
41 Elizabeth Catlett, "Responding to Cultural Hunger," in Mark O'Brien and Craig Little, eds., *Reimaging America: The Arts of Social Change* (Philadelphia, 1990), 244–249; quoted passage, 249.

SHAPING PUBLIC SPACE

1 True to form, Melanie Herzog covers this facet of Catlett's oeuvre in her monograph *Elizabeth Catlett: An American Artist in Mexico* (Seattle, 2000), 170–171.
2 Elizabeth Catlett, statement in *Art in Public Places* (Museum of African American Art, Los Angeles, 1987).
3 Patricia Cardona, "Homenaje a un Gran Músico," *El Día*, July 27, 1976.
4 Elizabeth Catlett, "La pintura mural en las calles de EUA," *Los Universitarios*, January 15–31, 1975, 7–8 (author's translation).
5 Catlett to Alonzo Davis and members of the Louis Armstrong Statue Committee, November 17, 1974, collection number LA MSS 0002, Los Angeles Public Library.
6 Harvey Siders, "Saying Thanks to Satchmo," *Los Angeles Herald—Examiner*, April 18, 1976.
7 Elizabeth Catlett papers, 1957–1980, press release for the unveiling of Elizabeth Catlett's sculpture *Students Aspire*, Archives of American Art, Smithsonian Institution.
8 *Chicago Tribune* staff, *Public Art in Chicago: Photography and Commentary on Sculptures, Statues, Murals and More* (Chicago, 2013), n.p.
9 Abigail Gruskin, "Keeping Black History Alive in Riverside Park," *Our Town* (Upper East Side, NYC), February 19, 2021, https://www.ourtownny.com/news/keeping-black-history-alive-in-riverside-park-DA1525353. See also Stephanie Anne Johnson, "Education, Art and the Black Public Sphere," *Africology: The Journal of Pan African Studies* (March 2019): 41–58.
10 For more information on these two commissions, see Schomburg Center: correspondence, press release, institutional history, 1986–1990, box 11, folder 1, Elizabeth Catlett Papers (addendum), Amistad Research Center, Tulane University; and Michele Helene Bogart, *Sculpture in Gotham: Art and Urban Renewal in New York City* (London, 2018), 219.

A WOMAN OF GREAT INTEGRITY, AND BRAVERY

1 Ellen Hopkins, "Blacks at the Top," *New York*, January 19, 1987, 20–31.
2 See Tricia Hersey, *Rest Is Resistance: A Manifesto* (New York, 1922).
3 Quoted in Karen Rosenberg, "Elizabeth Catlett, Sculptor with Eye on Social Issues, Is Dead at 96," *New York Times*, April 3, 2012.

CHRONOLOGY

1 United States Census 1910, National Archives and Records Administration, Washington, DC; John H. Catlett and Mary S. Carson, December 30, 1908, Lincoln, North Carolina County Marriages, 1762–1979, North Carolina State Archives Division of Archives and History.
2 *Elizabeth Catlett: Sculpting the Truth*, created and produced by Linda Freeman, written and directed by David Irving and Juan Mora Catlett, featuring Faith Ringgold (1997; Chappaqua, NY: L & S Video, 2006), DVD.
3 *Elizabeth Catlett: Sculpting the Truth*.
4 "Racial Violence and the Red Summer," National Archives, last modified July 24, 2020, https://www.archives.gov/research/african-americans/wwi/red-summer.
5 Elizabeth Catlett, oral history interview by Shawn Wilson, July 26–27, 2005, The HistoryMakers® African American Video Oral History Collection, Chicago, videocassettes.
6 Samella Lewis, *The Art of Elizabeth Catlett* (Claremont, CA, 1984), 8.
7 Melanie Anne Herzog, *Elizabeth Catlett: An American Artist in Mexico* (Seattle, 2000), 15.
8 Herzog, *Elizabeth Catlett*, 15.
9 "DC Society," *Afro-American*, August 8, 1931.
10 See Melanee C. Harvey's essay in this publication.
11 Elizabeth Catlett Howard University Transcripts, 1935, Rosenwald Collection, box 400, folder 7, John Hope and Aurelia E. Franklin Library Special Collections, Fisk University, Nashville. See Harvey's essay in this publication.
12 Exhibitions that EC likely saw at the Howard Gallery of Art in 1932 included *Exhibition of Paintings by Valentin de Zubiaurre* (April), *Exhibition of Paintings by Negro Artists* (May), and *Famous Woodcuts by Japanese Artists* (December). Lucinda H. Gedeon, ed., with Michael Brenson and Lowery Stokes Sims, *Elizabeth Catlett Sculpture: A Fifty-Year Retrospective* (Purchase, NY, 1998); Art Department Exhibitions 1931–1935, box 45, Howard University Archives, Moorland-Spingarn Research Center, Howard University, Washington, DC.
13 Dena Merriam, "All History's Children: The Art of Elizabeth Catlett," *Sculpture Review* 42, no. 3 (1993): 6–11.
14 Elizabeth Catlett, interview by Clifton Johnson, January 5, 1983, tape 1-01, Elizabeth Catlett Papers, Amistad Research Center, Tulane University.
15 "Number Thirteen Means Nothing to Delta Girls at H.U.: Sorority Has 13 Girls on Probation and 13 Freshmen Members of Pyramid Club," *Afro-American*, May 20, 1933.
16 Catlett, interview, tape 2-01. For more on Myers, see David Lucander, "'It is a new kind of militancy': March on Washington Movement, 1941–1946" (PhD diss., University of Massachusetts Amherst, 2010).
17 Florence Collins, "Federal Funds Provide Work for 10 Artists: Negro Theme Shown in Projects," *Afro-American*, February 10, 1934.
18 Camille Billops, "Interview with Elizabeth Catlett," *Artists and Influence* (1991): 18. Catlett also specifically mentions getting a book from the library about Diego Rivera's murals, which may have been Ernestine Evans's *The Frescoes of Diego Rivera* (New York, 1929). See *Elizabeth Catlett: Sculpting the Truth*; Catlett, interview.
19 *The Bison* (Howard University yearbook, Washington, DC, 1934), 54.
20 *The Hilltop*, October 19, 1936.

21 *The Bison*, 64.
22 *The Bison*, 76.
23 "Howard University Students Picket with Ropes Around Necks," *Afro-American*, December 22, 1934.
24 See Lewis, *Art of Elizabeth Catlett*, 10; Gedeon, *Elizabeth Catlett Sculpture*, 105; Herzog, *Elizabeth Catlett*, 17.
25 Exhibition pamphlet, Art Department Exhibitions 1931–1935, box 45, Howard University Archives.
26 Howard University Commencement Program, 1935.
27 Catlett, interview, tape 1-01.
28 Catlett, interview, tape 1-01.
29 Deborah Caplow, Helga Prignitz-Poda, Elizabeth Kathleen Mitchell, Arturo García Bustos, Pablo Mendez, and Michael T. Ricker, *El Taller de Gráfica Popular: Vida y Arte* (Athens, GA, 2015), 62.
30 Kathleen A. Edwards, "The Fine Art of Representing Black Heritage: Elizabeth Catlett and Iowa, 1938–1940," in *Invisible Hawkeyes: African Americans at the University of Iowa during the Long Civil Rights Era*, ed. Lena M. Hill and Michael D. Hill (Iowa City, 2016).
31 Gedeon, *Elizabeth Catlett Sculpture*.
32 Catlett, interview, tape 1-01.
33 See Edwards, "Fine Art of Representing Black Heritage."
34 Catlett, interview, tape 1-01.
35 Billops, "Interview with Elizabeth Catlett"; Alain Locke Papers, box 164-216, folder 16, Howard University Archives.
36 Herzog, *Elizabeth Catlett*, 25.
37 Catlett, interview, tape 1-01. See Alice Elizabeth Catlett, "Sculpture in Stone: Negro Mother and Child" (MFA thesis, State University of Iowa, 1940).
38 Edwards, "Fine Art of Representing Black Heritage," 51.
39 James A. Porter, *Modern Negro Art* (New York, 1943).
40 Herzog, *Elizabeth Catlett*, 23.
41 "Named Art Head at Dillard Univ," *Chicago Defender*, August 10, 1940; Catlett, interview, tape 2-01.
42 Billops, "Interview with Elizabeth Catlett," 8. See Sarah Kelly Oehler's essay in this publication.
43 Catlett, interview, tape 2-01.
44 Billops, "Interview with Elizabeth Catlett," 8; Herzog, *Elizabeth Catlett*, 24; Catlett, interview, tape 2-01.
45 Catlett, interview, tape 2-01.
46 "Local Artists Exhibit Works in New York," *Chicago Defender*, December 13, 1941.
47 Marriage Records, District of Columbia, Clerk of the Superior Court, Records Office, Washington, DC; Sarah Kelly Oehler and Esther Adler, eds., *Charles White: A Retrospective* (Chicago, 2018), 195.
48 Catlett, interview, tape 2-02; Oehler and Adler, *Charles White*, 195.
49 Billops, "Interview with Elizabeth Catlett," 20; Herzog, *Elizabeth Catlett*, 30.
50 Billops, "Interview with Elizabeth Catlett," 20; Herzog, *Elizabeth Catlett*, 30.
51 See June Levine and Gene Gordon, *Tales of Wo-Chi-Ca: Blacks, Whites and Reds at Camp* (San Rafael, CA, 2002), xi.
52 Billops, "Interview with Elizabeth Catlett," 21.
53 Bill Chase, "Meet Mr., Mrs. Charles White: An Interesting and Talented Combination," *New York Amsterdam Star-News*, September 5, 1942.
54 Oehler and Adler, *Charles White*, 195.
55 Herzog, *Elizabeth Catlett*, 34–35.
56 Catlett 1943 Rosenwald Application, Rosenwald Collection, box 400, folder 7, John Hope and Aurelia E. Franklin Library Special Collections, Fisk University.
57 Catlett 1943 Rosenwald Application, Rosenwald Collection, box 400, folder 7, John Hope and Aurelia E. Franklin Library Special Collections, Fisk University; Herzog, *Elizabeth Catlett*, 36.
58 Herzog, *Elizabeth Catlett*, 36–40; "Six Directors Quit the Carver School," *New York Times*, December 18, 1943.
59 Elizabeth Catlett, "The Negro Artist in America," *American Contemporary Art* 1, no. 2 (1944): 3–6.
60 Herzog, *Elizabeth Catlett*, 39. For more on the Jefferson School, see Marvin E. Gettleman, "'No Varsity Teams': New York's Jefferson School of Social Science, 1943–1956," *Science & Society* 66, no. 3 (2002): 336–359.
61 Charles W. White papers, 1933–1987, bulk 1960s–1970s, box 9, folder 30: Publications with Illustrations by White, Congress Vue, 1943–1946, Archives of American Art, Smithsonian Institution.
62 See Danielle L. McGuire, *At the Dark End of the Street: Black Women, Rape, and Resistance—A New History of the Civil Rights Movement from Rosa Parks to the Rise of Black Power* (New York, 2010).
63 Oehler and Adler, *Charles White*, 196.
64 George Washington Carver School course catalog, 1945–1946, Schomburg Center Clipping File, 1925–1974, Schomburg Center for Research in Black Culture, New York Public Library.
65 Catlett 1945 Rosenwald Application, Rosenwald Collection, box 400, folder 7, John Hope and Aurelia E. Franklin Library Special Collections, Fisk University. See Erik S. McDuffie, *Sojourning for Freedom: Black Women, American Communism, and the Making of Black Left Feminism* (Durham, NC, 2011); Dayo F. Gore, *Radicalism at the Crossroads: African American Women Activists in the Cold War* (New York, 2012).
66 Oehler and Adler, *Charles White*, 196.
67 Catlett's 1945 Registration Form, Archives of the Art Students League of New York.
68 Elizabeth Catlett, "Negro Artists," *New Masses* 58, no. 1 (January 1, 1946): 27–28.
69 Committee for the Detroit Art Exhibit to W. E. B. Du Bois, January 18, 1946, W. E. B. Du Bois Papers (MS 312), Special Collections and University Archives, University of Massachusetts Amherst Libraries.
70 "Mrs. Catlett to Speak at Art Symposium," *Daily Worker*, April 19, 1946.
71 Elizabeth Catlett, "Responding to Cultural Hunger," in *Reimaging America: The Arts of Social Change*, ed. Mark O'Brien and Craig Little (Philadelphia, 1990), 244.
72 Catlett, interview, tape 3-01; Herzog, *Elizabeth Catlett*, 47–50.
73 Catlett to Mr. William Haygood, c. August 1946, Rosenwald Collection, box 400, folder 7, John Hope and Aurelia E. Franklin Library Special Collections, Fisk University.
74 Catlett to Dorothy Elvidge, September 25, 1946, Rosenwald Collection, box 400, folder 7, John Hope and Aurelia E. Franklin Library Special Collections, Fisk University.
75 C. G. Woodson, review of *La Poblacion Negra de México, 1510–1810, Estudio Etnohistorico*, by Gonzalo Aguirre Beltran, *Journal of Negro History* 31, no. 4 (October 1946): 491–494.
76 Elizabeth Catlett, "Tribute to the Negro People," *American Contemporary Art* (Winter 1946): 17; Herzog, *Elizabeth Catlett*, 46.
77 See Theresa Avila, "El Taller de Gráfica Popular and the Chronicles of Mexican History and Nationalism," *Third Text* 28, no. 3 (2014): 311–321. Also see Jaime M. Pensado and Enrique C. Ochoa, eds., *México beyond 1968: Revolutionaries, Radicals, and Repression during the Global Sixties and Subversive Seventies* (Tucson, 2018), 297–320.
78 Caplow et al., *El Taller de Gráfica Popular*, 62.
79 Thalia Gouma-Peterson, "Elizabeth Catlett: 'The Power of Human Feeling and of Art,'" *Woman's Art Journal* 4, no. 1 (1983): 48–56.
80 "The Negro Woman: D.C. Art Show Theme," *New Journal and Guide*, December 20, 1947.
81 Caplow et al., *El Taller de Gráfica Popular*, 62.
82 Shifra M. Goldman, "Six Women Artists of Mexico," *Woman's Art Journal* 3, no. 2 (1982): 1–9.
83 Caplow et al., *El Taller de Gráfica Popular*, 63.
84 Pensado and Ochoa, *México beyond 1968*.
85 Germán Alburquerque Fuschini, "Pro-Soviet Movements and the War for Peace," in *La trinchera letrada: Intelectuales latinoamericanos y Guerra Fría* (Santiago, Chile, 2011).
86 Gedeon, *Elizabeth Catlett Sculpture*.
87 Margaret Burroughs, "A Woman's Viewpoint: Negro Artists Active in Mexico," *Philadelphia Tribune*, September 18, 1951.
88 Herzog, *Elizabeth Catlett*, 102–103.
89 See Michelle Chase, *Revolution within the Revolution: Women and Gender Politics in Cuba, 1952–1962* (Chapel Hill, NC, 2015).
90 Pensado and Ochoa, *México beyond 1968*, 297–320.
91 FBI, "Correlation Summary," October 20, 1970, NARA record number 124-10313-10012, https://www.maryferrell.org/showDoc.html?docId=232046. See Rebecca M. Schreiber, *Cold War Exiles in Mexico: U.S. Dissidents and the Culture of Critical Resistance* (Minneapolis, 2008), 27–57.
92 Herzog, *Elizabeth Catlett*, 117.
93 Herzog, *Elizabeth Catlett*, 124.
94 Gedeon, *Elizabeth Catlett Sculpture*.

95 Elena Poniatowska and Robert Alegre, *Railroad Radicals in Cold War Mexico: Gender, Class, and Memory* (Lincoln, NE, 2014); Pensado and Ochoa, *México beyond 1968*.
96 Catlett, interview, tape 4-01; FBI, "Correlation Summary," October 20, 1970.
97 Catlett, interview, tape 4-01; Herzog *Elizabeth Catlett*, 119.
98 Herzog, *Elizabeth Catlett*, 119.
99 Herzog, *Elizabeth Catlett*, 79.
100 Caplow et al., *El Taller de Gráfica Popular*, 63.
101 Elizabeth Catlett, "The Negro People and American Art," *Freedomways* 1, no. 1 (Spring 1961): 74–80. See Erin P. Cohn, "Art Fronts: Visual Culture and Race Politics in the Mid-Twentieth-Century United States" (PhD diss., University of Pennsylvania, 2010).
102 Herzog, *Elizabeth Catlett*, 131.
103 Herzog, *Elizabeth Catlett*, 79, 130.
104 FBI, "Correlation Summary," October 20, 1970.
105 Herzog, *Elizabeth Catlett*, 112.
106 Herzog, *Elizabeth Catlett*, 112.
107 Herzog, *Elizabeth Catlett*, 112.
108 See Ana Lau Jaiven, "La Unión Nacional de Mujeres Mexicanas entre el comunismo y el feminismo: Una difícil relación," *Revista de estudios de género* 5, no. 40 (Summer 2014), 165–185.
109 Pensado and Ochoa, *México beyond 1968*.
110 Gedeon, *Elizabeth Catlett Sculpture*.
111 Herzog, *Elizabeth Catlett*, 112.
112 Herzog, *Elizabeth Catlett*, 112.
113 See Peter B. Levy, "The Holy Week Uprising of 1968," in *The Great Uprising: Race Riots in Urban America during the 1960s* (New York, 2018), 153–188.
114 See J.V. Decemvirale's essay in this publication.
115 Elizabeth Catlett Curriculum Vitae, c. 1982, David C. Driskell Papers, box 6, folder 5, David C. Driskell Center for the Study of the Visual Arts and Culture of African Americans and the African Diaspora, University of Maryland, College Park.
116 Rebecca Zorach, "Interview with Barbara Jones-Hogu," *Never the Same*, https://never-the-same.org/interviews/barbara-jones-hogu/
117 "Freedomways," *Freedomways* 9, no. 4 (January 4, 1969).
118 Herzog, *Elizabeth Catlett*, 138.
119 Marc Crawford, "My Art Speaks for Both My Peoples," *Ebony*, January 1970, 94–101.
120 Herzog, *Elizabeth Catlett*, 147–148.
121 Herzog, *Elizabeth Catlett*, 149.
122 See Dalila Scruggs's essay in this publication.
123 Elizabeth Catlett Curriculum Vitae, c. 1982, David C. Driskell Papers, box 6, folder 5, David C. Driskell Center.
124 Kellie Jones, "Swimming with E. C.," in *Women and Migration: Responses in Art and History*, ed. Deborah Willis, Ellyn Toscano, and Kalia Brooks Nelson (Cambridge, 2019), 167–191.
125 Sarah J. Seidman, "Angela Davis in Cuba as Symbol and Subject," *Radical History Review* 2020, no. 136 (2020): 11–35.
126 Anne Brice, "Inside Rainbow Sign, a Vibrant Hub for Black Cultural Arts," *Berkeley News*, September 19, 2017.
127 See Herzog, *Elizabeth Catlett*, 214n66, for more details on where the show traveled.
128 Herzog, *Elizabeth Catlett*, 150–151.
129 Herzog, *Elizabeth Catlett*, 156; Elizabeth Catlett, "La pintura mural en las calles de EUA," *Los Universitarios*, January 15–31, 1975, 74.
130 Gedeon, *Elizabeth Catlett Sculpture*.
131 Gedeon, *Elizabeth Catlett Sculpture*.
132 Elizabeth Catlett, "The Role of the Black Artist," *Black Scholar* 6, no. 9 (1975): 10–14.
133 Colony Little, "Building Faith in the Future Part 2: Five Women of the Black Arts Movement in Los Angeles," *ARTnews*, July 11, 2023.
134 Herzog, *Elizabeth Catlett*, 157.
135 Herzog, *Elizabeth Catlett*, 163.
136 Gedeon, *Elizabeth Catlett Sculpture*. Floyd Levin, "The Seven-Year Challenge to Complete the Louis Armstrong Statue," in *Classic Jazz: A Personal View of the Music and the Musicians* (Berkeley, 2000), 302.
137 David C. Driskell, *Two Centuries of Black American Art* (Los Angeles, 1976).
138 Event pamphlet, Catlett Faculty—Staff File (1a), Howard University Archives.
139 Catlett, interview, tape 4-01.
140 Romare Bearden and Harry Henderson, *A History of African American Artists: From 1792 to the Present* (New York, 1993).
141 See J.V. Decemvirale's essay in this publication.
142 Exhibition brochure, Catlett Faculty—Staff File (2c), Howard University Archives.
143 *ICAA Documents Project Working Papers: The Publication Series for Documents of 20th-Century Latin American and Latino Art*, no. 1 (September 2007).
144 *ICAA Documents Project Working Papers*.
145 "New to the Collection," Stanley Museum of Art, https://stanleymuseum.uiowa.edu/new-collection.
146 Morton A. Kaplan, "Elizabeth Catlett: The Power of Form," *World and I* 13, no. 7 (1998): 118.
147 Gedeon, *Elizabeth Catlett Sculpture*.
148 Allen L. Edmonds to Catlett, 1983, Brandywine Workshop Artist Files.
149 Gedeon, *Elizabeth Catlett Sculpture*.
150 Gedeon, *Elizabeth Catlett Sculpture*.
151 Presented by the Office of Arts & Culture, City of Philadelphia Afro-American Historical and Cultural Museum and Brandywine Workshop, held at Drexel University on April 10, 1987.
152 "For My People," Limited Editions Club Newsletter 2, no. 567, series 53 (December 1992).
153 Gedeon, *Elizabeth Catlett Sculpture*, 112.
154 Gedeon, *Elizabeth Catlett Sculpture*, 113.
155 Melanie Anne Herzog, "Elizabeth Catlett (1915–2012)," *American Art* 26, no. 3 (2012): 105–109.
156 "Ralph Ellison Memorial Committee," Riverside Park Conservancy, n.d., https://riversideparknyc.org/ralph-ellison-memorial-committee/.
157 John Riehl, "True to Self," Graduate College News, University of Iowa, September 13, 2012.
158 See J.V. Decemvirale's essay in this publication.
159 "The Work of Elizabeth Catlett," Carnegie Library of Pittsburgh, n.d., https://www.carnegielibrary.org/staff-picks/the-work-of-elizabeth-catlett/.
160 Tom Patterson, "A Powerful Printmaker: Elizabeth Catlett and Maya Angelou Will Have a Conversation Surrounded by a Show of Catlett's Work at Delta Arts Center," *Winston-Salem Journal*, April 6, 2008.
161 "Stargazers: Elizabeth Catlett in Conversation with 21 Contemporary Artists," Bronx Museum, November 30, 2010, https://bronxmuseum.org/news/stargazers-elizabeth-catlett-in-conversation-with-21-contemporary-artists/.
162 Colleen Walsh, "Principled Expression," *Harvard Gazette*, April 22, 2011.

ACKNOWLEDGMENTS

In mounting this exhibition, the Brooklyn Museum and National Gallery of Art come belatedly to an art history built by historically Black institutions and Black woman art historians. Catlett's career was nurtured by these institutions and by Black scholars, gallerists, and collectors who recognized her gifts over the long decades of her life when the art world, along with the rest of the United States, was segregated. The groundbreaking art historian and teacher James A. Porter was perhaps Catlett's first patron. In one of his many prescient acts, he collected examples of artwork by his students, including Catlett, and as a result two of her rare charcoal life drawings reside in the Howard University Gallery of Art's collection. She maintained a lifelong relationship with her alma mater, where she is remembered as Mother Catlett to this day. Though scholars regularly acknowledge her foundational *Negro Woman* exhibition at the nation's first black-owned gallery, Barnett-Aden Gallery, in Washington, DC, her participation in Clark Atlanta University Atlanta Annuals is far less remarked upon.

We also recognize that the very foundation of art historical literature on Catlett rests on the work of Black women, including Frida High Tesaforgis, Lowery Stokes Sims, Kellie Jones, and most especially Samella Lewis, Catlett's close friend and the first Black woman to earn a PhD in art history in the US. As the market for her work expanded near the end of her life, Catlett chose to work primarily with Black woman gallerists, and June Kelly and Stella Jones continue to represent her estate to this day. We are honored to acknowledge this long history of Black scholarly production and art world patronage without which our book and the exhibition it accompanies would not be possible. Nor could we have realized this project without the scholarship and support of Melanie Anne Herzog and her foundational monograph—it serves as the authoritative source for titles and dates of works, and Herzog herself provided invaluable insight into Catlett's mentality and working process.

Bringing this exhibition and publication to fruition was an enormous undertaking and required no less than a village. First and foremost, we thank the Board of Trustees at both museums along with visionary directors Anne Pasternak and Kaywin Feldman, and their executives Sharon Matt Atkins (Brooklyn) and Kate Haw (National Gallery), as well as members of leadership including Brooklyn's KP Trueblood. We are indebted to the Mora Catlett family—especially Catlett's sons Francisco, Juan, and David—for trusting us to tell their mother's remarkable story and for providing significant loans of artwork to the exhibition.

Other lenders were equally generous in making their works available for this special project. We are indebted to the directors, curators, and administrative staff of the following museums and galleries: Academia des Artes, Mexico City; Amistad Research Center; Archives of American Art; Art Bridges Foundation; The Art Institute of Chicago; Baltimore Museum of Art; The Bronx Museum of the Arts Collection; Canton Museum of Art; Center for Southwest Research and Special Collections, University of New Mexico Libraries; Charles White Estate; Chicago Public Art Program and the Chicago Public Library, Legler Regional Library; Cincinnati Art Museum; City of Atlanta, Mayor's Office of Cultural Affairs; Clark Atlanta University Art Museum; Cleveland Museum of Art; Crystal Bridges Museum of American Art; Currier Museum of Art; Davis Museum at Wellesley College, Wellesley, MA; Detroit Institute of Arts; DuSable Black History Museum and Education Center; Hampton University Museum Collection; Howard University Archives; Howard University Gallery of Art; John Hope and Aurelia E. Franklin Library, Fisk University; The Johnson Collection, Spartanburg, SC; June Kelly Gallery; La Salle University Art Museum; Library of Congress; Los Angeles Public Library; Makey Twins Art Gallery, Inc.; Margaret Walker Center; The Metropolitan Museum of Art; Morgan Library & Museum; Mott-Warsh Collection; The Museum of Modern Art; The Museum of Modern Art Archives; National Gallery of Art; National Museum of Women in the Arts; National Portrait Gallery; New Orleans Museum of Art; New York Public Library; North Carolina Central University Art Museum; Pennsylvania Academy of the Fine Arts; Philadelphia Museum of Art; Princeton University Art Museum; Riverside Park Conservancy; Schomburg Center for Research in Black Culture; Sidney and Lois Eskenazi Museum of Art; Smithsonian American Art Museum; Smithsonian National Museum of African American History and Culture; Sragow Gallery; Stella Jones Gallery; Studio Museum in Harlem; Toledo Museum of Art; Universidad Iberoamericana; University of Iowa Art Library; University of Iowa Stanley Museum of Art; Wadsworth Atheneum Museum of Art; Whitney Museum of American Art; Williams College Museum of Art; and Yale University Art Gallery.

Equally generous have been a large number of private collectors, including Shahara Ahmad-Llewelyn, Reginald and Aliya Brown, Sheryll Cashin and Marque Chambliss, Collection of Helen Nitkin, The D. L. Demps Collection, Mrs. Thelma Driskell, Paula Gerson, David and Susan Goode, Linda Goode Bryant, Donald Hardy and P. Bruce Marine, Juanita and Melvin Hardy, Kyra E. Hicks, JLW Collection, Robert L. Johnson, Samella Lewis, Barbara Luke, Laura and Richard Parsons, Otis and Harryette Robertson, John W. L. Russell Jr. Living Trust, Peter Schneider and Susan DeJarnatt, Gabriel and Monilola Tenabe, Larry D. and Brenda A. Thompson, Dr. Sheila D. Wright, and other private collections.

We began working on this project in the early days of the COVID-19 pandemic, which brought the politics of representation and equity into sharp relief. Fittingly, our first conversations were with curators and archivists at HBCUs, institutions that had supported Catlett during her lifetime. Our deep thanks go to Maurita Poole (former), Clark Atlanta University Art Gallery; Vanessa Thaxton-Ward, Hampton University Art Museum; John Kennedy, Malik Bartholomew, and John Barnes, Dillard University; and Lisa Farrington (former), Abby Eron (former), and Scott Baker, Howard University Gallery of Art. We also shared our preliminary plans for the exhibition with participants of the 2021 Brooklyn Museum's Martin Luther King Day of Action education workshop on antiracist curatorial practice. We also thank the entire education division for their support of the project from its earliest iteration.

We would like to acknowledge the tireless work of our colleagues on Team Catlett—the many passionate individuals who helped bring the project to fruition. We want to especially thank our cocurator Mary Lee Corlett, whose veteran expertise in all aspects of printmaking media brought a depth and rigor worthy of a catalogue raisonné. She tapped many networks to locate artworks, establish provenances, and parse nuances in Catlett's process. Both before and after Mary Lee's retirement during the organization of the exhibition, Rashieda Witter went above and beyond her role as research assistant, offering invaluable insight on key conceptual decisions and becoming an essential member of the curatorial team. Throughout the planning of the exhibition, the team in Washington was led by E. Carmen Ramos and Shelley Langdale and supported by Rebecca Mei. We thank all those scholars, collectors, and curators who supported this work—particularly J.V. Decemvirale, who expertly facilitated and documented meetings with former Catlett printers Raul Cabello and Ana Iturbe in Mexico, Allen Edmunds at the Brandywine Workshop, as well as Esther Adler, Katherine Blood, Sarah Duke, Ruth Fine, Jane Glaubinger, Susan Goldman, Robin Holder, Christine M. Perry, Dafne Cruz Porchini, Maureen Turci, Joseph Kleineman, and our extremely diligent intern Ateret Sultan-Reisler.

It was a pleasure to watch this volume come to life under the expert guidance of Audrey Walen, Peggy Martin, Emiko K. Usui, Emily Zoss, Julie Warnement, Brad Ireland, and Christina Wiginton, with Magda Nakassis, Lisa Shea, Caroline Weaver, Nancy Eickel, Jasmine Lee, and Nicola Wood. The phenomenal design from Morcos Key brings a keen eye for historical detail to a decidedly contemporary book.

Many teams at both the Brooklyn Museum and the National Gallery deserve our heartfelt thanks for their meaningful contributions to this project. At the Brooklyn Museum, numerous colleagues have supported this project: in exhibitions Dolores Farrell and Gwen Arriaga; in curatorial Catherine Futter, Carla Forbes, and Jenee Daria Strand (former); in editorial Sophia Bruneau; in registration Katie Welty, Katrina Dumas, Cindy Ortiz, Filippo Gentile, and the art handling team; in digital services Taylor Catalana; in exhibition design Kyong Kim; in graphic design Adam O'Reilly and Bon Hae Koo; in public programs Lauren Zelaya, Margo Cohen Ristorucci, danilo machado, June Lei, and Enrique Mendía; in digital Brooke Baldeschwiler, Elise Beck, Holland Baker, Joelle Seligson, Kyle Thornburg, and Katie Yee; in marketing and communications Sofie Andersen and Miles Hicks; in libraries and archives Abigail Dansiger; in learning and social impact Adjoa Jones de Almeida (former) and Laval Bryant-Quigley; in DEIA Keonna Hendrick and Hannah Lawson; in development Judy Sussman, Shaquana Lee, Jane Asher, and Isabel Varban; in audiovisual Bob Nardi; and the many other experts who contribute across all departments. Since the Elizabeth A. Sackler Center for Feminist Art at the Brooklyn Museum opened its doors in 2007, every exhibition, project, program, and publication has reflected Elizabeth A. Sackler's vision and commitment to philanthropy driven by social action.

At the National Gallery we are grateful to numerous colleagues: in exhibitions Steven Mann, Lawrence Hyman, Abigail Clarke, and Naomi Remes; in interpretation Joanna Marsh and Lynn Matheny; in learning and engagement Damon Reaves; in public programs Grace Murray; in design Michael Lapthorn, Donna Kirk, Madeline Rikhoff, Jaime Lowe, Victoria Kaak, Bryant Johnson, Drew Watt, and Jane Grigg; in digital Nick Sharp, Annie Yi, and Scott Keiner; in registration and loans Theresa Beall; in conservation James Gleason, Michelle Facini, and Kyle Bauer; in diversity, inclusion, and belonging Mikka Gee Conway and Jeannette Shindell; in the office of the secretary and general counsel Julian Saenz; in imaging Barbara Wood; in communications Anabeth Guthrie, Laurie Tylec, and Sydni Meyers; in experience Paula Lynn; in development Sean O'Connor, Maria Bonta de la Pezuela, Sarah Hyde, Patricia Donovan, and Hilary Fry, and in special events Chelsea Souza and Kelly Scandone.

This project afforded us opportunities to consult with dozens of dynamic scholars, artists, and curators. We thank our exhibition advisors Julia Fernandez, Michael Brenson, John Ott, Linda Goode Bryant, Ariana Curtis, Sarah Kelly Oehler, Simone Leigh, Melanie Anne Herzog, and M. Scott Johnson. Meaningful ideas, suggestions, and approaches were offered by many people in the fields of modern and contemporary art, particularly those who participated in the exhibition's community label project. We are grateful to Terry Carbone, Connie Choi, Kathryn Coney-Ali, Lynne Cooke, Kaleta Doolin, Rupert Garcia, Linda Goode Bryant, Alan Govenar, Breea Govenar, Radiah Harper, Carmen Hermo, LaToya Hobbs, Perri Irmer, Kelly Jones, Lucy R. Lippard, Kelli Morgan, Lorraine O'Grady, Susanne Pfeffer, Richard Powell, Joel Rosenkranz, Cameron Rowland, Lowery Stokes Sims, Danielle Taylor, Michael Taylor, and Vanessa Thaxton Ward. Assistance came by more informal routes as well, including the Pca-l and Am-Art listservs. Our inquiries were received with an outpouring of insight and support from colleagues across the field. Other requests were also graciously met, and we extend our thanks to Lilia Rocio Taboada and Faythe Weaver for their timely assistance. We also thank the Terra Foundation International Research Travel Grant for US-based Scholars, which funded Dalila Scruggs's travel to Mexico, as well as all those who supported her field research in Mexico City, including Edgar Bobadilla, Renee Gonzalez de la Lama, Luis Héctor Inclán Cienfuegos, Carlos A. Molina, Norma Parra Martínez, and Cecilia Santacruz Langagne.

On a personal note, I (Dalila Scruggs) thank Lindsay C. Harris, Midrene Lamy, Christina Marinelli, Wendy Ikemoto, Michael Reback, Nia Smith, and Lea Scruggs for hours of emotional labor rendered over the course of the last four years; and I (Catherine Morris) acknowledge the loving support and notable patience of family—John Surface, Elizabeth MacGregor, Emily Belke, Thomas H. MacGregor, Ben Surface, Charlotte Surface, Ruby Koch-Feinberg, and the sustaining memory of Elizabeth Morris, Marianne Morris, Thomas P. Morris Sr. and Jr., and Billie MacGregor.

Dalila Scruggs
Catherine Morris

INDEX

Note: Page numbers in boldface type indicate illustrations. Unattributed works of art are by Elizabeth Catlett.

A

Abraham Lincoln Centre, Chicago, 79
abstraction, 12, 13, 15, 83, 84, 86, 188–191, 202, 245, 259. *See also* formal rigor in Catlett's work
Addams, Jane, 79
Aden, Alonzo, 81
African art, 13, 72, 73, 84, 188, 190–191, 249, 256, 257, 259
African Commune of Bad Relevant Artists (AfriCOBRA), 126, 264
"African Influences in Mexican Art" (lecture), 266
African Negro Art (exhibition), 257
Afro-American (newspaper), 72
Aguirre, Ignacio, 260; *Carter G. Woodson*, from *Against Discrimination in the US* series, **106**, 181
AIC. *See* Art Institute of Chicago
Albany Institute of History and Art, New York, 260
Alemán Valdez, Miguel, 260
Alfabetización, 138, **140**
Alston, Charles, 258
Alto a la agresión, **164**
Álvarez Amaya, Jesús, letter from Catlett to, 143, **143**, 268
American Contemporary Art (magazine), 259, 260
American Negro Art, 19th and 20th Centuries (exhibition), 83, 258
American Negro Exposition (Chicago, 1940), 80–82, 86, 258
...And a special fear for my loved ones, from *The Black Woman* series, **47**
Angela Libre, 132–134, **169**, **170–171** (detail)
Angelou, Maya, 265, 268
Anguiano, Raúl, 118, 257
anti-lynching movement, 199, 256, 257
Aptheker, Bettina, 130–131, 133
Aptheker, Herbert, 130
Arenal, Luis, 118, 257, 260
Army Nurse, **26**, 86
art deco, 193
Artes de Mexico (magazine), 181
Art Institute of Chicago (AIC), 78, 80, 258
Art Is a Weapon (symposium), 260
Artists and Models Ball, Chicago, 78, 80, 83
Arts Craft Guild, 80
Art Students League, New York, 179, 260
Associated Negro Press, 81
Association for the Study of Negro Life (now Association for the Study of African American Life and History), 73
Atlanta University Annual Exhibition, 262, 263
Attucks, Crispus, 82

B

Bailey, Radcliffe, **268**
Baldwin, James, 132, 265
BAM. *See* Black Arts Movement
Bañista Olmeca (Olmec Bather), **151**, 263, **263**, **269**
Barlach, Ernst, *Floating Angel*, 192, **193**
Barnes Collection, Merion, Pennsylvania, 256
Barnett, Claude, 81
Barnett-Aden Gallery, Washington, DC, 261
Barr, Alfred, 14
Barthé, Richmond, 82, 84
Bather, 263
Bauhaus, 141
Bearden, Romare, 258, 260
Beltrán, Alberto: *Nat Turner*, from *Against Discrimination in the US* series, **108**; *Untitled (Composition for a Peace Poster)*, **93**, 181
Beltrán, Gonzalo Aguirre, *La poblacion negra de México, 1510–1810*, 260
Bennett, Gwendolyn, 83–84, 200
Billops, Camille, 74
Black Arts Movement (BAM), 12, 13, 124, 203, 244, 263
Blackburn, Robert (Bob), 83, 179, 259, 266. *See also* Robert Blackburn Printmaking Workshop
Black Chicago Renaissance, 80, 258
Black feminism, 13, 15, 199, 201–204
Black Left, 13, 14, 201
Black Lives Matter, 15
Black nationalism, 133, 191, 201
Black Panther Black Community News Service (newspaper), 127–128
Black Panther Party, 127, 133
Black Power, 13, 124, 126–130, 133, 134, 191, 202, 263
The Black Scholar (journal), 265
Black Unity, **front cover**, **152**, **back cover**
The Black Woman series, **32–48**, 118–121, 124, 178–179, 180, 182, 259, 260, 267
Black Woman Speaks (lithograph), 182. *See also Cabeza de Negra*
Black Woman Speaks (sculpture), **158**, 182
Black women: Catlett's artistic engagement with, 13, 15, 75, 82, 86, 118–121, 179, 185, 188, 190–194, 198; societal challenges facing, 13, 75, 86
Black Women Artists for Black Lives Matter, 203–204
Bodet, Jaime Torres, **230**, 266
Bracho, Ángel, *Heroe negro (Crispus Attucks)*, from *Against Discrimination in the US* series, **106**, 181
Brâncuşi, Constantin, 13
Brockman Gallery, Los Angeles, 265
Bronx Museum of Art, New York, 268
Brooklyn Museum, New York, 203
Brooks, Gwendolyn, 258
Brown, Mamie, 200
Bryant, Roberta Wolfe, 202, **202**
Bryant Foundation, 180
Burnham, Louis E., 181
Burroughs, Margaret Taylor (Goss), 78–84, **79**, 179, 258, 261; *Sojourner Truth*, from *Against Discrimination in the US* series, **106**, 181
Bustos, Arturo García, *Peon acasillado*, from *Estampas de la revolución mexicana* series, 118–119, **119**

C

CAA. *See* College Art Association of America
Cabello, Raul, 141, 265
Cabeza de Negra, 182, **183**
Cabeza Indigena, **111**
Calderón, Celia, 141, 182, 200; *Ida B. Wells-Barnett*, from *Against Discrimination in the US* series, **107**
campesinos, 118–121
Campesinos, 119
Campesinos Mexicanos, **101**, 121
Caribbean Cultural Center / African Diaspora Institute, New York, 267
Carlos, John, 127
Carnegie Institute of Technology, 68, 256
Carnegie Mellon University, 268
Carson, Cera (grandmother), 256
Carson, Charles H. (grandfather), 256
Castro, Fidel, 201
Catlett, Cera L. (sister), 256, 264
Catlett, Elizabeth: appearance of, 13; art education and influences, 13–14, 68–75, 78–86, 179, 188–192, 249, 256–261; audience for the work of, 14, 15, 118, 124, 143, 178–180, 182, 198, 200, 203–204, 244–245 (*see also* public art); autobiographical narratives of, 12; awards and honors, 75, 80, 82, 86, 118, 258, 262, 263, 264, 267; birth and youth of, 12, 199, 256; and Black Power, 13, 126–128; Black pride of, 12–14; in Chicago, 78–83, 86, 258; death of, 12, 250, 268; exile from the US, 12, 14, 124–134, 191, 202, 248, 263; feminism of, 12, 13, 141, 198–204; at Howard University, 68–75, 81, 179, 256–257; legacy of, 15; Mexican citizenship of, 125, 201, 262, 263; in Mexico, 12, 13, 14, 86, 118–121, 124–134, 138–143, 189–190, 201–202, 260–268; in New York, 83–86, 200, 259, 266; photographs of, **14**, **71**, **75**, **79**, **84**, **257**, **259–264**, **266–269**; political engagement of, 12, 13, 78, 82, 85–86, 124–134, 140, 199–201, 256–257, 264; and printmaking, 178–185; professional name of, 13; racial background of, 13; and sculpture, 188–194; statements about art, 82–83, 86, 132, 179, 180, 185, 188–189, 198, 202–203, 244–245; subject matter of, 12, 13, 15, 82, 85–86, 118–121, 249, 258 (*see also* Black women: Catlett's artistic engagement with; motherhood, as subject matter for Catlett); as teacher and mentor, 13–14, 80, 82, 83, 84, 86, 128–129, 138–143, 200, 257–260, 265; US citizenship reinstated, 267
Catlett, John H. (father), 256
Catlett, John H., Jr. (brother), 256
Catlett, Louisa (Jamison) [grandmother], 256
Catlett, Mary S. (Carson) [mother], **14**, 68, 256, 262
Central American Says No!, **135** (detail), **164**, 184
Central Intelligence Agency (CIA), 134, 262
Change the Joke and Slip the Yoke (symposium), 249
Charlot, Jean, 258
Chicago Artists' Group Gallery, 80
Chicago Artists Union, 79
Chicago Defender (newspaper), 82, 83
Chicago Public Library, 82; Henry E. Legler Regional Branch, 192, 245
Chicano Movement, 133, 244
Chicano Mural Movement, 265

Childress, Alice, 200
Chile, 184, 265
China, 125, 134, 261, 265
Chisholm, Shirley, 265
civil rights, 126, 193, 198, 200, 201, 256, 267
Civil Rights Congress, 182
Civil Rights Congress, **104**, **116** (detail), 182
class, 13, 79, 84, 119–121, 191, 200–202, 259, 263
Cohen's Inc., 72
Cold War, 125–126, 128, 200, 201, 262
Colectiva Ira del Silencio, *Lienzo de Tlatelolco*, 142, **142**
Coleman, Floyd, 249
Collage Maquette for Father and Son, **221**
Collage Study for Vendedora de periódicos, **122** (detail), **174**
College Art Association of America (CAA), 69, 71
Comite Unificador Nacional de Mujeres (National Women's Unification Committee), Mexico City, 263
Committee for the Detroit Art Exhibit, 260
communism, 79, 127, 128, 129, 199, 256, 262
Communist Party, 79, 82, 84
Communist Party USA (CPUSA), 125, 130, 200, 259, 260
Conference on the Functional Aspects of Black Art (CONFABA), 12, 14, 129, 264
Congreso Mundial de Mujeres, 263
Congress of Women of the Americas (Cuba, 1963), 201, 263
Congress Vue (magazine), 13, 86, 259
Conwill, Houston, 245
Cooke, Marvel, 83, 259
Corcoran Gallery of Art, Washington, DC, 256
El Corneo Emplumado (*The Plumed Horn*) [journal], 133
Cortés Juárez, Erasto, *George Washington Carver*, from *Against Discrimination in the US* series, **107**
Cortor, Eldzier, 79, 80, 83, 258
A Courtyard Apart: The Art of Elizabeth Catlett and Francisco Mora (exhibition), 249
Covarrubias, Miguel, 257
COVID-19 pandemic, 245
CPUSA. *See* Communist Party USA
The Crisis (magazine), 69
Critchlow, Ernest, 83, 84, 259
Cuba, 125, 133, 182, 263, 265
Cuban Revolution, 133, 261, 263
cubism, 14, 84, 249

D

Daubers' Art Club, Howard University, 74, **75**, 256–257
Davis, Alonzo, 128
Davis, Angela, 129–133, 264
Dawson, Charles C., 79, 81; *Quadroon Madonna*, 72
Delano, Jack, 120
Delta Arts Center, Winston-Salem, North Carolina, 268
Delta Sigma Theta Sorority, 74, 75, 200, 256–257, 267
El Día (newspaper), 265
DIGAME: Elizabeth Catlett's Forever Love (exhibition), 268
Dillard University, New Orleans, 80, 82, 83, 249, 258–259
Divine Nine, 74
Domestic Worker, **63**
Dominican Republic, 263
Dorman, Cheryl Mason, 201–202, **202**
Douglas, Aaron, 260
Douglas, Emory, 133
Douglass, Frederick, 181, 256
Douglass, Haley, 256
Dow, Lorenzo, 72
Downtown Gallery, New York, 83, 179, 258
Drawing of Floating Family for Chicago Library, 245, **245**
Dress Model, 72, **73**
Driskell, David C., 265
Dumont, Hermie, 200

E

Early Sketchbook, 14, **30–31**
Early Sketch for Students Aspire, **209**
East Germany, 125, 133, 264
Ebony (magazine), 264
Elizabeth Catlett, Francisco Mora, & David Mora (exhibition), 267
Elizabeth Catlett: Artist as Activist (exhibition), 250
Elizabeth Catlett: Print Retrospective (exhibition), 267
Elizabeth Catlett: Prints and Sculpture (exhibition), 248, 265
Elizabeth Catlett Sculpture: A Fifty-Year Retrospective (exhibition), 267
Elizabeth Catlett: Sculpture and Graphics (exhibition), 266
Ellington, Duke, 259
Ellison, Ralph, 259
Elvira, **238**
Embree, Edwin, 81
Escobedo, Jesús, *La mortandad de niños por hambre y enfermedades en Nueva Rosita y Cloete es grande*, **92**
Escuela Nacional de Artes Plásticas. *See* Universidad Nacional Autónoma de México
La Esmeralda (Escuela Nacional de Pintura, Escultura y Grabado), 86, 184, 260, 261, 262
La Estampa Mexicana, *El Taller de Gráfica Popular*, 261
Evans, Walker, 120
Exhibition of Paintings by Negro Artists, 71
Exhibition of Works by Negro Artists, 73–74
Experienca Negra: Escultura y grabado de Elizabeth Catlett (exhibition), 264

F

Farm Security Administration, 120
Federal Art Project, 79; Community Art Center (CAC) program, 80
Federal Bureau of Investigation (FBI), 262, 264
feminism, 12, 141, 198–204; and aesthetics, 141; Black, 13, 15, 199, 201–204; first wave, 198; second wave, 15, 198, 202–203; third wave, 198; Third World, 201
feminist aesthetics, 141
Fiesta, 183, **184**
Figura, 263
Firmas para la Paz, **94**
first wave feminism, 198
Flashpoints: The Art of Social Upheaval (exhibition), 267
Floating Family, 192, **232–233**, 245
"The Focus on Women" (essay), 202
For Colored Only (drawing), **52**
For Colored Only (lithograph), **51**
formal rigor in Catlett's work, 12, 14, 15, 86, 188–189, 193–194, 244–245. *See also* abstraction
For My People: Singing Their Songs, 184
For My People: To Marry, 184
Foster, William Z., 260
450 años de lucha (exhibition), 262
Free Angela Davis campaign, 126, 129–133, 264
Freedom (magazine), 181
Freedom for Angela Davis and All Political Prisoners poster, 130–131, **131**
Freedomways (magazine), 262, 264, 265
French Relief Societies, 84
Frías, Óscar: *Benjamin Davis*, from *Against Discrimination in the US* series, **106**, 181; *Homenaje a Cárdenas*, **110**, 181
Friends, 85
fugitive pedagogy, 138–139

G

Gates, Henry Louis, Jr., 268
Gedeon, Lucinda H., 249
George Washington Carver School, Harlem, New York, 84, 86, 200, 249, 259–260, **260**
German expressionism, 13
Girls, **176** (detail), 183, **184**
global sixties, 126, 134
Glory, **217**, 266
Gogh, Vincent van, 69, 257
Gómez, Andrea, *Homenaje a Cárdenas*, **110**, 181
Goode Bryant, Linda, 201–202, **202**
Goss, Bernard, 80
Goss, Margaret Taylor. *See* Burroughs, Margaret Taylor (Goss)
Gossip, 184–185, **203**
Grabados y Esculturas de Elizabeth Catlett (exhibition), 263
Gregory, Montgomery, 257
Guatemala, 184, 262
Guevara, Ernesto "Che," 130, 133
Guggenheim Foundation, 119

H

Halpert, Edith, 179
Hammons, David, 201, **202**
Hampton Institute (now Hampton University), Virginia, 82, 259
Hancraft Studios, 266
Hansberry, Lorraine, 78
Harding, Florence, 202, **202**
Harlem Community Art Center, 84
Harlem Renaissance, 257
Harlem Woman, 184, **225**
Harmon Foundation, 71
Harper, William A., 79
Harriet, **175**
Harvard University, 249
Hats by Suzy White, **21**
Hayden, Palmer, 72

Haygood, William C., 180
Head (1944), 14, 84, **85**
Head (1947), **64**
Head (1960s), **147**
Head (Head of a Man), **24**, 83
Head of a Negro Woman, **56**, **58** (detail), **59** (detail)
Head of a Woman, **49**
Head of a Woman (Woman), **23**
Head of a Young Woman, **64**
Head of Kwan Yin, 75
Hemminghaus, Randy, 185
Hepworth Barbara, 13
Herring, James, 69, 72–74, 81
Hill, Anita, 198
Hillside High School, Durham, North Carolina, 257
The Hilltop (newspaper), 69, 75
Hoffman, Malvina, 84
Holder, Robin, 185
Homage to My Young Black Sisters, 126–127, **153**, **154** (detail), **155** (detail), 191, 201–204, 264
Homage to the Panthers, **163**
Homenaje a Cárdenas, **88** (detail), **110**, 181
Howard, Darnley, 69
Howard University, 13, 14, 68–75, 81, 179, 200, **200**, 244, 245, 256–257, 262, 265, 267
Howard University Choir, **18**, **66** (detail), 71
Hudson, Henry, 71, 74
Hughes, Langston, 83–84, 259
Hull-House, Chicago, 79

I

I am the Black Woman, from *The Black Woman* series (1946), **33**
I am the Black Woman, from *The Black Woman* series (1947), **34**, 184
I Have Always Worked Hard in America..., from *The Black Woman* series, **35**
I have given the world my songs, from *The Black Woman* series, **38**
I Have Special Reservations, from *The Black Woman* series, **45**
I Have Studied in Ever Increasing Numbers, from *The Black Woman* series, **43**
Indian Woman, **172**
In Harriet Tubman I Helped Hundreds to Freedom, from *The Black Woman* series, **40**
...In Other Folks Homes, from *The Black Woman* series, **37**
In Phillis Wheatley I Proved Intellectual Equality in the Midst of Slavery, from *The Black Woman* series, **41**
"Inside / Out Private Gallery Tour," 250
In Sojourner Truth I fought for the Rights of Women as well as Blacks, from *The Black Woman* series, **39**
Instituto Cubano de Amistad con los Pueblos (Cuban Institute of Friendship with the Peoples), 263
Instituto Mexicano del Seguro Social, Mexico City, 260
Instituto Politécnico Nacional (National Polytechnic Institute), Mexico City, 263
La Integración Racial en Cuba, **136** (detail), **148**
International Women's Day, 133, 265
International Workers Order, 84
intersectionality, 13, 198, 200
...In the Fields, from *The Black Woman* series, **36**, 120
Invisible Man: A Memorial to Ralph Ellison. See *Ralph Ellison Memorial*
Isaac Delgado Museum, New Orleans, 80, 249, 258. *See also* New Orleans Museum of Art
Iturbe, Ana, 141–143, 265

J

Jackson, George, 130, 132
Jackson, Jonathan, 130
Jackson, Mahalia, 193, 268
Jaime Torres Bodet and José Vasconcelos, **230**, 266
JAM. *See* Just Above Midtown
Jamaica Arts Center, New York, 267
Janson, H. W., 13, 258
Jefferson School of Social Science, New York, 200, 259
Jews, 79
Jim Crow segregation, 12, 69, 199
Jimenez, Ana Victoria, 129
John Reed Club, 79
Johnson, Sargent Claude, 82
Johnson, William H., 72
Jones, Loïs Mailou, 69, 71–74, **71**, 203, 256; *Ascent of Ethiopia*, 73; *Buddha*, 72
Jones-Hogu, Barbara, 126–127, 264; *Unite*, 126, **127**, 264
Julius Rosenwald Fund, 81, 83, 86, 118, 120, 178–180, 259, 260
June Kelly Gallery, New York, 248, 250, 267
Just Above Midtown (JAM), New York, 201–202, 204

K

Kennedy, John F., 134
Kersey, Joseph, 82
King, Martin Luther, Jr., 264
Kleinman, Joseph, 267
Kollwitz, Käthe, 13, 192
Korean War, 261
Kuan-Yin, an Outstanding Example of Chinese Sculpture (exhibition), 75

L

Lange, Dorothea, *Hoeing Cotton (A Negro tenant farmer and several members of his family hoeing cotton on their farm in Alabama)*, 120, **120**
Lanker, Brian, *Elizabeth Catlett*, **267**
Lawrence, Gwendolyn, 259
Lawrence, Jacob, 83, 259, 260
Learning, 180, **181**
Lee, Russell, 120
Leftist politics, 14, 78, 79, 80, 82, 84, 124–126, 129, 130, 132–134, 249. *See also* Black Left; New Left
Leigh, Simone, 203
Lenape people, 84
The Lesson, **91**, 180
letter to Jesús Álvarez Amaya, 143, **143**, 268
Lewis, Frederick, 131
Lewis, Norman, 83, 84, 85, 259, 260; *Woman with Yellow Hat*, 85
Lewis, Samella, 258; *The Art of Elizabeth Catlett*, 266
Liberal Club, Howard University, 74–75, 200, 257
liberation theology, 141
Life (magazine), 129
Limited Editions Club, 267
Links Together, **228**, **229** (detail)
linocuts, 179–180, 183
lithography, 184
Locke, Alain, 73, 81, 82, 121, 257
Louis Armstrong, 193, **208**, **242**, 244–245, 265
Lovey Twice, **212**, **214–215** (detail)
Lowenfeld, Viktor, 259
Luna, Francisco, *Unity of All Workers (Isaac Myers)*, from *Against Discrimination in the US* series, **109**

M

MacArthur Genius Grant, 249
Mackey, Howard H., 69
Madonna, **218**
maestras (women teachers), 138–143
Magic Mask, **159**
Mahalia Jackson, 193, **194**, 268
Malcolm X Speaks for Us, **4–5** (detail), 124, 134, **156**, 184, 263, 264
Man, **206** (detail), **210**
Margaret and Gayle, 83
Marshall, Thurgood, 257
Marxism, 84, 133, 259
Masilela, Nomaduma Rosa, 203–204
Mask, 127–128, **160**
Massacre of Tlatelolco (1968), 128–129, 142, 264
maternity. *See* motherhood
McBride, William, 258
McBrown, Gertrude P., 71
McCarthyism, 125
McKeown, Anne, 184
Méndez, Leopoldo, 118, 119, 180, 257, 260; *La mortandad de niños por hambre y enfermedades en Nueva Rosita y Cloete es grande*, **92**; *Motherhood*, 260; *Paul Robeson*, from *Against Discrimination in the US* series, **108**; *Pequeña maestra, ¡Que inmensa es tu voluntad!*, 138, **139**
Mesoamerican sculpture, 13
Mexiac, Aldolfo, Movimiento Estudiantil protest poster, 129, **129**
Mexican art, 13, 14. *See also* Mexican muralism; Pre-Encounter Mesoamerican art
Mexican muralism, 13, 71, 74, 257, 258, 265
Mexican Revolution, 13, 118–120, 128, 260, 261
Mexico: and the Cold War, 125, 128; social and political conditions in, 128, 141, 260, 261, 262; student protests in, 128–129, 263, 264. *See also* Catlett, Elizabeth: in Mexico
Mexikansk grafik, i samverkan med Mexikanska Legationen, Stockholm (exhibition), 261
Meyer, Hannes, 180
Miner Teachers College, Washington, DC, 257
Mis niños, **95**
Mississippi Museum of Art, 249
modernism, 14, 71, 73, 119, 140, 183, 188, 189, 193
Moore, Henry, 13, 189–190; *Seated Figure*, 189–190, **191**

Mora, Betty. *See* Catlett, Elizabeth
Mora, Francisco "Pancho," **14**, 141, 180, 249–250, 260–261, **261**, **262**, 263, 266, **266**, 267; *Mississippi/Ballot (Blanche K. Bruce)*, from *Against Discrimination in the US* series, **107**
Mora Catlett, David (son), 128–129, 249, 261, 262, 267
Mora Catlett, Francisco, Jr. (son), 261
Mora Catlett, Juan (son), 261; *Betty y Pancho*, 267
Moran's restaurant, New York, 250
La mortandad de niños por hambre y enfermedades en Nueva Rosita y Cloete es grande, **92**
Mother and Child (lithograph), **28**, 179
Mother and Child (sculpture, 1942–1944), 14, **55**
Mother and Child (sculpture, 1956), **76** (detail), **114**, 189
Mother and Child (sculpture, 1970), **167**, 191
Mother and Child (sculpture, 1983), 191
Mother and Child (sculpture, 1993), **186** (detail), 191, **192**, **219**
Mother and Child (watercolor), 179
Motherhood, 260
motherhood, as subject matter for Catlett, 72, 75, 82, 129, 189, 191–192, 201. *See also works titled* Mother and Child
Motley, Archibald, Jr., 79–81, 83; *Brown Girl after the Bath*, 71; *Uncle Bob*, 71
Movimiento Estudiantil (Student Protest Movement), 128–129, 134, 264
Movimiento Estudiantil C.N.H., *¡Detrás de cada estudiante muerto, hay una madre…que clama justicia!* poster, 129, **129**
Mujer, **150**, 190–191, 263
Mujer Cocinando (Woman Cooking), **96**
Mujer Negra, **16** (detail), **53**
Murales en las calle de Chicago (presentation), 265
murals, 244, 257, 265. *See also* Mexican muralism
Museum of African American Art, Los Angeles, 266
Museum of Modern Art, New York, 14, 80, 257
Mydans, Carl, 120
Myers, E. Pauline, 256
My reward has been bars between me and the rest of the land, from *The Black Woman* series, **44**
My right is a future of equality with other Americans, from *The Black Woman* series, **48**, **87** (detail), 182, **182**
My Role has been Important in the Struggle to Organize the Unorganized, from *The Black Woman* series, **42**

N

NAACP. *See* National Association for the Advancement of Colored People
Naima: My Granddaughter, **238**
National Association for the Advancement of Colored People (NAACP), 69, 199; Cultural Committee of the Washington Branch, 71
National Bloc of Revolutionary Women, 201
National Conference of Artists (Pomona, California, 1975), 265
National Conference of Negro Artists, 262
National Council of Negro Women, 266
National Gallery of Art, Washington, DC, 73
National Negro Congress (NNC), 13, 86, 260; Arts Committee, 259
National United Committee to Free Angela Davis (NUCFAD). *See* Free Angela Davis campaign
The Negro Artist Comes of Age (exhibition), 260
"The Negro Artist in America" (essay), 259
"Negro Artists" (essay), 260
Negro es Bello (Negro es Bello II), 124, 126–127, **144** (detail), **157**
Negro Girl, 258
Negro Mother and Child, 75, 80, **81**, 82, 189, 258
"The Negro People and American Art" (speech), 262
Negro Woman (lithograph), **29**, 179
Negro Woman (sculpture), **65**, 262
The Negro Woman series. See *The Black Woman* series
Neil, Frank, 258
Neuberger Museum of Art, Purchase, New York, 249, 267
New Left, 126, 128, 130, 133, 134
New Masses (magazine), 14, 260
New Negro Movements, 72
New Orleans, Louisiana, 14, 80, 249; Louis Armstrong Park, 193, 244, 268
New Orleans Museum of Art, 266. *See also* Isaac Delgado Museum, New Orleans
New Visions Gallery, Atlanta, 267
New York (magazine), 248
Niño Papelero, **90**, 182, **182**
Nixon, Richard, 134
NNC. *See* National Negro Congress
North Carolina Teachers Association, 257
Northwestern University, 12
NUCFAD. *See* Free Angela Davis campaign

O

Obama, Barack, 12
O'Grady, Lorraine, 198
O'Higgins, Pablo, 118, 180, 257, 260; *Frederick Douglass*, from *Against Discrimination in the US* series, **107**; *La mortandad de niños por hambre y enfermedades en Nueva Rosita y Cloete es grande*, **92**; *Motherhood*, 260
Olympic Games (Mexico City, 1968), 127, 128, 244, 264
Organization of Solidarity of the People of Asia, Africa & Latin America, 133
Ortega, Armando, 139–142
Ortiz, Tiburcio, 139
Oswald, Lee Harvey, 134
Owens, Andy, 201, **202**

P

Paintings, Sculpture, and Prints of the Negro Woman (exhibition), 261
Pan, **96**, **99** (detail)
Parks, Gordon, 120
Patterson, William L., 182
Paul, Alice, 199
Paul Laurence Dunbar High School, Washington, DC, 256
Pensive, **60**
People of Atlanta, **230**, 245
People's Voice (newspaper), 83, **84**
Perkins, Marion, 82
Phillis Wheatley, **173**, **246** (detail), 265
Picasso, Pablo, 14, 80, 249; *Les Demoiselles d'Avignon*, 80; *Guernica*, 14, 80
Picasso: Forty Years of His Art (exhibition), 14, 80, 258
Pinkett, Flaxie, 75
Playing, **220**, **222–223** (detail)
Political Prisoner, 132, **168**
Pollack, Peter, 80, 81, 83
Pollar, Mary Ann, 265
Pop art, 14, 132–133
Popular Front, 79, 133
Porfirio Díaz, José de la Cruz, 118–119
Porter, James A., 13, 69–74, 81, 256; *Reflections*, 72; *Twelfth Street YMCA Mural*, 74, **74**
Portrait, 182, **183**, **205** (detail)
Portrait sketches for "Military Equality—A Victory Demand," 86, **86**
Prairie View College, Texas, 258
Pre-Encounter Mesoamerican art, 188, 189, 249. *See also* Mexican art
Primer Congreso Nacional por la Paz (Mexico, 1951), 181, 261
Print Club of New York, 184
printmaking, 178–185
public art, 15, 74, 178, 191–194, 244–245. *See also* Catlett, Elizabeth: audience for the work of
Public Works of Art Project (PWAP), 74, 257

Q

Quander, Nellie M., 72
Quevedo, Mercedes, 141, 182

R

Rabel, Fanny, *Frances Ellen Watkins Harper*, from *Against Discrimination in the US* series, **108**
racism: in the American South, 119; in Chicago, 78–79; in Federal Art Project, 79; public discrimination and segregation, 13–14, 80, 249, 258; rejection from Carnegie Institute as instance of, 68, 256; in the US, 126, 256; and the war effort, 86
Rainbow Sign, Berkeley, California, 265
Ralph Ellison Memorial, **236**, 245, 267
Ramírez, Everardo, *La hora del almuerzo*, from the portfolio *Vida en mi barriada*, 119, **119**
Rare Negro Paintings (exhibition), 72
realism, 140, 245. *See also* social realism
Rebozo (1957), 189–190, **190**
Rebozo (1968), **166**
Red Cross Woman (Nurse), **27**, 86
Red Leaves, **195** (detail), **213**
Reginald F. Lewis Museum of Maryland African American History & Culture, Baltimore, 250
Relief Study (Sculpture Sketch of *People of Atlanta*), **231**
Rescatar y hacer validos los derechos de la mujer, **165**
Rich, Daniel Catton, 81, 83
Richards, Beah, 182
Ringgold, Faith, **267**
riot grrrl subculture, 198
Rivera, Diego, 71, 257; *La maestra rural*, 138

Robert Blackburn Printmaking Workshop, 185, 266, 267
Robeson, Paul, 259, 261
Rodriguez, Guillermo, *W. E. B. Du Bois (Black Reconstruction)*, from *Against Discrimination in the US* series, **109**
Roerich Museum, New York, 71
Rogers, Herman, *Wynona Wing*, 71, **71**
"The Role of the Black Artist" (speech), 265
Roosevelt, Eleanor, 83
Roosevelt, Franklin Delano, 86
Roots, **216**, **252–253** (detail)
Rostgaard, Alfredo, 133; *Che* poster, 133, **133**
Rothstein, Arthur, 120
Ruiz, José L., 189, 261, 262
Russian War Relief, 84, 200, 259
La Ruta de Amistad, 244
Rutgers Center for Innovative Print and Paper, 184

S

Saar, Alison, 245
Saar, Betye, 265
Sacramento, California, 193
SAIC. *See* School of the Art Institute of Chicago
Said, Edward, 125, 132, 134
Salón de la Plástica Mexicana, Mexico City, 141, 261
Sánchez, José, 184
Sanchez, Sonia, "6 haiku (for Elizabeth Catlett in Cuernavaca)," 143
Sapp, Delores, 75
Savage, Augusta, 82, 84
Schapiro, Miriam, 202–203
Schomburg Center, Harlem, New York, 245
School of the Art Institute of Chicago (SAIC), 78–79, 80, 83
Scott, William E., 72
Scottsboro Boys Trial, 75
sculpture, 188–194
Seated Figure with Hands to Head, **224**
Seated Woman, 191, **240**
Sebree, Charles, 80, 83, 258
second wave feminism, 15, 198, 202–203
Self-Portrait, **239**, **254** (detail)
Separation, 124, **125**
Shahn, Ben, 120
Sharecropper (color linocut), **103**, **116** (detail)
Sharecropper (linocut; Clark Atlanta University Art Museum), **103**, 182
Sharecropper (linocut; Davis Museum at Wellesley College), **103**
Sharecropper (male), **100**, 120
Sharecropper (painting), **102**
Shoeshine Boy, **96**
Simone, Nina, 265
Simpson, Lorna, 203
Sims, Lowery Stokes, 201, **202**
Singing Head, 190, **216**
Siqueiros, David Alfaro, 184, 260
Sketch for Louis Armstrong, **208**
Sketch for Sojourner, **234**
Smith, Tommie, 127
Smithsonian American Art Museum, 190
socialism, 79, 82, 86, 125, 256
social justice, 12, 79, 82, 86, 200, 203
social realism, 12, 82, 129. *See also* realism
Sojourner, 193, **235**, **251** (detail)
Soledad Brothers, 130
Solitude and Solidarity: The Art of Elizabeth Catlett (exhibition), 268
South Side Community Art Center (SSCAC), Chicago, 78, 80, 82, 83, 84, 200, 258
Soviet Union, 125, 128, 261, 265
...Special Houses, from *The Black Woman* series, **46**
Sragow, Ellen, 179
SSCAC. *See* South Side Community Art Center
Stargazer, 191, **241**
Stargazers: Elizabeth Catlett in Conversation with 21 Contemporary Artists (exhibition), 268
Stepping Out, 191
Sternberg, Harry, 179, 260
Stinson, Henry, 258
Struggle and Serenity: The Visionary Art of Elizabeth Catlett (exhibition), 267
Stryker, Roy E., 120
Students Aspire, **209**, 245, 265
Studio Museum, Harlem, New York, 124, 248, 250, 265
Study for Special Houses, **50**
Stylus Literary Society, Howard University, 74, 257
Synthesis: A combination of parts of elements into a complex whole (exhibition), 202

T

Taller de Gráfica Popular (TGP, People's Graphic Workshop), 13, 15, 82, 86, 118–121, 125, 126, 129, 141, 143, 178–183, 248, 257, 260–261, 263, 268; *Against Discrimination in the US* series, 181, 200, 261; *Estampas de la revolución mexicana*, 118–120, 261
Tanner, Henry Ossawa, 81
Tanner Art Galleries, American Negro Exposition, 81
Target Practice, **161**
Taylor, Recy, 259
Telesistema, 127
Terra-Cotta Head, **146**
Terrell, Mary Church, 72
Terry, **226**
TGP. *See* Taller de Gráfica Popular
There Is a Woman in Every Color, **211**
third wave feminism, 198
Third World, 14, 126, 133, 134, 140, 201
Third World feminism, 201
Thomas, Clarence, 198
Three Women of America, 182, **183**
Tinoco, Silvia, 141–143; *La Torre de la Plaza de las Tres Culturas*, from the series *Torres de Babel*, 141–142, **142**
Tired, **57**
Torso, **240**
Torso, Portrait of Joan, **115**, **196** (detail)
Torture of Mothers, 129, **162**, 201
transnational perspective, 13, 118–121, 124–126, 129, 132, 191, 200–201
"Tribute to the Negro People" (essay), 260
Tribute to the Negro People (exhibition), 260
Tricontinental (journal), 133
Trotter, William Monroe, 266
Trotter House, University of Michigan, 266
Truth, Sojourner, 82, 120, 193, 261
Tubman, Harriet, 120, 181, 245, 261
Turci, Maureen, 267
Turner, Nat, 261
Two Centuries of Black American Art (exhibition), 265

U

UNAM. *See* Universidad Nacional Autónoma de México
Unión Nacional de Mujeres Mexicanas (UNMM, National Union of Mexican Women), 129, 130, 133, 134, 182–183, 201, 263, 265
United Nations, 182, 261
Universidad Nacional Autónoma de México (UNAM), 14, 128, 139–141, 262–263, 265
University of Iowa, 13, 75, 80, 179, 191, 248, 258, 267, 268
UNMM. *See* Unión Nacional de Mujeres Mexicanas
Untitled (Composition for a Peace Poster), **93**, 181
Untitled (Harriet Tubman), from *Against Discrimination in the US* series, **10** (detail), **105**, 181
Untitled (Head of Woman), **113**
Untitled (Mother and Child), **96**, **98** (detail)
Untitled (painting, 1947), **54**
Untitled (pastel, c. 1935), **20**, 75
Untitled (student drawing—Standing Male Model), **19**
Untitled (Woman in a Yellow Hat), **25**, 85
Untitled (Wynona Wing Seated), 70–71, **70**
Untitled (Young Woman Looking Up), **112**
US State Department, 191

V

Vachon, John, 120
Van Scott, Glory, 202, 266
Vasconcelos, José, **230**, 266
Vermeer, Johannes, 69
Vietnam, 263
Vincent van Gogh (exhibition), 257
Virginia, 184, **227**

W

Walker, Kara, 249, **268**
Walker, Margaret, 258, 259, 265; *For My People*, 267
Warhol, Andy, 13, 132–133; *Gold Marilyn Monroe*, 132; *Marilyn Diptych*, 132
Waring, Laura Wheeler, 72
War Worker, **22**, 86
Watts/Detroit/Washington/Harlem/Newark, 129, **162**
Weaver, Faythe, 202, **202**
Webbed Woman, **237**
W. E. B. Du Bois Research Institute, Harvard University, 268
Weems, Carrie Mae, 203
Wells, Ida B., 199–200, 261
Wells, James, 69, 71–73, 75, 256; *Looking Upward*, 73; *Plowman*, 72
We Wanted a Revolution (exhibition), 203, **203**
Wheatley, Phillis, 120, 265

White, Charles, 79, 80, 82–86, **84**, 180, 249, 258–260; works by, 80, 85, **86**, 259, **259**
Wilberforce University, 69
Wing, Wynona, 71
Winter War (1939), 258
Wo-Chi-Ca. *See* Workers Children's Camp
Wofford, Tobias, 73–74
Wolcott, Marion Post, 120
Woman's Suffrage Procession (1913), 199
Woman with Oranges, **97**
Women of America, 134, **149**
Women's International Democratic Federation, 201
Wood, Grant, 13, 80, 82, 83, 179, 258
Woodruff, Hale, 260
Workers Children's Camp (Camp Wo-Chi-Ca), 84, 259, 260
working class. *See* class
Working Woman, **62**
World Congress of Women (Moscow, 1963), 182, 263
World War I, 192
World War II, 83–86, 118
Worldwide Congress of Women, Moscow, 134

X

X, Malcolm, 263

Y

Yampolsky, Mariana: *Guerillero negro*, from *Against Discrimination in the US* series, **108**; *Homenaje a Cárdenas*, **110**, 181
Young Girl, **61**
Your Heritage House, Detroit, 266, **266**

Z

Zadkine, Ossip, 83, 84, 259
Zalce, Alfredo, 180
Zedong, Mao, 130
Zehbrauskas, Adriana, Catlett at her home in Cuernavaca, **268**
Zorach, William, *Mother and Child*, 258
Zúñiga, Francisco, 189, 261; *Mujer sentada con las manos en el pelo*, 189, **189**

CONTRIBUTORS

Dalila Scruggs is Augusta Savage Curator of African American Art, Smithsonian American Art Museum.

Mary Lee Corlett is associate curator, modern prints and drawings (retired), National Gallery of Art.

J.V. Decemvirale is assistant professor of art history and global cultures, Cal State San Bernardino.

Julia Fernandez is assistant professor, department of art history and visual culture, Denison University.

Melanee C. Harvey is associate professor of art history, The Chadwick A. Boseman College of Fine Arts, Howard University, and 2023 Genevieve Young Writing Fellow, Gordon Parks Foundation.

Melanie Anne Herzog is professor emerita of art history, Edgewood College, Madison, Wisconsin.

Catherine Morris is Sackler Senior Curator, Elizabeth A. Sackler Center for Feminist Art, Brooklyn Museum.

Sarah Kelly Oehler is Field-McCormick Chair and Curator, Arts of the Americas, and vice president of curatorial strategy, The Art Institute of Chicago.

Lowery Stokes Sims is an independent curator and art historian, and curator emerita, Museum of Arts and Design, New York.

Rashieda Witter is curatorial assistant, modern prints and drawings, National Gallery of Art.

CREDITS

p. 14: Photographs and Prints Division, Schomburg Center for Research in Black Culture, The New York Public Library; p. 18: Davis Museum at Wellesley College, Wellesley, MA; pp. 19, 33, 40, 41, 43, 57, 70 (fig. 1, Photo by Jada A. Brooks), 71 (fig. 2): Howard University Gallery of Art, Washington DC / Licensed by Art Resource, NY; pp. 20, 21, 29, 44, 45, 217: © Jacob Fine Art 2023; p. 22: Image © the Johnson Collection; p. 23: Image copyright © The Metropolitan Museum of Art, Image source: Art Resource, NY; p. 24: The Art Institute of Chicago / Art Resource, NY; pp. 35, 210: Courtesy of The Cleveland Museum of Art; p. 38, 46, 54: photo Travis Fullerton © Virginia Museum of Fine Arts; p. 39: © Jacob Fine Art 2024; pp. 42, 94, 148: Jaime Alvarez; p. 49: The Morgan Library & Museum, New York; p. 50: Helen Nitkin; pp. 55, 73 (fig. 4), 104, 162 (bottom): Mark Gulezian/Quicksilver; p. 64 (left): Digital image © Whitney Museum of American Art / Licensed by Scala / Art Resource, NY; p. 71 (fig. 3): Photo from Tritobia H Benjamin, *The Life and Art of Loïs Mailou Jones* (San Francisco: Pomegranate Artbooks, 1994), 15, Courtesy the Estate of Tritobia Hayes Benjamin; pp. 74, 75, 257: Courtesy of the Howard University Archives, Moorland-Spingarn Research Center, Howard University, Washington DC; p. 81 (fig. 2): Photo General Collection, Beinecke Rare Book and Manuscript Library, Yale University; p. 86 (fig. 5): Copyright © The Charles White Archives; p. 86 (fig. 6): Photography by Dalila Scruggs; p. 91: Courtesy of the RISD Museum, Providence, RI; pp. 92, 119: Center for Southwest Research and Special Collections, University of New Mexico Libraries (p. 92: Latin American Ephemera Pictorial Collection, Series 7. PICT 999-006-0188; p. 119, fig. 2: PICT-999-011); p. 93: The Art Institute of Chicago / Art Resource, New York; pp. 96 (top, left), 150, 183 (fig. 4): photography by Axel Schneider; pp. 96 (top, right), 174, 190, 209 (left), 220, 221: photography by Carlos R. Montes de Oca/Inéditas Films; p. 102: Wes Magyar; p. 103 (top, left): Davis Museum at Wellesley College, Wellesley, MA; p. 103 (bottom, right): The Art Institute of Chicago / Art Resource, NY; pp. 106 (all), 107 (left), 108 (right and bottom, left:), 109 (left), 110: Images courtesy of the Prints & Photographs Division, Library of Congress; p. 106 (bottom right): © Estate of Margaret Burroughs; p. 112: John Woo, photographer; p. 114: Digital Image © The Museum of Modern Art/Licensed by SCALA / Art Resource, NY; p. 115: Image courtesy of Jonathan Boos, New York; p. 119 (fig. 1): Image copyright © The Metropolitan Museum of Art, Image source Art Resource, NY; pp. 120 (fig. 3), 140 (fig. 2): Images courtesy of the Prints & Photographs Division, Library of Congress; p. 127 (fig. 2): © Barbara Jones-Hogu; p. 129 (fig. 4, Adolfo Mexiac Calderón): © 2024 Artists Rights Society (ARS), New York / SOMAAP, Mexico City; p. 133 (fig. 6): © uneedyt.com; p. 139 (fig. 1): © 2024 Museum Associates / LACMA, Licensed by Art Resource, NY; p. 140 (fig. 2): Library of Congress, Washington, D.C. LC-DIG-ppmsca-35275; pp. 142 (fig. 3), 151: photography by Carlos R. Montes de Oca/Inéditas Films; p. 142 (fig. 4): photograph courtesy of Gogan Iturbe; p. 143 (fig. 5): photograph courtesy of J.V. Decemvirale; p. 143 (lines quoted from Sonia Sanchez, "6 haiku"): from *Collected Poems* by Sonia Sanchez, Copyright © 2022 by Sonia Sanchez, Reprinted with permission from Beacon Press, Boston, Massachusetts; pp. 146, 149: © Detroit Institute of Arts / Bridgeman Images; p. 147: James Prinz Photography; p. 152: Photography by Edward C. Robison III; p. 156: Digital Image © The Museum of Modern Art/Licensed by SCALA / Art Resource, NY; p. 158: Gregory R. Staley; p. 161: Courtesy of the Amistad Research Center, New Orleans, LA / Bridgeman Images; p. 164 (left): Digital Image © The Museum of Modern Art/ Licensed by SCALA / Art Resource, NY; p. 169: Neil Boyd Photography; pp. 172, 240 (left): Roz Akin, New York; p. 173: Photo © Cincinnati Art Museum / Museum Purchase / Bridgeman Images; p. 183 (fig. 5): © Elizabeth Catlett / Artists Rights Society (ARS), New York, Photo © President and Fellows of Harvard College, 2006.76; p. 184 (fig. 8): Courtesy of The Driskell Center at the University of Maryland, College Park; p. 189 (fig. 1): Photo courtesy of Fundación Zúñiga Laborde A.C.; p. 191 (fig. 3): © Henry Moore Foundation, Photo: AGO, Reproduced by permission of The Henry Moore Foundation; p. 192: Melanie Anne Herzog, *Elizabeth Catlett: An American Artist in Mexico* (Seattle, 2000); p. 168: © 2000. Reprinted courtesy of the University of Washington Press; p. 193 (fig. 5): Photo Art Resources; p. 194 (fig. 6): Photo ID 43585686 © Allenalo | Dreamstime.com; p. 200 (fig. 1): Photo by International News Photo Co. via Getty Images; p. 202 (fig. 2): Photograph courtesy Faythe Weaver, New York; p. 203 (fig. 4): Photograph courtesy Brooklyn Museum; pp. 208 (left), 234, p. 245 (fig. 1): Josh Brasted Photography; p. 208 (right): Photo Rubens Alarcon / Alamy Stock Photo; p. 209 (right): Images courtesy of the Prints & Photographs Division, Library of Congress, Photograph by Carol M. Highsmith; p. 224: Museum purchase with funds from Donald, Nicole, and Dexter Griffin; Janice and Mary Wiggins; and the Estate of Herman B Wells via the Joseph Granville and Anna Bernice Wells Memorial Fund, Photo credit: Eskenazi Museum of Art/Kevin Montague; p. 230 (top): Photography by GLR Estudio (Gerardo Landa & Eduardo López); p. 230 (bottom): © Elizabeth Catlett / Licensed by VAGA, New York, NY; p. 231: Photograph by Alan Harmon and Bruce Morton of City of Atlanta; pp. 232–233: Courtesy of the City of Chicago Public Art Collection and the Chicago Public Library, Legler Regional Library, Patrick L. Pyszka/City of Chicago; p. 236: Photo © Richard Levine / Alamy Stock Photo; pp. 237, 241: Vallarino Fine Art; p. 238 (right): John Wadsworth Photography; p. 240 (right): Allen Phillips/ Wadsworth Atheneum; p. 208: Photo Rubens Alarcon / Alamy Stock Photo; p. 257: Vallarino Fine Art; p. 259: courtesy of The Charles White Archives; p. 266 (bottom): Photo by Fern Logan; p. 267 (left): © Brian Lanker Archive; p. 268 (left): From the Kara Walker Archives, courtesy of Sikkema Jenkins & Co. and Sprüth; p. 268 (right): Photograph © Adriana Zehbrauskas

Elizabeth Catlett: A Black Revolutionary Artist and All That It Implies is organized by the Brooklyn Museum and the National Gallery of Art, Washington, in collaboration with the Art Institute of Chicago.

This exhibition is made possible through support from the Terra Foundation for American Art.

Leadership support for the exhibition and publication is provided by the Henry Luce Foundation.

Generous support for the Brooklyn Museum presentation is provided by Christie's, the Every Page Foundation, the Maurer Family Foundation, and the National Endowment for the Arts.

This publication is supported by an endowment for scholarly publications from the Mellon Foundation.

Exhibition dates:
Brooklyn Museum, September 13, 2024–January 19, 2025
National Gallery of Art, Washington, March 9–July 6, 2025
The Art Institute of Chicago, August 30, 2025–January 4, 2026

Published by the National Gallery of Art and the Brooklyn Museum

For the National Gallery of Art:
Managing Editor: Emily Zoss
Senior Editor: Julie Warnement
Design Manager: Brad Ireland
Production Manager: Christina Wiginton
Production Associate: Jasmine Lee
Production Assistant: Mariah Shay
Editing by Julie Warnement, with Magda Nakassis, Lisa Shea, Caroline Weaver, and Emily Zoss
Design by Morcos Key
Proofreading by Tanya Heinrich
Indexing by David Luljak
Rights clearance by Barbara Wood and Wordesign Services

For the Brooklyn Museum:
Director of Publications, Interpretation, and Editorial Services: Audrey Walen
Image Licensing Specialist: Taylor Catalana
Senior Museum Technician/Digital Imaging Technician: Danny Perez

Typeset in Canela and Graphik
Printed on GardaPat Kiara by Conti Tipocolor, Italy

Copublished by The University of Chicago Press, Chicago and London
press.uchicago.edu

ISBN-13: 978-0-226-83657-7 (cloth)
ISBN-13: 978-0-226-83658-4 (e-book)
DOI: https://doi.org/10.7208/chicago/9780226836584.001.0001

Library of Congress Control Number: 2024936694

Cover: *Black Unity* (p. 152, front and back)

Display illustrations (details):
pp. 4–5: *Malcolm X Speaks for Us* (p. 156); p. 10: *Untitled (Harriet Tubman)* (p. 105); p. 16: *Mujer Negra* (p. 53); pp. 58–59: *Head of a Negro Woman* (p. 56); p. 66: *Howard University Choir* (p. 18); p. 76: *Mother and Child* (p. 114); p. 87: *My right...* (p. 182, fig. 2); p. 88: *Homenaje a Cárdenas* (p. 110, upper right); p. 98: *Untitled (Mother and Child)* (p. 96, upper left); p. 99: *Pan* (p. 96, upper right); p. 116: *Sharecropper* (p. 103, bottom right); p. 122: *Collage Study for Vendedora de periódicos* (p. 174); p. 135: *Central America Says No!* (p. 164, left); p. 136: *La Integración Racial en Cuba* (p. 148); p. 144: *Negro es Bello II* (p. 157); pp. 154–155: *Homage to My Young Black Sisters* (p. 153); pp. 170–171: *Angela Libre* (p. 169); p. 176: *Girls* (p. 184, fig. 8); p. 186: *Mother and Child* (p. 219); p. 195: *Red Leaves* (p. 213); p. 196: *Torso, Portrait of Joan* (p. 115); p. 205: *Portrait* (p. 183, fig. 4); p. 206: *Man* (p. 210); pp. 214–215: *Lovey Twice* (p. 212); pp. 222–223: *Playing* (p. 220); p. 229: *Links Together* (p. 228); p. 242: *Louis Armstrong* (p. 208, right); p. 246: *Phillis Wheatley* (p. 173); p. 251: *Sojourner* (p. 235); pp. 252–253: *Roots* (p. 216, bottom); p. 254: *Self-Portrait* (p. 239); p. 269: Catlett working on *Bañista Olmeca* (p. 263)

10 9 8 7 6 5 4 3 2 1